The Other Canon of Economics

Anthem Press and The Other Canon Foundation are pleased to present the *Anthem Other Canon Economics* series. The Other Canon – also described as 'reality economics' – studies the economy as a real object rather than as the behaviour of a model economy based on core axioms, assumptions and techniques. The series includes both classical and contemporary works in this tradition, spanning evolutionary, institutional and Post-Keynesian economics, the history of economic thought and economic policy, economic sociology and technology governance, and works on the theory of uneven development and in the tradition of the German Historical School.

The *Anthem Frontiers of Global Political Economy and Development* series seeks to trigger and attract new thinking in the global political economy, with particular reference to the prospects of emerging markets and developing countries. Written by renowned scholars from different parts of the world, books in this series provide historical, analytical and empirical perspectives on national economic strategies and processes, the implications of global and regional economic integration, the changing nature of the development project and the diverse global-to-local forces that drive change. Scholars featured in the series extend earlier economic insights to provide fresh interpretations that allow new understandings of contemporary economic processes.

The Other Canon of Economics

Essays in the Theory and History of Uneven Economic Development

Volume 1

Erik S. Reinert
Edited by Rainer Kattel

ANTHEM PRESS

Anthem Press
An imprint of Wimbledon Publishing Company
www.anthempress.com

This edition first published in UK and USA 2024
by ANTHEM PRESS
75–76 Blackfriars Road, London SE1 8HA, UK
or PO Box 9779, London SW19 7ZG, UK
and
244 Madison Ave #116, New York, NY 10016, USA

British Library Cataloguing-in-Publication Data
A catalogue record for this book is available from the British Library.

Library of Congress Cataloging-in-Publication Data: 2022932210
A catalog record for this book has been requested.

ISBN-13: 978-1-83998-297-2 (Hbk)
ISBN-10: 1-83998-297-7 (Hbk)

This title is also available as an e-book.

Praise

"Reinert is one of the pioneers of a distinctly different narrative about economic development than has long occupied the commanding heights, with much more focus on politics and institutions and path-dependence. Anyone who enjoys the company of an articulate, off-beat, well-informed intelligence will want to read his collection – and perhaps pick a fight with it."

Robert H. Wade, Professor of Global Political Economy, London School of Economics, London, American Political Science Association Best Book or Article Award, 1989–91, Leontief Prize in Economics, 2008

"Over decades, Erik Reinert's profound and significant work has highlighted the importance of increasing returns for development—and the ways in which poor countries have been prevented from reaping the benefits of such technologies. This book, bringing together some of his most essential insights, is a treasure trove for anyone interested in understanding processes of development and global inequality, and also an essential instruction manual for what can be done."

Jayati Ghosh, Professor of Economics, University of Massachusetts Amherst, USA

"Development policy, like History, is written by those who won. But the recommendations of the successful countries paradoxically become 'do as I say, not as I did'. This book looks at the process of development from the perspective of the third-world countries to identify why their interests lie in alternative development strategies."

Jan Kregel, Adjunct Professor, Ragnar Nurkse Department of Innovation and Governance, Taltech, Estonia

"Sensitive to history, especially the development of ideas, and fluent in several key European languages, Erik Reinert is surely the most thoughtful, original and prolific muse of the Other Canon of economic development theory in our times. This tome of his wide-ranging work addresses contemporary development challenges by creatively interrogating received theory, especially informing investment and technology policy."

JOMO Kwame Sundaram, Visiting Senior Fellow at Khazanah Research Institute, Visiting Fellow at the Initiative for Policy Dialogue, Columbia University, and Adjunct Professor at the International Islamic University in Malaysia

CONTENTS

INTRODUCTION

These volumes represent the second and last installment of my collected papers and chapters on economics. The first installment – *The Visionary Realism of German Economics. From the Thirty Years' War to the Cold War* – was published in 2019, also then kindly collected and edited by Prof. Rainer Kattel of the Institute for Innovation and Public Purpose, University College London.

¡Viva el tercer extremismo! was once the only text in a mail I received from a Latin American friend: 'long live the third extremism'. My friend and I are both what you can call children of the Cold War, born at its start in the late 1940s and spending many formative and active years under its reign until 1989. His point was that my form of extremism, instead of becoming a rigid ideology, was a rather extreme attention to historical facts and the tools and mechanisms they revealed. Indeed, I was very pleased when I found that an influential German economist, Gustav Schmoller, had referred to communism and what was to become neoliberalism as 'twins of an ahistorical rationalism'[1]. My 'extremism' was intended to be the opposite, hopefully a 'historical rationalism', which by necessity had to be more complex than the simplistic solutions of the 'ahistorical twins' which dominated the Cold War view.

With time, I found that several approaches qualified as not belonging to any of the 'ahistorical twins' that dominated Cold War economics. I came to think of these as 'reality economics', but a philosophical discussion started within the group around 'reality' and we decided to adopt the term *The Other Canon of Economics*: the study of the economy as a real object, not defined in terms of the adoption of core assumptions and techniques. The end of this introduction provides a comparison between standard economics and The Other Canon, listing many economists who have provided input to The Other Canon. A family tree of The Other Canon is found here http://othercanon.org/family-tree/

The beginning of the Cold War brought a massive theoretical contradiction to the surface. We could call it Marshall vs. Samuelson. On June 5, 1947, US secretary of state George Marshall presented what was originally called 'The European Recovery Plan', later the 'Marshall Plan'. His speech at Harvard that day contained some interesting theoretical insights:

1. Schmoller, Gustav, *Wechselnde Theorien und feststehende Wahrheiten im Gebiete der Staats- und Socialwirtschaften und die heutige deutsche Volkswirtschaftslehre,* Berlin, Büxenstein, 1897, p. 22. Downloadable on http://othercanon.org/papers/

> 'There is a phase of this matter which is both interesting and serious. The farmer has always produced the foodstuffs to exchange with the city dweller for the other necessities of life. *This division of labor is the basis of modern civilization.* At the present time it is threatened with breakdown. The town and city industries are not producing adequate goods to exchange with the food producing farmer' (my italics).[2]

Just one year later, in 1948, resurrecting David Ricardo's 1817 theory of international trade US economist Paul Samuelson in a paper in *The Economic Journal* introduced the theory of *factor-price equalization*:[3] That the prices of identical factors of production, such as the wage rate or the rent of capital, will be equalized across countries as a result of international trade.

In other words, George Marshall insisted that manufacturing industry was needed to build 'modern civilization', while Paul Samuelson – building on Ricardo's 1817 theory that was meant to keep England the only industrialized country in the word – insisted that it does not matter what you produce. Somewhat contradictory, even though Ricardo's trade theory became the core trade theory of capitalism, it does not contain capital as a factor of production! The children of the Cold War experienced that George Marshall's theory dominated in practice up until and including Spain's integration in the European Union in the 1980s, while Paul Samuelson's theory gradually completely took over in the textbooks in economics.

George Marshall and Paul Samuelson both received a Nobel Prize for their work: Marshall received the Nobel Peace Prize in 1953 and Paul Samuelson received the Prize in Economics in 1970, the second year it was awarded (rather 'Sveriges Riksbank Prize in Economic Sciences in Memory of Alfred Nobel').

The Wikipedia entry for 'factor-price equalization' states: 'an often-cited example of factor prize equalization is wages. When two countries enter a free trade agreement, wages for identical jobs in both countries tend to approach each other.'

Growing up in egalitarian Norway, I was first exposed to abject poverty in Peru at the age of 18. This was 20 years after Marshall's Harvard speech, but only much later did I understand that my initial inquiry as to economic development went right into the confrontation between George Marshall's and Paul Samuelson's disagreement from the late 1940s. I had been invited by the Peruvian government as a representative of the Norwegian secondary school students who – with their Nordic counterparts – received one day off from school to work collecting money for building schools in the Andes.

The people I observed in Lima – be it the people working at the airport, the bus drivers, the waiters, or the barbers – had the same technical equipment as their Norwegian counterparts and were equally efficient, but their wages were only a fraction – perhaps 20 per cent – of their Norwegian counterparts. The baggage handling at the Lima airport at the time was more technically advanced than the one in Oslo, and Lima had

---

2. https://www.oecd.org/general/themarshallplanspeechatharvarduniversity5june1947.htm (accessed May 2, 2023).
3. Samuelson, Paul A. (1948). 'International Trade and the Equalisation of Factor Prices', *Economic Journal*, June, pp. 163–184.

new German-made buses of the Büssing quality brand. There was, I would gradually conclude, no sign of what Samuelson had 'proved' with his version of David Ricardo: that wages for identical jobs tended to approach each other. On the contrary, what seemed to be the case was that the wage level in 'normal' jobs tended to be determined by the wages in the industrial sector with whom they shared their labour market. Despite this, Ricardian trade theory to this very day seems totally to dominate not only the education of economists, but also the economic policies determined by the Washington Institutions, the International Monetary Fund and the World Bank.

My simple question at the age of 18 was: Why are the wages of people who are equally efficient and working with the same quality equipment paid so differently? Why were the real wages of Norwegian bus drivers up to 20 times higher than their Peruvian counterparts? Only decades later I understood that George Marshall and his argument based on *synergies between qualitatively different economic activities* was the correct approach, not Paul Samuelson's.

In his 1817 *Principles of Economics* David Ricardo 'proved' (interestingly enough in a theory which did not contain capital) that the optimal solution for world income was if every nation specialized according to its comparative advantage, i.e. in the product it was *least inefficient* compared to its competitors. Figure 0.1 below shows how this term was hardly used during the first 100 years after its discovery, but its use exploded at the beginning of the Cold War. The most surprising – and in my view disturbing – element here is that the use of the term 'comparative advantage' peaks in the year 1990, with the collapse of the Berlin Wall and the end of the Cold War. Economists used the term 'comparative advantage' when there was an important demand for the West to 'prove' that capitalism was the superior system to communism. When communism had collapsed the use of this term rapidly declined. As everyone else, *the economics profession geared their production towards what the market demanded.*

I was personally first introduced to the importance of demand in the development of economic theory when I defended my Ph.D. thesis – *International Trade and the Economic Mechanisms of Underdevelopment* – in 1980. My main advisor – Tom Davis, an expert on

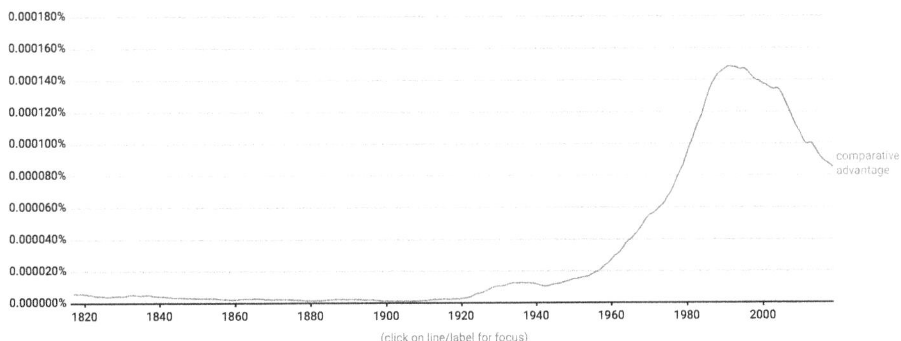

Figure 0.1 Frequency of the term 'comparative advantage' from 1817 until today. As is clearly shown the term was very little used for the first 100 years of existence, but the use of the term exploded with the start of the Cold War in the late 1940s.

Latin American economic history – explained to me that there was good news and there was bad news. The good news was that my theory provided an original and very important contribution to our understanding of poverty and underdevelopment. The bad news was that there was no demand for such a theory, so I would not get a job at a first-rate university. But, he said, since I also had an MBA from Harvard I would no doubt do well in life.

During my Ph.D. studies I had taken time to go through the history of economic thought searching for approaches that could satisfy my curiosity as to what determined the unequal development I had observed contrasting Peru with Western Europe. Based on my business experience and my MBA at Harvard I understood that economic activities were qualitatively different: what in neo-classical economics was called 'perfect competition' in business school language was called 'hostile markets'; a market a company ought to abandon. But what was the key factor determining the qualitative differences between economic activities? One day I found an 1804 reprint of one of the oldest economics books in the huge library at Cornell University: a book published in Naples in 1613 by a certain Antonio Serra.

Antonio Serra established two simple dichotomies in economics. The first one – the financial economy vs. the real economy – was there already in the Bible, where mammon represented the undesirable hoarding of unproductive money. The second dichotomy was new in 1613: the difference between economic activities subject to diminishing returns – where one factor of production is limited by nature (agriculture, mining and fisheries) – and activities without any such limit, where increasing returns would dominate. In nature-based activities, productivity increases would be limited to what John Stuart Mill had called 'a flexible wall' of diminishing returns.[4]

Using historical data, my thesis had shown that what had happened in Ecuador, Peru and Bolivia over the last decades, followed exactly what Antonio Serra had predicted in 1613. Nations specializing in diminishing returns activities would get poorer as they increased their specialization, because the cost of production would increase.[5] Back to Paul Samuelson: his de-facto promise that it did not matter what you produced became the *noble lie* of neo-classical economics. A *noble lie* was a term used by the Greeks for a myth, or a lie, knowingly propagated by an elite to maintain social harmony. During the Cold War communism promised 'from each according to his abilities' and 'to each according to his needs'. Neoliberalism could promise even more: everyone would become equally rich if only the market were allowed to take over. In its most extreme form, the result was *deadly truths* as 'bombing for democracy' became

4. '…a highly elastic and extensible band, which is hardly ever so violently stretched that it could not possibly be stretched any more, yet the pressure of which is felt long before the final limit is reached, and felt more severely the nearer that limit is approached.' Mill, John Stuart (1848), *Principles of Political Economy*, London: Parker, p. 177.

5. In a 2018 report on Chile, the country with the world's largest copper deposits, OECD reports that the mechanism identified by Antonio Serra is still at work there "…the fall of ore grades, which forces copper producers to process more ore to produce the same quantity of refined copper" (OECD Economic Surveys: Chile, February 2018, p. 43).

a reality, as in Iraq, Afghanistan and Somalia. Had the Western economics profession properly absorbed George Marshall's explanation of what defined Western Civilization, these extremely violent (and extremely costly) political blunders and many deaths would have been avoided.

The poverty I observed in Peru aroused my interest in the subject, to the extent that I soon was to spend a year there working for an international trade fair in Lima. One fortunate aspect was that when I subsequently studied economics – in Switzerland and in the United States – key professors had their education from before World War II: before Paul Samuelson had resurrected David Ricardo, when German – rather than mathematics – was the normal language requirement for US economics student, and when geography departments were still a standard feature at US universities.

When I asked them, important senior professors were only too happy to provide alternative trade theories, from that of Alexander Hamilton, the first US Secretary of the Treasury, and that of Frank Graham (1890–1949) among many other approaches. I found that if I had been born 100 years earlier than I was, my economic ideas would have been mainstream. That gave a certain hope that these less abstract theories could once again become mainstream, and with that abolish the poverty of the nations specialized in the production of natural resources with their diminishing returns and perfect competition (alias 'commodity competition')

The chapters in this volume are written over a period of 30 years. After having spent more than 20 years running my own industrial company – with branches in Italy, Finland and Norway – I sold the company in 1991 and went back to academia. My youthful intuition had been that the main problem with David Ricardo's 1817 trade theory was that all economic activities were treated as being qualitatively alike; represented by labour hours *void of any skills or qualifications.*

It seemed to me that when these same economists advised their own children they would follow a completely 'unprofessional' attitude. Economists do not say to their children: "My son, my daughter, observing your work at home it strikes me that you have a comparative advantage in washing dishes and making order in the kitchen. You should make a career in restaurant kitchens!" When advising their own children, economists envision hierarchies of skills, and they normally want them to make a career in prestigious professions, e.g. as medical doctors or lawyers. In private matters, economists understand that economically their children will do better as a mediocre lawyer in London than as London's most efficient dishwasher. Had they understood that, they might also have understood that a nation with a relatively inefficient manufacturing sector would be better off than one with no manufacturing sector at all.

We have decided to stick to the chronological sequence of the publications as the organizing principle of these volumes. This has the effect that the chapter best defining the history of The Other Canon only appears in Chapter 12. After having consulted the contrasting piece at the end of this introduction, the reader might want to read that chapter first.

In Chapter 1 of this book, I attempt to make a 'quality index' of economic activities from the point of view of a nation. At the 1993 conference where the paper was presented, I was worried what the reaction would be to such an heretic idea. However, at the conference I was pleasantly surprised by the positive reaction to this both from Stanford's Moses Abramovitz (1912–2000) and Sussex' Christopher Freeman (1921–2010), both of whom I very much respected. Backing up my conceptual 'quality index', I also used a 1942 graph from the US *National Bureau of Economic Research* ranking 51 different US industries in terms of change in physical output, number of wage earners employed and wage earners employed per unit of product (i.e. change in productivity) from 1899 to 1937. At that point I understood the old saying that there are two kinds of economics: measurement without theory and theory without measurement. I wanted to unite them.

Chapter 2 focuses on some trends in economics around 1990. There was a renewed interest in technology shown by OECD's TEP (Technology and Economy Programme), "new economic growth theory", and in the relationship trade and geography pioneered by Paul Krugman. We find that Krugman in two articles (1979 & 1980) had opened Pandora's box by including both increasing and diminishing returns in trade models but had been "sitting on the lid of the Pandora's box he opened" ever since. Again, the lack of demand seems to have prevented the further development of this model, which Krugman himself compares to that of traditional development economics, and even to Lenin's theory of imperialism.

When I studied at Harvard, my professor of history of economic thought was Arthur Smithies (1907–1981) who had probably been the closest friend Joseph Schumpeter (1883–1950) had at Harvard, and who also wrote his obituary.[6] Contrary to the intention of the faculty, Smithies' course almost entirely focussed on the theories of Schumpeter. Although my interest was underdevelopment, studying Schumpeter indirectly provided me with a new angle of development: nations where Schumpeter's creative destruction did not take place. This is the essence of Chapter 3. Later, when writing my Ph.D. thesis on Antonio Serra, I was pleased to find that according to Schumpeter, Antonio Serra: '..must, I think, be credited with having been the first to compose a scientific treatise, though an unsystematic one, on Economic Principles and Policy'.[7]

'Competitiveness' became one of the new buzzwords of economics in the 1990s, hotly contested by several mainstream economists. Chapter 4 analyzes the concept, which makes much sense at Harvard Business School where it originated, but is fundamentally incompatible with the core assumptions of neo-classical economics.

Chapter 5 returns to one of the key factors from my thesis: what specializing on diminishing returns activities means in practice, especially because these activities almost by definition are in conflict with the need for *sustainability*, a problem which was becoming important at the time. Chapter 6 is a brief piece contrasting Ricardian economics – fairly called 'the dismal science' – and the possibility of a 'never-ending frontier of knowledge' which was envisioned by President Eisenhower's science advisor Vannevar Bush. Where to apply the pessimistic and where the optimistic version?

6. *The American Economic Review*, Vol. 40, No. 4 (September 1950), pp. 628–648.
7. Schumpeter, Joseph (1954), *History of Economic Analysis* (1954), New York: Oxford University Press, p. 195.

Contrasting 'production capitalism' and 'financial capitalism' was the purpose of Chapter 7, produced for a 1998 conference. We have decided to include the extensive bibliography produced for the conference. Much of this literature, perhaps particularly the unique – but largely forgotten – theories of finance that originated between 1920 and the 1940s should be of interesting to today's scholars.

Chapter 8 originated at a 2000 meeting in Mongolia's capital Ulaanbaatar, to which I had been invited by the government. It shows the dramatic effects of the heavy de-industrialization to which Mongolia had been subject since the Fall of the Berlin Wall. Since then, Mongolia has been doing better, but countries like Ukraine and Georgia are poorer today than they were under communism. Chapter 9 contrasts the Morgenthau Plan – a 1943 plan to de-industrialize Germany as a punishment for having started the war – with the Marshall Plan in order to explain the mechanisms expanding the gap between wealthy and poor countries.

Starting in the 1990s, the concept of National Innovation Systems,[8] had become popular. In Chapter 10, with our youngest son Sophus, we analyzed Antonio Serra's 1613 work in this framework. Sophus had edited the first-ever English translation of Serra.[9] In Chapter 11 we extended this perspective in a paper for the 1st Globelics Conference, held in Rio de Janeiro in 2003, to a broader theoretical and historical framework on uneven development.

In Chapter 12, with Arno Daastøl, my 'extremism' is described: the production-based and fact-based Other Canon of economic theory, and its contrast with barter-based British economic theory presently expressed in mathematics. Chapter 13 is a case study of the Dutch Republic from 1500 to 1750, showing – using contemporary sources – how the goal of other European countries was to emulate the successful economic strategy of the Dutch.

Chapter 14 is another chapter written with Sophus Reinert, who is now a tenured professor at Harvard. Christopher Freeman had brought the idea of National Innovation Systems back to German economist Friedrich List (1789–1846),[10] in this chapter we analyze the Schumpeterian dynamics of capitalism as an innovation system even further back into the so-called mercantilist period.

Chapter 15 is a paper written for the United Nations on the problem of balancing aid and development assistance to prevent what Canadian anthropologist Robert Paine called 'welfare colonialism',[11] a system where the colonial dependence of ethnic groups still exists, but with the flow of funds being reversed.

---

8. Lundvall, Bengt-Åke, ed. (1992). *National systems of innovation: toward a theory of innovation and interactive learning*, London: Pinter, and Nelson, Richard R., ed. (1993). *National innovation systems: a comparative analysis.* New York: Oxford University Press,
9. Serra, Antonio [1613] (2011) *A short treatise on the wealth and poverty of nations*, Sophus A. Reinert, ed., London: Anthem.
10. Freeman, Christopher (1995). 'The "National System of Innovation" in historical perspective'. *Cambridge Journal of Economics*: Volume 19, Issue 1, February 1995, Pp. 5–24.
11. Paine, Robert (1977). *The White Arctic: anthropological essays on tutelage and ethnicity.* Institute of Social and Economic Research, Memorial University of Newfoundland. pp. 7–29.

The first chapter in volume 2, Chapter 16, continues on the fate of ethnic groups, in this case the Saami reindeer herders of Northern Norway. I had studied pre-capitalist economies at Cornell under the well-known anthropologist John Murra (1916–2006) and obtained an Adjunct Professorship in Reindeer Economics at the Saami University College in Kautokeino, Norway. The chapter describes the obstacles the Norwegian government put in the way of the reindeer herders.

Chapter 17 – commissioned by the EU Joint Research Center in Seville – extends the geographical perspective to the problems of European Union integration, focusing on what I had previously called a Schumpeterian icing (or rhetoric) on a thoroughly neo-classical cake (theory). These problems would later become more serious within the EU.

Chapter 18 – commissioned by the UNU World Institute for Development Economics Research (UNU-WIDER) in Helsinki – focusses on different schools of institutional economics and how they have handled uneven development.

Chapter 19, written with my editor Rainer Kattel, takes a rather grim view on how the abrupt integration of the former communist countries of Eastern Europe into world trade and the European Union has damaged the industrial structure of these countries.

Chapter 20 grew out my keynote speech at a conference on failed states organized by UNIDO (United Nations Industrial Development Organization) at their Vienna head-quarters. Rainer Kattel and Yves Ekoué Amaïzo, at the time an UNIDO employee, are my co-authors.

Chapter 21 takes a sweeping look at the history of economic *policy* (as opposed to the history of economic *thought*) and finds that economically successful countries had started by emulating economically successful countries (as shown in Chapter 13 with Holland) before they – once a manufacturing industry had been successfully established – would turn (with important exceptions) to the 'comparative advantage' that had been created in the process of emulation.

Chapter 22 – also commissioned by the UN Department of Social and Economic Affairs – looks at important turning points in the history of economic thought. One such year was 1848, when Ricardian economics was defeated for the first time. Standard economics came under attack that year not only by Marx – who had fled to England – with his 'Communist Manifesto', by the important English liberal John Stuart Mill who insisted that all countries needed 'infant industry protection' to become wealthy, but also by German economist Bruno Hildebrand who was so con-servative he had to flee to Switzerland.

Chapter 23, written with Rainer Kattel and Margit Suurna, takes a new look at the fate of the central and Eastern European countries since 1990.

Chapter 24 presents the dynamics of capitalism as understood at Harvard Business School, in connection with the 100th anniversary of that school.

Chapter 25, describing the economic destruction caused by neo-classical economics, was first published in Russian.

Chapter 26, with Rainer Kattel, follows up with a historical analysis of Russian economic history where successful periods of industrialization were created (1) by Peter the Great (1672–1725) – who spent much time studying the Dutch economy – and (2) by Sergei Witte (1849–1915), minister of finance under the last two Tsars, who recommended Russia to follow the theories of Friedrich List. His pro-industrial policy became the theory and policy adopted by the Soviet Regime. This chapter was simultaneously published in Moscow in Russian and English.

Chapter 27 – written for a conference at the Social Science Center in Berlin (WZB) – continues the analysis of the mechanisms creating the cyclicality in economic theories.

Chapters 28 and 29 look at economic theory from the point-of-view of the Norwegian-American economist Thorstein Veblen (1857–1929). With his family's roots in rural Norway – a country with no feudalism – chapter 28 analyzes Veblen's economic ideas, while chapter 29 compares 'economic greed' as understood by Veblen and by neoliberalism.

In chapter 30 Kattel and I look at the non-financial origins of what was normally analyzed as a financial crisis in the Baltic countries.

Chapter 31, written with Australian economist John Mathews, looks at sustainability and 'green growth' from the perspective of Antonio Serra and his followers: also in the energy sector increasing returns is a key element in order to achieve sustainability.

Chapter 32 compares the handling of the financial crisis in the United States in the 1930s, under Marriner Eccles as chairman of the Federal Reserve (1934–1948), with the handling of the latest financial crisis in Europe under Mario Draghi as head of the European Central Bank (2011–2019). It is argued that while Eccles achieved a good balance between the interests of financial capital and the real economy, Draghi to a large extent favoured the financial sector.

Chapter 33 addresses the growing inequalities that have been the result of neoclassical/neo-liberal economics as it developed during the Cold War. The final chapter 34 represents a thorough historical overview of industrial policy published in Oxford Handbook of Industrial Policy.

Another economist who has inspired me was my economics professor at Cornell in the late 1970s, Jaroslav Vanek (1930–2017). Born in Czechoslovakia, Vanek studied at Sorbonne in Paris and at the University of Geneva, receiving his Ph.D. in economics at MIT. He made important contributions to the international trade theory with the so-called Heckscher-Ohlin-Vanek theorem. Vanek was an inspiring professor also because of his strong ethics based on his Catholic faith. He introduced his students to Brazilian sociologist Gilberto Freyre and his *Pedagogy of the Oppressed* (1970) and to Iván Illich and his books *Deschooling Society* (1971) and *Tools for Conviviality* (1973). He taught us 'the other's shoe principle', that it was a human necessity to put oneself in the other person's situation.

One day – when Vanek had already passed 40 – he woke up to the fact that the trade theory he had worked on for years locked many poor countries into their 'comparative advantage' in being poor. He felt that he himself had contributed to the problem, and started writing academic articles proving the errors in his previous contributions to economics. Again I observed the demand factor at work in economics. When Vanek, the famous trade theorist, wrote theories that were not demanded by the Cold War 'conspiracy', his articles were only published in unknown journals in India, where there was indeed a demand for explanation of poverty.

I got to know Vanek well, also working for him as an interpreter during one of his visits to Peru working on his labour-managed systems. His idea was that the Ricardian trade theory was like a case of 'The Emperor's New Clothes': an uncorrupted soul would reveal that 'Emperor Ricardo' was naked. Swedish economist Gunnar Myrdal had similar ideas: this irrational economic theory could not last.

After finishing my thesis in 1980, I noted a professional academic loneliness that reminded me of Vanek's. I seemed to disagree with present economic theory both right and left. My friends observed that I appeared to be a 'necrophile' economist, all economists who agreed with me had been long dead. It was therefore natural to start collecting old economics books written by people who to a large extent agreed with me. During my studies at Harvard from 1974 to 1976, my wife Fernanda– a recent graduate of the Norwegian School of Library Science – worked at the Kress Library at Harvard Business School, a library specializing in economics books published before 1850. This was the library where Joseph Schumpeter had spent the war years, and which he called 'a scholar's paradise'. Ken Carpenter, Fernanda's boss, had been commissioned by the director of the HBS libraries to establish a list of historically bestselling economics books, defined as books that had been published in 10 editions or more before 1850. In 1975 an exhibition was held, showing the 40 bestselling books that fulfilled the requirements.[12]

Before the age of internet, Carpenter had invested much time and effort corresponding with academic libraries across the world to obtain data on books. When Carpenter retired, he transferred his notes to Fernanda and myself, and we continued his work. In 2017, we had arrived at 80 bestsellers fulfilling his criteria.[13] At the moment we are at 102 bestsellers, and preparing a book with our findings. This work will illustrate both the diversity and the changing and contrasting fashions through which the profession has passed. What is notable with the 102 economic bestsellers over almost 500 years is how economic activities vary in their level of abstraction. From the point of view of explaining uneven growth, accuracy is achieved at the cost of irrelevance. Schumpeter described this trade-off between accuracy and relevance very well: 'The general reader will have to make up his mind, whether he wants simple answers to his questions or useful ones – in this as in other economic matters he cannot have both.'[14] A high level of abstraction – as in neo-classical economics – in reality becomes an instrument of rent-seeking for the leading countries, an instrument for 'kicking away the ladder' for

---

12. Carpenter, Kenneth E., The Economic Bestsellers before 1850. A Catalogue of an Exhibition prepared for the History of Economics Society Meeting, May 21–25, at Baker Library, *Bulletin # 11, May 1975, of the Kress Library of Business and Economics, Harvard Business School.* Downloadable on www.othercanon.org
13. Reinert, Erik S., Ken Carpenter, Fernanda Reinert & Sophus A. Reinert (2017) '80 Economic Bestsellers before 1850: A Fresh Look at the History of Economic Thought' (with Kenneth Carpenter, Fernanda Reinert & Sophus Reinert), The Other Canon Foundation and Tallinn University of Technology Working Papers in Technology Governance and Economic Dynamics, No. 74. Downloadable on http://technologygovernance.eu/eng/the_core_faculty/working_papers/
14. Schumpeter in the introduction to Zeuthen, F., *Problems of Monopoly and Welfare*, London: Routledge, 1930, p. x (10).

latecomer nations. The language of mathematics thus easily becomes an instrument of rent-seeking. More than 25 years ago I remarked at a conference that explaining mathematics in economics is analogue to writing a thesis on snow in Swahili. My understanding is that Swahili has one word for snow, while one of my colleagues at Saami University College in Kautokeino in her thesis identified more than 300 words for snow in Saami, expressing the knowledge needed by reindeer herders in sometimes extreme Arctic climates.

The British economics tradition of Adam Smith and David Ricardo was based on barter and trade rather than on production. Not without reason German economists would criticize English-language economics for consisting of 'qualitätslose Grössen': concepts void of any qualities. Earlier in this introduction we observed how David Ricardo took for granted that all labour hours involved in international trade would be void of any qualities. One reason that such equality could be taken for granted may have been the efforts Adam Smith had put into this in his 1776 *Wealth of Nations*, where his insistence that more knowledge does not create higher wages today stands out as remarkable. Says Smith: 'Put your son apprentice to a shoemaker, there is little doubt of his learning to make a pair of shoes; But send him to study the law, it is at least twenty to one if he ever makes such proficiency as will enable him to live by the business.' He immediately continues: 'In a perfectly fair lottery, those who draw the prizes ought to gain all that is lost by those who draw the blanks.'[15]

Given this theoretical background from Smith's 1776 work it becomes more explicable that David Ricardo in 1817 makes manufacturing industry qualitatively equal to agriculture. This logical failure is the most devastating mistake made in the history of economics – it explains why so many countries stay poor – but at least it explains us how the 'equality assumption' was created already by Adam Smith. Today, the official policy of the Washington Institutions – the International Monetary Fund and the World Bank – is still dictating free trade to the poor countries that are more or less forced to accept their advice, while world powers like the United States, the European Union and China are tailoring increasingly sophisticated industrial policy for their own use. In a sense we are again in a de-facto colonial system: the economic core employs very selective policies, but the poor periphery is forced to employ so-called 'free trade'.

With the fall of the Berlin Wall, an unexpected window of opportunity opened for somebody, like Vanek and me, who were ideologically equidistant from communism and neoliberalism. The first World Bank economist who came on a mission to Estonia after the Cold War argued that the country would have a 'comparative advantage' in something that did not require higher education, so Estonia ought to close its universities. The Estonians, who had their first university in 1632 and since 1960 had been home for the Soviet Institute of Cybernetics, were not amused. A German colleague,

15. Smith, Adam, *Wealth of Nations* (1776), Chicago: University of Chicago Press, 1976, p. 118. The counterintuitive assumptions backing Smith's view on the equality of the professions are discussed in the Introduction to Reinert, Erik S. and Ingrid H. Kvangraven (eds.) *A Modern Guide to Uneven Economic Development*, Cheltenham: Edward Elgar, 2023, pp. 1–17.

Wolfgang Drechsler, was already in Estonia when I started teaching at Tallinn University of Technology in 2004, later becoming Professor of Technology Governance and Development Strategies. Under the leadership of Rainer Kattel our department was later named The Ragnar Nurkse Department of Innovation and Governance, after the Estonian pioneer development economist Ragnar Nurkse (1907–1959). Lately I have also found refuge as Guest Researcher at the Centre for the Study of the Sciences and the Humanities at the University of Bergen, and as an Honorary Professor at The Institute for Innovation and Public Purpose with Mariana Mazzucato and her colleagues at University College London.

According to my wife, who keeps track of this, my academic (and business) activities have taken me to 72 different countries for work. In addition, there are several countries we have only visited as tourists. With my Harvard Business School background, I subconsciously see each country as a case study. Drawing on the observations of all the case studies, in 2007 I published an English version of *How Rich Countries Got Rich... and Why Poor Countries Stay Poor.* According to NORLA, the association subsidizing the translation of Norwegian books, this book has been published in 25 different languages. It has been reprinted both in Chinese and Russian several times, but there are editions also in more exotic languages. Very soon there was a translation into Farsi, in Iran, and later into Serbian, Georgian, Arabic, Bahasa Malaysia, and presently a translation into Kreyól (Haiti) is being prepared. The government official who organized the conference in Mongolia later became his country's Ambassador to Cuba, and used part of his time there to translate my book into Mongolian. Relatively greatest has been the success in Ukraine, with two different translations and three different editions.

The present volumes include what in many cases has been the raw materials for *How Rich Countries Got Rich... and Why Poor Countries Stay Poor.* In addition to my editor Rainer Kattel, I would like to thank my other co-authors to the chapters in this book (in alphabetical order): Yves Ekoué Amaïzo, Arno Mong Daastøl, John Mathews, Sophus A. Reinert, Vemund Riiser and Margit Suurna. As usual my biggest debt is to Fernanda Aars Reinert, my wife, muse, librarian and proof reader for the last 50 years.

The original publication data for the chapters in this book is as follows:

Chapter 1. 'Catching-up from Way Behind - A Third World Perspective on First World History' in Fagerberg, Jan, Bart Verspagen and Nick von Tunzelmann (eds.) *The Dynamics of Technology, Trade, and Growth,* Aldershot, Edward Elgar, 1994, pp. 168–197, and as *Fremtek-Notat* No. 8/93, Royal Norwegian Council for Scientific and Industrial Research, Oslo.

Chapter 2. 'Recent Trends in Economic Theory - Implications for Development Geography' (with Vemund Riiser). *STEP Report,* Studies in Technology, Innovation and Economic Policy, Oslo, No. 12/94 and in Hesselberg, Jan (ed.) *Development Geography,* University of Oslo, Department of Human Geography, 1994. Vol. 1, pp. 1–18.

Chapter 3. 'A Schumpeterian Theory of Underdevelopment - A Contradiction in Terms?' *STEP Report* No. 15/1994 and as 'Symptoms and causes of poverty:

Underdevelopment in a Schumpeterian system' in *Forum for Development Studies*, Nr. 1-2, 1994, Norwegian Institute of International Affairs (NUPI), Oslo, pp. 73–109.

Chapter 4. 'Competitiveness and Its Predecessors – A 500-year Cross-national Perspective' in *Structural Change and Economic Dynamics*, Vol. 6, 1995, pp. 23–42. Special Issue on 'Changes in Long-term Competitiveness. A Historical Perspective', *STEP Report* No. 3, 1994. Also published in Brazil in *Arché Interdisciplinar,* Universidade Cândido Mendes Ipanema (UCAM), Rio de Janeiro, Vol VI, No. 15, 1997, pp. 5–34. Spanish translation: 'El concepto de "competitividad" y sus predecesores', *Socialismo y Participacion,* No. 72, Lima, Peru, December 1995, pp. 21–41.

Chapter 5. 'Diminishing Returns and Economic Sustainability: The Dilemma of Resource-based Economies under a Free Trade Regime' in Hansen, Stein, Jan Hesselberg and Helge Hveem (eds.) *International Trade Regulation, National Development Strategies and the Environment: Towards Sustainable Development?,* Oslo, Centre for Development and the Environment, University of Oslo, 1996, pp. 119–150.

Chapter 6. 'Economics: '*The Dismal Science*' or '*The Never-ending Frontier of Knowledge*'?. On Technology, Energy, and Economic Welfare' in *Norwegian Oil Review,* Vol. 22, No. 7, 1996, pp. 18–31.

Chapter 7. 'Production Capitalism vs. Financial Capitalism – Symbiosis and Parasitism'. An Evolutionary Perspective and Bibliography (with Arno Daastøl), *The Other Canon Foundation and Tallinn University of Technology Working Papers in Technology Governance and Economic Dynamics,* No 36, 2011. (Original 1998).

Chapter 8. 'Globalization in the Periphery as a Morgenthau Plan: The Underdevelopment of Mongolia in the 1990s' in Lhagva, Sakhia, *Mongolian Development Strategy; Capacity Building,* Ulaanbaatar, Mongolian Development Research Center, 2000, pp. 82–143. Also published in Reinert, Erik (ed.), *Globalization, Economic Development and Inequality: An Alternative Perspective,* Cheltenham, Edward Elgar, 2004, pp. 157–214.

Chapter 9. 'Increasing Poverty in a Globalized World: *Marshall Plans* and *Morgenthau Plans* as Mechanisms of Polarization of World Incomes' in Chang, Ha-Joon (ed.), *Rethinking Economic Development,* London, Anthem, 2003, pp. 453–478.

Chapter 10. 'An Early National Innovation System: The Case of Antonio Serra's 1613 *Breve Trattato*' (with Sophus Reinert) in *Institutions and Economic Development/ Istituzioni e Sviluppo Economico,* Vol. 1, No. 3, 2003, pp. 87–119.

Chapter 11. 'Innovation Systems of the Past: Modern Nation-States in a Historical Perspective. The Role of Innovations and of Systemic Effects in Economic Thought and Policy' (with Sophus Reinert). Paper prepared for the 1st Globelics Conference, Rio de Janeiro, November 2003, published in conference volume on CD-ROM and later the internet.

Chapter 12. 'The Other Canon: The History of Renaissance Economics. Its Role as an Immaterial and Production-based Canon in the History of Economic Thought and in the History of Economic Policy' (with Arno Daastøl). In Reinert, Erik (ed.), *Globalization, Economic Development and Inequality: An Alternative Perspective,* Cheltenham, Edward Elgar, 2004, pp. 21–70.

Chapter 13. 'Benchmarking Success: The Dutch Republic (1500–1750) as Seen by Contemporary European Economists'. SUM , Centre for Development and the Environment, University of Oslo. Working paper No. 1, 2004. Published as 'Emulating Success: Contemporary Views of the Dutch Economy before 1800', in Gelderblom, Oscar (editor), *The Political Economy of the Dutch Republic*, Aldershot, Ashgate, 2009, pp. 19–40.

Chapter 14. 'Mercantilism and Economic Development: Schumpeterian Dynamics, Institution Building and International Benchmarking' (with Sophus Reinert) in Jomo, K. S. and Erik S. Reinert (eds.) *Origins of Development Economics*, London, Zed Publications/New Delhi, Tulika Books, 2005, pp. 1–23. Published in Brazil with Portuguese abstract, *Oikos*, Vol. 10, No. 1, 2011, pp. 8–37.

Chapter 15. 'Development and Social Goals: Balancing Aid and Development to Prevent 'Welfare Colonialism' in *Post-autistic economics review*, issue no. 30, 21 March 2005, article 1, Complete version: United Nation Department of Social Affairs, DESA Working Paper No. 14, 2006, and in Ocampo, Jose Antonio, Jomo K. S. and Sarbuland Khan (eds.), *Policy Matters: Economic And Social Policies to Sustain Equitable Development*, Hyderabad, India: Orient Longman; London and New York: Zed Books; Penang, Malaysia: Third World Network. Published in association with the United Nations, 2006, pp. 192–221.

Chapter 16. 'The Economics of Reindeer Herding: Saami Entrepreneurship between Cyclical Sustainability and the Powers of State and Oligopolies', *British Food Journal*, Vol. 108, No. 7, 2006, pp. 522–540.

Chapter 17. 'European Integration, Innovations and Uneven Economic Growth: Challenges and Problems of EU 2005', Paper prepared for FISTERA (Foresight on Information Society Technologies in the European Research Area), in Compañó, R., C. Pascu, A. Bianchi, J.-C. Burgelman, S. Barrios, M. Ulbrich, I. Maghiros (eds.), *The Future of the Information Society in Europe: Contributions to the debate*, Seville, Spain, European Commission, Directorate General Joint Research Centre. Institute for Prospective Technological Studies (IPTS), 2006, pp. 124–152.

Chapter 18. 'Institutionalism Ancient, Old and New: A Historical Perspective on Institutions and Uneven Development'. Research Paper No. 2006/77, United Nations University, WIDER, Helsinki. Abbreviated version in Chang, Ha-Joon (ed.), *Institutional Change and Economic Development*, Tokyo, United Nations University Press & London, Anthem, 2007, pp. 53–72.

Chapter 19. 'European Eastern Enlargement as Europe's Attempted Economic Suicide?', with Rainer Kattel, *The Other Canon Foundation and Tallinn University of Technology Working Papers in Technology Governance and Economic Dynamics*, WP No. 14, 2007.

Chapter 20. 'The Economics of Failed, Failing and Fragile States: Productive Structure as the Missing Link', with Yves Ekoué Amaïzo and Rainer Kattel, *The Other Canon Foundation and Tallinn University of Technology Working Papers in Technology Governance and Economic Dynamics*, No 18, 2009. In Kahn, Shahrukh Rafi & Jens Christiansen, *Towards New Developmentalism: Market as Means Rather Than Master*, London, Routledge, 2010, pp. 59–86. A different version published as 'State Failure, Poverty and Productive Structure', in Mutis, Alicia Puyana and Samwel Ong'wen Okuro (eds.), *Strategies against Poverty. Designs from the North and Alternatives from the South*, Buenos Aires, CLACSO, 2011, pp. 325–347.

Chapter 21. 'Emulation vs. Comparative Advantage: Competing and Complementary Principles in the History of Economic Policy'. In Cimoli, Mario, Giovanni Dosi and Joseph Stiglitz (eds), *Industrial Policy and Development; The Political Economy of Capabilities Accumulation,* Oxford University Press, 2009, pp. 79–106

Chapter 22. 'The Terrible Simplifiers: Common Origins of Financial Crises and Persistent Poverty in Economic Theory and the New '1848 Moment', United Nations Department of Economic and Social Affairs, DESA Working Paper No. 88, December 2009, and in Jomo K.S. and Anis Chowdhury, *Poor Poverty. The Impoverishment of Analysis, Measurement and Policies,* London, Bloomsbury in association with The United Nations, 2011, pp. 11–37. Spanish translation: 'Los terribles simplificadores: orígenes comunes de la crisis financiera y la persistencia de la pobreza en la teoría económica y el nuevo 'momento 1848', *Revista de Trabajo,* Buenos Aires, Vol. 5 No. 7, July-December 2009, pp. 17–47

Chapter 23. 'Industrial Restructuring and Innovation Policy in Central and Eastern Europe since 1990', (with Rainer Kattel, and Margit Suurna). *The Other Canon Foundation and Tallinn University of Technology Working Papers in Technology Governance and Economic Dynamics,* No 23, 2009.

Chapter 24. 'Capitalist Dynamics. A Technical Note', Technical Note produced for the 100th Anniversary of Harvard Business School, September 2008. *The Other Canon Foundation and Tallinn University of Technology Working Papers in Technology Governance and Economic Dynamics,* No 26, 2009.

Chapter 25. 'Neo-Classical Economics: A Trail of Economic Destruction', in Russian, *Ekspert Magazine,* Moscow, No. 1, 2010, pp. 12–17. Enlarged English version: 'Neo-classical economics: A trail of economic destruction since the 1970s', real-world economics review, issue no. 60, 20 June 2012, pp. 2–17,

Chapter 26. 'Modernizing Russia: Round III. Russia and the Other BRIC countries: Forging Ahead, Catching Up or Falling Behind?', with Rainer Kattel. *The Other Canon Foundation and Tallinn University of Technology Working Papers in Technology Governance and Economic Dynamics,* No 32, 2010. Report for Global Policy Forum 'The Modern State: Standards of Democracy and Criteria of Efficiency', Yaroslavl, Russia, September 9–10, 2010. In *Modernization of the Russian Economy: from Theory to Practice,* pp. 2–33. Published in Russian and English, Moscow, 2010.

Chapter 27. 'Economics and the Public Sphere: The Rise of Esoteric Knowledge, Refeudalization, Crisis and Renewal', Paper presented for *The Public Mission of the Social Sciences and Humanities: Transformation and Renewal,* Social Science Research Center, Berlin (WZB). Published on the web by the Social Science Research Council, and by *The Other Canon Foundation Tallinn University of Technology,* WP 40, 2012. French translation: 'Economie et sphère publique: la montée en puissance du savoir ésorétique, le retour de la féodalité, la crise et le renouveau', in *Perspectives libres,* No 6, 2012, pp. 113–149. Special issue 'La crise de l'idéologie global'.

Chapter 28. 'Three Veblenian Contexts: Valdres, Norway and Europe; Filiations of Economics; and Economics for an Age of Crises', in Reinert & Viano, *Thorstein Veblen: Economist for an Age of Crises,* London, Anthem (The Anthem Other Canon Series), 2012, pp. 17–50.

Chapter 29. 'Civilizing Capitalism: "Good" and "Bad" Greed from the Enlightenment to Thorstein Veblen', *real-world economics review*, issue no. 63, 25 March 2013, pp. 57–72,

Chapter 30. 'Failed and Asymmetrical Integration: Eastern Europe and the Non-financial Origins of the European Crisis', with Rainer Kattel. *The Other Canon Foundation and Tallinn University of Technology Working Papers in Technology Governance and Economic Dynamics*, No. 49, 2013 and in Sommers, Jeffrey & Charles Wolfson (eds.), *The Contradictions of Austerity. The Socio-Economic Costs of the Neoliberal Baltic Model*, London, Routledge, 2014, pp. 64–86.

Chapter 31. 'Renewables, Manufacturing and Green Growth: Energy Strategies Based on Capturing Increasing Returns', with John Mathews, in *Futures*, Vol. 61, 2014, pp. 13-22.

Chapter 32. 'Financial Crises and Countermovements. Comparing the Times and Attitudes of Marriner Eccles (1930s) and Mario Draghi (2010s)', in Dimitri Papadimitriou (ed.), *Festschrift to Jan A. Kregel*, London, Routledge, 2014, pp. 319-344.

Chapter 33. 'The Inequalities That Could Not Happen: What the Cold War Did to Economics', in real-world economics review, No. 92, June 2020. Also as chapter 13 in Fullbrook, Edward & Jamie Morgan, *The Inequality Crisis*, World Economic Association Books, Bristol UK, 2020, pp. 387-430.

Chapter 34. 'Industrial Policy: A Long-term Perspective and Overview of Theoretical Arguments', in Arkebe Oqubay, Christopher Cramer, Ha-Joon Chang, and Richard Kozul-Wright (eds.), *The Oxford Handbook of Industrial Policy*, Oxford, Oxford University Press, 2020, pp. 319–344.

Two different ways of understanding the economic world & the wealth and poverty of nations.

STARTING POINT FOR THE STANDARD CANON:	*STARTING POINT FOR 'THE OTHER CANON':*
Equilibrium under perfect information and *perfect foresight*	Learning and decision-making under uncertainty (Joseph Schumpeter, John Maynard Keynes, George Shackle)
High level of abstraction	Level of abstraction chosen according to problem to be resolved
Man's wit and will absent	Moving force: *Geist- und Willenskapital:* Man's wit and will, entrepreneurship
Not able to handle *novelty* as an endogenous phenomenon	*Novelty* as a central moving force
Moving force: 'capital per se propels the capitalist engine'	Moving force: New knowledge which creates a demand for capital to be provided from the financial sector
Metaphors from the realm of physics	Metaphors (carefully) from the realm of biology
Mode of understanding:	Mode of understanding:
Mechanistic ('begreifen')	Qualitative ('verstehen'), a type of understanding irreducible only to numbers and symbols
Matter	*Geist* precedes matter

(*Continued*)

(Continued)

STARTING POINT FOR THE STANDARD CANON:	*STARTING POINT FOR 'THE OTHER CANON':*
Focused on *Man the Consumer* Adam Smith: 'Men are animals which have learned to barter'	Focused on *Man the Innovator and Producer.* Abraham Lincoln: 'Men are animals which not only work, but innovate'
Focused on static/comparative static	Focused on change (a movie of the world)
Not cumulative/history absent	Cumulative causations/'history matters'/backwash effects (Gunnar Myrdal, Nicholas Kaldor, Joseph Schumpeter, German Historical School)
Increasing returns to scale and its absence a non-essential feature	Increasing returns and its absence essential to explaining differences in income between firms, regions and nations (Nicholas Kaldor)
Very precise ('would rather be accurately wrong than approximately correct')	Aiming at relevance over precision, recognizes the *trade-off between relevance and precision* as a core issue in the profession (Joseph Schumpeter)
'Perfect competition' (commodity competition/price competition) as an ideal situation = a goal for society	Innovation- and knowledge-driven Schumpeterian competition as both engine of progress and ideal situation. With perfect competition, with equilibrium and no innovation, capital becomes worthless (Joseph Schumpeter, Friedrich von Hayek)
The market as a mechanism for setting prices	The market also as an arena for rivalry and as a mechanism selecting between different products and different solutions. (Joseph Schumpeter, Richard Nelson & Sidney Winter)
Equality Assumption I: No diversity	Diversity as a key factor (Joseph Schumpeter, George Shackle)
Equality Assumption II: All economic activities are *alike* and *of equal quality* as carriers of economic growth and welfare	Growth and welfare are *activity-specific* – different economic activities present widely different potentials for absorbing new knowledge
Both theory and policy recommendations tend to be *independent of context* ('one medicine cures all')	Both theory and policy recommendations highly *context dependent*
The economy largely independent from society	The economy as firmly embedded in society
Technology as a *free good*, as 'manna from heaven'	Knowledge and technology are *produced*, have cost and are protected. This production is based on incentives of the system, including law, institutions and policies
Equilibrating forces at the core of the system and of the theory	Cumulative forces are more important than equilibrating ones, and should therefore be at the core of the system
Economics as *Harmonielehre* I: An unregulated market will cause factor-price equalization – all wages globally will tend towards equality	The natural tendency of the market is to enlarge already existing differences (Gunnar Myrdal, Nicholas Kaldor)
Economics as *Harmonielehre* II: The economy as a self-regulating system seeking equilibrium and harmony	Economics as an inherently unstable and conflict-rich discipline. Achieving stability is based on Man's policy measures (Henry Carey, Karl Polanyi, Max Weber, John Maynard Keynes)

(*Continued*)

(Continued)

STARTING POINT FOR THE STANDARD CANON:	*STARTING POINT FOR 'THE OTHER CANON':*
Postulates the representative firm	No 'representative firm'. All firms are unique (Edith Penrose)
Static optimum. Perfect rationality	Dynamic optimization under uncertainty. Bounded rationality
No distinction made between real economy and financial economy	Conflicts between real economy and financial economy are normal and must be regulated (Hyman Minsky, John Maynard Keynes)
Saving caused by refraining from consumption and a cause of growth	Saving largely results from profits (Joseph Schumpeter) and saving *per se* is not useful or desirable for growth (John Maynard Keynes)

Chapter 1

CATCHING-UP FROM WAY BEHIND. A THIRD WORLD PERSPECTIVE ON FIRST WORLD HISTORY[1]

Schumpeter once said that 'the upper strata of society are like hotels which are ... always full of people, but people who are forever changing' (Schumpeter 1934: 156).[2] It is tempting to use the same metaphor on nations. Taking a long view, many nations have in sequence joined the upper strata hotel: Britain, the United States, Germany, Japan and others. Once there, however, they have tended to stay. The country occupying the best suites has changed, but all who ever moved into the hotel, still – compared to the Third World – 'constitute "the rich", a class ... who are removed from life's battles', to continue quoting Schumpeter on this issue (Schumpeter 1934: 156). These countries, however, are the home of only a minority of the world population.

The last 10 years have brought about a changing perspective on how economic growth actually happens. This improved understanding, however, has mainly evolved around the countries which are already living in Schumpeter's upper strata hotel – the Triad of Europe, Japan and the United States. In this chapter I shall mentally leave this hotel, and see the world from the Third World point of view. Unfortunately, the focus on the upper strata is somewhat in the spirit of the master himself. Schumpeter's own aristocratic manners, habits and tastes were not exactly compatible with viewing the world from the point of view of the 'losers' or laggards.

There is a second, and, less obvious, reason for studying the problems of the Third World. Understanding underdevelopment in the Third World can contribute effectively to a better understanding of the growth process in the industrialized countries. The economic problems of the industrialized world give weak and unclear symptoms, much in the same way that early stages of an illness produce general and unspecific symptoms: a fever or a headache. As the illness advances – as the patient gets sicker – stronger and more specific symptoms appear, making a diagnosis possible. My contention is that the study of the economically very sick nations can significantly contribute to the

1. The author is grateful to Daniele Archibugi, Charles Edquist, Keith Smith and the editors of this volume for helpful comments. The usual disclaimer applies.

2. This part has been added since the first German edition, Leipzig, Duncker & Humblot, 1912.

understanding of the developed world, for example the European Community running a slight fever.

We traditionally place the catching-up of the Third World in a different profession – that of development economics – from that of industrialized country catching-up. In doing this, we perpetuate a fragmentation of economic science which is instrumental in blocking our path towards a better understanding of the process of economic development.[3]

The long distance to be covered today by the Third World to get to the present theoretical possibility or frontier of living standards and technology is very similar to the long distances which in the past were faced – at different times in history – by countries like England and Japan. These countries, as did the United States and Germany, at some point in history went through remarkably successful catching-up processes starting from very far behind what was then the *avant garde* countries economically. For this reason history becomes a very useful laboratory, where successful strategies for catching-up from way behind can be studied. Economic ideologies of successful national take-off periods in different countries, although separated by centuries, have key common elements. These common elements also distinguish them as a group from the neoclassical economic policy which today is the foundation of the IMF and World Bank policy towards the Third World. My premise is that historically all *long-distance* catching-up processes have shared certain important elements. With marginal exceptions for tiny economic areas, there appears to be only *one* type of national strategy which has led to long-distance catch-up through the centuries. I shall call this the *List-cum-Smith* model. There is reason to believe that this will be the only possible strategy also in the future.

In this chapter I attempt to do the following: Part 1 focuses on the recent insights in the growth process, but looks at them from the point of view of the Third World. Part 2 looks at successful long-distance catch-up strategies from a historical perspective going back 500 years and more. A key insight provided by history is the view that economic development at any point in time is *activity-specific*. Historically, there has been a clear perception that only some activities induce growth – these are 'better' than normal economic activities. In Part 3 I attempt to isolate the factors causing some economic activities to be 'better' than others, and to provide a Quality Index or Quality Meter for ranking economic activities according to their potential for creating development with growth. Part 4 describes the diffusion process of gains from new technologies – why technological progress in some cases is appropriated by the producing nations, and sometimes spreads entirely to the consumers. The Clinton administration's emphasis on 'high-quality jobs' is an example of an intuitive approach to the same set of problems. At any point in time, the people and nations who capture the high-quality activities inhabit the top floors of Schumpeter's hotel.

3. In an earlier work (Reinert 1980), I have argued for studying underdevelopment in a framework including First World historical national strategies, technological change and industry analysis.

I argue that historically the common interventionist strategy of the industrialized world created a 'platform', above which the virtuous circles of development later became self-sustaining under a non-interventionist policy. I call this the *List-cum-Smith* strategy, because it combines the nurturing of 'superior' economic activities with competitive markets. Later 'path dependence' took off from these platforms, created by skilful use of both regulation and market. Below this platform, similar cumulative processes, in the form of vicious circles, work towards a convergence of the poor countries.[4] The Quality Meter and the alternative mode of productivity gains spread in the world economy, are mechanisms which create two convergence groups of nations – one rich and one poor – with a remarkable lack of *middle-class* countries.

1. THE VIEW OF THE VANQUISHED – A THIRD WORLD LOOK AT RECENT THEORETICAL INSIGHTS

Understanding the problems of *under*development is in a way a process of turning the many recent insights in the process of economic growth and development upside down. This often implies simply looking at the same evidence, but from the side of the loser, not the winner. Historically, a parallel to this can be found in the similarity of dynamic world view that underlies both Marx and Schumpeter, in spite of their very different conclusions. This similarity is readily admitted by Schumpeter,[5] who suggests that the similarities between Marx and himself are 'obliterated by a very wide difference in general outlook' (Schumpeter 1951: 161). Marx tended to see the destructive side of the capitalist system, while Schumpeter emphasized the creative aspect of that destruction. Schumpeter saw the rise of the cotton-textile mills in Manchester, Marx (1867: 389) saw the bones of the cotton weavers who previously supplied India and England 'bleaching the plains of India'. Similarly, Chandler, Porter, Lundvall/Nelson and Perez/Freeman emphasize the winners – the *star industries* in Porter's first book – without paying much attention to what happens to the losers – Porter's *dog industries* – that are necessarily a part of the same system. Their focus is on understanding the frontiers of technological development, as if all economic activities could be at that frontier. In the following examples I apply the view from the 'dog' industries – a *view of the vanquished* – to what are probably the six most significant new theoretical insights into the economic growth process of the industrialized world to have emerged during the last decade: 1) Chandler's 'scale and scope', 2) Porter's 'competitive advantage', 3) Lundvall and Nelson's 'national innovation systems', 4) Perez and Freeman's 'techno-economic paradigms', 5) Nelson and Winter's 'evolutionary theory', and 6) Chandler and Lazonick's 'organizational

4. Reinert (1980: 39 and 41) shows the characteristics of the two circles.
5. In the foreword to the Japanese edition of his *Theorie der wirtschaftlichen Entwicklung*, Schumpeter describes how he looked for 'a source of energy within the economic system which would of itself disrupt any equilibrium that might be attained .... It was not clear to me at the outset ... that the idea and the aim are exactly the same as the idea and the aim which underlie the economic teachings of Karl Marx' (Schumpeter 1951: 160)

capabilities'. All of these, although insightful, have the common feature that they only look at 'frontier' industries, the 'high-quality jobs' in Robert Reich's terms.

1. Alfred Chandler has given us a theory of the growth of big business which has greatly improved our understanding of the development of the industrialized world – the First World. In order to understand the Third World we must keep in mind that for every spectacularly successful US Steel Corporation, there was an equally spectacular failure of a US Leather Corporation which tried the same strategy as US Steel.[6] Understanding *development* means being able to pinpoint the potential US Steels out there, understanding *underdevelopment* is understanding *why US Leather Corporation failed* where US Steel succeeded.

2. Michael Porter's first book on industrial strategy (Porter 1980) is in many ways a list of recipes and prescriptions for avoiding being in a business where the assumptions of neoclassical economics are valid – how to avoid working where there are no barriers to entry, no economies of scale and where information is reasonably perfect. Understanding underdevelopment is understanding what happens to the industries where Porter's strategies don't work – the industries he tells his customers to keep away from, the 'dogs' in his classification (Porter 1980). In the Porter book which economists read – *The Competitive Advantage of Nations* – the author carries the conclusions drawn from the arena of industrial competition to the national level (Porter 1990). The core of the advice he gives to nations is essentially the same that he gives to corporations: grow 'star' industries – 'good' industries – and keep away from the 'dog' industries. However, aggregate world demand consists of products both from 'star' industries and 'dog' industries, thus opening up for a game with very variable payoffs. Limited by demand for 'star' industry products, the winners in Porter's game can only be a small fraction of the world population. What are the solutions for the rest, the vast majority of the world population? 'Competitiveness' in Porter's scheme consists of positioning your own country in the 'star' activities, where imperfect markets will shuffle wealth your way. The core of Porter's theory is like observing, correctly, that doctors make more money than lettuce pickers, and then recommend that the world population should consist exclusively of doctors. Later in the chapter I shall argue that Porter's national strategy recommendations are essentially a more sophisticated version of the recommendations of the dynamic part of two very old schools of economic thought the mercantilists and the cameralists.

3. A third important development is the research around the concept of *National Innovation Systems,* generally associated with Bengt-Åke Lundvall (1992) and Richard Nelson (1993). Interactive learning, research and development and the resulting innovation are, correctly in this writer's eyes, seen as crucial factors in explaining economic growth. If the 'national innovation system' approach is extended from being another recipe book for the growing of 'star' industries, into being a more generalized theory of economic development, it is haunted by an implicit assumption very similar to the one

6. The success of the trusts which sought static rents like the Leather Trust, part of the Beef Trust, was limited to the lobbying for tariffs.

which haunts Porter: it does not discuss sufficiently the fact that, at any time in history, economic activities possess widely different opportunities for learning. As long as there is demand also for goods in the non-learning areas, trade is no longer a win/win game. That would only happen if learning potential was the same in all activities – that one 'unit of learning' in every activity changes the output by the same quantity. The cumulative nature of knowledge is frequently, and correctly, pointed out. You are not likely to build a 747 if you have not built other, simpler aircraft previously. But there is more to it than that at any point in time: world learning focuses – is 'available' – only in a few out of the total spectrum of economic activities. We tend to name historical periods after the economic activities where learning took place at that time: in the stone-working industry in the Stone Age, in the bronze-working industry in the Bronze Age and in manufacturing industry in the Machine Age.

4. Radical changes in the technology systems, penetrating the majority of economic activities, were named changes in the 'techno-economic paradigm' by Perez (1983). The new technological paradigms, however, not only penetrate different industries to different degrees, new technology often 'hits' some activities in the *value chain*[7] of an industry and not others. In my student days in Cambridge, Massachusetts, this fact was visualized by a very old uniformed man from Western Union. He daily plodded across the Charles River bridge to deliver by hand international cables which at an incredible speed had been carried around the world by satellite – except for the last one mile. Today, thousands of people in Haiti are making a living producing baseballs using a needle-and-thread technology which has changed minimally over the last few hundred years, while golf balls are made with machines. The Machine Age came to the harvesting of wheat, but not yet to the harvesting of strawberries. The neglected historical *sequence of mechanization,* and the resulting trade patterns, has profound implications for explaining differences in GNP per capita. Understanding growth is understanding how to grab the activities which first create or benefit from the new techno-economic paradigms. Understanding poverty is understanding the trade patterns caused by the *sequence* in time and space of introduction of these new paradigms.

5. In their *Evolutionary Theory of Economic Change*, Nelson and Winter (1982) describe markets as a selection mechanism among firms. This selection is strongly influenced by the *capabilities of the firm*, in addition to the important effects of random events. Understanding the process of economic development and underdevelopment requires changing the unit of analysis; applying the analysis of the evolutionary selection process to what happens between *nations*, not firms. Markets are a selection mechanism by which different economic activities are distributed among nations, according to the capabilities of these nations. One key mechanism at work is that economic activities requiring few capabilities (needle-and-thread technology) are automatically shed by the rich countries to the poor. For this reason, among others, random events like production with new technologies are far from randomly distributed among nations. Through the logical selection process of the market, low wages – in short: being poor – become

7. Porter (1985) elaborates on the concept of 'value chains'.

the key success factor for Third World manufacturing businesses. A consequence of this strategy is that poor countries specialize in the economic activities where the industrialized countries have not found any scope for learning.

6. The final factor which I would like to discuss from the point of view of the Third World is Chandler's and Lazonick's (1991) view of *organizational capabilities* as the key to the success of a firm. Thomas McCraw of Harvard Business School suggests that the national counterpart of *organizational capabilities* in firms is the Listian concept of *National Productive Power*[8] (see McCraw 1993, addendum). In such a framework the national standard of living of a country – and indeed sometimes the physical survival of its inhabitants – will be determined by the same selection process as the one which determines the profit rate – or survival – of a firm. This is a potentially very useful connection between micro- and macroeconomic theory. To understand underdevelopment, the key question is not how to build *capabilities* and *productive power,* it is: what happens if you stick to your comparative advantage in an activity whose capabilities have become commonplace, with skills which have played out their course, in activities left over from exhausted techno-economic paradigms? What are the economic consequences of being a populous and skilled nation specialized in Stone-Age technology, if the rest of the world is far into the Iron Age already?

Faced with the compelling logic of the market, that activities which cannot be further mechanized should be carried out by cheap labour, any attempt at 'technology transfer' to the Third World tends to run against the extremely strong forces of the world market. 'Technology transfer' therefore becomes one of the slogans based more on wishful thinking than on any real understanding of the mechanisms at work, on a par with 'new world economic order'.

2. HISTORICALLY SUCCESSFUL LONG-DISTANCE CATCH-UP STRATEGIES: ECONOMIC DEVELOPMENT AS ACTIVITY-SPECIFIC

The striking contrast between the historically successful long-distance catching-up strategies – Britain, the United States, Germany, Japan – and today's economic theory is that these strategies were *activity-specific.* The solution to problems of economic development was to *get into the right business,* which almost inevitably meant manufacturing. This view is expressed in literally hundreds out of the thousands of mercantilist tracts written, particularly in Britain, Germany and France, starting in the early sixteenth century.[9] Following Adam Smith, today's studies of mercantilism have concentrated on the monetary aspects of their theories. I suggest that there is an important

8. This concept seems to have originated with Adam Müller. His 1809 book is the main work of a German school of economics which is sometimes referred to as the 'Romantic School'.
9. The bibliography of the German cameralist (mercantilist) literature (Humpert 1937) lists over 14,000 entries for Germany alone.

'*realökonomisch*-mercantilist' school, whose national economic strategies were responsible for a fairly even development within Europe, in contrast with that of the Third World.

To the early economists, all economic activities were different – much in the same way all professions today are different from an individual's point of view. To an individual, his choice of profession will to a large extent determine his future income and social standing. In pre-Ricardian times, society's future income and standing between nations was determined by its *choice* of economic activity. The neoclassical notion that 'all economic activities are alike' would be as meaningless to a pre-Ricardian economist as it is to a young person today facing the problem of choosing a profession. To a person, choosing a career of washing dishes in a restaurant provides a dramatically different future than deciding to become an engineer. Pre-Ricardian national strategy broadens this argument into one where a nation of engineers will be better off than a nation of dishwashers.

The *activity-specific* outlook on wealth creation can be traced back to the strategic importance the Venetians gave to their salt pans, already before the turn of the Millennium.[10] The strategic decision of being in the right business had to be backed up in the political and military spheres by protecting supplies and markets for the 'superior' and 'wealth-creating' activities. Use of force was needed to protect the static and dynamic rents created by *being in the right business.* Historian Frederic Lane (1979) – in a book venturing into economic theory – explains the rise of empires as a result of '*increasing returns* from the use of force as an economic service'.[11]

Following Venice, England presents the most spectacularly successful use of the *activity-specific* strategy. Daniel Defoe describes the English strategy in his *Plan of English Commerce* in 1728.[12] In the early fifteenth century, England was a poor country, heavily indebted to her Italian bankers. Her chief export was raw wool. Henry VII, who came to power in 1485, had lived in exile in wealthy Burgundy, where English wool was being spun into cloth. The Tudor strategy which started with him was to bring England into the wealth-creating downstream activities in wool manufacturing that Henry had observed abroad. The English strategy was gradual, starting with import substitution. In 1489 tariffs on cloth were increased, and local cloth manufacturing was encouraged. The Crown paid for foreign workers to be brought in, and businessmen were paid bounties for establishing textile manufacturing firms. When sufficient manufacturing capacity had been achieved, England prohibited all export of raw wool. This development paved the way for what has been called 'the closest approximation to a businessman's government' among the *ancien régimes* of Europe (O'Brien 1993: 125). As the wave of mechanization extended from wool to other areas of manufacturing, these new industries were in turn given the same preferential treatment given initially to the production of woollen cloth. Friedrich List (1844: 12) later put it this way: 'The

10. Hocquet (1990). In the early days of the Republic, much of the government revenue came from the sale of salt. See also Lane (1973: 58).
11. The parallel with more recent days is striking.
12. Palgrave regards Defoe as 'an important authority for economic history'. See Higgs (1963).

principle *sell manufactures, buy raw material* was during centuries the English substitute for an (economic) theory.'

Taking up the example set by England, the economic strategies of the great industrial nations in their pre-take-off period share a core theme of the *activity-specific* nature of growth.[13] This theme can be followed in economic writings from the early 1500s in Italy and England and France, a little later in the German cameralists. It is introduced to the United States through Alexander Hamilton[14] and his favourite economist, the English mercantilist Malachy Postlethwayt, and from Friedrich List's involuntary exile in the United States it is reinforced again in the Germany of the Zollverein. In Meiji, Japan, the *doitsugaku* school – favouring the German model – came to be the most influential for the building of society, at least until 1945 (Yage 1989: 29 and Bernd 1987). The Japanese took over the policies which dominated the German historical school: a basic distrust in free trade and an activity-specific attitude towards economic development, part of which was a belief in the superior 'productive powers' of manufacturing. In Japan, after 1883, 'a stream of German teachers of political economy and related disciplines continually flowed in' (Sugiyama and Mizuta 1988: 32). After World War II, the Japanese strategy was challenged by the American occupants, who suggested that the Japanese should specialize, according to their Ricardian comparative advantage, in cheap labour. Japanese policy-makers in that period strongly rejected what we today could call the World Bank / IMF strategy of a 'Ricardian' specialization in low-cost labour. The 'Asian Tigers' headed by South Korea have in their turn inherited much of their activity-specific philosophy from Japan. Freeman talks about the osmosis[15] in the development process from Japan to Korea, and Vogel (1991: 90) shows how 'the Japanese model was of great importance to Taiwan, South Korea, Hong Kong and Singapore'.

A common thread of successful long-distance catching-up through the centuries, is a shared distrust of free trade until the nation is firmly established in what were seen to be the *right* economic activities – the *specific activities* which gave the nation 'productive powers'. Somewhat paradoxically, while postwar United States rode on the crest of perhaps the strongest technological wave history has seen, in that same country the neoclassical paradigm, with no room for technology, was perfected. Doubly confident both in her economic power and in the intellectual underpinnings of the neoclassical paradigm (boldly so even in spite of its unrealistic assumptions), the United States unlearned the activity-specific economic strategy which had dominated the nation's policy over the last 100 years (although not always in the academic theory). The nation self-confidently

13. This is described in Reinert (1992).
14. It has been shown that Hamilton knew his Adam Smith, but rejected particularly the free trade conclusion. Excerpts from Postlethwayt's *Universal Dictionary of Trade and Commerce* were scattered through Hamilton's Army Pay Book, see Morris (1957). Hamilton's view on the English classical economists was similar to that taken 80 years later by the Japanese, see Morris-Suzuki (1989).
15. Personal communication.

faced the coming of a post-industrial society with the belief that the market can do no wrong. With the election of Bill Clinton, the United States is painfully rediscovering, now also in practical policy, that manufacturing matters, although there is little theoretical understanding as to why this is so. Interestingly, that manufacturing mattered was thoroughly accepted by the nineteenth-century policy-makers in the United States, this was precisely the essence of what was called The American System (Dorfman 1947, vol. 2: 566–97). Then, as today, there were 'high-quality jobs' and 'low-quality jobs' both from the point of view of the individual and from the point of view of a nation. These terms are Robert Reich's of today, but the same understanding was the foundation of the nineteenth-century 'American System', offering protection to manufacturing. In Part 3 of this chapter, I attempt to build a framework for understanding *high-quality* and *low-quality* jobs.

There was always a considerable lag in the economic understanding of *why* some economic activities created more wealth than others. If a remedy worked, it was not always considered important to understand *why*. The first to identify the qualities that made an activity 'good' for a nation was Antonio Serra in 1613.[16] Serra associated 'good' activities as being the result of *increasing returns,* and associated these primarily with manufacturing. Most early works on national trade strategies, however, merely list the characteristics of 'good' and 'bad' activities for a nation without giving any explanation as to *why.* One hundred years after Serra, Charles King's detailed list of 'good' and 'bad' trade was very influential. Exporting manufactures was 'good', importing them was 'bad', except when manufactured goods were traded for other manufactured goods which was 'to ... mutual advantage' of the trading nations (King 1721: 3). King gives no explanations as to why this is so, but if one associates manufacturing with Schumpeterian 'historical increasing returns', and non-manufacturing with diminishing returns, the strategy makes sense.

Moving on to the next century, it is perfectly clear that increasing returns, to quote Schumpeter, were 'an important feature of nineteenth-century analysis'.[17] Increasing returns are very much present until and including the early editions of Alfred Marshall's *Principles of Economics,* the first being in 1890. Marshall (1890: 452) emphasizes that national income may be increased by taxing commodities produced at diminishing returns and paying bounties to producers of commodities produced at increasing returns. This is probably the best description we shall ever get of Japanese growth strategy, but this key insight is lost in the later editions of *Principles.*

Marshall's dismissal of increasing returns from economic theory over the life of his *Principles,* starting in 1890, represents an important watershed in economic theory. Marshall thereby opened the way for the world of economic theory to be inhabited by

16. Serra's remarkable dynamic 'model' shows how wealth is created without the benefit of natural resources (Venice) on the one hand, and poverty remains in the midst of great natural resources (Naples) on the other. The parallel with modern Japan is interesting.
17. *History of Economic Analysis,* p. 259. The republishing of Serra's work in 1801 may, or may not, have influenced this.

clones of 'the representative firm' – a world view which lasts until this very day. The reason why increasing returns disappeared from mainstream economic theory is the same reason they were not allowed back after Frank Graham's article on the subject in 1923: they are not compatible with equilibrium (see e.g. Viner 1937: 475–82).

The *activity-specific* strategies common to all presently industrialized countries – protecting for centuries manufacturing as 'good' economic activities – created a common platform from which growth became self-sustaining. The remarkable lack of long-distance catch-up processes starting in the (neoclassical) twentieth-century seems to be associated with a lack of long-term *activity-specific* strategies in the presently underdeveloped world. Third World nations are stuck with what we later shall describe as 'growth-inhibiting' economic activities.

Graham's 1923 article represents an important conceptual bridge between pre-twentieth-century economic thought and today's gradual rediscovery of economies of scale and technical change – Schumpeter's 'historical increasing returns' – as important factors causing uneven economic growth. Crossing that bridge, First World historical growth strategies and today's theories and problems can be woven into a very meaningful whole. History starts to make more sense.

What kind of conclusions can we draw from the historical sequence of catching-up strategies of the presently developed countries? Most presently industrialized countries have through the centuries passed through two distinct stages: 1) A *List-cum-Smith stage* of strong intervention against free trade to establish the nation in the 'right' industries. 2) A pure *Smithian stage* emphasizing free trade. Sequentially – after Venice – England was the first country to reach an industrial plateau where free trade would lead to a higher welfare level than continued protectionism. This stage was reached much later by Germany, the United States and Japan, who in the meantime continued their *List-cum-Smith* strategies. Only long after it was possible to trade manufactures for manufactures, a free trade regime was established between the industrialized countries.[18]

I would suggest that history presents us with two important *stylized facts:*

1. No nation of any size has ever joined what today is the rich convergence group – inhabiting the upper strata hotel – without a prolonged Listian phase of economic policy. In a Listian system 'some economic activities are better than others'. In terms of the circular flow, the focus is on man as the *producer.*
2. Once world leadership has been achieved, the Smithian phase takes over in the successful catch-up country. In a Smithian system, 'all economic activities are alike'. In terms of the circular flow, the focus is on man as the *consumer.*

Growth theory in the 1990s is focusing, no doubt correctly, on technical change, innovation and learning – in addition to the traditional factor, capital. The enormous diversity of economic activity today obscures our view of what is a 'good' and 'bad'

18. This is the strategy recommended by King in 1721, and it also follows as the best strategy from Paul Krugman's 1979 and 1981 papers.

economic activity. Going back to fifteenth-century England it is possible to see things more clearly.

At the time of Henry VII, out of all existing human activities, only *one* experienced rapid technical change: the manufacturing of woollen textiles. All other activities were basically carrying on as before. This one activity absorbed capital, because only here were there large-scale investments to be made. This one activity had technical change and innovation. Only in this activity were there economies of scale and scope. Only this one activity offered any possibility for new learning. Only this activity created a *demand* for 'organizational capabilities'. At that moment in time it was clear that economic progress was *activity-specific* – it was basically taking place in one economic activity and not in any of the others. The basis for building a 'National Innovation System' was to protect and support the one economic activity where innovation was taking place.

Studies of patents confirm the idea that economic progress develops through changing 'focal points' of technological change (MacLeod 1988). The concentration of patenting in changing areas of manufacturing – and its almost complete absence in agriculture and services – give us a clue as to why the winning combination of *innovation* and *imperfect competition* is found mostly in manufacturing. The combination *innovation* + *imperfect competition* produces the kind of economic growth which 'sticks' in the producing nation.[19] The mercantilist 'national innovation system' achieved this combination by protecting any economic activity in the process of being mechanized – the 'good' economic activities. In the remainder of this chapter we discuss issues related to this:

- How to determine 'good' and 'bad' economic activities.
- The two modes of diffusion of the benefits of new technologies.

3. THE 'QUALITY' OF ECONOMIC ACTIVITIES AS A DETERMINANT FOR ECONOMIC DEVELOPMENT

The obstacle to our understanding the distribution of wealth and poverty between nations is embedded deeply in an economic theory which sees all economic activities as being alike. 'All Chinese look alike to me' is hardly a scientific approach to a study of China and Chinese culture. In neoclassical economic theory, on the other hand, the core assumptions make all economic activities 'alike'. In a world with perfect information, no scale effects and full divisibility of all factors, the outcome of increased world trade will be factor-price equalization. In the real world the gap between rich and poor nations is increasing steadily, in spite of huge increases in world trade. Clearly *relative efficiency* in the export sector is not a main determinant of wealth: the world's most efficient golf ball producer (in an industrialized country) receives a monetary wage 30 times higher than the world's most efficient baseball producer (in Haiti) – 30 cents an hour compared to a typical industrial country wage of 9 dollars an hour.

19. Innovations applied under near-perfect competition, like the invention of the container, tend to lower prices and GDP as measured, and therefore create 'Solow-Paradoxes'.

We have seen that the growth of the presently rich countries was based on a theory where economic development is *activity-specific:* it happens only in a small part of the whole spectrum of economic activities at any one point in time. Today, locating these 'superior' activities concentrated in any broad industrial category, as in the past, is difficult. Almost all activities and industries, even the most pedestrian ones, have some segments offering the winning combination of innovation and imperfect competition. The process is not fully understood until one reaches the product and brand level.

Economic development is a process which requires the presence of several *reactants*: capital, education, skills training, institutional factors (property, credit), entrepreneurship and a technological 'wave' or 'window of opportunity'. The absence of any of these reactants will impede the development process. The understanding of this process is difficult, because not only does the 'formula' – the right mix of reactants – for growth change over time but it also changes from industry to industry at any point in time. Growth-producing innovations have different 'fingerprints' in every industry. In a 1993 article, Moses Abramovitz enters into these important but neglected problems, but only on an aggregate national level. Further studies into the 'fingerprint' of innovation in different industries would be useful.

An innovation creates *a demand* for education, for skilled labour, for R&D and for capital. By identifying the economic activities which at any point in time were *in the process of being mechanized* – where new skills were in high demand – the 'primitive' industrial policy of mercantilists and cameralists managed to single out the 'winning' activities, those at the start of a steep learning curve.

Figure 1.1 shows the distribution of technological opportunities in 51 industrial sectors of the US economy from 1899 to 1937.[20] The growth in productivity rates varies enormously; although we can assume that the same capital, skills and institutional factors were present over the whole spectrum of activities. Clearly, the United States would not have taken world leadership if it had been only in industries 27–51. No amount of capital or learning would have achieved the results that in fact were achieved, without the industrial activities on the left side of the chart. Secondary effects spiral from the activities to the left: these activities are the 'wage setters' of the economy, and the upward pressure on wages in turn increases the use of capital in the rest of the economy at the expense of the increasingly more expensive factor, labour. Demand grows as the result of higher monetary wages. In the end, the multiplier effect of technological progress in 'wage setting activities' is formidable, and forms a core mechanism in the virtuous circles of development. We tend to forget, however, that technological change comes in focused 'clusters'; in the stone-working industry in the Stone Age, bronze-working industry in the Bronze Age, etc.

Uneven distribution of wealth seems to have the same basic causes nationally and internationally. Wage-level differences inside nations are caused by the same mixture of static and dynamic factors, which cause the polarization of the world in a rich and a poor

20. This chart is taken from Solomon Fabricant (1942).

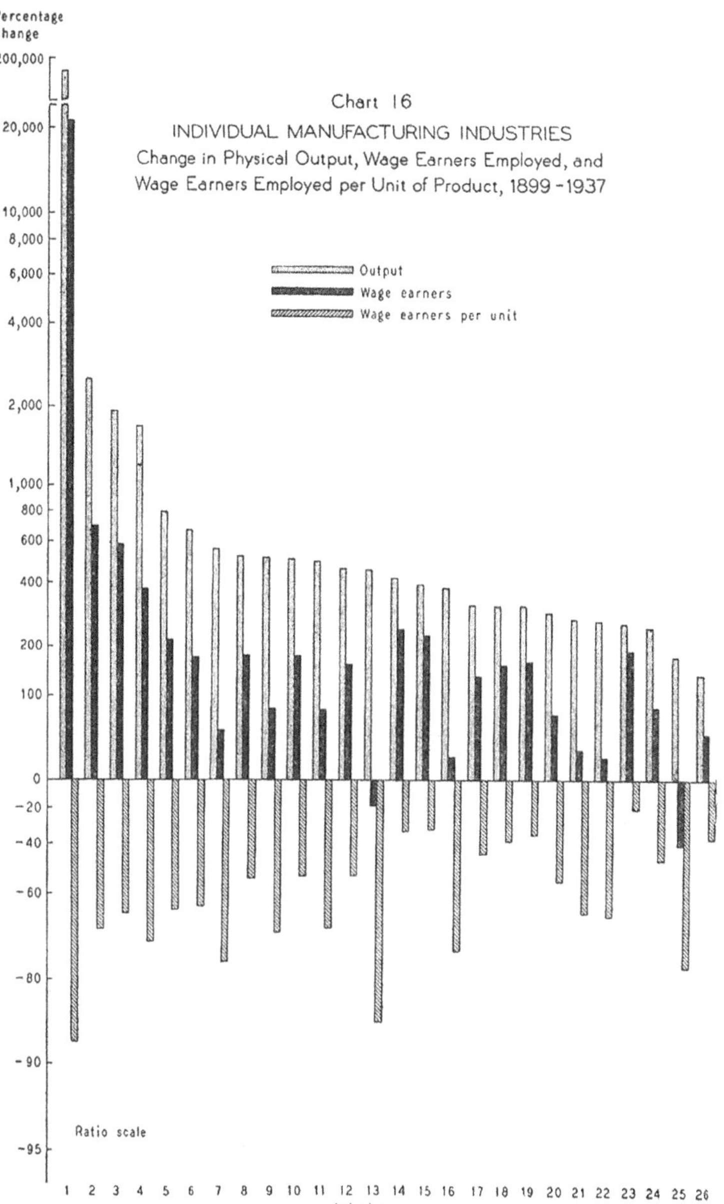

Figure 1.1 *Source*: Solomon Fabricant (1942).

convergence group. Interestingly, in the 1980s sociologists studied the US economy with a dual-economy approach, an approach used in development economics for a long time (see e.g. Tolbert et al. 1980, Hudson and Kaufman 1982). This resulted in a ranking

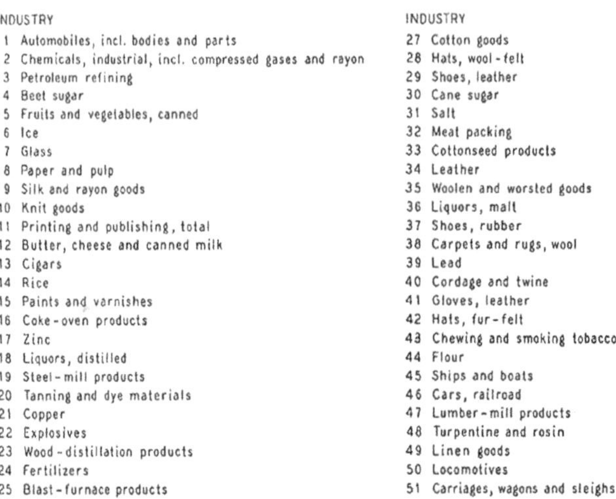

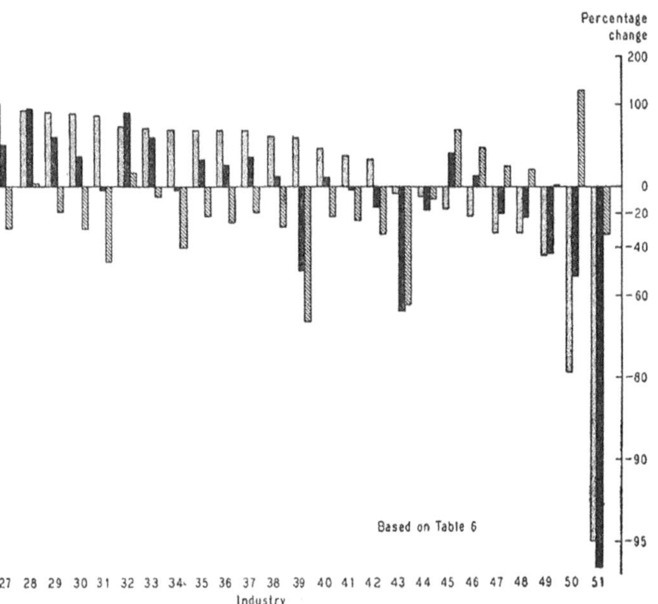

Figure 1.1 (Continued)

of economic activities similar to that in Figure 1.1 – from 'good' to 'bad' – which is inexplicable, or rather pure nonsense, from a neoclassical viewpoint.[21]

The challenge in economic theory is to find a level of abstraction, where useful generalizations can be made without making all economic activities either *all equal* or *all*

21. I am grateful to Tom McCraw of Harvard Business School for pointing these articles to me.

different. To a businessman, his firm is unique. The opportunity seen by an entrepreneur is a unique vision, if not in other ways, in the geographical location of his business. At this level of abstraction we are faced with billions of economic agents who are all *unique.* On the other extreme – in neoclassical theory – all economic activities are *equal.*[22] Case studies of firms, industries and nations are useful building blocks for theories, but a theory on a higher level of abstraction is needed.

What, then, are the characteristics of growth-inducing – 'good' – economic activities? Identifying these characteristics must be seen as a task comparable to the measuring of IQ – quantifying the unquantifiable. In economic theory we have defined two extremes of a continuum reasonably well: perfect competition and, at least statically, monopoly. Under perfect competition we would achieve factor-price equalization, we would all be equally rich. Under monopoly, we can predict high rents transferred to the monopoly holder from the rest of the world. A core problem in economic theory is that the profession has, at least until the recent events of new growth and trade theory, *little meaningful to say about varying degrees of imperfect competition,* the conditions under which virtually all economic activities produce and trade. The situation is similar to being able to measure two extremes, black and white, without having any way of measuring the various intermediary shades of grey. This is particularly bothersome in economics, where no activities over any length of time belong to either of the categories we have defined well. In terms of 'degree of perfect/imperfect competition', economic activities are scattered over the spectrum from almost white – where the assumptions of neoclassical theory are reasonably valid – to almost black, where the same assumptions are highly unrealistic. Game theory seems to be in a similar situation, having only the extremes, games with two players and infinite number of players, well defined.

Differences in wage levels, both nationally and between nations, seem to result from varying degrees of imperfect competition – caused by both static and dynamic factors. The factors at work have long been identified both by businessmen and in industrial economics, and they are correlated. In Figure 1.2, I attempt to create an area from light to dark grey where 'the quality' of economic activities at any time can be roughly plotted on a scale from white – 'perfect competition' – to black: 'monopoly'. The latter is only a temporary state, as new technologies fall towards a lower score as they mature. The upper part of the Quality Index corresponds to Schumpeter's metaphor of the upper strata of a market economy being like hotels which are indeed full of people, but people who are forever changing. Activities with a high score are *growth inducing,* activities with a low score are *growth inhibiting.* Jaroslav Vanek – in a comment to one of my earlier papers – suggests that the quality axis should be seen as a third dimension in the traditional geometrical presentation of trade theory.

The factors listed are correlated, but clearly not in any way perfectly so. The two lists of factors, those creating high-quality and those creating low-quality activities, exhibit a negative type of correlation: in their extreme form, the characteristics in the two

22. See, however, Lucas (1988, 1993) for examples of neoclassical models incorporating differences with regard to learning between activities.

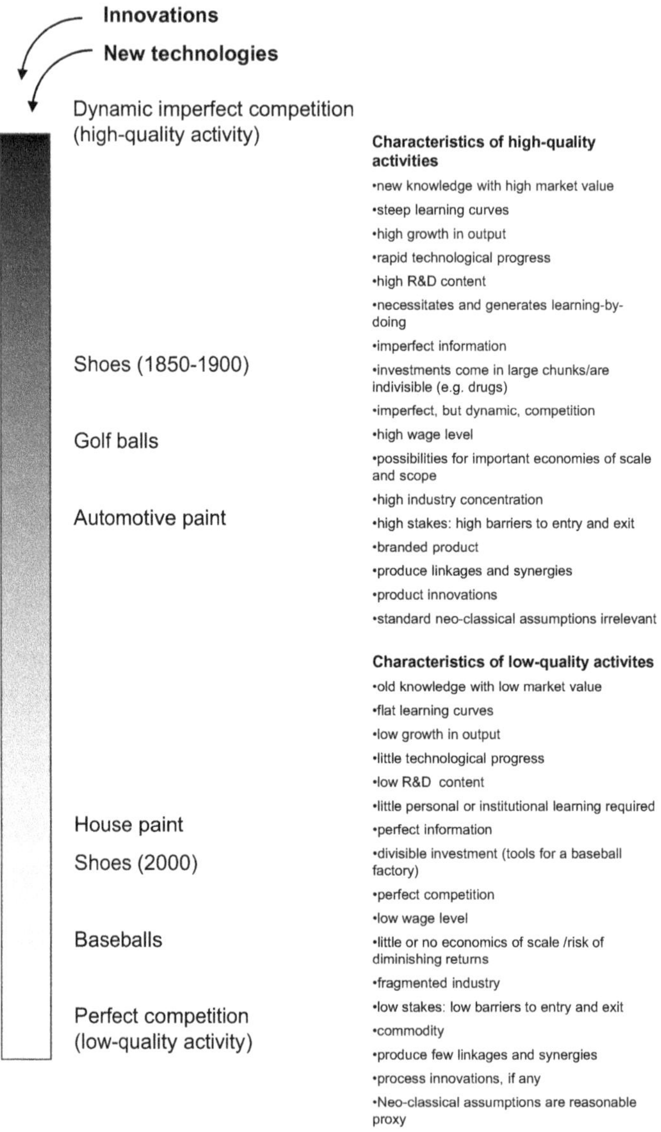

Figure 1.2 The Quality Index of Economic Activities.

groups are mutually exclusive. Each of the characteristics in one group is, in this form, incompatible with *all* characteristics in the other. The 'quality' of an economic activity for a nation, its ability to pay high wages and its potential for high profits, can be read off on this scale. High-quality activities carry with them high risks in innovation and new technologies, and high barriers to entry also carry with them high barriers to exit. Consequently, there is no direct relationship between the quality of an activity and its profit level, only its *potential* profit level. A high-quality activity can be ruined in shakeout periods by huge losses across the industry. These losses are caused by high barriers to exit. However, this normally does not drastically affect wage levels. In spite of the huge losses in the airline industry in recent years, wages of airline pilots are much higher than those of bus drivers. Airlines are still a high-quality economic activity for a country, due to their potential economies of scale.

As they are presented at the moment, the factors are a blend of causes and effects. I therefore choose to call them 'characteristics'. *Barriers to entry* boils down to being a common denominator of the forces at work. The system is a closed one, except for an opening at the top, in the black end. Here new knowledge – technological change – enters the system as a temporary monopoly, and then falls towards perfect competition over time at greatly differing speeds. Nathan Rosenberg's frequently used example of the innovation with shipping-containers fell reasonably fast on the scale towards perfect competition. Patented drugs fall more slowly. Patents are of course set up for this very reason, to keep profits up in order to encourage investment in research. Even when technological progress no longer takes place in an economic activity, static scale effects may give the activity in question a high-value score (= dark grey).

The gravity in the system – the speed with which economic activities fall from temporary monopolies to perfect competition – is also determined by the intensity of competition. More intense competition causes the gravitational power to increase, as we are experiencing in our time with successive generations of computers. A more rapid fall of innovations through the system – more perfect competition and more classical spread of benefits (next section of the chapter) – combined with wage and exchange rigidities, will by itself increase unemployment. This is, in my opinion, a relevant point for the present employment situation in Europe and the United States.

This Quality Meter is in my view useful in conceptualizing a number of issues in economics, old and recent: competitiveness, Porter's world view, Bill Clinton's crusade for high-quality jobs, national wage differentials and, most importantly, the clustering of the world in two groups of nations, the haves and the have-nots. Historically, the Quality Meter opens for an explanation as to why colonialism made sense to the colonial powers. This is not clear in neoclassical analysis, see e.g. Fitzgerald (1998). Colonial economic policy assured the mother-country exclusive access to the activities with the highest score on the Quality Meter. There is also considerable historical evidence that the colonial powers consciously pursued policies based on notions which are compatible with the Quality Index – that access to high-quality activities was prohibited in the colonies. The 'industricides' – the conscious killing off of advanced sectors in colonial economies – testify to this. Perhaps the clearest examples are from British colonial policy: the prohibition of the prosperous woollen industry in Ireland starting in 1699, described by Hely-Hutchinson (1779), and the destruction of the cotton-textile industry in India around 1814 (Chopra 1990). The prohibitions on the export of machinery, in force in Britain until 1843, also indicate an understanding of economic power which is compatible with the Quality Index. The machinery question is described in Berg (1980). All in all, the Quality Index is able to throw new light on why many *'realökonomisch'-oriented* mercantilists were essentially right, although often for the wrong reasons.

If the Marshall Plan worked wonders in a few years in postwar Europe, it was because the nations in question were brought back in the top-floor industries, where they were active before the war. The reason 'technical assistance' to the Third World – originally seen as an extension of the Marshall Plan – has failed so miserably in the Third World in general, is because these countries lacked everything the *List-cum-Smith* stage has given Europe, the United States and Japan. Most postwar attempts at Third World industrialization under protectionism, like in Mexico and India, did not develop well essentially because the competitive aspect – the *Smithian* element of *List-cum-Smith* – was missing. This led to static rent-seeking and very inefficient industries based on government industrial licences.[23]

4. THE CLASSICAL AND COLLUSIVE MODES OF DIFFUSION OF TECHNOLOGICAL GAINS

To the classical economists, productivity improvements would show up in the economy as lowered prices for the goods which experienced these improvements (see e.g. Smith 1776: 269, and Ricardo 1817: 46–47). At the time of Smith and Ricardo, the gold standard facilitated the result they predicted. In a closed economy, holding velocity of circulation constant, the increase of goods in the economy resulting from technological progress would chase only the same amount of bullion. Prices *would have to fall.* Rapid technological progress would therefore lead to deflation – which it in fact often did until the gold standard was abolished.

When the gold standard was abolished, people in the industrialized countries got rich in a different way than before – instead of seeing the price of industrial goods fall as it used to, they now saw their monetary income rise. Previously deflation had caused awkward social problems: it was difficult to convince people who had to take continuous pay cuts that, in spite of these pay cuts, they were still getting richer, because the price of the goods they purchased fell at an even faster rate than their wages. The monetary policy which followed after the gold standard was abolished became, from the point of view of the industrialized nations, a more sensible one: money supply kept rising with the amount of goods in the economy, or slightly faster, creating a small inflation which seems to have served to oil the machinery of development. Now the producer in an activity not exhibiting productivity improvements – e.g. the barber – got rich by raising his prices at the rate everybody else had their salaries raised, not only by having the price of manufactured goods lowered.

As shown in Figure 1.1, from 1899 through 1937, within the United States, labour productivity in the automotive industry increased by about 900 per cent, and many other industries recorded productivity improvements exceeding 100 per cent. However, in many US industries: meat packing, hats, railroad cars, lumber-mill products and

23. List was writing on Germany, where he wanted free trade established between more than 30 small states, each with high tariff barriers. That ferocious competition would erupt once these barriers were removed goes without saying.

others, labour productivity did not change at all in the same period.[24] Yet, the workers in the industries which had no productivity increase at all over this 40-year period had their good share in the unprecedented growth in the US economy over that period. But, as opposed to what was expected in the classical model, this did not come through an improvement in their terms of trade. The increase in real wages came essentially through increased monetary wages as the national stock of money grew, not through improvements in the terms of trade in the 'dog' industries. In this way the huge productivity advances in the 'star' industries spread to a much larger extent *inside the producing nation* than to customers abroad. A similar view on wage determination is held by the French regulation school (see Boyer 1988).

Terms of trade between developed and developing countries seem to have changed very little, in spite of the widely different changes experienced in productivity between industries within each nation (Figure 1.1). This observation would support the impression that each country keeps its 'average' productivity increase in the form of a higher standard of living. This again suggests that the *choice of economic activity* is strategically crucial to a nation.

The benefits of technology clearly spread in the economy in a different pattern from what the classical and neoclassical economists expect. I call this the *collusive*[25] mode of diffusing the benefits from technological change: the benefits are divided among the capitalists, the workers and the government *in the producing nation*. (The word collusive does not imply a conspiracy. This collusion comes about by the normal working of the economic, social and political forces.) Inside a nation, social and democratic forces, labour mobility and the distributive effects of a huge government sector ensure that the wage level and standard of living in the 'dog' industries do not lag too far behind those of the 'star' industries. Interindustry differences are, of course, much greater in a society like the United States than in a 'wage solidarity' culture like the Scandinavian, but the same mechanisms are at work.

Faced with a *collusive spread*, the United States during the period covered in Figure 1.1 would grow richer if it could move workers from the hat industry to the automotive industry. Importing hats and exporting cars will – under the collusive diffusion of technological improvements that in fact happened – improve the US welfare position as compared to autarky. This opportunity is created by the fact that not all economic activities are mechanized at the same time and to the same extent. Things would look different, as US economist Henry Vethake said in 1844, 'if improvement in all the arts were to take place *at the same rate*'.[26] This is clearly not the case. A more realistic picture is the one given by Kodama: 'It is more like the principle of surf-riding; the waves of innovation come one after another and you have to invest to ride the waves; if you miss, you are out of the game' (Kodama 1991).

24. Data from Fabricant, op. cit, pp. 90–91.
25. This matter is discussed more in detail in Reinert (1990).
26. Italics in original.

A *classical* spread is the result of the usual assumptions in neoclassical economics. However, in a Schumpeterian world view, a purely classical spread is hardly plausible. The dynamics of the system are generated by the technological change which creates disequilibria – and the higher profits created in the industries experiencing technological change are necessary in order to draw capital to these higher-risk and more capital-intensive activities. In addition, a classical spread of the benefits – only in the form of price reductions to customers at home and abroad – would not be seen as fair and democratic in the producing country. That industrialized country workers receive their share in the productivity improvements in terms of higher wages is an integral part of the credo of industrialized societies.

In the late 1930s, the Brookings Institution published a series of books aiming at 'nothing less than a general re-examination, in the light of modern developments, of the operation of the capitalistic system of wealth production and distribution' (Bell 1940). The studies conclude that the benefits of technological progress may be spread in the US economy in two different ways:

1. *Raising money wages (my collusive mode)*. 'The most obvious method by which the income of the masses might be expanded... it is the method which has been steadfastly pursued by labor organizations... and it is the method which has been officially experimented with under the auspices of the National Recovery Administration' (Moulton 1935). It is recognized, however, that this gives a disproportionate wage lead for manufacturing and railway workers.
2. *Price reductions (my classical mode)*. The series of studies concluded that 'the *most advantageous* means of broadly distributing the benefits of technological progress was by reducing prices in line with increasing efficiency in production' (Bell 1940). The practical difficulties in achieving this were outlined in a third volume in the series: *Industrial Price Policy and Economic Progress* (Nourse and Drury 1938). The conclusion was that in a market where both the industry in question and the labour unions charge what the market can take for products and labour, respectively, a large amount of what from an international trade point of view is a 'collusive spread' is inevitable in a market economy.

Clearly, in most industries, the benefits of technological development spread with elements of both modes. Distribution problems *within* a nation, which was the object of the Brookings Institution study, will be alleviated through competition in the labour market, through labour mobility, through the high government share in GNP, through the relocation of industry to areas in the country with less expensive labour and, particularly in the case of Europe, through the 'wage solidarity' of labour unions. Internationally, these mechanisms work in a very limited way, as does the huge redistributive machinery of national governments. The inevitability of a 'collusive spread' makes a nation's *choice of economic activity* so crucial. As a result of the collusive spread of technological progress, the world's most efficient baseball producer makes 30 US cents an hour in Haiti, and the world's most efficient golf ball producer makes 30 times as much in an industrialized country, as noted above.

Table 1.1 Characteristics of the two modes of diffusion of productivity improvements.

	The Collusive Mode	*The Classical Mode*
Characteristics of Mode		
Divisibility of investments	Indivisible, comes in 'chunks'	Divisible Perfect
Degree of perfect information	Imperfect (e.g. patents, internal R&D)	(competitive market for technology itself)
Source of technology from user company point of view	Internal, or external in big chunks = high degree of economies of scale	External
Barriers to entry	Increase	No change
Industry structure	Increases concentration	Neutral
Economies of scale	Increase	No change
Market shares	Very important	Unimportant
How Benefits Spread		
GNP as measured	Highly visible	Tends not to appear (Solow-paradoxes)
Profits level	Increases stakes: possibilities for larger profits or losses	No change
Monetary wages	Increase	No change
Real wages (nationally)	Increase	Increase
Price level	No change	Decreases
Terms of trade	No change	Turns against industries experiencing technological progress
Examples of innovations in the two groups	New pharmaceuticals, main-frame computers, automotive paint production	Electricity, telephones, sewing machines, use of PCs, dispersion paint production, containers
Where found	Mainly in industry, in recent products and processes	In primary and tertiary industry, use of new basic technologies, mature industry

Hans Singer, a former student of Schumpeter, raised the distribution issue of technological progress in his paper at the 1949 meeting of the American Economic Association. Singer[27] pointed out unquantifiable factors, however, and his important insight drowned in the attention paid to the terms of trade argument presented by Prebisch. Measuring prices – terms of trade – appealed to the traditions and static world view of the economics profession. The remarkable lack of change in terms of trade between industrialized and primary-producing nations over time, shown by Kindleberger and others, really served to reinforce Singer's point: each group of nations is able to keep its own productivity improvements as an increase in national welfare.

Table 1.1 shows the characteristics of the *classical* mode (price reduction) and the *collusive* mode (raising money wages). In a truly classical spread, the innovation immediately

27. Published as Singer (1950).

falls to the lower level of the Quality Index in Table 1.1. The use of containers could be an example of such an innovation. The two modes are not mutually exclusive – in most cases they are both present to some degree. Under autarky, it makes no immediate difference to GNP whether the benefits spread in a classical or in a collusive way. In an open economy with restricted labour mobility it makes all the difference in the world.

5. REDISCOVERING OLD STRATEGIES FOR DEVELOPMENT IN A NEW ECONOMIC PARADIGM

The neoclassical paradigm in economics is being challenged by new theoretical approaches. A central feature in a Kuhnian change in paradigm is a 'Gestalt-switch', that the object of study – in this case the economy – starts to be perceived as a different *Gestalt.* If economics is to make progress towards understanding the causes of national wealth and poverty, it is necessary to dispense with the view of the world economy as a *Gestalt* consisting of a mass of undifferentiated 'representative firms', all operating under perfect information and competition. The implicit assumption that 'all economic activities are alike' will have to be abandoned. A new and more relevant economic theory will have to consider the differences between economic activities – their use of factors like fixed costs, scale and knowledge – and the cumulative effects of these factors over time. The description of this new multifaceted world-economy *Gestalt* will require new, but unfortunately less accurate tools than those presently used. The Quality Index of economic activities is one example of such a tool. Simple and absolute 'truths' – like the absolute superiority of free trade under all circumstances – will yield to much more complex, but also more useful, views. Readers who are worried about this development may find some consolation in Schumpeter's words: 'The general reader will have to make up his mind, whether he wants *simple* answers to his questions or *useful* ones – in this as in other economic matters he cannot have both.'[28]

The evolutionary paradigm will be able to throw new light on mercantilist industrial policy. A new understanding of pre-twentieth-century industrial policy is seeping even into neoclassical economics, without the authors being aware of it old practices are being restored, without any historical references, and only used for First World consumption, not for the Third World.[29] The best *realökonomisch*-oriented mercantilists can be seen as having built efficient national innovation systems. Today the goal of enlightened industrial policy is to create an innovation-driven society: positioning the nation in the upper echelons of the Quality Index where growth-inducing activities carried out under imperfect competition create wealth. The economics profession knows, in some place in the right part of the brain – where intuition is seated – that Japan would never have made her way to international economic leadership if she had concentrated on

28. Schumpeter in his foreword to F. Zeuthen (1930) and Schumpeter (1954).
29. Paul Krugman of MIT, whose contributions to the rediscovery of increasing returns has already been mentioned, with hindsight now approves of Canada's protectionist policies (Krugman 1992: 42). See also endnote 31.

pyjama production instead of car production and electronics. However, the profession as a whole refuses to build this 'knowledge' into the models produced by the left side of their brains. The Quality Index or Quality Meter for economic activities is intended as a device to connect the two parts.

The mercantilists – English, German and French in particular – identified superior economic activities with the use of machinery.[30] In a world where very few economic activities had been mechanized, the use of new machinery was synonymous at once with innovation, technological change, learning, imperfect competition, high profits, high wages and national welfare. Today the economists who were associated with the most spectacular catching-up operations in human history, England starting in the late fifteenth century, the United States and Germany starting in the nineteenth century, are not even mentioned in the textbooks. A basic reason for this, of course, is that the strategic factors used to create and maintain wealth historically, contradict the very foundations of the neoclassical theoretical construction: perfect information and the absence of increasing returns to scale.

If a nation's economic activities historically are concentrated in the lower area of the Quality Index, the workings of the market will reinforce this position by assigning only mature products, produced with common knowledge and technology, to the poor nation. As the pressures of an increasingly perfect competition weigh on a product, cheap and unskilled labour becomes a key success factor for companies. Therefore, the production of a product like baseballs – until now unmechanized – is farmed out to Haiti, while the mechanized production of golf balls and tennis balls is kept in the industrialized countries.[31] As a result, the Third World receives the activities working under perfect competition and a *classical spread* of benefits, while the First World monopolizes the upper part of the Quality Index, the top floor of Schumpeter's capitalist hotel. The Third World mainly receives the destructive part of the Schumpeterian *creative destruction* – the destruction of the existing non-market economies. The invisible hand tends to shuffle the gains from technological progress to the industrialized countries in the form of rents, through the mechanisms described in this chapter. An understanding both of the historical strategies of the First World, and of the differing 'qualities' of economic activities are necessary ingredients in the economic strategies of poor nations facing a long-distance catching-up process.

References

Abramovitz, M. (1993), 'The Search for the Sources of Growth: Areas of Ignorance, Old and New', *Journal of Economic History*, Vol. 53, No.2, 217–43.

Bell, S. (1940), *Productivity, Wages and National Income*, Washington, DC: The Brookings Institution, 3.

Berg, M. (1980), *The Machinery Question and the Making of Political Economy 1815–1848*, Cambridge: Cambridge University Press.

30. This policy is being rediscovered in the United States; see De Long and Summers (1991).
31. This argument can be seen as an extension of the product life-cycle effects associated with Raymond Vernon and Lou Wells, see Vernon (1966) and Wells (1972).

Boyer, R. (1988), 'Technical Change and the Theory of "Règulation"', in G. Dosi et al., *Technical Change and Economic Theory*, London: Pinter, 67–94.

Bernd, M. (ed.) (1987), *Japans Weg in die Moderne. Ein Sonderweg nach deutschem Vorbild*, Frankfurt: Campus Verlag.

Chopra, P.N. (1990), *The Gazetter of India*, Vol. 2, New Delhi: Ministry of Education and Social Welfare, 613–15.

Clemence, R.V. (ed.) (1951), *Essays of J.A. Schumpeter*, Cambridge, MA: Addison – Wesley Press, 160.

Defoe, D. (1728), *Plan of English Commerce*, London: C. Rivington.

De Long, B. and L. Summers, (1991), 'Equipment Investment and Economic Growth', *Quarterly Journal of Economics*, Vol. 106, May, 445–502.

Dorfman, J. (1947), The *Economic Mind in American Civilization*, Vol. 2, London: George Harrap.

Fabricant, S. (1942), *Employment in Manufacturing. An Analysis of its Relation to the Volume of Production*, New York: National Bureau of Economic Research, 90–1.

Fitzgerald, E.P. (1998), 'Did France's Colonial Empire Make Economic Sense? A Perspective from the Postwar Decade', *Journal of Economic History*, Vol. 48, No. 2, 373–85.

Graham, F.D. (1923), 'Some Aspects of Protection Further Considered', *Quarterly Journal of Economics*, Vol. 37, February, 199–227.

Hely-Hutchinson, J. (1779), The *Commercial Restraints of Ireland Considered, in a Series of Letters to a Noble Lord, Containing an Historical Account of the Affairs of that Kingdom, so far as they Relate to this Subject*, Dublin: William Hallhead. (All copies of this book were ordered to be burned by the Dublin hangman on publication, few escaped).

Higgs, H. (ed.) (1963), *Palgrave's Dictionary of Political Economy*, Vol.1, New York: Kelley, 535.

Hocquet, J.-C.(1990), *Il, Sale e la Fortuna di Venezia*, Rome: Jouvence.

Hudson, R. and R. Kaufman, (1982), 'Economic Dualism: A Critical Review', *American Sociological Review*, Vol. 47, 727–39.

Humpert, M. (1937), *Bibliographie der Kameralwissenschaften*, Köln: Schroeder.

King, C. (1721), *The British Merchant; or, Commerce Preserved*, London: John Darby, Vols 1, 3. This part of the book was first published in 1713.

Kodama, F. (1991). 'Changing Global Perspective: Japan, the USA and the New Industrial Order', *Science and Public Policy*, Vol. 8, No. 6, 388.

Krugman, P. (1992), *Geography and Trade*, Cambridge, MA: MIT Press, 92.

Lane, F. (1973), *Venice. A maritime Republic*, Baltimore: Johns Hopkins, 58.

Lane, F. (1979), *Profits from Power. Readings in Protection Rent and Violence – Controlling Enterprises*, Albany: State University of New York Press, 45–8.

Lazonick, W. (1991), *Business Organization and the Myth of the Market Economy*, Cambridge: Cambridge University Press.

List, F. (1844), *Das Nationale System der politischen Oekonomie*, Basel: Kyklos, 1959, 12.

Lucas, R.E. (1988), 'On the Mechanics of Economic Development', *Journal of Monetary Economics*, Vol. 22, 3–42.

Lucas, R.E. (1993), 'Making a Miracle', *Econometrica*, Vol. 61, No. 2, 251–72.

Lundvall, B.-Å.(ed.) (1992), *National Systems of Innovation*, London: Pinter.

Macleod, C. (1988), *Inventing the Industrial Revolution. The English Patent Systems, 1660–1800*, Cambridge: Cambridge University Press.

Marshall, A. (1890), *Principles of Economics*, London: Macmillan, 452.

Marx, K. (1867), *Das Kapital*, Vol. 1, page numbers quoted refer to the reprinted version published by Ullstein: Frankfurt, Ullstein, 1967, 389.

McCraw, T. (1993), 'Adam Smith and Friedrich List: The Invisible Hand Versus Industrial Policy', Paper presented at the Business History Conference, Harvard Business School, March 19–21.

Moulton, H.G. (1935), *Income and Economic Progress*, Washington, DC: The Brookings Institution, 102.

Morris, R.B. (1957), *Alexander Hamilton and the Founding of the Nation*, New York: Dial Press, 285.

Morris-Suzuki, T. (1989), *The History of Japanese Economic Thought*, London: Routledge.

Muller, A. (1809), *Elemente der Staatskunst*, Vol. 5, Berlin: J.D. Sander.

Nelson, R. (ed.) (1993), *National Innovation Systems*, New York: Oxford University Press.

Nelson, R. and S. Winter (1982), *An Evolutionary Theory of Economic Change*, Cambridge, MA: Harvard University Press.

Nourse, E.G. and H.B. Drury (1938), *Industrial Price Policy and Economic Progress*, Washington, DC: The Brookings Institution.

O'Brien, P.K. (1993), 'Political Preconditions for the Industrial Revolution', in P.K O'Brien and R. Quinault, *The Industrial Revolution and British Society*, Cambridge: Cambridge University Press, 125.

Perez, C. (1983), 'Structural Change and the Assimilation of New Technologies in the Economic and Social System', *Futures*, Vol. 15, 357–75.

Porter, M. (1980), *Competitive Strategy. Techniques for Analyzing Industries and Competitors*, New York: Free Press, 362–3.

Porter, M. (1985), *Competitive Advantage*, New York: Macmillan.

Porter, M. (1990), *The Competitive Advantage of Nations*, London: Macmillan, 552–6.

Reinert, E. (1980), *International Trade and the Economic Mechanisms of Underdevelopment*, Ann Arbor: University Microfilm Publications, 237–9.

Reinert, E. (1990), 'How do Productivity Improvements Become Visible in Economic Data – Or: is the *Solow Paradox* a Paradox at All?', mimeo.

Reinert, E. (1992), 'Thoughts before Takeoff. Hva mente økonomene I de nåværende iland om næringspolitikk og økonomisk vekst før disse landene le rike?', Parts 1 and 2 Oslo, STEP-Group, mimeo.

Ricardo, D. (1817), *Principles*, London: Dent, reprinted 1973 (page numbers refer to the reprint).

The Royal Tropical Institute, Amsterdam (various authors) (1961), *Indonesian Economics. The Concept of Dualism in Theory and Policy*, The Hague: van Hoeve, 1961.

Schumpeter, J.A (1934), *The Theory of Economic Development*, Cambridge, MA: Harvard University Press, 156.

Schumpeter, J.A. (1951), Foreword to the Japanese edition of *Theorie der wirtschaftlichen Entwicklung*, Reprinted in: Clemence, R.V. (ed.), *Essays of* J.A. Schumpeter, Cambridge, MA: Addison-Wesley Press.

Schumpeter, J.A. (1954), *History of Economic Analysis*, New York: Oxford University Press.

Serra, A. (1613), *Breve trattato delle Cause che possono far abbondare li Regni d'Oro e Argento dove non sono miniere. Con applicazione al Regno di Napoli*, Naples: Lazzaro Scorriggio.

Singer, H. (1950), 'The Distribution of Gains between Investing and Borrowing Countries', *American Economic Review, Papers and Proceedings*, Vol. II, No. 2, May.

Smith, A. (1776), *Wealth of Nations*, Chicago: University of Chicago Press, reprinted 1976 (page numbers refer to the reprint).

Sugiyama, C. and H. Mizuta (1988), *Enlightenment and Beyond. Political Economy Comes to Japan*, Tokyo: University of Tokyo Press.

Tolbert, C. et al. (1980), 'The Structure of Economic Segmentation: A Dual Economy Approach', *American Journal of Sociology*, Vol. 85, March, 1095–116.

Vernon, R. (1966), 'International Investment and International Trade in the Product Cycle', *Quarterly Journal of Economics*, Vol. 80, May, 190–207.

Vethake, H. (1844), *The Principles of Political Economy*, 2nd Edition, Philadelphia: J.W. Moore, 95.

Viner, J. (1937), *Studies in the Theory of International Trade*, New York: Harper, 475–82.

Vogel, E. (1991), *The Four Little Dragons. The Spread of Industrialization in East Asia*, Cambridge, MA: Harvard University Press.

Wells, L. (ed.) (1972), *The Product Life Cycle and International Trade*, Boston: Harvard Business School.

Yage, K. (1989), 'German Model in the Modernization of Japan', *The Kyoto University Economic Review*, Vol. 29, No. 1–2, April-October, 29.

Zeuthen, F. (1930), *Problems of Monopoly and Economic Welfare*, London: Routledge.

Chapter 2

RECENT TRENDS IN ECONOMIC THEORY — IMPLICATIONS FOR DEVELOPMENT GEOGRAPHY

With Vemund Riiser

'About a year ago I more or less suddenly realised that I have spent my whole professional life as an international economist thinking and writing about economic geography, without being aware of it.'

Paul Krugman, Professor at MIT, leading US economist[1]

1. Introduction

Development geography and mainstream economic theory have for many years lived separate lives. Especially so since the downfall of development economics, an academic subject which has repeatedly been pronounced dead by one of today's leading US economists.[2] The geographical dimension - the location of production in space - has completely disappeared from neo-classical economic theory. This is, in one sense, curious, because the 'founding father' of neo-classical economic theory - the Englishman Alfred Marshall - is still an important figure in economic geography through his *industrial districts.* We shall return to 'the two Marshalls' later in this chapter. Another vintage economist used in modern economic geography, Alfred Weber, with his Location Theory (Standorttheorie)[3] belongs to a school of economics which virtually died out: The Historical School, of German origin.

However, economic theory is itself changing rapidly at the moment - and interestingly one of the new developments is that the ideas of the German Historical School are coming back into economic theory. In contrast to modern economic theory, in the holistic Historical School of Economics, both time (history) and place (geography) play a

1. In: *Geography and Trade*, Louvain, Belgium, Louvain University Press and Cambridge, MA, London, England, MIT Press, 1991, p. 1.
2. Krugman, Paul, 'Toward a Counter-Counterrevolution in Development Theory', in *Proceedings of the World Bank Annual Conference on Development Economics 1992*, Washington, DC, World Bank, 1993, p. 15.
3. Weber, Alfred, 'Industrielle Standortlehre. Allgemeine und kapitalistische Theorie des Standortes', in *Grundriss der Sozialökonomik*, Tübingen, J.C.B. Mohr, 1914. Vol. VI, pp. 54–82.

natural part.[4] In this chapter we shall analyze the recent main trends in economic theory, and attempt to assess the implications of these changes for development geography. Especially, we shall discuss the possibilities for a process of convergence between the discipline of development geography and parts of economic theory.

In economic theory there are three main developments which we find are of potential importance to development geography: **First** of all, the mainstream neo-classical paradigm is being challenged from a growing school under the heading 'Evolutionary' or 'Schumpeterian' economics, with roots in the German Historical School. This group is gaining prominence within the OECD and the EU. **Secondly**, from inside the neo-classical school, a 'new growth theory' is evolving. It is not clear whether this new theory will reform the neo-classical paradigm from within, or whether it indirectly attacks the very foundations of the neo-classical system in such a way that in the long run it may bring down the whole neo-classical framework. The **third** development, perhaps the one with the most immediate implications for development geography, is the change which has taken place in international trade theory over the last 10–12 years.

Before treating these three developments in separate sections, we shall look at the background and timing of the changes presently taking place in economic theory.

> 'I foresee that within the next ten or twenty years the now fashionable highly abstract analysis of conventional economists will lose out. Though its logical base is weak - it is founded on utterly unrealistic, poorly scrutinised, and rarely even explicitly stated assumptions - its decline will mainly be an outcome of the tremendous changes which, with crushing weight, are falling upon us.' Gunnar Myrdal, 1976.[5]

2. Counter-factual assumptions - how neo-classical economics 'lost' the causes of uneven growth

From the point of view of a geographer, historian, or business theorist, economic theory has worked at a very high level of abstraction. The mathematical accuracy of neo-classical economics has been achieved at the cost of 'assuming away' factors which to other disciplines were crucial variables. To many development economists - Gunnar Myrdal being a prime example[6] - the irrelevant basic assumptions of neo-classical theory are at the core of the problems of the Third World. The most important of these assumptions are 'perfect information', 'constant returns to scale' and 'full divisibility of all factors'. These assumptions form the very foundations of the theoretical structure we call neo-classical economic theory.

---

4. The part geography played in German economic theory is expressed in the monumental *Grundriss der Sozialökonomik*, edited by Max Weber and Joseph Schumpeter among others, in the article 'Die geographische Bedingungen der menschlichen Wirtschaft', by Alfred Hettner, in Vol. II, pp. 1–31, Tübingen, J.C.B. Mohr, 1914.
5. *The Meaning and Validity of Institutional Economics*, in Dopfer, K. (Ed.), *Economics in the Future*, London, Macmillan.
6. See e.g. his *Development and Underdevelopment. A Note on the Mechanism of National and International Economic Inequality*, Cairo, National Bank of Egypt, 1956, pp. 11–15.

The three core assumptions describe the necessary conditions for perfect competition. The assumptions are not there because they reflect observations of the real world. They are merely there to keep the theoretical structure intact. The time factor disappeared from neo-classical economic theory sometime in the 1930s, and the present theory assumes instant adjustments in the economic system. An unintended by-product of this set of assumptions is that *all economic activities become alike.* A shoe-shine boy in Quito, Ecuador, and IBM both become 'representative firms'. All variables which make these two firms differ are each and every one assumed not to exist. The mathematical accuracy of neo-classical economics is achieved at the cost of assuming away all factors which cause a geographically uneven distribution of economic growth. From the point of view of explaining uneven growth, the accuracy of neo-classical economic theory is achieved at the cost of irrelevance. Schumpeter described this trade-off between accuracy and relevance very well: 'The general reader will have to make up his mind, whether he wants *simple* answers to his questions or *useful* ones - in this as in other economic matters he cannot have both'.[7] Neo-classical economics opted for simple and accurate answers, at the cost of neglecting the factors which cause both uneven growth and, and to large extent, growth itself.

There is a total neglect of the problem of uneven development in neo-classical economics. The theory of which economists normally have been most proud - international trade theory - shows decisively that with increasing international trade we shall all be equally rich. Paul Samuelson 'proved' with two articles in 1949 and 1950 that under the usual assumptions of neo-classical economic theory, everybody would be equally rich with more international trade. *Under the assumptions,* no doubt Samuelson is correct. The problem is, however, that by assuming away increasing returns to scale, diminishing returns and imperfect competition, the main factors causing uneven development have been excluded from his analysis.

Excluding the key factors which skew income distribution has a long history in economics. The roots of the problem lie already in Adam Smith's treatment of the process of economic growth. Smith describes the division of labour - which is crucial to modern society - but he refuses to go into the organizational changes which necessarily follow. Adam Smith is committed to the study of the *individual,* and totally neglects the organizational changes which follow as the natural result of his celebrated division of labour.[8] Smith accurately observes that the division of labour '*so far as it can be introduced,* occasions, in every art, a proportionable increase of the productive powers of labour'.[9] On the same page he observes that the textile industry allows many divisions of labour, whereas agriculture does not. If division of labour causes wealth, can we understand from this that industry is more likely to cause national wealth than agriculture? Later

7. Schumpeter in the introduction to Zeuthen, F., *Problems of Monopoly and Welfare,* London, Routledge, 1930, p. x (10).
8. Adam Smith's deficiency as a student of human organizations is very well pointed out in McCraw, Thomas, 'The Trouble with Adam Smith', *American Scholar,* Vol. 61, No. 3, Summer 1992, pp. 353–73.
9. *Wealth of Nations* (1776), Chicago, University of Chicago Press, 1976, p. 9. Our italics.

in book one, on the single occasion Adam Smith uses the term 'an invisible hand'[10] he argues for the protection of national industry. On the other hand, only agriculture was 'natural' to him. There are observations in the *Wealth of Nations* - an embryo of a theory - that economic activities are different because they allow for different degrees of division of labour. However, these observations are completely lost in the main thrust of his work: A celebration of the 'natural order' of things. To Smith, industry produces the organizations and institutions which he so abhors because they invariably distort 'the natural course of things'. Adam Smith has no theory of organization, seemingly because he deeply distrusted all human institutions.

There is a profound contradiction in Adam Smith: The source of wealth, to him the division of labour, is also the source of large-scale organizations which he so despised. Without a division of labour, there is little reason why firms should exist at all. If markets are perfect, why do we need firms? Clearly because of the division of labour among men. The difference in size and power of firms is then also a result of larger or smaller divisions of labour. To this very day, economic theory has no 'theory of the firm', a fact which is observed with increasing uneasiness in the profession.

Neo-classical economic thought carries on Smith's tradition of neglecting the organizational consequences of economic development - all economic activities become alike. Since the early seventeenth century, one factor has been described as being important in making some activities better than others as carriers of economic growth: *increasing returns to scale*, or, as the phenomenon is called in business theory, *economies of scale*. **Increasing returns to scale** is the one factor which is common to the three changes in economic theory which we are looking at in this chapter: Evolutionary/ Schumpeterian, new growth theory and new trade theory.

The importance of this factor was long recognized in economic theory, until it was forced out of economic theory due to the mathematization - modelled on physics - which took place towards the end of the nineteenth century. As far back as in 1613 Antonio Serra noted that one nation could grow richer than others by specializing in activities where costs decreased in a less than proportionate way as the volume of production increased - a phenomenon he indicated was largely limited to industry.[11] To Antonio Serra the unprecedented wealth of the Republic of Venice was to a large extent to be attributed to increasing returns. Adam Smith does not mention this phenomenon, although scale effects follow naturally as a consequence of his praised division of labour - or rather their effects are what make a division of labour more profitable and 'competitive' than previous forms of production. Economies of scale were central to the nineteenth-century theories of economic growth which led - protected by high tariffs - to the industrialization of the United States, Germany and other European nations, and Japan. The founder of neo-classical economics, Alfred Marshall, in the early editions of

10. Ibid., p. 477.
11. Serra, Antonio, *Breve Trattato delle Cause che possono far abbondare li Regni d'Oro e Argento dove non sono miniere. Con applicazione al Regno di Napoli,* Naples, Lazzaro Scorrigio, 1613.

his celebrated *Principles of Economics*,[12] clearly recognized that a nation could improve its position by subsidizing economic activities subject to increasing returns, and tax those subject to diminishing returns (e.g. agriculture).

During the last decades of the nineteenth century, economic theory was formalized to the model of the physics science of that period.[13] *Increasing returns to scale*, which up until then had played an important role in economic policy-making, was not compatible with the concept of *economic equilibrium* which came to form the centrepiece of the new theory. The gradual disappearance of *increasing returns* can be studied over the eight editions of Marshall's *Principles*,[14] as economic theory moved towards mathematization in the style of late nineteenth-century physics, and the theory acquired its essential features, which are still retained today. There are in a sense two Marshalls, the early Marshall who thoroughly understands industry and to whom 'the Mecca of the Economist lies in Economic Biology', and the later Marshall who is remembered for the mechanical principles in the appendices of his *Principles*.[15] The later Marshall won the day, and during this transition economic theory 'lost' the factors which cause uneven geographic development.

Later, some economists insisted on the importance of *increasing returns* in explaining both economic growth as such (Young 1928[16]) and - working in conjunction with diminishing returns - in explaining international maldistribution of income (Graham 1923[17]). However, these very important insights were disregarded by the majority of the economics profession for one simple reason: The existence of *increasing* and *diminishing* returns was not compatible with what had come to be the core credo of economics: general equilibrium.[18]

3. Economic theory - why a radical change now?

The main body of economic theory has lived with irrelevant assumptions for 100 years. A few economists have protested - the most famous ones being Joan Robinson, Nicholas Kaldor and Wassily Leontief. Although they criticized the assumptions of economic

12. Marshall, Alfred, *Principles of Economics*, London, Macmillan, 1890 (1st edition), p. 452.
13. This extremely interesting account is found in Mirowski, Philip, *More Heat than Light. Economics as Social Physics, Physics as Nature's Economics*, Cambridge, Cambridge University Press, 1989, and in De Marchi, Neil (Ed.), *Non-Natural Science: Reflecting of the Enterprise of 'More Heat than Light'*, Durham, Duke University Press, 1993.
14. These changes can be studied in the Ninth (Variorum) Edition, 2 Volumes, London, Macmillan for the Royal Economic Society, 1961.
15. For an account of this, see Niman, Neil B., 'Biological Analogies in Marshall's Work', *Journal of the History of Economic Thought*, Vol. 13, No. 1, Spring 1991, pp. 19–36.
16. Young, Arthur, 'Increasing Returns and Economic Progress', *Economic Journal*, Vol. 38, pp. 527–42.
17. Graham, Frank, 'Some Aspects of Protection Further Considered', *Quarterly Journal of Economics*, Vol. 37, pp. 199–227.
18. A typical example showing this line of argument is found with Jacob Viner, the main trade theorist of the period, in his *Studies in the Theory of International Trade*, New York, Harper, 1937, pp. 475–82.

theory, development economists surprisingly did not pick up the issue of increasing and diminishing returns. Myrdalian vicious and virtuous circles could easily be explained by their existence. Reinert (1980[19]) shows the extent and importance of diminishing returns in the main export products of Bolivia, Ecuador and Peru. However, when the issue of scale economics returned to economic theory later in the 1980s, only the variant of importance to the industrialized world - increasing returns - was resurrected. Diminishing returns in real life is - despite its importance in the Third World - still not a part of the economics debate.

Why have these protests been ignored for so many years, and now suddenly are taken seriously? As usual in economic theory, there is a demand side and also a supply-side answer to this question. To a nation engaged in activities with 'historical increasing returns' - technical change and increasing returns - excluding scale effects will not harm economic performance - on the contrary, the country will greatly benefit from a world trading system where scale effects are ignored. The diminishing 'competitiveness' of the United States in world trade in the late 1970s - especially *vis a vis* Japan - led to a demand for theories which could provide an explanation for this. The American public now demanded the relevance which Myrdal had demanded decades earlier. Myrdal's prophesies quoted above came true. The key economist in the resurrection of *increasing returns*, Paul Krugman, emphasizes the importance of *new economic tools* as the key factor for the changes. His colleague Joseph Stiglitz stresses what in our opinion is the most important source of the change: It was the demand for new and different ideas that was crucial.[20]

After the fall of the United States from the summit of world economic power, a new generation of US economists was forced to re-examine the basic assumptions of neoclassical theory. They succeeded in developing mathematical tools to handle the problem of increasing returns to scale. In doing this, these economists unintendedly again introduced the issues of spatial income distribution, thereby reopening possibilities of communication between economics and geography.

The new demand led to a perusal of these assumptions, and also to the rediscovery of geography. As Paul Krugman puts it: 'The neglect of spatial issues in economics arises for the most part from one simple problem: how to think about market structure. Essentially, to say anything useful or interesting about the location of economic activity in space, it is necessary to get away from the constant-returns, perfect-competition approach that still dominates most economic analysis. As long as economists lacked the analytical tools to think rigorously about increasing returns and imperfect competition, the study of economic geography was condemned to lie outside the mainstream of the profession. Indeed, as standards of rigor in economics have risen over time, the study of location has been pushed further and further into the intellectual periphery.'

19. Reinert, Erik, *International Trade and the Economic Mechanisms of Underdevelopment*, Ann Arbor, University Microfilms, 1980.
20. Stiglitz, Joseph, 'Comment on "Toward a Counter-Counterrevolution in Development Theory", by Krugman', in *Proceedings of the World Bank Annual Conference on Development Economics*, Washington, DC, World Bank, 1993, p. 42.

When Krugman refers to the lack of analytical tools, he intends the mathematical toolbox of neo-classical economics. The importance of increasing and diminishing returns to the spatial distribution of wealth was clearly shown by Graham in his 1923 article, using numerical examples.

4. Trend 1: The evolutionary challenge to neo-classical economics

The evolutionary or Schumpeterian school of economics is based on the writings of the Austrian Harvard economist Joseph Alois Schumpeter. In a Schumpeterian system, the world is driven forward by technical change and innovations. These changes and innovations break down the existing structures of production in a process which Schumpeter dubbed 'schöpferische Zerstörung' or *creative destruction*. This dynamic world view contrasts sharply with the neo-classical model of the world economy, in which the central feature is the static equilibrium of supply and demand. Table 2.1 shows a comparison between evolutionary and neo-classical economics.

Schumpeter's world view is extremely different from that of today's Anglo-Saxon mainstream economics, but his views are much less original in the context of the German Historical School of Economics. Of Schumpeter's many books and articles, the central piece which contained the seeds of most of his later work was first published in German in 1912,[21] and in English as *The Theory of Economic Development*[22] in 1932. Schumpeter's view on the dynamic role of technology has much in common with Marx's, a similarity Schumpeter readily admitted to.[23]

The key book resurrecting Schumpeterian economics is Nelson and Winter's *An Evolutionary Theory of Economic Change*[24] from 1982. Lately Schumpeterian and evolutionary economics have been used by the OECD in analyzing economic growth in the so-called TEP-programme (Technology and Economy).[25] Evolutionary economics, with its emphasis on technical change and innovation as the factors creating economic growth, opens up a widely different arena for public policy than neo-classical economics does. In the neo-classical paradigm, fiscal and financial policies are virtually the only variables of government policy.

Schumpeterian economics has from its beginnings - starting with the master himself - been focused on the side of the 'winners' in the system - those 'inhabiting the top floor of the first class hotels'. The Schumpeterian school has emphasized the *creative* side of the creative destruction, not the destructive side. In our view Schumpeterian economics can - and should - also be used in explaining the more destructive sides of the world economic system. It is not clear that all Schumpeterian destructions are equally creative. It is not clear that the creation and the destruction - although related - take place in the same

---

21. *Theorie der wirtschaftlichen Entwicklung*, Leipzig, Dunker & Humblot, 1912.
22. Cambridge, MA, Harvard University Press.
23. See e.g. 'Preface to the Japanese *Theorie der wirtschaftlichen Entwicklung*', in Clemence, Richard V. (Ed.), *Essays of J.A. Schumpeter*, Cambridge, MA, Addison-Wesley, 1951, 160–61.
24. Nelson, Richard and Winter, Sidney, Cambridge, MA, Harvard University Press, 1982.
25. The main report is *Technology and the Economy. The Key Relationships*, Paris, OECD, 1992.

Table 2.1 Neo-classical and Evolutionary Economics - a brief comparison.

NEO-CLASSICAL THEORY	*EVOLUTIONARY THEORY*
USE OF PHYSICAL METAPHORS	USE OF BIOLOGICAL METAPHORS
'EQUILIBRIUM' AS A CENTRAL CONCEPT	EMPHASIS ON FACTORS CAUSING DISEQUILIBRIUM
STATIC/COMPARATIVE STATICS	DYNAMIC
HIGH DEGREE OF PRECISION	LESS PRECISE, OPEN TO NON-QUANTIFIABLE FACTORS
ASSUMES PERFECT INFORMATION	SYSTEM OPERATES UNDER UNCERTAINTY
TIME NOT AN ISSUE	TIME AS IMPORTANT FACTOR 'HISTORY MATTERS'
ENTREPRENEURSHIP UNIMPORTANT	ENTREPRENEURSHIP CENTRAL FACTOR
'ALL ECONOMIC ACTIVITIES ARE EQUAL' (POTATO CHIPS, WOOD CHIPS AND COMPUTER CHIPS)	ECONOMIC ACTIVITIES ARE DIFFERENT BECAUSE INNOVATION 'FOCUSES' AT ANY POINT IN TIME
POSTULATES 'THE REPRESENTATIVE FIRM'	'THE REPRESENTATIVE FIRM' DOES NOT EXIST
THE MARKET AS PRICE SETTER	THE MARKET ALSO AS A SELECTION MECHANISM AMONG FIRMS
TECHNOLOGY AS A FREE GOOD 'MANNA FROM HEAVEN'	TECHNOLOGY AS AN IMPORTANT FACTOR IN WEALTH CREATION AND DISTRIBUTION
'THE MARKET IS ALWAYS RIGHT'/ LAISSEZ-FAIRE	OPENS FOR A MORE ACTIVE ECONOMIC POLICY

geographical area. (Indian indigo producers and German producers of synthetic dyes). The technological 'frontier', where creative destruction takes place, moves ahead very unevenly across industries, creating the opportunity for backwardness caused by technological lock-in effects, to occur (being an efficient Stone-Age producer in the Bronze Age).

Diminishing returns to natural resources in the Third World is to some extent being counteracted by technological change - but what is the end effect on national income? In Schumpeterian economics all economic activities are qualitatively not alike from the point of view of creating wealth and poverty.

If economic activities are not 'alike', then how do they differ? To any entrepreneur his business - product and/or location, service, personnel or clientele - is unique. The real world gives us hundreds of millions of different firms; economic theory, for all practical purposes, tells us they are all alike. How can we find an intermediate level of abstraction, one where economic activities can be ranked according to their importance

Table 2.2 The Quality Index of Economic Activities.[1]

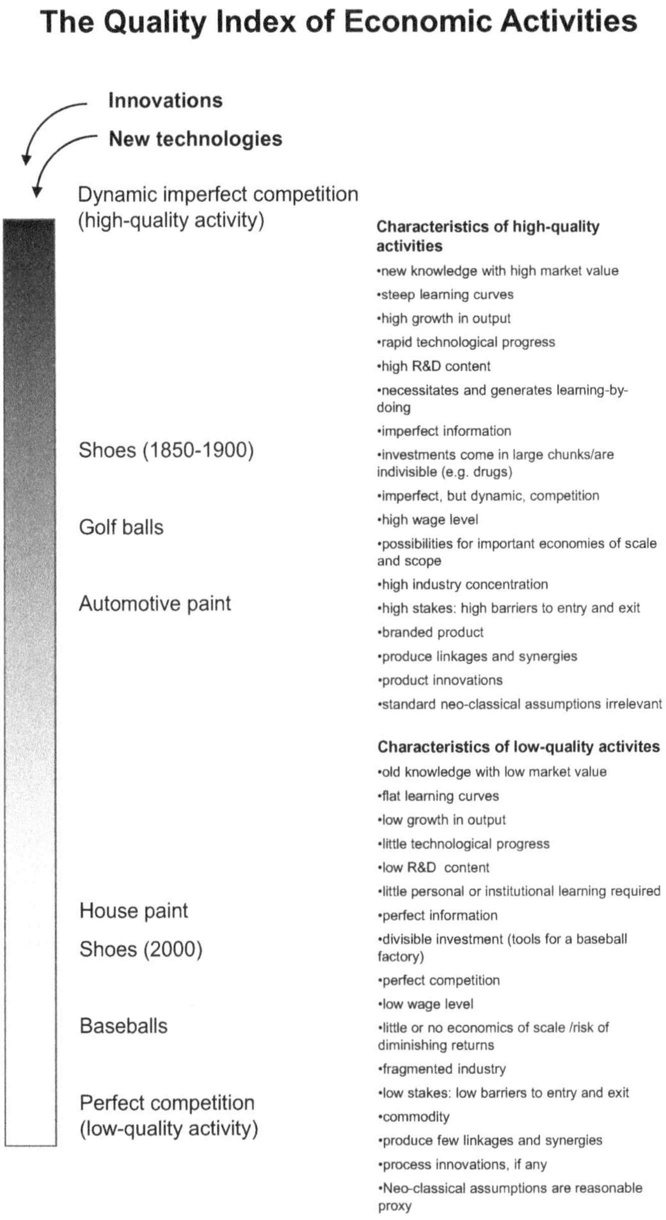

The Quality Index of Economic Activities

Innovations

New technologies

Activity scale	Characteristics
Dynamic imperfect competition (high-quality activity)	**Characteristics of high-quality activities**
	•new knowledge with high market value
	•steep learning curves
	•high growth in output
	•rapid technological progress
	•high R&D content
	•necessitates and generates learning-by-doing
	•imperfect information
Shoes (1850-1900)	•investments come in large chunks/are indivisible (e.g. drugs)
	•imperfect, but dynamic, competition
Golf balls	•high wage level
	•possibilities for important economies of scale and scope
	•high industry concentration
Automotive paint	•high stakes: high barriers to entry and exit
	•branded product
	•produce linkages and synergies
	•product innovations
	•standard neo-classical assumptions irrelevant
	Characteristics of low-quality activites
	•old knowledge with low market value
	•flat learning curves
	•low growth in output
	•little technological progress
	•low R&D content
	•little personal or institutional learning required
House paint	•perfect information
Shoes (2000)	•divisible investment (tools for a baseball factory)
	•perfect competition
	•low wage level
Baseballs	•little or no economics of scale /risk of diminishing returns
	•fragmented industry
Perfect competition (low-quality activity)	•low stakes: low barriers to entry and exit
	•commodity
	•produce few linkages and synergies
	•process innovations, if any
	•Neo-classical assumptions are reasonable proxy

[1] *Source*: Reinert, 'Catching-up from Way Behind - A Third World Perspective on First World History'.

to what we measure as economic growth? In Table 2.2 we attempt to construct an index where economic activities may be ranked according to their potential of contributing to economic growth. The 'high-quality' activities are those which give nations 'competitiveness': activities which enable nations to raise their national wage level and still be able to sell their products on the international market. Underlying the index is that the activities with a high score collect an 'industry rent' which is distributed between capital, labour and national governments. A core mechanism for capital allocation in market societies is that risk capital is attracted to the activities with a high rate of technical change and a high rate of innovations - those with a high score on the quality index. The imperfect competition which exists at the top level of the quality index - showing the characteristics which are listed - attracts necessary risk capital, but the benefits accrued from being in these activities are also divided with labour, and ultimately with the nation through the creation of a higher tax base.

The main export activities of developing countries achieve a low score on the quality index. They consist of raw materials or mature industrial products. In the production of raw material - due to more perfectly working markets - technical change tends to be taken out as lowered prices, and not as higher wages. Mature industries, like the production of baseballs with a needle and thread technology, are farmed out to the poor countries through the working of the market. Such activities become labour intensive, in the sense that low labour cost becomes the most critical factor of production.

The Schumpeterian system - exemplified in the Quality Index of Economic Activities - presents development geographers with a theoretical framework in which the study of uneven economic growth can be placed. This set of theories could serve as a unifying theory to the many case studies in the field of development geography. They offer an alternative theoretical 'peg' on which case studies may be appended.

5. Trend 2: 'New Economic Growth Theory'

5.1. The 'residual' and the origins of doubt

From being a theory where economic growth was caused merely by the addition of more capital to each unit of labour, economic growth theory has, over the last four decades, moved on to take account also of other factors. The origin of this change lies in the so-called 'residual debate' in the late 1950s, associated with Moses Abramovitz and Robert Solow. In his 1957 paper 'Technological Change and the Aggregate Production Function',[26] Solow compares a model based on the standard aggregate production function to the actual figures in the US economy.[27] His surprising result is that only 12.5 per cent of economic growth in the period studied can be attributed to the increase of

26. Solow, Robert, 'Technical Change and the Aggregate Production Function', in *Review of Economics and Statistics*, August 1957.
27. The aggregate production function sees the amount of produced goods in a society as a function of the total amount of labour and capital in society. An increase of the total production (measured by GDP) in a society must therefore be explained by an increase of the amount of capital or labour (or both) in production. This means that if one can measure the increase of labour and capital during a period, it should be possible to calculate growth of GDP fairly accurately.

labour and capital. A 'residual' of 87.5 per cent of overall growth has to be explained by some other factor. Solow therefore introduces a third factor labelled 'technical change'.

A year earlier Moses Abramovitz had published a paper with a slightly different methodology. He obtained similar results: Only a small part of the growth in the national income could be explained by the growth of the traditional production factors labour and capital. The remainder - the huge 'residual' - was impossible for Abramovitz to explain by traditional economic theory. He saw the size of the residual as 'a measure of our ignorance about the causes of economic growth'.[28]

Both Solow and Abramovitz pointed out that in order to explain economic growth, a new and third factor had to be included in the traditional neo-classical production function: The concept of technology. But a consequence of doing this is to question a fundamental condition in all neo-classical theory: The condition of no increasing returns to scale.

Anyone who has opened an introductory text in economics will remember that the idea of supply and demand being equal is at the core of economic theory. A French physicist-turned-economist, Leon Walras, showed towards the end of the nineteenth century, by mathematical deduction, that in economic equilibrium free competition was what later came to be called 'Pareto optimal': Any deviation from the situation of free competition - i.e. general equilibrium - would lead to a welfare loss. Challenging the notion of constant returns on an aggregate level therefore not only threatens the 'scientificness' of the economic science but also the ideological basis of today's world economic system. Liberating economic theory from the straitjacket of constant returns also opens up for explaining uneven growth.

5.2. *Saving the model - achieving perfect competition* and *increasing returns*

Technology was clearly a factor which differed from those hitherto employed in neo-classical theory: Labour and capital. A 1962 article by Kenneth Arrow discusses *information* as a commodity, and his analysis can also be extended to be valid for the *commodity* technology.[29] Arrow shows that unlike traditional commodities such as labour and goods, information has some special qualities: (a) Once produced it is difficult to shield from others, and (b) There is often no cost associated with sharing information with others. Knowledge - and in many instances technology - can be labelled as a public good.

This basic insight from Arrow was used by the founder of what is now called the new neo-classical growth theory, Paul Romer,[30] when discussing technological change and increasing returns. Romer sets up two sets of dichotomies: First he distinguishes

28. Abramovitz, Moses, 'Resource and Output Trends in the United States since 1870', in *American Economic Review, Papers and Proceedings*, May 1956.
29. Arrow, Kenneth, 'Economic Welfare and the Allocation of Resources for Invention', in *The Rate and Direction of Inventive Activity*, Princeton, Princeton University Press, 1962.
30. Romer, Paul, 'Are Nonconvexities Important for Understanding Growth', in *American Economic Review, Papers and Proceedings*, May 1990.

between what he calls *rival* and *nonrival* goods, with *nonrival* meaning that 'it can be used simultaneously by arbitrarily many different firms and people'. The use of a car is *rival* - using the knowledge to produce a new fishing hook is *nonrival.* To Romer, 'a nonrival input has a high cost of producing the first unit and a zero cost of producing subsequent units'. Romer explicitly mentions inputs like production design, which can also be extended to mean technology. The second dichotomy established by Romer is *excludability* and *nonexcludability*. Excludability is: 'if someone with a property right can exclude others from taking advantage of it.' As an example, a car is rival and excludable, computer software is excludable (by copy protection) but nonrival because the same knowledge is being used by subsequent users. If a good is nonrival, it produces what Romer calls *nonconvexity*: If the input of rival goods which are used in the production process is doubled, then the production doubles. But, the nonrival product technology does not have to be doubled in order to achieve this. The nonrival input can (by definition) be used again, in this model virtually cost free.

Technology, being a nonrival factor of production, does not have to be doubled in order to double production. This effect will produce increasing returns, since doubling of output does not depend on doubling of all the inputs (only on doubling of capital and labour). US mathematician Paul Romer - in his PhD dissertation from 1983 - managed to introduce technology into economic theory again, bringing growth back into the mainstream of economic debate. In this way technology was introduced as a major factor of growth, but the assumption of perfect information and the general equilibrium were saved. Romer has elegantly included the technology variable, but by making technology a public good he continues to exclude all economic factors which cause uneven development.

The new growth models treat technical change as an *endogenous* - or internal - factor. Solow's model of aggregate growth includes a factor representing technical change over time. This helps Solow fit the model to his data, but many economists have found his approach rather unsatisfactory. It looks like technical change is *exogenous* - as if it were generated outside the economic system itself. Romer and other writers in the new neo-classical growth tradition have shown how this change can itself be generated as a product of economic activity.

A 1986 article by Romer[31] is mainly concerned with the question of externalities and increasing returns. Romer distinguishes between two different forms of knowledge: Specific knowledge for the firm, and the general level of knowledge in society. This general level of knowledge in society equals the sum of the knowledge of individual companies. This means that if one company increases its level of knowledge, the general level of knowledge in society increases. Clearly Romer here maintains the assumption of perfect information, which in the end would mean that all human beings know exactly the same. Other companies will gain from the production of knowledge in a firm, implying that knowledge production has externality effects. Following the excludability and rivalry discussions above, the growth of an economy is determined by the

31. Romer, Paul, 'Increasing Returns and Long-Run Growth', *Journal of Political Economy*, 1986.

growth of knowledge. Romer has elegantly made increasing returns and externalities compatible with 'competitive equilibrium'.

One interesting aspect is that Romer shows how market forces by themselves do not necessarily lead to optimal welfare. His model shows that government action may produce positive welfare effects. To each individual firm the most profitable strategy may be to use existing knowledge. On the other hand, knowledge produced in individual firms will spill over to the rest of society, thereby increasing economic growth and welfare. This has, of course, long been recognized outside the circles of neo-classical economists.

5.3. Opening up for uneven growth

In 1988 Robert Lucas, Jr. published an article entitled 'On the Mechanics of Economic Development'.[32] Here he attempts the task of 'constructing a neo-classical theory of growth and international trade that is consistent with some of the main features of economic development'. His main concern with neo-classical economics is 'its apparent inability to account for observed diversity across countries, and its strong and counterfactual prediction that international trade should induce rapid movement towards equality in capital-labour ratios and factor prices'. By introducing accumulation of human capital (learning) which is constant independently of the level of achieved knowledge (no diminishing return on knowledge production), Lucas is able to make a much more realistic model of the economy. In his model the production of knowledge takes place either as a result of intentional practice or as a by-product of other activities. ('learning by doing'). The fact that knowledge can be produced in activities not intended directly for knowledge production, was pointed out by Kenneth Arrow in 1962.[33] In Lucas' model, if a country has a large part of production that generates 'learning by doing', this country will achieve a higher growth because of the higher accumulation of knowledge. As opposed to Romer, Lucas opens up a new growth theory for the study of uneven development.

The general conclusions of the most realistic models in the new neo-classical growth theory are twofold: (1) that there is a role for a government industrial policy, and (2) that, following Lucas, countries with different initial conditions can face two different paths of development depending on the initial conditions. These models can produce a general equalization of the growth levels of the rich countries - there will be a catching-up of the least rich of the rich towards the richest. Among the poorest countries there will be convergence where the poorest countries will be lagging more and more behind - a polarization of the world into two groups, the have's and the have not's.

32. Lucas, Robert Jr. 'On the Mechanics of Economic Development', *Journal of Monetary Economics*, Vol. 22, pp. 3–42.
33. Arrow, Kenneth, 'The Economic Implications of Learning by Doing', *Review of Economic Studies*, Vol. 29, pp. 155–73.

6. Trend 3: Trade and geography - the return of increasing returns

Forcing the issue slightly, the history of economic thought can be divided into three periods: The *Age of Discovery* (from the beginnings of the science in the sixteenth century until the 1890s), the *Age of Formalization* (1870–1980s) and the *Age of Rediscovery* (starting in the 1980s). In the Age of Rediscovery, economists are putting back into economic theory important factors - described and used for economic policy centuries ago - which were excluded from economic theory during the period of mathematization based on nineteenth-century physics. As a result, economic theory is lowered several notches in terms of the level of abstraction. Consequently, it also reopens for including the factors which cause uneven growth.

The key factor being put back into trade theory is, again, increasing returns, and the key person in the process of rediscovery is MIT's Paul Krugman. Krugman correctly observes that economic theory 'has followed the perceived line of least mathematical resistance'.[34] He claims that the reason scale effects were excluded was that the profession was unable to express these mathematically. Starting in 1979 Krugman published a series of articles introducing increasing returns in international trade theory. His 1979 and 1980 articles[35] model a world where an initial discrepancy in capital-labour ratio exists between two countries or groups of countries. A period of increasing international trade follows, where only the industrial sector works under increasing returns to scale. The result of this is a world divided into two groups, a rich industrialized centre and a poor underdeveloped periphery. In these papers, Krugman refers to Myrdal, Frank, Baran, Wallerstein and even Lenin.

This breakthrough in international trade theory was the result of using models originating in the study of imperfectly competitive markets in the field of industrial economics. Krugman inadvertently opened a Pandora's box, where international markets no longer are fully competitive, and where countries may grow poorer in the presence of free trade than under autarky. Paradoxically, the wave of Reaganomics free market policies, which hit the developing countries in the early 1980s, coincided with the first proof of neo-classical trade theorists that government intervention really *could* improve the free trade situation of a poor country.[36] Krugman's conclusions are no more precise than were Marshall's in 1890: That a country can be better off subsidizing its increasing return activities and taxing those under diminishing returns. However, Krugman does not refer to this. His history of increasing returns starts with Graham's 1923 article, and he has no mention of the long history of increasing returns - going back to 1613 - as a cause of imperfect competition and consequently as a factor determining economic policy, especially the support and protection of national industry.

One important problem is that the existence of increasing returns provides an argument both for free trade and protection. When commodities are traded at the same

34. Krugman, Paul, *Rethinking International Trade*, Cambridge, MA, MIT Press, 1990, p. 4.
35. Reproduced in *Rethinking International Trade*.
36. A collection of papers on this subject is in Grossman, Gene (Ed.), *Imperfect Competition and International Trade*, Cambridge, MA, MIT Press, 1992.

'level' or 'degree' of increasing returns, the new theory is an argument for more free trade. When trading is between nations producing goods at different degrees of scale effects, the benefits of international trade accrue more, or in some cases exclusively, to the nation producing with the highest degree of economies of scale. In a dynamic framework, when goods produced at increasing returns are sold in exchange for goods produced with diminishing returns, it can be shown, as Graham did in 1923, that the country producing at diminishing returns will actually grow poorer with trade than under autarky. We can compare these cases with what the dependency school referred to as 'symmetrical' and 'asymmetrical' dependency.

The understanding we express here differs crucially from Krugman's. Krugman's mental scheme seems to operate with broadly based sectors, containing homogenous activities from the point of view of scale effects. His conclusion is therefore that what he calls intraindustry trade - trading inside the same product groups, trading cars for cars - is necessarily mutually beneficial to both trading countries. Krugman's approach, using homogenous sectors, excludes the possibility that within the same sector or industry only *some* economic activities are subject to increasing returns. The very same differences he assumes *between* economic sectors, also exist *within* sectors, industries and even within companies. Within the industry producing balls for sports, the most efficient golf ball producers live in the industrialized countries and make about 10 dollars hourly, while the world's most efficient baseball producers make 30 US cents an hour in Haiti. Both the US golf ball producers and the Haitian baseball producers are the most efficient in the world, given the present state of technology. The difference between the two industries is that golf balls are produced with increasing returns to scale and high barriers to entry, whereas the baseball-producing industry operates under conditions of nearly constant returns to scale and low barriers to entry (needle and thread technology).

Krugman's distinguished career 'has been ... confined geographically to the Northeast corridor' (of the United States).[37] His imaginative models have extended to 'a clever paper on interstellar trade, where goods are transported from one stellar system to another at speeds close to that of light; the resulting relativistic correction to time entails different interest rates in different frames of reference'.[38] The problem in today's economic theory is that writing a model of a phenomenon proves next to nothing. Any good graduate student in economics can write a model showing his pet theory. The problem lies in verifying the models, and deciding which ones contain elements which point at important relationships in the real world. After siding with the dependency school, and with Lenin, in his 1979 and 1980 articles, Krugman has been sitting on the lid of the Pandora's box he opened. In his latest book[39]- aimed at a wider audience than his other book - Krugman's trade theory is again reduced to Ricardo's static gains from 1817. The new insights are - inexplicably, in our opinion - lost. The 1979 and

---

37. Dixit, Avinash, 'In Honor of Paul Krugman: Winner of the John Bates Clark Medal', *Journal of Economic Perspectives*, Vol. 7, No. 2, Spring 1993, p. 173.
38. Ibid., p. 173.
39. *Peddling Prosperity*, New York, Norton, 1994.

1980 articles, which in our view provided very important insights into the structure of North-South trade, have been relegated to the same level as the interstellar paper - a clever use of mathematics with no practical consequences. Krugman's emphasis has been on the existence of increasing returns as an argument for *more* free trade, which is the case with 'symmetrical' relationships. This may, of course, be because he is afraid that the scale argument may be used to reinforce the already strong protectionist sentiments in his own country. The fact that neither Krugman nor his colleagues use actual economic data from either industrial countries or from the Third World to verify their models, effectively blocks his important insights from being used in economic policy.

It may also seem as if Krugman sees scale effects for poorer countries only in a framework of *the infant industry or infant nation argument.* His treatment of Canada - a rare case of historical examples in Krugman's work, illustrates this point. Krugman seemingly accepts the argument that the historical lag and smaller scale of the Canadian economy warranted protection: 'it seems reasonable to argue that Canada's nationalistic economic policies were the key factor in creating this (industrial) strength[40].' Krugman goes out of his way to show that the Canadian case - the only empirical case he uses - is different to that of other periphery nations. His argument is that since the United States and Canada in the period in question were competing for immigrants, 'they could do something that similar policies elsewhere cannot: by protecting the domestic market, they could also extend it'. We have two problems with this argument: First of all, it is difficult to understand why it only applies to Canada and the United States, and not all the other nations which at the same time were 'competing' for immigrants: Australia, New Zealand, Argentina and many others. Secondly, there are more ways to expand markets than by encouraging immigration. Increasing per capita production and consumption by entering into activities exhibiting Schumpeterian 'historical' increasing returns, or achieving the winning combination of learning by doing and imperfect information, can be done equally well with a fixed population.

The core of nineteenth-century protectionism is exactly what Krugman points out: By protecting the national market for national industries, the market was extended, because the increasing returns which accrued to new industries more than outweighed the initial increase in price caused by the protection. A higher initial price for industrial goods was traded off for an even higher increase in real wages and profits in the protecting nation[41] - a phenomenon which is inexplicable without the existence of imperfect competition and/or increasing returns.

A thorough understanding of the scale argument leads to the possibility of recommending lasting protection of certain industries, especially if the alternative free trade leads to lock-in effects in natural resource–based industries which by their very nature lead into production with diminishing returns. This is the core of the Australian

40. *Geography and Trade*, p. 92.
41. For a discussion of this, see Reinert, Erik, 'Competitiveness and its Predecessors - A 500-year Cross-National Perspective', Oslo, STEP-Group, STEP-Report No. 3, 1994, pp. 11–12

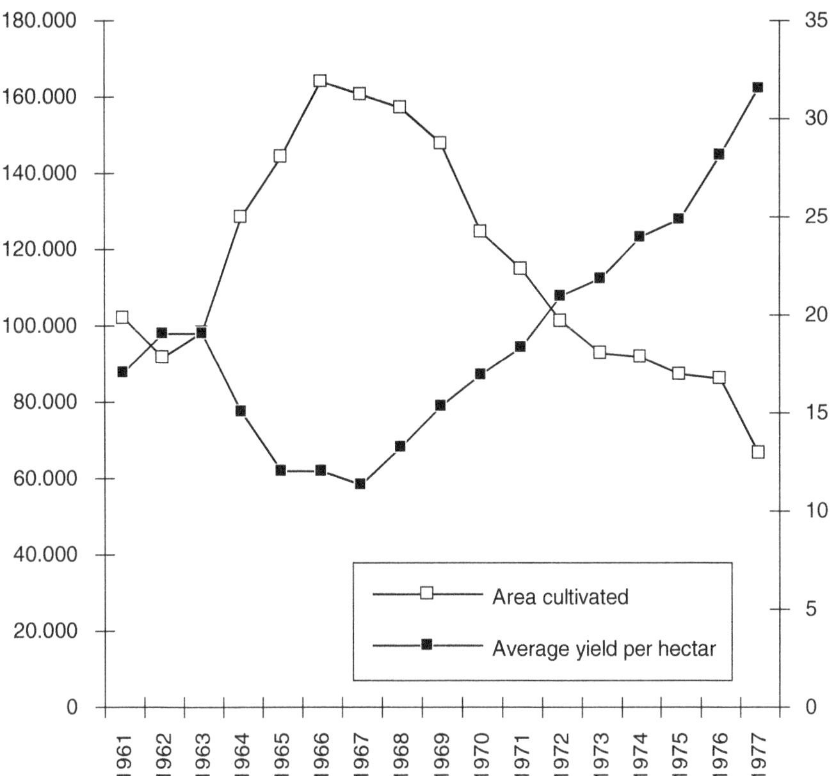

Figure 2.1 Ecuador, Banana Production 1961–1977: Area Cultivated and Yield per Hectar.

strategy historically. As already mentioned, Krugman has only resurrected *half* of Frank Graham's 1923 paper, the part dealing with increasing returns, which is the part of interest to the United States today. Graham also showed how production under diminishing returns would lead to underdevelopment, implicitly also if the industrial country only produced under constant returns to scale. An example of how the effect of diminishing returns contributes to underdevelopment - the case of banana production in Ecuador - is shown in Figure 2.1.

7. Conclusion - towards a *rapprochement* between economics and development geography

Development geography has, since the heyday of development economics in the 1950s and 1960s, lived in a world with relatively little theoretical development on the macro-level. One may say that the field of development geography has suffered from a *case-study syndrome* - many case studies and little unifying theory. The need is clearly there to tie the case studies together with theories on a higher level of abstraction.

The field of economics, on the other hand, has until recently disregarded - assumed as non-existent - all the factors which cause differences in economic growth. As described in this chapter, the recent revival of interest in the process of economic growth is about to free economic theory from its most restrictive assumptions. This process has brought new theoretical insights in three broad areas: Schumpeterian Economics, New Neo-classical Growth Theory and New Trade Theory. The use of the new insights from these areas is, to a surprising degree, only confined to the OECD countries. While the OECD countries apply the new knowledge on how imperfect markets distribute growth in favour of certain industries, the Second (ex-communist) and Third World are being treated to a 'restructuring' exercise which leaves the majority of them largely de-industrialized and considerably poorer than they were when the process started. The exceptions to this are the South-East Asian countries which pick up the 'cascade' of maturing industrial products which successively are farmed out for production from the industrial growth engines of Japan, Taiwan and Korea.

Today the only area where neo-classical economics is used exclusively as a basis for economic policy is in the Third World. The ignorance in the IMF and in the World Bank of the insights used by the OECD and the EU is, in our opinion, a case of what Myrdal used to call 'opportunistic ignorance'. The challenge for development geography as a profession is in our view to apply the new knowledge generated about the First World growth processes for use in the Second and Third World.[42] Case studies from developing countries and comparisons of First and Third World historical experiences, analyzed in the perspectives of Schumpeterian economics, could prove exceedingly useful in furthering the understanding of underdevelopment. Development policy would take a radically new turn if only the insights used by the OECD were to be integrated into the policies of the World Bank and the IMF - the last fortresses of applied neo-classical economics.

---

42. An attempt at this is Reinert, Erik, 'Catching-up from Way Behind - A Third World Perspective on First World History', in Fagerberg, Jan et al. (Eds.), *Catching up, Forging Ahead, and Falling Behind. On the Dynamics of Technology, Trade, and Growth*, London, Edward Elgar. Chapter 1 in this volume.

Chapter 3

A SCHUMPETERIAN THEORY OF UNDERDEVELOPMENT - A CONTRADICTION IN TERMS?

The aim of this chapter is to show that the dynamics of Schumpeterian economics, in addition to explain the creation of wealth, also implicitly contain the elements of a theory of relative poverty. It is argued that the German tradition of economics, of which Schumpeter is a part, has always encompassed the necessary elements of a theory of *uneven* growth. List, Marx, and Schumpeter have all emphasized different aspects of this uneven growth. This contrasts sharply with the Anglo-Saxon tradition which, particularly since the 1890s, has produced theories of growth and trade which imply an even, converging distribution of world activity and income.

The organization of the chapter is as follows: **Section 1** contrasts Anglo-Saxon and German economic traditions from the point of view of theories of *uneven* growth vs. theories of *even* growth. **Section 2** raises the question of the relationship between technical change and underdevelopment, and identifies two key mechanisms which create uneven distribution of the gains from technical change. The two are (I) the consequences of the extremely uneven advance of the 'technological frontier' and (II) *Classical* and *Collusive* spreads of technological gains. **Section 3** shows how these mechanisms work to create three cases of 'Schumpeterian underdevelopment' in the Caribbean. In **Section 4** it is claimed that the factors identified in Section 2 may create conflicting interests between the two parts that every individual plays in economic life, that of *producer* and that of *consumer.* It is claimed that these are identical only under the assumptions of neo-classical economics and in special cases of what is labelled *symmetrical* trade. Finally, in **Section 5**, the policy conclusions of these findings are discussed. It is showed how the conflicting interests of man-the-consumer and man-the-producer, produced by *classical* and *collusive* spreads of technical change, were central to the creation of US industrial policy in the early nineteenth century.

1. Anglo-Saxon vs. German economics: Theories of even vs. theories of uneven growth

Friedrich List, Karl Marx and Joseph Alois Schumpeter are the German economists who have had a major influence on economic policy outside the German-speaking area. The theories of Marx and Schumpeter are deeply rooted in the traditions of the German Historical School of Economics, and although Friedrich List antedates what is generally seen as the starting point of the older historical school, his approach is clearly that of a 'proto-historical school'. The roots of this line of thought go back to the times of the cameralists, at least as far back as Philipp von Hörnigk's work of 1684.[1] All three authors - List, Marx and Schumpeter - share an essentially very similar dynamic view of economic development. This is especially evident when their theories are contrasted with the Anglo-Saxon economic traditions, the tradition which provides the foundation for our present world economic order. The German tradition produces theories of *uneven* growth; Anglo-Saxon neo-classical economics tends to produce theories of *even* growth. This is particularly true when neo-classical economics is translated into international economic policy, and the finer points of the theory are lost. In terms of economic policy, a key difference between these two bodies of thought is that whereas in Anglo-Saxon economic theory the location of production in space is not an issue, this location is often crucial to economic wealth in German economic policy. Anglo-Saxon economics is primarily a theory of *exchange*, whereas German economic theory, to a much larger extent, involves *production*. In German theory, differences in circumstances of production translate into differences in wealth.

Prior to Adam Smith, many English theories of growth were also theories of uneven growth. I have argued elsewhere that the mercantilist view was that economic growth was *activity-specific*, that it took place in some economic activities and not in others.[2] It should also be noted that in nineteenth-century United States the economic theories which served as guidance for economic policy (as opposed to what was often thought at 'ivy league' universities) were 'German-type' theories. Friedrich List's prolonged stay in the United States in the 1820s clearly provided a cross-fertilization of German theories and US Hamiltonian thoughts on the matter of economic policy. Similarly, in Japan, the economic theories adopted after the Meiji Restoration were specifically based on German *national*ökonomische theories, openly rejecting the *cosmo*political aspects of English economic theory.

The similarities of Marx and Schumpeter are readily admitted by Schumpeter, most clearly so in the foreword to the Japanese version of the *Theorie der wirtschaftlichen Entwicklung*. Schumpeter explains here how he was looking for 'a source of energy within the economic system, that would of itself disrupt any equilibrium that might be attained ...It was not clear to me at the outset ..that the idea and the aim are exactly the

1. *Österreich über alles wann es nur will,* Nürnberg, 1684.This important work appeared in 16 editions between 1684 and 1784, all in German. This was considerably more than the most famous English economists at the time. Mun's *England's Treasure* from 1664 reached eight editions in English and six in translations, Child's *Brief Observations* of 1690 reached ten editions in English and two translations. Anthem published an English translation of von Hörnigk's work as 'Austria Supreme (if it so wishes). A strategy for European Economic Supremacy' in 2018.
2. Reinert, Erik S. 'Catching-up from Way behind, A Third World view Perspective on First World History', Chapter 1 in this volume.

same as the idea and the aim which underlie the teachings of Karl Marx'.[3] The similarities in the two systems are, Schumpeter says, 'obliterated by a very wide difference in general outlook'.[4] Many authors, starting in the late 1940s, have compared Marx and Schumpeter. A bibliography of 'Works on Schumpeter' lists 77 works treating both Marx and Schumpeter (of a total of 1916 entries).[5]

In spite of their similarities, the 'wide difference in general outlook' between the two economists has continued with their modern disciples. A special division of labour of Schumpeter's *creative destruction* has taken place between Schumpeterians and Marxists: The Schumpeterians explain the *creative* part, e.g. the growth of the English cotton textile industry, whereas the Marxists concentrate on the *destructive* part: The bones of the Bengali weavers, the previous suppliers of the same product to the English and Indian markets, 'whitening the plains of India'. Schumpeterians produce theories of *development,* Marxists produce theories of *underdevelopment.* Both these sets of theories, however, intrinsically contain the elements of the opposite view. Marxian economics (as distinguished from Marxist economics) produces a dynamic theory of development,[6] albeit uneven, where the 'bourgeoisie cannot exist without constantly revolutionising the instruments of production'. The uneven distribution of wealth is kept up by, among other factors, the imperfect competition produced by constant innovations.

A similar picture of Schumpeter's *dynamic income inequalities* can be found in his *Theory of Economic Development*: Schumpeter recognizes that 'the upper strata of society are like hotels which are always full of people, but people who are forever changing'.[7] As opposed to Marx, Schumpeter's interest in the fate of the groups not living in this upper-class hotel, however, is very limited. The key factor which unites Marx and Schumpeter - and distinguishes both these approaches from Anglo-Saxon economic theory - is that theirs is essentially a theory of *uneven growth.* For this reason, in any 'German-type' theoretical approach, problems of income distribution are implicit in the system, whereas this type of problem is non-existent at the paradigm level in Anglo-Saxon economics.

If we compare the world of today with the world in which Marx wrote, two important developments have taken place, especially since World War II. These developments have changed the geographical setting of distributional problems, from being essentially *national* to being *international* problems: (i) Successful mechanisms for income redistribution in most industrialized countries have alleviated national problems of income

---

3. Reproduced in English in Clemence, Richard V., *Essays of J.A. Schumpeter,* Cambridge, MA, Addison-Wesley Press, 1951, p. 160.
4. Ibid., p. 161.
5. Augello, Massimo M., *Joseph Alois Schumpeter. A Reference Guide,* Berlin, Springer-Verlag, 1990. The largest numbers of publications comparing Marx and Schumpeter have appeared in Italian books and journals, a total of 23. The second most frequent nation is Japan.
6. For a comment on this see e.g. Rosenberg, Nathan, 'Marx on the Economic Role of Science', in his *Perspectives of Technology,* Cambridge, Cambridge University Press, 1976, pp. 126–138.
7. Schumpeter, Joseph A., *The Theory of Economic Development,* Cambridge, MA, Harvard University Press, 1934, p. 156. This part is not found in the first German edition, Leipzig, Duncker & Humblot, 1912.

distribution, and (ii) 'globalization' has substituted the present international division of labour for the previous national one, also in manufacturing goods, thus moving the distributional conflicts more and more from the national (between 'classes') to the international arena (between nations). National problems of income distribution, in the sense of poverty alleviation, have to a large extent been solved in the industrial countries, particularly in Europe and Japan. The enormous costs involved in this redistribution with the industrial nations are rarely debated, least of all on a theoretical level.

Since Adam Smith, Anglo-Saxon economics has been *cosmo*political economy. In English classical theory, as opposed to in economic policy, distributional issues were not a core issue. In classical and neo-classical theory, national and international distributive issues have been assumed away through the inclusion of simplifying assumptions. Over time these simplifications crystallized into the two key assumptions of neo-classical economics: perfect information and the absence of increasing returns. It is the inclusion of these two assumptions - both counterfactual - which have created the blind spot of neo-classical economics: the inability to account for the extremely different levels of development between the nations of the world. With the assumptions of perfect information and constant returns to scale in place, any theory of economic growth automatically becomes a theory of *even* growth. These assumptions seem to remove the reasons for a Smithian 'division of labour': differences in human knowledge and fixed costs in specialized machinery. Perfect information seems difficult to reconcile with a notion of 'human capital'. Constant returns to scale seems difficult to reconcile with the existence of fixed costs, which create varying degrees of 'minimum efficient size'. These two assumptions - implicit or explicit - turned English economics into a *cosmo*political school of economics. As a reaction to this, nineteenth-century German economics became *National*ökonomie and *Volks*wirtschaft - terms which stick to this very day both in Germany and in Scandinavia. Here, less restrictive assumptions were made.

What Marx and Schumpeter have in common are strong roots in the German Historical School of Economics. These roots are not clear to the observer of today, for at least two reasons. First of all, the German historical tradition is hardly known outside the German-speaking world, very few works have been translated[8] and secondly the followers of both Schumpeter and Marx have, for different reasons, consciously and/or unconsciously cultivated the originality of their leading man. In the communist bloc, Marx's doctrine was cultivated as being the product of what in another religion is called an 'immaculate conception': Marx could not be seen as having borrowed from despicable bourgeois economists. The fact is that Marx borrowed heavily from the founder of the German historical school, Wilhelm Roscher.[9]

8. Two volumes of Wilhelm Roscher's works were published in English in Chicago, 1882. We should also keep in mind that Schumpeter's first book, on methodology, was only published in English in 2010, whereas there were Japanese translation already in 1936, 1950, and 1983/84.

9. Roscher, Wilhelm, *Die Grundlagen der Nationalökonomie*, Stuttgart, Cotta, 1854.

Together with Charles Babbage[10] and Andrew Ure,[11] whom he quotes several times, Roscher was probably the first economist to fully understand the economics of mass production: 'He (Roscher) created the image of large-scale industry whose essential feature is increasing returns or decreasing costs.'[12] Roscher also specifically pointed to the existence of increasing returns in research. Whereas Babbage and Ure wrote specialized treatises on the economics of large-scale industry, Roscher incorporated these insights into a holistic economic theory. Roscher's work was to be the standard textbook for a generation of Germans, appearing in 26 editions. Marx differed from the rest of the German school by subscribing to Ricardo's labour theory of value, which to Roscher and to the German historical tradition was un-German and 'typically English'. The importance given to economies of scale in German economics goes back before Roscher to previous works by Hufeland[13] and Hermann.[14] Roscher also refers several times to Serra, whose 1613 treatise was the first to associate national welfare with increasing returns, and national poverty with the lack of it.[15]

Schumpeter's originality in the Anglo-Saxon environment was clearly, to a large extent, also a product of the ignorance, outside Germany, of the traditions on which he built. Most Schumpeterians, especially non-Germans, would probably be surprised by a recent German book that describes Schumpeter's 1942 book *Capitalism, Socialism and Democracy*[16] as essentially a reworking of a German debate which had taken place decades earlier, where, the author carefully points out, Schumpeter neither refers to the debate itself nor to its protagonist Werner Sombart.[17] (Perhaps a wise thing to do considering the year of publishing.)

10. Babbage, Charles, *On the Economy of Machinery and Manufactures,* London, Charles Knight, 1832.
11. Ure, Andrew, *The Philosophy of Manufactures, or, an Exposition of the Scientific, Moral, and Commercial Economy of the Factory System of Great Britain*, London, Charles Knight, 1835.
12. Streissler, Erich W., *Increasing Returns and the Prospects of Small-scale Enterprise,* Paper presented at the Sixth Annual Heilbronn Symposium in Economics and the Social Sciences, 'Wilhelm Roscher (1817–1894). A Centenary Reappraisal', June 1994, p. 1.
13. Hufeland, Gottlieb, *Neue Grundlegung der Staatswirthschaftskunst, durch Prüfung und Berichtigung ihrer Hauptbegriffe von Gut, Werth, Preis, Geld und Volksvermögen mit ununterbrochener Rücksicht auf die bisherigen Systeme*, Giessen and Wetlar, Tasche & Müller, 1807.
14. Hermann, Friedrich B.W., *Staatswirtschaftliche Untersuchungen,* München, A. Weber, 1832. Stuttgart, Cotta, 1854.
15. Serra, Antonio, *Breve trattato delle cause che possono far abbondare li regni d'oro e argento dove non sono miniere*, Naples, Lazzaro Scoriggio, 1613.
16. New York, Harper.
17. 'Ohne auf Sombart und die allgemeine Literatur der zwanziger und dreißiger Jahre hinzuweisen, bot Schumpeter (*in Kapitalismus, Sozialismus und Demokratie*) im wesentlichen nur daß, was bereits Jahrzehnte zuvor in den deutschen Diskussionen über die 'Zukunft der Kapitalismus' geschrieben und gesagt worden war, wobei er freilich die gesellschaftlich konservativen Folgerungen, die bei Sombart in der Forderung nach Reagrarisierung und Autarkie gipfelten, nicht übernahm.' In: Appel, Michael, *Werner Sombart. Theoretiker und Historiker des modernen Kapitalismus,* Marburg, Metropolis, 1992, p. 260.

All of this is in sharp contrast to the Anglo-Saxon tradition. Adam Smith provided great insight into the importance of 'division of labour', but he failed to see the organizational implications of this division of labour. Adam Smith assumed markets would continue to function as perfectly as the agricultural markets of his time. On the other hand, he specifically states that the lack of progress of agriculture at the time of his writing was probably due to the 'lack of scope for the division of labour'. Adam Smith goes half way to see the connection between 'lack of division of labour' and perfect competition, but not quite. The differences in organization of production have been left out in neo-classical theory, as has any follow-up of the consequences of various degrees of 'division of labour'. Neo-classical economics is essentially a theory of the exchange of goods already produced, taking no account of the diversity of conditions of production and their influence on pricing behaviour. Neo-classical theory is, it seems, a theory which cannot accommodate for the existence of fixed costs, since these create increasing returns. We are, seemingly, still victims of Adam Smith's inability to see the necessary organizational consequences of his key insight of the importance of division of labour. The division of labour will create firms organized around the combining of tasks into which the manufacturing, assembly and sale of a final product have been divided. The fixed costs invested in machinery and equipment will by definition create a minimum efficient size, increasing returns, barriers to entry and imperfect competition. The understanding of this is traditionally part of German economics, but since the early 1890s definitely not of the paradigm of Anglo-Saxon economics.[18]

For this reason, a most significant long-term pattern of economic policy emerges: 'German-type' theories of uneven growth dominated the take-off stage of all industrialized countries, including England, from the late 1400s up until the late 1800s. The economic policies of these nations have gradually changed to 'English-type' theories as they, one by one, reached the 'technological frontier'. At that point increasing returns in industrial activities turn from being a barrier to growth (for nations not engaged in such activities) into a mechanism where international trade is beneficial to both trading partners. In the early stages, increasing returns creates a barrier to development and is an obstacle, as the economy industrializes the same factor becomes an important ally. As a consequence of this, to a poor country with an economy based on natural resources, free trade was seen as a poverty-trap (due to the existence of diminishing returns and perfect competition). To a nation engaged in increasing returns activities, the existence of these factors becomes yet another reason for free trade.[19] In a successful strategy, increasing returns must be part of economic growth theory in the early take-off stage. Therefore a 'German-type' theory has

---

18. For a recent treatment of the consequences of 'division of labour' in the history of economics, see, Rosenberg, Nathan, *Exploring the Black Box. Technology, Economics, and History,* Cambridge, Cambridge University Press, 1994. Chapter 2 'Charles Babbage: Pioneer Economist', pp. 24–46.
19. The earliest clear statement of this is probably found in Charles King's 1721 book, *The British Merchant or Commerce Preserv'd,* London, John Darby, 1721, 3 Vols, Vol. 1, p. 3.

always been present at an early stage in all industrialized countries. Once a nation is established in a virtuous circle of increasing returns activities and dynamic imperfect competition, leaving increasing returns out of economic theory is not harmful on a short-term basis. Consequently, the successful former laggard countries all convert to Anglo-Saxon type theories - especially with respect to international trade - without any short-term damage.

In Anglo-Saxon economics all economic activities are 'alike'; they are all equally suited to promote national welfare. In German economic theory some economic activities are 'better' than others: Those exhibiting dynamic imperfect competition produced by 'historical increasing returns'. Engaging in these 'better' activities is a necessary requirement if a country is to 'catch-up' with the leading nations of the world.

'German' economic theory has been the basis of the economic policies of the 'laggards', including England when she was a laggard. Anglo-Saxon economics has been the theory of the 'leaders' - the theory embarked upon when 'German' theory has brought a nation into international leadership. For this reason, all rich countries have attempted to export 'Anglo-Saxon' ideas, whereas they themselves have stuck to 'German' ideas. The policy of the United States imposing free trade on Japan and Latin America, while still engaged in extremely heavy-handed protection of national industry at home, is but one example. Today's *managed free trade* is an attempt to achieve the same thing: The advantages of 'German' theories for home use combined with Anglo-Saxon for the rest of the world.

The basic difference between a rich and a poor nation in the world of today, is that whereas *all* rich nations - except some small city-states - have been through a long stage of 'German' economic policy (combining competition *and* protection), in most cases lasting at least 100 years. It is difficult to find a poor nation which has been through this stage.

2. Technological change and Schumpeterian underdevelopment

As stated in the previous section, in German economic theory, some economic activities are 'better' than others, in the sense that they produce dynamic technical change and increasing returns. English economic theory tended to neglect these factors, and, for this reason, for the purposes of economic growth, all economic activities became 'alike'. This was a necessary condition for equilibrium. Increasing returns was, however, still important in the first edition, but not in the later, of Alfred Marshall's *Principles*. Marshall, consequently, is able to give us a formula for an excellent industrial policy: 'A tax ...on the production of goods which obey the Law of Diminishing Return, and devoting the tax to a bounty on the production of those goods with regard to which the Law of Increasing Returns acts sharply.'[20] This insight had to be sacrificed in later editions, since the existence of increasing returns was incompatible with equilibrium.

---

20. Marshall, Alfred, *Principles of Economics*, London, Macmillan, 1890, p. 452.

What in Marshall's early writings start out as a 'Law' (with a capital 'L') of increasing returns, is reduced to being a 'tendency' in subsequent editions, later to disappear from mainstream theory altogether with John Hicks. Today, new trade theory and new neo-classical growth theory are about to rediscover the impact of increasing (but not diminishing) returns.[21] Their policy conclusions are no different from Marshall's in 1890, Roscher's in the 1850s or Serra's in 1613.

Schumpeter's dynamic system, with the role of 'historical increasing returns', retains the characteristics of other authors of the German school, and therefore of a system which produces uneven growth. My notion of Schumpeterian underdevelopment relates to two aspects of technological change, I and II below. Both of these mechanisms are based on the existence of increasing and diminishing returns, imperfect information, barriers to entry and resulting imperfect competition:

I. **The uneven advances of the 'technological frontier'.** It is often visualized that technological knowledge moves forward in the form of a technological 'frontier' of knowledge. The word 'frontier' conveys a notion of a fairly orderly and even progress, where a borderline is being pushed ahead, somewhat reminiscent of the 'frontier' being pushed from the East to the West coast in US history. I feel our understanding of wealth and poverty is hampered by this vision of an orderly 'frontier'. The historical patterns of technological change look more like a scatter diagram than an orderly frontier. Technical change happens very fast in some areas, dragging with them others, but in some areas the 'frontier' hardly moves at all for centuries. At any particular time both the search for new technologies and technological change itself are - in Nathan Rosenberg's words - 'focused'[22] on specific areas of technological problems and opportunities. In the Stone Age, technical change was concentrated in the stone implements industry, in the Bronze Age in bronze implements and in the Machine Age in the activities which were being mechanized. Even today, 200 years into the Machine Age, some activities are still not mechanized - cutting hair, picking strawberries or sewing baseballs.

'If improvements in all the arts were to take place *at the same rate*, they would obviously have no effect to alter the exchangeable value of things', said US economist Henry Vethake in 1844.[23] In a system with perfect information and constant returns to scale,

21. An excellent survey of these models is found in Verspagen, Bart, 'Endogenous Innovation in Neoclassical Growth Models: A Survey', *Journal of Macroeconomics,* Fall 1992, Vol. 14, No. 4, pp. 631–662. See also Romer, Paul M., 'The Origins of Endogenous Growth', *Journal of Economic Perspectives,* Vol. 8, No. 1, Winter 1994, pp. 3–22.
22. See Rosenberg, Nathan, 'The Direction of Technological Change: Inducement Mechanisms and Focus Devices', Chapter 6 in *Perspectives on Technology,* Cambridge, Cambridge University Press, 1976.
23. Vethake, Henry, *Principles of Political Economy,* 2nd edition, Philadelphia, J.W. Moore, 1844, p. 95.

the sequence of technological change makes no difference to the distribution of wealth. On the other hand, in a system with increasing and diminishing returns and imperfect competition, *choosing economic activity* becomes a crucial strategic decision. Where your activities are in the sequence of technological waves - what technological vintage they are - consequently becomes important. We shall see examples of this from the Caribbean in Section 3 of this chapter. A formal model in which learning takes place at different rates in different sectors of the economy is contained in a 1988 paper by Robert Lucas.[24] As to the practical consequences of uneven learning, Lucas provides an unusually candid remark from a formal economist: 'The consequences for human welfare involved in questions like these are simply staggering: Once one starts to think about them, it is hard to think about anything else.'

II. **The two alternative ways in which the benefits from technical change spread.** Under perfect competition, the advances from technical change will spread in the economy in the form of lowered prices to the end user. As I discuss in chapter 1 of this book, this is the assumption made by both Adam Smith and David Ricardo. In the same chapter I have argued that the benefits from technological change always will be distributed in one of the following ways:

- *To the customers* buying the product in the form of lowered prices and/or better quality. I call this the ***classical*** form of distribution of the gains from technological change, because Adam Smith and David Ricardo both state that this will be the effect of technical improvements. This mechanism will operate when conditions of production and markets are similar to those assumed in neo-classical theory.
- *To the owners and workers* in the producing firm, and later to the *government* of the producing country in the form of higher taxable income. I call this the ***collusive*** form of distribution of the gains from technical change, because the forces of the producing country (capital, labour and government) in practice - although not as a conspiracy - 'collude' to appropriate these gains. This mechanism will operate if the technical change is accompanied by the creation of barriers to entry, where increasing returns is a key mechanism.

A typical example of the ***collusive*** form would be 5 January 1914, when Henry Ford increased the wages of his workers from an average of 2.34 dollars for a nine-hour day to 5 dollars for an eight-hour day.[25] A typical example of a ***classical*** distribution would be the employment of bar code readers in supermarkets. This technological improvement would not show up as higher wages for the store staff. Harvard's Zvi Griliches uses this case to show what I call 'invisible economic growth', those cost-cuts and quality

24. Lucas, Robert, 'On the Mechanisms of Economic Development', *Journal of Monetary Economics*, Vol. 22, 1988, pp. 3–42.
25. For an account of this see Raff, Daniel M.R., 'Wage Determination Theory and the Five-Dollar Day at Ford', *The Journal of Economic History*, Vol. 43, No. 2, June 1988, p. 387.

improvements which never show up in any statistics: 'For example, more and more supermarkets have installed bar code readers in their checkout lines, making them faster and more accurate. Yet these gains to consumers do not show up in the government's numbers.'[26] For a closer comparison of the two modes, see chapter 1.

Most technical changes contain an element of both *classical* and *collusive* distribution of the benefits from technical change. What we measure as economic growth is largely the *collusive* mode. *Collusive* technical change is accompanied by the creation of higher barriers to entry, more imperfect competition, and it normally affects the minimum efficient size of an operation. The effects of *classical* technical change 'fall through' the producing organization without changing the structure of the firm or the industry, and is visible mainly as lower prices of the end product. This *classical* technical change does not affect the bargaining power of labour. *Classical* technical change takes place under conditions that do not strongly violate the neo-classical assumptions of perfect competition, and is most frequently found in agriculture and in the traditional service sector. Typically an invention initially creates a temporary monopoly which allows for *collusive* spread of benefits, but as the technique in question becomes commonplace, its benefits will spread more and more as lower prices, not as higher wages and profits. Table 3.1 illustrates the characteristics of classical and collusive spread of technical change.

In a typical industrialized country, 70 per cent of GNP are payments to factor labour, i.e. wages. What we measure historically as growth in GNP is to a large extent the impact of technical change on monetary wages. *Classical* technological change tends to leave fewer traces. When, as in the last decade, an increasing percentage of GNP growth takes place in the service sector - following Petty's Law - the *classical* type spread of technical change becomes more dominant in the economy. Because of the decentralized nature of service production (the classical definition is that a service product must be produced where it is consumed), economies of *scope* in multi-site operations is more of a success factor in the service industry than traditional economies of *scale*, typical of a fordist-type factory. This, combined with the use of technology to *replace* and not *enhance* labour skills in the traditional service sector, allows for a *classical* rather than a *collusive* spread of the benefits of technical change in this sector. An important part of the explanation of the 'Solow paradox' - that computers are visible everywhere except in government statistics - clearly lies in the combination of the huge measurement problems in the service sector combined with the *classical* spread of technological change in this area.

The two phenomena - the classical spread of technological gains and the measurement problems - are closely intertwined. A considerable portion of the lower growth in what we measure as GNP in most industrialized countries over the last decade, is most likely the result of increasing employment in the traditional service sector which produces 'invisible growth' (lowered transaction costs in grocery purchases due to checkout scanners, etc. etc.) However, the subject of this chapter is not the measurement problems of GNP caused by technical change but the effects of technical change on income distribution among nations.

---

26. 'America's New Growth Economy', *International Business Week*, 16 May 1994, s. 47.

Table 3.1 Characteristics of the Two Modes of Diffusion of Productivity Improvements.

CHARACTERISTICS OF MODE	*THE COLLUSIVE MODE*	*THE CLASSICAL MODE*
Divisibility of Investments	Indivisible, comes in *chunks*	Divisible
Degree of Perfect Information	Imperfect (e.g. patents, internal R&D)	Perfect (competitive market for technology itself)
Source of Technology from user company point of view	Internal, **or** External in *big chunks* = high degree of economies of scale	External
Barriers to Entry	Increase	No change
Industry Structure	Increases Concentration	Neutral
Economies of Scale	Increase	No change
Market Shares	Very important	Unimportant
How benefits spread		
Gnp as measured	Highly visible	Tends not to appear ('Solow-paradoxes')
Profit Level	Increases Stakes: Possibility for larger profits or losses	No change
Monetary Wages	Increase	No change
Real Wages (nationally)	Increase	Increase
Price Level	No change	Decreases
Terms of Trade	No change	Turns *against* industry experiencing technological progress
Examples of Innovations in the two Groups	New pharmaceuticals, mainframe computer production, automotive paint production	Electricity, telephones, sewing machines, use of pcs, dispersion paint production, containers
Where found	Mainly in industry, in recent products and processes	In primary and tertiary industries, *use* of new basic technologies, mature industry

In the collective bargaining process, the *collusive* mode is traditionally seen as being 'fair'. If a company improves its labour productivity, part of the benefits of this should go to labour *in that firm*. The phenomena which I describe as the *classical* and *collusive* modes of distributing the proceeds from technical change were thoroughly discussed in a 'comprehensive series of investigations of the relation of the distribution of income to economic progress'[27] by the Brookings Institution. These investigations led to the publishing of a series of books between 1935 and 1940, several of which directly address the way benefits from technological change spread in the economy.[28] In the framework of the Brookings Institution, my ***classical*** spread is called 'distributing income through price reductions' and the ***collusive*** spread is called 'distributing income through raising money wages'. In general the Brookings studies find that, although the *classical* way of distributing gains from technological progress is the preferred one from the point of view of society as a whole, the imperfectly competitive markets for goods and labour in industry make this impossible to achieve. These studies point, however, to the serious problems of income distribution caused (within the United States) by the *collusive* spread of the benefits from technical change in industry and the *classical* spread in agriculture. In a paragraph entitled 'The conflict between wage earners and farmers', Moulton has the following comments as to the national income distribution resulting from *collusive spread* of gains. We ask the reader also to study the paragraph substituting the US farmers for a Third World nation producing raw materials or mature industrial products under conditions of near-perfect competition:

- In considering the price-reduction method (our *classical* mode) as an alternative to wage increases (our *collusive* mode), attention should also be called to a broad social consequence of the latter that has apparently seldom been recognized. The disparities in the income and purchasing power of the industrial and agricultural populations resulting from the wage-increasing method create a basic maladjustment between two great divisions of our economic life and imposes a serious barrier to economic progress. It is apparent that there would be a growing disparity in the economic position of the agricultural and industrial populations even if prices of industrial products showed no tendency to rise as wages rose:[29] the income of the urban population would be increasing while that of the agricultural population would be stationary. In practice there is, however, a tendency for industrial prices to rise somewhat as wages are increased, and the consequence is that the purchasing power of the farm tends to be actually reduced. The consequent inability of the

27. Bell, Spurgeon, *Productivity, Wages, and National Income*, Washington, DC, The Brookings Institution, 1940, p. 3.
28. Among them are Bell, *Productivity, Wages, and National Income*, Moulton, Harold, G., *Income and Economic Progress*, Washington, DC, The Brookings Institution, 1935, and Nourse, Edwin and Drury, Horace, *Industrial Price Policies and Economic Progress*, Washington, DC, The Brookings Institution, 1938.
29. This statement should be compared with the terms-of-trade debate following the Prebisch-Singer argument in the early 1950s. Moulton shows a mechanism where one group grows rich and the other poor with *Terms of Trade unchanged.* My **collusive** spread and Moulton's argument reflect the views of Singer rather than Prebisch, see Singer's 1949 paper 'The Distribution of Gains between Investing and Borrowing Countries'. This paper is reproduced in Singer, Hans, *International Development. Growth and Change*, New York, McGraw-Hill, 1964, pp. 161–72.

> agricultural population to buy ever-increasing quantities of industrial products limits the scale on which industrial establishments can operate.
>
> The struggle to obtain higher living standards through the medium of higher money wages has been the cause of a long and deep-seated conflict between the agricultural and urban populations. The people of the cities have fought for higher wages even though it has meant somewhat higher prices for industrial products. The farmers have long fought for lower prices on the commodities they have to buy. The struggle underlies the so-called Granger Movement of the 1870s; it explains the traditional opposition of the agricultural South to high protective tariffs; and it lies at the basis of farmer opposition to trusts, monopolies and combinations in all their forms.[30]

These paragraphs describe the problems of income distribution between two groups within the same nation, both producing at what was then the *technological frontier*: Both the US farmers and the US industrial population were the most productive in the world. Yet, one group got rich and the other group stayed poor. At about the same time another US author tried to explain the same phenomenon from a leftist point of view in a book called *Why Farmers are Poor.*[31] I would argue that the reason for this poverty *of the world's most efficient farmers on the world's probably most fertile soil* is this:

- The productivity increases of the farmers are taken out in the form of lowered prices, in the ***classical*** way, whereas the productivity increases of their trading partners producing industrial goods are taken out ***collusively***, in the form of higher wages. In a neo-classical world of perfect information and no economies of scale, this would of course not be a problem, because the individual farmers would all produce the tractors and all the other industrial implements in their own backyard without any loss of efficiency compared to industrial production. In real life, however, the farmers were facing high barriers to entry - the 'perfect information and constant returns to scale option' is of course non-existent. The farmers of the United States in the 1930s suffered from 'Schumpeterian underdevelopment'.

If we now place these two groups in two different countries, an industrial country and an agricultural country, and open for trade, we would have achieved a much bigger gap in the standard of living than the one which so much worried the Brookings Institution in the late 1930s. Placing the two groups of producers in two different countries would have eliminated important distributive mechanisms that existed within the United States. Migration of surplus labour from the farms to the industrial districts as farming demanded less labour and more capital was an important distributive mechanism, as was the pressure from alternative employment in the cities on farm wages. The government

30. Moulton, *Income and Economic Progress*, pp. 124–25.
31. Rochester, Anna, *Why Farmers are Poor. The Agricultural Crisis in the United States,* New York, International Publishers, 1940.

tax base was much larger in the cities and in industrial areas, so infrastructure, schools and other government services in the farming areas were clearly heavily subsidized by the industrial districts. Last but not least, the farmers, in spite of their steadily declining numbers, did have political power. Moulton mentions the Granger Movement which started just after the Civil War, whose activities served as the basis for later legislation affecting income distribution within the United States: Railroad and public utility regulations, antitrust laws and measures establishing a postal savings bank and parcel post on government hands. Our basic point is this:

- Had the industrial population and the agrarian population in the United States been living in two different nations, we would have found a deeply impoverished agricultural nation and an extremely wealthy industrial nation. Both would have been the world's most efficient, but one would still have suffered from Schumpeterian underdevelopment.

This is but one example. Using other examples from the Caribbean later in the chapter, I shall argue that wealth is not caused by relative efficiency but by *imperfect competition*. From the point of view of both an individual and a nation, the choice of economic activity is much more important than the degree of efficiency. There is, for nations as well as for individuals, an optimization process available.

As Moulton correctly points out, the poverty of the farmer hampers the wealth development of the rich. The lack of purchasing power of the farmers hampers the growth of the industrialists. This same argument is found in a different context as an argument for the protection of US manufacturing industries in the 1820s: If the United States are allowed to build their own industries, British trade will not suffer. In the long run the increase of national demand caused by industrialization of the United States will increase and upgrade the US demand for British industrial goods. Increasing the size of the cake for the weaker trading partner benefits everybody. The same argument is again found in the EU of 1994: the implicit social contract of the EU aims at 'competitiveness' to industry, simultaneously with a 'social cohesion' created by increasingly massive *collusive* transfers to the non-industrial regions. Also, here the argument is that the poor must get transfers in order to create markets for industry.

Inside the rich economies themselves lies a perfect illustration of the mechanisms of uneven economic growth: imperfect competition and ***collusive*** spread of benefits from technical change on the one hand and perfect competition and ***classical*** spread of the benefits from technical change on the other. The problem is that this mechanism is never discussed on a theoretical level. The rich countries, like the EU, simply pay and protect the farmers as a matter of political necessity without ever asking ***why***. Inefficiency is clearly not the problem; on the contrary the farmers of the industrialized world are so efficient that, in spite of their low numbers, they produce more than the industrialized countries can consume, causing huge payments to be made for those who keep their land uncultivated and huge amounts of food to be given as 'aid' to poor countries, causing the collapse of farm prices there.

The high-tech industries and, in general, those activities working under imperfect competition are the national wage leaders. This causes the phenomenon of 'industry rent' in labour economics: certain industries, usually the same industries all over the world, pay much higher wages than others. The size of the industry rent, however, varies with the political setting (big in the United States, small in Scandinavia), although the rank of the industries tends to stay the same. The industries working under what Schumpeter called 'historical increasing return' become the wage leaders, while the traditional service sectors are 'wage followers'. If we assume that the price of capital is relatively constant in the long run, this upward pressure on the wage level from the 'wage-leading industries' will make labour-saving devices more profitable also in other economic activities. The upward pressure on wages from wage leaders can be seen as an initial turn on the screw of virtuous circles which makes labour a more costly factor of production than capital, triggering an upward spiral of continuous substitution of capital and new technologies for labour-intensive technologies - the very essence of economic growth.

One definition of a poor country is that - to its average inhabitants - everything is expensive, except labour. Because of this, the costs of traditional inexportable services vary wildly. A haircut in industrialized Europe costs 20 times more than the same quality haircut in Peru or Bolivia. This is because in industrialized countries, the traditional service sector collusively shares in the 'industry rent'.

The distribution of wealth between rich and poor *within* a nation will, as Moulton pointed out, also affect the size of the market and the scale of operations of the increasing returns sector. The failure to raise wages of large groups of the population will cause a vicious circle with suboptimal scale of industrial production and lack of national competition to stall growth, even if a nation is in the 'right' industry. Several Latin American countries seem to fall in this category.

3. Three cases of Schumpeterian underdevelopment in the Caribbean

The case of serious maldistribution of income in the United States between the agricultural and industrial sectors - both the world's most efficient at the time - opens up for an understanding that being wealthy is not so much a matter of being efficient, it is more ***what one chooses to be efficient in.*** Schumpeterian underdevelopment happens if a nation chooses to be efficient *in the wrong industry*. This mechanism works similarly as with individuals: the most efficient dishwasher in the country has a much lower income than the most efficient lawyer.

There are two mechanisms which come together to cause this: The uneven advance of the phenomenon which by a misnomer is called The Technological Frontier, and the ***collusive vs. classical*** spread of the benefits from technical change. These mechanisms are able to operate because of what Schumpeter called 'historical increasing returns' - the fact that the technological change that we measure as economic growth has been accompanied by higher fixed costs creating greater economies of scale. This 'visible' (as opposed to the often invisible growth in the traditional service sector) technological change consequently operates under very imperfect competition protected by two important sets of barriers to entry: Scale-based and knowledge-based, which interact and cumulate in creating Myrdalian vicious circles.

One important feature of neo-classical economics is that, under its standard assumptions, all economic activities become 'alike'. In neo-classical economics, a faster technological change in one industry than in another is neutralized by instant adjustment, provided by 'perfect information', 'perfect foresight', and 'constant returns to scale'. In real life the existence of huge differences in knowledge and information, 'bounded vision' and huge increasing returns to scale combine to chain nations to the trajectories they have historically embarked upon, or in the case of the Caribbean, those they *have been* embarked upon. In the following examples we shall observe how, in the case of three Caribbean islands, Schumpeterian underdevelopment develops. In all three cases the choice of economic activity, rather than the efficiency, determines wealth or poverty.

3.1. Cuban counterpoint of tobacco and sugar

In 1940 the foremost Cuban social scientist in this century, Fernando Ortìz, published a book[32] with a fascinating account of how Cuban society and history have been shaped in very different ways by tobacco and sugar, 'two gigantic plants, two members of the vegetable kingdom which both flourish in Cuba and are both perfectly adapted, climatically and ecologically, to the country. The territory of Cuba has in its different zones the best land for the cultivation of both plants. And the same happens in the combinations of the climate with the chemistry of the soil.'[33]

From an economic point of view, Cuba clearly has an absolute advantage in the production of both crops. But to Cuba, one crop - tobacco - produced wealth, the other -sugar - poverty. The counterpoint between tobacco and sugar is a parallel to the uneven wealth creation we witnessed in a previous paragraph, between the industrial and the agricultural sectors in the United States. Both in the US and Cuban cases we are studying *the most advanced production in the world,* both in the activities which produced wealth and the activities which produced poverty. The difference is here that we are studying two agricultural products which both are being industrialized. We must, then, go beyond the standard categorizations of agriculture as being 'bad' and industry as being 'good', to find the mechanisms at work.

In Cuban society tobacco was the hero, sugar the villain. Tobacco - predominantly grown on the Western part of the island - created a middle class, a free bourgeoisie.

---

32. *Contrapunteo Cubano del Tabaco y el Azúcar,* Havana, Jesus Montero, 1940. There is another edition in Biblioteca Ayacucho, Caracas, 1978. The book was published in English in 1947 by Knopf, superbly translated by Harriet de Onìs. The well-known anthropologist Bronisław Malinowski provided an introduction to the English edition. Knopf and Onìs were also behind the English publication of most of the best Latin American fiction at the time. *Cuban Counterpoint. Tobacco and Sugar,* New York, Alfred A. Knopf, 1947.
33. Ibid., English edition, p. 7.

Sugar - grown on the rest of the island - created two classes of people: masters and slaves. The cultivation and picking of tobacco created a demand for specialized skills: Tobacco leaves were harvested individually, and the market price of the product depended on the skill of the picker. Tobacco breeded skills, individuality and modest wealth. 'Sugar was an anonymous industry, the mass labor of slaves or gangs of hired workmen, under the supervision of capital's overseers.'[34]Where tobacco required skill, care and judgement, sugar only required brute force in cutting the cane. Tobacco was individuality and division of labour, sugar was bulk and commodity. Tobacco carries its origins with it as a brand name, 'sugar comes to the world without a last name, like a slave'.[35] Tobacco is stable prices, sugar is wildly fluctuating prices. A skilled tobacco selector can distinguish 70 or 80 different shades of tobacco, but all saccharose is the same. Timing is crucial in the harvesting of tobacco, for the cutting of cane, timing is not important. Tobacco is delicately cut leaf by leaf with a small sharp knife, making sure that the rest of the plant survives. The sugar plant is brutally slashed with a big machete. Working with sugar is a trade, working with tobacco an art.

As a result of this, Ortìz says, the tobacco worker is not only wealthier than the destitute sugar workers, 'he is better mannered and more intelligent'.[36] Tobacco is wealth and intelligence, sugar is poverty and ignorance. Sugar is foreign capital, tobacco is predominantly national capital. 'In the history of Cuba sugar represents Spanish absolutism; tobacco, the native liberators. Sugar has always stood for foreign intervention.'[37] 'Sugar has always preferred slave labour; tobacco free men. Sugar brought in Negroes by force; tobacco encouraged the voluntary immigration of white men.'[38]

Differences in barriers to entry are clearly a key factor producing the differences in production and marketing which created the Cuban counterpoint. Cuban tobacco was one of the few cases of brand-name products from the Third World. Cuba had an absolute advantage in the world in both products, but one brought wealth and the other poverty. This is a parallel case to the Brookings Institution study from the United States in the 1930s, which showed a US 'counterpoint' similar to the Cuban: The United States had both the world's most efficient farmers and the world's most efficient industry. But - the farmers stayed poor and the industrial workers got rich. Both in the United States and in Cuba, world-level efficiency led to wealth for those who specialized in one product, and poverty for those who specialized in another. We are facing cases of ***classical*** spread of the gains from technological change in the case of the US farmers and the Cuban sugar workers, and ***collusive*** spread in the case of US industry and Cuban tobacco production. It is also worth noting that in spite of a much larger technological change in sugar refining than in cigar making, the cigar makers were consistently wealthier than their sugar-producing colleagues. From the point of view of the nation involved, imperfect competition and no technical change are infinitely better

34. Ibid., p. 65.
35. Ibid., p. 42.
36. Ibid., p. 40.
37. Ibid., p. 71.
38. Ibid., p. 81.

than technical change and perfect competition. Farming in the United States and sugar in Cuba led to Schumpeterian underdevelopment, industry and tobacco did not.

Fifty years after the original publication of *Cuban Counterpoint*, a Cuban author in exile dedicated his book *La Isla Que Se Repite* - 'The Island Which Repeats Itself' - to its author, Fernando Ortìz.[39] The title of the book says it all: In spite of a change in political paradigm, the qualities inherent in sugar production - not only in Cuba but anywhere - continue to shape Cuba and determine its economic faith.

Two years ago, two US political scientists and Latinamericanists published a study of the political and economic structure of two Caribbean islands: The Dominican Republic and Jamaica.[40] In spite of the extremely different historical and administrative backgrounds of the two islands; one coming from the Spanish tradition and one from the English, the authors found both nations had very similar political and economic structures and the same set of problems. Again, their conclusion is, without referring to Ortìz, that the fate of both islands is shaped by the economic forces of sugar production. No matter your past, producing the same thing will make you alike.

Many modern studies point to the extreme poverty of the world's most efficient sugar producers. The titles indicate the social concerns which prompted their publication: *The Hunger Crop. Poverty and the Sugar Industry*[41] and *Bitter Sugar.*[42] The policies of the industrialized countries subsidizing their own inefficient sugar production - beet sugar in Europe and cane sugar in the United States - plus the increased competition from corn-based sweeteners just add to the desolation of this 'lock-in effect'. In 1985 *The Economist* dedicated a cover story - 'Enslaved by Subsidies' - to the sugar policies of the industrialized nations, calling it 'a case study in taxing the rich to ruin the poor'.[43]

Studying the sugar industry makes one understand the intuitive approach to industrial policy used by the early mercantilists. The starting point of the British ascent to world power was the economic policy of the Tudors. In 1485 Henry VII embarked on a programme to convert England from being a producer of raw wool to being a producer of woollen textiles. His logic stemmed from his travels in France and England, where he observed that all wool producers were poor, whereas all producers of woollen cloth were rich. We could call it 'Henry VII's counterpoint'.

3.2. Haiti - economic counterpoint in baseballs and golf balls

Today the unchallenged position at the bottom of the sugar hierarchy is held by the Haitian seasonal workers in the sugar fields of the Dominican Republic.[44] But, the

39. Benítez Rojo, Antonio, *La isla que se repite,* Hanover, New Hampshire, Ediciones del Norte, 1989.
40. Hillman, Richard S. and D'Agostino, Thomas J., *Distant Neighbours in the Caribbean. The Dominican Republic and Jamaica in Comparative Perspective*, New York, Praeger, 1992.
41. Coote, Belinda, *The Hunger Crop. Poverty and the Sugar Industry*, Oxford, Oxfam, 1987.
42. Lemoine, Maurice, *Bitter Sugar,* London, Zed Books, 1985.
43. *The Economist*, August 10, 1985.
44. See Lemoine, *Bitter Sugar.*

Republic of Haiti also dominates the world market for a manufactured product: Baseballs, produced mainly for the US market, provide a classical case of Schumpeterian underdevelopment.

Economists make sense of the enormous variations of industries by placing them in groups according to a standard industrial classification. Even seemingly homogeneous groups, however, may contain enormous diversity in the economic conditions individual products create in the country of production. The world's most efficient golf ball producers are located in industrialized countries and make a normal industrial wage of 9 dollars per hour. The world's most efficient baseball producers are in Haiti, working 10 hours per day for an hourly wage of 30 US cents. The wage ratio between the two groups of workers, both in the same industry and both being the most efficient in the world, is about 30 to 1.

Why is there no factor-price equalization with the industry producing balls for various sports? The technological explanation is: The Machine Age has not yet reached the production of baseballs; they have to be hand-sewn, even in the United States. The currents of creative destruction have not yet penetrated this little industry. The baseball-producing industry is a relic from an otherwise extinct techno-economic paradigm, to use the terms of Perez/Freeman.

As in sugar production, the *characteristics of the product* 'baseballs' itself contains the elements of poverty and underdevelopment. No new skills are developed because there is no *demand* for new skills. No learning-by-doing takes place in Haiti, because there is no learning taking place in baseball production *anywhere.* The Haitians are not working with capital and machines, because not even all the capital of the United States has managed to mechanize baseball production. The mercantilists told us that economic growth was *activity-specific* - it happened in some industries and not in others. And they were right.

When Haiti sells baseballs to the United States and buys golf balls back, one hour of labour in the United States is exchanged for 30 hours of labour in Haiti. This in spite of the fact that US baseball sewers are *not* more efficient than the Haitians. These are the 'unequal exchange' effects of Schumpeterian underdevelopment.

3.3. The Dominican Republic and technological change in pyjamas production

The Dominican Republic scores considerably higher in terms of GNP per capita than Haiti. As we have seen, the Dominican Republic can afford to import labour which is even cheaper than her own, for the *zafra* - the sugar harvest. Over the last decade more than 400,000 new manufacturing jobs have come to the Dominican Republic. Most people expected economic growth and higher wages to result from manufacturing; after all, wasn't the wealth of the United States built on manufacturing?

Much to the surprise of everybody, the 400,000 manufacturing jobs did not increase welfare to any measurable extent. The explanation lies in the way the market mechanisms of Schumpeterian underdevelopment assign production processes with and without technical change. The Dominican Republic produces garments made from imported fabrics. Pyjamas bought in the United States 15 years ago would have a label reading: 'Fabric made in the US, cut and assembled in the Dominican Republic.' About 10 years ago, the labels were changed. They now read: 'Fabric made **and cut** in the US, assembled in the Dominican Republic.' What had happened?

About 10 years ago a new technology - laser cutting - hit the garment industry. As a result of this, the labour content in this operation fell dramatically, and the cost of labour was no longer a strategic factor in the cost of the final product. The cutting operation was therefore taken back to the United States when the new technology appeared.

As long as the frontier of technological change moves forward extremely unevenly in a world with imperfect competition, free trade will lead to Schumpeterian underdevelopment in parts of the world economy. Production processes with no technological development, with no creative destruction, will, by the logic of the market, be farmed out to the poor nations. In some cases, where a huge closed market absorbs one small and relatively poor nation, this 'farming out' of products with less technical change may have beneficial effects on both trading partners. The inclusion of small and relatively poor Portugal in the EU can prove beneficial to all, just as the import of a few Third World citizens to wash dishes in the First World can be to the benefit of all parties.[45] However, the number of poor compared to the number of rich in the world today makes this 'absorption' to make the poor nations rich not a viable strategy. The extremely high costs faced by West Germany in absorbing relatively the rich and much smaller East Germany testifies to this.

4. The circular flow and the two economic roles of man

If the world is a stage where each must play his part, we are all - in an economic sense - playing two different roles: That of the producer and that of the consumer. On the one hand we produce goods (man-the-producer), and on the other hand we consume goods (man-the-consumer) which are exchanged for the ones we produce. What counts as GNP is limited to production where these roles are ***separated***, where the producer is not the consumer. The economics profession has abdicated from the study of situations where the roles of producer and consumer of a good are played by the same person. These cases of household economies have been left to economic anthropology: It is the *exchange*, and not the production, which is at the very heart of modern economics.

A special feature of neo-classical economics is the perfect harmony of interest between these two roles of man (or woman). Man-the-producer never has any conflict of interests with his other self – man-the-consumer. Individual human beings, during their life span, face a similar situation as that of society as a whole. But, individuals have possibilities to optimize their strategies, a path which today is difficult for a nation. For the individual, who consciously or unconsciously selects a profession, the two roles of

45. In the summer of 1994, the Tamil refugees in Switzerland, who are threatened with expulsion, have one political ally: The association of restaurant owners who depend on them for dishwashing.

consumer and producer imply trade-offs. The individual can embark on a path which optimizes his income. One can easily imagine man-the-consumer rejecting the suggestions of his producer-self that present consumption has to be reduced in order to attend law school. A reasoned discussion between man-the-consumer and man-the-producer, both inhabiting the same individual, may lead to the conclusion that the individual in question would be better off quitting the job as a dishwasher and going to law school, i.e. foregoing consumption now for more prestige and consumption in the future. Among thousands of different professions, individuals are able to ***optimize*** their situation. Normally this optimization carries with it a trade-off between present and future income. This optimization between professions is clearly recognized also by economists, on a practical level or in the guise of 'human capital'. Certainly no economists, not even traditional trade theorists, tell their children to stick to the job washing dishes because 'factor-price equalization is just around the corner' - the time when people washing dishes will make the same amount of money as lawyers. Indeed, it would be easy to produce a convincing Ricardian-style argument for the would-be lawyer, that the world would be richer if he sticks to washing dishes and does not try to become a lawyer.

Why does this ***optimization*** option apply to individuals and not to nations? We all agree that our children should rather become lawyers than wash dishes in a restaurant. Why is it conceptually impossible for an economist to extend this argument to apply to a nation specializing in dishwashing trading with a nation of lawyers? Why is a certain path obviously an ***optimizing*** path to an individual, but not to a collection of individuals like a region or nation? Why do economists make opposite recommendations to one individual than to a *group* of individuals facing the same options? Why would we never dream of recommending to nations whose part in the international division of labour is similar to washing dishes that they can optimize by changing into a different profession?

The answer is relatively simple: Neo-classical theory has abstracted from - assumed as not existing - all the characteristics which distinguish a job of washing dishes from the job of being a lawyer. Under conditions of perfect competition and perfect information with constant returns to scale, lawyers and dishwashers would make the same salaries. Under these conditions all individuals in an economy would have the same salaries, and no trade-offs and no optimizations would be possible.

Individual wage differences and differences in industry profitability are caused by a package of factors which carry the collective label 'barriers to entry' - fixed costs and increasing returns, imperfect competition, speed of technological change and many others. In previous STEP-Reports, I have published the Quality Index of Economic Activities.[46] The Quality Index represents a continuum from perfect competition to monopoly, on which any economic activity conceptually can be plotted. The score on this index reflects the degree to which an activity can support a high wage for the individual and a high standard of living for the nation exporting this good. In other words, the score of the Quality Index shows the degree of 'industry rent' available to the individual or to the nation. Schumpeter's

46. E.g. in 'chapter 1, 'Catching-up from Way behind, A Third World view Perspective on First World History'.

'historical increasing returns' - the interplay of scale and technological change over time - is an important factor creating high-quality activities.[47] Schumpeterian underdevelopment is the result of a specialization, within the international division of labour, in activities with a low score on the Quality Index of Economic Activities.

The national strategies under mercantilism and cameralism shared the view of economic growth being ***activity-specific***; it took place in some economic activities and not in others.[48] In order to get rich, a nation had to engage in the activities which gave the nation *productive powers* or *nationale Produktivkraft*, the equivalent of today's 'competitiveness'.[49] In practice, this was the core of English economic policy from the late 1400s and in the economic policies of France (starting in the 1600s), Germany (from its cameralist past and with the Zollverein in the 1830s), the United States (starting in 1820) and Japan (after the Meiji Restoration). In practical terms this meant engaging in the economic activities which at any point in time were in the process of being mechanized, through bounties, subsidies and protection. By singling out the activities which at any point in time were in the process of being mechanized, this 'mercantilist' trade policy developed a 'national innovation system'. Seen from a slightly different angle, the slopes of the national learning curves were maximized. The scale effects and the barriers to entry created in these activities secured the creation of 'industry rent', which produced the gap in standards of living between the European countries and their colonies. The exceptions were formed by the 'white' colonies - those which in the early UN statistics were grouped under the heading 'areas of recent settlement'. These nations followed the former strategies of the metropolis countries, protecting and supporting local industry even from that of the mother country.

The Ricardian trade theory excludes all the factors which cause 'industry rent'. Our personal 'gut feelings' when we give our children or others advice on what profession to seek takes the industry rents in our own economies into account. When we analyze the relationship between nations, this tacit knowledge is automatically blocked off, and we return to Ricardo and a world where all the factors creating uneven wealth within a nation are assumed not to exist. But, why are Ricardo and Samuelson able to convince us that a nation of dishwashers will be equally rich as a nation of lawyers when we intuitively know that each individual lawyer will be much richer than each individual person making a living washing dishes?

In a world where the division of labour causes different degrees of imperfect competition, scale effects and - in general - a different market value on different types of knowledge, an uneven income distribution is bound to be found. It is not the existence of increasing returns and barriers to entry *per se* that causes this maldistribution, but the fact that **different economic activities embody these characteristics to varying degrees**. Relative wealth and poverty are created by the *asymmetry* between

47. The 'Quality Index' can be seen as an attempt to explain Robert Reich's 'high-quality jobs' and 'low-quality jobs'. A nation specializing in 'low quality jobs' - like Haiti - will suffer from Schumpeterian underdevelopment.
48. See chapter 1.
49. This is discussed in chapter 4.

different degrees of imperfect competition, not by imperfect competition in and of itself. In the very hypothetical case that all activities had the same degree of imperfect information and increasing returns, we could still have an even income distribution. On the Quality Index this would correspond to persons or nations trading in professions with the same score on the Quality Index - the case of the lawyer going to the doctor. This case was specifically recognized in the most important work on 'national strategy' in eighteenth-century England, when Charles King explicitly lists among 'good trade' the exchange of manufactured goods for other manufactured goods.[50] Paul Krugman's conversion from free-trade scepticism after he rediscovered increasing returns - and consequently an important mechanism of uneven development - in the late 1970s[51] to advocating free trade across the board today[52] seems to be based on this 'special case': When nations trade at the same degree of increasing returns - or at the same degree of imperfect information for that matter - the existence of increasing returns and imperfect information is correctly seen as *an additional argument for free trade.* This is, however, only a special case - e.g. that of Germany and France trading large cars, or that of the lawyer visiting the doctor: Both benefit mutually from the specialization of the other (essentially from the saving of fixed costs and from having better information), and income distribution is not affected. This case - lawyers and doctors exchanging services in activities with the same score on the Quality Index - we shall refer to as *symmetrical* trade. However, if two nations previously under autarky, both consisting of lawyers and people washing dishes, suddenly open up for trade in a way that one country specializes in legal matters and the other specializes in washing dishes, we have the case of an *asymmetrical* specialization which will have serious effects on income distribution: One nation will be much richer than before and one will be much poorer. This, in a very simplified form, is what has caused the GNP per capita in Eastern Europe to fall between 30 and 50 per cent in three years. This is what Friedrich List saw happening in France after the fall of Napoleon, and what converted him from being a free trader to being a promoter of industrialization and of the somewhat vague concept of *Nationaler Produktivkraft,* normally as ill-defined as the concept of 'competitiveness' today.

The nation in the losing end of this deal, the nation who is specializing in the activity with no 'historical increasing returns' and no 'industry rent', will be poor. Adam Smith's 'division of labour' is free of distributional effects on income only when all the economic activities created by the division of tasks are 'alike', when they have the same degree of scale effects, imperfect information, barriers to entry etc. The spectrum of economic activities which surrounds us is clearly extremely divergent in terms of these

50. See King, *The British Merchant or Commerce Preserv'd.*
51. Krugman, Paul, 'Increasing Returns, Monopolistic Competition, and International Trade', *Journal of International Economics,* Vol. 9, No. 4, November 1979, pp. 464–79, and 'Trade, Accumulation, and Uneven Development', *Journal of Development Economics,* Vol. 8, 1981, pp. 149–61.
52. See e.g. his *Peddling Prosperity, Economic Sense and Nonsense in the Age of Diminished Expectations,* New York, Norton, 1994.

characteristics, and consequently an increasing division of labour also opens up for increasing divergence of income levels, both inside nations and between nations.

The specialization in activities not containing Schumpeterian 'creative destruction', and consequently not enjoying the industry rent which comes with it, leads to what I call 'Schumpeterian underdevelopment'. This is distinguished from 'classical underdevelopment' because the nations suffering from 'Schumpeterian underdevelopment' are participating in the international division of labour. The Shipibo Indians of the Amazon live with 'classical underdevelopment', whereas the baseball producers, pyjama sewers and sugar producers in the Caribbean suffer from 'Schumpeterian underdevelopment'. Their activities either (a) suffer from little technical change and, in the case of sugar, from diminishing returns, or (b) suffer from perfect competition which causes technical improvements to be reflected as falling prices on the world market, not as higher national wages, profits and tax base, or (c) from a combination of both.

5. Schumpeterian underdevelopment: Policy conclusions past and present

The rediscovery of the effects of increasing returns in new trade theory and new growth theory are made without any references to the economic thinking and to economic policies of past centuries. The new theories open up for an understanding of uneven growth, but they are hardly translated to practical policy, least of all in the policies of the First World towards the Third World, which is where they would have had the most impact. The editor of the Papers and Proceedings of the 1993 Annual Meeting of the American Economic Association appropriately heads the section on new trade theory: 'Free Trade: A Loss of (Theoretical) Nerve?'[53]

One basic reason for this is the unwillingness to test the theoretical models in economics with observable economic facts. The practical relevance of a theoretical economic model is hardly ever tested with actual observations of how the world economy operates. Paul Krugman's 1981 paper, quoted in the previous section, actually contains a relevant description of how international trade creates wealth on one side and poverty on the other. Without knowing it, Krugman rediscovered and mathematized the principal nineteenth-century argument for protection of industry which made his own country rich. This is only one of Krugman's models. Another - early - model is in 'a clever paper on interstellar trade, where goods are transported from one stellar system to another at speeds close to that of light; the resulting relativistic correction to time entails different interest rates in different frames of reference'.[54] One of these theories is very important to human welfare, the other is not. In which of these categories does Paul Samuelson's proof of *factor-price equalization* belong - the serious one or the irrelevant and clever one? In the institutions which are responsible for Third World development, the proof of *factor-price equalization* with free trade seems to be taken as a foundation

53. *American Economic Review*, Vol. 83, No. 2, May 1993, p. iv.
54. Dixit, Avinash, 'In Honor of Paul Krugman: Winner of the John Bates Clark Medal', *Journal of Economic Perspectives*, Vol. 7, No. 2, Spring 1993, p. 173.

for economic policy. A verification of the economic history of the industrialized world shows that factor-price equalization probably should be relegated to the same category as Krugman's paper on interstellar relativistic trade. As long as verification in the real world is not part of economic modelling - and cleverness and not relevance tends to be a main criterion for success - these theories are all part of what essentially is a purely theoretical intellectual game. On one level, there is nothing wrong with this. Playing simulation games, like chess, is perfectly legitimate. Problems arise only if the general public, in particular those responsible for the economic policy of the Third World, are led to believe that there is any direct relationship between economic modelling and what goes on in the world economy.

Here the laments of Colin Clark, in the foreword to his 1940 book *The Conditions of Economic Progress*, are even more valid now than at the time of his writing:

> 'I have left the academic world with nothing but regard for the intellectual integrity and public spirit of my former colleagues in the ...Universities; but with dismay at their continued preference for the theoretical rather than the scientific approach to economic problems. Not one in a hundred - least of all those who are most anxious to proclaim the scientific nature of Economics - seem to understand what constitutes the scientific approach, namely, the careful systematisation of all observed facts, the framing of hypotheses from these facts, prediction of fresh conclusions on the basis of these hypotheses, and the testing of these conclusions against further observed facts. It would be laughable, were it not tragic, to watch the stream of books and articles, attempting to solve the exceptionally complex problems of present-day economics by theoretical arguments, often without a single reference to the observed facts of the situation.....The hard scientific discipline has yet to be learned, that all theories must be constantly tested and retested against observed facts, and those which prove wrong ruthlessly rejected.'[55]

The observed or 'stylized' facts are that an increasing international division of labour is accompanied by an increasing gap in income between poor and wealthy nations, with little movement between the two groups. The same effect is also found within the EU: Larger markets require more redistribution. Every year the European Union increases the amount of money flowing through its enormous redistributional machinery, which adds to the redistribution which already absorbs around 50 per cent of GNP in the industrialized nations. Another key stylized fact is that economic welfare seems to be much less a product of the *efficiency* of a nation in its specialization, but much more the product of the *choice* of economic activity. The cases where nations are efficient in their production compared to world 'best-practice', but are still poor, I have labelled Schumpeterian underdevelopment.

The policy implications which slowly emerge from new neo-classical growth theory and new trade theory are in principle not different from those of Serra, Roscher or the early Marshall; authors writing from 1613 to 1890. These new theories rediscover the essence of mercantilist industrial policy: In a world inhabited by economic activities

55. Clark, Colin, *The Conditions of Economic Progress,* London, Macmillan, 1940, pp. vii–viii.

with different potentials for raising national income, there are **optimizing** paths. These insights are being used in the industrial policies of the First World, but they are absent from the policy of the First World towards the Second (previously communist) and the Third World, which is where they would have the most effect.

In any country, a mediocre lawyer has a much higher income than the most efficient dishwasher in a restaurant. For a person washing dishes, studying to become a lawyer is an *optimizing* path, one which will maximize future income compared to a do-nothing (laissez-faire) option: 'My comparative advantage in society, due to my low wages, is to wash dishes.' A similar situation faces nations stuck in Schumpeterian underdevelopment. Haiti could, instead of exchanging 30 hours of labour producing baseballs for export for 1 hour of US labour in imported golf balls, optimize national welfare by producing golf balls less efficiently than the United States. Even if the United States managed to stay ten times as efficient as Haiti producing golf balls, the Haitian would, in terms of balls at today's prices, still be three times as rich under autarky in golf balls than under specialization and free trade. Under autarky in sporting balls, Haiti could improve its position compared to free trade. How would Haiti get the capital? Presumably the same way our law student will: Taking up a loan and paying it back from his future 'industry rent'.

In any system with differing degrees of increasing returns and a mixed pattern of *collusive* and *classical* distribution of gains from technical progress, some nations will be better off under autarky than under free trade. This is the basic reason why most of the German historical economists, including the dean of the historical school, Werner Sombart, were fundamentally critical of free trade between nations at different levels of development. The Haitian example, far from being a far-fetched theoretical argument, was at the core of the optimizing path embarked upon by the United States in the 1820s: The American System of Industrial Protection, which in a period of less than 100 years made the United States into the world's powerhouse.

The economist who, next to Alexander Hamilton, was the spiritual father of the North American protection to industry, Daniel Raymond, compared the situation of individuals to that of nations: 'If an individual can do this, so may a nation.'[56] The core of Raymond's argument was one of optimization: The increased prices paid in the United States for industrial products under protection would be more than compensated by the increase in wages, since industrial workers everywhere had so much higher wages than farm labour.[57]In the case of the nineteenth-century US economy, the trade-off between man-the-consumer and man-the-producer led to the conclusion that, there and then, free trade was a suboptimal option. Both the Second (former communist) World and the Third present many cases of Schumpeterian underdevelopment where there are similar optimizing paths to be explored. Exploiting these requires more 'theoretical nerve' from economists, and a conscious move into what Colin Clark would have called 'factual and scientific investigations' to complement the theoretical ones which dominate today.

56. Raymond, Daniel, *Thoughts on Political Economy*, Baltimore, Fielding Lucas, 1820, p. 115.
57. This wage difference is well documented in Clark, *The Conditions of Economic Progress*, where he finds e.g. that in Norway agricultural wages were only 8 per cent of industrial wages.

Chapter 4

COMPETITIVENESS AND ITS PREDECESSORS - A 500-YEAR CROSS-NATIONAL PERSPECTIVE

Competitiveness - 'corporate graffiti' invades economic theory

Even a casual observer of the practice and science of management will not fail to notice how a continuous flow of new concepts are born, become fashionable and then disappear from management jargon. A recent article in *Financial Times* (Ref. 1, p. 10) suggests the term 'corporate graffiti' - or 'management graffiti' - to describe the unthinking use of buzz-words. Management language is 'opaque, ugly, and cliché-ridden', FT claims. 'Management graffiti' is intended as the catch-phrase to end all catch-phrases.

Clearly these 'corporate graffiti' are important not only to the world of business but also to the rest of society - largely due to the influence wielded by the people who employ them. Michael Porter, himself a contributor to corporate graffiti, has issued a warning to managers against paying too much attention to the fads - against what he calls single-issue management. Luckily, most management graffiti live and die without ever leaving the spheres of management. Exceptionally, however, the term competitiveness has taken the leap from management theory to the field of economics and public policy. Does this mean that public policy theory is starting to be subject to the same fads as management theory? Apparently, some mainstream economists are of this opinion. However - although most of the time ill-defined - the term competitiveness seems to fill a need in public discourse. Does the need for such a concept reflect a new situation in the world economy? Do we need the term competitiveness in order to come to grips with increasing globalization (another graffiti term), or is this a new term for a set of problems which have been around for a long time?

In this chapter I shall argue that, although often misused and mostly ill-defined, the term competitiveness properly used does describe an important feature in the world economy. This concept scratches the surface of important issues which are central for understanding the distribution of wealth, both nationally and globally. In spite of its fairly recent appearance on the scene, the term competitiveness in my view addresses issues which have been central in public policy at least during the last 500 years, albeit under different headings. I shall also argue that competitiveness - properly used - exposes important weaknesses in the neo-classical economic paradigm. This could then account for the vehemence with which some mainstream economists attack the use of the term.

If competitiveness is almost universally regarded as a formula for growth, another related term - picking winners - carries with it basically negative connotations. I shall attempt to show that both the above terms may be new, but that the underlying issues and the practice behind them are older than economic theory - perhaps as old as international trade itself. I shall also try to show that the discredited idea of picking winners is closely connected to the highly fashionable term competitiveness.

In the parlance of today's economic policy-making, competitiveness is like motherhood and apple-pie - few people in their right mind would argue against it. Opposition to the term competitiveness seems to fall into two categories: The first group questions competitiveness as the basis for the world economic system. The second questions the validity of the concept as such. The first category is represented by the 'Group of Lisbon' - 19 scientists who have put together an interesting document entitled 'Limits to Competition' (Ref. 2). The Group of Lisbon raises several questions on the long-term feasibility of a planet governed by what one of them calls 'The Gospel of Competitiveness' (Ref. 3). The second category group consists mostly of neo-classical economists who see the term as meaningless.

The use of the word competitiveness flourishes on both sides of the Atlantic. The term also starts to show up in the Third World - it is in the process of being 'globalized'. The overall strategy of the European Union (EU) seems to be centred around three buzz-words: Competitiveness - conveying a notion of continued wealth creation, cohesion - the EU term for income distribution and subsidiarity - the democratic dimension, implying that decisions should be taken at the lowest possible level in the hierarchy. Also in the United States, competitiveness is decidedly 'in'. In the United States, however, opposition to the use of the term brings together unexpected allies. The Clinton administration brought with it what to an outsider looks like the first non–neo-classical economic advisors to the Presidency for several decades. Predictably - friction between the neo-classical camp and the 'newcomers' appeared. Robert Reich's 'high-quality jobs' and 'low-quality jobs' are not exactly meaningful terms to neo-classical economists. In a paper presented at the 1993 Annual Meeting of the American Economic Association, MIT's Paul Krugman twice refers to Robert Reich as a 'pop internationalist', and somewhat unacademically condemns his Harvard colleague's notion of 'high-value sectors' as a silly concept (Ref. 4). Faced with such an unusual degree of academic animosity, it is surprising to find that Krugman and Reich share the same negative view on the term competitiveness - a term everybody else seems to love. In his review of Michael Porter's *The Competitive Advantage of Nations* (Ref. 5), Robert Reich opens with a broadside: 'National competitiveness is one of those rare terms of public discourse to have gone directly from obscurity to meaninglessness without any intervening period of coherence' (Ref. 6). In Krugman's article quoted above, he concludes that in international economics 'the essential things to teach students are still the insights of Hume and Ricardo', and 'if we can teach undergrads to wince when they hear someone talk about "competitiveness", we will have done our nation a great service'. The 'pop internationalist' and the defender of neo-classical economics have found a rare common ground in their shared dislike of the term competitiveness.

Competitiveness as a term in international economics

The macro-economic use of the word competitiveness is often not properly defined. In a micro world, the term is fairly straightforward. A standard definition would be that competitiveness refers to the capacity of a firm to compete, grow and be profitable in the marketplace. At the macro level, however, the concept becomes more elusive. Porter (Ref. 5, p. xii) comments that there is no accepted definition of competitiveness, and later says that 'The only meaningful concept of competitiveness at the national level is national productivity' (Ref. 5, p. 6). This is hardly an operational definition, since - as we shall see later - there is sometimes little relationship between absolute level of productivity and national wealth. A 1993 book carrying the title *European Competitiveness* (Ref. 7, p. 1) sees two distinct uses of the word: on the one hand, it refers to relative efficiency (dynamically or statically), on the other, to relative international trade performance (market shares, revealed comparative advantage). Also these definitions seem unsatisfactory. In a 1985 book on *US Competitiveness in the World Economy,* Bruce Scott provides the following definition: 'National competitiveness refers to a nation state's ability to produce, distribute, and service goods in the international economy in competition with goods and services produced in other countries, *and to do so in a way that earns a rising standard of living*' (Ref. 8, p. 15, italics added). The OECD Programme on 'Technology and the Economy' provides the following definition: '(Competitiveness) may be defined as the degree to which, under open market conditions, a country can produce goods and services that meet the test of foreign competition *while simultaneously maintaining and expanding domestic real income*' (Ref. 9, p. 237, my italics).

In this chapter I shall use the Scott/OECD definition of competitiveness. By this definition, national competitiveness is limited to activities where 'being competitive' in the micro sense simultaneously increases the national standard of living. This is in my view the core of the argument. We may thus say that 'competitiveness' is achieved only when the neo-classical 'law' of factor-price equalization (Refs. 10, 11) is being defied. Competitiveness is in my view divorced from the issues of productivity or efficiency as such. Although it is difficult to be competitive if you are not efficient and have a high productivity, it is by no means obvious that being the most efficient producer of an internationally traded product makes a country competitive - i.e. enables it to raise the standard of living. Some very efficient producers and nations are desperately poor - they are efficient in products which do not provide competitiveness in the income-raising meaning of the word. Taking an example: The most productive manufacturers of base-balls in the world are Haitians. They earn 30 cents an hour. Although the US firms which have their base-balls produced in Haiti are competitive in the micro-economic sense, base-ball production does not make the Haitian economy more competitive in our macro-economic use of the word. In spite of its absolute efficiency and large market share in producing base-balls with the state-of-the-art technology (needle and thread), Haiti's standard of living does not increase.

We can observe that high relative or absolute productivity levels do not necessarily lead to competitiveness. However, fast changes in the level of productivity do tend to lead to competitiveness. Behind competitiveness there is a key element of imperfect competition, and it is of course this imperfect competition which prevents factor-price equalization. That a firm is competitive in the micro-economic sense does not mean that all its activities make the nations where it operates more competitive in the income-raising macro-economic sense of the term. Being the most efficient in the 'wrong' activities - the opposite of national competitiveness - leads to 'negative development'.

The conflict between 'competitiveness' and neo-classical theory - or: How the world got rich in the 'wrong' way

Why does a prominent mainstream international economist like Paul Krugman want all US undergraduates to wince at the mention of the term competitiveness? The term seems to provoke in him something more than indifference. Why this strong visceral reaction? One explanation could be the frequently uncritical and ill-defined use of competitiveness in public discourse. However, I think there are more profound reasons. The very idea of a nation lifting itself to higher levels of living standards through competitiveness - being engaged in activities that raise the national living standards more than other activities - goes directly against the assumptions and beliefs which form the foundations of the neo-classical economic edifice. This is not the way economic growth is supposed to take place in the neo-classical model. The strong reaction against the term seems to be there because the implicit assumptions behind competitiveness contradict the very core of neo-classical economic thought. In a world inhabited by 'representative firms' operating under perfect information and with no scale effects - the classical assumptions of neo-classical theory - the term competitiveness is absolutely meaningless. Thus Krugman's view of a 'high-value sector' is being silly. Competitiveness is caused by factors which neo-classical economics traditionally has assumed away - the term must therefore seem meaningless.

Both high-value sectors and competitiveness come alive, however, in a world where imperfect information and huge economies of scale create cumulative causations, path-dependent development and lock-in effects. Economies of scale are at the core of globalized competition. Indeed, under the standard assumptions of neo-classical economic theory it is difficult to find reasons why firms exist at all, even more so for globalized firms. So, in spite of the often vague and cliché-like use of the term competitiveness, the word carries with it a core of intuitive understanding which challenges the very paradigm on which the world economic order rests.

An important problem facing the standard economic theory of today is that the countries which grew rich did so in the wrong way. In the neo-classical world, additional created wealth is supposed to spread through lowered prices. In a world with perfect information and no economies of scale, there is no room for wealth to be taken out in any other way. New technology in the form of added capital per worker increases the output of the economy, and - under the standard assumptions - this spreads through the world economy in the form of lowered prices. Both Adam Smith (Ref. 12, p. 269) and David Ricardo (Ref. 13, pp. 46–47) explicitly state that this would be the effect of improved techniques - prices would fall.

However, as technology progresses a nation can get rich in two very different ways. One is the mechanism suggested by Smith and Ricardo: technological change only causes prices to fall. The other way, which is not discussed outside the field of labour economics, is that an important portion of the benefits from technological change is being distributed inside the producing nations through higher profits, higher wages and higher taxable income overall. I call the first mechanism the *Classical Mode* of distribution of economic growth, and the second the *Collusive Mode* of distribution. When the first mechanism operates, the benefits of technical change are spread exclusively to the consumers of goods produced. When the second mechanism operates, the producer (company and nation) of goods retains an important part of the benefits of improved productivity (see chapter 1 for a discussion of this). Only when the second system is at work - when there is a collusive spread of economic growth - is there a possibility for discussing competitiveness. Competitiveness in this way can be seen as the consequences on a national level of what labour economists refer to as 'industry rent'. The core of the competitiveness strategy is to locate industries where high industry rents exist - where there is a collusive spread of economic growth in my terminology. Competitiveness - the income-rising effect - is essentially achieved through appropriation of this rent.

In the static system of neo-classical economics, rent-seeking is seen as a negative term. In a world where increasing returns to scale, imperfect information and huge barriers to entry dominate all industries of any importance, dynamic rent-seeking seems to be a key factor for economic growth and competitiveness. Being micro-economically competitive in an industry with perfect information, perfect divisibility of factors of production and no scale effects leads to poverty - regardless of the level of productivity - as we have shown in the Haitian example. High-tech protectionism is a part of this rent-seeking. The existence and national appropriation of this rent is the core of competitiveness. This 'industry rent' is also a central feature of the mechanisms which prevent factor-price equalization to take place in the world, and it gives us a hint at why increased globalization seems to be accompanied by larger income inequalities. Inside the EU this tendency is confirmed; at present more than 60 per cent of EU territory receives subsidies due to their 'underdevelopment'. This amount comes in addition to the huge redistributional effects of national economic budgets. The quest for competitiveness seems to necessitate increasing flows of funds for social cohesion. Originally one main argument for the internal European market was the reaping of economies of scale. Not unexpectedly, this seems to lead to a concentration of production - creating fewer centres and more peripheries, thus increasing the need for redistribution.

If the increased wealth produced with new technology is, even to a small extent, kept in the producing country in the form of higher wages and profits, the logical foundation of our world economic system today would seem to face a serious challenge. Given that technological progress at any point in time is very unevenly distributed among different economic activities, the logical result of this is the high-tech protectionism that we see in practice. Nations attempt to pick winners, i.e. those activities with the highest potential for an increase in productivity and sales[1], assuming that increasing returns and imperfect information will cause the 'industry rent' to stick. Probably the static Ricardian-type benefits from trade are more than outweighed by dynamic 'industry rent' effects, caused e.g. by increasing returns. On the other hand, if both trading partners work under increasing returns, this would again make an even stronger argument for free trade. It

1. I assume that Verdorn's law will very often be at work.

is, however, quite easy to envision situations where free trade would no longer be the preferred solution.

Recent developments of mainstream economic theory - 'New Growth Theory' and 'New Trade Theory' - are approaching an understanding of the very same factors we discuss here, but from a different angle. As the father of the 'New Growth Theory' Krugman himself has resurrected a key concept from nineteenth-century national economic policy[2] - economies of scale (Ref. 15). In my view the findings of these 'new' schools are absolutely compatible both with 'high-value sectors' and 'competitiveness'. If Krugman were to see the quest for competitiveness and for high-value sectors as being the result of the **uneven spread across industries** of economies of scale, endogenous technical change and consequently of positive hysteresis effects, he would, in my opinion, find that both Robert Reich, the reasoned competitiveness school, and 'New growth theory' and 'New Trade Theory' are indeed addressing the same issues. One barrier to this theoretical convergence and mutual understanding is that in spite of the resurrection of economies of scale as an important factor determining the distribution of world income, Krugman and other 'new trade theorists' so far seemingly avoid facing the practical consequences of their own theories. It is easy to have an understanding for their reluctance. Incorporating the conclusions of 'new trade theory' would require a complete overhaul of the world trading system, and make painfully clear the imperfections of what one US writer refers to as GATTism (Ref. 16). With a view to the problems of the Third World, and now also the fast erosion of the living standards of the Second World, it still seems pressing to make this overhaul.

Graffiti from the past - historical equivalents of competitiveness

Competitiveness in a Schumpeterian framework

Between the Anglo-Saxon economic theory which presently rules the world and its predecessors - the theories which in turn built the industrial powers of England, the United States, Germany and Japan - there is a very fundamental difference: the desirability of perfect vs. imperfect competition.

In the Anglo-Saxon neo-classical theory, perfect competition is - at the same time - a core assumption of the system and a prerequisite for the system to deliver what it promises: factor-price equalization under a system of world free trade. In neo-classical theory economic activities are 'alike' - all equally good as carriers of economic development from a nation's point of view. This is a logical consequence of the key assumptions of perfect information and constant returns to scale, and a condition for general equilibrium. The stated goal is that of perfect competition. The Anglo-Saxon paradigm is neo-classical economics, whereas the alternative Schumpeterian or evolutionary economics has its roots in the German Historical Tradition.

2. Although Krugman seems unaware of its former importance. He only tracks the term back to a 1924 article.

One economist - Joseph Alois Schumpeter - provides a bridge from the German historical school to the world of Anglo-Saxon economic theory. In Anglo-Saxon economics Schumpeter stands out as being much more original than he is to someone who has a knowledge of the German historical school of economics. Today Schumpeterian or evolutionary economics challenges neo-classical economics as an alternative basis for economic policy-making. Its breakthrough on the policy-making level was the Technology and Economy Programme (TEP) recently carried out by the OECD, where the aim was to create a better understanding of the relationship between technological change and economic growth. In Schumpeter's process of 'creative destruction', waves of innovation hit different industries at different points in time - providing widely differing entrepreneurial profit across industries. The industries where high degrees of entrepreneurial profits exist will also be the activities which provide competitiveness as this entrepreneurial profit is spread in a collusive mode and 'trickles down' in the producing nation. In this way a reasoned use of the term competitiveness is perfectly compatible with a Schumpeterian world view.

In the empire-building economic paradigms of the past, economic development was seen as 'activity specific' - some economic activities were seen to bring economic development, others not (see chapter 1). Economic development in this system was - stated in today's terms - caused by engaging in the economic activities which provided dynamic imperfect competition. The Schumpeterian creative destruction which caused growth was historically clustered around a few activities at any point in time - in stone working activities in the Stone Age and in bronze working activities in the Bronze Age. Since the 1500s the implicit or explicit assumption in economic thinking was that if a country engaged in the activities experiencing technical change, the technological advances would not all have to be given away to customers abroad, much of it could be kept in the producing nations as profits and higher real wages which gave a higher standard of living. This reasoning is evident in the *realökonomisch*-oriented mercantilists both in England and France, in the philosophy behind the arguments used by the German cameralists, in the 'American System' starting around 1820, and in the German historical school. In a Kaldorian sense, the development economics in the growth period of all the presently industrialized countries was 'economics without equilibrium' - a system where shifting clusters of disequilibrium-producing technical change provided growth. The goal of economic policy - mostly implicit - was a search for dynamic imperfect competition. In this connection various concepts or buzz-words - of the likes of competitiveness - were in use. We shall return to this later in this section, where English, US, German and Japanese experiences are treated separately.

The historical economic growth of nations is hardly a history of free trade or perfect markets. Even though historically natural protection in the form of very high transportation costs has served as a natural deterrent to trade, no doubt tariffs and import and export prohibitions have been the most used tools of economic policy in history. Tariffs were clearly important sources of revenue, but they were also tools for a wider economic policy.

Using the word 'strategy' for economic policies of past centuries is perhaps an overly ambitious term, but for hundreds of years nations have possessed beliefs and ideologies on what promoted national welfare. Based on these beliefs' economic policy, heavy interventions in the working of the market were carried out. Just as the ideology of free trade has been seen as the key mechanism in promoting universal economic welfare since the Second World War, other concepts have dominated earlier. Often the expression of the policies to follow was as nebulous as today's competitiveness - often they were more specifically targeted. Our understanding of these past policies tends to be built on stereotypes. Hundreds of years of economic history and economic thought are usually lumped together under the - mostly derogatory - term 'mercantilism'. Unfortunately - following the example set by Adam Smith - we tend to discuss only the monetary aspects of mercantilism and other pre-classical schools of economic thought. The teaching of history of economic thought seems to lose out in Western countries - unlike in Japan - and what is left of the subject tends to become the history of neo-classical economics. The economists who were actually important for policy-making in the past are mostly lost to us in the pursuit of the genealogy of neo-classical thought. In the following section we shall look at the *realökonomisch* (non-monetary) aspects of pre-classical - and later 'anti-classical' - economic thought in some of the largest and most successful economies.

England and the theories of 'good' and 'bad' trade

Towards the end of the fifteenth century, England was a poor nation, heavily indebted to her Italian bankers. Her main produce was wool. Over a relatively short period, England went from being a poor periphery of Europe to being what we today would call the world's superpower: From being a poor farming country to possessing a world empire where the sun never set. England's competitiveness increased enormously - she increased production and exports and raised the standard of living considerably, although unevenly.

This development was not a result of macro-economic 'laissez faire'. It was seemingly based on a perception of the economic growth process very different from today's; I would even venture to call it a strategy. Seemingly, economic growth was seen as being activity-specific, it happened in some activities and not in others. It was a world where 'good' activities caused national wealth - not a world where an abstract 'economy' grows by percentage points. In a less complex environment - without the bewildering array of new products and new technologies facing us today - I find this view plausible. Merchants and workers in some activities were wealthier than others, and pre-Ricardian common sense seems to have reasoned that if lawyers make more money than lettuce-pickers, a nation of lawyers will be richer than a nation of lettuce-pickers. Increasing national wealth - competitiveness - was tied to being active in the 'good' activities. Exporting certain goods was 'good trade' - a term which recalls Robert Reich's 'high-quality jobs'. The economy consisted of activities which were potentially different - good, bad, so-so. The economy was far from being a black box inhabited by 'representative firms'.

The core of the English strategy is well captured by German economist Friedrich List: 'The principle "sell manufactured goods, buy raw materials" has during centuries been the substitute for a whole theory' (Ref. 17, my translation). Manufacturing was seen as bringing competitiveness - raw materials not. From a neo-classical point of view this is of course nonsense, but it is difficult to refuse the results of this strategy - the industrial revolution. Looking at the English cult of manufacturing and the concepts of 'good' and 'bad' trade in the light of modern innovation theory, the strategy seems to make sense. The industrial revolution can be visualized as a process where, following woollen textiles, more and more processes, one by one in a sequence, were being mechanized, and more and more differentiated products appeared. The English seem to have picked up the new industries during the period of transition from being a handicraft into being a manufacturing industry. In this way they would run down the learning curves faster than their later-starting competitors, achieve important economies of scale, learning-by-doing, and would build important barriers to entry for foreign competitors. By concentrating on manufacturing early in the industrial age, the English created an unrivalled national innovation system (Refs. 18, 19). As a result, pockets of activities working under imperfect competition clustered in different parts of England as 'growth poles' or Marshallian industrial districts.

Daniel Defoe - who is normally seen as a reliable source in English history - gives us his account of the origins of England's take-off in his 'Plan of English Commerce' of 1728. By his account, the Tudors - especially Henry VII and Elizabeth I - are to be credited for England's ascent. Defoe describes how Henry VII - who came to power in 1485 - had spent his childhood in Burgundy. The wealth he observed there contrasted sharply with the poverty he later found in England. But, the Prince observed, the wealth in Burgundy depended totally on the import of English raw materials: wool and Fuller's earth.[3] When he came to the throne of England, Henry employed the pre-Ricardian logic which during later centuries seems to have dominated, not only in England but also on the Continent: (Woollen) manufacturers are rich, producers of raw materials (wool) are poor. Therefore, to get rich and develop the country, we must promote the production of (woollen) manufactures. Selling manufactures is 'good' trade - in today's lingo: it makes us competitive. The methods used to start the production of woollen textiles in England starting in 1489 are the same which later became standard features in all presently industrialized countries: The king 'secretly procured a great many Foreigners, who were perfectly skill'd in the Manufacture, to come over and instruct his own People here in their Beginnings', bounties were paid to entrepreneurs, import duties were raised for textiles, export duties for raw wool were kept high, and finally, when the English production capacity was sufficient, the export of raw wool was prohibited.

The theories of 'good' and 'bad' trade probably reached their perfection in the eighteenth century. Three volumes published in 1721 by Charles King under the title 'The British Merchant; or, Commerce Preserv'd' (Ref. 21) were extremely influential in the eighteenth century. King gives an elaborate list of 'good' and 'bad' trade - of what makes a country competitive. The list is long and detailed, but a basic message is that selling manufactures is 'good' trade, importing them is 'bad' trade (Ref. 21, Vol. 1, pp. 1–14). Selling raw materials - commodities - to import manufactures is 'bad' trade. 'Bad' trade today finds its counterpart in Boston Consulting Group's and Michael

3. Silicate of alumina, used in cleansing cloth.

Porter's 'dog industries', activities characterized by fragmented market shares and no growth, i.e. where there is perfect competition. Here Marx, Schumpeter and Porter meet: perfect competition does not lead to wealth.

Interestingly in Charles King's scheme, exchanging manufactures for other manufactures is specifically seen as being beneficial to both trading countries. In a world where commodities are produced under conditions of diminishing returns, and where manufactured goods are produced under conditions of increasing returns, King's recommendation would make sense. During the last 10 years 'The New Trade Theory' has - indirectly and without referring to it - reconfirmed the validity of this old 'unscientific' and 'superstitious' economic policy. We should also note that an Italian economist - Antonio Serra - already in 1613 had identified the existence of increasing returns as an important source of Venetian wealth (Refs. 22, 14).

The English emphasis on manufacturing consisted not only of promoting own manufacturing, it was important to stop other nations from manufacturing when this was feasible. In most cases the manufacturing-centred strategy involved preventing the birth of manufacturing industries in the colonies, which could be done without causing too much political uproar. However, on some occasions it was seen as necessary actively to destroy foreign manufacturing in order to promote important English interests. Prohibiting the prosperous woollen textile manufacturing in Ireland starting in 1699 and the destruction of the Bengali weaving industry in the early nineteenth century are particularly dramatic examples - both with very serious social consequences - of this side of the strategy. In terms of today - getting rid of the Irish woollen industry and the Indian cotton weavers made English industry more competitive. This aim was also achieved by prohibiting the emigration of skilled workers - a practice already used by the Venetians under threat of death penalty - and through prohibiting the export of machinery from England until the 1830s.

It may be said that the English policies on economic growth truly created a 'national innovation system'. In a period of time when innovation materialized as a sequence of mechanizations of manufacturing processes, one very efficient way of maximizing innovation was to pay bounties to the producers of goods for which production was in the process of being mechanized, and to raise the duties of these goods. We often also find a high-tech bias in tariff schedules, even today. In the United States of the 1920s German dolls with heads made from modern synthetic material were subject to much higher duties than traditional dolls. Similar patterns are frequently found both in Japan and elsewhere, but this phenomenon needs to be studied more. Today the EU external tariff still maintains the basic characteristics of the English mercantilists: raw material can be imported free of duty, manufactured goods often not. Fish as a raw material can be imported duty free to the EC, however once breaded, cured or smoked, it has to pay duty.

'The American System'- productive capacity and competitiveness

By the time the early economic policies of the United States were being formed, the English policy had shifted away from previous strategies. Alexander Hamilton - in his 1791 'Report on Manufactures' - has clearly read Adam Smith and knows the free trade arguments, but comes down on the side of the previous English strategy: manufactures are to be encouraged. Hamilton was clearly much more influenced by the late English mercantilist Malachy Postlethwayt than by Adam Smith. Although Hamilton provided a favourable attitude towards the protection of manufactures, tariffs as a permanent 'American System' only started in 1819. Seemingly the 'involuntary protection' experienced by the United States by being largely cut off from trade with Europe during the blockades during the War of 1812 encouraged enough manufacturing activity to achieve a critical mass of political pressure for tariffs. This 'involuntary protection' seems to have a parallel in Latin America during the Second World War.

In this 'American System of Manufactures' Daniel Raymond's 'Thoughts on Political Economy' provided the first theory (Ref. 23). Here tariffs were a permanent part of the system, not an incidental temporary aid to infant industry. Raymond elaborated much around the concept of 'productive capacity'. Productive capacity seems to have been the buzz-word of the day, a parallel to the concept of National Productive Power which was used in Germany during the same period. Some activities provided more 'productive capacity' and 'productive power' than others - like competitiveness it is not present to the same degree in all activities. Raymond specifically complains that 'In the *Wealth of Nations* agriculture, commerce and manufactures are all jumbled together' (Ref. 23, p. 132). Just as Serra did in 1613, Raymond implies that different natural laws apply to different activities.

Raymond points out that England did not get rich by following Adam Smith's prescriptions, but that it would be in their interest to have other nations following them: 'That policy which Adam Smith reprobates, and which England has adopted, must then be considered the cause which has produced the unexampled wealth and power of England' (Ref. 23, p. 136). 'It might answer a very good purpose for them, to cry up his (Adam Smith's) system, that other nations might be gulled by it, but they never choose to be gulled by it themselves' (Ref. 23, p. 134).

Responding to the argument that tariffs would raise prices, Raymond claimed that this was no argument for the nation as a whole. The high prices and favourable profits would both stimulate businessmen and increase the demand for labour far beyond the difference in price. We here encounter an important argument which became part of the eighteenth-century reasoning: The increase in prices caused by tariffs on manufactures is more than compensated by the increase in profits and wages in the protecting country. Man's two economic roles - as consumers and producers - are weighed against one another, in a circular-flow type of reasoning. If man-the-wage-earner is compensated more as a result of the tariff than what man-the-consumer has to spend additionally on the protected goods, the net effect to him of the tariff is positive. This argument would be valid if technological developments spreads collusively - see above - as the result of imperfect competition, externalities, and/or scale effects. Typically, present economic thinking - having internalized the standard assumptions of neo-classical theory - focuses exclusively on the interests of man-the-consumer, which only under perfect competition are identical to those of man-the-wage-earner.

The literature around the issues of protection of manufactures in the United States is enormous. Many economists deserve to be mentioned, Matthew and Henry Carey,

John Rae - perhaps the first author to emphasize invention and technical change - and Friedrich List, the German political refugee who later was to export 'The American System' so successfully to Germany. The result of the debates was a considerable fluctuation in the level of tariffs during the nineteenth century, in the United States as in Europe. This lack of consistency in the tariff level may be seen as a weakness, but in fact Friedrich List came to recommend this strategy. Turning protection on and off would keep the local manufacturers 'on their toes', under constant pressure to improve both their products and their methods of production. We could say that such a system insured a continuous flow of process and product innovations. List's argument recalls Porter's emphasis on the need for competition and demanding customers.

Tariffs and protection were by some - including Friedrich List both during his period in the United States and later - seen as a temporary measure, a measure needed in order to catch up with England and later forge ahead. Dorfman expresses this vision particularly well, partly using quotes from List and partly using his own words as follows:

> '...free trade is the ideal, and the United States will proclaim the true cosmopolitan principles when the time is ripe. This will be when the United States has a hundred million people[4] and the seas are covered with her ships; when American industry attains the greatest perfection, and New York is the greatest commercial emporium and Philadelphia the greatest manufacturing city in the world; and 'when no earthly power can longer resist the American Stars, then our children's children will proclaim freedom of trade throughout the world, by land and sea'. (Ref. 24, p. 581)

In this prophetic statement, the English strategy for growth is recreated. If the United States had the courage to follow the strategy that England had followed, and not the one she preached at the moment, in the end the United States would surpass the old master, England.

Germany: Cosmo-political economic theory vs. 'National productive power'

Whereas early recruitment to the economics profession in England came from the merchants, the ranks of economists were filled from the public sector in Germany. German cameralists - the equivalent of mercantilists - were generally employed as keepers of the treasury or *Schatzkammer* - therefore the term cameralists.

The German cameralist literature is huge, but largely unknown outside Germany. Like the English mercantilists, the cameralists favoured the protection of manufacturing. An early book recommending the protection of manufacture - a contemporary of Mun's and Child's tracts in England - was Philipp von Hörnigk's *Österreich über alles wann es nur will,* first published in 1684. This book went through 16 editions, more than both Mun and Child. In contrast to England, however, it is important to notice that Germany

4. The population of the United States passed the 100 Million mark around 1915.

consisted of many states, some of them very small. By the early nineteenth century, Germany consisted of about 32 states, each one extremely protectionist.

Already from the seventeenth century we find that English economics books are translated to many languages including German, but the German books are hardly ever translated to foreign languages. This means that German economists have access to - and comment extensively on - both English and French economists, but not vice versa. There were seven German editions of *Wealth of Nations* before 1850, but in spite of this large diffusion, Smith's influence on trade and manufacturing policy was, as in the United States, limited.

Friedrich List was the man to provide the theory which led to the economic unification of Germany, carried out under the leadership of the Prussian bureaucrats. Originally a preacher of the doctrines of Adam Smith and J.B. Say, List had witnessed first-hand both the 'admirable' effect of Napoleon's 'Continental System' and of the 'American System of Manufactures'. He had also seen the destructive effects of free trade in France after the fall of Napoleon (the 'herbicide effect' of free trade, see chapter 1). To List, Smith was not altogether wrong, but to him the English economists failed to distinguish between national and universal interests. Their political economy was a cosmo-political economy, but nations needed to build a national system of political economy. To this very day, macro-economics is called *Volkwirtschaftslehre* or *Nationaløkonomie* in Germany and Scandinavia as a result of this reaction to English cosmo-political economics.

List's version of competitiveness was the term 'National Productive Power', originating from the German economist Adam Müller (Ref. 25). Nations must build Productive Power, and List gives examples on how manufacturing creates these powers and agriculture does not, but he essentially fails to explain why. Using today's buzz-words, List clearly explains that 'manufacturing matters', but he fails to explain why this is so. According to List, to free the national productive powers the internal tariffs in Germany had to be abolished and an external tariff established. In Germany, List is therefore seen as a free-trader; while in the Anglo-Saxon world he is seen as the incarnation of protectionism. List's argument for free trade in a larger geographical area suggests an understanding of the importance of scale in manufacturing. In order to create national productive power, List insisted on the importance of building railways, using much of the same reasoning now used in the United States in arguments for an electronic superhighway. Thus, in Germany, List is seen as the 'father of the national railway system'.

German political economy continued its 'one-way mirror' relationship with the rest of the world, virtually until the end of the Second World War. Exceptions were provided by the international spread of List's ideas, by a number of American teachers of economics who had studied in Germany, but above all by the very strong influence of German political economy in Japan.

Japan: Doitsugaki *economics beats* Eigaku *economics - twice!*

There are two crucial points in the history of Japanese economic policy, two points in time where a choice of economic strategy has decided the quality of her future: The Meiji restoration in 1868 and the end of the Second World War in 1945. In both cases the country has faced a strategic choice between following the recommendations of one of two schools of economic thought - between what the Japanese used to call the *Eigaku* (English) School - or the German - or *Doitsugaki* School. Remarkably, in both cases the German school of thought won the day. On the first occasion the most influential German economist was Friedrich List, on the second occasion it was the Austrian Joseph Alois Schumpeter.

Also in Japan the cosmopolitan universality of the English political economists came under criticism. British economists looked for economic laws that were as universal as those of the physical sciences, the German historical school accepted that social and economic sciences were specific to a given time and place. At the time, List's Japanese translator, Oshima Sadamasu, put it this way:

> 'If all apples fall to the ground in England, we can presume that all apples will fall towards the ground in every country of the world. But in the case of politics, law, or economics, what is suitable to England may not be applicable to France, for nations may be old or new, strong or weak, and their position, climate, customs and etiquette are also interconnected' ...... (quoted in Ref. 26)

In the founding manifesto of the Japanese National Economic Association from 1890 we again find expressed the importance of building national productive power', recalling the German and American strategies. Oshima saw the logical extension of Ricardian trade theory that 'agricultural nations must stay agricultural, and industrial nations must stay industrial' (Ref. 26, p. 61). However, no fundamentally agricultural nation had ever managed to build 'productive power'. In the end, productive power was seen as closely tied to that of national independence. The conclusion was that manufacturing had to be encouraged.

It was 55 years later, at the end of the Second World War, that Japan again entered into an intense debate as to her future economic strategy. The officials of the Bank of Japan were of the opinion that Japan should cultivate low-technology industries and seek competitive advantage through her low labour costs, following the standard recommendations of neo-classical economics. The officials of the Ministry of Industry and Trade (MITI) - armed with the writings of Schumpeter - argued that Japan should build high technology industries. Again German economic theory - with its model of imperfect competition as the engine of economic growth at its core - won the day. Schumpeterian economics and competitiveness converge around this core of imperfect competition. In the way competitiveness visualizes growth, the imperfect competition element is implicit, in Schumpeterian economics it is explicit.

No country has embraced Schumpeter like the Japanese have. Schumpeter's first book - *Wesen und Hauptinhalt der theoretischen Nationalökonomie* (Ref. 27) from 1908 - has appeared in three Japanese editions, the first in 1936. There was no English translation until 2010, and the only other translation is an Italian one from 1982. When Schumpeter was unable to find a job in Europe in the early 1930s, he was offered a job in Japan. Before leaving for Japan, however, he was offered another job at the University of Bonn, which he accepted. But he never forgot the Japanese job offer. Schumpeter's own library is now housed in the Hitotsubashi University in Tokyo - formerly Tokyo School of Commerce - which was established towards the end of the last century with the Hochschule für Welthandel in Schumpeter's Vienna as a model. Thus, today the two periods of *doitsugaki* economic influence in Japan meet in Schumpeter's library.

Measuring potential for competitiveness - The Quality Index of Economic Activities

Historically the presently developed nations have built their competitiveness above all on manufacturing. In the past, as we have seen, this was achieved by protecting and aiding manufacturing activities in various ways, thus building a 'national innovation system' where industry rent could be appropriated by the nation-state. There is, of course, nothing which makes manufacturing per se valuable. The key lies in the dynamic imperfect competition which sustains growth, which historically has been more present in manufacturing than in other economic activities. Today, many manufacturing industries fail to build competitiveness. On the other hand, many services - such as engineering and banking - can build competitiveness, as well as some agricultural products. In the United States rice seems to be one example. Historically, however, the superior economic activities - those providing 'national productive power', 'productive capacity' and competitiveness - have overwhelmingly come from the manufacturing sector.

In neo-classical economic theory - as a result of its core assumptions - all economic activities become 'alike'. The world is inhabited by 'representative firms'. From the individual entrepreneur's point of view, his firm is unique, at the very least through its geographical location. There is in my view a challenge to find an intermediary level of abstraction between these two extremes - that economic activities are either 'all equal' or 'all unique' - where economic activities may be grouped or categorized by common characteristics. The 'Quality Index' of economic activities in Table 4.1 is an attempt at achieving this goal. The 'Quality Index' ranks economic activities by their ability to provide competitiveness: their ability to increase a nation's standard of living while being micro-economically competitive in an open economy. The higher the score on the Quality Index, the higher the ability of an activity to raise a nation's standard of living. In Robert Reich's terms, the index ranks jobs from 'low quality' at the bottom to 'high quality' on the top.

The workings of an economic system under perfect competition is described well by current economic theory. There are also reasonably good theories of monopoly behaviour. However, in the real world, these two situations hardly ever exist. Economic theory has little meaningful to say about varying degrees of oligopoly, although this is clearly an important issue. In my view, this is like having defined well two extremes, black and white, whereas we have no way to define the intermediary tones of grey. Most economic activities operate under varying degrees of imperfect competition, varying degrees of grey to use my analogy. The Quality Index attempts to establish shades of grey - degrees of ability to raise national standards of living. Robert Reich's high-quality jobs are clustered towards the top. The 'dog' industries in Michael Porter's and Boston Consulting Group's portfolio concepts are found at the bottom. This low-quality area is

Table 4.1 The Quality Index.

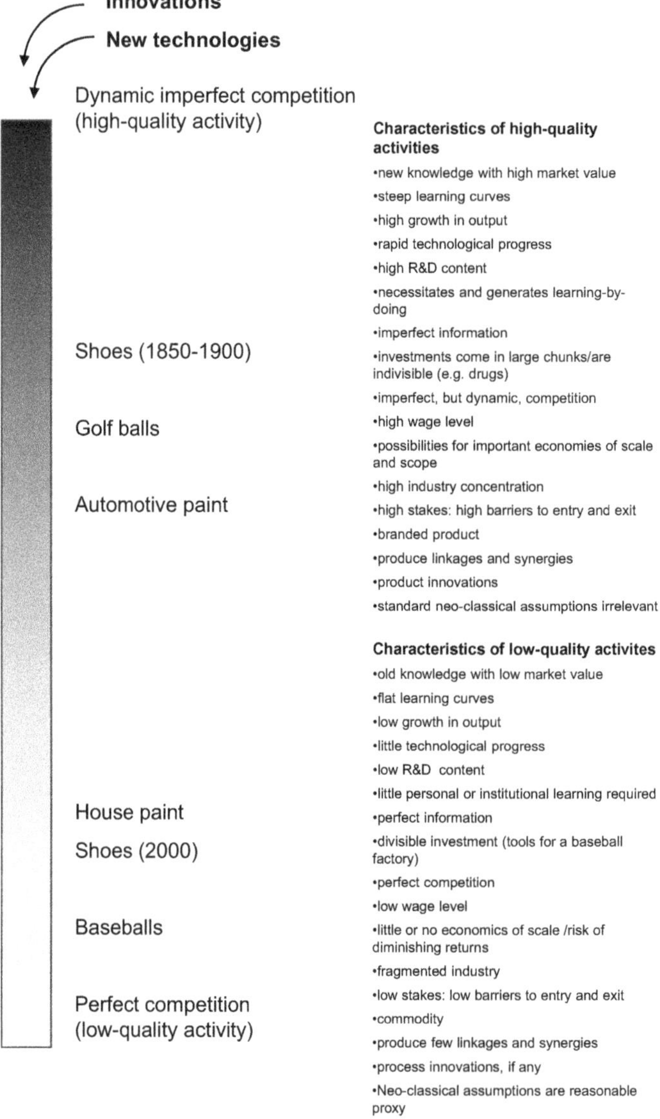

inhabited by what Tom McCraw calls peripheral firms, 'labor intensive, managerially thin, and bereft of scale economies' (Ref. 28, p.73). These low-score industries are often important employment-creating industries, but the top-score industries are the wealth-creating industries from the nation's point of view. For a further discussion of the index, see chapter 1.

The system must be visualized as a closed one where new activities enter at the top through new technologies or other forms of innovation. These innovations then fall towards perfect competition with varying speeds - as a result of variable gravitational pull. The gravity is also determined by purely static effects, like static economies of scale, which may make an activity 'stick' at a high level of quality even in the absence of new technology. Using an example: From 1850 to 1900 the US shoe industry experienced a very high productivity increase: man-hours employed per pair of medium-grade welt oxford shoes fell from 15.5 in 1850 to 1.7 in 1900 (Ref. 29, p. 271). At this point in time the shoe industry gets a high score on the Quality Index. As a result of this steep learning curve, the shoe industry provided competitiveness to the US economy: Real wages rose considerably, but the country was still able to compete. The nation's labour-hour terms of trade improved - more hours of labour from abroad could be exchanged for a smaller number of hours worked at home. Later, the score of the shoe industry on the Quality Index falls markedly. From 1900 to 1923, man-hours employed per pair fall only from 1.7 to 1.1, and from 1923 to 1936 further from 1.1 to 0.9. This is clearly a very meagre productivity increase compared to the development from 1850 to 1900. Even though the commodity shoes slowly ceased to be a high-quality activity after 1900, there are still today high-quality niches in the shoe industry. The high scores on the Quality Index of the niches in the shoe industry are based on factors like style, fashion, brand, design or innovations like in golf shoes or ski boots. 'Shoes the commodity', however, is now a low-quality activity which has been farmed out to poorer countries. This analysis has of course much in common with Vernon's product life cycle model.

The Quality Index represents an attempt to measure, though imperfectly, how economic activities differ, and to be able to outline the macro-economic consequences of these differences. At the same time the Index highlights the factors and mechanisms which cause competitiveness to exist; the factors which enable some nations to increase their standard of living markedly compared to others under a system of free trade, contrary to the predictions of mainstream economic theory. Said simply, the Quality Index measures the degree of imperfect competition - the degree to which an 'industry rent' may be achieved and temporarily appropriated by a nation-state.

Conclusion - Competitiveness as a proxy for the pursuit of dynamic imperfect competition

The roots of the competitiveness controversy are already present in Adam Smith. On the one hand Smith's ideal was agriculture - only there did he see markets working nearly perfectly. On the other hand he saw in his age more technical change in manufacturing, and he speculates that the cause of this may be 'the impossibility of making so complete and entire a separation of all the different branches of labour employed in agriculture' (Ref. 12, p. 10). Unfortunately Smith fails to see the organizational and distributional implications of this difference in the potential for division of labour. The very division of labour seems to be a key factor in causing economies of scale, barriers to entry, imperfect competition and consequently variations in the 'quality' of economic activities. A high degree of 'division of labour' causes imperfect competition - the very foundation for competitiveness the way the term is used today.

In contrast to Anglo-Saxon mainstream economics, German economics generally allowed for economic activities to be different. Because some activities provided 'National Productive Power' or 'Competitiveness' more than others, nineteenth-century economists both in Germany, the United States and Japan saw the need for a 'National System of Political Economy' as opposed to the English system which they labelled 'Cosmo-Political Economy'. The underlying reasoning for this distinction is the same as the reasoning underlying the contemporary use of the term competitiveness, i.e. the quest for the imperfect-competition activities - present in some economic activities and not in others - which raise the standard of living collusively (not only through falling prices). In a world where economic activities are qualitatively different, seeking competitiveness is an optimization process for the nation-state.

All presently industrialized countries, starting with England, seem to have grown with a specific ideology or strategy where the activities providing imperfect competition have been singled out and protected. These 'good' activities provided wealth which trickled down to the rest of the nation - they provided 'national productive power', 'productive capacity' or - as we call it today: 'competitiveness'. The successful colonies also embarked on the same strategy, often in sharp contrast to the official policies of the mother countries. All nations tended to prohibit manufacturing in the colonies, maximizing the competitiveness of the metropolis in its trading relations. In the nineteenth century, England, who came to dominate all the 'high-quality activities', gradually converted to free trade. A New Zealand colonist remarks in 1897 that 'The British colonist is scarcely seated in the saddle (before he) discards all theories of free trade with the outer world and levies high import duties on every product which his colony is capable of supplying in adequate quantity for his own needs. He levies these duties even on the products of the country under whose flag he lives. He believes that only in this way can his new land be made ..prosperous.., and that prosperity so large as this aim implies will not be attainable while subject to unrestricted competition with the great Capital...' (Ref. 30, pp. 41–42).

Up until after WW II, nations tended to secure competitiveness - access to the high-quality activities - through the protection of manufactures. The success of the theories of free trade in the economics profession was not matched in business and political circles until then. In today's world with managed free trade, the goals are the same, but the means more subtle, at least among the triadic countries: Europe, Japan and the United States. Typically, however, the industrialized countries have mechanisms both to protect activities with a high score on the Quality Index and some of those with a low score, particularly agriculture and fisheries, but for opposite reasons. In the name of competitiveness - raising national incomes through imperfect competition - the European Union (EU) supports the Airbus project. In the name of cohesion (income distribution) the same EU supports its farmers who are engaged in activities operating closer to perfect competition, unshielded by 'industry rents' the way their compatriots in the manufacturing industry are. I have previously referred to this as 'aggressive' and 'protective' protectionism

- apparently the same type of economic policy which in fact is carried out as the result of two entirely different types of economic and political pressures (Ref. 31).

Although the term competitiveness is a fairly new one, it is basically only a new term for a long-standing 'winner-picking' exercise, a quest for activities operating under imperfect competition which can be traced at least as far back as England in the late fifteenth century. The tariff policies and other economic measures taken by the Republic of Venice show the same characteristics even in earlier centuries. Until fairly recently the basic mechanism used to climb the Quality Index was tariffs. However, once nations have achieved competitiveness in activities with high scores on the Quality Index, they have (sensibly) turned to free trade. Due to economies of scale, free trade is clearly beneficial to both parties when products from 'high-quality activities' are exchanged for others with the same score on the Quality Index, just as Charles King was claiming in 1721.

The Quality Index attempts to illustrate why manufacturing matters. The whole process of economic development can be pictured as an ascent towards dynamic imperfect competition and 'rents' on the Quality Index. A similar view is embedded in the theories of such diverse authors as Michael Porter, Karl Marx and Joseph Schumpeter. Recently we have seen how some nations have achieved high growth by climbing very fast up the Quality Index with export-oriented production - Korea and Taiwan would be examples of this. These Asian countries have climbed towards increased wealth emphasizing exports, to a large extent based on the electronics industry. If we are to consider the present acute situation of the de-industrializing Eastern block and the increasing poverty in much of the Third World, what would be the policy implications of the historical strategies for competitiveness? The successful export-oriented high-growth countries of South East Asia only represent about 2 per cent of the Third World population. It seems doubtful that the remaining 98 per cent - billions of people - in the Third World will be able to climb the Quality Index by exporting electronics or other high-tech products to the industrialized world. The historical growth strategies of the presently industrialized countries - how they climbed the Quality Index and achieved national productive power and competitiveness - are clearly also worth studying as an alternative strategy.

References

1. 'Time to Walk the Talk', *Financial Times*, February 4, 1994, p. 10.
2. The Group of Lisbon, *Limits to Competition*, Lisbon, Gulbenkian Foundation, 1993.
3. Petrella, Riccardo, 'L'evangile de la competitivite', *Le Monde Diplomatique,* Paris, September, 1991.
4. Krugman, Paul, 'What do Undergrads Need to Know About Trade?', *The American Economic Review, Papers and Proceedings,* May 1993, pp. 23–26.
5. Porter, Michael, *The Competitive Advantage of Nations,* London, Macmillan, 1990.
6. Reich, Robert, 'But Now we're Global', *The Times Literary Supplement*, August 31–September 6, 1990.
7. Hughes, Kirsty S. (editor), *European Competitiveness*, Cambridge, Cambridge University Press, 1993.

8. Scott, Bruce and George Lodge (editors), *US Competitiveness and the World Economy*, Boston, Harvard Business School Press, 1985.
9. OECD/TEP - The Technology/Economy Programme, *Technology and the Economy. The Key Relationships*, Paris, OECD, 1992.
10. Samuelson, Paul A., 'International Trade and the Equalization of Factor Prices', *Economic Journal*, Vol. 58, June 1948.
11. Samuelson, Paul A., 'International Factor-Price Equalization once Again', *Economic Journal*, Vol. 59, June 1949.
12. Smith, Adam, *Wealth of Nations* (1776), Chicago, University of Chicago Press, 1976.
13. Ricardo, David, *On the Principles of Political Economy and Taxation* (1817), London, Dent, 1973.
14. Reinert, Erik, 'Catching-up from Way Behind - A Third World Perspective on First World History', Chapter 1 in this book.
15. Krugman, Paul, *Rethinking International Trade*, Cambridge, MA, MIT Press, 1990.
16. Prestowitz, Clyde V., Jr., et al., 'The Last Gasp of GATTism', *Harvard Business Review*, March–April, 1991.
17. List, Friedrich, *Das Nationale System der Politischen Ökonomie* (1841), Basel, Kyklos, 1959.
18. Lundvall, Bengt-Åke (editor), *National Systems of Innovation*, London, Pinter, 1992.
19. Nelson, Richard (editor), *National Innovation Systems*, New York, Oxford University Press, 1993.
20. Defoe, Daniel, *A Plan of English Commerce*, London, C. Rivington, 1728.
21. King, Charles, *The British Merchant; or, Commerce Preserved*, London, John Darby, 1721. 3 Volumes.
22. Serra, Antonio, *Breve trattato delle Cause che possono far abbondare li Regni d'Oro e Argento dove non sono miniere. Con Applicazione al Regno di Napoli*, Naples, Lazzaro Scorriggio, 1613.
23. Raymond, Daniel, *Thoughts on Political Economy*, Baltimore, Fielding Lucas Jr., 1820.
24. Dorfman, Joseph, *The Economic Mind in American Civilisation*, Vol. 1, London, Harrap & Co., 1947.
25. Müller, Adam, *Elemente der Staatskunst*, Vol. 5, Berlin, J.D. Sander, 1809.
26. Morris-Suzuki, Tessa, *A History of Japanese Economic Thought*, London, Routledge, 1989.
27. Schumpeter, Joseph Alois, *Wesen und Hauptinhalt der theoretischen Nationalökonomie*, Leipzig, Duncker & Humblot, 1908.
28. McCraw, Thomas K., *Prophets of Regulation*, Cambridge, MA, Harvard University Press, 1984.
29. Stern, Boris, 'Labor Productivity in the Boot and Shoe Industry', *Monthly Labor Review*, February 1939.
30. (Moss, F.J.), *Notes of Political Economy by a New Zealand Colonist*, London, Macmillan, 1897.
31. Reinert, Erik S., *International Trade and the Economic Mechanisms of Underdevelopment*, Ann Arbor, University Microfilm, 1980.
32. von Hörnigk, Philipp, *Österreich über alles wann es nur will*, first published in 1684.

Chapter 5

DIMINISHING RETURNS AND ECONOMIC SUSTAINABILITY: THE DILEMMA OF RESOURCE-BASED ECONOMIES UNDER A FREE TRADE REGIME

'And the land was not able to bear them, that they may dwell together ...'

Genesis XIII, 6.

(quote used by Alfred Marshall, *Principles of Economics*, London, 1890, in order to emphasize the role of Diminishing Returns as a fundamental factor in human history.)

'I apprehend (the elimination of Diminishing Returns) to be not only an error, but the most serious one, to be found in the whole field of political economy. The question is more important and fundamental than any other; it involves the whole subject of the causes of poverty;...and unless this matter be thoroughly understood, it is to no purpose proceeding any further in our inquiry.'

John Stuart Mill, *Principles of Political Economy*, 1848.

This chapter explores the impact of Diminishing Returns on world poverty and sustainable growth. Diminishing Returns is an economic factor which not only heavily influences the behaviour of costs, wages and standard of living in any resource-based economy - particularly in Third World economies - but, I shall argue, this factor is the key to understanding the concept of sustainability. This chapter argues that the strong warning from John Stuart Mill quoted above is as valid today as it was almost 150 years ago. Mill's warning has, however, been largely ignored, almost completely so in the period following World War II.

Part one of the chapter traces how Diminishing Returns disappeared from economic theory as neo-classical economics and general equilibrium analysis took over from other, less abstract, economic paradigms. Part two discusses the impact of Diminishing Returns vs increasing returns if they were to be reintroduced in international trade theory. Part three describes how 'The Triple Curse' of Diminishing Returns, perfect competition and price volatility combine and mutually reinforce each other in maintaining vicious circles of poverty and unsustainable growth. Part four describes how a few resource-rich nations - Australia and Canada taken as examples - managed to escape the 'Triple Curse' which threatens all resource-based economies. The concluding part discusses the need for a wide-ranging overhaul of the World Economic Order, an overhaul which once again incorporates the lock-in effects created by Diminishing Returns in resource-based economies. The most important conclusion is that perhaps a key building block of the present international economic order - *the absolute supremacy of free trade under any circumstances* - will have to be modified when the effects of both Diminishing and Increasing Returns are again incorporated into international trade theory.

1. Diminishing Returns, or, How our Oldest Economic Law was Forced out of International Economic Theory

Diminishing Returns is the oldest of all economic laws known to mankind. It was first described by the Greek philosopher Xenophon - the man who also coined the term economics - around 550 BC. Diminishing Returns is the main factor behind most, if not all, mass migrations of human history. Diminishing Returns was the reason why Abraham and Lot parted - after a strife between their respective herdsmen - as the quote from *Genesis 13* at the beginning of this chapter reminds us. We would claim that many Third World problems today - like the apparent tribal problems in Rwanda - are caused by nations being ***locked into*** comparative advantages in economic activities subject to Diminishing Returns with their population rising.

Diminishing Returns occur when one factor of production is held constant, while the other factors of production are expanded. As a consequence of the one factor being held constant, the increased input of the other factors yield less and less benefit. In general terms, any company or nation could be subject to Diminishing Returns in any economic activity. If Microsoft had not extended their office space as the company grew, they, too, would have suffered from Diminishing Returns as more and more personnel would have to work more and more cramped in the same small office area. Of course, there is no reason why Microsoft (or any other economic activity not based on natural resources) should refrain from buying more office space or more of any input as their production expands. In 'normal' economic activities these new inputs are available, as output grows, at commercial terms - price and quality - which are *not inferior* to what they already have.

Here lies the basic difference between resource-based economic activities and all other economic activities: When output is increased in any resource-based activity - agriculture, fishing and mining - there is always one point, after which the crucial resource is no longer available at the same quality or in the same quantity as the previous 'unit' of the same resource. If specialized in agriculture, a nation will sooner or later have to resort to inferior land - if Norway specialized only in growing carrots, we would in the end have to grow carrots on top of the mountains. If specialized exclusively in fisheries, the nation would fish the oceans empty. If specialized in mining, the nation would have to mine deposits with decreasing quality of ore. As a result, the resource-based nation is locked into an economic activity which yields less and less as its specialization in the resource-based activity deepens. The more such a nation produces of the specific resource-based product, the poorer it gets, and the more the environment suffers. This is what I call *the double trap of resource-based nations*: **poverty and economic degradation increase hand in hand as the nation continues to specialize according to its comparative advantage in international trade.**

Historically, there have been two ways of escaping the trap of Diminishing Returns:

1. The first way to escape the trap of Diminishing Returns is the one given in the Bible. Abraham and Lot solved their problems by Lot taking his huge herds Eastward into the plains of Jordan and Abraham taking his herds to the land of Canaan. This is the first and most 'primitive' logical response to Diminishing Returns: to move on as long as there is uninhabited land to move on to. This is of course the way of life of all nomadic tribes. Consequently, as the father of neo-classical economics, Alfred Marshall, pointed out, Diminishing Returns is 'the cause of most migrations of which history tells'.[1] This includes the huge nineteenth- and twentieth-century migrations from Europe to North America and Australia. Diminishing Returns has always been an important fact of life, and has, until this century, always been present in more or less rudimentary economic theory all through human history.
2. The second, more sophisticated way of avoiding the trap of Diminishing Returns was discovered during the Renaissance. This strategy consisted in building what Michael Porter would call a *created comparative advantage* in activities not subject to Diminishing Returns. The basis for the economic changes of the Renaissance was a new interpretation of the Holy Scriptures. Man's duty was no longer seen as living in the product of God's Creation. Since Man was created in God's image - and God was the Creator of the Universe - Man consequently also had a duty to God to create, to learn, to innovate and to invent.[2] Founded on this new way of thinking, the economic strategies of European nations starting in the late fifteenth century were based on building science and knowledge, on developing manufacturing industry which could add value to national resources, on the use of machinery in more and more activities, on innovations,[3] on creating economic empires where the colonies provided the raw materials and constituted markets for increasing returns (i.e. manufactured) goods, and where the European mother country provided knowledge and manufacturing. Important philosophers and 'statesmen of science' behind these knowledge-based strategies were Henry VII, Elisabeth I and Francis Bacon in England; Gottfried Wilhelm von Leibniz and Christian Wolff in Germany; and

1. Marshall, Alfred, *Principles of Economics,* London, Macmillan, 1890, p. 201.
2. This development is discussed in Reinert, Erik and Arno Daastøl, 'Exploring the Genesis of Economic Innovations: The Religious Gestalt-Switch and the Duty to Invent as Preconditions for Economic Growth', *European Journal of Law and Economics*, Vol. 4, No. 2/3, 1997, and in Christian Wolff, *Gesammelte Werke, Materialien und Dokumente*, Hildesheim, Georg Olms Verlag, 1998, pp. 233–83.
3. Francis Bacon (1561–1626) wrote both *An Essay on Innovations* and *The Advancement of Learning,* The latter published in 1605.

> Jean-Baptiste Colbert in France. This was a system where ideas flowed freely, but where each European nation nursed the creation of its own manufacturing industry. In this way the European nations created a comparative advantage inside a social framework receptive to new knowledge and new technologies, in activities subject to what Schumpeter called *historical increasing returns* - a dynamic combination of increasing returns and technical change. The enduring success of the economic policies of the Renaissance can best be understood by contemplating that the nations which were to be made rich through this policy - the European powers - are still rich, whereas the areas which were to be poor, the colonies, are still poor after several hundred years.

To Third World countries today, the first option is no longer *physically* feasible, due to the lack of empty land. The second option is not *politically* feasible because it invariably also involves measures which violate the principle of free trade; the principle which forms the very foundation of the present world economic order. As a consequence, many of the poorest Third World nations face the double curse of acute poverty and ecological disaster. I would claim that if we study how resource-rich nations - the United States, Australia, Canada - have escaped the trap of Diminishing Returns only by *consciously* building industrial strength outside the resource-based activities, do we find a solution to the problems of the Third World. In nineteenth-century United States, the strategy for economic development was based on the wise slogan 'Do what the English did (starting in 1485), don't do what the English tell us to do.' Today, the slogan for the Third World ought to be: 'Do what the United States did, not what the United States tell you to do.'

The United States is a good example of how a nation locked in raw material production escaped the trap of Diminishing Returns. As a young republic the United States had its *comparative advantage* in the cotton-and-slave business, and only escaped this trap through huge efforts and high tariffs. Well-known men in the United States, who spoke up against specializing in resource-based activities, are Alexander Hamilton, Benjamin Franklin, Abraham Lincoln, Andrew Jackson and Thomas Jefferson - all of them personalities whose portraits today adorn the US dollar bills. They all saw the problems of a United States locked into only exploiting its natural resources, and promoted industrialization behind tariff barriers until sufficient industrial strength had been built.

The US arguments were based more on the superiority of the 'productive powers' of industry than on the inferiority of resource-based activities - but the message about their inferiority was always clear. Consequently, in nineteenth-century United States theories of free trade were seen as most harmful until the nation had built what was then called 'productive powers' - a term related to today's term 'competitiveness'. The English free-trade doctrines were the doctrines of the slave-owners.[4] In an attempt to

4. The most complete account of the economic theory of the slave-owners is contained in *Cotton is King, and Pro-Slavery Arguments,* Augusta, Georgia, Pritchard, Abbot & Loomis, 1860. This is a massive tome of 908 pages, where the core of the economic arguments against the industrialization of the United States are found on pages 19–226.

keep the free trade doctrines of the English economists out of the nation, US president Thomas Jefferson also tried, in vain, to stop the publication of David Ricardo's *Principles of Economics* in the United States. The showdown between the two schools of economic thought came with the Civil War: The free trade and resource-based Confederate South fighting the protectionist and industrializing North.[5]

The Third World continues to specialize in resource-based activities subject to Diminishing Returns. In many Third World countries - particularly in Latin America - we find the same nineteenth-century conflict as in the United States, between the 'industrialists' (the North in the US Civil War) and the raw material producers (the South in the US Civil War). The difference is that in Latin American countries, the 'South' won their version of the Civil War, and industrialization was truncated. Economic actors whose vested interests lay in the exploitation of natural resources - not in industrialization - won the political battle. This aspect of Latin American history - the 'modernization schemes' which failed - is a seriously underresearched area.[6]

As we shall discuss more in detail in Part three of this chapter, technical change in resource-based activities carries with it completely different effects than it does in normal manufacturing (Increasing Returns) activities: Technical change increases the pressure on the natural resources by making commercially profitable the exploitation of resources further into the realm of Diminishing Returns. New equipment makes it possible to catch the 'last fish in the ocean'. The wage-rising effect, which accompanies technical change in manufacturing industry, does not result, therefore, from technical change in Diminishing Return activities. Technical change in Diminishing Returns (resource-based) activities also tends to come embedded in new machinery, not as a result of knowledge created near the resource itself. As a result of this, there are few spillover effects to the rest of the economy from knowledge created in the resource-based sector.

The position of Diminishing Returns in today's economic theory in no way reflects its practical importance, probably because the founding father himself - Adam Smith - did not take the phenomenon into consideration. Indeed, Adam Smith, heavily influenced by the French physiocrats, saw agriculture, subject to Diminishing Returns, as the only 'natural' state of affairs. A basic assumption for Adam Smith, as well as for neo-classical economic theory, is that perfect competition, as in agriculture, is the ideal situation. To the alternative economic tradition the world moved forward as a result of human learning, innovations and *dynamic imperfect competition*.

To most economists today, economics started with Adam Smith. For this reason, today's most influential economist, Paul Samuelson, makes the mistake of stating, in the

5. For an account of this, see Salisbury, Allen, *The Civil War and the American System. America's Battle with Britain, 1860–1876*, New York, Campaigner Publications, 1978, and Draper, John William, *History of the American Civil War*, New York, Harper, 1867. 3 volumes.
6. Two interesting studies have appeared on this aspect of Peruvian history: Gootenberg, Paul, *Between Silver and Guano, Commercial Policy and the State in Postindependence Peru*, Princeton, Princeton University Press, 1989, and McEvoy, Carmen, *Un proyecto nacional en el siglo XIX, Manuel Prado y su visión del Perú*, Lima, Universidad Católica, 1994.

chapter of his influential textbook where the history of economic thought is outlined, that 'In the half-century after (Smith's) *Wealth of Nations,* the law of Diminishing Returns was discovered'.[7] Samuelson assumes that what Adam Smith does not mention was not known at that time. In fact, the devastating effects of Diminishing Returns have been known since biblical times. We shall see that a similar mistake is made by a presently prominent US economist, Paul Krugman, when it comes to understanding Increasing Returns, the mirror image of Diminishing Returns.

Diminishing Returns is a term often introduced at an early stage to students of economics. In Samuelson's classic textbook, the concept of Diminishing Returns is introduced early as 'a famous technological economic relationship'.[8] But most students of economics will go through their studies, even up to a PhD, without ever encountering a practical example where Diminishing Returns is found in some activities (resource-based), and its mirror image, Increasing Returns in others (manufacturing). Neo-classical production-possibility curves may contain Diminishing Returns and Increasing Returns, but when it comes to practical policies, the implications of having one group of nations specialize in Diminishing Returns activities (Traditional Third World) and one in Increasing Returns activities (First World) are never discussed. Paul Samuelson excludes this Diminishing Returns/Increasing Returns counterpoint in his most famous theoretical work, the one proving factor-prize equalization in international trade.[9] In his perhaps most famous work, Samuelson shows that if free trade is introduced, everybody in the world will in the end be equally rich. This theory is based on the standard assumptions of neo-classical theory, which does not take into consideration that some activities are produced under Diminishing Returns while others obey the laws of its mirror image, Increasing Returns.

To the English classical economists, Diminishing Returns was a very important factor. Indeed, Diminishing Returns underlies Malthus' dismal view of world population growing much faster than world food production. Since land is of different quality, and Malthus assumes that the best land is cultivated first, 'the productive powers of labour as applied to the cultivation of land must gradually diminish and as a given quantity of labour would yield a smaller and smaller return, there would be less and less produce to be divided.'[10] To Nassau Senior, an economist who was important in England in his day, Diminishing Returns was one of the 'four fundamental axioms of Political Economy'. As early as in 1613 the Italian economist Antonio Serra pointed out the importance of Diminishing Returns in explaining the relative poverty of Naples compared to the wealth of Venice, which he saw as a result of Increasing Returns.[11] To German authors the principle of Diminishing Returns was equally important. In

7. Samuelson, Paul, *Economics*, 1976, 10th edition, p. 841.
8. Ibid., p. 24.
9. Samuelson, 1949 and 1950.
10. Malthus, Thomas Robert, *Principles of Political Economy,* 2nd Edition, London, Pickering, 1836, pp. 273–74.
11. Serra, Antonio, *Breve trattato delle cause che possono far abbondare li regni d'oro e argento dove non sono miniere*, Naples, Lazzaro Scoriggio, 1613.

the 1850s, Wilhelm Roscher discussed Diminishing Returns and related this to the 'bearing capacity' or 'carrying capacity' of lands and nations - terms strikingly close to today's 'sustainability'.[12] In the nineteenth century, only American authors - faced with the enormous prairies still to be cultivated - paid little attention to Diminishing Returns.

As we briefly mentioned initially, Alfred Marshall - the founder of today's neo-classical economic theory - emphasizes the importance of the 'Law of Diminishing Returns' in the first edition (1890) of his main work *Principles of Economics.* Marshall leaves no doubt about the importance of this economic factor: 'This tendency to a Diminishing Return was the cause of Abraham's parting from Lot,[13] and of most of the migrations of which history tells. And wherever the right to cultivate land is much in request, we may be sure that the tendency to a Diminishing Return is in full operation.' There is all reason to believe that Diminishing Returns plays an equally important role in the Third World today. Later in this chapter we shall attempt to show this, using data from Bolivia, Ecuador and Peru. In today's economics profession - which is completely cast in the mould of equilibrium analysis - the counterpoint of Increasing and Diminishing Returns is not part of the professional toolbox. In my personal opinion this has devastating results for poverty and environment alike.

A succinct recommendation for economic policy can be found in this first edition of Marshall's *Principles*: Tax economic activities subject to Diminishing Returns and give bounties to activities subject to Increasing Returns.[14] Yet Marshall is the person who must carry the main responsibility for leaving out Increasing and Diminishing Returns from economic theory. Over the eight editions of his Principles, we can observe how the importance of Diminishing Returns is reduced in Marshall's mind. From being listed in the index as a *Law* of Diminishing Returns, in the eighth edition we find it listed as a *tendency.* The fact that Marshall in the eighth edition no longer capitalizes the first letters in Diminishing Returns (but writes diminishing returns) could be from purely orthographic considerations, but we note that the first letters in 'Capital Goods' are still capitalized.

Why did Diminishing Returns and its mirror image, Increasing Returns, disappear as a counterpoint in economic theory? Why do famous economists like Marshall and Samuelson on the one hand acknowledge the transcendental importance of Diminishing Returns in human history, but quietly leave this factor out when they construct the economic theories on which our World Economic Order presently rests? In today's standard economics encyclopaedia, *The New Palgrave,* Diminishing Returns (decreasing returns) is only briefly discussed under the heading of 'Economies and diseconomies of scale'. One explanation for the lack of interest in the subject could be that this factor no longer awakens any interest in the First World, where economic theory is being

12. Roscher, Wilhelm, *Principles of Political Economy,* Chicago, Callaghan, 1882.
13. 'The land was not able to bear them that they might dwell together; for their substance was great so they could not dwell together', Genesis xii 6.
14. Marshall, *Principles of Economics*, p. 452.

produced. There is no *demand* for theories involving Diminishing Returns. In my view the answer lies more on the supply side: Diminishing Returns does not 'fit' the choice of methodology and language used in the profession. I shall attempt to explain this in the following paragraphs.

With neo-classical economics, economic theory came to be modelled after late nineteenth-century physics - economics became 'social physics'. Mathematizing the profession required making certain fundamental assumptions, and as a result of these assumptions, economic activities - for all practical purposes - came to be seen as being 'alike'. This was the price paid for achieving 'general equilibrium'. As was repeatedly and consistently pointed out by the majority of nineteenth-century German and American economists, English classical theory suffered from the fundamental weakness of being a theory of *exchange*, not of *production*.[15] Before the classical theory, the different circumstances under which production took place in different industries were seen as having great influence on national standards of living. Not only were some economic activities seen as being 'better' than others, but achieving a harmonious balance between the different sectors of an economy was seen as being of great importance. In neo-classical general equilibrium analysis - analyzing the economy as a 'black box' inhabited by clones of 'representative firms' - these considerations disappeared from the mainstream of the economy.

In order for economics to become a 'true science', economists had to assume away the Increasing/Diminishing Returns dichotomy, since its existence was not compatible with general equilibrium. For all practical purposes all economic activities became 'alike' in that they were all generally assumed to operate under perfect information and under constant returns to scale. The choice of methodology - comparative statics based on nineteenth-century physics - meant that all factors which were not compatible with equilibrium had to be left out of the theory. As Paul Krugman succinctly put it: 'Economic theory came to follow the path of least mathematical resistance.'[16] The choice of tools came to determine what was included and what was excluded in economic theory. Whether the factors excluded were important in real life or not was, after an initial period of soul-searching doubt by people like Marshall, no longer an issue. David Ricardo was at one point faced with the objection that his theories were not relevant: The map did not correspond with the real world. To this Ricardo is supposed to have replied that this was 'so much the worse for the real world'. Nowhere in the history of economics is this description more fitting than when it comes to the exclusion of Increasing and Diminishing Returns from economic theory in the late 1800s.

Alfred Marshall knew of the importance of Increasing Returns from what he himself called his 'Wanderjahre' in industry, and, as we have shown above, he knew about the historical importance of Diminishing Returns. Yet, he must take the main responsibility for leaving these crucial factors out of modern economic theory, as they

15. See Reinert, Erik, 'Symptoms and Causes of Poverty: Underdevelopment in a Schumpeterian System', *Forum for Development Studies*, No. 1-2, 1994, pp. 73–109.
16. Krugman, Paul, *Rethinking International Trade*, Cambridge, MA, MIT Press, 1990.

violated the concept which came to be the centrepiece of economic theory: General Equilibrium. The particular physics-based mathematical language chosen as the means of communication in the economics profession brought with it the assumption of constant returns. This happened not because anybody at that time thought these assumptions to be realistic, they came purely as a necessary by-product of *the choice of tools* made collectively by the profession.

Marshall was indeed very worried about excluding Increasing and Diminishing Returns. His own attempt to defend leaving Increasing Returns out of economic theory is remarkable. Marshall here introduces a biological analogy where firms are seen as trees in a forest, where old ones die out only to be replaced by new ones. Since 'after a while, the guidance of the business falls into the hands of people with less energy and less creative genius', the monopolizing tendencies of Increasing Returns would be counteracted. This may be true from the point of view of firms, but, in my view, definitely not of nations. From an evolutionary or Schumpeterian point of view, the opposite could be argued: Since knowledge is very cumulative, the succession of firms operating under Increasing Returns, each growing and dying as Marshall implies, could explain the creation of a virtuous circle, which leads one nation to 'forge ahead' of other nations.

One important result of Marshall's attempt to solve the problem of Increasing Returns, was that he assumed the existence of the 'representative firm' - that 'average' which in today's economic theory is assumed to be the sole inhabitant of the economic world. All economic activities, and all firms, came in this way to be 'alike' in today's standard economic theory. Our lack of understanding of unequal economic growth is fundamentally a result of this *equality assumption.* The equality assumption, which is built into neo-classical theory, almost by definition produces theories of *even* economic growth. In Figure 5.1, I have schematically outlined the genealogy of theories which explain why economic growth is so *unevenly* distributed. In these non-equilibrium theories, Increasing and Diminishing Returns play important roles, explicitly or implicitly. The theoretical lines in Figure 5.1, with the exception of evolutionary economics, have virtually died out. Evolutionary economics has very little representation in European or US economics departments, but is used in policy formulation in the EU and the OECD. Evolutionary economics has, in my view, enormous potential in exploring the links between underdevelopment and sustainability. Unfortunately, very few attempts have been made in this direction.[17]

Nobel Prize winner in economics, James Buchanan, puts the fundamental problem which has trapped neo-classical economics in the *equality assumption* as follows, under the heading of *Equality as Fact and Norm*:

17. See Reinert, 'Symptoms and Causes of Poverty'.

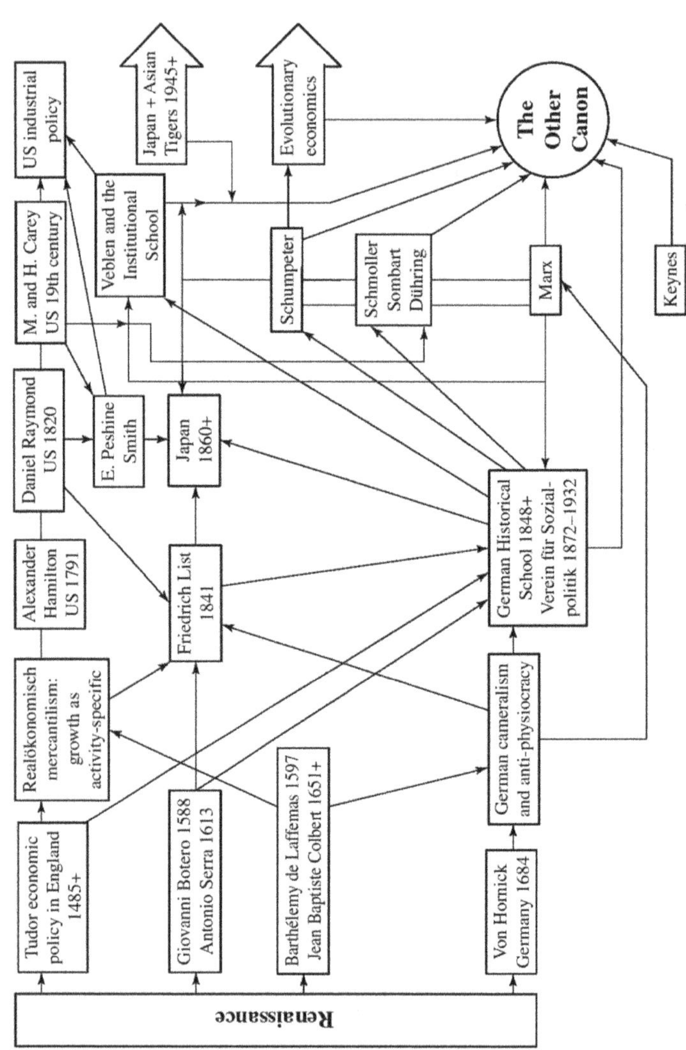

Figure 5.1 The Knowledge- and production-based Other Canon of Economics.

- 'Any generalised prediction in social science implies at its basis a theoretical model that embodies elements of an *equality assumption*. If individuals differ, one from the other, in all attributes, social science becomes impossible.'[18]

The rise of the economics profession to being a 'true science' was thus achieved at the cost of ignoring any impact of the diversity of economic activities on the economy. Only by assuming away any such diversity between economic activities, did Paul Samuelson reach his conclusion that we would all be equally rich if the world adopted free trade.

However, in the real world, Increasing and Diminishing Returns continued to operate as before, in many ways these factors had higher impact than before 1900. Huge trusts and multinational enterprises developed, and in the last decades we are witnessing an increasing globalization of the economy. The basic moving factor both behind the multinational corporations and the process of globalization is basically only one: A dynamic and knowledge-based version of Increasing Returns to scale - what Schumpeter called *historical increasing returns*. Assuming this factor away reduces the explanatory power of economic theory to virtually zero when it comes to understanding the distribution of wealth both nationally and globally.

Seen in a micro-perspective, the fundamental problem arising from the basic assumptions of constant returns - in the general equilibrium approach and of standard international trade theory - is that the assumption of constant returns to scale in effect removes any fixed costs in the economy. In an economy where all production takes place with constant returns to scale over all ranges of output for all goods, there would be no trade at all. Each person would become 'a microcosm of the whole society', as Buchanan puts it.[19] We are faced with the fundamental paradox that with the standard assumptions underlying Samuelson's pro-free trade proof - perfect information and constant returns to scale - all trade would cease to exist! Every individual on earth would be completely self-sufficient. In order to explain why trade exists at all, we have to introduce factors which violate the assumptions which prove that we shall all be equally rich if we only let free trade be the governing principle of the world economic order! The very factors which cause international trade are the very reasons that we live in a world where economic development is uneven. Two fundamental factors at work here are the dynamic and cumulative effects of Diminishing and Increasing Returns to scale.

---

18. Buchanan, James, *What Should Economists Do ?*, Indianapolis, Liberty Press, 1979, p. 231. Italics added.
19. Ibid., p. 236.

2. Diminishing Returns and Trade Theory

Today's world economic order rests on the Ricardian trade theory and Samuelson's proofs from 1949 and 1950, where the Increasing/Diminishing Returns dichotomy is excluded, and where all economic activities are 'alike'. The standard Ricardian trade theory which proves that the world will be richer if each nation sticks to its comparative advantage is outlined in Figure 5.2.

In the nineteenth century, German, American and Japanese economists almost in one voice criticized Ricardo and the English economists for 'jumbling all economic activities together as if they were alike'. There are, in the view of these economists,

A static comparison of costs of production in England and Portugal:

Labour cost of production (in hours)

	1 unit of wine	1 unit of cloth
Portugal	80	90
England	120	100

In England more labour is needed to produce wine than cloth - consequently the price of wine must be higher than the price of cloth:
1 unit of wine = 1.2 units of cloth

In Portugal the price of wine will be lower than the price of cloth:
1 unit wine costs 80/90 = 0.89 units of cloth

We open up for trade and assume that the price will establish itself at 1 cloth for 1 wine. In this way it will pay for both countries to trade.

We assume:
England has 60.000 labour hours at her disposal, Portugal 72.000

Specializing in wine, Portugal will be able to produce 900 wine units, England 500.

Specializing in cloth, Portugal will be able to produce 800 cloth units, England 600.

If each country puts half of the labour force at work in each industry, world production will be:
Portugal 450 wine + England 250 wine = 700 wine
Portugal 400 cloth + England 300 cloth = 700 cloth. **Total 1400 units.**

Under specialization production will be 900 wine + 600 cloth = **1.500 units.**

Conclusion: The world is 100 units richer with free trade than without.

Figure 5.2 Ricardo's theory of comparative advantage.

important differences between economic activities. ***It is in these differences between economic activities***, argued seventeenth- to nineteenth-century non-English economists following on Serra, ***that we find the reasons as to why some nations are rich and some are poor***. I have elsewhere[20] argued that this *activity-specific* view of economic growth was the basis for the industrialization of the First World - that this is essentially why the North got rich and the South stayed poor. Perusing today's textbooks in development economics, one finds that both the issue of Diminishing Returns and of the activity-specific aspect of development are completely absent.[21] Present development economics seems to reflect the 'averaging' argument which is at the core of neo-classical analysis. Therefore, I have argued, our policies towards the Third World tend to address *symptoms* rather than *causes* of underdevelopment.[22]

On the intuitive level, the activity-specific argument for wealth goes like this: We know that in Norway the pay of the average lawyer is about 600.000 NOK.[23] The average pay of a person washing dishes or washing floors is about 120.000 NOK, or 1/5 of that of a lawyer, before taxes. Let us put all the lawyers in one country, where they pay their taxes, and all the people doing washing jobs in another country, paying their taxes in that second country. Now, they start trading, each specializing according to their comparative advantage. We intuitively understand that the 'lawyer nation' will be richer than the 'washer nation', both in terms of private wealth and in terms of public wealth from the taxes collected. Still today's world economic order fundamentally rests on Samuelson's elegant mathematical proofs that these nations will become equally rich. How does this happen? Simply by Samuelson having assumed away - like most of economic theory - any differences between the profession of law and the profession of washing dishes.

The seventeenth- to nineteenth-century argument for an *activity-specific* view of economic growth resulted in policies helping industrialization in the nations of the present 'North'. They also formed the basic rationale for prohibiting manufacturing in the colonies. It is remarkable how the majority of economists before 1900 - with the exception of most, but not all, English classical economists - were fully aware of the fact that colonies, by supplying raw materials in exchange for manufactured goods, were getting a bad deal, that they, in today's terms, were being 'underdeveloped'. That exporting raw materials in order to import manufactured goods was 'bad trade' leading to poverty was common knowledge before Ricardo - both in England and elsewhere. This knowledge was part of the mercantilist belief system, an economic system which grew out of the Renaissance policy of *promoting and protecting new knowledge* was an important part of government policy.[24] Later in this chapter we shall discuss the reasons

20. Reinert, 'Symptoms and Causes of Poverty'.
21. Meyer, Gerald, *Leading Issues in Economic Development,* Sixth Edition, New York, Oxford University Press, 1995.
22. Reinert, 'Symptoms and Causes of Poverty'.
23. *Dagens Næringsliv*, 15 September 195, p. 5.
24. This is discussed in Reinert and Daastøl, 'Exploring the Genesis of Economic Innovations'.

why the realökonomisch-oriented mercantilists - under certain conditions - were right in their policy towards raw materials.

In this context, it is extremely important to note that the famous repeal of the corn-laws in 1846 - which is normally seen as the break-through for free trade - was not at all in conflict with the old mercantilist economic theory. No longer protecting English agriculture would - also in the pre-Ricardian philosophy - be an advantage to England. She would now export more manufactured goods in order to import her corn - a classical example of 'good' trade. The repeal of the corn-laws was just as much a confirmation of the old role - punish the producers of raw materials and give bounties to manufacturing industry (see quote from Marshall above) - as it was a victory for free trade.

In international trade theory the confirmation that exporting raw materials was 'bad' trade finds its best expression in a 1923 article by US economist Frank Graham.[25] A simplified version of Graham's argument is reproduced in Figure 5.3. Graham here provides a numerical example of how and why a country producing raw materials may be better off under autarky or by protecting industry, than under free trade. Graham gives a more accurate rendering of Antonio Serra's theory and of why Marshall was right in his recommendation of taxing activities subject to Diminishing Return industries (agriculture, fisheries and mining) in order to give bounties to activities produced under Increasing Returns (industrial goods).

Reinert (1980) provides a discussion of the role of Increasing and Diminishing Returns in economic theory. In addition, this book presents three case studies, showing how the historically most important export industries of Ecuador, Bolivia and Peru - bananas, tin and cotton - are constantly producing under extreme conditions of Diminishing Returns. In other words: In all these countries, the cost of producing one extra unit of export product was found to be considerably higher than the average costs at the present volume of activity. The empirical findings - and additional data from the Cuban sugar industry - strongly suggest that Diminishing Returns as described by the Graham model is actually a *normal state of affairs in Third World raw materials exports*, and that this model is indeed a realistic representation of the economic forces which created - on a global level - a rich North and a poor South. Numerical examples from Reinert (1980), corresponding to Graham's thesis, are shown in Charts 5.1. through 5.5. This work suggests that the averaging out of all economic activities, which characterizes neo-classical economic theory - the fact that factors Increasing and Diminishing Returns have been excluded - is a main reason for our failure to understand the uneven growth of the North and South. As already indicated, it is argued that this is particularly so if the term Increasing Returns is defined as Schumpeterian *historical increasing returns* - a term which includes static increasing returns, as well as the technological change which has accompanied the industrial activities operating under Increasing Returns.

International trade theory - and indeed today's Economic World Order - implicitly assumes that all economic activities are 'alike'. Based on this assumption, standard trade theory predicts a world of 'factor-price equalization': that all nations will be

25. Graham, Frank, 'Some Aspects of Protection further considered', *Quarterly Journal of Economics*, Vol. 37, 1923, pp. 199–227.

Increasing and Diminishing Returns in International Trade - a Numerical Example

STAGE 1: World income and its distribution before trade:

Country A				Country B			
Man-days	Output per man-day	Production		Man-days	Output per man-day	Production	
200	**4**	**wheat**	**800**	**200**	**4**	**wheat**	**800**
200	**4**	**watches**	**800**	**200**	**3**	**watches**	**600**

World production: 1.600 wheat + 1.400 watches. In wheat equivalents: 3.200

Country A's income in wheat equivalents: 1.714 wheat
Country B's income in wheat equivalents: 1.486 wheat

Price: 4 wheat = 3,5 watches

STAGE 2: World income and its distribution after each country specializes according to its comparative advantage:

Country A				Country B			
Man-days	Output per man-day	Production		Man-days	Output per man-day	Production	
100	**4,5**	**wheat**	**450**	**300**	**3,5**	**wheat**	**1050**
300	**4,5**	**watches**	**1.350**	**100**	**2**	**watches**	**200**

World production w. trade: 1.500 wheat + 1.550 watches. In wheat equivalents: 3.271

Country A's income in wheat equivalents: 1.993 wheat
Country B's income in wheat equivalents: 1.278 wheat

Figure 5.3 Graham's dynamic theory of uneven economic growth.

equally rich. In the real world, however, different economic activities give rise to different standards of living. From a theoretical trade-theory point of view, we can divide all economic activities into three groups:

1) Activities subject to Increasing Returns to Scale, typically manufacturing industry. We shall call these '**positive**' variants.
2) Activities which are neutral to scale, typically the traditional service sector. We shall call these '**neutral**' variants.
3) Activities subject to Diminishing Returns, comprising all resource-based activities. We shall call these '**negative**' variants.

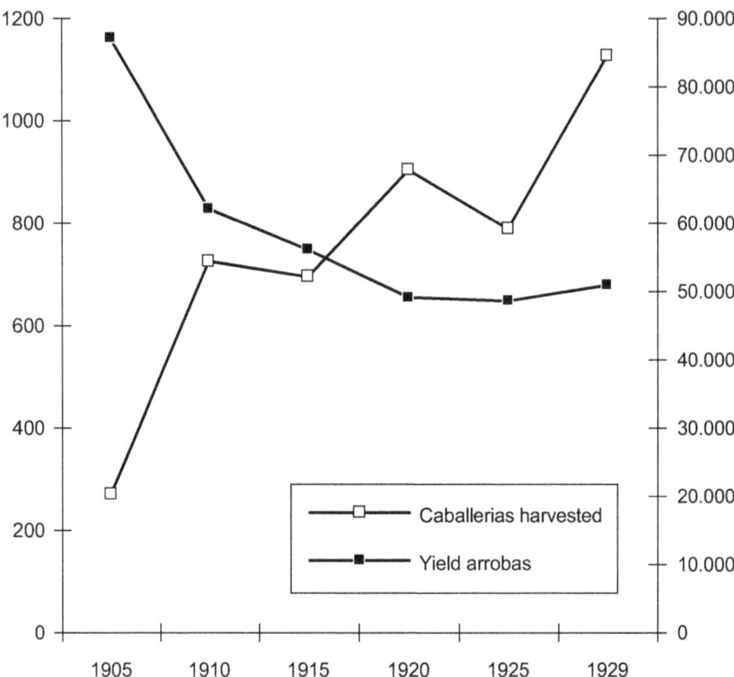

Chart 5.1 Cuba: Diminishing Returns in the Banes Division of United Fruit, 1905–29. *Source*: Reinert 1980, page 228. Area and yield: United Fruit. Banes Division. Agricultural Department, Operating Statistics (1905–50).

The theory which forms the basis for the present world economic order - where Samuelson's proof of factor-price equalization is the crowning achievement - assumes that all economic activities are of the 'neutral' variant. To the industrialized countries, whose activities are 'positive' variants - subject to increasing returns - this theory is **irrelevant but helpful**. They are much better off than what the theory assumes. To the resource-based nations, whose activities are 'negative' variants - subject to Diminishing Returns - this theory is **irrelevant but harmful**. These nations are much worse off than what the theory assumes.

Industrialized countries have come to specialize in activities based on human knowledge - both in traditional industry and in a growing knowledge-based service sector. The nations whose comparative advantage has led them to specialize in natural resources (Diminishing Returns activities) are locked into a historical trajectory where technical advances are fighting a losing battle against Diminishing Resources in the export sector. The resulting downward pressure on wages and employment in its turn leads to more pressure on the natural resources, by desperate human beings in the informal sector trying to carve out a miserable living from nature. The result of both pressures - in the export sector and in the informal poor sector - is unsustainable development.

The 1980s provided a minor revolution in international trade theory. Under the heading of 'New Trade Theory' US economist Paul Krugman reintroduced Increasing

Returns to trade theory.[26] A fundamental problem of this revolution - from the point of view of the Third World - is that Krugman correctly sees that the 'neutral' variety in our scheme above is not very significant in real life, but he only brings in the 'positive' variants into the discussion - Increasing, and not Diminishing Returns. His conclusions for trade policy are therefore exactly the opposite of those which are valid for the Third World. By only including the 'positive' variations from the standard model, and not the 'negative' ones, Krugman concludes that this is yet another argument for free trade.

Krugman traces the origin of this idea back to Frank Graham's 1923 article. He does not seem to be aware that Graham's presentation, rather than being the first to identify the issues raised by the 'New Trade Theory', is the *last* statement of a major nineteenth-century debate. This debate was a key factor in creating 'The American System of Manufacturing', a system which protected US industry for about 100 years in spite of its inefficiency compared to English industry. The US argument was that it was better to be less efficient than England in Diminishing Returns activities, than to be the world's most efficient producer of raw materials, e.g. cotton.

As we have discussed, this issue of protection or free trade was a key issue in the US Civil War, where the protectionist North won over the free trade South.

In chart 5.1. we can observe how an extension of the area under cultivation drastically decreases the yield of sugar as a result of Diminishing Returns. This tendency is particularly strong early in the period. After World War I we can only assume that technical change, fertilizers etc. keep the tendency towards Diminishing Returns at bay.

Chart 5.2. shows the Diminishing Returns to labour productivity in Peru's main export product in the period in question - 1916 through 1949. The chart shows the typical 'mirror image' *of intensity of exploitation of a natural resource* and *productivity*. If production ***increases***, the productivity of labour ***decreases.*** This is the opposite phenomenon of what is normally observed in the manufacturing industry, where Increasing Returns to scale produces the exact opposite effect. The counterpoint of *Increasing Returns* in manufacturing, and *Decreasing Returns* in resource-based activities is the mechanism which Antonio Serra pointed to in 1613 when he explained the wealth of the Republic of Venice - having no natural resources - and the poverty of the Kingdom of Naples and The Two Sicilies - being very rich in natural resources.

Chart 5.3. shows abnormal cost developments in the main export product of Bolivia at the time - tin - due to strong effects of Diminishing Returns. The Great Depression caused the demand for tin to decrease - and consequently also the production. As a result of the contraction in volume of production, the cost of producing one ton of tin decreased considerably. Again, this is exactly the opposite of what would happen in the manufacturing industry under the same circumstances. In manufacturing, the amount of fixed costs involved would cause unit costs to skyrocket as a result of a similar

26. Krugman, *Rethinking International Trade.*

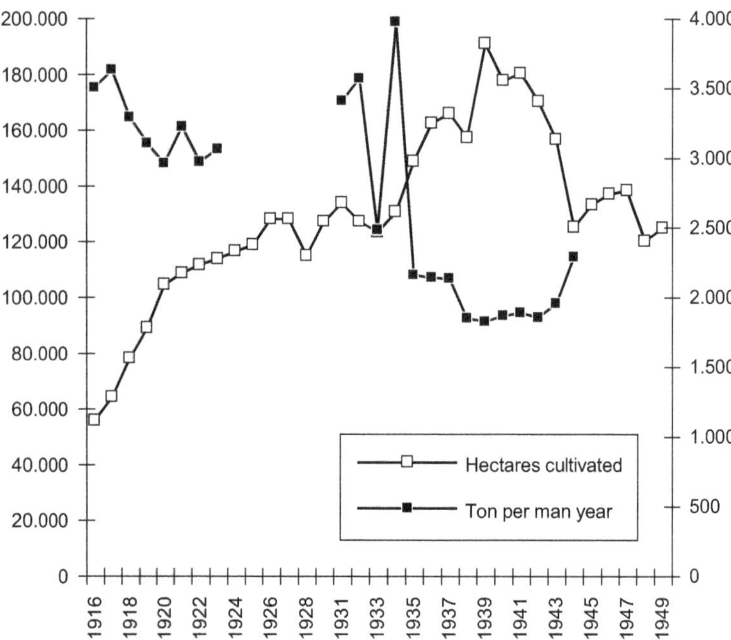

Chart 5.2 Peru: Diminishing Returns to Labour Productivity in the Cultivation of Cotton. *Source*: Reinert 1980, page 215. 'Anuario Estadistico del Peru', and 'Extracto Estadistico del Peru', various years. Apparently official statistics lack one year's data.

decrease in output. In mining and agriculture, a cut in production will put the least efficient mines and the least efficient plots of land out of production first, and unit costs will therefore *decrease* instead of *increase* when production is contracted. Malthus, in his *Principles of Political Economy*, describes this mechanism very well, particularly on pp. 178–79.[27]

Chart 5.4 again presents the typical 'mirror image' of *increasing production* and *decreasing productivity* resulting from Diminishing Returns. This is an essential element of the mechanisms which lock resource-based nations into a low-productivity and low-wage trap - leading to unsustainable development. Being free from the Sigatoka Disease which had invaded Central American banana plantations in the early 1960s, Ecuador saw a golden opportunity to develop the nation based on an absolute advantage in banana production. However, the more bananas Ecuador produced, the poorer the banana producers got. The reason why this specialization in international trade led to more poverty, can be understood from this chart, which was assembled from unpublished data.

Chart 5.5 visualizes one aspect of the lock-in effects created by dependency on natural resources. We can observe how, over a period of 30 years, the average concentration of ore in the tin mined in Bolivia is reduced by 50 per cent. More efficient machinery

27. Malthus, *Principles of Political Economy.*

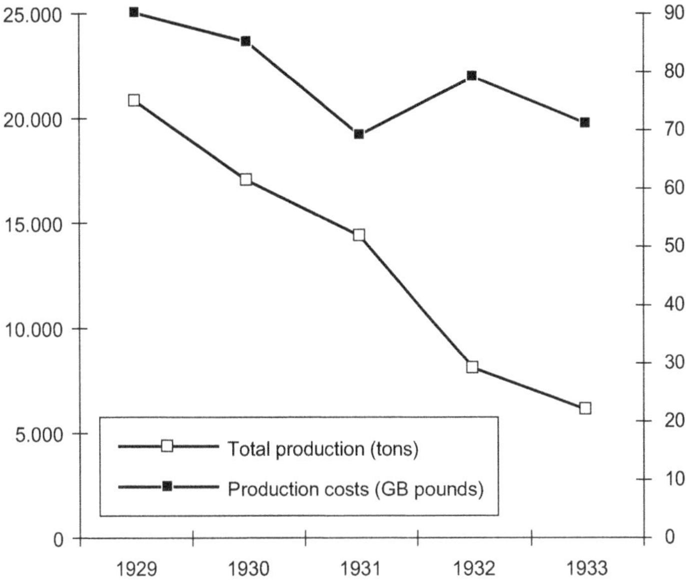

Chart 5.3 Bolivia: Reversal of Diminishing Returns Effects by Contraction of Production Due to the Great Depression. Tin Mining: Production Costs for One Ton of Fine Tin, Delivered in Catavi. *Source*: Reinert 1980, page 194. 'Foreign Minerals Quarterly', vol. 2, No. 4. Quoted in: Gutierrez Guerra, Rene; 'Situacion Economica y Financiera de Bolivia', La Paz, Editorial Universo, 1940, page 18.

to some extent compensates for this, but there is a continual fight between technical progress and Diminishing Returns which leaves no room for the wage increases which accompany technical change in manufacturing industry. Being completely uncompetitive in manufacturing industry, Bolivia is permanently trapped in poverty created by an exclusive dependency on natural resources.

From the point of view of the Third World, today's fashionable 'New Trade Theory' suffers from an inexcusable omission. Krugman and his colleagues only resurrect half of Frank Graham's argument, the part which is relevant for the First World - i.e. Increasing Returns - and leave out the other half of the argument which is of crucial importance to the Third World, i.e. Diminishing Returns. This is also the case in the paper where Krugman specifically argues for New Trade Theory from a Third World perspective. 'Trade, Accumulation, and Uneven Development'.[28] By ignoring Diminishing Returns, the New Trade Theory distorts the theoretical discussion in the following ways:

28. Published in the *Journal of Development Economics*, Vol. 8, 1981, pp. 149–61. Reproduced as Chapter 6 in Krugman, *Rethinking International Trade*.

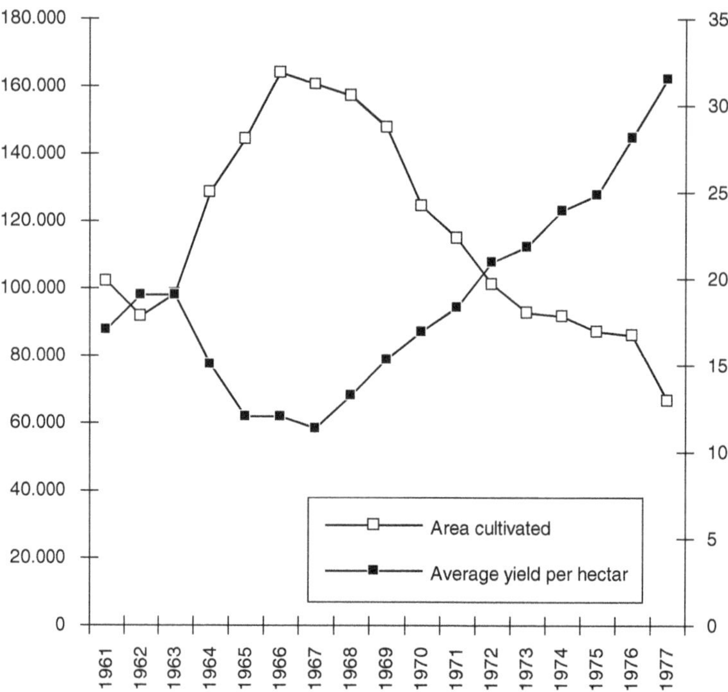

Chart 5.4 Ecuador: Diminishing Returns in Banana Production 1961-1977. *Source*: Reinert 1980, page 175. Programa Nacional del Banano y Frutas Tropicales, Guayaquil. Unpublished data.

1. In Krugman's eyes, the non-constant returns argument essentially becomes yet another argument for free trade. It is true, as Charles King argued already in 1721,[29] that trading manufactured goods for other manufactured goods is beneficial to both trading nations. This assumes, however, that the goods are subject to the same degree of increasing returns - that the trade is 'symmetrical'.
2. By not differentiating between *degrees* of increasing returns, he ignores the very different roles played by different manufacturing industries.
3. By essentially continuing a static analysis, Krugman leaves out the complex cumulative dynamics of technical change and path dependency.
4. By leaving out Diminishing Returns, the New Trade Theory leaves out both the main factor locking in the greater part of the Third World in a Myrdalian vicious circle and also a key mechanism which prevents sustainable growth in resource-based economies.

29. King, Charles, *The British Merchant or Commerce Preserv'd*, London, John Darby, 1721. 3 Vols., Vol. 1, p. 3.

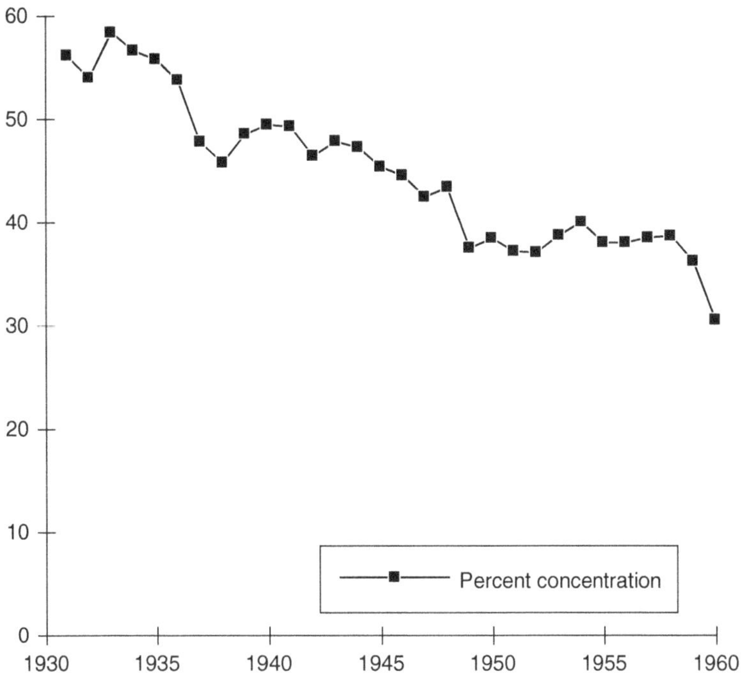

Chart 5.5 Bolivia: Diminishing Returns Due to Falling Average Concentration of Tin in Ore. *Source*: Reinert 1980, page 191. Bolivia. Ministerio de Planificacion. 'Tablade Concentracion Media del Estano Exportado', elaborated by Juilo Garcia. Quoted in: Gomez, Walter: 'La Minería en el Desarrollo Economico de Bolvia', La Paz, 1952, page 242.

3. The 'Triple Curse of Natural Resources', Path Dependence and Unsustainable Development

- *'It's the eternal paradox - the poor live in nations which are rich from Nature's bounties'*, José Cecilio del Valle, economist and vice president of the short-lived Central American Republic. About 1830.[30]
- *'The higher the civilization of a people, the less does it depend on the nature of the country'*, Wilhelm Roscher, German economist and inspirer of Marx and Schumpeter, founder of the 'New Historical School' of Economics in Germany. About 1860.[31]

30. The best edition of Valle's works is published as *Obras de Don José Cecilio del Valle*, Ciudad de Guatemala, Tipografía Sanchez & de Guise, 1930. 2 Volumes.
31. Roscher's four-volume *Grundlagen der Nationalökonomie* appeared in 26 editions, the first edition in 1854. This work formed a school of thought which was to dominate German economic and industrial policy until World War II. Roscher was the first economist to incorporate Increasing Returns and mass production in an economic textbook. His dynamic world view formed a platform for later dynamic theories, of economists with such diverse views as Marx and Schumpeter. The quote is taken from the US edition of his textbook: *Principles of Political Economy*, Chicago, Callaghan and Co., 1882, Volume 1, p. 137.

Economic literature is surprisingly full of references to *lack of natural resources* as an important factor in explaining economic growth. We have already mentioned Antonio Serra, who explained the wealth of Venice as coming from being forced by lack of natural resources into Increasing Returns activities. Due to Increasing Returns, the Venetians could produce the minor miracle of selling their products cheaper than anybody else, while at the same time they could pay their workers higher wages than anybody else. And, in today's terms, both the volume of production and the dynamic learning effects achieved by the Venetians provided extremely high *barriers to entry* for would-be competitors.

Serra's 1613 analysis is extremely persuasive in analysing *why* the natural resources of Naples were an impediment to economic growth. Other authors comment on this phenomenon, but give less complete explanation as to why the 'curse of the resources' occurs.

Often the lack of natural resources has been seen as an advantage for a nation. The lack of natural advantages leads the population to rely on acquiring skills, not on Nature's bounties. The old saying is that 'Necessity is the mother of invention', and the assumption is that one lives better off inventions than off the land. Holland's wealth was seen as partly resulting from their 'establishing themselves in a swampy little corner' in a seventeenth-century economic tract,[32] and thus becoming traders, manufacturers and bankers for the rest of Europe. The argument that the lack of natural resources is important for wealth creation is found also in the discussion of Japan and modern Italy - 'we cannot live off the natural resources, so we have to create a living by transforming the raw materials of others'. On the other hand the contrast between natural wealth and human poverty is also a frequent object of comment, as with José Cecilio del Valle above. Similarly a nineteenth-century French traveller, Alcides d'Orbigny, commented in the 1840s that Bolivia was 'like a beggar sitting on a throne of gold'.

From an economic point of view, are there any reasons why nations which specialize in making a living from their natural resources should be poor? Isn't it a gigantic paradox, like José Cecilio del Valle pointed out? In my view, the 'resource paradox' is of a complex nature, where three economic factors combine to create what I choose to refer to as ***'The Triple Curse of Natural Resources'***. These are three purely economic factors, which interact among themselves and with other socio-economic variables creating the vicious circles which characterize underdevelopment.

'The Triple Curse of Natural Resources' stems from three factors which all are in the blind spots created by equilibrium analysis:

1) Diminishing Returns
2) Perfect Competition
3) Price Volatility

The effects of **Diminishing Returns** have been discussed earlier in this chapter.

32. 'An Inquiry into the Connection between the present Price and Provisions...', p. 63.

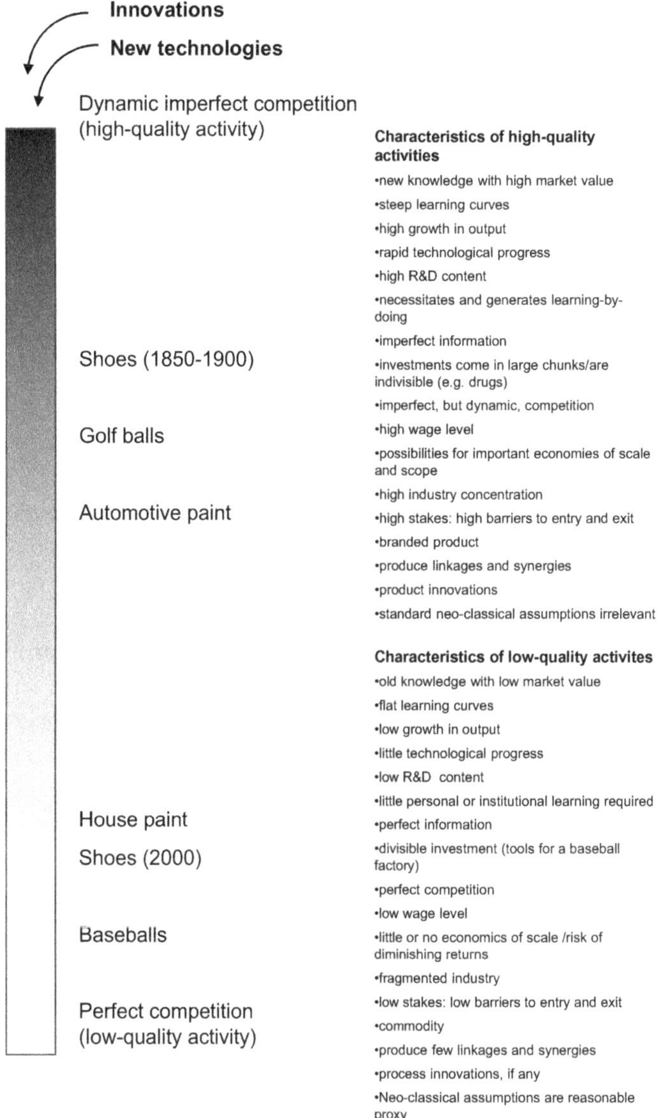

Figure 5.4 The 'Quality Index' of economic activities.

Perfect Competition is in many ways seen at the same time as being an assumption and an implicit goal of neo-classical economic theory. However, as I have discussed in chapter 1 and chapter 4[33] the historical economic strategies of First World nations

33. Reinert, Erik, 'Catching-Up from Way behind. A Third World Perspective on First World History', in Fagerberg, Jan et al. (Eds.), *The Dynamics of Technology, Trade and Growth,*

and the very essence of strategies of any corporation - national or multinational - are to *avoid* perfect competition. Indeed, under true perfect competition there is no profit to be made at all, and there is an enormous downward pressure on wages. I have argued elsewhere that the present competitiveness debate in the industrial world is in reality a systematic search for imperfect competition.[34] To Marx the collapse of the whole capitalist system under falling rates of profits would come as a result of perfect competition. Michael Porter of Harvard Business School uses the term 'dog industries' to describe the industries subject to perfect competition - industries where he advises his customers to stay out. Here we find a case of complete agreement between Karl Marx and Harvard Business School, which, surprisingly, is not the only one. Marx and Porter both share the same view of the dynamics of technological change as being crucial in maintaining wealth in a capitalist system. The dynamics of how it is *imperfect* - not perfect - competition which is the true source of what we call economic development, is a complex one which I have tried to outline in the other chapters referred to. A summary of the factors at work is found in Figure 5.4. - The Quality Index of Economic Activities, where most raw materials get a very low score as 'low-quality activities'. We shall see in Section 4 how this score may be improved.

Price Volatility is important to an economy in many ways. Company owners who know that the price level of their products is subject to sudden reversals through mechanisms which are totally out of their control, will be very reluctant to give wage rises. Indeed, in industries subject to large price fluctuations, the owners who have *not* given wage rises will often be the only ones which survive a prolonged crisis. Furthermore, in industries suffering from high price fluctuations, the profitability of a company will depend more on the owner's skill in *timing sales* than on his skills in producing and running his business efficiently. This encourages a 'casino economy', where building knowledge bases and production skills will play an inferior role to that of 'gambling'.

A very important feature of monoculture resource-based economies, is that the national wage level and level of economic activity in general tend to fluctuate with the world market price of their commodity. Real wages are reversible, if not in terms of local currency, then in terms of real wages, with massive devaluations being the ultimate mechanism which brings real wages down. When prices boom again, the general sense that 'this cannot last' prevents spending on assets which could build a viable economy. This boom and bust pattern is well known in most Third World countries.

Extreme **price volatility** is, generally, a phenomenon observed only in raw materials. Manufactured goods may often fall in price, but they rarely rise again (unless their quality has been radically changed). Figure 5.5 shows how, in principle, price fluctuations decrease with increasing refinement. The left-hand and fluctuating part of

Aldershot, Edward Elgar, 1994, and 'Competitiveness and its Predecessors – A 500-year Cross-National Perspective', *Structural Change and Economic Dynamics,* Vol. 6, 1995, pp. 23–42. (chapters 1 and 4 in this book)

34. Reinert, 'Competitiveness and its Predecessors – A 500-year Cross-National Perspective'. (chapter 4 in this book)

Price fluctuations and value added
(left: coffee beans | right: instant coffee)

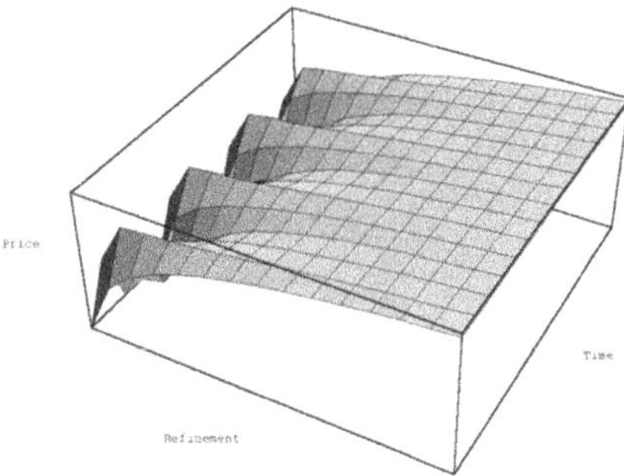

Figure 5.5 Price fluctuations with respect to grade of refinement and time The low refinement regime is dominated by perfect competition, low and unstable prices, and reversibility of real wages. The high refinement regime is dominated by imperfect competition, 'stickiness' of wages and prices, high stable prices and large barriers to entry.

the graph can be seen as cocoa beans, coffee or fresh salmon. The right-hand part of the graph can be read as respectively: milk chocolate, Nescafé or smoked salmon.

Together the elements of 'The Triple Curse' combine to reinforce one another. They create lock-in effects in positions of ecological unsustainability - there is simply no other means of subsistence available to many people than that of carving out a living from destroying nature. Destroying nature is the logical *individual* response to one's survival being challenged - creating problems for the *collective*. In spite of the strength of 'The Triple Curse' in creating and strengthening mechanisms of vicious circles, some nations have escaped the curses and are rich in spite of the fact that their main export earnings come from natural resources. How did they achieve this? We shall look at the solution to this in the next section.

4. Escaping the Resource Paradox into Sustainability - the Lessons from Australia and Canada

We can divide all economic activities in the world into two broad categories:

a) Activities where the supply of one factor of production is limited in quantity and/or quality by nature. These are resource-based activities which are all subject to Diminishing Returns. Nations dependent on Diminishing Return activities - *and where little alternative employment exists* - may find that they are *locked into* a dependence upon these raw materials, that the *barriers to exit* from this dependency are enormous. Under these circumstances the nation may, in effect, be locked into a situation where the only possible livelihood for a large part of its inhabitants is to carve out a living destroying the environment (burning rain forests, polluting rivers with chemicals needed for washing gold, etc.) In manufacturing industries their skills lag so far behind those of the advanced countries, and their markets for such goods are so small, that they are effectively locked out of manufacturing in a free-trade regime.

b) Activities where the supply of all factors of production is expandable at the same or lower unit costs (with the exception of temporary bottlenecks). Nations who have a large part of their economy within such activities - including a manufacturing sector- will find that, even though Diminishing Return activities may account for the bulk of their exports, the unsustainable pressure on their national resources is of a much less serious nature, and - due to a lack of absolute poverty - much more easily controlled by legislative measures.

Many countries have historically been in the situation of being exclusively in Diminishing Returns industries, but through conscious counter-market activities, they have got their resource situation under control, while still depending on raw materials for a large part of their exports. Two prominent examples are Australia and Canada, and in my view the only way to achieve a sustainable economic development in resource-based Third World countries is by following the examples of these two nations.

The Australian and Canadian strategies to escape the 'resource curse' carry with them many elements for the 'disequilibrium economists' who are shown in Figure 5.1. The basic element in the strategy is the following reasoning, taking the example of Australia: According to Ricardian trade theory, Australia should have specialized completely in the production of wool, where the nation not only has a comparative advantage but also an absolute cost advantage in the world. Yet, in spite of this clear recommendation, the two main government reports on economic policy in Australia in the 1900s - the Brigden Report[35] and the Vernon Report[36] - both see the dangers of specializing according to their comparative advantage, which today is the standard solution for all resource-based Third World nations. The Australian argument is very similar to the arguments forwarded by the influential Canadian economist Harold Innes (1894–1952),[37] and indeed the industrial and trade policies of Australia and Canada have been remarkably similar. Both these countries, however, went completely against the recommendations which the First World today gives to Third World countries in the situation where Australia and Canada once were.

The Australian (and Canadian) argument, starting in the late nineteenth century, is, in practice, a copy of the strategy previously employed by the United States to get out of its dependence on raw cotton. The Australian and Canadian arguments for embarking on the strategy are slightly different than the US arguments, however, based as they are more on the danger of the 'inferiority' of raw material production, than on the 'superiority' of manufacturing, the key argument used in the United States. This is the essence of the Australian argument:

35. Brigden, J.B. et al., *The Australian Tariff: An Economic Inquiry*, Melbourne, Melbourne University Press, 1929.
36. Vernon, J. et al., *Report of the Committee of Economic Inquiry,* Canberra, Commonwealth Government Printing Office, 1965.
37. For a representative selection of Innes' writings, which are also very relevant to Third World problems, see Innes, Harold, *Staples, Markets, and Cultural Change. Selected Essays.* Edited by Daniel Drache, Montreal, McGill-Queen's University Press, 1995.

- **If our nation specializes completely in one resource-based product, e.g. wool, two things will happen which will for ever prevent us from getting into the club of wealthy nations. First, the price of wool will fall, because we shall be producing so much of it. Second, and more important, having no other alternative source of mass employment, we shall be taking our wool production into areas of Diminishing Returns, to places where productivity will be much lower than in our best areas. There will be no natural checks - no deterrents - to this process of taking the whole nation into producing massively under Diminishing Returns. An automatic consequence of this process will be that wages will have to fall as population increases. In short: An exclusive dependence on natural resources will lead us into a poverty trap.**

The solution to this dilemma was to build an alternative source of employment, an industrial sector which would establish an alternative source of employment and a 'natural' level of high wages. With the new source of employment in place, an alternative employment opportunity and wage level would prevent wool production from getting into Diminishing Returns. The wool industry would simply not be able to pay high enough wages other than in the most productive areas for wool. In less efficient areas wool production will no longer be profitable.

However, both Canadians and Australians knew that their industry for a small market could never compete with English industry. In spite of this, they reasoned that having an industrial sector - in a competitive local market - would be better than having no industrial sector at all. Being a relatively inefficient lawyer was seen as better than being the world's most efficient washer of dishes, to revert to an example used earlier in this chapter.

5. Conclusions

This chapter confirms and reinforces an important conclusion - with significant practical consequences for poverty and sustainable growth - which was arrived at in Reinert (1980). This conclusion has been confirmed by recent experiences in resource-based economies, and historically by the experiences of the United States, Australia and Canada:

> **...economic activities subject to Diminishing Returns will never by themselves - in the absence of a manufacturing base - be able to raise a country out of poverty ...**[38]

---

38. Reinert, Erik, *International Trade and the Economic Mechanisms of Underdevelopment,* Ann Arbor, University Microfilm, 1980, p. 148.

The actions of individual human beings, who, like in Rwanda, feel the consequences of Diminishing Returns threatening their physical survival, bring with them disasters of biblical proportions, just as the quote from Genesis used by Alfred Marshall, the father of neo-classical economics, alludes to. Wilhelm Roscher associates the existence of Diminishing Returns with what he already in 1881 called 'the carrying capacity' or the 'bearing capacity' of a nation. Roscher - in many ways the spiritual forefather both of Marx and Schumpeter - thus anticipated what we today refer to as sustainability. Philosopher and economist John Stuart Mill says that unless we thoroughly understand Diminishing Returns, 'it is to no purpose proceeding any further in our inquiry' of wealth and poverty.

In spite of this, today's economics profession has placed its analysis at a level of abstraction where the Increasing/Diminishing Returns counterpoint in international trade is not discussed at all. The Increasing/Diminishing Returns issue is neither compatible with General Equilibrium nor with the political demands of the First World for theories supporting free trade. The perverse effects of nations being forced deeper and deeper into Diminishing Returns can be seen in the violence of Rwanda, in the 'technological retrogression' ably described in a 1995 PhD thesis at the University of Oslo[39] and in the way sustainable development is within reach in some rich nations, but seems contrary to the 'natural order' in many poor nations. We see the symptoms, but - since the 2.000-year-old basic factor is not part of today's economic theory - we fail to understand **the most fundamental underlying mechanisms of poverty and environmental degradation in the Third World**. As a natural consequence, we are utterly unable to do something to stop both poverty and environmental degradation in the countries which are locked in the trap of Diminishing Returns. Instead, we continue to treat the symptoms of poverty, and not the causes.

The basic obstacle to improving the situation of nations in the trap of 'Diminishing Returns' is that any serious efforts at building skills outside the natural resource area will enter into conflict with the principle of universal free trade. All presently industrial nations, when they escaped the resource trap, only did so through conscious policies of moving their economies away from dependence on natural resources. In all cases, this strategy included a period where the principle of free trade was sacrificed. Only when, and if, the presently industrialized world can be brought to understand that the core of a strategy to overcome ***the dual trap of poverty and environmental degradation*** must incorporate the key elements of what used to be *their own* economic strategies - those employed historically by the First World - only then is there any hope for solving today's problems of poverty and sustainable development. As long as the present world economic order prohibits the poor Third World countries from adopting the historically successful strategies of the First World, we are going to see ever more Rwandas and ever more Somalias.

39. Endresen, Sylvi, *Technological Retrogression*, University of Oslo, Department of Geography, 1995.

Chapter 6

ECONOMICS: 'THE DISMAL SCIENCE' OR 'THE NEVER-ENDING FRONTIER OF KNOWLEDGE'? ON TECHNOLOGY, ENERGY AND ECONOMIC WELFARE

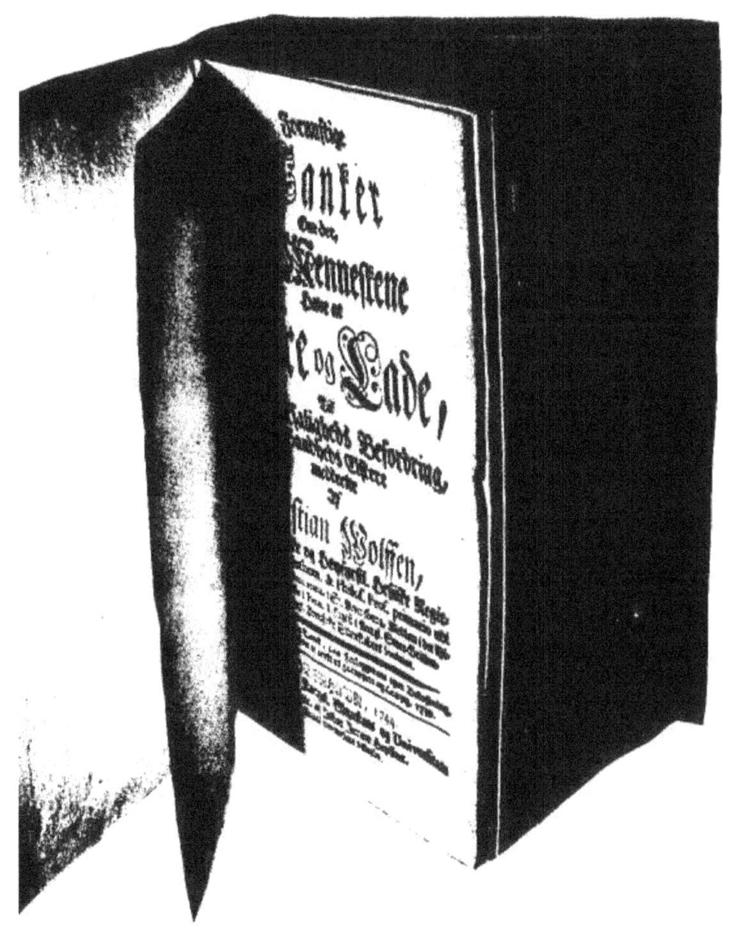

Christian Wolff's works were enormously influential in Scandinavia, and furthered the thought that it was Man's pleasurable duty continuously to create new knowledge.

'Smith and Ricardo were our best allies in the cold war against central planning – but that battle is over and won, and we are now facing other challenges where other prophets will better serve Society's needs.'

'Neo-classical economics fundamentally lacks a theory of economic development beyond seeing it as a process of adding capital to labour.'

'The "Green Movement" has done us all a great favour by pointing to the severity of the problems of environment and sustainability. But, although they are not aware of it, their solutions to these problems are framed in the static and barter-centred theories of Smith, Malthus and Ricardo.'

'All levels of knowledge carry with them their own limits to ecological sustainability. For this reason, the habit of making predictions holding the level of knowledge constant produces curious and overly pessimistic results.'

The work of the 1997 Bergo Commission is based on today's standard economic theory, the economics of Adam **Smith** and David **Ricardo.** The theories of Smith and Ricardo were our best allies in the cold war against central planning but that battle is over and won, and we are now facing other challenges in areas which these authors ignored. We shall argue in this chapter that today's mainstream economic theory – because of its basic structure – contains important 'blind spots' when it comes to the role of knowledge, technology and energy for the welfare of nations. We further argue that the monopoly of this type of economic theory, based on the 'dismal science' of Adam Smith, Thomas **Malthus** and David Ricardo, is a fundamental source of inspiration for the techno- and eco-pessimism which dominated the *Zeitgeist* of the late 1990s. The same production functions predicting diminishing returns which gave birth to Malthus' dismal predictions of disaster, are still at the very core of the tool-box of today's standard economic theory.

We here suggest an alternative tradition in economic theory which can help us find our place in the knowledge-based society of the future. Where Smith and Ricardo focused on *barter and exchange,* other economists have focused on *knowledge, production and the harnessing of energy,* and produced theories which in our opinion will better serve us as guides for today's challenges. In this alternative body of theories, the underlying production function is characterized by the *increasing* returns which is the fundamental property of human knowledge: The more it is used, the more it grows.

'Adam Smith's Enemies'. In most academic disciplines the canonical texts – the 'true' texts – are periodically revised. Traditional historiography which centred on 'the achievements of great men' has given way to a richer and more varied perspective. Physics has been through several scientific revolutions, and even in literary sciences the authority of the great 'classics' has been challenged. Economics, however, is almost totally unaffected by such revisionism, and the fall of the centrally planned economies has even reinforced the canonical sequence: Adam Smith, who was inspired by the French physiocrats, found the promised land and wrote the 'Bible' – The Wealth of Nations – in 1776, the start of the new era. David Ricardo wrote a more accurate map (1817). Then, in 1890, Alfred **Marshall** started the job of translating the Bible from the clumsy and inaccurate English language into the much more accurate mathematical language. In the opinion of many economists, the crowning achievement of the profession is **Paul Samuelson's** work on perfectioning Ricardo's trade theory in 1949/50. Samuelson proved that if only all nations would open up to free trade, the invisible hand would provide 'factor-price equalization' – all wage earners of the world would become equally rich. This theorem is also the starting point for the Bergo Commission when discussing the effects of internationalization on the Norwegian economy.

The adherence of virtually the whole profession to the same canonical texts greatly simplifies the debates on economic policy. The picture of who constitutes a hero and who constitutes a villain is shared by everyone. The report of the Bergo Commission is efficiently defended by one of its members (*Dagens Næringsliv,* July 6th, 1996) by conjuring up pictures of such heroes and enemies: The heading of the article reads: 'The Enemies of Adam Smith', accompanied by a picture of the cover of a recent edition of *The Wealth of Nations*. A subheading gives the picture of the enemy: 'Mercantilist special treatment of single industries is not the way to go.' This is effective rhetoric: No economist in his right mind would dream of *criticizing* Adam Smith or *defend* the mercantilists.

We find ourselves in the world of the novels written for the youngsters of yesteryears – already on the cover it is evident to the reader who is to be the crook and who the hero. In this writer's opinion this state of affairs subsists because economics still suffers from an overdose of 'Cold War Economics' – the ideological battle between two Utopias, the friends and the enemies of the market: The Communist Utopia which promised to pay everyone according to need, and the neo-classical Utopia which promised even more than that: The market would make all wage earners of the world *equally rich* if only barriers to trade were removed – i.e. Samuelson's and the Bergo Commission's factor-price equalization. This result, however, was achieved at the expense of removing from economic theory the very mechanisms which create economic wealth. At a closer look, the mathematical rigour of the analysis proves to be a *rigor mortis* – the fundamental driving forces of society have been lost.

The Untapped Potentials of Factor-price Equalization?

We are tempted to put some irreverent questions to the honourable commission. If factor-price equalization will take place in international trade, it is tempting to ask why the Bergo Commission has not used this knowledge to solve other important problems of Norwegian society. A perennial problem is that some economic groups – e.g. farmers and people washing dishes in restaurants – consistently have a much lower income than other groups, e.g. lawyers and stockbrokers. International trade theory makes it clear that these problems of inequitable distribution can be solved elegantly in a relatively simple way. To illustrate the logic of this theory: If we just put the farmers in one separate nation, and the stockbrokers in another nation, and then open up for free international trade between the two nations, *the invisible hand will make farmers and stockbrokers equally rich* – it will produce *factor-price equalization!*

International trade theory cannot tell us what the new equilibrium wage, common to farmers and stockbrokers, will be. But, whatever it will be, we will have solved the problem of inequalities in national income distribution forever. Why did we not think of this before: If we just put people of different professions in different countries, they will all be equally rich. After all, Samuelson got a Nobel Prize in economics for this discovery, and this theory is the very foundation – not only of the Bergo Commission but of our present world economic order. Although resulting from the commonly accepted assumptions of economic theory, *factor-price equalization* is clearly a case where economic theory consciously walks away from the facts. For this reason some economists take only limited pride in this particular theoretical achievement, and do not push this theory for use in the 'real world'.

It is therefore all the more remarkable that the Bergo Commission confidently uses *factor-price equalization* and its underlying assumptions as the starting point for their recommendations for Norwegian economic policy: 'Assume that all knowledge is commonly known and that everybody has the same productivity" (page 29–30). The problem of the economics profession is that *factor-price equalization* represents the only theory of worldwide income distribution which is available to us – there are no alternatives except in the despised "mercantilist' tradition. In this alternative tradition *relative levels of knowledge and skill,* in a framework of dynamic imperfect competition, determine world income distribution, and – at any point in time – different economic activities present widely different *windows of opportunity* for introducing such skills. For this reason economic growth is *activity specific* – it is available in some economic activities rather than in others. (We intuitively know that the Japanese could not have achieved their welfare by supplying the world with inexpensive shirts, rather than with inexpensive cars and electronics. This intuitive knowledge cannot, however, be captured in today's economic theory.)

However, we do suspect that the members of the Bergo Commission secretly practice 'mercantilism' in the sphere of their own domestic economy. We find it unlikely that they recommend their children to choose a profession which does not require a degree of formal education. Contrary to their teachings, neo-classical economists do not tell their children that it's just as well to take a job washing dishes in a restaurant, because factor-price equalization is just around the corner anyway.

Anleitung
zur
Technologie,
oder
zur Kentniß
der
Handwerke, Fabriken und
Manufacturen,
vornehmlich derer, die mit der
Landwirthschaft, Polizey und
Cameralwissenschaft
in nächster Verbindung stehn.

Nebst
Beyträgen zur Kunstgeschichte.
Von
Johann Beckmann
Hofrath und ordentl. Prof. der Oekonomie in Göttingen.

Dritte, verbesserte und vermehrte Ausgabe.
Mit einer Kupfertafel.

Göttingen,
im Verlag der Vandenhoeckschen Buchhandlung. 1787.

At the time Adam Smith created his economic theory based on barter, German economists, like professor Johann Beckmann of Göttingen, were writing about the importance of technology for national welfare. The first academic chair in economics was established in Germany 100 years earlier than in England, and nineteenth-century US economics was to find its inspiration in Germany rather than in England.

In this way they exhibit 'a mercantilist preference for one economic activity above others' which, according to professor Victor Norman of the Bergo Commission, is a main characteristic of Adam Smith's enemies. Why is it that what is common sense in a family economy automatically becomes despicable mercantilism when brought to the national level? This is because the incomplete notions of production in today's economic theory assume that the same amount of human capital can be profitably added to a person washing dishes as to a lawyer – that all economic activities are 'alike' in the sense that they present the same windows of opportunity for expanding welfare.

'Powerful assumptions produce powerful conclusions', says US economist Robert Solow. In order to achieve factor-price equalization, economic trade theory assumes that all persons on the planet possess exactly the same knowledge and skills, i.e. that we

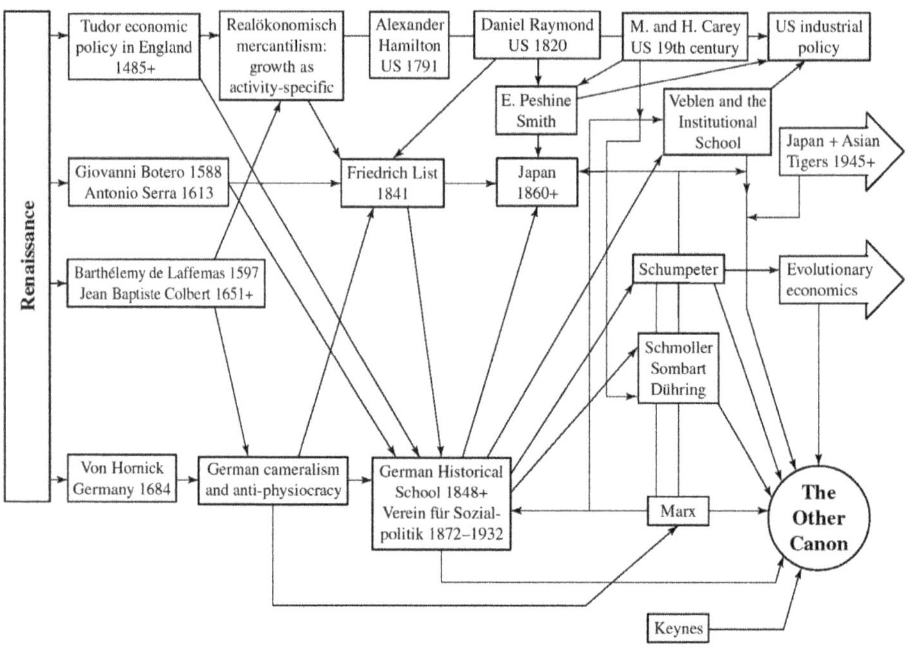

Figure 6.1 Genealogy of theories of technology, knowledge and economics.

are all clones, and that there are no economies of scale, i.e. no fixed costs. But, if we all know the same and there are no fixed costs, this describes the complete do-it-yourself society. We would all build our own Mercedes in the back yard from iron ore as cheaply as the Stuttgart factory! The curious effect of the assumptions of today's theory of international trade is that it takes away the existence of that most important insight of Adam Smith: The Division of Labour.

This example uncovers one of the important blind spots of neo-classical economic theory: The theory only produces *even* economic growth – it gives no clues whatsoever as to what causes wealth to be unevenly distributed. This makes this theory singularly unsuited as a basis for national economic policies. A common theme of 'Adam Smith's enemies' – listed in the alternative genealogy in Figure 6.1 – is the relatively simple proposition that income distribution *between* nations is caused by the same factors which cause income distribution *within* nations, i.e. that farmers and stockbrokers will not get the same salary even if they are put in different nations. With today's free trade and full mobility of resources, there is no reason why a theory of international trade should differ from a theory of *national* trade. This point – which I refer to as pre-Ricardian common sense – has, since Adam Smith's Bible, been referred to as 'mercantilism'. The alternative family tree consists of economists who are not opposed to the market – although Marxism after Marx developed into such a position – they just disagree with Adam Smith that there is any automatism either in economic growth as such or in any 'natural' equitable income distribution. The disagreement is founded in different conceptions of what creates economic growth.

Exploring the Causes of Economic Growth and Forever Finding New Ones

Underlying the disagreement between Adam Smith and the alternative school chartered in Figure 6.1 are fundamental philosophical reasons as to what causes economic growth and welfare. In other words, what brought mankind – and not the other species – out of the cold and draughty caves into modern society? Adam Smith's theory focuses on the role *of barter*, whereas the alternative tradition focuses on *production*. It is only by focusing on *barter and exchange*, with *an insufficient theory of production*, that Adam Smith's friends today produce the counterintuitive mathematical 'proof' that farmers and stockbrokers will be equally rich if we just put them in two different nations.

STATEMENT

OF SOME

NEW PRINCIPLES

ON THE SUBJECT OF

POLITICAL ECONOMY,

EXPOSING THE FALLACIES OF THE SYSTEM OF

FREE TRADE,

AND OF SOME OTHER DOCTRINES MAINTAINED

IN THE "WEALTH OF NATIONS."

BY JOHN RAE.

When we reason upon general subjects, one may justly affirm, that our speculations can scarce ever be too fine, provided they be just.—Hume, Essay on Commerce.

BOSTON:

HILLIARD, GRAY, AND CO.

1834.

John Rae introduces the role of technology in English-speaking economics. To Rae, both capital accumulation ('savings') and economic progress are fundamentally caused and driven by imperfect competition created by new technologies. The United States would therefore stay poor if it kept to its comparative advantage of picking cotton by hand, a process then not yet mechanized.

Should the reader be interested in seeing what 'Adam Smith's enemies' looked like, a good way to start is by looking at the gallery of portraits on US dollar bills. Here is an unusual collection of persons from Franklin through Washington, Hamilton, Jefferson, Jackson and Lincoln who – although acutely aware of the importance of markets and competition – all fundamentally disagreed with Adam Smith's theories and their policy implications. We therefore let Abraham Lincoln represent 'Adam Smith's enemies' as the contrasting view on what brought mankind out of the caves:

The barter-centred theory of development:

> *'The division of labour arises from a propensity in human nature to truck, barter and exchange one thing for another. It is common to all men, and to be found in no other race of animals, which seem to know neither this nor any other species of contracts.... Nobody ever saw a dog make a fair and deliberate exchange of one bone for another with another dog.'*
>
> (Adam Smith, Wealth of Nations (1776), Chicago Edition, p. 17.)

The reply from the production-centred theory of development:

> *'Beavers build houses; but they build them nowise differently, or better, now than they did five thousand years ago. Man is not the only animal who labours; but he is the only one who* ***improves*** *his workmanship. These improvements he effects by* ***Discoveries*** *and* ***Inventions****....'*
>
> (Abraham Lincoln, Speech of the 1860 Presidential Campaign.)

The roots of the problems of today's mainstream economics can be traced back to these conflicting views on Man. Neo-classical economics fundamentally lacks a theory of economic development beyond seeing it as a process of adding capital to labour. In 1956 Stanford economist Moses **Abramovitz** showed that capital accumulation only accounted for 10–20 per cent of US economic growth – which he then referred to as 'a measure of our ignorance about the causes of economic growth'. Adam Smith's nineteenth-century enemies in the United States would ask how Adam Smith's theory explains economic growth. How, would his 'enemies' ask, do you get more bones into the economy by teaching dogs to barter and to make contracts? And, how do you explain with Adam Smith's theory why dogs today eat canned dog food and not bones? Although Adam Smith sees a 'general tendency of things to improve' in the background, these improvements descend on mankind as 'manna from heaven' – not as a result of organized conscious effort – and hit everybody at the same time.

What are the forces creating welfare? It seems that the search process for the approximate causes of growth follows the path of Ibsen's Peer Gynt, to whom the onion – and his inner self – only revealed layer after layer, but no core. Modern economics has been uncovering layers this way:

1. **Markets**
2. **Capital**
3. **Technology (the *techno*part: new hardware/tools)**
4. **Technology (the *-logy* part: new human skills and new knowledge)**

5. **The attitude to new knowledge (persons' and nations')**
6. **Man's rational will ('wit and will')**

The problem with today's mainstream economic theory – and the Bergo Commission – is that they limit themselves to *the first two factors only*. Mankind did not get out of their caves only by starting to barter and by 'getting the prices right'. These are clearly necessary, but far from sufficient, building blocks for a theory of economic growth. New research, sponsored by the OECD under the title TEP – Technology and Economy Programme – also includes factor 3, and increasingly factor 4. Through the TEP programme the Schumpeterian message is slowly sinking in: The driving forces of the economic system are innovations created by new knowledge. Nations who stop innovating do not keep their standard of living, they lose their standard of living even though they keep the same efficiency. This research – most relevant for economic policy – is seemingly completely unknown to the Bergo Commission.

What Brought Mankind Out of the Caves?

Modern society started with the Renaissance, when neo-Platonist ideas from the Byzantine Empire reached the Academy of Florence in the early fifteenth century. Before this time, Man saw himself as the caretaker of God's creation – a creation which was finished by the Lord on the 6th day. To Mediaeval Man all knowledge worth knowing – and all knowledge allowed for him to seek – was contained in the Holy Scriptures and in the writings of **Aristotle.** During the Renaissance, Man came to see himself in a different light. In the Mediaeval world view, new thinking and 'innovations' were considered heresies. In fact, Roger **Bacon** was jailed in Oxford in 1271 for 'suspicious innovations'. The basis for our modern society lies in a new interpretation of the Holy Scriptures. The new argument went like this: Man was created in the image of God. But, what characterizes God above anything else? It has to be His enormous creativity. Then – if Man was created in the image of God – then Man should also be creative.

In the time following the Renaissance 'explosion', bartering raw materials increasingly gave way to the production of manufactured goods. In the process, the value added to the raw materials of nature was seen as imputable to human knowledge – to 'the Soul of Man' – which distinguished him from beasts. Importantly – to the observers of the day – *these new and knowledge-based economic activities were seen as bringing more wealth, as being more profitable, than the old resource-based activities.* Therefore Renaissance economic policy supported the manufacturing industries at the expense of resource-based industries – *encouraging and protecting new knowledge, e.g. through the establishment of a patent system.* A list of economic policies of the Renaissance is found on the next page.

Out of this line of reasoning, *Man's duty to invent* and to *create new knowledge* is born. But, this duty was a pleasurable one. The argument seems to have gone like this: It is Man's duty to people the Earth, therefore God made the duty of procreating a joyous one. Similarly, because it was Man's duty to create, to invent and to discover was also a joyous duty. In England Francis **Bacon** – statesman under Elizabeth I – was the carrier of these ideas, and wrote *An Essay on Innovations* around 1605. In Germany the philosophers **Leibniz** and **Wolff** later represented the same philosophical tradition. 'Some people collect knowledge like other people collect money', says Christian Wolff. Economic growth is achieved by putting the two types together.

In Adam Smith's work there is an automatic 'general tendency for things to improve', but in a sense his causal arrows are reversed. The economists focusing on invention would see the division of labour as a result of new inventions; Adam Smith took the view that *trade alone* would have this effect. That this is more than a chicken-and-egg problem is evident when the policy recommendations are studied. In the alternative tradition, exemplified by **Lincoln,** the fundamental cause of economic growth is 'Man's rational will' – his ability to make hypotheses and to generate new knowledge. With this knowledge Man develops a never-ending chain of new knowledge, which manifests itself in new processes, products and tools.

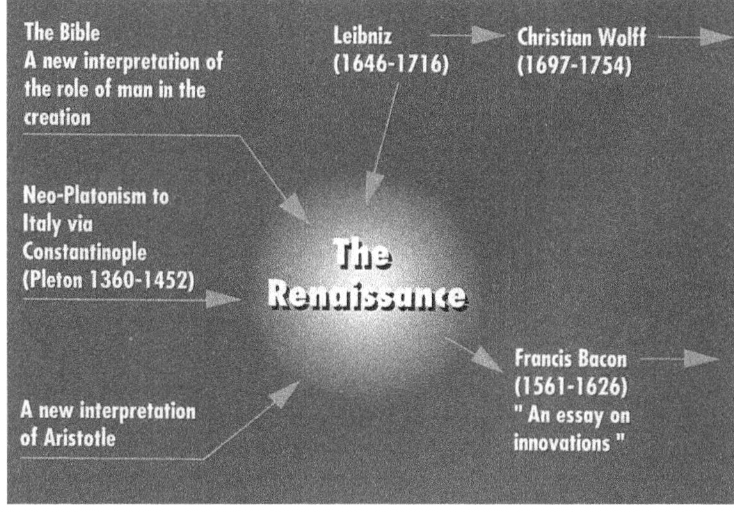

Figure 6.2

Economics and Sustainability: 'The Dismal Science' vs. 'the Never-Ending Frontier of Knowledge'

The focus of neo-classical theory on the barter aspects of economic life, rather than on production, is the single most important underlying factor of the technology-pessimism which is an important feature of the *Zeitgeist* towards the end of the century. The mood of the day is a curious mixture of two sets of credos which at first sight seem to be extremely contradictory: Economic theory predicts that if we just keep our hands off, things will go fine and we will all be equally rich. On the other hand, since we see that this is not happening, then this must be due to 'faith' and 'destiny'. The recommended economic strategy in both cases is 'passivity' – just 'get the prices right', do nothing and leave things to the invisible hand/destiny. However, the apparently contradictory beliefs originate from the same philosophy, shared with neo-classical economic theory: Man's creative powers are assumed away, in a static model of a world of barter, not production.

In contrast, the message of the Renaissance philosophers and economists was an extremely optimistic one. But the men of the Renaissance were acutely aware that their optimistic visions could only be carried out by wise and active economic policies and through the conscious will of man. Francis Bacon – the statesman under Elizabeth I – foresaw a never-ending frontier of knowledge in Man's future. As Leonardo da **Vinci** described aeroplanes and helicopters**,** Bacon describes and initiates inventions and reforms of society, leading to economic welfare.

His inventions include the telescope, microphone, explosive material, flying machines, engines with air and water power, chemical discoveries, better culture of plants and animals, telephones and cars. But, whereas Leonardo and the other artists of the Renaissance are considered heroes today, Bacon and other economist-statesmen of his time – due to the influence of Adam Smith – today fall into the despicable category of 'mercantilists'.

The Renaissance pulled Mankind out of a miserable life tilled with ignorance and superstition. This was not a product of Adam Smith's invisible hand of natural harmony, but of Man's rational will and strong economic policies. As seventeenth-century Italian philosopher Giambattista **Vico** put it, 'Human history differs from natural history in this, that we have made the former, but not the latter.' History is produced by Man's 'wit and will'**.**

Today's production functions in economic theory are still those produced by David Ricardo for his 'corn economy' – reflecting the diminishing returns which will occur with static knowledge in agriculture, rather than the increasing returns found in industry. Over time, with new knowledge, farming is also subject to increasing returns. After David Ricardo, economics rightly came to be called 'the dismal science'. The 'Green Movement' has done us all a great favour by pointing to the severity of the problems of environment and sustainability. But, although they are not aware of it, their *solutions* to these problems are framed in the static and barter-centred theories of Smith, Malthus and Ricardo. In our opinion, this heritage is the reason why environmentalism is so often synonymous with techno-pessimism. There is no invisible hand which will get us out of these problems. Technological development is shaped by society – by Man's knowledge and attitudes – not by the invisible hand of 'Destiny'.

One important inheritance from Adam Smith and neo-classical economics is the tradition of evaluating problems of population independent of the level of knowledge. For the same reason, the standard reply to problems of ecology and technology is 'freeze society as it is' – or even 'reverse it' – rather than 'apply more knowledge to solve our present problems'. The lack of dynamics in economic theory seems to carry over to the *Zeitgeist.* Optimization in neo-classical theory is a static concept. Optimization in the alternative tradition includes cumulative increases in the stock of knowledge, and is therefore only an ever-moving target on the horizon.

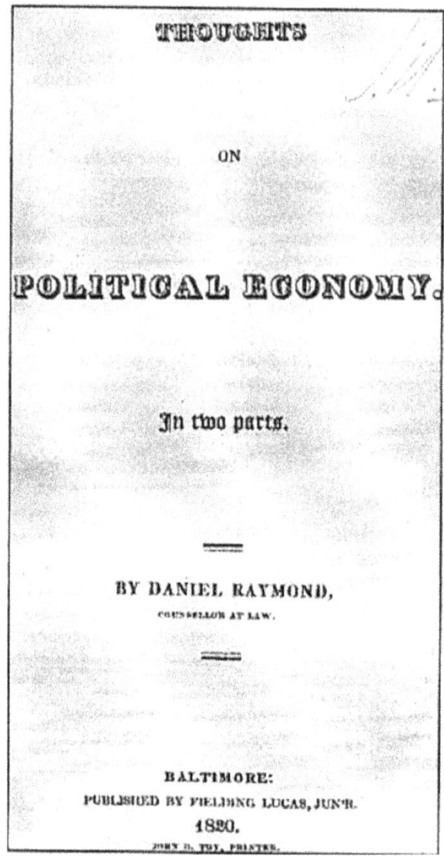

THOUGHTS

ON

POLITICAL ECONOMY.

In two parts.

BY DANIEL RAYMOND,

COUNSELLOR AT LAW.

BALTIMORE:

PUBLISHED BY FIELDING LUCAS, JUN'R.

1820.

JOHN D. TOY, PRINTER.

Daniel Raymond, a lawyer and economist from Baltimore, provided perhaps the most important basis for economic policy in nineteenth-century United States – the 'American System of Manufactures' and 'the High Wage Strategy'. His is the simple and intuitive notion that the standard of living of a nation – just like the standard of living of a person – will above all be determined by its choice of profession and the skill level required by this profession. Therefore there is no tendency towards equalization of wages between nations engaged in professions requiring very different skill levels.

All levels of knowledge carry with them their own limits to ecological sustainability. For this reason, predictions holding the level of knowledge constant produces curious results. The sustainability of Stone Age society was limited by the supply of flintstone. Extrapolating the population assuming static stock of knowledge was a sure prediction of disaster. Extrapolating the traffic increase in the cities of the late nineteenth century, one could predict the year when the city would drown in horse manure. This dire prediction, we have to add, was made by Stanley **Jevons,** one of the founding fathers of today's neo-classical economic theory. The same economist, true to his Physiocratic legacy, attributed the fluctuation in human economic activities – the business cycles – to fluctuations in sun-spot activities.

However, the most serious results of today's barter-based economic theory appear in our relationship to the Third World, as was evident in the conclusion of last year's population conference in Cairo: A virtually unanimous industrialized world agreed that the main development problem is the population explosion. No one asks the question why we are convinced that the poverty problem of Bolivia – with 5 persons per square km – or Peru – with 15 persons per square km – has its roots in overpopulation. Why are their levels of population not 'sustainable', whereas a population density of 350 persons per square km in Holland is 'sustainable'? In effect many poor nations today are underpopulated, like Norway after the Black Death. In effect, the nineteenth-century US economists, here exemplified by Henry **Carey** (1851), firmly rejected this sort of economic theory: 'Overpopulation is the ready excuse for all the evils of a vicious system, and so it will continue to be until that system shall see its end.'

E. Peshine Smith – Energy as the Fundamental Driving Force of Economics

As already mentioned, nineteenth-century German and American economists claimed that the fallacies of the English classical economics were rooted in the fact that English theory formed their theories 'upon the supposition that men are merely vendors and purchasers, and not producers'. This criticism could be voiced equally well against today's neo-classical theory, whose 'production functions' – where technological change appears like 'manna from heaven' – utterly fail to grasp the realities behind technological change.

Consequently these alternative economists developed theories of 'productive powers'. Whereas English classical economics, after Ricardo, deservingly earned its name 'the dismal science', American economics, in particular, developed into a very optimistic science. American economics was to be a science based on facts, not on assumptions. As in the German philosophical tradition of **Leibniz and Wolff,** the driving force of the economy was seen as the domination of Man's mind over physical matter. The two fundamental driving forces of history were Man's 'wit and will' – the *wit* to extend the frontiers of technological ability, and the *will* of society to provide adequate inducements anti-incentives to invest in this technological potential. This 'American System' of political economy can be traced back to the thoughts of Benjamin **Franklin;** it dominated US economics well into this century – being the doctrine of the North against the English doctrines of the South during the Civil War. This tradition completely died out after World War II – under the crossfire of mathematization and the Cold War demand for 'perfect markets'.

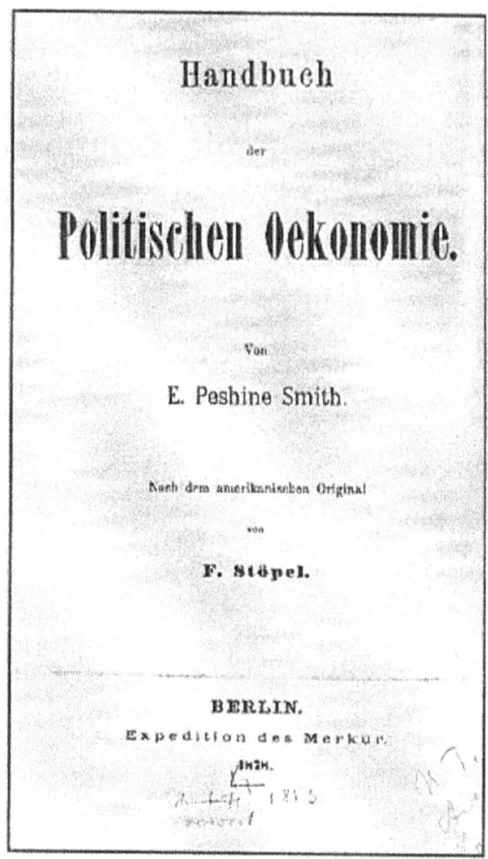

Handbuch

der

Politischen Oekonomie.

Von

E. Peshine Smith.

Nach dem amerikanischen Original

von

F. Stöpel.

BERLIN.

Expedition des Merkur.

1878.

E. Peshine Smith is unique in the history of economic thought in having produced a theory of economic growth entirely on energy – on Man's ability to harness the forces of nature. Just like Raymond and Rae, Peshine Smith was of the opinion that the United States, until it had reached the level of knowledge of England, should protect the activities which used new knowledge and machinery.

American economists who deserve to be resurrected due to their relevance for economic policy include Daniel **Raymond**, whose reply to English trade theory (1820) was the proposition that the forces which determined the income distribution *between* nations are caused by the same factors which cause income distribution *within* nations, i.e. that farmers and stockbrokers will *not* get the same salary even if they are put in different nations. To Raymond, skills and knowledge were the most important factors determining the wealth of a nation. These factors were excluded by Adam Smith in his trade theory – in fact Adam Smith goes out of his way to prove that education is of no value to the individual or to society, because the higher gains from more knowledgeable persons are 'no greater than what is sufficient to compensate the superior expense of their education'. Another American, John Rae, introduced the role of technology into English-speaking economic theory (1834). Friedrich **List** – a German political refugee in the United States – carried these ideas to the European Continent, where they merged into the German historical tradition in economics.

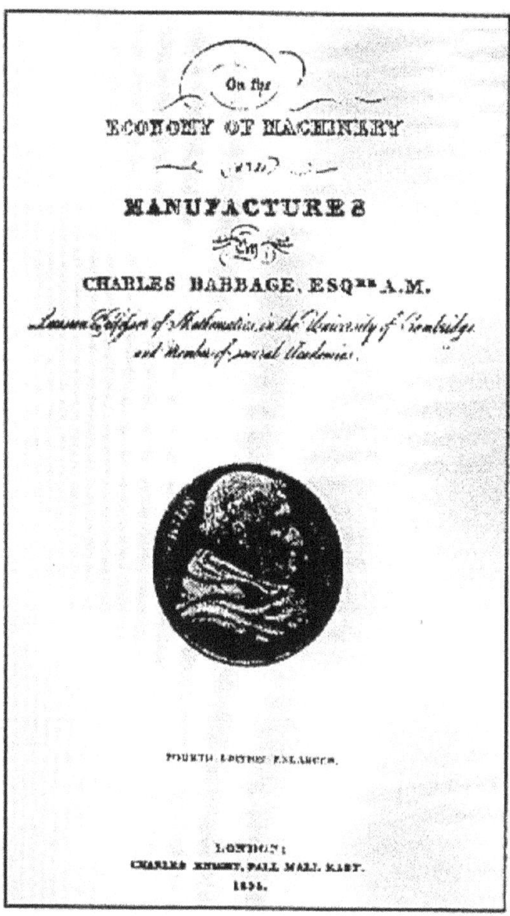

On the
ECONOMY OF MACHINERY
and
MANUFACTURES
by
CHARLES BABBAGE, ESQ.RE A.M.
Lucasian Professor of Mathematics in the University of Cambridge
and Member of several Academies.

FOURTH EDITION ENLARGED.

LONDON:
CHARLES KNIGHT, PALL MALL EAST.
1835.

Whereas the English exported the theories of Adam Smith and David Ricardo, their own industrial policy was led by the theories of Charles Babbage, the inventor of the theory of the computer. Babbage emphasized the role of knowledge embedded both in machinery and in new scientific discoveries.

Erasmus Peshine **Smith** (1814–1882) was the economist who above anyone else placed *Man's harnessing of Nature's energy* as the main moving force of the economy. To Peshine Smith, Nature's resources, especially her energy resources, have an infinite potential, in sharp contrast to the pessimistic 'scarcity' economics of British Ricardian orthodoxy. Whereas the theories of Adam Smith developed into pessimistic Malthusianism, Peshine Smith's theories kept alive the spirit of the Renaissance and of Man's undeveloped potentials.

Peshine Smith sought to develop economics into a quantitative engineering science: 'to construct a skeleton of political economy upon the basis of purely physical laws.' He believed all economic laws to have their counterparts in those of the natural sciences, and proceeded to characterize the reproduction of wealth as a vast energy-transfer system within Nature's overall equilibrium, the basic question being the extent to which Man would proceed to exploit Nature's latent wealth. He wrote to Henry **Carey,** a fellow economist: 'The entire universe then *is* motion, and the only point is how much of the universal and ceaseless motion we shall utilise, and how much we shall permit to be working against us.' His holistic view of the planet as described in the 'Law of Endless Circulation in Matter and Forces' is decidedly both 'modern' and 'ecological'.

The increased wealth produced by increased productivity was to Peshine Smith a product of the forces of nature – harnessed by Man – substituting for manual labour. 'Twenty years ago', says Smith, 'a paper box of matches sold for a shilling. Now as many matches, of superior quality, are sold for a halfpenny' – i.e. the price had been reduced to 1/24. '...in the meantime, by improved chemical and mechanical combinations, twenty-five boxes had come to be made by the same expenditure of human labour as one match required in its day.' In a box with twenty-five matches, says Peshine Smith, *twenty-four* may be regarded as the contribution from Man's harnessing of Nature – a Nature who gives her aid, and asks no recompense – and *one,* as the result of muscular action.

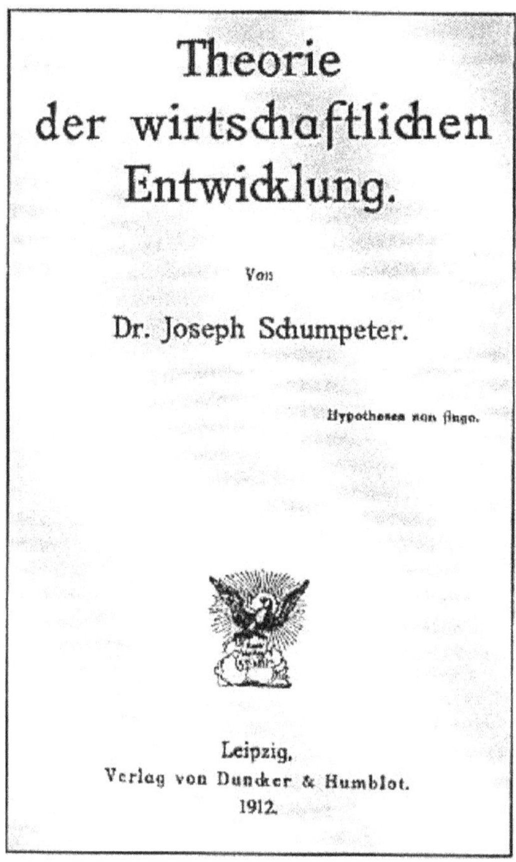
Theorie der wirtschaftlichen Entwicklung.

Von

Dr. Joseph Schumpeter.

Hypotheses non fingo.

Leipzig,
Verlag von Duncker & Humblot.
1912.

Austrian-born Harvard economist Joseph Alois Schumpeter shared Marx's view that inventions and innovations were the main forces 'propelling the capitalist engine'. He spent his life trying to integrate this vision into the body of neo-classical economics – and failed. Schumpeter is the starting point for today's 'evolutionary economics' which is very influential in the OECD, but is not considered at all by the Bergo Commission on Norwegian industrial policy.

The policy implications of the nineteenth-century US economists differed from that of Adam Smith. Because they saw knowledge in harnessing nature and technology as the main moving force of welfare, it was crucial to Peshine Smith and his colleagues to move the US economy into the limited number of economic activities where mechanization took place at the time. For 300 years English commercial policy had favoured manufacturing exports – goods made with new technology and new knowledge. Now English economists recommended the United States to stick to its comparative advantage in picking cotton, an activity where no technical change took place. 'The English have found national wealth', US economists said, and they are now 'trying to pull up the ladder' – using the theories of Smith and Ricardo in order to convince the rest of the world to stick to our comparative advantage of being poor and ignorant. To nineteenth-century US economists, every nation tended to keep its productivity advances in the form of higher wages. Knowledge – assumed away in English theory – was the most important factor of production. Therefore, for a period, until they had reached the level of technical knowledge of the English, the United States had to protect their knowledge and industries from the more advanced English industries. This conclusion was evident from theory based on production, but not from a theory based only on barter.

Early in his career as a lawyer, Peshine Smith joined the law firm of William Henry **Seward** in Rochester, N.Y. Seward later became governor of the state of New York, a US senator, the leader of the Republican Party in its early years, and Lincoln's secretary of state; Peshine Smith's *Manual* appeared in 1853, one year before the Republican Party was founded, and came to provide the ideological basis for that party and for the Civil War reconstruction effort. The US economists of the period, who saw knowledge as the moving factor of welfare, observed with horror the fact that the slave-owners took great care in preventing their slaves from learning how to read and write – 'knowledge unfits a person to be a slave'. They found a parallel to this way of thinking in the suffering of the United States 'from the policy of Great Britain in checking our industrial and mechanical aspirations, and keeping us a buying instead of a making people.'

In 1871 – four years after the Meiji Restoration – the Japanese government requested from the government of the United States an advisor in international law. The secretary of state recommended Peshine Smith, who was to spend eight years in Japan as the first US citizen to serve the Japanese government in an official capacity. When he left, he proudly commented that the 'American System' of economic theory – as opposed to English theory – had become 'common thinking among Japanese statesmen, government officials and philosophers'.

Nine editions of Peshine Smith's *Manual of Political Economy* appearing in the United States between 1853 and 1897 testify to his influence, and his book was translated into French, German and Italian. In spite of this, and in spite of his strong influence on American economic policy, Erasmus Peshine Smith remains virtually unrecognized in the history of economic thought, not being mentioned in any of the standard histories of the subject. The nineteenth-century evolutionary and history-based branches of economics died out with the formalization of classical economics into neo-classical economics. The history of economic thought has, since then, been monopolized into a history of the predecessors of neo-classical theory. The alternative production-based theories and the theories which were important for economic policy, all have virtually disappeared.

The Historical Techno-Economic Paradigms

PERIOD FROM-TO	NAME OF PERIOD	IMPORTANT INDUSTRIES	INEXPENSIVE RESOURCE	INFRASTRUCTURE
1. 1770–1840	*Early mechanization*	*Textiles Wool*	*Water power Cotton*	*Canals Roads*
2. 1830–90	*Steam and railway*	*Iron Transportation*	*Steam Coal*	*Railroad Steam ships*
3. 1880–1940	*Electricity and heavy industry*	*Electr. machinery Chemical ind..*	*Electricity Steel*	*Ships, Roads*
4. 1930–90	*Mass production (Fordism)*	*Cars Synthetic matter.*	*Oil*	*Roads, Planes, Cables*
5. 1990–?	*Information and communication*	*Data/Software Bio-technology*	*Micro-electronics*	*Digital telecom Satellites*

Source: Carlota Perez.

Energy and the Techno-Economic Paradigms

Erasmus Peshine Smith clearly shows how the different sources of energy carry the various industrial periods. These are the periods which we today call *techno-economic paradigms*.

Traditionally we divide the history of Mankind into historical periods named after the technologies which dominated the period: e.g. stone cutting technology in the Stone Age and iron technology in the Iron Age. The gradual shift from one period to the next radically changes Man's way of life. These historical periods may be looked upon as different modes – different methods – of increasing Man's material standard of living. Towards the end of each period, it becomes increasingly clear that the previous technology is 'used up', its potentials are exhausted. There is no more room for improvements along the previous technological path – the world does not change anymore without fundamental changes to the technological base. Such periods are closely related to the long waves in economic history.

In modern history, we distinguish between five such different ways of increasing the standard of living, all of which dominated a long historical period. Above we show, after Carlota **Perez** and Christopher **Freeman**, an overview of these periods, and the various sources of energy which fed each technological development: Perez and Freeman have shown that techno-economic paradigm shifts not only lie in a cluster of new and radical innovations but also in the universal and low-cost availability, in large quantities, of a key factor or a combination of factors. The source of energy here is such a key factor distinguishing each techno-economic paradigm. We are now moving into a paradigm which solves some of our past problems, but which, no doubt, also produces new and different challenges.

The fundamental driving force behind the world economy is the changing level of Man's knowledge. Only by assuming away this factor, neo-classical economics produces factor-price equalization. Part of an alternative theory based on this vision is also the fact that nations exporting products based on old and commonplace knowledge will have a lower standard of living than nations exporting products containing advanced, new and scarce knowledge – regardless of their relative efficiency. The world's most efficient producers of baseballs for the American sport, who are in Haiti, make 30 US cent per hour. They are the world's most efficient producers in an industry which all the capital of the United States has not managed to mechanize. Baseballs are sewn by hand everywhere. The world's most efficient producers of golf balls – made by machines – have a nominal wage which is about 30 times higher. The uneven advances of mechanization produce huge inequities in world income, and lock many poor nations into a comparative advantage of being poor and ignorant. This fact was not lost on US economists and politicians of the nineteenth century, but today its absence forms the most important blind spot on the cornea of mainstream economic theory. Until we include knowledge – Man's 'wit and will' – as a factor in economic theory, we shall continue, in vain, to throw money at the *symptoms* of poverty, rather than address its *causes.*

Today mainstream economic theory continues to play Hamlet without the Prince – theorizing about economic welfare without considering the huge, but uneven, advances of human knowledge which – through innovations, new technologies and new products – provide the real engine fuelling human welfare. Today's limited understanding of how the market system creates and so unevenly distributes the fruits of these processes would be enormously helped by researching the insights of nineteenth-century production-based economics. These theories, or their modern versions sponsored by the OECD, are not taught anywhere in the Norwegian university system. We are, in terms of economic theory, stuck in the paradigm of 'Cold War Economics'. A better understanding of the mechanisms at work would not only improve the debate on Norwegian economic policy – it would above all benefit the Third World which is trapped in its Ricardian comparative advantage of being poor and ignorant.

Chapter 7

PRODUCTION CAPITALISM VS. FINANCIAL CAPITALISM – SYMBIOSIS AND PARASITISM. AN EVOLUTIONARY PERSPECTIVE AND BIBLIOGRAPHY

Bibliography by Arno Mong Daastøl

This chapter presents a note and an extensive bibliography on the relationship between production capitalism and financial capitalism. The document was produced for a conference held at Leangkollen outside Oslo on 3–4 September 1998. The background for the conference was the Asian financial crisis that started in July 1997. The massive Russian financial crisis had started a few days before the conference, on 17 August 1998, and the Russian participant, Professor Vladimir Avtonomov, brought fresh news from these dramatic events.

The global financial crisis that started in 2008 – ten years after this conference – vindicated the perspectives presented here, and prompted the wish to make the note and the very extensive bibliography of relevant, but mostly forgotten, literature on the relationship between the production sector and the monetary sector of the economy. The conference programme is found at the end of the chapter.

Financial issues are far from being at the core of evolutionary economics. The evolutionary focus has been on the production of goods and services (on what Schumpeter called the *Güterwelt*), not on money. This has, no doubt, been the right emphasis, particularly as much of our economic policy – both in the First and in the Third World – is still based on what Schumpeter called 'the pedestrian view that it is capital *per se* which propels the capitalist engine'. The view of evolutionary economics on finance has tended to be in line with what the same author, Schumpeter, saw as one conclusion from Antonio Serra's 1613 book: 'If the economic process as a whole functions properly, the monetary element will take care of itself and not require any specific therapy.' However, in the context of the late 1990s, the financial system seems to intrude into the economic process in a way that is qualitatively different from before. This, we feel, raises the need to discuss the relationship between evolutionary economics and finance.

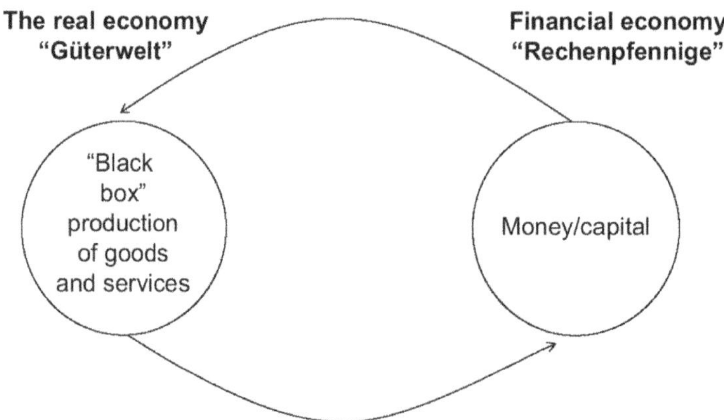

Traditionally, evolutionary economics deals with the dynamics within the black box of production (the *Güterwelt*). The dynamics of the *Güterwelt* require, however, a financial scaffolding in order to develop. At the best of times, then, there is a healthy symbiosis between the two worlds, between the **real economy** and the **financial economy**. The workshop is dedicated to the relationship between the two spheres above, between **production capitalism** and **financial capitalism**, between the sphere of *goods* and the sphere of *money*, between *innovation* and *finance* – in all its aspects, e.g. historical, theoretical, technological, or in terms of its effect on the distribution of income or on the clustering of innovations, within nations or internationally. This discussion is an old one, but of renewed relevance.

The relationship between *production capitalism* and *financial capitalism* is reflected in the old German distinction between 'schaffendes Kapital' (creative capital) and 'raffendes Kapital' (grabbing capital). Hilferding's *Finanzkapital* from 1912 is a classic in this field. This same issue was also much discussed in nineteenth-century United States, when foreign (i.e. English) capital tended to be 'bad' capital and domestic capital was 'good' capital. South East Asians today will probably share this view on the roles of foreign vs. domestic capital. In his *Treatise on Money* (1931), Keynes sees depressions as arising when money is shifted from 'industrial circulation' into 'financial circulation'. This is again an observation that seems to fit the present situation as well. A few years later, in 1936, Harold Macmillan complained about his own party being dominated by *Casino Capitalism*. Later a similar distinction is found in Bill Lazonick's 'wealth creation' vs. 'wealth extraction'. At the same time, the English *Telegraph* recently estimated the market for financial derivatives as around twice the world GNP in size. Other estimates are even higher. Perhaps this is a good time to reread Keynes.

The aim of the conference is to contribute to public policy by attempting to answer some fundamental questions regarding the relationship between financial capitalism and production capitalism:

1. What can theory and history contribute in terms of an **operational delimitation** between 'Production Capitalism' and 'Financial Capitalism'?

2. What have been the most efficient **policy measures** – in tax policy, industrial policy or otherwise – in channelling financial flows into 'industrial circulation' (of course also including services) rather than into 'financial circulation'?
3. **To what extent is the present Asian crisis a 'typical' bubble?** (The term *bubble* was coined during the financial crisis in 1720, which was the first truly international financial crisis.) What is new about today's situation, and what are recurrent elements of all financial crises through the ages?
4. What are the relationships between **discontinuities in technological change** – systemic paradigm shifts – **and financial crisis?** Do financial bubbles tend to appear at a similar point in the technological trajectory? If so, what are the mechanisms at work?
5. How do financial cracks change **the distribution of income and wealth** – nationally and internationally? The 1929 crack provides an interesting case on how different sectors are affected in very different ways. In the United States, industrial labour kept their wages, and the crisis was taken out in terms of unemployment. As a result, labour's share of GNP actually rose in the United States during the depression, whereas in agriculture the price and wage level fell by around 50 per cent. During recent Latin American crises, whole national wage levels behave more like the US agricultural sector than like the US manufacturing sector during the Great Depression. In many nations, the financial adjustment policies have led to a radical redistribution of GNP away from labour and the self-employed towards profits and the financial sector. In the 1930s labour's share of GNP was around 70 per cent in the United States. In Peru in 1996 profits and the financial sector amounted to about 53 per cent of GNP. What can be learned from the US experience in terms of protecting real wages during a financial crisis?

Capitalism is, of course, a name for our whole economic system. From the standpoint (of one branch) of evolutionary economics, it could be considered a misnomer. The name does seem to confirm the already quoted 'pedestrian view' that capital *per se* is at the core of the system. The term 'capitalism' was first used by the enemies of the system – by German socialists – as a derogatory term. Was the term chosen as a protest against financial speculation? In the spirit of evolutionary economics, a more fitting term would perhaps have been **idea-ism**: a system which is driven by human ideas and human will, based on conscious rationality, intuition, perceptiveness and leadership. The *demand* for capital is created by these innovative ideas and this human will. Without new ideas, in a state of equilibrium, there would – as Schumpeter pointed out – not be any demand for capital (beyond that covered by depreciation). Capital would have no value and pay no interest. Ideas, then, must come first in order to give capital its value. Thus, the term **idea-ism** would seem to take priority over **capital-ism**.

There are times in the history of economics when the profession has attempted to look through 'the veil of money' (This was the title of Pigou's 1949 book, see bibliography) to capture the real economic forces. Before WWI metaphors like 'money is a wrapper in which goods come to you' or 'money is the garment draped around the body of economic life' were common. First after the violent disturbances in prices and exchange rates following WWI and then again during the depression of the 1930s, money – the passive veil – 'took on the appearance of an active and evil genius' (Pigou). 'Money, after being little or nothing, was now everything.' Although during WWII emphasis was on the real world of equipment, organization and production, the last 50 years of abstract and formal 'neo-classical synthesis' in economics has again covered the world of ideas, leadership, intuition, knowledge and human will in a fairly impenetrable 'veil of money'. How can the real forces be unveiled and understood to prevent money from again becoming 'an active and evil genius' which causes *the real economy* to collapse?

Production capitalism depends on a working financial system, and clearly innovation in finance often accompanies innovations of products and processes. There is, then, often a healthy symbiosis between the worlds of production and finance. However, at certain points in history, this relationship seems to take on a parasitic quality: the financial sector, as compared to the real economy, enters a stage of explosive and disproportionate growth and – as this bubble later bursts – the financial sector severely reduces the size and virility of its 'host', i.e. of the real economy (the production of goods and non-financial services). In the serious cases, the national standards of living collapse simultaneously with the collapse of the financial sector. In the United States, GNP/capita did not reach its 1928 level again until the middle of WWII.

In the United States, probably more money has been made through the appreciation of real estate than in any other way. What are the long-term consequences if an increasing percentage of savings and wealth, as it now seems, is used to **inflate the prices of already existing assets** – real estate and stocks – instead of to create new production and innovation? On the other hand, access to production credit is an important problem for the poor in the Third World. This has given rise to microenterprise finance among the poor as a business and as an incipient field of academic inquiry that will be covered at the conference.

As a result of the tendency towards savings being used to prop up the value of already existing assets, do we need a different theory of saving? Ragnar Frisch – who in 1969 shared the first so-called Nobel Prize in economics – claimed that 'saving' from the point of view of a nation was so different from private savings that a new and different term ought to be invented. 'A nation', said Frisch, 'can only save through arrangements in the productive sphere.' This would open up for a differentiation between two kinds of savings and capital accumulation – one adding to the 'real world' of goods and services, the other just inflating the value of already existing assets. A most important issue is this: What can be learned from previous efforts aiming at taxing financial operations leading towards bubbles, while sheltering productive investment? Is the Tobin tax one answer to our problems? What, if anything, can we learn from the different schemes of the 1930s which attempted to force savings into productive schemes only, like e.g. Silvio Gesell's 'stamped money' which decreased in value if not productively invested or used for consumption?

Like theories of trade, theories of banking seem to lend themselves to an analysis contrasting the Continental (German) approach and the English approach. This contrast in approach between English and Continental theories also applies to 'the social question' which seems to recur – in slightly different versions – with every financial crisis.

Financial bubbles seem to appear in historical periods that are characterized by a *zeitgeist* giving priority to monetary goals above goals in the real economy, in periods when the tail (the monetary economy) is allowed to wag the dog (the real economy). One example: In the UK after WWI, it was decided to put the pound back on pre-war parity with the dollar. In order to achieve this, UK wages were deliberately forced down in an attempt to make wages match the deflated level of prices. This move caused Keynes for the first time to question the sanity of economic theory, and made him fire the first shot, in 1922, of what was to become the Keynesian Revolution. At one point – in order to introduce a common currency – the European Community has set a completely arbitrary figure of 3 per cent budget deficit for nations to qualify. The economies ruled by old-fashioned Latin American dictators – like Stroessner and Duvalier – would have been the first to qualify for the criteria for the European common currency. Just like after WWI in the UK, we seemed not to mind adjusting people's standard of living downwards in order to achieve a monetary goal which has been chosen in a completely arbitrary manner. The fact that the economy is in the middle of a technological revolution, which creates a strong deflationary tendency, makes a policy fundamentally based on the fear of inflation all the more questionable.

The relationship between money and production also raises important philosophical and historical – even anthropological – issues. To German speakers there are, as always, treasures to be rediscovered in the almost forgotten German economic tradition. What did Roscher, Schmoller and Sombart have to say about this problem? Georg Friedrich Knapp and Karl Elster (*Die Seele des Geldes* – 'The Soul of Money', 1920) combine economic theory and monetary theory, finance, law and philosophical/theoretical issues with political science ('Das Geld ist ein Geschöpf der Rechtsordnung'). Schumpeter also contributed to this debate in 1917 with a paper called 'Das Sozialprodukt und die Rechenpfennige' and in his book *Das Wesen des Geldes* ('The Nature of Money'), written in the late 1920s, but only published in 1970. Schumpeter here discusses the relationship between the monetary economy and the real economy – between *the sphere of money* (Geldgrössen und monetäre Vorgänge) and *the sphere of goods and services* (Güterwelt). His theoretical approach here is very much in line with Schmoller's – with the holistic tradition of the German historical school.

The history of finance and production goes back to the Codes of Hammurabi in ancient Mesopotamia, where sporadic debt cancellation was an institutionalized mechanism for preventing an increasing concentration of land into a few hands. In modern times there is plenty of literature pointing to financial bubbles and their follies. The famous Dutch tulip mania of 1636–37 is well documented. Often already the titles of the contemporary books say much: In 1688 a book appeared describing the Amsterdam stock exchange, which was then the world's leading financial centre. The book, entitled 'Confusion de Confusiones', was written in Spanish by a Portuguese Jew, Joseph de la Vega, and published in Amsterdam. In 1720 – after the South Sea Bubble in England and the Mississippi Bubble in France – appeared, among many others on the subject, a large and extravagant book with many plates, under the title 'The Great Mirror of Folly'. An important nineteenth-century contribution to this literature – 'Extraordinary Popular Delusions and the Madness of Crowds' by Charles Mackay – appeared in 1841, and was republished in 1980.

The crisis of 1929 was not the last financial crisis which brought down the real economy with it. There are many worrisome signs which point to the need for a better understanding between *the sphere of money* and *the sphere of real goods and services.* The standard of living of the average Mexican fell drastically as the result of a financial collapse, the 'tequilazo'. After the fall of the Berlin wall, capitalism came to Albania in the form of a financial pyramid game, which no one seemingly tried to stop, bringing ruin to a nation which already was the poorest country of Europe by far. The official figures show that the 'real economy' in Russia (GNP/capita) has been more than halved since the fall of the Berlin wall, accompanied by a measurable fall in life expectancy. Real wages in Lima, Peru, have been reduced by between 40 and 60 per cent since 1983, in private and public sectors, respectively. Income distribution in the industrialized world is worsening almost everywhere. Schumpeter's 'creative destruction' also takes on a new meaning – one of *financial* ***creativity*** combined with *the* ***destruction*** *of real wealth.* One example is buyouts aimed at dismembering assets, running down plant and equipment, 'dressing up' earnings; all in the expectation that stock markets will continue to rise so that the assets again can be unloaded.

The relationship between production capitalism and financial capitalism through history can be seen as one of ebbs and flows, of periods of industrial capitalism maturing into financial capitalism, at one point causing a financial crack which prompts the creation of a more restrictive system aimed at reconstructing the 'real' economy, thus starting the cycle all over again. The high tides of financial crises are accompanied by a similar tidal wave of literature. The first truly international financial crash in 1720 caused the production of economic books to increase by a factor of 10 in one year. No doubt the Asian crisis will produce a similar tidal wave. The aim of this workshop-conference is to maximize the learning effects of previous financial crises, minimizing the number of wheels that have to be reinvented.

BIBLIOGRAPHY, by Arno Mong Daastøl.

FOREWORD

Compiling a bibliography of the relationship between production capitalism and financial capitalism – on how to divert investment from speculation to production – is a complex task. The problem is related to a multitude of other questions of larger or smaller nature. In the more narrow sense of economics it is related to not only finance and manufacturing but also to theories of business cycles, of investment, taxation, growth, stage theories, planning, public goods, infrastructure, value, credit (-creation), debt, rent, money, risk, stability, international banking, globalisation, protection, international politics, power, currency policy, international seniorage, balance of trade, etc. Financial regulations in periods of war are particularly interesting in this regard, since in times of war these regulations tend to focus intensely on production. Finance has often been seen as the ultimate instrument of power in periods both of war and of peace.

Although any definition is subjective, we suggest the following definition of speculation: Speculation is selling and buying for profits detached from real production. This contrasts to the hedging deals in currency trade as a part of a transaction of real products and services.

Under financial capitalism, finance regulates itself and national authorities are more prone to follow the dictates of the financial interests: bankers, fund managers etc. Under industrial capitalism, finance is under the dictates of national political authorities, democratically elected or not, through regulations of various kinds. On the theoretical level this regulation blocks the efficiency of the financial system itself. However, in real terms successful regulations increase the efficiency of the **total** socio-economic system since the efficiency of production is increased by directing capital away from short term financial investments towards long term investments in productive assets. In other words, regulation may push investments away from pure and sterile financial investments or consumption and into long term 'real' productive investments in activities related to production, communication, infrastructure, research, education, and health. From the standpoint of political economy or 'nationalist economics' the former type would represent zero-sum investments whereas the latter would represent positive sum investments.

This problem is an old one. In order to rescue the Roman Empire from moral decay and physical deterioration, Caesar and Augustus severely restricted speculation, interest and the activities of finance in general, through waves of political reforms, in the 1st century BC and AD. Louis XI and Henry VII were to follow their example 14 centuries later, and F.D. Roosevelt another 5 centuries after that. Today the Asian crisis again raises these same questions.

ON CLASSIFICATION OF LITERATURE

The classification of literature below is intended to point out important literature in the field concerning the problem of diverting investment from speculation to production, as well as to establish a systematic perspective referring to historical periods. As noted, the categories 'financial' and 'industrial' capitalism are terms that refer to how strong financial affairs are regulated by national political authorities. Using time as the classification criterion therefore points to the changing character of this debate through the past centuries.

The first category is split chronologically in order to highlight the fluctuations in the production of literature. The delineation of periods is based on the dominating trend within the global financial system.

The second major category, 'new monetary system movements', could largely be grouped into the chronological section 1918-1945 but constitutes a tradition which stands out by itself and breaks this chronological categorization. We believe a better perspective of this tradition is gained by separating this tradition from the rest of the literature. The reason is that on several points these movements converge. Not only do they all intend to solve the post WW I economic crisis of instability, unemployment and social misery and strife. They do also propose more or less similar solutions to this prolonged crisis. It turns out that the most famous of these reformers, J.M. Keynes, was more the visible surface of a great wave than the originator of the wave itself. The reformers saw the problem as primarily connected to the monetary system, concerning in particular credit. The titles of three books are revealing of the general intent of the general movement: Robert Eisler's *Stable Money* (1932), Brynjolf Bjørseth's *Distribute or Destroy* (1934) and Major Douglas' *The Monopoly of Credit* (1931). The depression was seen as a kind of constipation of the economy caused by a lack of proper circulation of credit and money as lubricants in the economic machinery. The solution was seen as a politically administrated distribution of these lubricants to the public in general. The differences between the various reformers reflect the different suggestions of how to carry this out in practice.

LANGUAGES:

For practical purposes the literature is classified into different language groups. The subsection *Scandinavia* is a reflection of the ethnocentricity of this author The classification into languages is, of course, also a classification in terms of cultural areas. In particular the European continental nations have a different, more nationalistic tendency (favouring political control), whereas the Anglo-Saxon countries have a more market-oriented policy (favouring banking control). The latter is the normal and accepted view today. However – from an historical point of view – this is a fairly recent phenomenon, indeed a post WW II and even a post 1970s phenomenon. In particular, the United States followed a much more nationalist policy during periods of the 19th century and in the 1931-1963 era. This goes for Britain as well in several periods, the last being the partly successful attempt to revive mercantilism a century ago and to some degree Labour dominated post-WW II period.

CHRONOLOGY:

Chronologically, important watersheds in this century are 1931 and 1971. Before 1931, we find a system dominated by financial capitalism but with important islands of industrial capitalism, for instance in the US, Germany, Russia, and Japan. The years 1931 to 1971 are characterized as a period of industrial capitalism, starting with New Deal in the US and ending with the downfall of the Bretton Woods system.

The year 1918 is also chosen as a dividing line, since this year too changes the nature of some of the islands of industrial capitalism: Russia, and Germany. Whereas the typical credit policy of production capitalism lost weight in the USA with the assassination of President McKinley in 1901, Japan kept following this policy practically to this day, or perhaps until the late 1980s. The period 1918-1931 is characterised as a period of financial capitalism with an intense debate around the question of the very structure of the financial system itself. Since this debate does not stop in 1931 but continues until WW II, the end of the category is for practical reasons chosen as 1945.

The years 1931-1971 were a period of industrial capitalism under various political regimes. The literature in the period 1931-1940 (1945), however, continues the debate from the preceding years and it is therefore convenient to group these sub-periods together.

Literature in the period 1945-1971 is generally dominated by a discussion within the frames of the Bretton Woods system. This focused on the necessity of regulation based on the experience with unregulated markets before the crash of 1929 and the devastating consequences to real production and consumption as well as to international peace.

Increasingly, however, the urge to liberalize markets was to make its way. Internationally this was brought about by actions of the French and British governments, in particular. This led to the establishment of offshore dollar markets outside national control during the 1960s. The downfall of Bretton Woods in 1971 was only the most visible sign of the increased focus on liberalisation. As the period comes closer to the time of writing (1998), the principles of financial capitalism are increasing their influence. Financial capitalism is again on top. Concerning the literature, however, 1982 is chosen as a more appropriate dividing line since the effects of the new international regime took time to manifest themselves. Accordingly, neither did the literature react instantly. A better delineation of categories is reached with the Peso-crisis in Mexico in 1982, since this also more closely corresponds to the first effects of the free-trade, free-capital flow policy of the Thatcher and Reagan revolutions.

What is particularly striking about the literature is, firstly, the great flood of literature on monetary and financial issues in the period between the world wars, between 1918 and 1935, in particular. Secondly, what is striking is the increasing amount of literature after the debt crisis hit Mexico in 1982 and again after Black October on Wall Street in 1987, Tokyo early 1990s, Mexico 1994, Barings, Schneider, Orange County, Credit Lyonnais etc., all of the early 1990s. The recent 1997-1998 Southeast Asian crisis – in particular in Thailand, Korea, the Philippines, and Malaysia – is sure to leave the same marks in any list of literature on financial and monetary issues. This is a repetition of the flow of literature after any such event throughout history such as the (more or less international) financial crises in 241 BC, 50 BC, 1345 AD, 1637, 1720, 1858, 1873, 1890, 1907, 1924, 1929, 1958, 1973 etc. The titles we would specifically recommend are marked with an asterisk (*).

1) BOOKS OF GENERAL INTEREST IN THE FIELD

After the 1929 crash, a massive bibliography was assembled by Prof. Mitsuzo Masui of Kobe University: *A Bibliography of Finance*, Kobe University of Commerce, 1935. The work consists of 1,614 pages + an authors' index filling 105 pages.

A) BEFORE 1918: FINANCIAL CAPITALISM.

I) LITERATURE IN ENGLISH BEFORE 1918

Early financial literature can be found in the printed catalogues of the Kress Library at Harvard Business School (4 volumes) and of the Goldsmiths Library at the University of London (5 volumes). Both libraries contain economic literature published before 1850. The entries are chronological, and financial literature is listed annually under that heading.

References

Ainsworth, William Harrison. (1868). *The South-Sea Bubble: a tale of the year 1720*. Leipzig: Tauchnitz. (Collection of British authors, vol. 989–990).

Alvord, Clarence Walworth. (1917). *The Mississippi Valley in British politics: a study of the trade, land speculation, and experiments in imperialism culminating in the American Revolution*. Cleveland: Arthur H. Clark Company.

Andreades, Andreas. (1909). *History of the Bank of England*. London: King & Son.

Angell, Norman. (1912). *The money game: how to play it: a new instrument of economic education*. London: Dent.

Ashburton, Lord Alexander. (1847). *The financial and commercial crisis considered*. London: John Murray.

Ashley, William James. (1903). *The Tariff problem*. London: King.

*Ashley, William James. (1912). *Gold and prices*. London: Green & Co.

Atkey, Bertram. (1908). *Easy money: the genuine book of Henry Mitch, his diligent search for other folk's wealth, and his urgent fear of the feminine*. Illustrated by G.L. Stampa. London: Grant Richards.

Attfield, James B. (1893). *English and Foreign Banks*. London: Wilson.

*Bagehot, Walter. (1869). *A practical plan for assimilating the English and American money as a step towards a universal money*. London: Longmans, Green, Reader, and Dyer.

*Bagehot, Walter. (1873). *Lombard Street: a description of the money market*. London: Henry S. King.

Bagehot, Walter. (1875). 'A new standard of value.' *The Economist*, November 20, reprinted in the *Economic Journal*, volume 2 (1892).

Bastable, Charles Francis… [et al.]. (1924). *The money problems of the world: course of reading on money exchange and finance*. London: Encyclopaedia Britannica, (The Britannica Home University, first series, 2).

*Beccaria, Cesare (1769). *A discourse on public economy and commerce*, by the Marquis Caesar Beccaria Bonesaria. London: Dodsley.

*Bell, Gavin M. (1840) *The philosophy of joint stock banking*. London: Longman, Orme, Brown, Green, and Longman's.

*Botero, Giovanni. (1606). *A treatise concerning the causes of the magnificency and greatnesse of cities*. Divided into three books by Sig. Giovanni Botero in the Italian tongue, now done into English by Robert Peterson. London: Thomas Purfoot.

*Bowen, Francis. (1870). *American Political Economy*. New York: Scribner.

*Brace, Harrison H. (1913). *Valuation of organized speculation*. Boston: Houghton Mifflin.

Bryce, Viscount James. (1893). *The American commonwealth*. New York: Macmillan.

Carey, Henry Charles. (1837). *Principles of political economy*. Philadelphia: Carey, Lea & Blanchard.

*Carey, Henry Charles. (1838). *The credit system of France, Great Britain, and the United States*. Philadelphia: Carey, Lea & Blanchard.

Carey, Henry Charles. (1848). *The past, the present, and the future*. London: Longman, Brown, Green, and Longman's.

Carey, Henry Charles. (1851). *Harmony of interests*. Philadelphia: Skinner.

Carey, Henry Charles. (1858–1859). *Principles of social science*, 3 vols. Philadelphia:, Lippincott.

*Carey, Henry Charles. (1864). *Financial crises: their causes and effects*. Philadelphia: Baird.

*Child, Josiah. (1668). *Brief observations concerning trade and interest of money*. London: Printed for Elizabeth Calvert at the Black-spread Eagle in Barbican, and Henry Mortlock at the Sign of the White-Heart in Westminster Hall.

Circulating capital (1885): being an inquiry into the fundamental laws of money. An essay by an East India merchant, author of 'The Homology of Economic Justice' (1884). London: Kegan Paul & Trench.

City Man, a. (see: Meason, Malcolm R.L).

*Clare, George. (1891). *A Money Market Primer*. London: Wilson.

Conant, Charles A. (1905). *The principles of money and banking*. New York: Harper.

Conway Jr., Thomas. (1911). *Investment and speculation: a description of the modern money market and analysis of the factors determining the value of securities.* New York: Alexander Hamilton Institute.

Cortelyou, Geo B. et al. (1908). 'Lessons of the financial crisis.' Philadelphia: *American Academy of Political and Social Science*, vol. 31, no. 2.

Crump, Arthur. (1874). *The theory of stock speculation.* New York: Longmans, Green, Reader, and Dyer.

Cunningham, Audrey. (1910). *British credit in the last Napoleonic war*, with an appendix containing a reprint of *Des finances de l'Angleterre* by H. Lasalle. Cambridge: Cambridge University Press (Girton college studies no. 11).

Cunningham, William. (1891). *The use and the abuse of money.* London: University Extension Manuals.

*Cunningham, William. (1905). *The rise and decline of the free trade movement.* Cambridge: Cambridge University Press.

Cunningham, William. (1909). *The moral witness of the church on the investment of money and the use of wealth: an open letter addressed to his Grace the Archbishop of Canterbury, President of the Convocation of the Province of Canterbury.* Cambridge: Cambridge University Press.

*Easton, Harry T. (1896). *Banks and banking.* London: Wilson.

*Easton, Harry T. (1900). *The works of a bank.* London: Wilson

Emery, Henry Crosby. (1896). *Speculation on the stock and produce exchanges of the United States.* New York: Columbia University (Studies in history, economics and public law, Faculty of Political Science, vol. 7, no. 2).

*Evans, David Morier. (1861). *Speculative notes and notes on speculation, ideal and real.* London: Groombridge & Sons.

*Fawcett, Henry. (1863). *Manual of Political Economy.* London: Macmillan.

*Fisher, Edmund D. (1918). *After war credit: an outlook.* Detroit: Bank of Detroit.

*Fisher, Irving. (1914). *Why is the dollar shrinking?* New York: Macmillan.

Fowler, William. (1866). *The crisis of 1866: a financial essay.* London: Longmans, Green.

Gervaise, Isaac. (1720). *The system or theory of the trade of the world. Treating of the different kinds of value of the ballances of trade of exchange of manufactures of companies and shewing the pernicious consequences of credit, and that it destroys the purpose of national trade.* London: Printed by H. Woodfall.

Giffen, Robert. (1880–1890). *Essays in finance*, 1st ser. London 1880, 2nd ser. London 1890.

*Giffen, Robert. (1904). *Economic inquiries and studies*, 2 vols., London: Bell & Sons.

Gibbons, James S. (1858). *The banks of New York: their dealers, the clearing house, and the panic of 1857, with a financial chart.* New York: Appleton & Co.

*Gilbart, James W. (1856). *A practical treatise on banking*, I-II, 6th ed. London: Longman, Brown, Green & Longman's.

*Gilbart, James W. (1871). *Principles and practice of banking*, I-II, 7th ed. London: Bell & Daldy.

*Hamilton, Alexander. (1791). *The reports of Alexander Hamilton*, I-IV, edited by E. Cooke. New York: The University Library, Harper & Row, 1964, Part I: *Report Relative to a Provision for Support of Public Credit*, January 1790, Part II: *The Second Report of the Further Provision Necessary for Establishing Public Credit (Report on a National Bank)*, December 13, 1790, Part III: *Opinion on the Constitutionality of the Bank*, February 23, 1791, Part IV: *Report on Manufactures*, December 5, 1791.

Hamilton, Alexander, James Madison, and John Jay. (1791). *The federalist.* Chicago: Great Books of the Western World, no.43, Encyclopaedia Britannica Inc., 1952.

Hammurabi. (2500 BC). *The code of Hammurabi*, translated by L.W. King, with commentary from Charles F. Horne, Ph.D. (1915) and The Eleventh Edition of the Encyclopaedia Britannica, 1910- by the Rev. Claude Hermann Walter Johns, M.A. Litt.D. The Code of Hammurabi Introduction Charles F. Horne, Ph.D. 1915.

*Hardcastle, Daniel. (1842). *Banks and bankers.* London: Whittaker & Co.

Hartnoll, John Hooper. (1853). *A letter to the Right Hon. E. Cardwell M.P., President of the Board of Trade, on the inoperative character of the joint stock companies' registration act, as a means of preventing the formation of bubble assurance companies, or of regulating the action of those honourable and legitimately instituted*, 2nd ed. London: W.S.D. Pateman.

Harvey, James. (1865). *The exchequer note versus the sovereign: the great want of the country, a state paper money expanding with population and wealth.* Liverpool: Howell [etc.].

Henry, Francois (1942). *The theory of money, or it is a fine day to-day.* London: King.

*Hewins, William A.S. (1892). *English trade and finance, chiefly in the seventeenth century.* London: Methuen.

*Hewins, William A.S. (1901). *Imperialism and the probable effects of the commercial policy of the United Kingdom.* London and Germany.

*Hewins, William A.S. (1919). *The apologia of an imperialist: forty years of empire policy (1889–1929)*, 2 vols. London: Constable.

*Hilferding, Rudolf. (1912). *Finance capital: a study of the latest phase of capitalist development.* London: Routledge & Kegan Paul. (Orig. title *Das Finanzkapital).*

Hobson, John A. (1889). *Physiology of industry* (with A.F. Mummery). London: Murray.

Hobson, John A. (1890). *The economics of distribution.* New York: Macmillan.

Hobson, John A. (1894). *The evolution in modern capitalism.* London: Walter Scott.

*Hobson, John A. (1901). *The social problem.* London: Nisbet.

*Hobson, John A. (1902). *Imperialism, a study.* London: Nisbet.

Hobson, John A. (1909). *The crisis of liberalism*, ed. by P.F. Clarke. Brighton: Harvester Press.

*Hobson, John A. (1909). *The industrial system, an inquiry into earned and unearned income.* London: Longman.

Hobson, John A. (1911). *The science of wealth*, 4th ed., with preface by R.F. Harrod. Oxford: Home University Library.

Hobson, John A. (1911). *An economic interpretation of investment.* London: Financial Review of Reviews.

Hobson, John A. (1914). *Work and wealth, a human valuation.* London: Macmillan.

*Hobson, John A. (1916). *The new protectionism.* New York: Putnam's Sons.

*Hobson, John A. (1915). *Towards international government.* London: Allen & Unwin.

Hoyle, Edmund. (1802). The new pocket Hoyle, containing the games of whist, quadrille … and speculation: accurately displaying the rules and practice, as admitted and established by the first players in the Kingdom. London: Wynne & Scholey.

*Hume, David. (1752). 'Essay on commerce'. In his *Essays and Treatises on Several Subjects*, part II. London: Millar, 1764.

*Hume, David. (1752). 'Of money.' In his *Essays and Treatises on Several Subjects*, part II. London: Millar, 1764.

*Hume, David. (1752). 'Of interest' In his *Essays and Treatises on Several Subjects*, part II. London: Millar, 1764.

*Hume, David. (1752). 'Of the balance of trade.' In his *Essays and Treatises on Several Subjects*, part II. London: Millar, 1764.

*Hume, David. (1752). 'Of taxes.' In his *Essays and Treatises on Several Subjects*, part II. London: Millar, 1764.

Ingram, John Kells. (1886). *A history of political economy.* Edinburgh: Black.

Jevons, W. Stanley. (1875). *Money and the mechanism of exchange.* Boston: Appleton. (23th ed. London: Kegan Paul, Trench, Truebner (The international scientific series, vol. 17).

*Keynes, J.M. (1914). 'War and the financial system.' *The Economic Journal*, vol. XXIV, August, pp. 460–486.

*Kirkaldy, Adam W. (1915). *Credit, industry, and the war*: being reports and other matter presented to the section of economic science and statistics of the British association for the advancement of science. London: Pitman.

*Lauderdale, James Maitland, Lord. (1804). *An inquiry into the nature and origin of public wealth and into the causes of its increase.* Edinburgh: Constable/London: Reeman & Rees, 1804.

Lenin, Vladimir I. (1917). *Imperialism: the highest stage of capitalism.* Reprint. Moscow: Foreign Languages Publishing House, 1959.

List, Friedrich. (1827). *Outlines of American political economy*, Philadelphia: Samuel Parker.

*List, Friedrich. (1837). *The natural system of political economy.* Philadelphia: Lippincott, 1856.

[Liverpool, Robert Banks Jenkinson, Lord] (1822). *A letter to Lord Liverpool, on the fallacy of considering the late and present extensive shipments of British-manufactured goods as indicative of anything else than a spirit of speculation in our merchants, which will speedily produce ruin to our manufacturers.* London: Whittaker.

Locke, John. (1691). *Some considerations of the consequences of the lowering of interest and the raising the value of money.* In a letter sent to a Member of Parliament. London: Printed for Awnsham and John Churchill.

Locke, John. (1695). *Further considerations concerning raising the value of money wherein Mr Lowndes's arguments for it in his late report concerning an essay for the amendment of silver coins, are particularly examined,* To the Right Honourable Sir John Sommers, Kt. Lord Keeper of the great Seal of England, and one of His Majesties most Honourable Privy Council. London: A. & J. Churchill.

*Longfield, Samuel Mountifort. (1834) *Lectures on political economy.* Dublin: Milliken & Son.

*Mackay, Charles. (1841). *Memoirs of extraordinary popular delusions and the madness of crowds.* London: Richard Bentley.

*Macleod, Henry D. (1855–1856). *The theory and practice of banking,* I-II. London: Longmans, Green & Co.

*Macleod, Henry D. (1896). *A History of banking in all the leading nations.* I-IV, Vol. II *Great Britain.* London: Wilson.

Maitland, James (see: Lauderdale, James Maitland, Lord).

Malthus, Thomas R. (1815). *An inquiry into the nature and progress of rent, and the principles by which it is regulated.* (By Rev. T.R. Malthus, Professor of History and Political Economy in the East India College, Hertfordshire.) London: Printed for John Murray.

Malynes, Gerard de. (1622). *The maintenance of free trade, according to the three essentiall parts of traffique; namely commodities, moneys, and exchange of moneys, by bills of exchanges for other countries. Or answer to a Treatise of Free Trade, or the meanes to make Trade flourish, lately published. Contraria iuxta se Pofita magis Elucescunt.* London: Printed by I.L. for William Shefford.

Mar, Alexander Del. (1885). *A history of money in ancient countries from the earliest times to the present.* London: Bell.

Mar, Alexander Del. (1886). *Money and civilization: or A history of the monetary laws and systems of various states since the Dark Ages, and their influence upon civilization.* London: Bell.

[Meason, Malcolm R.L.]. (1865). *The bubbles of finance: joint-stock companies, promoting of companies, modern commerce, money lending, and life insuring, by a city man.* London: Sampson Low, Son, and Marston.

*McKinley, William. (1896).*Tariff in the days of Henry Clay and since, an exhaustive review of our tariff legislation from 1812–1895.* New York: H. Clay.

*Michie. (1882). *The history principles and practice of banking,* 2nd ed. London: Bell.

*Minor, Ursa [D.C. Itzkowitz]. (1891). *On the science and practice of stock exchange speculation.* London: Gibbings.

Mises, Ludwig von. (1912). *The theory of money and credit.* London: Jonathan Cape, 1924. (Orig. title *Theorie des Geldes und der Umlaufsmittel).*

Misselden, Edward. (1622). *Free trade or, the meanes to make trade Florish. Wherein, the causes of the decay of trade in this Kingdome, are discovered: and the remedies also to remoove the same, are represented. Propertius, nauita de ventis, de tauris narrat arator: Enumerat miles vulnera, pastor oues.* London: Printed by John Legatt, for Simon Waterson.

*Moore, Henry L. (1914). *Economic cycles: their law and cause.* New York: Macmillan.

*Moxon, Thomas B. (1894). *English practical banking.* Manchester: Heywood.

Mun, Thomas. (1621). *Englands treasure by forraign trade. Or the balance of our forraign trade is the rule of our treasure.* [Now published for the Common good by his son John Mun of Bearsted in the County of Kent, Esquire]. London: Printed by J.G. for Thomas Clark, 1664.

Newton, Isaac. (1712–1717). *Representations on the subject of money. Representation first to the right honourable the Earl of Oxford and Earl of Mortimer, Lord High Treasurer of Great Britain. May it please Your Lordship.*

North, Dudley. (1691). *Discourses upon trade, 1691: principally directed to the cases of the interest, coynage, clipping, increase of money.* London: Basset. (Baltimore: Johns Hopkins Press, 1907).

Orage, Alfred Richard. (1917). *An alphabet of economics.* London: T. F. Unwin, Ltd.

*Patten, Simon N. (1885). *The premises of political economy being a re-examination of certain fundamental principles of economic science.* Philadelphia: Lippincott.

Osborne, Algernon Ashburner (1913). *Speculation on the New York Stock Exchange, September 1904-March 1907.* New York: Columbia University Press.

Petty, William. (1662). *A Treatise of taxes & contributions, the nature and measures of crown lands, assessments, customs, poll-money, lotteries, benevolence, penalties, monopolies, offices, tythes, raising of coins, harth-money, excize, etc. With several intersperst discourses and digressions concerning warres, the church, universities, rents & purchases, usury & exchange, banks & lombards, registries for conveyances, beggars, ensurance, exportation of money & wool, free-ports, coins, housing, liberty of conscience, etc. The same being frequently applied to the present state and affairs of Ireland.* London: Printed for N. Brooke.

Petty, William. (1682). *Quantulumcunque concerning money. To the Lord Marquess of Halyfax.* London: Churchill [1695].

Pigou, Arthur C. (1905). *Principles & methods of industrial peace.* London: Macmillan.

Pigou, Arthur C. (1912). *Wealth and welfare.* London: Macmillan.

Pigou, Arthur C. (1913). *Unemployment.* London: Williams & Norgate.

Pigou, Arthur C. (1916). *The economy and finance of the war: being a discussion of the real costs of the war and the way in which they should be met.* London: Dent.

Pike, James S. (1867). *The financial crisis: its evils and their remedy.* New York: [s.n.], From: *New York Tribune.*

*Price, Hilton. (1876). *Handbook of London bankers, with some account of their predecessors, the early goldsmiths.* London: Chatto & Windus.

*Proudhon, Pierre J. (1840). *What is property?* English translation 1898, reprinted in London: William Reeves, 1969.

Quelch, Harry. (1895). *The bimetallic bubble.* London: Twentieth Century.

Rae, John. (1834). *The sociological theory of capital*, ed. with biographical sketch and notes, by Charles Whitney Mixter, Ph.d. Reprinted New York: Macmillan, 1905.

*Roscher, Wilhelm. (1857). *Principles of economics.* New York: Holt, 1878.

*Ruskin, John. (1857). *The political economy of art, unto this last, essays on political economy.* London: Smith, Elder & Co.

*Seligman, Edwin R.A. (1908). *The crisis of 1907 in the light of history: introduction to the currency problem and the present financial situation.* New York: Columbia University press.

Simmel, Georg. (1900). 'A chapter in the philosophy of value.' *American Journal of Sociology*, vol. 5, no. 5, pp. 577-603.

*Simmel, Georg. (1907). *The philosophy of money.* Boston: Routledge, 1978, 1982.

*Sinclair, Upton. (1908). *The money-changers.* New York: Dodge & Co.

*Smith, James W. (1892). *A Handy Book on the law of banker and customer.* London: Wilson.

*Steuart, Sir James. (1767). *An inquiry into the principles of political economy being an essay on the science of domestic policy in free nations. In which are particularly considered population, agriculture, trade, industry, money, coin, interest, circulation, banks, exchange, public credit, and taxes.* Ore trabit quodcumque potest atque addit acervo. Hor. Lib. I. Sat. 1 in 2 volumes. London: Printed for A. Millar, and T. Cadell.

Stilwell, Arthur E. (1912). *Cannibals of finance: fifteen years' contest with the money trust.* Chicago: Farnum Publ. Co.

*Swift, Jonathan. (1732). *A proposal for an act of parliament, to pay off the debt of the nation, without taxing the subject, by which the number of landed gentry, and substantial farmers will be considerably encreased and no one person will be the poorer, or contribute one Farthing to the Charge. By A—- P—-, Esq.* Dublin: Printed in the Year MDCCXXXII.

Swift, Jonathan. (1736). *Reasons why we should not lower the coins now current in this Kingdom*, Occasioned by a Paper Entitled, Remarks on the Coins current in this Kingdom. To which is added, The Rev. Dean Swift's Opinion, Delivered by him, in an Assembly of above One hundred and fifty eminent Merchants who met at the Guild Hall, on Saturday the 24th of April, 1736, in order to draw up their Petition, and Present it to his Grace the Lord-Lieutenant against lowering said Coin. Dublin: E. Waters.

*Thorpe, C.A. (1901). *How to invest and how to speculate.* London: Richards.

Turgot, Anne-Robert Jacques. (1774). *Reflections on the formation and distribution of wealth.* London: E. Spragg, 1793.

*Weyl, Walter E. (1912). *The new democracy.* New York: Macmillan.

*Wilson, Alexander J. (1897). *Practical hints to investors and some words to speculators.* London: Wilson.

Zimmern, Alfred Eckhardt. (1918). *The economic weapon against Germany.* London: Allen & Unwin.

II) LITERATURE IN CONTINENTAL LANGUAGES BEFORE 1918

Bachmann. (1898). 'Die Effektenspekulation mit besonderer Berücksichtigung der Ergebnisse der deutschen Börsenenquete.' Sonderabdruck aus der *Zeitschrift für schweizerische Statistik.*

*Basch, Julius. (1900). *Wirtschaftliche Weltlage, Börsen- und Geltmarkt im Jahre 1899*, 10. Folge. Berlin: Prager.

*Becher, Ernst. (1868). *Der Kredit und seine Organisation.* Pest: Hartleben.

*Becher, Johann Joachim. (1673) *Politischer Discours.* Frankfurt: Zunner.

*Belot, Emile. (1885). *La révolution économique et monétaire qui eut lieu à Rome du III siècle avant l'ère chrétienne.* Paris: Leroux.

*Bondi, Felix. (1897). *Die Berufspflichten des Bankiers auf Grund der neuesten Gesetzgebung.* Berlin: Heymanns.

Christians, Wilhelm. (1893). *Die deutschen Emissionshäuser und ihre Emissionen in den Jahren 1886–1891.* Berlin: Schneider.

Cohn, Gustav. (1868). *Die Börse und die Spekulation.* Berlin: Lüderitz (Sammlung gemeinverständlicher wissenschaftlicher Vorträge, 3. Serie, H. 57).

*Cohn, Gustav. (1895). *Beitrage zur deutschen Börsenreform.* Leipzig: Duncker & Humblot.

*Cohn, Gustav. (1898). *Nationalökonomie des Handels- und Verkehrswesens* (System, vol.III, p. 550 ff). Stuttgart: Encke.

*Cohn, Gustav. (1901). *Welche sind die Ursachen den gegenwärtigen Krisen.*

*Coquelin, Charles. (1859). *Le Crédit et les Banques.* Paris: Guillaumin.

*Courcelle-Seneuil. (1899). *Les Opérations de Banque*, 8th ed., Paris: André Liesse.

*Eberstadt, Rudolf. (1901). *Der deutsche Kapitalmarkt*, p. 105 ff. Leipzig: Duncker & Humblot.

*Ehrenberg, Richard. (1883). *Die Fondsspekulation und die Gesetzgebung.* Berlin: Springer.

*Endemann, Adolf. (1895). *Das moderne Börsenkommisionsgeschäft im Effektenverkehr.*

*Deloume, Antonin. (1892) *Les manieurs d'argent a Rome.* Paris: Thorin.

*Doering, Valentin. (1913). *Die Ansichten deutscher Kameralisten des 18. Jahrhunderts über das Kredit- und Bankwesen*, Dissertation Erlangen. Bamberg.

Dubost, Christopher. (1818). *The elements of commerce: or treatise on different calculations, operations of exchange, arbitrations of exchange, speculations in exchange and banking operations, exchange circulations, operations of specie and bullion, pars of exchange and of coins, practical speculations in merchandize, description and tables of monies, weights and measures, and tables of logarithms, being a complete system of commercial calculations.* 2nd ed. London: Boosey & Sons.

*Duchêne, Georges. (1867). *La spéculation devant les tribunaux: pratique et théorie de l'agiotage*. Paris: Librairie Centrale.

Fallon, Valère. (1914). *Les plus-values et l'impôt: plus-values des terrains: villes, campagnes, spéculation, monopole foncier, concentration, la terre et le droit de proprieté, Henry Georges, single-taxers, Bodenreformer, imposition de la rente et des plus-values, législation*. Bruxelles: Van Fleteren; Paris: Rousseau.

*Ferraris, Carlo. (1892). *Principi di scienza bancaria*. Milan: Hoepli.

*Fichte, Johann Gottlieb. (1800). *Der geschlossene Handelsstaat*. Leipzig: Philip Reclam.

Gareis, Karl. (1874). 'Die Börse und die Gründungen.' *Deutsche Zeit- und Streitfragen*, Vol. 41.

Geffroy, M.A. (1888). *Du role de la richesse dans l'ancienne Rome sous la République*. Paris: Revue des deux mondes.

Geyer, Philipp. (1865). *Banken und Krisen*. Leipzig: Weigel.

Gotthelf, Jeremias [Bitzius, Albert]. (1844). *Geld und Geist, oder, Die Versöhnung*. Solothurn: Jent & Gassmann.

Gruntzel, Josef. (1914). *Wert und Preis. Eine theoretische Untersuchung nach realistischer Methode*. Munich and Leipzig: Duncker & Humblot.

*Guillemot, Pierre. (1906). *La spéculation financière: sa fonction économique*. Dissertation Paris, Paris.

*Helfferich, Karl. (1910). *Geld und Banken*, (Hand- und Lehrbuch der Staatswissenschaften, Bd. 8), Teil: *Das Geld*. Leipzig: Hirschfeld.

Hildebrand, Richard. (1867). *Das Chequesystem und das Clearinghouse in London*. Jena: Mauke.

*Hilferding, Rudolf. (1912). *Das Finanzkapital*. Vienna: Brand.

*Hochstetter, Franz. (1933). *Geld und Kredit. Als störer der moderner Tauschwirtschaft*. Berlin: Militär-Verlag.

*Hocker, Nikolaus. (1858). *Sammlung von Statuten aller Actien-banken Deutschlands*. Cologne: Greven.

*Ischenhäuser. (1898). 'Bankkraft Berlins', *Gegenwart*. Leipzig.

Jannet, Claudio. (1892). *Le capital, la spéculation et la finance au XIXe siècle*. Paris: Plon, Nourrit et Cie.

Jastrow, Ignaz. (1915). 'Geld und Kredit im Kriege.' Jena: Fischer (*Weltwirtschaftliches Archiv*. Ergänzungsheft/Universität Kiel. Institut für Weltwirtschaft und Seeverkehr, 1).

*Justi, Johann Heinrich Gottlob von. (1755). *Staatswirtschaft*. Leipzig: Breitkopf.

*Justi, Johann Heinrich Gottlob von. (1760). *Die Grundfeste zu der Macht und Glückseeligkeit der Staaten oder ausführliche Vorstellung der gesamten Polizeywissenschaft*. Leipzig, Königsberg: Hartungs Erben.

*Justi, Johann Heinrich Gottlob von. (1766). *System des Finanzwesens*. Halle: Renger.

Kautsch, Jacob. (1901). *Handbuch des Bank- und Börsenwesens*, 2nd ed. Berlin: Simon.

*Knies, Karl. (1858). 'Das heutige Bank- und Kreditwesen'. *Gegenwart*, Band XI, p. 294 ff. Leipzig.

*Knies, Karl. (1873–1876). *Geld und Kredit*, I-II, especially vol. II. Berlin: Weidmann.

Lefebvre, Pierre. (1899). *Du fonctionnement de la spéculation sur les valeurs de bourse*. Dissertation Université de Nancy.

Lefevre, H. (1870). *Traité des valeurs mobilières et des opérations de bourse: placement et spéculation*. Paris: Lachaud.

Leist, Emil. (1914). *Der internationale Kredit- und Zahlungsverkehr*. Leipzig: Glöckner.

Lexis, Wilhelm. (1914). *Das Kredit- und Bankwesen*. Berlin: Göschen (Sammlung Göschen, 733).

*List, Friedreich. (1827). *Grundriss der amerikanischen politischen Ökonomie*, Wiesbaden: Böttinger, 1996. (English title *Outlines of American Political Economy*).

*List, Friedrich. (1841). *Das nationale System der politichen Ökonomie*. Stuttgart: Cotta.

List, Friedrich. (1927–1936). *Schriften, Reden, Briefe*, 10 vols. Berlin: Hobbing.

*Loeb, Ernst. (1897). 'Die Wirkungen des Börsengesetz auf das Bank und Börsengeschäft'. *Jahrbücher für Nationalökonomie und Statistik* (Conrads Jahrbücher), III Folge. Bd. XIII, p. 725 ff.

*Loeb, Ernst. (1902). 'Das Institut des Aufsichtsrats.' *Jahrbücher für Nationalökonomie und Statistik* (Conrads Jahrbücher), III Folge. Bd. XXIII, p. 1 ff.

*Lotz, Walther. (1890). *Technik des Emissionsgeschäft*. Erweiterter Sonderabdruck aus Schmoller's 'Jahrbuch', vol. XIV, Heft 2, Leipzig.

*Lumm, Karl von. (1891). *Die Entwicklung des Bankwesens in Elsass-Lothringen seit der Annexion* ('Staatswissenschaftliche Studien', ed. Dr. Ludwig Elster, Vol. III, Heft 7). Jena: Fischer.
*Luxemburg, Rosa. (1913). *Die Akkumulation des Kapitals.* Berlin: Singer.
*Marco De Viti, Antonio de. (1898). *La Funzione della Banca.* Rome: Accademia dei Lincei.
*Marx, Karl. (1894). *Das Kapital*, I-II, Vol. I, Ch. 29. Hamburg: Meissner.
*Mayer, Bruno. *Die Emission von Wertpapieren.* Vienna: Hölder.
Merten, Francois. (1867). *Cours de sciences commerciales. Rédigé conformement au programme du Gouvernement: comprenant tout ce qui concerne les institutions et les places de commerce, la correspondance commerciale, la comptabilité, les operations de banque, des établissements de prévoyance, calles de bourse, du commerce de spéculation, etc., etc.* Gand: Hoste.
Michaelis, Otto. (1873). *Volkswirtschaftliche Schriften*, Vol. I, p. 237 ff, Vol. II, p. 3 ff, 198 ff, 301 ff., and 322 ff. Berlin: Herbig.
*Mises, Ludvig von. (1912). *Theorie des Geldes und der Umlaufsmittel*, 2nd ed. München: Duncker & Humblot, 1924. English transl. 1934.
Mises, Ludvig von. (1918). 'Zur Klassifikation der Geldtheorie'. *Archiv für Sozialwissenschaft und Sozialpolitik*, vol. XXXIX, pp. 174–186.
Mises, Ludvig von. (1924). 'Über Deflationspolitik'. *Mitteilungen des Verbandes österreichischer Banken und Bankiers*, vol. 6, no. 1/2, pp. 13–18.
*Model, Paul. (1896). *Die grossen Berliner Effektenbanken.* Jena: Fischer.
*Mommsen, Theodor. (1854). *Römishce Geschichte.* Leipzig: Weidmann.
Müller, Adam. (1808–1809). *Elemente der Staatskunst.* Meersburg: F.W. Hendels Verlag.
*Müller, Adam. (1816). *Versuch einer neuen Theorie des Gelde*s. Leipzig: Brockhaus.
*Müller, Adam. (1812). *Vom Geiste der Gemeinschaft.* Leipzig: Kröner.
Neumann-Hofer. (1894). *Depositengeschäfte und Depositenbanken.* Leipzig: Winter.
*Obst, Georg. (1898). *Der Depositen- und Kontokorrentverkehr.* Leipzig: Poeschel
*Obst, Georg. (1899). *Theorie und Praxis des Checkverkehrs.* Stuttgart: Strecker & Moser.
*Obst, Georg. (1900). *Lehrbuch des Geld-, Bank- und Börsenwesens.* Stuttgart: Strecker & Moser.
*Patoux, A. (1899). *De la liquidation par filières des marches en spéculation sur marchandises.* Dissertation Paris, Paris.
*Patterson., Robert (1867). *Der Krieg der Banken.* Berlin: Springer.
*Perrot, Franz. (1873). *Der Bank-, Börsen- und Aktienschwindel.* Rostock: Kuhn.
Petrazycki, Leon von. (1906). *Aktienwesen und Spekulation: eine ökonomische und rechtspsychologische Untersuchung.* Trans. from Russian to German. With author's foreword. Berlin: Müller.
Pfleger, Franz Josef and Ludwig Gschwindt. (1896–1897). 'Börsenreform in Deutschland'. *Münchener volkswirtschaftliche Studien*, Vol. 15, 16, 22.
*Phillipovich, Eugen von. (1899). *Grundriss der politischen Ökonomie*, 1. & 2, 1. Part, p. 280, Freiburg im Breisgau: Mohr.
*Price, Bonamy. (1877). *Geld und Bankwesen.* Berlin: Springer.
Roscher, Wilhelm. (1874). *Geschichte der National-Ökonomie in Deutschland.* München: Oldenbourg.
*Roscher. (1881). *System der Volkswirtschaft.* 2nd ed., Vol. III, p. 275 ff, Stuttgart: Cotta.
*Rössig, K.G. (1781). *Versuch einer pragmatischen Geschichte der Ökonomie, Polizey und Kameralwissenschaft.* Leipzig: Weidmanns Erben.
*Rota, Pietro. (1872). *Principi di scienza bancaria.* Milan: Agenzia internazionale.
*Sattler, Heinrich. (1890). *Die Effektenbanken.* Leipzig: Winter.
Sayous, Andre-Émile. (1900). *La spéculation sur les fanons et l'huile de baleine en Hollande, au XVIIe siècle: mémoire lu a l'Académie des sciences morales et philosophiques dans la séance du 7 juillet 1900.* Paris: Pigelet. Compte rendu de l'Académie des sciences morales et politiques.
*Sayous, André-Émile. (1901). *Les Banques de Depôt.* Paris: Larose.
*Schäffle, Albert. (1873). *Das gesellschaftliche System der menschlichen Wirtschaft*, I-II, 3rd ed., vol. II, p.143 and 146 ff. Tübingen: Laupp.
*Scharling, William. (1900). *Bankpolitik.* Jena: Fischer.

Schaub, Franz. (1905). *Der Kampf gegen den Zinswucher, ungerechten Preis und unlautern Handel im Mittelalter.* Freiburg im Breisgau: Herder.

*Schmoller, Gustav. (1909). 'Skizze einer Finanzgeschichte von Frankreich, Östereich, England und Preussen (1500–1900), Historische Betrachtungen über Staatenbildung und Finanzentwicklung.' Sonderandruck aus dem *Jahrbuch für Gesetzgebung, Verwaltung und Volkswirtschaft in Deutschen Reich,* Vol. XXXIII, no. 1. Leipzig: Duncker und Humblot.

*Schnapper, Eduard. (1900). *Zur Entwicklung des englischen Depositenbankwesens.* Zürich: Leemann.

*Schönberg, Gustav von. (1898). *Handbuch der politischen Ökonomie,* Vol. I. Tübingen: Laupp.

*Schraut, Max von. (1883). *Die Organisation des Kredits.* Leipzig: Duncker & Humblot.

Schumpeter, Josef A. (1908). *Das Wesen und der Hauptinhalt der theoretischen Nationalökonomie,* Berlin: Duncker & Humblot.

*Schumpeter, Josef A. (1917). *Das Sozialprodukt und die Rechenpfennige.* Tübingen: Mohr.

*Schwarz, Otto. (1911). *Diskontpolitik: Gedanken über englischen, französische und deutsche Bank-, Kredit- und Goldpolitik.* Leipzig: Duncker & Humblot.

*Serra, Antonio. (1613). *Breve trattato delle cause che possono far abbondare li regni d'oro e argento dove non sono miniere. Con applicazione al Regno di Napoli.* Naples: Lazzaro Scoriggio.

*Seyd, Ernst. (1874). *Das Londoner Bank-, Check-, und Clearinghouse-System,* German edition by Otto Sjöström. Leipzig: Hartung.

*Siemens, G. (1883). *Die Lage des Chequewesens in Deutschland.* Berlin: Springer.

*Simmel, Georg. (1900). *Philosophie des Geldes.* Leipzig: Duncker & Humblot.

Sombart, Werner. (1913). *Krieg und Kapitalismus.* Munich and Leipzig: Duncker & Humblot.

*Sombart, Werner. (1916). *Der moderne Kapitalismus,* I-IV. Munich and Leipzig: Duncker & Humblot.

*Sonnenfels, Joseph von. (1767). *Grundsätze der Polizey, Handlung und Finanzwissenschaft.* Vienna: Kurzböck.

Steinberg, Julius. (1915). *Geld und Kredit im Kriege,* Bonn: Marcus & Weber.

*Struck, Emil. (1881). *Die Effektenbörse. Eine Vergleichung deutscher und englischer Zustände ('Staats- und sozialwissenschaftliche Forschungen',* ed. Gustav Schmoller, Vol. III, no. 3). Leipzig: Duncker & Humblot.

*Telschow, R. (1889). *Der Geschäftsverkehr mit der Reichsbank.* 2nd ed. Berlin: Dieckmann.

*Vega, Joseph de la. (1688). *Confusion de Confusiones,* Amsterdam (English ed.: *The Great Mirror of Folly*).

Vesanis, Sotirios. (1895). *Über das Verhältnis der Vermehrung der Zinskapitalinhaber und der Zinskapitalien.* Berlin: Puttkammer & Mühlbrecht.

*Vosberg. (1901). 'Die Katastrophe in unseren Aktienunternehmung und die Gesetzgebung über deren Reservefonds.' *Gegenwart,* p. 177 ff., Leipzig.

*Vuitry, Adolphe. (1885). *Le désordre des finances et les excès de la spéculation a la fin du règne de Louis XIV et au commencement du règne de Louis XV.* Paris: Lévy.

*Wachtel, Adolf. (1899). *Bank und Börsenverkehr.* Vienna: Manz'sche Verlag.

*Wagner, Adolf. (1899). *Finanzwissenschaft.* Leipzig: Winter.

*Wagner, Adolf. (1901). 'Bankbrüche und Bankkontrollen' *Deutsche Monatsschrift für das gesamte Leben der* Gegenwart. Berlin.

Wagner, Adolph D.H. (1912). *Finanzwissenscaft, Britische Besteuerung im19. Jahrhundert und bis zu Gegenwart 1815–1910.* Vol. 2(3), 2. ed. Leipzig: Winter.

Waltershausen, A. Sartorius, Freiherr von. (1907). *Kapitalanlage im Auslande.* Berlin: Georg Reimer.

*Weber, Adolph. (1902). *Depositenbanken und Spekulationsbanken. Ein Vergleich deutschen und englischen Bankwesens.* Leipzig: Duncker & Humblot.

Weber, Adolph. (1910). *Der Kampf zwischen Kapital und Arbeit.* Tübingen: Mohr.

*Weishut, Albert. (1898). *Der Effektenumsatz und die Börsengeschäfte,* 2nd ed. Leipzig: Breitenstein.

*Wirth, Max. (1870). *Handbuch des Bankwesens.* Cologne: Mont-Schanberg.

III) LITERATURE IN SCANDINAVIAN BEFORE 1918

*Aschehoug, Thorvald. (1903, 1905 and 1908). *Socialøkonomik, En videnskabelig fremstilling af det menneskelige samfunds økonomiske virksomhed*, I-III. Kristiania: Aschehoug & Co.

*Carey, Henry Charles. (1853 and 1855). *Grunderna af Nationalekonomien I & II*. Uppsala: Wahlstrøm & Co.

Einarsen, Einar. (1895). 'Begrebet "Kapital" i økonomien', Kristiania: Aschehoug (Supplement to: *Statsøkonomisk Tidsskrift*.

Einarsen, Einar. (1904). *Gode og daarlige tider: en undersøkelse med særligt hensyn til den økonomiske udvikling i Norge og Danmark i den sidste menneskealder*. Kristiania: Gyldendal.

Hertzberg, Ebbe. (1877). *Om kredittens begreb og væsen*. Kristiania: Malling.

*Hilferding, Rudolf. (1912). *Finanskapitalen*. Copenhagen: Rhodos, 1976. (Orig. title *Das Finanzkapital)*.

Lenin, Vladimir I. (1917). *Imperialismen* som kapitalismens høyeste stadium. Oslo: Elan 1969.

List, Friedrich. (1840). *Innförselsfrihet och skyddsförfattningar, betraktade från erfarenhetens och historiens synspunkt*. Stockholm: Norstedt & Söner.

List, Friedrich. (1840). *Om Vigten och Betydelsen af Sløjder och Manufakturer för et Samhälle*. Stockholm: Hörbergska Boktrykkeriet.

*List, Friedrich. (1888). *Det nationella nationalekonomiska systemet*. Stockholm: Carlson.

*Luxemburg, Rosa. (1913). *Kapitalens akkumulasjon*. Copenhagen: Rhodos, 1976. (Orig. title *Die Akkumulation des Kapitals*).

Scharling, Wilhelm. (1900). *Bankpolitik*. Copenhagen: Gad.

*Scharling, Wilhelm. (1907). *Samfundsproduktionen med særlig henblikk på dens historiske udvikling*, 2 vols., Copenhagen: Gad.

*Snellmans, Johan Vilhelm. (1894–1898). *Samlade Arbeten*, Vol. I-X, Helsingfors (Helsinki): Helsingfors Central-Tryckeri (especially vol. V-VI).

Wicksell, Knut. (1906). *Föreläsningar i nationalekonomi*, Lund: Berlingska Boktryckeriet.

Wulff, Nic. Hertel. (1912). *Penge. En populær fremstilling af pengenes tilblivelse og virken i nutidens samfund*. Copenhagen and Kristiania: Gyldendalske Boghandel Nordisk Forlag.

B) BETWEEN 1918 AND 1931 (1945): FINANCIAL CAPITALISM

II) LITERATURE IN ENGLISH, 1918–1945

Allen, Frederick Lewis. (1938). *The Lords of creation. The story of the great age of American finance*. London: Hamish Hamilton.

Anderson, Benjamin McAlester. (1919). *Effects of the war on money, credit, and banking in France and the United States*. New York: Oxford University Press.

*Atwood, Albert W. (1919). *The exchanges and speculation*. New York: Alexander Hamilton Institute. (Modern business, vol. 20).

Baruch, Bernard M. (1921). *American industry in the war, A Report of the War Industries Board*. New York: Prentice-Hall.

Bogart, Ernest L. (1921). *War costs and their financing*. New York: Appleton.

Brand, R.H. (1921). *War and International Finance*, London: Edward Arnold.

*Canadian Cooperative Wheat Producers. (1931). *Grain futures and speculation*. Winnipeg: Canadian Wheat Pool.

*Canney, Ernest E. (1930). *Monetary reform. What money scarcity means to you: its effects on industry, agriculture, trade, works and wages*. 2nd ed. Manchester: Canney.

*Chamberlain, Lawrence and Will Wren Hay. (1931). *Investment and speculation*. New York: Holt.

Clark, J. Maurice, Walton H. Hamilton, and Harold G. Moulton. (eds). (1918). *Readings in the economics of war*, Chicago: University of Chicago Press.

Cole, George D.H. (1935). *Economic planning.* New York: Knopf.

*Committee on Finance and Industry. (1931). *Minutes of evidence taken before the Committee on finance and industry.* London, 2 Vols.

Commons, John R. (1939). *Legal foundations of capitalism.* New York: Macmillan.

Corti, Egon Caesar. (1928). *The rise of the house of Rothschild.* New York: Cosmopolitan Book Corp. (Orig. title *Der Aufstieg des Hauses Rotschild, 1770-1830*).

Dalton, Hugh... [et al.]. (1934). *Unbalanced budgets: a study of the financial crisis in fifteen countries.* London: Routledge.

Dubois, Armand Budington. (1938). *The English business company after the Bubble act, 1720–1800.* New York: The Commonwealth Fund; London: Humphrey Milford, Oxford University Press.

Fisher, Irving. (1920). *Stabilizing the dollar: a plan to stabilize the general price level without fixing individual prices.* New York: Macmillan.

Fisher, Irving. (1920). *The purchasing power of money: its determination and relation to credit interest and crises.* New York: Macmillan.

*Fisher, Irving. (1928). *The money illusion & related writings.* London: Allen & Unwin.

Fisher, Irving. (1930). *The stock market crash – and after.* New York: Macmillan.

Fisher, Irving. (1933). *Inflation?* London: Allen & Unwin.

Fisher, Irving. (1933). *Booms and depressions.* London: Allen & Unwin.

*Fisher, Irving. (1934). *Mastering the crisis. With additional chapter on stamp scrip.* London: Allen & Unwin.

Fisher, Irving. (1935). *Stabilised money: a history of the movement.* London: Allen & Unwin.

Fisher, Irving. (1935). *100 % money. Designed to keep the checking banks 100% liquid; to prevent inflation and deflation; largely to cure or prevent depressions; and to wipe out much of the national debt.* New York: Adelphi.

*Fisher, Irving. (ed.). (1935). *The meaning of money, (Irving Fisher's world authorities on...),* Consumer Guild of America. New York: Empire Books.

Frisch, Ragnar. (1934). 'Circulation Planning.' *Econometrica*, pp. 258–336.

*Foxwell, Herbert Somerton. (1919). *Papers in Current Finance.* London: Macmillan.

*Gordon, Robert Aaron. (1952). *Business fluctuations.* New York: Harper & Brothers.

*Hauser, Henri. (1930). 'The European financial crisis of 1559'. *Journal of Economic and Business History,* Vol. 2 (1929-30), pp. 241-55.

*von Hayek , Frederick A. (1939). *Profits, interest and investments.* London: Routledge & Kegan Paul.

*von Hayek , Frederick A. (1933). *Monetary theory and the trade cycle.* London: Jonathan Cape.

*Hecht, John S. (1920). *The real wealth of nations or a new civilization and its economics foundations.* London: Harrap.

*Heckscher, Eli. (1933). 'Importance of the financial forces of a country for carrying on war. Possibility of Credits Abroad', in *What Would Be the Character of a New War?* Enquiry organized by the Inter-Parliamentary Union, Geneva and New York.

*Herzog, Peter W. (1928). *The Morris plan of industrial banking.* Chicago: Shaw.

Hicks, John. (1939). *Value and capital: an inquiry into some fundamental principles of economic theory.* Oxford: Clarendon Press.

Hobson, John A. (1918). *Richard Cobden: the international man.* London: J.M. Dent.

Hobson, John A. (1919). *Taxation in the new state.* London: Methuen.

Hobson, John A. (1926). *Free thought in the social sciences.* London: Allen & Unwin.

Hobson, John A. (1929). *Wealth and life.* London: Macmillan.

*Hobson, John A. (1938). *Confessions of an economic heretic,* with an introduction by M. Freeden. Brighton: Harvester Press.

Holmes, George J. (1930). *Investment and speculation in theory and practice.* London: Macmillan and Eyre & Spottiswoode.

House of Representatives. (1928). *Stabilization: hearings before the committee on banking and currency,* 17th congress, 1st session on H.R. 11806: (Superseding H.R. 7895, 69th congress): a bill to amend the act approved December 23, 1913, known as the Federal Reserve Act; to define certain policies toward which the powers of the Federal Reserve System shall be directed; to further promote the maintenance of a stable goldstandard; to promote the stability of commerce, industry, agriculture, and employment; to assist in realizing a more stable purchasing power of the dollar; and for other purposes. Washington: United States Government Printing Office.

*Inouye, Junnosuke. (1927). *The financial crisis in Japan*. Honolulu, Prelim. paper prepared for 2nd General session of the Institute of Pacific Relations.

Josephson, Matthew. (1934). *The Robber Barons*. New York: Hartcourt, Brace and Co.

Kempster, John W. (1932). *Banking, credit, and the crisis*. London: London General Press.

*Keynes, John M. (1923). *A tract on monetary reform*. London: MacMillan.

Keynes, John M. (1926). *The end of Laissez-Faire*. London: Leonard & Virginia Woolf.

*Keynes, John M. (1930). *A treatise on money*, 2 Vols. London: MacMillan.

Keynes, John M. (1933). *The means to prosperity*. London: Macmillan.

Keynes, John M. (1939). 'The income and fiscal potential of Great Britain'. *Economic Journal*, vol. 49, no. 196, pp. 626-39.

Keynes, John M. (1940). *How to pay for the war*. New York: Macmillan.

*Kindleberger, Charles Poor. (1937). *International short-term capital movements*. New York: Columbia University Press.

*Kirkaldy, Adam W. (1917). *Industry and finance: war expedients and reconstruction, being the results of enquiries arranged by the section of economic science and statistics of the british association during the years 1916 and 1917*. London: Pitman & Sons.

*Knight, Frank. (1921). *Risk, uncertainty and profit, thesis*. Boston: Houghton Mifflin.

**Labour Research*, (1929, 1937–1939). London (magazine).

*Laughlin, J. Laurence. (1919). *Credit of the nations: a study of the European war*. New York: Scribner's Sons.

*Levy, Hermann. (1936). *The new industrial system: a study of the origin, forms, finance, and prospects of concentration in industry*. London: Routledge.

*Martin, H.S. (1919). *The New York stock exchange: a discussion of the business done: its relation to other business, to investment, speculation and gambling: the safequards provided by the exchange and the means taken to improve the character of speculation*. New York: Fitch.

*McGrane, Reginald. (1924). *The panic of 1837: Some financial problems of the Jacksonian era*. Chicago: University of Chicago Press.

*McVey, Frank L. (1918). *The financial history of Great Britain 1914-1918*. New York: Oxford University Press.

Melville, Lewis. (1921). *The South Sea bubble*. London: O'Connor.

Mendershausen, Horst. (1940). *The economics of war*. New York: Prentice-Hall.

Michelson, Alexander, Paul Apostol and Michael Bernatzky. (1928). *Russian public finance during the war*. New Haven: Yale University Press; London: Milford, Oxford University Press. ('Bevat: revenue and expenditure' by Alexander M. Michelson, with introd. by V.N. Kokovzov, 'Credit operations' by Paul Apostol, 'Monetary policy' by Michael W. Bernatzky).

Miller, Margaret S. (1926). *The economic development of Russia, 1905–1914: with special reference to trade, industry, and finance*. London: Routledge.

Mises, Ludvig von. (1929). 'Verstaatlichung des Kredits?' *Zeitschrift für Nationalökonomie*, vol. I, no. 3, pp. 430–439.

*Mitchell, Wesley Clair. (1927). *Business cycles, the problem and its setting*. Cambridge, MA: National Bureau of Economic Research.

Moon, Parker Th. (ed.). (1930). *Business, speculation, and money*: a series of addresses and papers presented at the annual meeting of the Academy of political science, November 22, 1929. New York (*Proceedings of the Academy of Political Science, Columbia University, New York*, vol. 13, no. 4).

Moon, Parker Th. (ed.). (1932). *The crisis in world finance and trade*: a series of addresses and papers presented at the semi-annual meeting of the Academy of Political Science, April 13, 1932, New York (*Proceedings of the Academy of Political Science*, vol. XV, no. 1).

*Moore, Henry L. (1923). *Generating economic cycles*. New York: Macmillan.

*Mottram, Ralph H. (1929). *A history of financial speculation*. London: Chatto & Windus.

*Nadler, Marcus and Jules I. Bogen. (1934). *The banking crisis*. London: Allen & Unwin.

Nurkse, Ragnar. (1933). *The problem of capital formation in underdeveloped countries*. New York and Oxford: Blackwell.

O'Reilly, G.A. (1918). *The relation of industrial chemistry to banking*. New York: Irving National Bank. (Vol. 2, no. 3).

*Oudard, Georges. (1928). *The amazing life of John Law, the man behind the Mississippi bubble*. New York: Payson & Clarke.

*Owens, Richard N. and Charles O. Hardy. (1925). *Interest rates and stock speculation: a study of the influence of the money market on the stock market*. London: Macmillan.

Parker, William. (1920). *The Paris Bourse and French finance: with reference to organized speculation in New York*. New York: Longmans, Green.

*Peel, George. (1925). *The financial crisis of France*. London: Macmillan.

Pigou, Arthur C. (1920). *The economics of welfare*. London: Macmillan.

Pigou, Arthur C. (1920). *A capital levy and a levy on war wealth*. London: Humphrey Milford.

Pigou, Arthur C. (1921). *The political economy of war*. London: Macmillan.

Pigou, Arthur C. (1927). *Industrial fluctuations*. London: Macmillan.

Pigou, Arthur C. (1929). *A study in public finance*. London: Macmillan.

Pigou, Arthur C. (1933). *The theory of unemployment*. London: Frank Cass.

Pigou, Arthur C. (1937). *Socialism versus capitalism*. London: Macmillan.

Pigou, Arthur C. (1945). *Lapses from full employment*. London: Macmillan.

*Robbins, Lionel. (1939). *The economic causes of war*. London: Jonathan Cape.

Ross, James A.R. (1938). *Speculation, stock prices and industrial fluctuations: a study of the effects of stock speculation on stock price movements and the influence of these movements on production and business*. New York: Ronald Press.

Rostow, Walt W. (1941). 'Business cycles, harvests, and politics.' *Economic History Review*, vol. 1, no. 16, pp. 206–221.

Rowe, Leo S. (1918). *Early effects of the European War upon the finance, commerce, and industry of Chile*. New York: Oxford University Press.

Rowe, Leo S. (1920). *Early effects of the war upon the finance, commerce, and industry of Peru*. New York: Oxford University Press.

Saulnier, Raymond J. (1940). *Industrial banking companies and their credit practices*. New York: National Bureau of Economic Research.

*Schumpeter, Joseph Alois. (1934) *The theory of economic development. An inquiry into profits, capital, credit, interest, and the business cycle*. Cambridge, MA: Harvard University Press.

Schumpeter, Joseph Alois. (1942). *Capitalism, socialism, and democracy*. London: Harper & Brothers.

*Shortt, Adam. (1918). *Early economic effects of the European war upon Canada*. New York: Oxford University Press.

*Smith, Vera C. (1936). *The rationale of central banking and the free banking alternative*. London: King.

Sakolski, Aaron M. (1932). *The great American land bubble: the amazing story of land-grabbing, speculations, and booms from colonial days to the present time*. New York: Harper.

Staley, Eugene. (1935). *War and the private investor*. Chicago: Chicago University Press.

Taussig, Frank W. (1911/1939). *Principles of economics*. 2 vols. New York: Macmillan.

Thomas, S. Evelyn. (1931). *British banks and the finance of industry*. London: King.

Viner, Jacob. (1920). 'Who paid for the war?' *Journal of Political Economy*, vol. 28, no. 1, pp. 46-76.

*Wade, Arthur S. (1926). *Modern finance and industry: a plain account of the British financial systems and of its functions in relation to industry and commerce*. London: Pitman & Sons.

Wagemann, Ernst. (1930). *Economic rhythm: a theory of business cycles*. New York: McGraw-Hill.

III) LITERATURE IN CONTINENTAL LANGUAGES, 1918–1945

Aboul-Ela, Hanafi. (1930). *La spéculation en Bourse: son influence économique et morale.* Dissertation Paris. Paris: les Presses universitaires de France.

*Backes, Gert. (1940). *La spéculation financière: essai sur sa nature, ses abus et sa réglementation par l'État.* Dissertation Geneva, Lugano.

Bark, Georg R. (1930). *Boden als Geld: ein Beitrag zur Geschichte des Papiergeldes.* Berlin: Emil Ebering.

*Beckert, Werner. (1935). *Banknoten-Monopol und Kredit-Krise: (ist die Monopolstellung der Reichsbank für den Zusammenbruch des deutschen Kreditapparates mitverantwortlich zu machen?).* Dissertation Munich. Ochsenfurt am Main: Fritz & Rappert.

Bonn, M.J. (1927). *Geld und Geist: vom Wesen und Werden der amerikanischen Welt.* Berlin: Fischer.

Boven, Pierre. (1924). *Le prix normal: essai sur la lutte contre les crises économiques et la spéculation illicite.* Paris: Payot.

*Capdeville, Robert. (1920). *L'accaparement et la spéculation illicite.* Bordeaux: Imprimerie de l'Université.

*Cazes, Daniel. ((1919). *Le délit de spéculation illicite.* (Art. 10 de la loi du 20 avril 1916). Lille: Robbe.

Eheberg, Karl Theodor von. (1926). *Grundriss der Finanzwissenschaft.* Leipzig: Deichart.

*Elster, Karl. (1920). *Die Seele des Geldes.* Jena: Fischer.

*Eucken, Walter. (1940). *Die Grundlagen der Nationalökonomie.* Jena: Fischer.

Gotthelf, Jeremias (Bitzius, Albert). (1941). *Geld und Geist. – Der Geltstag.* Naunhof: Hendel. (Grosse deutsche Ausgabe, ed. Hans Loewe, 9).

Hahn, L. Albert. (1924). *Geld und Kredit: gesammelte Aufsätze,* I-II. Tübingen: Mohr.

Hahn, L. Albert. (1931). Kredit und Krise: ein Vortrag über Aufgaben und Grenzen der Monetären Konjunkturpolitik. Tübingen: Mohr.

*Halm, Georg. (1935). *Geld – Kredit – Banken.* Munich: Duncker & Humblot.

Heymann, Hans. (1921). *Die Welt-Kredit- und – Finanzreform: ein Aufruf zum Solidarismus.* Berlin: Rowohlt.

Honegger, Hans. (1929). *Der schöpferische Kredit.* Jena: Fischer.

*Jastrow, J. (1919). *Geld und Kredit.* Berlin: de Gruyter.

*Köppel, Wilhelm and Hans Paschke. (1923). *Devisennotverordnung: Verordnung gegen die Spekulation in ausländischen Zahlungsmittels vom 12. Oktober 1922.* Berlin: Spaeth & Linde.

*Lautenbach, Wilhelm. (1937). *Über Kredit und Produktion.* Frankfurt am Main: Societäts-Verlag.

*Leiskow, Hanns. (1930). *Spekulation und öffentliche Meinung in der ersten Hälfte des 19. Jahrhunderts.* Jena: Fischer.

*Lewinsohn, Richard and Franz Pick. (1933). *La bourse: les diverses formes de la spéculation dans les grandes bourses mondiales.* Paris: Payot.

*Marmion, Jean. (1925). *Étude sur le projet de loi relatif a la spéculation illicite vote par la Chambre des deputés le 15 mars 1924.* Dissertation Paris. Paris: Jouve.

*Martin, Charles. (1922). *La spéculation illicite sur les denrées et marchandises: législation, jurisprudence, réformes en préparation.* Dissertation Dijon. Dijon: Berthier .

*Mary, Jules. (1923). *Étude juridique du délit de spéculation illicite sur denrées et marchandises et de la réforme des articles 419-420 du Code penal.* Toulouse Dissertation. Poitiers: Societé Francaise d'Imprimerie.

*Maurice, Xavier. (1922). *La spéculation sur les loyers.* Dissertation Paris. Paris: Tenin.

*Mises, Ludvig von. (1929). 'Verstaatlichung des Kredits?' *Zeitschrift für Nationalökonomie,* vol. I, no. 3, pp. 430–439.

*Nonaka, Tetsuya and Hans Müller. (1925). *Vom Wesen und Wert des Geldes: die psychische Natur des Geldes und der Einfluss der Spekulation auf seinen Wert. Berlin: Eberin.*

Obst, Georg. (1921). *Das Bankgeschäft,* 1.Band*: Verkehrstechnik und Betriebseinrichtungen,* 2. Band: *Bankpolitik,* 1st ed. 1914. Stuttgart: Carl Ernst Pöschel Verlag.

Ortega y Gasset, José. (1942). *Das Wesen geschichtlicher Krisen.* Stuttgart: Deutsche Verlags-Anstalt.

Owesny, Hans. (1924). *Geld und Geldwesen der Geld- (Kredit-) Wirtschaft.* Leipzig: Drugulin.

*Päch, Georg. (1931). *Kreislauf: Konjunktur und Kredit.* Berlin: Spaeth & Linde.

Pella, Vespasien V. (1920). Le délit de spéculation illicite, avec preface de Alfred Le Poittevin. Paris: Sagot & Cie.

Priester, Hans Erich. (1936). *Das deutsche Wirtschaftwunder.* Amsterdam: Querido.

Prion, Willi. (1938). *Das deutsche Finanzwunder. Die Geldbeschaffung für den deutschen Wirtschaftaufschwung,* Berlin-Wilmersdorf: Franke & Co.

Rathenau, Walter. (1922). Schriften und Reden, Auswahl und Nachwort von Hans Werner Richter. Frankfurt am Main: Fischer Verlag, 1964, in particular p. 398: Produktionspolitik.

Röpke, Wilhelm. (1937). *Die Lehre von der Wirtschaft.* Vienna: Springer.

*Royal Treasury. (1931). *Report committee on finance and industry, presented to Parliament by the financial secretary to the Treasury by command of His Majesty, June, 1931.* (The Macmillan Report) London: His Majesty's Stationary Office.

Schmölders, Günter. (1938). *Geld und Kredit: Probleme der Wirtschaftspolitik.* Leipzig: Bibliographisches Institut.

*Schmoller, Gustav. (1923). *Grundriss der Allgemeinen Volkswirtschaftslehre,* I-II. Berlin: Duncker & Humblot.

*Schreiber, Hans. (ed.). (1910). *Wie schützt sich der Kapitalist vor Verlusten an der Börse?: ein unentbehrlicher Ratgeber für Kapitalanlage und Spekulation.* Berlin: Patria.

Schumpeter, Josef A. (1929). *Das Wesen des Geldes.* Göttingen: Vandenhoeck & Ruprecht, 1970.

*Schwenk, Ernst. (1937). *Kredit-, Lohn- und Investitionskontrolle: ein Beitrag zur Konjunkturpolitik.* Dissertation Tübingen. Tübingen: Becht.

Terhalle, Fritz. (1936). *Leitfaden der deutschen Finanzpolitik.* Munich and Leipzig: Duncker & Humblot.

Tinbergen, Jan. (1934). 'Der Einfluss der Kaufskraftsregulierung auf den Konjunkturverlauf.' *Zeitschrift für Nationalökonomie,* Vol. 5 (3), pp. 289-319.

*Wagemann, Ernst. (1940). *Wo kommt das viele Geld her? Geldschöpfung und Finanzlenkung in Krieg und Frieden.* Düsseldorf: Völkischer Verlag.

*Wasserman, Max J. (1925). *L'oeuvre de la Federal Trade Commission: la dernière phase de la législation américaine contre les trusts, la spéculation illicite et les pratiques commerciales déloyales,* avec une préface de Edouard Lambert. Paris: Giard.

Weber, Adolf. (1929). *Ende des Kapitalismus. Die Notwendigkeit freier Erwerbswirtschaft.* Munich: Max Hueber Verlag.

Weber, Adolf. (1939). *Geld, Banken, Börsen.* Munich: Richard Pflaum Verlag.

Weber, Adolf. (1947). *Die neue Weltwirtschaft.* Munich: Richard Pflaum Verlag.

Wiriath, Marcel. (1924). *La spéculation et les troubles monetaires.* Paris: Les presses universitaires de France.

IV) LITERATURE IN SCANDINAVIAN, 1918–1945

Aakerman, Johan. (1928). *Om det ekonomiska livets rytmik.* Stockholm: Nordiska Bokhandeln.

Aarum, Thorvald. (1918). *Penge, kredit og priser. En utredning om aarsakene til pengeverdiens fald.* Kristiania: Aschehoug.

*Aarum, Thorvald. (1924 and 1928). *Læren om samfundets økonomi,* I-II, Bind I, *Teoretisk Socialøkonomik,* Kristiania: Det Mallingske Bogtrykkeri 1924 og Bind II, *Næringspolitik og socialpolitik.* Oslo: Norli.

Bauer, Fritz. (1944). *Pengar, igår, idag och imorgon.* Stockholm: Natur och Kultur.

*Brøgger, Kristian Fredrik. (1926–1928). *Kredittlivets utvikling og nutidens forretningsbanker,* I-II. Oslo: Aschehoug.

Brøgger, Kristian Fredrik. (1928). *Realkredittens organisasjon. En orientering i anledning av det nye hypotekinstitutt for næringslivet.* Oslo: Aschehoug.

Brøgger, Kristian Fredrik. (1930). Aktiespekulasjon. Børs og samfundsliv i Rom for 2000 år siden. Oslo: Aschehoug.

Brøgger, Kristian Fredrik. (1932). *Gullfeber. En advokats opptegnelser fra siste jobbetid.* Oslo: Aschehoug.

Brøgger, Kristian Fredrik. (1938). *Når aksjespekulasjonen raser i samfundet.* Oslo: Aschehoug.

Brøgger, Kristian Fredrik. (1941). *Romerske Finansbaroner og kurtisaner på Ciceros tid.* Oslo: Jacob Dybwad

Brøgger, Kristian Fredrik. (1942). *Pengefyrsten.* Oslo: Nasjonalforlaget.

Frisch, Ragnar. (1932). *Statens plikt til circulasjonsregulering* (Written in a hurry, December 10-12, 1932), Memorandum from the Department of Economics, University of Oslo, January 11,1951.

Frisch, Ragnar. (1933). *Sparing og cirkulasjonsregulering.* Oslo: Fabritius & Sønner.

Hoffstad, Einar. (1928). *Det norske privatbankvesens historie.* Oslo: Forretningliv.

*Keilhau, Wilhelm. (1933). *Overgang til ny pengeenhet: rettsøkonomisk utredning utarbeidet efter oppdrag av pengekomiteen.* Oslo: Aschehoug.

Nielsen, Axel. (1930). *Bankpolitik.* Copenhagen: Hagerup.

Ræstad, Arnold. (1934). *Penger, valuta og gull.* Oslo: Aschehoug.

Schønheyder, Kristian. (1927). 'Productionscyklerne og kriserne.' *Statsøkonomisk Tidskrift,* 1/1927, pp. 57-116.

Sinding, Thomas. (1935). *Socialøkonomisk teori.* Oslo: Tanum.

Sinding, Thomas. (1938). *Pengevesen og konjunktur.* Oslo: Tanum.

Vogt, Johan. (1937). *Dogmenes sammenbrudd innenfor den socialøkonomiske vitenskap.* Oslo: Aschehoug.

C) BETWEEN (1931) 1945 AND (1971) 1982: INDUSTRIAL CAPITALISM (BRETTON WOODS)

I) LITERATURE IN ENGLISH, 1945–1982

Aliber, Robert. (1969). *Choices for the Dollar.* Washington, DC: National Planning Association.

Andvig, Jens Christopher. (1980). *Ragnar Frisch and monetary reform movements in the thirties.* Memorandum. Oslo: University of Oslo, Institute of Economics.

Arai, Masao. (1958). *Development of local banking in Japan: period of development of industrial capitalism.* Tokyo: [Government Printing Bureau].

Argy, Victor. (1981). *The postwar international money crisis. An analysis.* London: Allen & Unwin.

Artis, Michael (1978). 'Monetary policy: part II.' In *British Economic Policy 1960–1974,* ed. F.T. Blackaby, Cambridge: Cambridge University Press.

*Aubrey, Henry G. (1964). *The Dollar in world affairs. An essay in international financial policy.* Published for the Council on Foreign Relations. New York and Evanston: Harper & Row.

Aubrey, Henry G. (1969). 'Behind the veil of international money.' In *Essays in international finance,* No. 71, January 1969. Princeton: Princeton University Press.

Balassa, Bela. (1980). *The process of industrial development and alternative development strategies.* Washington DC: World Bank.

Baran, Paul A. (1957). *The political economy of growth.* New York: Monthly Review Press.

Barker, Bernard. (1979). *The great crash: America 1920–1923.* Oxford: Blackwell.

Basu, Saroj Kumar. (1961). *Industrial finance in India: a study in investment banking and state-aid to industry with special reference to India,* 4th rev. ed. Calcutta: University of Calcutta. .

Becklake, J.T. (1963). *From real to rand: the story of money, medals, and mints in South Africa.* Johannesburg: Central News Agency.

Bennett, Edward W. (1962). *Germany and the diplomacy of the* financial crisis, 1931. Cambridge, MA: Harvard University Press.

Bloomfield, Arthur I. (1963). *Short-term capital movements under the pre-1914 gold standard.* Princeton, NJ: Princeton University.

Borer, Mary Cathcart. (1977). *The city of London. A history.* London: Constable.

Born, Karl Erich. (1977). *International banking in the nineteenth and twentieth centuries.* Warwickshire: Berg Publisher, 1983. (Orig. title *Geld und Banken im 19. und 20. Jahrhundert.* Stuttgart: Kröner, 1977).

Boyle, Andrew. (1967). *Montague Norman.* London: Cassell.

Brooke, Christopher N.L. (1975). *History of London: London 800-1216: the shaping of a city.* Berkeley: University of California Press.

Cairncross, Frances and Hamish McRae. (1975). *The second great crash: how the oil crisis could destroy the world's economy.* London: Methuen

Calleo, David P. (ed.) with Harold van B. Cleveland, Charles P. Kindleberger and Lewis E. Lehrman. (1976). *Money and the coming world order.* New York: New York University Press.

Carswell, John. (1960). *The South Sea Bubble.* London: Cresset Press.

Clay, Sir Henry. (1957). *Lord Norman.* London: Macmillan.

Commerce and Industry Department of the Hong Kong Government. (1964–1965). *Commerce, industry and finance directory: an official guide and directory, Hong Kong/* publ. by the Commerce and Industry Department of the Hong Kong Government. 1964 – 1965. Hong Kong: Commerce and Industry Department, Hong Kong Government, Also: CIF directory of Hong Kong.

Commission on Money and Credit. (1962). *The commercial banking industry: a monograph prepared for the commission on money and credit.* Englewood Cliffs, NJ: Prentice-Hall.

Commission on Money and Credit. (1964). *Private capital markets, a series prepared for the Commission on Money and Credit,* by Irwin Friend, Hyman P. Minsky, and Victor L. Andrews. Englewood Cliffs, NJ: Prentice-Hall.

Coombs, Charles A. (1976). *The Arena of international finance.* New York: Wiley Interscience.

Cowing, Cedric B. (1965). *Populists, plungers, and progressives: a social history of stock and commodity speculation, 1890–1936.* Princeton: Princeton University Press.

Cowles, Virginia. (1960). *The great swindle: the story of the South Sea Bubble.* London: Collins.

Crowther, Geoffrey. (1945). *An outline of money.* London: Thomas Nelson.

Day, Alan C. L. (1959). *The economics of money.* London: Oxford University Press.

Deane, Roderick S. (1972). *Papers on monetary policy, credit creation, economic objectives, and the Reserve Bank.* Wellington: Wellington Reserve Bank of New Zealand.

De Cecco, Marcello. (1974). Money and empire: the international gold standard, 1890–*1914.* Oxford: Blackwell.

Dent, Julian. (1973). *Crisis in finance: crown, financiers, and society in seventeenth-century France.* Newton Abbot: David & Charles.

Dines, James. (1975). *The invisible crash: what it is, why it happened, how to protect yourself against it.* New York: Random House.

Dobb, Maurice. (1963). *Studies in the development of capitalism.* London: Routledge & Kegan Paul.

*Dorfman, Joseph. (1959). *The economic mind in American civilization.* New York: Viking Press.

Egom, P. Alex. (1977). *Money in the theory of international economic activity: an inquiry into the nature and causes of the wealth and poverty of nations.* Nordborg [Egen Kirkevej 6]: Adioné Inc.

Enthoven, Adolf J.H. (ed.) (1980). *Accounting and auditing for industrial development banking in the 1980's*: results of a seminar on accounting at the Global symposium on development banking in the 1980's, organized by the UNIDO and the World Bank. Dallas: University of Texas, Center for International Accounting Department.

Erdman, Paul E. (1976). *The crash of '79.* New York: Simon and Schuster.

*Eucken, Walter. (1950). *The foundations of economics: history and theory in the analysis of economic reality.* Berlin and New York: Springer.

*Fenstermaker, Joseph van. (1965). *The development of American commercial banking, 1782–1837.* Kent, OH: Kent State University.

Floyd, John E. and J. Allan Hynes. (1972). *The contribution of real money balances to the level of wealth.* Toronto: University of Toronto. From *Journal of Money, Credit and Banking,* 4 (May 1972), pp. 260–271.

Frisch, Ragnar. (1967). 'A multilateral clearing agency'. *Economics of Planning*, vol. 7, no. 2, pp. 97-105.

Furness, Eric L. (1975). *Money and credit in developing Africa.* London and Nairobi: Heinemann Educational Books.

*Galbraith, John Kenneth. (1954). *The great crash of 1929.* Boston: Houghton Mifflin.

Galbraith, John Kenneth. (1975). *Money. Whence it came. Where it went.* Boston: Houghton Mifflin.

Galbraith, John Kenneth. (1977). *The age of uncertainty.* London: Jolly & Barber.

*Galbraith, John Kenneth. (1980). *The crash and the coming crisis.* Plymouth: Northcote House.

Gasparian, Fernando and Ingo Walter. (1970). *Excess industrial capacity and supplementary economic assistance for developing countries.* New York: New York University, Center for International Studies.

Goldberg, Lawrence G. and Lawrence J. White. (eds). (1979). *The deregulation of the banking and securities industries,* Papers presented at a conference. Lexington MA: Lexington Books.

Gordon, Robert Aaron. (1974). *Economic instability and growth: the American record.* New York: Harper and Row.

Grampp, William D. (1965). *Economic liberalism,* vol. I, *The Beginnings,* vol. II, *The classical view.* New York: Random House.

Grampp, William D. and Emanuel T. Weiler (eds). (1953). *Economic policy, readings in political economy.* Homewood, IL: Richard D. Irwin, Inc.

Grubel, Herbert G. (1966). *Forward exchange, speculation, and the international flow of capital.* Stanford: Stanford University Press.

Haavelmo, Trygve. (1960). *A study in the theory of investment.* Chicago: The University of Chicago Press.

Haberler, Gottfried. (1946). *Prosperity and depression. A theoretical analysis of cyclical movements.* 3rd ed. Lake Success: United Nations. (Orig. 1937, Geneva: League of Nations.)

*Hammer, Frederick S. (1964). *The demand for physical capital: application of a wealth model.* Englewood Cliffs, NJ: Prentice-Hall.

Harris, Laurence. (1981). *Monetary theory.* New York: McGraw-Hill.

*Harrod, Roy. (1965). *Reforming the world's money.* London: Macmillan.

Hawkins, Robert G. and Ingo Walter. (1972). *The United States and international markets; commercial policy options in an age of controls.* Lexington: Lexington Books.

Haxey, Simon. (1939). *Tory M.P.* London: Victor Gollancz.

von Hayek , Frederick A. (1952) *The counter-revolution of science. Studies on the abuse of reason.* Indianapolis: The Free Press.

von Hayek , Frederick A. (1960). *The constitution of liberty.* London: Routledge.

*von Hayek , Frederick A. (1976). *Denationalisation of money. – the argument refined.* London: The Institute of Economic Affairs.

Hayter, Teresa. (1971). *Aid as imperialism.* Harmondsworth: Penguin.

Heilbroner, Robert L. (1976). *Business civilization in decline.* London: Marion Boyers.

Heilbroner, Robert L. (1978). *Beyond boom and crash.* New York: Norton.

Henderson, Ronald F. (1951). *The new issue market and the finance of industry.* With a foreword by Henry Clay. Cambridge: Bowes & Bowes.

Hicks, John. (1965). *Capital and growth.* Oxford: Clarendon Press.

Hicks, John. (1967). *Critical essays in monetary theory.* Oxford: Clarendon Press.

*Hicks, John. (1969). *A theory of economic history.* Oxford: Oxford University Press.

Hirsch, Fred. (1967). *Money international.* London: Allen Lane and the Penguin Press.

Hirst, Francis W. (1948). *The stock exchange: a short study of investment and speculation,* 4th ed. London: Oxford University Press.

Hoff, Trygve J.B. (1949). *Economic calculation in the socialist society.* London: Hodge and Co. (Orig. title *Økonomisk kalkulasjon i socialistiske samfund,* Oslo: Aschehoug, 1938).

*Hudson, Michael. (1968). *Super imperialism. The economic strategy of American Empire.* New York: Holt, Rhinehart and Winston.

Huff, Charles and Barbara Marinacci. (1980). *Commodity speculation for beginners: a guide to the futures market.* New York: Macmillan, London: Collier Macmillan.

International Monetary Fund. (1981). *International capital markets: recent developments and short-term prospects, 1981,* by a staff team headed by Richard C. Williams with G.G. Johnson and including Ulrich Baumgartner... [et al.]. Washington: I.M.F.

Jensen, Finn B. and Ingo Walter. (1965). *The common market; economic integration in Europe.* Philadelphia: Lippincott.

Johnson, Harry G. (1967). *Nationalism in old and new states.* Chicago: Chicago University Press.

Katz, Samuel I. (1961). *Sterling speculation and* European convertibility, 1955–*1958.* Princeton: Princeton University, Department of Economics, International Finance Section.

*Keilhau, Wilhelm. (1951). *Principles of private and public planning. A study in economic sociology.* London: Allen & Unwin.

Kennedy, Susan Estabrook. (1973). *The banking crisis of 1933.* Lexington: University Press of Kentucky.

Kent, Richard J. (1980). 'Credit rationing and the home mortgage market'. *Journal of Money, Credit and Banking,* vol. 12, pp. 488–501.

Kidwell, David S. and Richard L. Peterson. (1981). *Financial institutions, markets and money,* Hinsdale: Dryden Press.

*Kindleberger, Charles P. (1950). *The dollar shortage.* Boston: MIT Technology Press.

Kindleberger, Charles P. (1963). *Foreign trade and the national economy.* New Haven: Yale University Press.

Kindleberger, Charles P. (1966). *Europe and the dollar.* Cambridge, MA: The MIT Press.

Kindleberger, Charles P. (1967). *The politics of international money and world language.* Princeton: Princeton University Press.

Kindleberger, Charles P. (1969). *American business at home.* New Haven: Yale University Press.

*Kindleberger, Charles P. (1970). *Power and money: the economics of international politics and the politics of international economics.* London: Macmillan.

Kindleberger, Charles P. (1974). *The formation of financial centers: a study in comparative economic history.* Princeton: Princeton University, International Finance Section.

Kindleberger, Charles P. (1974). *Keynesianism vs. monetarism and other essays in financial history.* London: Allen & Unwin.

*Kindleberger, Charles P. (1978). *Manias, panics and crashes: a history of financial crises.* New York: Basic Books.

Knudsen, Odin and Andrew Parnes. (1975). *Trade instability and economic development: an empirical study.* Lexington: Lexington Books.

Koss, Stephen E. (1970). *Sir John Brunner. Radical Plutocrat.* Cambridge: Cambridge University Press.

Kouwenhouven, John A. (1969). *Partners in banking ... brown brothers Harriman.* Garden City: Doubleday & Co.

Labys, Walter C. and Clive W.J. Granger. (1970). *Speculation, hedging, and commodity price forecasts.* Lexington: Heath Lexington Books.

Laffer, Arthur B. (1975). *Private short-term capital flows.* New York: M. Dekker.

Levien, J.R. (1966). *Anatomy of a crash, 1929.* New York: Traders Press.

Lindholm, Richard W. (1949). *Public finance of air transportation: a study of taxation and public expenditures in relation to a developing industry,* Columbus, OH: Ohio State University.

Lundberg, Ferdinand. (1969). *The rich and the super-rich. A study of the power of money today.* London: Nelson.

Lyle, Robert. (1976). *Real money.* Garden City, NJ: Anchor Books.

*Machlup, Fritz. (1964). *International payments, debts and gold.* New York: Scribner.

Mayer, Helmut. (1979). *Credit and liquidity creation in the international banking sector.* Basel: Bank for International Settlements.
Mayer, Martin. (1959). *Wall Street: the inside story of American Finance.* London: The Bodley Head.
Mayer, Martin. (1974). *The bankers.* New York: Weybright and Talley.
Mayer, Martin. (1980). *The fate of the dollar.* New York: Times Books, A Truman Tally Book.
Meeks, Gay. (1979). *Public money in private industry*, prepared for the [Open University, D323] Course Team by Gay and Geoff Meeks. Milton Keynes: Open University Press. With answers. Social sciences, a third level course: political economy and taxation.
*Mendelsohn, Stefan. (1980). *Money on the move: the modern international capital market.* New York: McGraw-Hill.
Minsky, Hyman P. (1965). *Poverty: the aggregate demand solution and other non-welfare approaches.* Los Angeles: University of California, Institute of Government and Public Affairs.
Minsky, Hyman P. (1975). *John Maynard Keynes.* New York: Columbia University Press.
*Minsky, Hyman P. (1978). *The financial instability hypothesis: a restatement.* London: Thames Polytechnic.
*Mises, Ludvig von. (1947). 'We must control credit', in a symposium on 'Can an economic depression be avoided?' *New York Times* (Sunday Magazine), pp. 7 and 71–75. April 13.
Mises, Ludvig von. (1953). 'Gold vs. paper.' *The Freeman*, vol. 3, no. 21, pp. 744–746. July 13.
Moggridge, Donald E. (1971). *The 1931 financial crisis – a new view.* Cambridge (Reprint series/ University of Cambridge. Department of Applied Economics, 327). From: the banker, August 1970.
*Morgenthau, Hans J. (1948). *Politics among nations.* New York: Knopf.
Morton, Frederic. (1961). *The Rothschilds. A family portrait.* London: Curtis Publ. Co.
Murdock, Steve H. and F. Larry Leistritz. (1988). *The farm financial crisis: socioeconomic dimensions and implications for producers and rural areas.* Boulder, CO: Westview Press.
*Murray, Alex. (1986). *Great financial disasters.* London: Weidenfeld & Nicolson.
*Newlyn, Walter T. (1967). *Money in an African context.* Oxford: Oxford University Press.
Newlyn, Walter T. (1968). *Finance for development: a study of sources of finance in Uganda with particular reference to credit creation.* Nairobi: East African Publishing House.
*Newlyn, Walter T. (1971). *Theory of money.* Oxford: Clarendon Press.
Newman, Peter C. (1978). *Bronfman Dynasty, The Rothschilds of the New World*, Toronto: McClelland and Stewart.
Norton, Michael. (ed.). (1981). *Raising money from industry.* London: Directory of Social Change.
Nurkse, Ragnar. (1959). *Patterns of trade and development.* Stockholm: Wicksell.
Oliver, Robert W. (1975). *International economic cooperation and the World Bank.* London: Macmillan.
Ostas, James R. and Frank Zahn. (1975). 'Interest and non-interest credit rationing in the mortgage market'. *Journal of Monetary Economics*, vol. 1, no. 2, pp. 187–201.
Owen, Roderic. (1957). *The golden bubble: Arabian Gulf documentary.* London: Collins.
Pesek, Boris P. and Thomas R. Saving. (1967). *Money, wealth, and economic theory.* New York: Macmillan; London: Collier-Macmillan.
*Pigou, Arthur C. (1949). *The veil of money.* London: Macmillan.
*Pilkington, Alastair. (1981). *Industry: men, money, and management.* London: Heinemann Educational Books.
Pool, James E. III and Suzanne Pool. (1978). *Who financed Hitler. The secret funding of Hitler's rise to power, 1919–1933.* London: Futura.
Prasad, Bisheshwar (ed.), Nirmal C. Sinha and Pran N. Khera. (1962). *Indian war economy: (supply, industry and finance).* (Official history of the Indian armed forces in the Second World War 1939–1945). Bombay: Orient Longmans.
Pressnell, Leslie S. (1956). *Country banking in the industrial revolution.* New York: Oxford University Press.
*Quigley, Carroll. (1966). *Tragedy and hope, a history of the world in our time.* New York: Macmillian.

Quigley, Caroll. (1949). *The Anglo-American establishment.* New York: Books in Focus, 1981.
Riencourt, Amaury de. (1968). *The American Empire.* New York: Dial.
Riley, James C. (1980). *International Government Finance and the Amsterdam capital market 1740–1815.* Cambridge: Cambridge University Press.
Röpke, Wilhelm. (1951). *The problem of economic order.* Cairo: National Bank of Egypt, Fiftieth anniversary commemoration lectures.
Röpke, Wilhelm. (1963). *Economics of the free society.* Chicago: Regnery. Orig. title *Die Lehre von der Wirtschaft.* Vienna: Springer, 1937.
*Röpke, Wilhelm. (1963). *A world without a world monetary order.* Johannesburg: University of Witwatersrand, Jan Smuts House.
Rolfe, Sidney E. (1966). *Gold and world power.* New York: Harper and Row.
Rose, Richard and Guy Peters. (1978). *Can governments go Bankrupt?* New York: Basic Books.
Schacht, Hjalmar. (1967). *The magic of money.* London: Oldbourne Books.
Schreiber, Bernhard. (1975). *The men behind Hitler: a German warning to the world.* London: H & P. Tadeusz.
*Schuker, Stephen A. (1976). *The end of French predominance in Europe: the financial crisis of 1924 and the adoption of the Dawes plan.* Chapel Hill: University of North Carolina Press.
Schumpeter, Josef A. (1954). *History of economic analysis.* New York: Oxford University Press.
Scitovsky, Tibor. (1969). *Money and the balance of payments.* Chicago: Rand-McNally.
Schwarzenberger, Georg. (1964). *Power politics: a study in world society.* London: Stevens & Sons.
Smith, Gordon W. (1977). *Commodity instability and market failure: a survey of issues.* Houston: William Marsh Rice University, Program of Development Studies.
Smyth, David J. (1966). 'Short-term capital movements and the stability of flexible exchange rates.' *Metroeconomica,* 19, October 1967. Birmingham: University of Birmingham.
*Sobel, Robert. (1973). *The money manias: the eras of great speculation in America, 1770–1970.* New York: Weybright & Talley.
Steuber, Ursel. (1976). *International banking: the foreign activities of the banks of principal industrial countries.* Leyden: Sijthoff.
Supple, Barry E. (1959). *Commercial crisis and change in England 1600–1642: a study in the instability of a mercantile economy.* Cambridge: Cambridge University Press.
Sutton, Anthony. (1976). *Wall Street and the Rise of Hitler.* Seal Beach: Seal Beach Press.
*Swoboda, Alexander K. (1980). *Credit creation in the Euromarket: alternative theories and implications for Control.* New York: Group of Thirty.
Thomas, Gordon and Max Morgan-Witts. (1979). *The day the bubble burst: a social history of the Wall Street crash of 1929.* Garden City, NY: Doubleday.
*Tinbergen, Jan and Jacques J. Polak. (1950). *The dynamics of business cycles.* Chicago: University of Chicago Press.
Tortella-Casares, Gabriel. (1972). *Banking, railroads, and industry in Spain, 1829-1874.* 2 vols. Madison, WI.: University of Wisconsin.
Triffin, Robert. (1960). *Gold and the Dollar Crisis.* New Haven: Yale University Press.
UNCTAD Secretariat. (1976). *Money and finance and transfer of real resources for development*: report by the UNCTAD secretariat [at the] fourth session [of the] United Nations conference on trade and development, Nairobi, Kenya, 5 May 1976, item 11 of the provisional agenda, 2 parts.
Venkataramanan, Lalgudi S. (1965). *The theory of futures trading: hedging speculation and storage in organised commodity markets.* London: Asia Publishing House.
Volpe, Paul A. (1945). *The international financial and banking crisis 1931–1933.* Washington, DC: Catholic University of America Press.
Walter, Ingo. (1967). *The European Common Market; growth and patterns of trade and production.* New York: Praeger.
Walter, Ingo. (1968). *International economics; theory and policy.* New York: Ronald Press.
Walter, Ingo. (1973). *U.S. trade policy in a changing world economy.* Tübingen: Mohr.

Walter, Ingo. (1975). *International economics*. New York: Ronald Press.
Walter, Ingo and Hans C. Vitzthum. (1967). *The Central American Common Market; a case study on economic integration in developing regions*. New York: New York University, Institute of Finance.
Wechsberg, Joseph. (1966). *The Merchant Bankers*. Boston: Little Brown and Company.
Wee, Herman van der. (1977). 'Monetary, credit and banking systems.' *Cambridge Economic History of Europe*, Vol. V, Cambridge: Cambridge University Press, pp. 290–393.
Whyte, William Foote... [et al.]. (1955). *Money and motivation: an analysis of incentives in industry*. New York: Harper & Brothers.
Wilson, Sloan J. (1963). *The speculator and the stock market: a study of speculation margin accounts volume of transactions and movements of the averages*. New York: Investors' Library Publication.
Wiseley, Will. (1979). *A fool of power. The political history of money*. New York: Wiley Interscience.

II) LITERATUéE IN CONTINENTAL LANGUAGES, 1945–1982

*Allais, Maurice. (1943). *Traité d'économie pure*. Paris: Imprimerie Nationale.
Allais, Maurice. (1943). *T. II: La dynamique du déséquilibre*. Paris: Imprimerie Nationale.
*Allais, Maurice. (1946). *Abondance ou misère: propositions hetérodoxes pour le redressement de l'économie francaise*. Paris: Librairie de Médicis.
Allais, Maurice. (1960). *L'Europe unie: route de la prospérité*. Paris: Calmann-Levy.
Allais, Maurice. (1972). *La libéralisation des relations économiques internationales*, pref. de Andre Piatier. Paris: Gauthier-Villars.
*Born, Karl Erich. (1931). *Die deutsche Bankenkrise*. Munich: Piper.
*Born, Karl Erich. (1977). *Geld und Banken im 19.und 20. Jahrhundert*. Stuttgart: Alfred Kröner.
Bowers, Q. David. (1975). *Wertvolle Münzen als Geldanlage: Spekulation oder finanzielles Ruhekissen?* Munich: Battenberg.
Chouraqui, Jean-Claude. (1972). *La spéculation et la politique de défense des monnaies*. Paris: Presses universitaires de France.
Ehrlicher, Werner. (ed.). (1981). *Geldpolitik, Zins und Staatsverschuldung*. Berlin: Duncker & Humblot.
Erhard, Ludvig. (1962). *Deutsche Wirtschaftspolitik. Der Weg der Sozialen Marketwirtschaft*. Düsseldorf: ECON Verlag.
*Eucken, Walter. (1959). *Grundsätze der Wirtschaftspolitik*. Tübingen: Mohr.
*Forstmann, Albrecht. (1952). *Geld und Kredit*, I-II. Göttingen: Vandenhoeck & Ruprecht.
Freund, Winfried. (1980). *Adelbert von Chamisso 'Peter Schlemihl': Geld und Geist: ein bürgerlicher Bewusstseinsspiegel, Entstehung, Struktur, Rezeption, Didaktik*. Paderborn: Schöningh.
Gestrich, Hans. (1944). *Kredit und Sparen*. Jena: Fischer.
Goldscheid, Rudolf and Joseph Schumpeter. (1976). *Die Finanzkrise des Steuerstaats: Beiträge zur politischen Ökonomie der Staatsfinanzen*. Frankfurt am Main: Suhrkamp.
Guggenheim-Grünberg, Florence. (1980). *Geist und Geld im Judendorf*. [Published by Schweizerischer Israelitischer Gemeindebund]. Zürich: Verlag Florence-Guggenheim-Archiv.
Hahn, L. Albert. (1960). *Geld und Kredit: Währungspolitische und Konjunkturtheoretische Betrachtungen*. Frankfurt am Main: Knapp.
Haller, Heinz. (1957). *Finanzpolitik. Grundlagen und Hauptprobleme*. Tübingen: Mohr.
Laffargue, Jean-Pierre. (1976). *Spéculation déstabilisante en régime de change flexible: une approche d'équilibre général*. Paris: Centre d'Études Prospectives d'Économie Mathématique Appliquées à la Planification.
*Lautenbach, Wilhelm. (1952). *Zins, Kredit und Produktion*. Tübingen: Mohr.
Mandel, Ernest. (1972). *Der Spätkapitalismus. Versuch einer marxistischen Erklärung*. Frankfurt am Main: Suhrkamp.
Meinhold, Wilhelm. (ed.). (1961). *Internationale Währungs- und Finanzpolitik*. Berlin: Duncker & Humblot.

Müller, Rudolf W. (1981). *Geld und Geist: zur Entstehungsgeschichte von Identitätsbewusstsein und Rationalität seit der Antike.* Frankfurt am Main: Campus-Verlag.
*Muthesius, V. (1961). *Geld und Geist: kulturhistorische und wirtschaftspolitische Aufsätze.* Frankfurt am Main: Knapp.
Möller, Hans. (1948). *Aktuelle Fragen der Wärungsreform.* Siegburg: Industrie-Verlag.
Neidig, Walter. (1961). *Die Spekulation in der Industrie.* Dissertation Mannheim.
Neumark, Fritz. (1961). *Wirtschafts- und Finanzprobleme des Interventionsstaates.* Tübingen: Mohr
Peyrelevade, Jean. (1978). *L'économie de spéculation*, Paris: Seuil.
Puhani, Josef. (1973). *Spekulation am Warenterminmarkt: unter besonderer Berücksichtigung des Porkbelly-Marktes.* Dissertation Munich.
Raddatz, Fritz J. (1980). *Von Geist und Geld: Heinrich Heine und sein Onkel, der Bankier Salomon: eine Skizze*, mit sechs Radierungen von Günter Grass. Cologne: Bund-Verlag.
Rechtenwald, Horst Claus. (1969). *Finanzpolitik.* Cologne: Kiepenheuer & Witsch.
Röpke, Wilhelm. (1932). *Weltwirtschaft: eine Notwendigkeit der deutschen Wirtschaft*, ein Vortrag von Tübingen: Mohr (Recht und Staat in Geschichte und Gegenwart: eine Sammlung von Vorträgen und Schriften aus dem Gebiet der gesamten Staatswissenschaften, 92).
*Röpke, Wilhelm. (1937). *Die Lehre von der Wirtschaft.* Vienna: Springer.
Röpke, Wilhelm. (1965). *Die Bank in unserer Zeit.* Zürich: Vortrag anlässlich des Festaktes zum 75 jährigen Bestehen des Bankhauses Julius anlässlich des Festaktes zum 75 jährigen Bestehen des Bankhauses Bär & Co., Zürich 1890-1965 im Kasino Zürichhorn am 7. Oktober 1965.
Roesler, Konrad. (1967). *Die Finanzpolitik des Deutschen Reiches im Ersten Weltkrieg.* Berlin: Duncker und Humblot.
Schmalenbach, Eugen. (1933). *Kapital, Kredit und Zins in betriebswirtschaftlicher Beleuchtung.* Leipzig: Gloeckner.
*Schmölders, Günter. (1955). *Finanzpolitik.* Berlin: Springer.
Schmölders, Günter and Wlhelm Röpke. (1964). *Währungspolitik in der europäischen Integration.* Baden-Baden: Nomos (Schriftenreihe zum Handbuch für Europäische Wirtschaft, Vol. 29).
Schomaker, Hanspeter. (1971). *Gibt es gewinnbringende destabilisierende Spekulation?: eine theoretische Untersuchung mit Simulationsversuchen.* Dissertation. Freiburg im Breisgau: Krause.
*Steinmann, Gunter. (1970). *Theorie der Spekulation.* Tübingen: Mohr.
Vicarelli, Fausto. (1977). *Keynes, l'instabilità del capitalismo.* Milan: Etas Libri
Walker, Karl. (1962). *Neue Europäische Währungsordnung: Indexwährung, flexible Wechselkurse, Euro-Mark: eine kritische Untersuchung und ein Vorschlag.* Nürnberg: Zitzmann.
Weber, Adolf. (1939). *Geld und Kredit, Banken und Börsen.* Leipzig: Quelle & Meyer.

III) LITERATURE IN SCANDINAVIAN, 1945–1982

Andvig, Jens Christopher. (1980). *Ragnar Frisch and monetary reform movements in the thirties.* Memorandum, Oslo: Institute of Economics, University of Oslo
Anikin, Andrej V. (1988). *Den gule djevel. Gull og kapitalisme.* Oslo: Falken; Moskva: Progress.
Commission on Rent Policy. (1979). *Report by the Commission on Rent Policy*, appointed by Royal decrees of July 14th, 1978, led by Peter Jacob Bjerve, submitted to the Ministry of Finance and Customs January 30, 1980. Oslo: Government Administration Services, Government Printing Service, Norwegian Official Reports NOR 1980: 4E. Norwegian version: NOU 1980: 4E.
Dobb; Maurice. (1975). *Kapitalismens udvikling.* Copenhagen: Rhodos.
*Frisch, Ragnar. (1947). *Noen trekk av konjunkturlæren.* Oslo Aschehoug.
Frisch, Ragnar. (1961). 'Det uopplyste pengevelde.' *Sosialøkonomen*, vol. 7/61, pp. 2-3.
Galbraith, John Kenneth. (1973). Det store krakket 1929. Oslo: Gyldendal. (Orig. title *The Great Crash, 1929*). (1954).

Galbraith, John Kenneth. (1978). *Usikkerhetens tidsalder.* Oslo: Dreyer. (Orig. title *The age of uncertainty* (1977).

Hanisch, Tore Jørgen. (1979). 'Oskar Jægers «Finanslære»., De norske sosialøkonomene og den økonomiske politikken før Frisch og Keynes.' *Sosialøkonomen*, vol. 2, pp. 11-15, 22.

Hayter, Teresa. (1971). *Pengemakt og avmakt. Verdensbankens og pengefondets rolle i U-landshjelpen.* Oslo: Gyldendal. (Orig. Title *Aid as Imperialism*).

Hoff, Trygve J.B. (1945). *Fred og fremtid. Liberokratiets vei.* Oslo: Aschehoug.

Isachsen, Arne Jon. (1977). *Inflasjon, et uløselig problem?* Oslo: Tanum-Norli.

Johansen, Leif. (1956) 'Bankenes rolle i en makroøkonomisk modell.' Reprint from *Statsøkonomisk Tidsskrift* no. 4, 1956. Oslo: Universitetsforlaget.

*Keilhau, Wilhelm. (1951). *Principles of private and public planning. A study in economic sociology.* London: Allen & Unwin.

Keilhau, Wilhelm. (1953). *Riktig og gal planøkonomi.* Oslo: Aschehoug.

Mandel, Ernest. (1976). *Senkapitalismen.* Oslo: Gyldendal. (Orig. title *Der Spätkapitalismus,* 1972).

Morton, Frederic. (1963). *Huset Rothschild.* Oslo: Gyldendal. (Orig. title *The Rothschilds. A family portrait,* 1961).

Munthe, Preben. (1978). *Penger, kreditt og valuta.* Oslo: Universitetsforlaget.

Nossum, Rolf H. (1952). *Fra statsdirigering til statsbankerott. Skremmende spor fra monopolenes århundreder.* Oslo: Laboremus.

Ortmark, Åke. (1981). *Skuld och makt: en kapitalistisk historia. Medici, Rotschild, Rockefeller, Wallenberg.* Stockholm: Wahlström & Widstrand.

Rose, Richard and Guy Peters. (1979). *Kan regjeringer gå konkurs?* Oslo: Gyldendal.

D) AFTER 1982:TOWARDS FINANCIAL CAPITALISM (AFTER BRETTON WOODS)

I) LITERATURE IN ENGLISH, AFTER 1982

*Abramson, Rudy. (1992). *Spanning the century. The Life of Avarell Harriman.* New York: William Morrow.

Ahmad, Ehtisham, Gao Qiang, and Vito Tanzi. (1995). *Reforming China's public finances.* Washington, DC: International Monetary Fund.

Ahmed, Shaghil. (1993). *Money and output: the relative importance of real and nominal shocks.* Philadelphia: Federal Reserve Bank of Philadelphia (Working paper, No. 93-20).

*Albert, Michel. (1993). *Capitalism vs. capitalism: how America's obsession with individual achievement and short-term profit has led it to the brink of collapse.* New York: Four Walls Eight Windows. (Orig. title *Capitalisme contre capitalisme*).

*Aliber, Robert Z. (1973). *The international money game.* London: Macmillan.

Allen, George C. (1972). *Japan and the crisis in international finance.* London: Economic Research Council.

al-Sultan, Fawzi H. (1989). *Averting financial crisis—Kuwait.* Washington, DC: Office of the Executive Directors, World Bank, (Policy, Planning, and Research working papers, WPS 243).

Ames, Brian. (1984). *Empirical review of the financial crisis in Mexico.* Geneva: UNCTAD.

Andvig, Jens Christopher. (1981). 'Ragnar Frisch and Business Cycle Research during the Interwar Years.' *History of political economy,* Vol. 13, no. 4, pp. 695-725.

Arbel, Avner and Albert E. Kaff. (1989). *Crash: ten days in October...will it strike again?* Chicago: Longman Financial Services Publishing.

Baestaens, Dirk J.E. (1991). *The concept of economic instability: a source structuralisation attempt.* Rotterdam: Erasmus University (Report/Centre for Research in Business Economics, Department of Business Finance and Portfolio Investment).

Bain, Trevor. (1992). *Banking the furnace: restructuring of the steel industry in eight countries.* Kalamazoo, MI: W.E. Upjohn Institute for Employment Research.

Bandow, Doug and Ian Vaquez (eds). (1982). *Perpetuating poverty. The World Bank, the IMF and the developing world.* Washington, DC: Cato Institute.

Bank of England. (1982). 'The supplementary special deposits scheme.' *Quarterly Bulletin*, vol. 22, no. 1, pp. 74–85.

Barsky, Robert B. and J. Bradford De Long. (1993). 'Why Does the Stock Market Fluctuate?' *Quarterly Journal of Economics*, vol. 108, no. 2, pp. 291–312. (Earlier version issued as National Bureau of Economic Research [NBER] working paper no. 3995, February 1992.)

Barth, James R., R. Dan Brumbaugh Jr., and Robert E. Litan (1990). *The banking industry in Turmoil.* Washington, DC: US Government Printing Office, December.

*Bartlett, Sarah. (1991). *The money machine: how KKK manufactured power & profits.* New York: Beard Books.

Bates, David S. (1997). *Post-'87 crash fears in S & P 500 futures options.* Cambridge, MA: National Bureau of Economic Research.

*Baumgartner, Ulrich and Guy Meredith. (1995). *Saving behavior and the asset price 'bubble' in Japan: analytical studies*, with a staff team comprising Juha Kähkoenen... [et al.]. Washington, DC: International Monetary Fund.

Bean, Charles. (1988). *Europe after the crash: economic policy in an era of adjustment.* Brussels: Directorate-General for Economic and Financial Affairs.

Becht, Marco and Carlos Ramirez. (1993). *Financial capitalism in pre-World War I Germany: the role of the universal banks in the financing of German mining companies 1906–1912.* Florence: European University Institute.

Becker, William H. and Samuel F. Wells (eds). (1984). *Economics and world power: an assessment of American diplomacy since 1789.* New York: Columbia University Press.

Beckman, Robert. (1988). *Crashes. Why they happen – what to do.* With introduction by Lord Rees-Mogg. London: Sidgwick & Jackson.

Bederman, David J. (1988). *The Bank for International Settlements and the debt crisis: a new role for the central bankers' bank?* Berkeley, CA: University of California, Boalt Hall School of Law.

Benink, Harald A. (ed.). (1996). *Coping with financial fragility and systemic risk.* Amsterdam: Kluwer Academic Publisher.

Bernanke, Ben and Harold James. (1990). *The gold standard, deflation, and financial crisis in the great depression: an international comparison.* Cambridge, MA: National Bureau of Economic Research.

Bhattacharya, Utpal and Paul Weller. (1992). *The advantage to hiding one's hand: speculation and central bank intervention in the foreign exchange market.* London: Centre for Economic Policy Research.

Bjanger, Thomas and Kjell Hagen. (1993). *Operative options under asset volatility and limited asset observability*, Sandvika: Forfatterne. [The Authors].

Blanchard, Ian, Anthony Goodman, and Jennifer Newman. (eds). (1992). *Industry and finance in early modern history*: essays presented to George Hammersley to the occasion of his 74th birthday, Stuttgart: Franz Steiner (*Vierteljahrschrift für Sozial- und Wirtschaftsgeschichte.* Beihefte, No. 98).

Bloch, Ernest. (1988). *How the investment banking industry keeps changing (again).* New York: New York University, Salomon Brothers Center for the Study of Financial Institutions, Graduate School of Business Administration.

Bordo, Michael D. and Forrest Capie. (eds). (1993). *Monetary regimes in transition.* Cambridge and New York: Cambridge University Press.

*Bordo, Michael and Richard Sylla. (eds). (1996). *Anglo-American financial systems: institution and markets in the twentieth century.* New York: Irwin.

Bosworth, Barry P. (1993). *Saving and investment in a global economy.* Washington, DC: The Brookings Institution.

*Braudel, Fernand. (1985). *Civilisation and capitalism.* 15th–18th *century*, I-III. London: Fontana. (Orig. title *Les Temps du Monde,* 1979).

*Brett, Edwin A. (1983). *International money and capitalist crisis. The anatomy of global disintegration.* Boulder, CO: Westview Press.

Brianza, Tiziano, Louis Phlips and Jean F. Richard. (1990). *Futures markets, speculation, and monopoly pricing.* Florence: European University Institute.

Brimmer, Andrew F. (1985). *The world banking system: outlook in a context of crisis.* New York: New York University Press.

Brown, Brendan. (1983). *The forward market in foreign exchange: a study in market-making, arbitrage, and speculation.* London: Croom Helm.

Calder, Kent E. (1993). *Strategic capitalism: private business and public purpose in Japanese industrial finance.* Princeton: Princeton University Press.

Callinicos, Alex, John Rees, Chris Harman, and Mike Haynes. (1994). *Marxism and the new imperialism.* London: Bookmarks Publisher.

Capie, Forrest. (1983). *Depression and protectionism: Britain between the wars.* London and Boston: Allen & Unwin.

Capie, Forrest. (1990). *Directory of economic institutions.* New York: Stockton Press.

Capie, Forrest. (ed.). (1991). *Major inflations in history.* Aldershot, Hants; Brookfield, VT: Elgar.

Capie, Forrest. (1994). *Tariffs and growth: some illustrations from the world economy, 1850–1940,* Manchester and New York: Manchester University Press; New York: Distributed exclusively in the USA and Canada by St. Martin's Press.

Capie, Forrest and Alan Webber. (1982). *Bank deposits and the quantity of money in the U.K., 1870–1921.* London: City University, Centre for Banking & International Finance.

Capie, Forrest and Alan Webber. (1984). *A survey of estimates of U.K. money supply and components, 1870–1982.* London: City University, Centre for Banking and International Finance.

Capie, Forrest and Alan Webber. (1985). *A monetary history of the United Kingdom, 1870–1982.* London, Boston: Allen & Unwin.

Capie, Forrest and Geoffrey E. Wood. (eds). (1985). *Financial crises and the world banking system.* New York: St. Martin's Press.

Capie, Forrest and Geoffrey E. Wood. (eds). (1986). *Financial crises and the world banking system.* London: Macmillan Press in association with City University, Centre for Banking and International Finance.

Capie, Forrest and Geoffrey E. Wood. (1989). *Monetary economics in the 1980s: the Henry Thornton lectures,* numbers 1–8, London: Macmillan Press in association with City University, Centre for Banking and International Finance.

Capie, Forrest and Geoffrey E. Wood. (eds). (1991). *Unregulated banking: chaos or order?* foreword by Gordon Pepper. New York: St. Martin's Press, and London: Macmillan.

Carmoy, Hervé de. (1988). *Stratégie bancaire: le refus de la dérive.* Paris: Presses universitaires de France.

*Carmoy, Hervé de. (1990). *Global banking strategy: financial markets and industrial decay.* Oxford and Cambridge, MA.: Blackwell.

Carmoy, Hervé de. (1995). *La banque du XXIe siècle.* Paris: Editions O. Jacob.

Carosso, Vincent P. (1987). *The Morgans: private international bankers 1854–1913,* (Harvard Studies in Business History, No 38), Cambridge, MA: Harvard University Press.

*Cassis, Youssef. (1995). *City bankers, 1890–1914.* Cambridge: Cambridge University Press.

Cauvin, Raoul and Berck [Arthur Berckmans]. (1989). *Crash à Wall Street.* Charleroi: Dupuis.

Caves, Richard E., Jeffrey A. Frankel, and Ronald W. Jones. (1990). *World trade and payments. An introduction.* 5th ed. New York: Harper Collins.

Central Planning Bureau. (1987). *The oil price crash of 1986 and some possible future developments of crude oil prices.* The Hague: Centraal Planbureau.

*Cerny, Philip G. (ed.) (1993). *Finance and world politics. Markets, regimes, and states in the post-hegemonic era.* Aldershot: Elgar.

*Chandler, Alfred. (1977). *The Visible Hand. The managerial revolution in American business.* Cambridge, MA: The Belknap Press of Harvard University Press.

Chandler, Alfred D. Jr. and Takasi Hikino. (1990). *Scale and scope: the dynamics of industrial capitalism.* Cambridge, MA: The Belknap Press of Harvard University Press.

Chapman, Stanley D. (1988). 'Venture capital and financial organisation: London and South Africa in the Nineteenth Century.' In Stuart Jones (ed.), *Banking and business in South Africa.* New York: St. Martin's Press, pp. 27–45.

Cheng, Elizabeth. (1983). *Debt crisis?: a situation discussion on the state of global monetary and financial affairs, in the context of world development and the developing world.* Hong Kong: Asian Regional Exchange for New Alternatives.

*Chernow, Ron. (1993). *The global Warburgs: the twentieth-century odyssey of a remarkable Jewish family.* New York: Random House.

Clark, E. Ritchie. (1985). *The IDB. A history of* Canada's *industrial development bank, federal business development bank.* Toronto: University of Toronto Press.

Clay, Charles J.J., Bernard S. Wheble and Leonard H.L. Cohen. (eds). (1983). *Clay and Wheble's modern merchant banking: a guide to the workings of the accepting houses of the city of London and their services to industry and commerce*, 2nd ed. Cambridge: Woodhead-Faulkner.

Cleveland, Harold van B., Charles P. Kindleberger, Lewis E. Lehrman, and David P. Calleo, (eds). (1976). *Money and the coming world order.* New York: New York University.

Clews, Henry. (1980). *Fifty years in Wall Street.* Hoboken: John Wiley & Sons.

Coakley, Jerry and Laurence Harris. (1983). *The city of capital. London's role as a financial centre.* Oxford: Blackwell.

*Cohen, Bernice. (1997). *The edge of Chaos: financial booms, bubbles, crashes, and chaos.* Hoboken, NJ: John Wiley & Sons.

Collier, Peter and David Horowitz. (1976). T*he Rockefellers. An American Dynasty.* New York: Holt, Rhinehart and Wilson.

Commission on the Banking Crisis. (1992). *Report by the commission on the banking crisis*, appointed by Royal decrees of October 4th, 1991, led by prof. Preben Munthe, submitted to the Ministry of Finance and Customs August 31st, 1992. Oslo: Government Administration Services, Government Printing Service, Norwegian Official Reports NOR 1992: 30E.

*Corbett, Jenny and Tim Jenkinson. (1994). *The finance of industry, 1970–1989: an international comparison.* London: Centre for Economic Policy Research.

Cottrell, Peter L. (1980). *Industrial finance, 1830–1914: the finance and organization of English manufacturing industry.* London: Methuen.

Cottrell, Peter L., Håkan Lindgren, and Alice Teichova. (eds). (1992). *European industry and banking between the wars: a review of bank-industry relations.* Leicester: Leicester University Press.

Coulbeck, Neil. (1984). *The multinational banking industry.* London: Croom Helm.

Cox, Andrew. (ed.). (1986). *State, finance and industry: a comparative analysis of post-war trends in six advanced industrial economies.* Brighton: Wheatsheaf.

Crabtree, John, Gavan Duffy, and Jenny Pearce. (1986). *The great tin crash: Bolivia and the world tin market.* London: Latin American Bureau.

Cremer, R.D. and Raymond A. Zepp. (1987). *Stock market crash 1987: a Hong Kong perspective.* Hong Kong: UEA Press.

Cukierman, Alex, Sebastian Edwards, and Guido Tabellini. (1990). *Seignorage and political instability.* London: Centre for Economic Policy Research.

Danaher, Kevin. (ed.). (1994). *50 years is enough. The case against the World Bank and the international monetary fund.* Boston: South End Press.

Davidson, Paul. (1972). *International money and the real world.* London: Macmillan.

*Davidson, Paul (ed.). (1983). *Can the free market pick winners? What determines investment.* Armonk, NY: Sharpe.

Davis, E. Philip (1992). *Debt, fragility and systemic risk.* Oxford: Clarendon Press.

Darwiche, Fida. (1986). *The gulf stock exchange crash: the rise and fall of the Souq Al-Manakh.* London: Croom Helm.

Dawson, Frank Griffith. (1990). *The first Latin American debt crisis: the city of London and the 1822-25 loan bubble.* New Haven, CT: Yale University Press.

De Cecco, Marcello. (ed.). (1983). *International economic adjustment: small countries and the European monetary system.* Oxford: Blackwell.

De Cecco, Marcello. (1987). (ed.). *Changing money: financial innovation in developed countries,* Oxford and New York: Blackwell.

De Cecco, Marcello and Jean-Paul Fitoussi. (eds). (1987). *Monetary theory and economic institutions*: proceedings of a conference held by the International Economic Association at Fiesole, Florence, Italy. New York: St. Martin's Press.

De Cecco, Marcello and Alberto Giovannini. (eds). (1989). *A European central bank?: perspectives on monetary unification after ten years of the EMS.* Cambridge and New York: Cambridge University Press.

De Cecco, Marcello, Lorenzo Pecchi, and Gustavo Piga. (eds). (1997). *Managing public debt: index-linked bonds in theory and practice.* Brookfield: Elgar.

Delamaide, Darrell. (1984). *Debt shock: the full story of the world credit crisis.* Garden City, NJ: Doubleday.

De Long, J. Bradford. (1990). *Did J.P. Morgan's men add value?, a historical perspective on financial capitalism.* Cambridge, MA: National Bureau of Economic Research.

De Long, J. Bradford. (1992). 'Bull and bear markets.' In John Eatwell, Murray Milgate, and Peter Newman (eds), *New Palgrave dictionary of money and finance.* London: Macmillan.

De Long, J. Bradford. (1992). 'Growth, industrialization, and finance.' *NBER Reporter* (Summer), pp. 5–11.

De Long, J. Bradford. (1993). 'Very long-run economic growth, ca. 1870–1990.' In Horst Siebert (ed.), *Economic growth in the world economy.* Kiel: Institute for World Economics.

*De Long, J. Bradford. (1995). 'Können Finanzmärkte zu liquide sein?: Gefahr der Verstärkung von Kurseinbrüchen.' *Neue Zürcher Zeitung: Elektronische Borse Schweiz,* December 5, p. B 14. (English title 'Can a Financial Market Be Too Liquid and Too Efficient?' Berkeley, CA, 1995).

De Long, J. Bradford. (1996). 'Is the Stock Market Overvalued?' *Slate,* December 21.

De Long, J. Bradford and Barry Eichengreen (1993). 'The Marshall plan: history's most successful structural adjustment programme.' In Rüdiger Dornbusch, Wilhelm Nölling, and Richard Layard (eds). *Postwar economic reconstruction and lessons for the East today.* Cambridge, MA: MIT Press, pp. 189–230. (Earlier version issued as HIER working paper no. 1576, October 1991).

De Long, J. Bradford and Andrei Shleifer. (1990). *The bubble of 1929: evidence from closed-end funds.* Cambridge, MA: National Bureau of Economic Research.

De Long, J. Bradford and Andrei Shleifer. (1993). 'Princes and merchants: city growth before the industrial revolution.' *Journal of Law and Economics,* vol. 36, pp. 671–702.

De Long, J. Bradford and Lawrence H. Summers. (1986). 'Are Business Cycles Symmetrical?' In Robert J. Gordon (ed.), *The American business cycle: continuity and change.* Chicago, IL: University of Chicago Press for the National Bureau of Economic Research, pp. 166–178.

De Long, J. Bradford [et al.]. (1989). *Positive feedback investment strategies and destabilizing rational speculation.* Cambridge, MA: National Bureau of Economic Research.

Dillon, Gadis J. (1984). *The role of accounting in the stock market crash of 1929.* Atlanta: Georgia State University, College of Business Administration.

Dobilas, Geoffrey. (1988). *Information technology and simultaneous financial markets: the crash of October 1987.* London: London School of Economics and Political Science, School of Geography.

*Donaldson, A.R. (1989). 'The World Bank on trade liberalisation.' *South African Journal of Economics,* Vol. 57, no. 1, pp. 54-59.

Dooley, Michael P. (1994). *A retrospective on the debt crisis.* Cambridge, MA: National Bureau of Economic Research.

Dooley, Michael, Eduardo Fernandez-Arias, and Kenneth Kletzer. (1994). *Is the debt crisis history?: Recent private capital inflows to developing countries.* Washington, DC: World Bank, International Economics Department.

Dowd, Kevin. (ed.). (1992). *The experience of free banking.* London and New York: Routledge.

Dymski, Gary and Robert Pollin. (eds). (1994). *New perspectives in monetary macroeconomics: explorations in the tradition of Hyman P. Minsky.* Ann Arbor, MI: University of Michigan Press.

Edwards, Franklin R. and Frederic S. Mishkin. (1995). *The decline of traditional banking: implications for financial stability and regulatory policy.* Cambridge, MA: National Bureau of Economic Research.

Eichengreen, Barry. (1989). *International monetary instability between the wars: structural flaws or misguided policies?* Cambridge, MA: National Bureau of Economic Research.

Eichengreen, Barry. (1990). *Elusive stability: essays in the history of inter*national finance, 1919–*1939.* Cambridge: Cambridge University Press.

Eichengreen, Barry. (1992). *Golden fetters: the gold standard and the great depression, 1919–1939.* New York and Oxford: Oxford University Press.

*Eichengreen, Barry. (1996). *Globalizing capital: a history of the international monetary system.* Princeton: Princeton University Press.

Eichengreen, Barry and Peter H. Lindert (eds). (1989). *The international debt crisis in historical perspective.* Cambridge, MA: MIT Press.

Eijffinger, Sylvester C.W., Marco Hoeberichts, and Eric Schaling. (1997). *Why money talks and wealth whispers: monetary uncertainty and mystique.* Tilburg: Tilburg University.

Engdahl, F. William. (1993). *A century of war, Anglo-American oil politics and the new world order.* Wiesbaden: Böttinger Verlag.

Erdman, Paul. (1988). *What's next?: How to prepare yourself for the crash of '89 and profit in the 1990's.* New York: Doubleday.

*Evans, David and Ian Goldin. (1991). 'Trade reform and structural adjustment.' *South African Journal of Economics,* Vol. 59, no. 3, September, pp. 141-151.

Eyre, Samuel R. (1978). *The real wealth of nations.* London: Edward Arnold.

Fallon, Peter R. (1993). 'The implications for South Africa of using World Bank facilities.' In Pauline H. Baker, Alex Boraine, Warren Krafchik and David Philip (eds). *South Africa and the world economy in the 1990s.* Cape Town and Johannesburg; The Brookings Institution: Washington, DC in association with IDASA and the Aspen Institute, 1993, pp. 205–211.

Farmer, Roger E.A. (1997). *Money in a real business cycle model.* London: Centre for Economic Policy Research.

Fay, Stephen. (1982). *The great silver bubble.* London: Hodder and Stoughton.

Fazzari, Steven and Dimitri B. Papadimitriou. (eds). (1992). *Financial conditions and macroeconomic performance: essays in honor of Hyman P. Minsky.* Armonk, NY: Sharpe.

Flannery, Mark J. (1982). 'Deposit insurance creates a need for bank regulation.' *Federal Reserve Bank of Philadelphia Business Review,* January-February, pp. 17–20.

*Flood, Robert P. and Peter M. Garber. (1994). *Speculative bubbles, speculative attacks, and policy switching.* Cambridge, MA: MIT Press.

*Freyer, Tony A. (1994). *Producers versus capitalists. Constitutional conflict in Antebellum America.* Charlottesville: University Press of Virginia.

*Frieden, Jeffry A. (1987). *Banking on the wold. The politics of American international finance.* New York: HarperCollins.

Friedman, Benjamin M. (1990). *Views on the likelihood of financial crisis.* Cambridge, MA: National Bureau of Economic Research.

Furtado, Celso, Lal Jayawardena, and Masaru Yoshitomi. (1989). *The world economic and financial crisis.* [Helsinki]: World Institute for Development Economics Research United Nations University. Papers originally presented at a Symposium on World economic and financial crisis, held on the occasion of the 31st session of the Council of the United Nations University in Brasilia, June 28, 1988. The revised version of the third paper was presented at the Development policy forum on Structural changes in the world economy and development cooperation, Tokyo, 25 October 1988.

Gabas, Jean-Jacques. (1986). *Foreign aid and financial crisis in the CILSS member states.* [Paris]: OECD.

Galletly, Guy and Nicholas Ritchie. (1986). *The big bang: the financial revolution in the city of London and what it means for you.* Plymouth: Northcote House.

Gavin, Michael and Dani Rodrik. (1995). *The World Bank in historical perspective.* AEA Papers and Proceedings, vol. II, no.2, p. 329.

George, Susan. (1988). *A fate worse than debt. A radical new analysis of the Third World debt crisis.* London: Penguin.

*George, Susan. (1994). *Faith and credit. The World Bank's secular empire.* London: Penguin.

*Ghosh, S. et al. (1987). *Stabilizing speculative commodity markets.* Oxford: Oxford University Press.

*Gibson, Donald. (1995). *Battling Wall Street: The Kennedy presidency.* New York: Sheridan Square Press.

Gideon, Shirley J. (1997). 'The modern free banking school: a review.' *Journal of Economic Issues,* vol. XXXI, no.1, pp. 209–222.

Gilbert, Christopher L. and Celso Brunetti. (1997). *Speculation, hedging and volatility in the coffee market, 1993–1996.* London: University of London, Queen Mary and Westfield College.

Goldsbrough, David and Iqbal Zaidi (eds). (1989). *Monetary policy in the Philippines during periods of financial crisis and changes in exchange rate regime: targets, instruments, and the stability of money demand.* Washington, DC: International Monetary Fund.

Goldsmith, James. (1993). *The trap.* London: Macmillan.

Gonzalez, Justo L. (1990). *Faith and wealth: a history of early Christian ideas on the origin, significance, and use of money.* San Francisco: Harper & Row.

*Greider, William. (1997). *One world, ready or not: the manic logic of global capitalism.* New York: Simon & Schuster.

Greider, William. (1997). *The Levy Report Interview,* with William Greider, author and national editor of *Rolling Stone* magazine, Discusses Contradictions in the Global Economic System, Corporate Responsibility, and Progressive Policy. With Assistant Director Sanjay Mongia on June 16.

Grou, Pierre. (1985). *The financial structure of multinational capitalism.* New York: St. Martin's Press. (Orig. title *La structure financière du capitalisme multinational).*

Gual, Jordi and Damein Neven. (1992). *Deregulation of the European banking industry (1980–1991).* London: Centre for Economic Policy Research.

Guha, Amalendu and Gheorghe Zaman. (1994). *Credit productivity?: creating stability power in international financial market.* Stockholm: Bethany Books.

Hama, Noriko. (1995). *Japan after the bubble economy: price destruction and what lies beyond,* for the Dujat symposium, April 27, 1995.

Haner, Frederick T. (1985). *Financial crisis: causes and solutions.* New York: Praeger.

Haraf, William S. and Rose Marie Kushmeider (eds). (1988). *Restructuring banking and financial services in America.* Washington, DC: American Enterprise Institute.

Hardouvelis, Gikas A. (1990). *Stock market bubbles before the crash of 1987?* New York: Federal Reserve Bank.

Harman, Chris. (1995). *Economics of the madhouse. Capitalism and the market today.* London: Bookmarks Publishers.

Hart, Albert G. and Perry Mehrling. (1995). *Debt, crisis and recovery: the 1930s and the 1990s.* Armonk, NY: Sharpe (Columbia University seminar series).

Hartlyn, Jonathan and Samuel A. Morley. (eds). (1986). *Latin American political economy: financial crisis and political change.* Boulder, CO: Westview Press.

Hawawini, Gabriel A. and Itzhak Swary. (1990). *Mergers and acquisitions in the U.S. banking industry: evidence from the capital markets.* Amsterdam and New York: North-Holland.

*Heilbroner, Robert L. (1988). *Behind the veil of economics. Essays in the worldly philosophy.* New York and London: Norton.

Heilbroner, Robert L. (1972 and 1989). *The making of economic society*, revised for the 1990s, 8th ed. Englewood Cliffs, NJ: Prentice-Hall.

Highham, Charles. (1983). *Trading with the enemy.* New York: Delacorte Press.

*Hoffman, Paul. (1984). *The dealmakers: inside the world of investment banking.* New York: Doubleday.

Horiuchi, Toshihiro. (1994). *Japanese public policy for cooperative supply of credit guarantee to small firms: its evolution since the post war and banks' commitment.* Florence: European University Institute.

Houston, William. (1993). *Meltdown. The great '90s depression and how to come through it a winner.* With introduction by Lord Rees-Mogg, London: Warner.

Hudson, Michael. (1992). *Trade, development, and foreign dept. A history of theories of polarisation and convergence in the international economy.* Volume I: *International Trade.* Volume II: *International Finance.* London: Pluto Press.

Hughes, Steward. (1987). *The capital market and finance of industry in the UK.* York: Longman.

Hunt, Edwin. (1994). *The medieval super-companies: a study of the Peruzzi company of Florence.* London: Cambridge University Press.

*Ingham, Geoffrey. (1984). *Capitalism divided. The city and industry in British social development.* London: Macmillan.

International Monetary Fund. (1991). *Determinants and systemic consequences of international capital flows.* A Study by the Research Department of the International Monetary Fund. Washington, DC.: International Monetary Fund.

Isaacson, Walter and Evan Thomas. (1986). *The Wise Men. Six friends and the world they made – Acheson, Bohlen, Harriman, Kennan, Lovett, McCloy.* New York: Simon & Shuster.

Jastram, Roy W. (1977). *The golden constant. The English and American experience, 1560–1970.* New York: Wiley Interscience.

*Jensen, Michael C. (1976). *The financiers: the world of the Great Wall Street investment banking houses.* New York: Weybright & Talley.

Joffe, Avril, David Kaplan, Raphael Kaplinsky, and David Lewis. (1993). 'Meeting the global challenge: a framework for industrial revival in South Africa.' In Pauline H. Baker, Alex Boraine, Warren Krafchik, and David Philip (eds). *South Africa and the world economy in the 1990s.* Cape Town, Washington DC: The Brookings Institution in association with IDASA and the Aspen Institute, pp. 91–126.

Jones, Stuart. (1994). 'The apogee of the imperial banks in South Africa: Standard and Barclays, 1919–1939.' In *Multinational and international banking.* International Library of Macroeconomic and Financial History, no. 2, Aldershot: Elgar; distributed in North America by Ashgate, Brookfield, VT, 1992, pp. 353–377. Previously published 1988.

Jones, Stuart. (1994). 'Origins, growth and concentration of bank capital in South Africa, 1860–1892.' *Business History*, vol. 36, no. 3, pp. 62–80.

Kane, Edward J. (1985). *The gathering crisis in federal deposit insurance.* Cambridge, MA: MIT Press.

Kasahara, Shigehisa. (1994). *A rescue plan for the post-bubble Japanese economy: the establishment of the cooperative credit purchasing company.* Geneva: UNCTAD.

Kaushik, S.K. (ed.). (1985). *The debt crisis and financial stability: the future*: proceedings of a conference held at Pace University, New York City, in March 1985. New York: Pace University, Papers from the Conference on International Banking.

Keen, Steve. (1996). 'The chaos of finance: the chaotic and Marxian foundations of Minsky's "Financial Instability Hypothesis".' *Économies et Sociétés*, vol. 30, no. 2–3, pp. 55–82.

*Kenen, Peter B. 'Role of the Dollar as an International Currency', in Kenen, Peter B. (ed.), et al. (1996). *From Halifax to Lyons: what has been done about crisis management?* Princeton, NJ: Princeton University .

*Khoury, Sarkis J. (1990). *The deregulation of the world financial markets. Myths, realities, and impact.* London: Pinter Publishers.

Kindleberger, Charles P. (1973). The world in depression, 1929–*1939.* Berkeley, CA: University of California Press.

Kindleberger, Charles P. (1984). *A financial history of Western Europe.* London: Allen & Unwin.

Kindleberger, Charles P. (1988). *The international economic order: essays on financial crisis and international public goods.* New York: Harvester Wheatsheaf.

Kindleberger, Charles P. (1995). *The world economy and national finance in historical perspective.* Ann Arbor, MI: University of Michigan Press.

*Kindleberger, Charles P. (ed.), Wilfred J. Ethier, Richard C. Marston, et al. (1985). *International financial markets and capital movements*: a symposium in honor of Arthur I. Bloomfield. Princeton, NJ: Princeton University.

Klausner, Michael and Lawrence J. White (eds). (1993). *Structural change in banking.* Homewood, IL: Business One Irwin; New York: New York University.

Klingaman, William K. (1989). *1929: the year of the great crash.* New York: Harper & Row.

*Krainer, Robert E. (1992). *Finance in a theory of the business cycle.* Cambridge, MA and Oxford: Blackwell, 1994.

Krause, Laurence A. (1991). *Speculation and the dollar: the political economy of exchange rates.* Boulder, CO: Westview Press.

Kress Library of Business and Economics, Baker Library. (1986). *Catalogue of an exhibition of prints from the Bleichroeder Collection.* Boston: Baker Library, Harvard Business School.

Krugman, Paul. (1996). 'How is NAFTA doing? It's been hugely successful - as a foreign policy.' *The New Democrat*, May/June.

Kurtzman, Joel. (1988). *The decline and crash of the American economy.* New York: Norton.

Lamfalussy, Alexandre. (1992). *The restructuring of the financial industry: a central banking perspective.* Tilburg: Société Universitaire Européenne de Recherches Financières. Text of the first SUERF lecture held at the City University, London, on March 5, 1992.

*Lane, Frederick C. (1985). *Money and banking in Medieval and Renaissance Venice*, Baltimore: Johns Hopkins University Press.

Langholm, Odd. (1983). *Wealth and money in the Aristotelian tradition: a study in scholastic economic sources.* Bergen: Universitetsforlaget; New York: Distribution office, U.S. and Canada, Columbia University Press.

Langholm, Odd. (1992). *Economics in the medieval schools: wealth, exchange, value, money, and usury according to the Paris theological tradition, 1200–1350.* Leiden: Brill.

Le Fort, Guillermo R. (1989). *Financial crisis in developing countries and structural weaknesses of the financial system.* Washington, DC: International Monetary Fund.

Leger, Kathryn. (1995). 'Chretien to urge G-7 economic co-operation,' Toronto. *Financial Post*, Weekly edition, Thursday, 15 June, p. 7.

Lessard, Donald R. and John Williamson. (1985). *Financial intermediation beyond the debt crisis.* Washington, DC: Peterson Institute for International Economics.

Lever, Harold and Christopher Huhne. (1985). *Debt and danger: the world financial crisis.* Harmondsworth: Penguin.

Lewis, Michael. (1989). *Liar's Poker. Two cities, true greed.* London: Coronet.

Lipsky, Seth (ed.). (1978). *The billion dollar bubble... and other stories from the Asian Wall Street Journal.* Hong Kong: Dow Jones Pub. Co. (Asia).

Litan, Robert E. (1987). *What should banks do?* Washington, DC: Brookings Institution.

Ljungqvist, Lars. (1992). *Destabilizing exchange rate speculation: a counterexample to Milton Friedman.* Stockholm (Seminar paper/Stockholm University. Institute for International Economic Studies, 525).

Llewellyn, David T. and Mark Holmes. (1991). *Competition or credit controls?* Hobart Paper no. 117. London: Institute of Economic Affairs.

Lomax, David. (1986). *The money makers: six portraits of power in industry.* London: BBC, From the BBC TV-serial The Money Makers.

Long, David. (1996). *Towards a new liberal internationalism: the international theory of J.A. Hobson.* Cambridge: Cambridge University Press.

*Lottman, Herbert R. (1995). *The French Rothschilds: the great banking dynasty through two turbulent centuries.* New York: Crown.

Lund, Diderik. (1985). *Compromising on rent tax neutrality to ensure economizing behavior.* Oslo. (Memorandum from Department of Economics, University of Oslo.)

*MacEwan, Arthur. (1990). *Debt and disorder: international economic instability and U.S. imperial decline.* New York: Monthly Review Press.

Maddison. Angus. (1982). *Phases of capitalist development.* Oxford and New York: Oxford University Press.

Mainwaring, Lynn. (1995). 'Tugan's "Bubble": underconsumption and crises in a Marxian model.' *Cambridge Journal of Economics*, vol. 19, no. 2, pp. 305–321.

Malkin, Lawrence. (1987). *The national debt.* New York: Mentor.

Martin, Philippe and Carol Ann Rogers. (1995). *Long-term growth and short-term economic instability.* London: Centre for Economic Policy.

Mathur, Purushottam N. (1987). A perspective on productivity, wages, and income in developing countries after the commodity price crash of the 1980s. *London: University College London, Department of Economics.*

*Mayer, Martin. (1955) *Wall Street: men and money.* New York: Harper & Brothers.

*Mayer, Martin. (1969). *New breed on Wall Street.* New York: Macmillan.

*Mayer, Martin. (1975). Conflicts of Interest: Broker-dealer firms. *New York: Twentieth Century Fund.*

*Mayer, Martin. (1978). The builders. New York: Norton.

*Mayer, Martin. (1980). The fate of the dollar. New York: Times Books.

*Mayer, Martin. (1983) has published non-fiction books). *The Diplomats.* New York: Doubleday.

Mayer, Martin. (1984). The money Bazaars. Understanding the banking revolution around us. *New York: Dutton.*

*Mayer, Martin. (1988). *Markets: who plays, who risks, who gains, who loses.* New York: Simon & Schuster.

*Mayer, Martin. (1992). *Stealing the market.* New York: Basic Books.

*Mayer, Martin. (1993). *Nightmare on Wall Street.* New York: Simon & Schuster.

*Mayer, Martin. (1997). *The bankers: the next generation. The new worlds of money and banking in an electronic age.* New York: Truman Talley Book / Dutton.

McKenzie, George and Stephen Thomas. (1992). *Financial instability and the international debt problem.* Hampshire: Macmillan, in association with the Centre for International Economics, University of Southampton. - Includes bibliographical references and index.

Melnik, Arie L. and Steven E. Plaut. (1991). *The short-term euro-credit market.* New York: New York University.

Melvin, Michael. (1989). *International finance and finance*, New York: Harper & Row.

Mikdashi, Zuhayr. (ed.). (1993?). *Financial strategies and public policies: banking, insurance, and industry.* New York: St. Martin's Press.

Miller, Merton H. (1991). *Financial innovations and market volatility.* Cambridge, MA: Blackwell.

*Millman, Gregory. (1995). *The Vandals Crown. How rebel currency traders overthrew the world's central banks.* New York: The Free Press.

Mills, Mark P. and Thomas R. Stauffer with Frank H. Lennox. (1986). *The crash in world oil prices: an analysis of market pressures on world oil prices.* Washington, DC: U.S. Committee for Energy Awareness.

*Minsky, Hyman P. (1982). *Can 'It' happen again?: essays on instability and finance.* Armonk, NY: Sharpe.

*Minsky, Hyman P. (1982). *Inflation, recession, and economic policy.* Armonk, NY: Sharpe; London: Wheatsheaf.

*Minsky, Hyman P. (1986). *Stabilizing an unstable economy.* New Haven: Yale University Press.

Minsky, Hyman P. (1995). 'Foreword'. In Ronnie J. Phillips (ed.), *The Chicago plan & New Deal banking reform.* Armonk, NY: Sharpe.

Mishkin, Frederic S. (1986). *The economics of money, banking, and financial market.* Boston: Little, Brown.

Mishkin, Frederic S. (1990). *Anatomy of a financial crisis.* Cambridge, MA: National Bureau of Economic Research.

Mishkin, Frederic S. (1990). *Asymmetric information and financial crises: a historical perspective.* Cambridge, MA: National Bureau of Economic Research. Prepared for the National Bureau of Economic Research's Conference on Financial Crisis, March 22-24, 1990 in Key Biscayne, Florida.

Mishkin, Frederic S. (1990). *Financial innovation and current trends in U.S. financial markets.* Cambridge, MA: National Bureau of Economic Research.

Mishkin, Frederic S. (1994). *Preventing financial crises: an international perspective.* Cambridge, MA: National Bureau of Economic Research.

Mishkin, Frederic S. (1996). *Understanding financial crises: a developing country perspective.* Cambridge, MA: National Bureau of Economic Research.

*Moffitt, Michael. (1983). *The World's money: international banking from Bretton Woods to the brink of insolvency.* New York: Simon & Schuster.

Muldur, Ugur. (1992). Towards a European banking competition policy: some lessons from an industrial analysis of French banking. Brussels: Centre for European Policy Studies.

Nascimento, Jean-Claude. (ed.). (1990). *The crisis in the financial sector and the authorities' reaction, the case of the Philippines.* Washington, DC: International Monetary Fund.

*Neal, Larry. (1990). *The rise of financial capitalism: international capital markets in the age of Reason.* New York: Cambridge University Press.

Nellis, Joseph and Rodney Thorn. (1983). 'The demand for mortgage finance in the UK.' *Applied Economics*, vol. 15, pp. 521–529.

*Newton, Maxwell. (1983). *The FED. Inside the federal reserve, the secret power centre that controls the American Economy.* New York: Times Books.

Obstfeld, Maurice. (1988). *Competitiveness, realignment, and speculation: the role of financial markets.* Cambridge, MA: National Bureau of Economic Research.

OECD. (1989). *Competition in banking.* Paris: OECD.

O'Hara, Phillip A. (1995). *The financial instability hypothesis and Australia's economic experience of the 1980s and early 1990s: an endogenous source of turbulence?* Perth, W.A.: Curtin University of Technology, School of Economics and Finance.

Organization of American States. (1984). *The economy of Latin America and the Caribbean: analysis and interpretations prompted by the financial crisis.* Washington, DC: Organization of American States, General Secretariat.

Palomino, Frederic. (1993). *Informed speculation: small markets against large markets.* Florence: European University Institute.

Patrick, Hugh T. and Yung Chul Park. (1994). *The financial development of Japan, Korea, and Taiwan. Growth, repression, and liberalization.* New York and Oxford: Oxford University Press.

Pauly, Louis W. (1997). *Who elected the bankers?: Surveillance and control in the world economy.* Ithaca, NY: Cornell University Press.

Peet, Richard (ed.). (1987). *International capitalism and industrial restructuring: a critical analysis.* Boston: Allen & Unwin.

Petzinger, Thomas. (1987). *Oil and honour.* New York: Putnam.

Phillips, Ronnie J. (1995). *The Chicago plan & New Deal banking reform*, foreword by Hyman P. Minsky. Armonk, NY: Sharpe.

Pirrong, Stephen Craig. (1996). *The economics, law, and public policy of market power manipulation.* New York: Springer.

*Plosser, Charles I. (1990). *Money and business cycles: a real business cycle interpretation.* Cambridge, MA: National Bureau of Economic Research.

Porter, Andrew N. and Robert F. Holland. (eds). (1985). *Money, finance, and Empire.* London: Frank Cass.

*Porter, Michael E. (1990). *The competitive advantage of nations.* London: Macmillan.

Portes, Richard and Alexander K. Swoboda. (1987). *Threats to international financial stability.* Cambridge: Cambridge University Press.

Ramirez, Carlos and J. Bradford De Long. (1996). 'Banker influence and business economic performance: assessing the impact of depression-era financial reforms.' In Michael Bordo and Richard Sylla (eds). *Anglo-American financial systems: institution and markets in the twentieth century.* New York: Irwin, pp. 161-178.

Rappoport, Peter and Eugene N. White. (1991). *Was there a bubble in the 1929 stock market?* Cambridge, MA: National Bureau of Economic Research.

Reid, Margaret. (1982). *The secondary banking crisis, 1973–1975: its causes and course.* London: Macmillan.

Rich, Bruce. (1994). *Mortgaging the earth. The world bank's environmental impoverishment and the crisis of development.* Boston: Beacon Press.

*Roberts, Richard and David Kynaston. (eds). (1995). *The bank of England. Money, power, and influence 1694–1994.* Oxford: Clarendon Press.

Romer, Christina D. (1988). *The great crash and the onset of the great depression.* Cambridge, MA: National Bureau of Economic Research.

Rossi, Salvatore. (1983). *Foreign exchange speculation in the very short run: a theoretical hypothesis and some preliminary empirical results.* Rome: Banca d'Italia, Research Department.

Ruigrok, Winfried. (1993). *When the bubble burst...: Japanese internationalisation strategies and the management of international dependencies.* Rotterdam: Erasmus Universiteit/Rotterdam School of Management.

Sachs, Jeffrey. (1991). 'Robin Hoods: How the big banks spell debt "Relief"'. In Steven L. Spiegel (ed.), *At issue. Politics in the world arena* 6th ed. New York: St. Martin's Press, pp. 293–299.

Saint Phalle, Thibaut de. (ed.). (1983). *The international financial crisis: an opportunity for constructive action.* Washington, DC: Georgetown University, Center for Strategic & International Studies.

*Sampson, Anthony. (1981). *The Money Lenders.* London: Hodder & Stoughton.

Sampson, Anthony. (1989). *The Midas touch. Why the rich nations get richer and the poor stay poor.* New York: Truman Talley/Plume.

Saunders, Anthony. (ed.). (1992). *Recent developments in finance.* New York: New York University, Salomon Center, Leonard N. Stern School of Business; Homewood, IL: Business One Irwin.

Saunders, Anthony. (1994). *Financial institutions management: a modern perspective.* Burr Ridge, IL: Irwin.

Saunders, Anthony. (1996). *Financial institutions management.* Chicago, IL: Irwin.

Saunders, Anthony and Lemma W. Senbet. (1992). *Financial research on Africa: a financial theory perspective.* New York: New York University Salomon Center.

Saunders, Anthony and Ingo Walter. (1994). *Universal banking in the United States: what could we gain? what could we lose?* New York: Oxford University Press.

*Saunders, Anthony and Ingo Walter. (eds). (1996). *Universal banking: financial system design reconsidered.* Chicago, IL: Irwin.

Saunders, Anthony, Gregory F. Udell and Lawrence J. White. (eds). (1992). *Bank management and regulation: a book of readings*. Mountain View, CA: Mayfield Pub. Co.

Saunders, Anthony and Berry Wilson. (1995). *Contingent liability in banking: useful policy for developing countries*. Washington, DC: World Bank, Policy Research Department.

Schiller, Robert J., Fumiko Konya, and Yoshiro Tsutsui. (1988). *Investor behavior in the Oktober 1987 stock market crash: the case of Japan*. Cambridge, MA: National Bureau of Economic Research.

Schuker, Stephen A. (1988). *American reparations to Germany, 1919–1933: implications for the third world debt crisis*. Princeton, NJ: Princeton University.

Schwert, G. William. (1989). *Stock volatility and the crash of '87*. Cambridge, MA: National Bureau of Economic Research.

Shelton, Judy. (1989). *The coming of the Soviet crash: Gorbachev's desperate pursuit of credit in Western financial markets*. London: Duckworth.

*Shepherd, William F. (1994). *International financial integration. History, theory, and applications in OECD countries*. Aldershot: Avebury.

Shields, Jon (1988). 'Controlling household credit.' *National Institute Economic* Review, vol. 125, pp. 46–55.

Smith, Roy. (1990). *The money wars*. New York: Dutton.

Sobel, Robert. (1988). *Panic on Wall Street: a classic history of America's financial disasters – with a new exploration of the crash of 1987*. New York: Truman Talley Books.

*Solomon, Steven. (1995). *The confidence game: how unelected central bankers are governing the changed global economy*. New York: Simon & Shuster.

Spotton, Brenda. (1997). 'Financial instability reconsidered: orthodox theories versus historical facts.' *Journal of Economic Issues*, vol. XXXI, no.1, March 1997, pp. 175–195.

Steinherr, Alfred and Pier-Luigi Gilibert. (1989). *The impact of financial market integration on the European banking industry*. Brussels: Centre for European Policy Studies.

Stokes, Peter. (1992). *Ship finance: credit expansion and the boom-bust cycle*. London: Lloyd's of London Press.

*Strange, Susan. (1986). *Casino capitalism*. Oxford: Blackwell.

Surajaras, Patchara and Richard J. Sweeney. (1991). *Profit-making speculation in foreign exchange markets*. Boulder, CO: Westview Press.

Sutton, Anthony. (1986). *An introduction to the order*. Billings, MT: Liberty House Press.

Swary, Itzhak and Barry Topf. (1992). *Global financial deregulation. Commercial banking at the crossroads*. Cambridge, MA and Oxford: Blackwell.

Taniguchi, Tomohiko. (1993). *Japan's banks and the 'bubble economy' of the late 1980s*. Princeton, NJ: Princeton University, Center of International Studies, Program on U.S.-Japan Relations.

Tanzi, Vito. (ed.). (1992). *Fiscal policies in economies in transition*. Washington, DC: International Monetary Fund.

Tanzi, Vito. (ed.). (1993). *Transition to market: studies in fiscal reform*. Washington, DC: International Monetary Fund.

Tanzi, Vito. (1995). *Taxation in an integrating world*. Washington, DC: Brookings Institution.

Teichova, Alice, Terry Gourvish, and Agnes Pogany. (eds). (1994). *Universal banking in twentieth century: finance, industry and the state in North and Central Europe*. Aldershot: Edward Elgar.

*Teweless, Richard J. et al. (1989). *The futures game: who wins? who loses? why?* New York: McGraw-Hill.

Thomas, William A. (1978). The finance of British industry, 1918–*1976*. London: Methuen.

Toporowski, Jan. (1993). The *economics of financial markets and the* 1987 Crash. Aldershot and Brookfield, VT: Edward Elgar.

Train, John and Pierre Le-Tan (Illustrator). (1985). *Famous financial fiascos*. New York: C.N. Potter.

UNIDO. (1983). *Types of finance for industry*. Vienna: UNIDO, Sectoral Studies Branch, Division for Industrial Studies.

*Vaga, Tonis. (1994). *Profiting from chaos: using chaos theory for market timing, stock selection, and option valuation.* New York: McGraw-Hill.

Van Helten, Jean-Jacques and Youssef Cassis. (eds). (1990). *Capitalism in a mature economy: financial institutions, capital exports and British industry, 1870–1939.* Aldershot: Elgar.

Velasco, Andres. (ed.). (1988). *Liberalization, crisis, intervention: the Chilean financial system, 1975-1985.* [Washington, D.C.]: International Monetary Fund. Central Banking Dept.

Viane, Jean-Marie. (1991). *Real effects of the 1992 financial deregulation.* European Research Workshop in International Trade. Stockholm: Institute for International Economic Studies.

*Vicarelli, Fausto. (1984). *J.M. Keynes, the instability of capitalism.* Philadelphia: University of Pennsylvania Press. (Orig. title *Keynes, l'instabilità del capitalism,* Milan: Etas Libri, 1977).

*Vincent, Isabel. (1997). *Hitler's silent bankers: how the Swiss Banks bankrolled the Nazis and their final solution against the Jews.* New York: William Morrow.

Volcker, Paul and Toyoo Gyohten. (1992). *Changing fortunes. The world's money and the threat to American leadership.* New York: Times Books.

Vries, Margaret Garritsen de. (1986). *The IMF in a changing world.* Washington, DC: International Monetary Fund.

Walker, Robert and Gillian Parker. (1988). *Money matters: income, wealth, and financial welfare.* London: Sage.

Walter, Ingo. (1985). *Secret money. The world of international financial secrecy.* London: Allen & Unwin.

*Watchel, Howard. (1986). *The money mandarins. the making of a supranational economic order.* New York: Pantheon Books.

Weitz, John. (1997). *Hitler's banker: Hjalmar Horace Greeley Schacht.* Boston: Little, Brown.

Weymark, John A. (1980). Money and Locke's theory of property. *History of Political Economy,* vol. 12, no. 2, pp. 282-290.

White, Eugene. (ed). (1990). *Financial panics in historical perspective.* New York: Dow-Jones-Irwin.

White, Lawrence J. (1992). *Why now? Change and turmoil in U.S. banking. Causes, consequences and lessons.* Washington, DC: Group of Thirty.

White, Lawrence H. (ed.). (1993). *The crisis in American banking.* New York: New York University Press.

Wigmore, Barrie A. (1985). *The crash and its aftermath: a history of securities markets in the United States, 1929-1933.* Westport, CT: Greenwood Press.

Williamson, Oliver E. (1985). *The economic institutions of capitalism. Firms, markets, relational contracting.* New York: The Free Press. Macmillan.

Wood, Christopher. (1992). The bubble economy: Japan's extraordinary speculative boom of the '80s and the dramatic bust of the '90s. New York: Atlantic Monthly Press.

World Bank. (1993). *The East Asian Miracle. Economic growth and public policy,* A World Bank Research. Washington, DC: The International Bank for Reconstruction and Development/ Oxford University Press.

Wright, Vincent. (1995). *Industrial and banking privatization in Western Europe: some public policy paradoxes.* Florence: The Robert Schuman Centre at the European University Institute.

Yao-Su Hu. (1984). *Industrial banking and special credit institutions: a comparative study.* London: Policy Studies Institute.

Zepeda Miramontes, Eduardo. (1988). *Internationalization, dollarization and the roots of financial crisis in Mexico.* Ann Arbor, MI: University Microfilms International - 3 microfiches, Dissertation University of California, Riverside.

*Zweig, Phillip L. (1996). *Wriston: Walter Wriston, Citibank, and the rise and fall of American financial supremacy.* New York: Crown.

II) LITERATURE IN CONTINENTAL LANGUAGES, AFTER 1982

Altmann, Jörn and Udo E. Simonis. (1983). *Entwicklungsländer in der Finanzkrise: Probleme und Perspektiven.* Berlin: Duncker und Humblot.

Austrup, Jürgen. (1994). *Zinsbesteuerung.* Frankfurt am Main: P. Lang.
Beijer, Carola. (1993). *De 'bubble' economie: oorzaken en gevolgen van de speculatiekoorts in Japan.* Rotterdam: Erasmus Universiteit.
Borchert, Manfred. (1982). *Geld und Kredit. Eine Einführung in die Geldtheorie und Geldpolitik.* Stuttgart: Verlag W.Kohlhammer.
Braudel, Fernand. (1985). *La dynamique du capitalisme.* Paris: Les Editions Arthaud.
*De Long, J. Bradford. (1995). 'Können Finanzmärkte zu liquide sein?: Gefahr der Verstärkung von Kurseinbrüchen.' *Neue Zürcher Zeitung: Elektronische Borse Schweiz,* December 5, p. B 14. (English title 'Can a Financial Market Be Too Liquid and Too Efficient?'.)
Dun, Frank van. (1988). *Crash en depressie.* Doetinchem: KNO, Kritische Nederlandse Ondernemers; Brussel: Stichting Ludwig von Mises.
*Hansen, Reginald. (1996). *Die praktischen Konsequenzen des Methodenstreits. Eine Aufarbeitung der Einkommensbesteuerung.* Berlin: Duncker & Humblot.
Herr, Hansjörg. (1986). *Geld, Kredit und ökonomische Dynamik in marktvermittelten Ökonomien (die Vision einer Geldwirtschaft).* Munich: Verlag Florentz.
Moers, Luc A.M. (1994). *Welke lessen trekt Japan uit de 'bubble'?* Amsterdam: De Nederlandsche Bank. From: *Bank- en effectenbedrijf.* vol. 43, no. 6, pp. 26–29.
North, Michael. (1994). *Das Geld und seine Geschichte: vom Mittelalter bis zur Gegenwart.* Munich: Beck.
Reuveni, Amnon. (1994). *In Namen der 'Neuen Weltordnung'. Vom unzeitgemässen Herrschaftswillen und seinen Trägern in der Weltpolitik.* Dornach, CH: Verlag am Goetheanum.
Vollkommer, Max. (ed.). (1989). *Der Zins in Recht, Wirtschaft und Ethik.* Atzelsberger Gespräche 1988: drei Vorträge. Erlangen: Universitätsbund Erlangen-Nürnberg.

III) LITERATURE IN SCANDINAVIAN, AFTER 1982

Andresen, Trond. (1991). 'Bank- og verdenskrise.' *Klassekampen,* October 28.
Andresen, Trond. (1991). 'Regulert frihandel?' *Klassekampen,* November 5.
Andvig, Jens Christopher. (1983). 'Ragnar Frisch and business cycle research during the interwar years,' *History of Political Economy,* Vol. 13, no. 4, pp. 695-725.
Aslaksen, Iulie. (1991). 'En kritisk vurdering av Margrit Kennedys "Det nye pengesystemet".' *Sosialøkonomen,* no. 4, pp. 26-29.
Batra, Ravi. (1988). *Den store depresjonen i 1990.* Oslo: Mercur Media forlag. (1985).
Bonné, Bjarne. (1990). *Verdensbanken og IMF. En kritisk grundbog.* Skive: Mellomfolkeligt Samvirke.
Braudel, Fernand. (1986). *Kapitalismens dynamikk.* Oslo: ARS. (Orig. title *La dynamique du capitalisme.*)
Castro, Fidel. (1986). *Verdens sosiale og økonomiske krise.* Report to the 7th top meeting of the Alliance-free nations. Oslo: Falken. (1983)
Commission on Money and Credit Policy. (1989). *Report by the commission on money and credit policy,* appointed by Royal decrees of June 5th, 1987, led by Per Kleppe, submitted to the Ministry of Finance and Customs February 15th, 1989, Oslo: Government Administration Services, Government Printing Service, Norwegian Official Reports NOR 1989: 1E. Norwegian version: NOU 1989: 1.
Commission on the Banking Crisis. (1992). *Report by the commission on the banking crisis,* appointed by Royal decrees of October 4, 1991, led by prof. Preben Munthe, submitted to the Ministry of Finance and Customs August 31. Oslo: Government Administration Services, Government Printing Service, Norwegian Official Reports NOR 1992: 30E. Norwegian version: NOU 1992: 30.
George, Susan. (1989). *En skjebne verre enn døden. Gjeldskrisen I den tredje verden.* Oslo: Cappelen.
Isachsen, Arne Jon. (ed.). (1984). *Penger, kreditt og valuta. En artikkelsamling.* Oslo: Universitetsforlaget.
Lewis, Michael. (1990). *Wall Street Poker. Historien om de grådige småbymeglerne.* Oslo: Hjemmets Bokforlag.

Vastrup, Claus. (1983). *Penge, spekulation og beskæftigelse*. Copenhagen: Jurist-Ökonomforbundets Forlag. English summary.
Vermnes, Thomas. (1990). Frihandel er en fare for jordas miljø. Intervju med Trygve Haavelmo. Klassekampen: November 3.

2) NEW MONETARY SYSTEM MOVEMENTS (1920–1940, in particular): TECHNOCRACY-, SOCIAL CREDIT-, AND FREE MONEY

The classics in this field are, in particular (in alphabetical order), Bertram Dybwad Brochmann (1881-1956) (N), Clifford Hugh Douglas (1879–1952) (GB), Robert Eisler (1882-1949) (A), Silvio Gesell (1862-1930) (B), Arthur Kitson (1859-1937) (GB), Howard Scott (1880-1970) (US), Frederick Soddy (1877-1956) (GB) and Rudolf Steiner (1861-1925) (D). Chronologically, Arthur Kitson, Silvio Gesell and Rautenstrauch would have to be put first.

A thorough bibliography on the Technocracy movement can be found in Akin, William E. (1977) below.

I) LITERATURE IN ENGLISH

Adams, W. (1925). *Real wealth and financial poverty: a study of the present financial system as a monopoly of money, and its relation to productive industry, social poverty, and economic war, from the point of view of the Douglas credit analysis*. London: Palmer
Adamson, Martha and Raymond A. Moore. (1934). *Technocracy: some questions answered*. New York: Technocracy Inc.
*Akin, William E. (1977). *Technocracy and the American dream: the technocrat movement, 1900–1941*. Berkeley, CA: University of California Press.
All American Technology Society. (1933). *Manless machines and workless man*. Chicago: All American Technology Society.
Allen, Robert C. and Gideon Rosenbluth. (1986). *Restraining the economy: social credit, economic policies for B. C. in the eighties*. Vancouver: New Star Books.
Arkright, Frank. (1933). *The ABC of technocracy based on authorized material*. New York: Harper.
Baker, Charles. (1932. *Pathways back to prosperity*. New York: Funk & Wagnalls.
Barr, John J. (1974). *The dynasty: the rise and fall of social credit in Alberta*. Toronto: McClelland and Stewart.
Beard, Charles A. (1930). *The American Leviathan: the republic in the machine age*. New York: Macmillan.
Beard, Charles A. (1932). *America faces the future*. Boston: Houghton Mifflin.
Bell, Edward Allan. (1993). *Social classes and social credit in Alberta*, foreword by Maurice Pinard, Montreal. Buffalo: McGill-Queen's University Press.
Blanshard, Paul. (1933). *Technocracy and socialism*. New York: League for Industrial Democracy.
Boudreau, Joseph A. (1975). *Alberta, Aberhart, and social credit*. Toronto: Holt, Rinehart, and Winston.
Brandon, Joseph. (1933). *Technocracy or democracy: which shall govern our industries*. Hollis, NY: C.A. Baker.
Brochmann, Bertram Dybwad. (1953). *World economy problems in the light of modern psychology. New orientation. New acknowledgement. New life's program*. To the Universal Holy Realm Congress, Paris, December 1953. Bergen.
Burnham, James. (1941). *The managerial revolution*. New York: John Day.

Chaplin, Ralph. (1948). *The rough-and-tumble of an American radical.* Chicago, IL: University of Chicago Press.

Chase, Stuart. (1925). *The tragedy of waste.* New York: Macmillan.

Chase, Stuart. (1930). *Men and machines,* illustrated by W.T. Murch. New York: Macmillan.

Chase, Stuart and Frederick J. Schlink (1931). *Your money's worth: a study in the waste of the consumer's dollar.* New York: Macmillan.

Chase, Stuart. (1931). *Out of the depression and after a prophecy.* New York: John Day.

*Chase, Stuart. (1932). *A new deal.* New York: Macmillan.

Chase, Stuart. (1933). *Technocracy: an interpretation.* New York: John Day.

Chase, Stuart. (1933). *Technocratie: het probleem der machinale productie.* Amersfoort: Valkhoff.

*Chase, Stuart. (1934). *The economy of abundance.* New York: Macmillan.

Chase, Stuart. (1936). *Rich land, poor land: a study of waste in the natural resources.* New York: McGraw-Hill.

*Cheadle, John B., Howard O. Eaton, and Cortez A.M. Ewing. (1934). *No more unemployed.* Norman, OK: Oklahoma University Press.

*Cole, George D.H. (ed.). (1933). *What everybody wants to know about money: a planned outline of monetary problems,* by nine economists from Oxford. London: Gollancz.

Cole, George D.H. (ed.). (1944). *Money: its present and future.* London: Cassell.

Cole, George D.H. (ed.). (1954). *Money: trade and investment.* London: Cassell. Completely rev. ed. of: *Money, its present and future* (1944).

Committee on Elimination of Waste in Industry of the Federated American Engineering Societies. (1921). *Waste in Industry.* New York: McGraw-Hill.

Continental Committee on Technocracy. (1933). *Plan of Plenty.* New York: Continental Committee on Technocracy.

*Davis, J.Ronnie (1971). *The new economists and the old economists.* Ames, IA: Iowa State University.

Director, Aron. (1933). *The economics of technocracy.* Chicago: University of Chicago Press.

Douglas, Clifford H. (1920). *Credit-power and democracy: with a draft scheme for the mining industry.* London: Cecil Palmer.

Douglas, Clifford H. (1924). *Social credit.* London: Palmer.

*Douglas, Clifford H. (1931). *The monopoly of credit.* London: Chapman & Hall.

Douglas, Clifford H.). (1969). *The development of world dominion*; published for the Social Credit Secretariat. Sydney: Tidal Publications; London: H.R.P. Publications.

*Eisler, Robert. (1932). *Stable money: the remedy for the economic world crisis: a programme of financial reconstruction for the international conference 1933.* With a preface by Vincent C. Vickers. London: The Search Publishing Co.

Field, Arthur N. (1932). *The truth about the slump.* Nelson, New Zealand: A.N. Field.

Finlay, John L. (1972). *Social credit; the English origins.* Montreal: McGill-Queens University Press.

Foster, William. (1933). *Technocracy and communism.* New York: Workers Library Publication.

Frederick, Justus G. (1933). *For and against technocracy.* New York: Business Bourse.

Gesell, Silvio. (1929). *The natural economic order.* Berlin: Neo-Verlag.

Grace, Alonzo G. et al. (1933). *Technocracy: fad, fallacy, or fact?* Rochester, NY: University of Rochester.

Graham, Frank D. (1932). *The abolition of unemployment.* Princeton University Press.

*Graham, Frank D. (1942). *Social goals and economic institutions.* Princeton: Princeton University Press.

Haldane, J.B.S. (1928). *Possible worlds. (And other essays).* New York and London: Harper & Brothers.

Hallgren, Mauritz. (1933). *Seeds of revolt: a study of American life and the temper of the American people during the depression.* New York: Knopf.

Hancock, A.E. (1973). *Social credit: a plan for Alberta.* Lethbridge, Alta.: Insight Pub. Co.

Hardorp, Benediktus. (1958). *Elemente einer Neubestimmung des Geldes und ihre Bedeutung für die Finanzwirtschaft der Unternehmung,* Dissertation Freiburg im Breisgau.

Harrison, John F.C. (1969). *Quest for the new moral world.* New York: Scribner.

Hattersley, Charles Marshall. (1922). *The community's credit: a consideration of the principles and proposals of the social credit movement.* London: Credit Power Press.

Hattersley, Charles Marshall. (1929). *This age of plenty: its problems and their solution.* London: Pitman.

Hawkins, Williard. (1934). *Castaways of plenty: a parable of our times.* Denver, CO: Rocky Mountain Division of the Continental Committee on Technocracy.

Henderson, Fred. (1931). *Economic consequences of power production.* London: Allen and Unwin.

Holder, William. (1933). *Simplified technocracy.* Salt Lake City: Pyramid Press.

*Hollis, Christopher. (1934). *The breakdown of money: an historical explanation.* London: Sheed & Ward.

Hollis, Christopher. (1935). *The two nations: a financial study of English history.* London: Routledge.

Hollis, Christopher. (1949). *Can parliament survive?* London: Hollis & Carter.

Hollis, Christopher. (1973). *Parliament and its sovereignty.* London: Hollis and Carter.

Hoogendijk, Willem, Hans C. Binswanger and Henk A. Plenter. (1995). *Money, from master to servant: about the liberation of productivity and the road towards genuine and just sustainability.* Utrecht: PROMODECO.

Hubbert, M. King. (1936). *Man-hours and distribution.* New York: Technocracy Inc.

Hutchinson, Frances and Brian Burkitt. (1997). *The political economy of social credit & guild socialism.* New York: Routledge.

Johnson, Julia Emily. (1933). *Selected articles on capitalism and its alternatives.* New York: Wilson.

Jones, Bassett. (1933). *Debt and production: the operating characteristics of our industrial economy.* New York: John Day.

Kennedy, Margrit. (1987). *Interest and inflation free money.* Steyerberg: Permaculture Institute.

*Kitson, Arthur. (1895). *A scientific solution of the money question.* Boston: Arena Publishing.

Kitson, Arthur. (1904). *A corner in gold.* London: King & Son.

Kitson, Arthur. (1910). *Usury (payment for the use of things) the prime cause of want and unemployment*: an address delivered by Mr. Arthur Kitson at the Sesame Club, London, May 2nd, 1910. London: Frank Palmer.

Kitson, Arthur. (1917). *Trade fallacies: a criticism of existing methods and suggestions for a reform towards national prosperity.* London: King & Son.

Kitson, Arthur. (1917). *A fraudulent standard: an exposure of the fraudulent character of our monetary standard, with suggestions for the establishment of an invariable unit of value.* London: King & Son.

Kitson, Arthur. (1921). *Unemployment, the cause and a remedy.* London: Cecil Palmer.

*Kitson, Arthur. (1933). *The bankers' conspiracy which started the world crisis.* Oxford: Alden Press.

Kixmiller, William. (1932). *Can business men produce a great age: an answer to technocracy.* New York: Commerce Clearing House.

Laing, Graham A. (1933). *Toward technocracy.* Los Angeles: Angelus Press.

Lardner, John and Tomas Surgue. (1933). *The crowning of technocracy.* New York: McBride.

Leech, Harper. (1932). *Paradox of plenty.* New York: McGraw-Hill.

Ligue du crédit social de la province de Québec. *Cahiers du crédit social.* Gardenvale, Québec: Ligue du crédit social de la province de Québec.

Loeb, Harold. (1933). *Life in a technocracy: what it might be like.* New York: Viking Press.

Loeb, Harold. (1946). *Full production without war.* Princeton, NJ: Princeton University Press.

Loeb Harold. (1959). *The way it was.* New York: Criterion Books.

Loeb, Harold et al. (1935). *The chart of plenty: a study of America's product capacity.* New York: Viking Press.

Mallory, James R. (1976, c1954). *Social credit and the federal power in Canada, its background and development.* Toronto: University of Toronto Press.

Mark, Jeffrey. (1934). The modern idolatry. An analysis of usury and the pathology of debt. London: Chatto and Windus.

Mayers, Henry. (1932). *The what, why, who, when, and how of technocracy.* Los Angeles: Angelus Press.

Melchett, Lord. (1931). *Why the crisis?* London: Gollancz.

Meulen, Henry. (1909). *Banking and the social problem.* London: Meulen.

Meulen, Henry. (1917). *Industrial justice through banking reform.* London: R.J. James.

Monahan, Bryan W. (1967). *An introduction to social credit.* London: K.R.P. Publications; Sydney, Tidal Publications.

Montgomery, Richard. (1995). *Disciplining or protecting the poor?: avoiding the social costs of peer pressure in solidarity group micro-credit schemes.* Swansea: University of Wales, Centre for Development Studies.

*Myers, Margaret G. (1940). *Monetary proposals for social reform.* New York: Columbia University Press.

New York City Housing Authority. (1935). *Report of the national survey of potential production capacity.* New York: New York City Housing Authority.

New Zealand Social Credit Political League. (1972?). *General policy.* Wellington: The League.

Nichols, Herbert Edward. (1900). *A handbook of social credit.* Toronto: The Social Credit Association of Canada.

North, Gary. (1993). *Salvation through inflation: the economics of social credit.* Tyler, TX: Institute for Christian Economics.

Osborne, J. Stephen and J. Tom Osborne. (1986). *Social credit for beginners: an armchair guide.* Vancouver: Pulp Press Book Publishers.

Parrish, Wayne. (1933). *An outline of technocracy.* New York: Farrar & Rhinehart.

Persky, Stan. (1989). *Fantasy government: Bill Vander Zalm and the future of social credit.* Vancouver: New Star Books.

Porter, Henry A. (1932). *Roosevelt and technocracy.* New York: Farrar & Rhinehart.

Pound, Ezra. (1935). *Social credit: an impact.* London: S. Nott.

President's Research Committee on Social Trends. (1933). *Recent social trends in the United States.* New York: McGraw-Hill.

*Rautenstrauch, Walter. (1934). *Who gets the money?: a study in the economics of scarcity and plenty.* New York: Harper & Brothers.

Rautenstrauch, Walter. (1939). *The economics of business enterprise.* New York: John Wiley & Sons.

Rautenstrauch, Walter. (1940). *Industrial surveys and reports.* New York: John Wiley & Sons.

Raymond, Allen, (1933). *What is technocracy?* New York: Whittlesey House of McGraw-Hill.

*Reeve, Joseph E. (1943). *Monetary reform movements. A survey of recent plans and panaceas.* Washington, DC: American Council on Public Affairs.

Rose, William C. (1968). *Social credit handbook.* Toronto, Montreal: McClelland and Stewart.

Rugg, Harold. (1933). *The great technology: social chaos and the public mind.* New York: John Day.

Scott, Howard. (1933). *Science versus chaos.* New York: Technocracy Inc.

*Scott, Howard and others. (1933). *Introduction to technocracy,* with an introductory statement by the Continental Committee on Technocracy and a selected reading list for laymen from the literature of science. New York: John Day.

Slocomb, Whitney. (1932). *How to put technocracy into practice.* Los Angeles: Oxford Typesetting Co.

Smalley, Jack. (1933). *The technocrats' magazine.* Minneapolis: Graphic Arts Corp.

Smyth, William H. (1932). *Technocracy: four pamphlets.* Berkeley, CA: Fernwald Press.

Smyth, William H. (1933). *Coming events cast their shadows before.* Berkeley, CA: privately printed.

Smyth, William H. (1933). *Technocracy explained by its originator.* Berkeley: privately printed.

Social Credit Association of Canada. (1964). *Social credit explained.* Ottawa: Social Credit Association of Canada.

Social Credit Co-ordinating Centre. (1969). *Fifty years of social credit, 1919–1969: C.H. Douglas.* Mexborough (Yorkshire): Social Credit Co-ordinating Centre.

Social Credit Secretariat. *Social credit,* [microform]. London, Social Credit Secretariat.

*Soddy, Frederick. (1926). *Wealth, virtual wealth, and debt: the solution of the economic paradox.* London: Allen & Unwin.

Soddy, Frederick. (1931). *Money versus man.* London: Matthews and Marrot.
*Soddy, Frederick. (1934). *The role of money. What it should be, contrasted with what it has become.* London: Routledge.
Soddy, Frederick. (1950). *Money reform as a preliminary to all reform*: an address by Frederick Soddy, read Before the Birmingham Paint, Varnish & Lacquer Club on the occasion of the 21st anniversary of the founding of the club, January 12.
Stein, Michael B. (1973). *The dynamics of right-wing protest: a political analysis of social credit in Quebec.* Toronto: University of Toronto Press.
*Steiner, Rudolf. (1956). *World economy.* London: Rudolf Steiner Press. (Orig. title *Nationalökonomischer Kurs,* 1921).
Technocracy, Inc. (1933–1936). *Technocracy study course.* New York: Technocracy, Inc.
Technocracy, Inc. (1934). *Technocracy: some questions answered.* New York: Technocracy, Inc.
Thomas, Lewis H. (ed.). (1977). *William Aberhart and social credit in Alberta,* Toronto: Copp Clark.
Veblen, Thorstein Bunde. (1899). *The theory of the leisure class.* New York: Macmillan.
Veblen, Thorstein Bunde. (1920). *The vested interest and the common man.* New York: B.W. Huebsch.
Veblen, Thorstein Bunde. (1921). *The engineers and the price system.* New York: Huebsch.
Whitaker, Thomas K. (1947). *Financing by credit creation.* With an introduction by Ch. Hollis. Dublin: Clonmore & Reynolds.
Willyams, Albert E. (1953). *Social credit is for me.* Christchurch, NZ: Pegasus Press.
Wilson, Robert McNair. (1933). *Understanding technocracy.* San Diego, CA: New Era Publications.
Wilson, Robert McNair. (1956). *Promise to pay: an inquiry into the principles and practice of the latter-day magic called sometimes high finance.* London: Routledge.
Young, Walter D. (1969). *Democracy and discontent; progressivism, socialism, and social credit in the Canadian west.* Toronto: Ryerson Press.

Magazines and periodicals:

Alberta social credit chronicle [microfilm]. (1934-1938). Calgary: Glenbow-Alberta Institute, Commonwealth Microfilm Products.
BC on the move: social credit news & views. Vancouver: On the Move Publications (1987–1988?)
British Columbia Social Credit Party. (1988-). *Party-link.* Richmond, BC: BCSC Publications.
The Canadian Social Crediter [microform]. Edmonton, Social Credit Association of Canada.
Focus, [microform], Ottawa [etc.], Social Credit Association of Canada.
Regards. (1977). (Athabaska, Quebec). Regards [microform], Montréal: Société canadienne du microfilm Huronia News Services.
Messenger, Wasaga Beach, Ont.: Huronia News Services.
The Social Credit Messenger. Wasaga Beach, Ontario: Grey-Simcoe (federal) Riding Association, 1976–1977.

II) LITERATURE IN CONTINENTAL LANGUAGES

(Mainly on Gesell and Steiner)

Belte, Theodor. (1974). *Die menschenwürdige Gesellschaft.* Frankfurt am Main: Vittorio Klostermann.
Binswanger, Hans C. (1985). *Geld und Magie: Deutung und Kritik der modernen Wirtschaft anhand von Goethes Faust.* Stuttgart: Weitbrecht.
Canal, Georg Freiherr von. (1992). *Geisteswissenschaft und Ökonomie.* Schaffhausen CH: Novalis Verlag.
Creutz, Helmut. (1994). *Das Geldsyndrom - Wege zu einer krisenfreien Marktwirtschaft.* Frankfurt am Main: Ullstein.

Gesell, Silvio. (1891). *Die Reformation in Münzwesen als Brücke zum Sozialen Staat.* Buenos Aires: S. Gesell.

Gesell, Silvio. (1897). *Die Anpassung des Geldes und seiner Verwaltung an die Bedürfnisse des modernen Verkehrs.* Buenos-Aires: Herpig & Stoeveken.

Gesell, Silvio. (1898). *La razon economica del desacuerdo chileno-argentino.* Buenos Aires: 'La Buenos Aires'.

Gesell, Silvio. (1906). *Die Verwirklichung des Rechtes auf den vollen Arbeitsertrag durch die Geld- und Bodenreform.* (*Zugleich eine Erledigung der Interessen-Politik und der Volkswirtschafts-Wissenschaft*). Leipzig: Hermann.

Gesell, Silvio. (1911). *Die neue Lehre vom Geld und Zins: eine Zusammenfassung, Läuterung und Vervollständigung früherer Schriften des Verfassers.* Leipzig: Hermann.

*Gesell, Silvio. (1916). *Die natürliche Wirtschaftsordnung durch Freiland und Freigeld.* Berlin: Blumenthal.

Gesell, Silvio. (1920). *Das Reichswährungsamt.* Rehbrücke bei Postdam: Freiland-Freigeld-verlag.

Gesell, Silvio. (1920). *Internationale valuta-assoziation.* Sontra in Hessen: Freiwirtschaftlicher Verlag..

Gesell, Silvio. (1922). *Denkschrift an die deutschen Gewerkschaften.* Potsdam: Müller.

Gesell, Silvio. Edited by H. Sveistrup. (1931). *Die Freiwirtschaftslehre als Wissenschaft, Weisung und Technik*: Rede, gehalten zum Gedächtnis an Silvio Gesell am 11. März 1931 im Lessing-Museum zu Berlin. Lauf bei Nürnberg: Zitzmann.

Gesell, Silvio. (1960). *Silvio Gesell: Zeitgenössische Stimmen zum Werk und Lebensbild eines Pioniers,* Beiträge von Hans Blüher, Werner Schmid, B. Uhlemayer [et al.]. Lauf bei Nürnberg: Zitzmann.

Gesell, Silvio. (1988). *Gesammelte Werke in 18 Bänden.* Lütjenburg: Gauke-Verlag, 1988 – ca. 1997.

Hegge, Hjalmar. (1992). *Freiheit, Induvidualität und Gesellschaft.* Stuttgart: Verlag Freies Geistesleben. (Orig. title *Frihet, individualitet og samfunn*).

Herrmanstorfer, Udo. (1992). *Scheinmarktschaft. Die Unverkäuflichkeit von Arbeit, Boden und Kapital.* Stuttgart: Verlag Freies Geistesleben.

Kennedy, Margrit. (1987). *Geld ohne Zinsen und inflation.* Steyerberg: Permaculture Institute.

Kennedy, Margrit. (1991). *Geld ohne Zinsen und Inflation – Ein Tauschmittel, das jedem dient.* Munich: Goldmann Verlag.

Leverkus, Erich. (1990). *Freier Tausch und fauler Zauber: vom Geld und seiner Geschichte.* Frankfurt am Main: Knapp.

Scharmer, Claus Otto. (1991). *Ästhetik als Kategorie strategischer Führung. Der ästhetische Typus von wirtschaftlichen Organisationen. Die künstlerische Perspektive als Ausgangspunkt der ökonomische Theorie. Auf der Suche nach der gegenwartfähigen Universität.* Stuttgart: Ursachhaus.

Schärrer, Markus. (1983). *Geld- und Bodenreform als Brücke zum sozialen Staat: die Geschichte der Freiwirtschaftsbewegung in der Schweiz (1915–1952).* Dissertation Zürich. Zürich University: Zentralstelle der Studentenschaft.

Schönmann, Ernst. (1952). *Karl Marx / Das Kapital: die wirtschaftlichen Lehren von Karl Marx aufs Neue dargeboten und einer Auswahl kritischer Stimmen,* von Thomas G. Masaryk, Karl Kautsky und Silvio Gesell, Affoltern am Albis: Ähren Verlag.

Schweppenhäuser, Hans G. (1969). *Arbeit, Lohn und Preis in ihrem Zusammenhang.* Dornach, CH: Verlag am Goetheanum.

Schweppenhäuser, Hans G. (1971). *Das Kranke Geld. Vorschläge für eine soziale Geldordnung von Morgen.* Stuttgart: Radius Verlag.

Senf, Bernd. (1996). *Der Nebel um das Geld.* Lütjenburg: Gauke Verlag.

Smundt, Wilhelm. (1968). *Der soziale Organismus in seiner Freiheitsgestalt.* Dornach, CH: Philosophisch-Antroposophischer Verlag.

Smundt, Wilhelm. (1973). *Revolution und Evolution.* Achberg bei Lindau: Verlag Edition dritter Weg.

Steiner, Rudolf. (1905–1906). *Geisteswissenschaft und soziale Frage* (Org.: Theosophie und soziale Frage). Dornach, CH., 1957.

Steiner, Rudolf. (1920). *Die Kernpunkte der soziale Frage in den Lebensnotwendigkeiten der Gegenwart und Zukunft.*
*Steiner, Rudolf. (1921). *Nationalökonomischer Kurs.* Dornach, CH.: Steiner.
Suhr, Dieter. (1975). *Bewusstseinsverfassung und Gesellschaftsverfassung: über Hegel und Marx zu einer dialektischen Verfassungstheorie.* Berlin: Duncker & Humblot.
Suhr, Dieter. (1988). *Alternes Geld. Das Konzept Rudolf Steiners aus geldtheoretischer Sicht.* Schaffhausen, CH.: Novalis Verlag.
Suhr, Dieter and Hugo Godschalk. (1986). *Optimale Liquidität: eine liquiditätstheoretische Analyse und ein kreditwirtschaftliches Wettbewerbskonzept.* Frankfurt am Main: Knapp.
Werner, Hans-Joachim. (1990). *Geschichte der Freiwirtschaftsbewegung - 100 Jahre Kampf für eine Marktwirtschaft ohne Kapitalismus.* Münster: Waxmann.
Wilken, Folkert. (1976). *Das Kapital und die Zukunft. Sein Wesen seine Geschichte und sein Wirken im 20. Jahrhundert.* Schaffhausen, CH: Novalis Verlag.
*Wilken, Folkert. (1981). *Das Kapital und das Geld. Die Wirtschaft als Geldorganismus.* Schaffhausen, CH: Novalis Verlag.
Wilken, Folkert. (1981). *Das Kapital und die Zukunft. Die assoziative Bedarfsdeckungswirtschaft.* Schaffhausen, CH: Novalis Verlag.
Witzenmann, Herbert. (1995). *Geldordnung als Bewusstseinsfrage.* Krefeld: Gideon Spicker.

Magazines:

Der dritte Weg - Zeitschrift für die natürliche Wirtschaftsordnung, Erftstr. 57, 45219 Essen.
Die natürliche Wirtschaftsordnung im World Wide Web / http://www.nwo.de/.
Zeitschrift für Sozialökonomie, Gauke Verlag, Postfach 1320, 24319 Lütjenburg.

III) LITERATURE IN SCANDINAVIAN

*Bjørset, Brynjolf. (1934). *Efter oss kommer overfloden: kan den utnyttes og fordeles rasjonelt?: aktuelle forslag og forsøk: en oversikt og en sammenligning.* Oslo: Aschehoug.
Bjørset, Brynjolf. (1936). *Distribute or destroy.* London: Stanley Nott. (Orig. title *Efter oss kommer overfloden,* Oslo 1934).
*Bjørset, Brynjolf, Hans J. Utne, and Henrik Palmstrøm. (1937). *Fra kriser til kredittkontroll.* Oslo: Tanum.
*Bonde, Gjert E. (1934). *Den nye tids økonomi. Totalitetsøkonomien.* Bergen: Det frie samfunds forlag.
Bonde, Gjert E. (1936). *Totalitetsøkonomi. En populær fremstilling av samfundslivets nye evangelium, B. Dybwad Brochmann's livssyn og samfundslære.* Bergen: Bondes forlag.
Brochmann, Bertram Dybwad. (1920). *Veien til det nye land. (Aandsrevolusjonen).* Bergen: private printing.
Brochmann, Bertram Dybwad. (1934). *Fandens efterlatte Papirer.* Bergen: Det frie samfunds forlag.
Brochmann, Bertram Dybwad. (1956). *Realøkonomi kontra fiktivøkonomi. Sparing i overflodens tidsalder. Hvorfor Norge spiller fallitt.* Bergen: Det frie samfunds forlag.
Brochmann, Bertram Dybwad. (1959). *Eksakt vurdering og Verdilære.* Bergen: eget forlag (private printing).
*Colbiørnsen, Ole and Axel Sømme. (1933). *En norsk 3-aarsplan.* Oslo: Det norske arbeiderpartis forlag..
Eivindson, Solveig. (1983). 'Fra fiktivøkonomi til realøkonomi.' in: Anders Ryste et al, *Fredens sosiologi.* Ørsta: Bonde-Lanser forlag.
Førre, Ingvald. (1939). *Det nye pengesystem.* Oslo: Oslo Industritrykkeri.
*Hegge, Hjalmar. (1988). *Frihet, individualitet og samfunn. En moralfilosofisk, erkjennelsesteoretisk og sosialfilosofisk studie i menneskelig eksistens.* Oslo: Universitetsforlaget.

Holbæk-Hanssen, Leif. (1976). *Metoder og modeller i markedsføringen*, I-III, part III: *Planlegging, budsjettering og styringssystemer*, chapter 4: Det selvstyrte samfunn som fremtidsbilde. Oslo: Tanum-Norli.

Holbæk-Hanssen, Leif. (1984). *Et samfunn for menneskelig utvikling. Bidrag til tenkingen om alternativ framtid.* Oslo: Tanum-Norli.

Kennedy, Margrit. (1991). *Det nye pengesystemet. Veiviser til en økonomi uten renter og inflasjon.* Oslo: Cappelen. (Orig. title *Geld ohne Zinsen und Inflation*, 1987).

Lange, Sven. (1941). *Teknokratiet: en kortfattet orientering.* Bergen: [S. Lange]. Utredning - Norges handelshøyskole, høsten 1941.

Millar, Robert and Hj Murstad. (1933). *Økonomisk frigjørelse: en oversikt over Douglas-planen for social kreditt og velstand for alle.* Oslo: Tanum.

Pfeiffer, Eduard. (1933). *Boken om teknokratiet*, bearbeidet for utgivelse på norsk ved Ernst Zychner, forord av Øyvind Lange. Oslo: Nasjonalforlaget.

Sømme, L.J. (1933). *Det gamle negative pengesystems undergang.* Oslo: private printing.

Sømme, L.J. (1942). *Det positive pengesystem.* Oslo: private printing.

Sømme, L.J. (1942). *Verdenskapitalismen og vi.* Oslo: Norsk Rikskringkastings serieforedrag no. 28.

Sømme, L.J. (1944). *Fra åger til samarbeide.* Oslo: private printing.

Sømme, L.J. (1948). *Krisenes oppklaring: tidens finanspolitikk er håpløs, men det er en vei ut av krisen.* [Stavanger?]: [L.J. Sømme].

Steiner, Rudolf. (1919–20). *Kjernepunktene i det sosiale spørsmål. Livsnødvendigheter I nåtid og fremtid, fritt selvforvaltende åndsliv, demokratisk rettssystem, assosiativt selvstyrende næringsliv.* Bergen: Forlaget de tre funksjoner, 1969.

Steiner, Rudolf. (1919–20). *De tre funksjoner og systemer i den sosiale organisme og deres livs-betingelser. Hvorfor -et fritt selvforvaltende åndsliv, -et demokratisk rettsystem, -et assosiativt selvstyrende næringsliv kan gi grunnlaget for sunne forhold i det sosiale liv.* Bergen: Forlaget de tre funksjoner. 1968. (Orig. articles in the magazine *Dreigliederung des sozialen Organismus*).

Steiner, Rudolf. (1922). *Samfundsøkonomi.* Oslo: private printing. (Orig. title *National-ökonomischer Kurs).*

Stenberg, Sig. (1933). *Teknokratin och krisen: en orientering i ett aktuellt problem.*Stockholm: Federativ.

Utne, Hans. (1929). *Et nyt skattesystem.* Bergen: n.p.

Winter-Hjelm, Thorolf. (1920). *Pengenes socialisering og kapitalrentens avskaffelse.* Kristiania: Det Norske arbeiderpartis forlag.

*Winter-Hjelm, Thorolf. (1930). *Kapitalrente og ågerrente.* Oslo: Arbeidernes aktietrykkeri.

Further Reading: Technocracy.

http://en.wikipedia.org/wiki/Technocracy_movement

The technocracy movement, starting in the 1930s, attempted to create a non-monetary society. The technocrats proposed replacing politicians and economists with scientists and engineers who had the technical expertise to manage the economy.

> *'Essentially Technocracy is a soundly scientific effort to restate economics on a purely physical basis.'*
>
> H.G. Wells

This is the current technocracy website: http://surepost.com/igdtech/technocracy/index.php

Production Capitalism vs. Financial Capitalism - Symbiosis and Parasitism.

An Evolutionary Perspective.

A Workshop/Conference organised by Norsk Investorforum, Oslo & SUM – Centre for Development and the Environment, University of Oslo.
September 3-4, 1998.
Leangkollen Hotel, Bleikeråsen 215, N-1370 Asker.

PROGRAMME.

Thursday, September 3.

10.00 Welcome and presentation of the participants.
10.15 Erik Reinert (Oslo): 'Production vs. Finance = 'Good' Capitalists vs. 'Bad' Capitalists: An Historical Overview of a Recurrent Theme in Economic History and Economic Theory.'
10.50 Wolfgang Drechsler (Tartu, Estonia): 'Money as Myth and Reality.'
11.30 Leonardo Burlamaqui & Carlos Fernando Lagrota (Rio de Janeiro): 'Evolutionary Macrofinance: Evolutionary Economics and Minsky's Macroeconomics.'
12.15 Lunch
14.15 Carlota Perez (Caracas/Sussex) & Christopher Freeman (Sussex): 'Paradigm Shifts and the Changing Relationship between Financial and Productive Capital.'
15.30 Coffee.
16.00 Comments and Introduction to Debate: Ha-Joon Chang (Cambridge UK) Jan Fagerberg (Oslo)
19.30 Dinner.

Friday, September 4.

08.30 Michael Hudson (New York): 'The New Financial Capitalism and the Previous Ones.'
09.10 Jürgen Backhaus (Maastricht): 'Finance Capital vs. Production Capital in the German Tradition.'
09.50 Lars Mjøset (Oslo): 'International Financial Regimes during British and US Hegemony – a Comparison.'
10.30 Coffee.
11.00 Michael Chu (Cambridge, Mass.): 'Destructive and Creative Destruction – From Wall Street Leveraged Buyouts to Third World Microfinancing.'
11.40 Hans Sjøgren (Linköping): 'Financial Growth and Financial Crisis 1760-1995: a test of a cycle and stage model'.

12.20 Lunch.

The Asian Crisis and the Real Economy – Aftermath and Repercussions:

14.30 Dieter Ernst (Copenhagen): 'Destroying or Upgrading the Engines of Growth? The Reshaping of the Electronics Industry in East Asia after the Crisis.'

15.10 Ha-Joon Chang (Cambridge UK): ' The Korean Case.'

15.50 Coffee

16.15 Presentations and Panel Discussion: 'The Impact of the Asian Crisis.'
Vladimir Avtonomov (Academy of Sciences, Moscow)
Gabriel Palma (Cambridge, UK)
Antonio Barros dc Castro (Rio de Janeiro)
Santiago Roca (Lima)

19.30 Dinner.

Chapter 8

GLOBALIZATION IN THE PERIPHERY AS A MORGENTHAU PLAN: THE UNDERDEVELOPMENT OF MONGOLIA IN THE 1990S

'I apprehend [the elimination of diminishing returns] to be not only an error, but the most serious one, to be found in the whole field of political economy. The question is more important and fundamental than any other; it involves the whole subject of the causes of poverty ... and unless this matter be thoroughly understood, it is to no purpose proceeding any further in our inquiry.'

(Mill 1848)

'Woe to the vanquished' – a saying of the ancient Romans – came to mind when I attended a conference in the Mongolian Parliament building in March 2000.[1] As the only non-Asian I participated in a forum addressing the severe economic problems of the country. The local newspapers vividly reported that not far away from the snug heat of Parliament, an estimated 2 million animals pasturing on the plains were starving to death in the bitter cold. Permanent desertification threatened the country, and it was clear that this disaster was manmade. What was not reported was the important fact that the 2 million animals dying during the winter of 1999–2000 were only the increase in the animal population over the previous two or three years. The fundamental cause of the disaster was the same type of diminishing returns that has afflicted mankind since biblical times: too much economic pressure on one factor of production, land, the supply of which was fixed. Rooted in this phenomenon, vicious circles of poverty were already well established.

In terms of economic theory, the Mongolian situation takes us back to economics as the 'dismal science', to Thomas Malthus (1820), John Stuart Mill (1848) and even Alfred Marshall (1890). In spite of the recurrence and description of these phenomena since the biblical Genesis, the mechanisms at work in Mongolia during the 1990s apparently were not recognized, even when the disaster was a consummated fact. The underlying cause was clearly not global warming, as the Western press reported.

The more I studied Mongolia in the months that followed, the clearer it became that this nation, vanquished in the Cold War, for all practical purposes was being subjected to a Morgenthau Plan (Morgenthau 1945). The subjugated Germany of the

1. The author gratefully recognizes the partial financing of this project from the Royal Norwegian Ministry of Foreign Affairs. The opinions expressed in this essay are, however, his own, and do not necessarily reflect the views of the ministry.

Second World War was, according to this plan, to be deindustrialized and made into an agricultural and pastoral nation. Early in 1947, in an astonishing mental and political turnaround, the United States ditched the Morgenthau Plan when former president of the United States Herbert Hoover reported back from Germany: 'There is the illusion that the New Germany left after the annexations can be reduced to a "pastoral state". It cannot be done unless we exterminate or move 25000000 out of it' (Hoover's report no. 3, 18 March 1947, quoted in Baade 1955). Secretary of State George Catlett Marshall announced the Marshall Plan, which had precisely the opposite objective of that of the Morgenthau Plan, during a speech at Harvard on 5 June 1947. According to the Marshall Plan – officially the Economic Recovery Program – the industrial production of Germany should, as soon as possible and at all costs, be brought back to its 1936 level, the last year that was considered 'normal' (Economic Cooperation Administration 1949, Balabkins 1964).

During the 50 years preceding the reforms of 1991, Mongolia slowly but successfully built a diversified industrial sector. The share of agriculture in the national product had declined steadily from 60 per cent in 1940 to about 16 per cent in the mid-1980s (International Monetary Fund 1991, p. 13). However, the de facto Morgenthau Plan proved exceedingly successful in deindustrializing Mongolia. In Mongolia 50 years of industry building was virtually annihilated over a period of only four years, from 1991 to 1995, not to recover again. In a majority of industrial sectors, production is down by more than 90 per cent in physical volume since the country opened up to the rest of the world, almost overnight, in 1991 (see Tables 8.2–8.4 in Appendix 2).

An unexpected effect of the Morgenthau Plan in Germany was that a reduction in agricultural productivity paralleled the decline in industrial production (Balabkins 1964, p. 87). This phenomenon – which would not have surprised nineteenth-century economists – was extremely strongly felt in Mongolia, as well. The jobless industrial workers were forced to take up the pastoral way of living of their ancestors, adding 8 million pasturing animals during the 1990s. This depressed productivity and strongly increased the ecological pressure on the pastures of the sub-Arctic steppe (Tables 8.7–8.8). The productivity decline in agriculture is even more notable. Since 1991, average yields for all crops are down by more than 50 per cent, and in the case of the most important fodder crop, the reduction in yield per hectare is an impressive 71 per cent (Tables 8.5–8.6). Real wages are difficult to estimate meaningfully, since a shrinking number of people have 'real' jobs. It has been estimated, however, that the purchasing power of the average Mongolian has been roughly halved since 1991 (Malhotra 1998). Already in 1996, before the last decline started, 36 per cent of the Mongolian population lived below the weighted national poverty line of US$17 per month (World Bank 2000b).

The Mongolian balance-of-payment deficit equals 50 per cent of annual exports. Still, the normal market mechanisms which, in the textbooks, are supposed to correct this situation have not been allowed to do their job. An artificially overvalued currency coupled with a real interest rate of 35 per cent make it impossible for the productive structure to regain international competitiveness. Priority is given to short-term financial stability, a choice which, at the next turn of the screw, will hit the financial sector again as the real economy deteriorates even more.

The causal roots of Mongolia's unrestrained economic decline can, however, no longer be traced through the normal sources in the West, since the industrial statistics provided by the Washington institutions – the International Monetary Fund (IMF) and the World Bank – only start in 1994 or 1995 (International Monetary Fund 2000). By then most of the economic damage had already been done. The picture of deindustrialization *à la* Morgenthau becomes clear only when we study the official Mongolian statistics (National Statistical Office of Mongolia 1999). IMF data after 1994 appear consistent with the data provided by the National Statistical Office of Mongolia, which is the source used by the IMF. There is therefore no reason to distrust these important data that the IMF chooses not to publish.

Mongolia only has 2.5 million people, so the disaster is not of the magnitude of the spectre of 25 million human beings exterminated or forced into migration. The matter-of-fact and pragmatic way in which Herbert Hoover presented this drama to the United States had a remarkable impact on Allied economic policy towards the loser of the Second World War. But the fundamental forces behind the drama of Germany in 1945 and the drama of Mongolia in 2001 were the same: the carrying capacity – in terms of both number of human beings and ecological sustainability – is infinitely higher in an industrialized nation than in an agricultural nation. Even a relatively inefficient manufacturing sector provides much greater welfare to a nation than having no manufacturing sector at all. The important synergies between manufacturing and agriculture, as made visible by the collapse of Mongolian agriculture, are but one reason for this. The solution is the same as it was in post-war Germany: the only way to save both the people and the ecology of Mongolia is reindustrialization with a prolonged transition period before free trade is introduced.

The big difference is that today there is no Herbert Hoover, no person or institution with the common sense and authority to overcome what Hoover managed to overcome in 1947: 'all the fallacies of logic, the evasion of issues, and the deliberate disregard of essential economic relationships' (Balabkins 1964, p. 13). The same type of zealots who today fight for instant free trade at any cost also propelled Morgenthau's strategy. Balabkins describes the fanatics then, who 'freely substituted normative views for positive propositions, and out of this mixture arose [a] "scientific" mixture for the treatment of post-war Germany' (ibid.). The economic theory behind the deindustrialization of Mongolia and large parts of the Second and Third Worlds is mostly concerned with the manipulation of monetary phenomena, with a very limited regard for the whole productive apparatus of which these monetary phenomena are but superficial ripples.

Imagine national economies as vehicles moving ahead at different growth rates. A parable for the management of the Second and Third Worlds since the early 1990s would be that of someone who has learned a theory on how to steer the US economy like a vehicle. Then this person attempts to apply the same steering principles to the economies of Mongolia, but without having given any thought whatsoever to what forces actually propel the vehicle. It is taken for granted that a production system like that of the United States and Europe – which has needed centuries of conscious and deliberate cultivation – with all its knowledge and all its technologies will appear spontaneously with 'the market'.

This is the type of problem that the Stanford economist Moses Abramovitz called to the attention of the profession in 1956: standard economic theory explains only a fraction of the economic growth actually observed (Abramovitz 1956). Only about 10 to 15 per cent of economic growth can be explained by the traditional factors of production; the balance became the unexplained 'residual' that Abramovitz called 'a measure of our ignorance about the causes of growth'. Many years later, Abramovitz returned to the same argument. His comment on the progress of economic science since 1956 was not positive:

> '[T]he old primitive Residual is really an understatement, a lower-bound measure of our ignorance about the sources of growth ... Perhaps some of you are thinking, "If we are already ignorant of 90 percent of the sources of per capita growth, how much worse can it be? Can it be worse than 100 percent?" In a sense, it can . . . "It ain't what we don't know that bothers me so much; it's all the things we do know that ain't so." That is really the nub of the matter.' (Abramovitz 1993)

Abramovitz points to the shaky theoretical foundations on which the uncompromising policies imposed on Mongolia rest. 'Laying the policy foundations for sustained growth' in Mongolia (World Bank 2000a, p. 2) has, in practice, meant eliminating many institutions without putting anything in their place. Economically, a belief in 'spontaneous order' has produced something closer to spontaneous chaos.

The structure of the rest of this chapter is as follows: section 1 outlines the basic mechanisms that created the vortex of economic contraction in Mongolia starting in the early 1990s. Section 2 discusses how economic theory lost the categories needed in order to explain both economic growth and economic contraction. Section 3 explains the synergies between increasing- and diminishing-return activities. These synergies were reversed in Mongolia in the 1990s. The collapse of the industrial sector starting in 1990 led to a partial and parallel collapse of the agricultural sector as well. I describe in theory the causal mechanisms leading into this vicious circle. Section 4 gives a description of the Mongolian setting, history and economy. Section 5 discusses in detail how the vicious circles described in theory in section 4 developed, interacted and reinforced each other in Mongolia during the 1990s. Section 6 argues that the Washington institutions have failed to meet the challenges that the Mongolian economy presents, using policies that effectively block the market mechanisms that, in theory, are supposed to bring relief. Section 7 discusses the mismanagement of the Mongolian economy by the Washington institutions. Finally, section 8 discusses the implications for the global periphery as a whole and outlines a way out.

Appendix 1 gives an account of the theory of economic thought as it applies to the understanding of uneven economic development, a theory that is highly relevant to this case. Appendix 2 gives statistical data for the Mongolian economy from 1989 to 1998. These data, taken from the records produced by the National Statistical Office of Mongolia, are of great importance, since the official IMF data have eliminated all documentation on the collapse of the manufacturing sector that took place from 1990 to 1995 (International Monetary Fund 2000). Appendix 3 gives a numerical example of one of the main mechanisms at work in Mongolia during the 1990s from an article published in 1923 by Frank Graham, and Appendix 4 gives a stylized version of the vicious circles at work.

1. THE BASIC MECHANISMS AT WORK

The mechanisms at work in Mongolia are the same that have reduced the standard of living during the 1990s in a number of countries, particularly in the former communist countries and in Latin America. According to the United Nations Conference on Trade and Development, 90 nations were poorer in 1997 than they had been in 1990. Thirty-seven of them were poorer in 1997 than they had been in 1970. Mongolia is a typical, but in many ways, extreme case. Mongolia's economy is not very complex, which makes it a good case for illustration purposes. Comparing the post-Cold War economic policies with the policies implemented after the Second World War, I argue that Mongolia and large parts of the Second and Third Worlds have, in effect, been subjected to a Morgenthau Plan rather than to a Marshall Plan. The core of the Marshall Plan was not the transfer of funds; it was the reconstruction of the manufacturing industry and a strategy focused on increasing the productivity of this industry.

Successful economic policy since the Renaissance had recognized the fundamental difference between diminishing-return industries, in which specialization increases unit costs, and increasing-return industries, in which specialization decreases unit costs. A policy basing a national strategy on the distinction between these two categories of goods has been successfully practised at least since 1485 in England (chapter 1 in this book). A remarkably clear statement of the theory and the vicious and virtuous mechanisms that emanate from the two types of economic activities was published in 1613 (Serra 1613). This type of consideration dominated the nineteenth-century discourse on economic policy (Schumpeter 1954, p. 259). The importance of these mechanisms was reiterated by Alfred Marshall (Marshall 1890, p. 452) and shown in a numerical example by Frank Graham, a president of the American Economic Association (Graham 1923; see also Appendix 3 in this chapter).

In the history of economic thought over the last 500 years, the dichotomy of increasing versus diminishing returns as a proxy for good versus bad exports was absent in economic theory for only a brief period, from the mid-1930s until the late 1970s. In the 1930s the Harvard economist Jacob Viner eliminated the concept of increasing returns from international trade theory because it was not compatible with equilibrium (Viner 1937, pp. 475–82). Thus a real-world phenomenon that economists for centuries had seen as a key to explaining wealth was sacrificed in order to maintain the 'purity' of the model. A key aspect of the economic terrain was airbrushed out of all maps in order to accommodate the weaknesses of the technical tools that the mapmakers insisted on using. The logical alternative would have been to change tools, but this would have meant sacrificing the assumption of equilibrium and opening up economic theory to a type of market that not only no longer created harmony but also potentially created disharmony. The abstract principles of the profession created an analytical framework in which the factor left out, increasing returns, was crucial in explaining the growth of welfare. It was indeed a paradox that this happened in the middle of the ascendancy of the 'Fordist' paradigm, which placed increasing returns at the core of the wealth-creating economy.

The attitude of Viner and his followers – that is, virtually all neoclassical economists – was very different from the attitude of the founder of neoclassical economics, Alfred Marshall. In his celebrated *Principles of Economics*, Marshall clearly recognizes that a nation could improve its position by subsidizing economic activities subject to increasing returns and taxing those subject to diminishing returns, such as agriculture (Marshall 1890, p. 452). During the twentieth century, neoclassical economics slid away from its founder into Ricardian and Walrasian models. When the concept of increasing returns was brought back into the theory, it formed a new fashion in economics modelling (Krugman 1980, 1988, 1996). This economic fashion had no influence whatsoever on the policy recommendations of the Washington Consensus, however, which had a devastating effect on Mongolia's economy.

The loss of increasing returns activities has often been observed in nations that have lost wars. After wars, 'Morgenthau Plans' may occur spontaneously. The devastating effects of deindustrialization in France after the Napoleonic Wars convinced the young Friedrich List – previously a free trader – of the need to build a national industry before the final goal of global free trade could be achieved. In 1947, Herbert Hoover was rephrasing what economists had known since the sixteenth century: a pastoral nation could not come close to supporting as dense a population as an industrial/agricultural/pastoral state. If industry is killed off, a nation's ability to support its population is seriously curtailed.

The economic mechanisms set in motion by the free trade shock in Mongolia were the same as those normally observed when free trade is suddenly opened between a relatively advanced nation and a relatively backward one. Experience shows that the first casualty of free trade, the first industry to close, tends to be the most advanced industry in the least advanced country. This was the case, for example, in the nineteenth-century unification of Italy and in the Czech computer industry after the fall of the Berlin Wall. Reinert has described this as the 'winner-killing effect' and Jaroslav Vanek has called it 'the herbicide effect of international trade' and 'destructive trade' (Reinert 1980). This 'Vanek–Reinert' effect is fully compatible with standard international trade theory: under free trade each nation reinforces its comparative advantage – the wealthy First World reinforces its comparative advantage in higher skills in increasing-return industries, while poor nations fall back on their comparative advantage in diminishing-return industries. A comparative advantage in a diminishing-return activity is a 'natural advantage' based on nature's bounty, whereas a comparative advantage in an increasing-return activity is a 'created advantage', based on human innovation and skill.

The problems facing a nation specializing in diminishing-return industries with a relatively weak industrial sector, such as Mongolia, can be observed in Appendix 3 of this chapter. This primary or 'first-round' effect is followed by secondary effects which tend to reinforce each other, creating a downward spiral of underdevelopment. We shall return to these secondary effects and the vicious circles in the case of Mongolia.

2. KNOWLEDGE LOST: NEOCLASSICAL ECONOMICS AND EARLY MEDICINE

'Just as we may avoid widespread physical desolation by rightly turning a stream near its source, so a timely dialectic in the fundamental ideas of social philosophy may spare us untold social wreckage and suffering.'

(Foxwell 1899)

A striking feature of the economic theory followed by the Washington institutions in the 1990s is that, implicitly and explicitly, all economic activities are considered to be qualitatively alike in terms of creating economic development. This is the outgrowth of an economic theory that increasingly came to focus on monetary and trade phenomena at the expense of the real economy producing goods and services. Periodic crises in the economy had apparently been brought under control through the fine-tuning of monetary factors, and the fundamental engine of economic wealth – the growth of new knowledge and technology – became marginalized in theory. Controlling the ripples of the economic cycles of the industrial world gave the economics profession the illusion of having understood and controlled the extremely complex and varied underlying productive machinery.

The productive machinery underlying industrial economies is, however, propelled by factors that are all external to standard economic theory: new knowledge, technical change under enormous scale effects, and human initiative. All these 'true' factors of production were excluded from the neoclassical production function. Economic theory thus came to externalize the real factors that create economic wealth and to focus on superficial monetary factors. The 'real economy' of production of goods and services was tucked away in a black box, the content of which was assumed to be completely homogeneous, devoid of scale effects and fully accessible to all individuals inhabiting the planet (under the assumption of 'perfect information'). The illusion after the Cold War was that 'perfect' markets – 'getting the prices right' – and 'sound fiscal and monetary policy' would automatically fill the black box of production of goods and services in poor nations. Paradoxically, the enormous productive powers of capitalism were taken for granted by capitalist theory; the focus was on superficial movements of trade and of monetary quantities. Mainstream economics and the Washington Consensus suffered from 'the pedestrian view that it is the accumulation of capital per se that propels the capitalist engine' (Schumpeter 1954, p. 468). A naive view of the economy as automatically creating harmony led to a disregard for the productive apparatus in the Second and Third Worlds.

This reduction of economics to monetary and trade phenomena was not harmful in the industrialized world, where the 'true' factors of production were in abundant supply. But for nations with weak or non-existent industrial sectors it created a dangerous and enduring illusion that economic development could be produced by adding capital to labour in a process analogous to adding water to instant coffee. The activity-specific element of economic welfare, the fact that all rich nations were riding on an industrial wave in which rapid innovation and increasing returns were the key factors, was forgotten. The mature economic activities pursued in poor countries did not present attractive investment opportunities. In other words, these nations could not absorb capital in a profitable way and therefore ceased to attract capital. Having lost touch with the real economy of production, many mistook the symptom of capital shortage as the root cause of their lack of development. The causal arrows of economic change had been inverted; the agent was considered the cause.

In this chapter, I apply to the Mongolian case a set of principles different from those of standard economic theory – the principles of the 'Other Canon' of economics (see Chapter 13). I shall attempt to show how development policies based on the principles of the Other Canon would have prevented the poverty, social suffering and environmental degradation that haunt Mongolia. The principles of the Other Canon were applied by the United States during its period of spectacular catching up from 1820 until the First World War. I am, in a sense, holding up the economic policy theories of Abraham Lincoln as the example to follow for the poor world, rather than those of the IMF, the World Bank and the present US Treasury.

A key stumbling block in mainstream economics is the loss of categories. The fact that all economic activities are seen as being qualitatively alike represents a curious break with long-standing scientific tradition. Early scientists saw it as their main task to order observable objects and phenomena into categories and components. Classification put an end to an impression of chaos, creating perceived order in the world. Starting in the Renaissance, scientists embarked on a huge but slow project of mapping and classifying the natural world. Linnaeus's classification of the world of plants is a well-known example. The completion of mapping the human genome in 2000 can be seen as a milestone in this project of classification of nature.

Medicine and economics are the two sciences that most acutely affect human welfare. Medical science and, thus, human welfare benefited enormously from the early classification project. Symptoms were described and classified into different illnesses or syndromes. This classification was a prerequisite for the later development of medicines directed specifically at specific clusters of symptoms. Our great advances in medicine would not have been possible without a prior project of classification of medical symptoms. Here mainstream economics of the 1990s again differed: the same medicine was prescribed for all nations, regardless of their different symptoms and degrees of poverty.

Traditional medicine depended on centuries of experience, as when, starting in the twelfth century, lemons and oranges were used against scurvy in the Mediterranean. The scientific explanation for why lemons prevented scurvy was found only with the discovery of vitamin C in the late 1920s. In economic policy as in medicine, remedies were used without knowing why they worked. As the English economist Edward Misselden put it in 1622, 'Before we knew it by sense; now we know it by science.'

By dividing all economic activities into two categories – those subject to increasing versus those subject to diminishing returns – Antonio Serra in 1613 did for economics what Linnaeus did for botany. It was crucial for a nation to understand whether costs would increase if it specialized in a certain activity (diminishing returns) or whether costs would decrease and create formidable 'barriers to entry' in its favour (increasing returns). In practice, however, the targeting of increasing-return activities had already been going on for centuries before Serra.

In the eighteenth century when Captain Cook sailed around the world, scurvy was again the biggest threat to long voyages. Knowledge of traditional medicine had been lost. Generic 'cure-all' medical treatment such as bleeding had come to dominate medicine. This was, in a sense, a 'Dark Age', when useful traditional knowledge had been lost and before 'scientific' medicine had developed.

Today's debate on the benefits of 'open economies' is similar to the long European debate about bleeding sick patients. In his treatise on bleeding, economist and physician François Quesnay (1750) praises the great curative effects of bleeding on most diseases, including inflammatory diseases and fevers. The discussion then was not whether to bleed sick patients but how to bleed them – how much, where, when. The principle of bleeding was not questioned. In much the same way, the principle of 'openness' of all national economies is not questioned today.

In the other canon tradition from Serra all the way up to the Second World War, it was accepted that no nation could ever grow out of poverty without an increasing-return sector. Only when the increasing-return sector was firmly established should the nation 'graduate' to free trade. As the twentieth century advanced, the habit of dividing economic activities into two categories disappeared from economic theory, essentially because the dichotomy between increasing and decreasing returns was incompatible with equilibrium. The true engine of development – technological change under increasing returns (Schumpeter's historical increasing returns) – was thrown out because it did not fit the tools of textbook economics.

Today we observe the clustering of the world's nations in two convergence groups, one rich and one poor. This process can never be understood as long as the Washington institutions insist on using an economic theory that is devoid of categories of economic activity, a theory in which all economic activities are qualitatively alike as carriers of economic development. Everyone intuitively understands that a nation of stockbrokers will be richer than a nation of people specialized in washing dishes. Pre-Serra economic policy was based on this intuition, that of Henry VII of England (from 1485) being a prime example. However, this insight is not compatible with the theory on which the world economic order rests. The increasing poverty of the 'middle-income nations', which got poorer during the 1990s, is directly related to the enforcement of neoclassical economics in these nations. The middle-income nations had some manufacturing activities, but these were too inefficient to survive the sudden shock of open markets. In many former planned economies, managers in charge of these increasing-return industries probably did not even have time to figure out what their real costs were before their firms were wiped out.

With the loss of categories in economics, depth and quality of understanding are also lost. Antonio Serra's simple model gave him the extremely important insight that the very same economic policy can have very different effects in different industries: 'like the sun which makes clay hard but makes wax soft, like a low whistle which irritates the dog but quiets the horse' (Serra 1613). In Mongolia this insight that specializing in pastoral activities would have a very different outcome than specializing in manufacturing would have spared the country much damage. Standard economics works under what the Nobel laureate James M. Buchanan calls the 'equality assumption' and its models operate in a straitjacket: The theory can only operate at a level of abstraction where all economic activities are assumed to be identical.

The foundations of the present world economic order's theories are fundamentally ahistorical, devoid of any categories that would help in understanding economic phenomena. The underlying theory is, in Kuznets's term, not a 'tested theory'. Too often the main variable discussed is the relative openness of the economy, in a setting where the beginning of time is around 1973. In its simplest form, the argument is that rich countries are open economies; therefore openness is the key to riches. This kind of reasoning is typical of scientific scholasticism (see Reinert 2000b for a discussion). What the Washington institutions fail to recognize is that this combination of wealth and openness is, without exception, the result of a prolonged period of conscious building of increasing-return activities, under whatever name. In the next section we shall see how a simple system of dividing economic activities into two categories provided important policy guidance in Europe for centuries.

3. DEVELOPMENT SYNERGIES: HOW THE PRESENCE OF INCREASING-RETURN ACTIVITIES BENEFITS DIMINISHING-RETURN ACTIVITIES

'Promoting husbandry ... is never more effectually encouraged than by the increase of manufactures' wrote David Hume, Adam Smith's close friend, in his *History of England* (Hume 1768, vol. 3, p. 65). The economic changes which have taken place in the Republic of Mongolia in the 1990s show us that the reverse is also true: the destruction of animal husbandry and agriculture is never more effectually ensured than by the destruction of manufacturing. The application of the standard economic theory of the Washington Consensus in Mongolia in the 1990s has given us a chance to observe – as in a laboratory experiment – how the classic vicious circles of poverty and environmental degradation set in and reinforce each other in a downward spiral of underdevelopment. The Mongolian experience is almost a textbook case for the theoretical framework in Reinert (1980).

During the early industrialization of Europe, agriculture and industry were often seen as being in competition. The first economist who expressed Hume's view of the complementarity of national investments in agriculture and manufacturing was Gottfried Wilhelm von Leibniz (Roscher 1874, p. 337). This view, later spread by authors as different as Johan Peter Süssmilch, James Steuart and Hume, was to influence profoundly both economic policy and economic development all over Europe. Later, Mathew Carey, starting in 1820, propagated the same basic view in the United States: the synergistic effect of manufacturing and agriculture in a nation. This idea made US industrial policy acceptable to US farmers throughout the rest of the nineteenth century. Leibniz's insight had an enormous impact on nineteenth-century economic policy. For centuries, undoing these synergies – as in Mongolia in the 1990s – would have been seen as a recipe for economic disaster. Just as knowledge of the simple cure for scurvy of eating lemons disappeared, so did this long-tested economic knowledge. The Mongolians are in the same situation as

Captain Cook's sailors were: they must suffer because age-old knowledge has been forgotten.

Building the complementarity of agriculture and manufacturing from a purely agricultural nation required a period of protecting and nurturing manufacturing. The principle 'import raw materials, export manufactured goods' for centuries took the place of economic theory in England, as Friedrich List correctly observed (List 1841, Reinert 1998). This principle had been applied in economic policy since Henry VII came to power in England in 1485. In England one important theoretical foundation was Charles King's (1721) three-volume work, *The British Merchant, or Commerce Preserved*. To King and his contemporaries, exporting raw materials was 'bad trade', whereas exporting manufactured products was 'good trade'. Interestingly, trading manufactured goods for other manufactured goods was also considered 'good trade'.

In fact, King's recommendations make excellent sense if we assume that raw materials are produced subject to diminishing returns, whereas manufactured goods are produced under increasing returns. In Germany a stream of authors consistently presented the same conclusions on this issue. Johann Friedrich von Pfeiffer's (1764–78) monumental five-volume *Lehrbegriff sämmtlicher Ökonomischer und Cameralwissenschaften* is one example. All European nations, large and small, attempted to follow these same principles for centuries. As Alfred Marshall (1890) points out, the forces of diminishing returns, presently at work producing increasing poverty in Mongolia, are clearly set forth in the Bible: 'The land was not able to bear them that they might dwell together; for their substance was great so they could not dwell together' (Genesis 13:6).

I suggest that the decline in living standards experienced in many nations since the 1990s is a result of fundamental flaws in the economic models that support the Washington Consensus and consequently the management of the economies of the Third World. As indicated, the core ideas of this chapter are that economic activities are qualitatively different and that economic development therefore is highly activity-specific. Some economic activities create development, others do not. And to complicate the matter, some types of economic activities create wealth only if other activities are present, as the quotation from David Hume at the beginning of this section suggests.

The role of increasing and diminishing returns in creating self-reinforcing cycles of, respectively, wealth and poverty also gives us a clue to one of the major puzzles confronting the economics profession: how was it possible for the notoriously inefficient centrally planned economies to produce standards of living that were considerably higher – in the case of Russia and Mongolia two times higher – than the living standards produced under capitalism today? The theoretical framework used here was first published in Reinert (1980) and later discussed and elaborated in Reinert (chapters 1 and 5 in this book, and 1996, 1998).

I also claim that evolution of the institutions enabling development is activity-specific. It is the presence of certain economic activities that gives birth to institutions (a view that represents the mid-eighteenth-century consensus in European economic policy). Insurance was created around 2000BC because camel caravans and sea trading created demand for such a financial tool and the institutions that provided it, not the other way around. Getting the causal mechanisms of this apparent chicken-and-egg problem right is highly significant. Today there is a tendency to try to create in poor countries, based on traditional agriculture, institutions that are the product of centuries of advanced manufacturing and commercial activities. As it was put in a German price essay written for the king of Prussia in 1749: 'It is not that a primitive people civilise, later to introduce manufacturing. It is the other way around' (see Reinert 2000b). Understanding this causality is indispensable to understanding economic development. In this chapter, using Mongolia in the 1990s as an example, I try to explain why.

Continuing a long economic tradition starting with Antonio Serra in 1613, I claim that economic wealth and poverty can be understood only if 'Malthusian activities' (subject to diminishing returns with international specialization) are separated from 'Schumpeterian activities' (subject to increasing returns with international specialization). 'New trade theory' in the early 1980s (Krugman 1980) essentially resurrected the existence of increasing and diminishing returns, an argument that had been important, if not crucial, to economic policy through the nineteenth century. However, in new trade theory the dichotomy between increasing versus diminishing returns was, for all practical purposes, lost: the 'equality assumption' in neoclassical theory – the fact that all economic activities are seen as qualitatively alike – overruled any other tendency in economic theory.

The elements in each of the two columns reinforce each other and create the virtuous and vicious circles of development and underdevelopment, respectively. In Mongolia, the de facto Morgenthau Plan started in 1991 virtually wiped out the Schumpeterian activities that had slowly been built up over 50 years, and the Malthusian mechanisms took over.

Antonio Serra pointed out these mechanisms when he explained the relative poverty of Naples compared to the wealth of Venice, which he saw as a result of increasing returns. To German authors the principle of diminishing returns was equally important. In the 1850s, Wilhelm Roscher highlighted diminishing returns and related them to the 'bearing capacity' or 'carrying capacity' of lands and nations – terms strikingly close to today's 'sustainability' (Roscher 1882, Reinert 1996a). Not only do different economic activities at any point in time present widely different potentials for economic growth, the presence of some types of activities is also crucial to the development of others, as David Hume claimed. The principles of increasing returns and cumulative causations now underlie the theories of W. Brian Arthur (1994) (Table 8.1).

Indirectly we also revisit the 'golden age' of development economics of the 1950s and 1960s, with its 'vicious circles' and 'perverse backwashes', of which Gunnar Myrdal (1956) gives perhaps the most concise expression. I claim that at the core of the mechanisms causing Myrdalian virtuous circles are increasing returns, and at the core of vicious circles are diminishing returns. Curiously, like Friedrich List (1841), Myrdal describes the effects of diminishing returns without pinpointing the core mechanisms themselves.

Table 8.1 'Good' and 'bad'; economic activities from the point of view of a nation-state.

Characteristics of Schumpeterian activities ('good' export activities)	*Characteristics of Malthusian activities ('bad' export activities unless a Schumpeterian sector is present)*
Increasing returns	Diminishing returns
Dynamic imperfect competition	Perfect competition ('commodity competition')
Stable prices	Extreme price fluctuations
Irreversible wages ('stickiness' of wages)	Reversible wages
Technical change leads to higher wages for the producer ('Fordist wage regime')	Technical change tends to lower price to consumer
Create large synergies (linkages, (linkages, clusters)	Create few synergies

4. MONGOLIA: A BRIEF DESCRIPTION

4.1 The Mongolian Setting

Ulaanbaatar, the capital of Mongolia, is nestled in a spacious valley at 1300 metres above sea level. Its 650 000 inhabitants do not come close to filling the valley. The country's average altitude is 1600 metres. At this altitude and latitude (about 48 degrees north) the landscape is bleak and nature seems fragile as in the sub-Arctic, where the tracks of a car remain visible for centuries. Mongolia's highest mountain, Khuiten, rises to 4374 metres above sea level.

When one arrives in Ulaanbaatar, the association that comes to mind is an Andean mining town at 4000 metres altitude. The German geographer Karl Troll once described the climate in the high Andes as 'winter every night and summer every day'. This description fits the extreme continental climate of the Mongolian *altiplano*. When I visited during late March, night temperatures still fell below minus 20 degrees Centigrade, rising to a few degrees above zero during the daytime. Because the country is shielded from the oceans by high mountain chains, its climate is very dry, so the cold, though bitter, is less unpleasant than a clammy cold would be.

Mongolia is blessed with an enormous variety of natural landscapes, ecosystems and fauna. The climate ranges from the Gobi Desert, through steppe and *taiga* (cedar and larch forests), to the sub-Arctic mountain world of glaciers and frozen rivers. The country is inhabited by 665 species of vertebrates.

On the steppe, only July is frost-free, but the dry climate still offers unique possibilities for herding and raising animals. The animals graze outside all year on grass that appears to have been naturally freeze-dried on the root. The little snow that falls in flurries is extremely light and tends to blow away from the plains. The total population of 2.5 million Mongolians shares an enormous territory of 1.5 million square kilometres, more than the combined territories of Italy, France, Germany, Austria and Great Britain. In 1998 the 2420500 Mongolians shared their land with 32897500 domesticated animals: 356500 camels, 3059100 horses, 3725800 cattle, 14694200 sheep and 11061900 goats.[2] In 1998 animals outnumbered people by a

2. 1998 figures are from National Statistical Office of Mongolia 1999, unless otherwise noted.

ratio of 14 to 1. The precipitous deindustrialization of the 1990s was accompanied by a human population growth of 16 per cent and an animal population growth of 33 per cent.

The Mongolian sky is an intense blue and the sun shines about 250 days a year. The dark blue sky in this dry climate is almost like a second national symbol. However, on the outskirts of Ulaanbaatar this image is tarnished by symbols of industrialization: four gigantic smokestacks spew smoke. The smokestacks belong to four power plants that provide electricity and heat to the city. Heating is by hot water, distributed through a citywide system of water pipes. The different plants produce smoke in varying shades of brown, testifying to different generations of technology and thus to the age of each plant. The World Bank recommendation is to privatize the most modern plant, the one which produces the least brown smoke. This is a truly 'Fordist' and centralized heating system. For the newly poor of the 1990s, the heating conduits that run underground through the city provide shelter from the bitter cold at night. Here is where the growing number of homeless children finds refuge. The Japanese social workers call them 'manhole children', from their dwellings.

4.2 Brief History

After having spent ten years uniting the tribes of Mongolia, Genghis Kahn proclaimed the Mongolian Empire in 1206. Under his grandson Kublai Khan (1215–1294) the Mongolian Empire reached its largest territorial extension, including a large part of the former Soviet Union, China, Korea, Turkey and Persia. In Europe the Mongols penetrated far into Poland. The Venetian Marco Polo stayed in the old capital of Kharakhorum from 1236 to 1240 and wrote a good description of life in old Mongolia.

Like the Vikings, the Mongolians ended their period of colonizing hundreds of years before Europe's colonial period started. The Mongolian Empire deteriorated after the Chinese invasions starting in 1380, and in 1691 Mongolia became itself a colony of the Manchu Empire. Eastern and Western Mongolia split up, and the Western Mongolian state later joined the Chinese Empire. This part, Inner Mongolia, today forms the Autonomous Republic of Inner Mongolia in China. When the Russian tsars invaded Siberia, Outer Mongolia remained relatively independent. What I refer to here as Mongolia is in fact Outer Mongolia.

In December 1911, Manchu domination ended and Mongolia was declared an independent kingdom. Ten years later, in 1921, a communist revolution led to the establishment of a socialist republic that lasted until 1990. During the Second World War, Soviet-Mongolian troops fought against the Japanese. Prisoners taken in this war built the huge building which today houses both Parliament (the Great Hural) and the government offices in the present-day capital, Ulaanbaatar. This is the building where the economics conference took place in March 2000.

Communism was the first foreign-induced shock to twentieth-century Mongolia. The communist purges in Mongolia in the 1930s were brutal. Buddhist temples and statues were destroyed and monks massacred. The communists outlawed the traditional Mongolian script and substituted the Cyrillic alphabet that is still used today to write the Mongolian language. Mongolians also lost their family names and thereby their traditional clan identity because the communist rulers believed that clan identification could constitute a threat to the system. Only in 1999 were new last names officially put back into use.

4.3 The Economy

The traditional Mongolian lifestyle is that of a nomadic herder who gets all of his essentials from his animals. Nomadic life in Mongolia is organized around five species of animals: sheep, goats, cattle, horses and camels, the largest number being sheep, the smallest number being camels. The traditional household follows the livestock along the vast steppes in search of new pastures and water. Even today, only 4 per cent of rural Mongolian households have access to electricity.

The traditional Mongolian house is the *ger*, a round tent with a wooden frame covered with animal felt. Though it appears smallish from the outside, the *ger* is surprisingly spacious inside. The growing shantytowns of Ulaanbaatar consist of a mixture of traditional shantytown buildings and *gers*.

Traditional Mongolian food is the food of the herdsmen. Meat – predominantly mutton – is the staple diet. Tea with milk and salt is a traditional drink, while the favourite drink is *airag*, fermented mare's milk, which is generously served at weddings, parties and ceremonies. Horse milk is very rich in vitamin C, which compensates for the lack of vegetables in the diet. Vegetables such as cucumbers are grown in small greenhouses surrounding Ulaanbaatar. The true Mongolian barbecue – as opposed to the mock Mongolian barbecue that has spread in the Western world in recent years – consists of whole animals roasted over the fire. The special local feature is that boiling hot stones are added inside the animal in order to cook the meat from both sides. The hot stones from this process are given to the arriving guests so they can warm up.

The Soviets carried through an ambitious industrialization programme in Mongolia. The country was to convert its raw materials into finished products: canned and other processed meat, leather products (jackets, boots and so on), and wool products such as carpets, mostly machine-made but also some handmade. Luxury products processed from mohair goat wool and camel hair are also traditional export items. In addition, typical import substitution industries – from soap to clothing and matches – were set up. The non-luxury items were largely traded within the former communist countries which made up the Council for Mutual Economic Cooperation (COMECON), which had an advanced division of labour. The machinery used in Mongolian industry came mainly from Czechoslovakia and East Germany. This policy considerably reduced Mongolia's dependence on husbandry and agriculture. The share of agriculture in the gross domestic product (GDP) was reduced from more than 60 per cent in 1940 to about 16 per cent in the mid-1980s.

5. MEETING THE 'FLEXIBLE WALL': MONGOLIA AND THE VICIOUS CIRCLES OF THE 1990s

In 1990, Mongolia embarked on two simultaneous transitions, one economic and one political. In this sense, Mongolia is more similar to most Eastern European countries than to the former planned economies in Asia. While the People's Republic of China and Vietnam essentially started with an economic transition only, Mongolia – true to tradition – looked west rather than south. In 1991 Mongolia embraced democracy and a minimalist *laissez-faire* market economy, in strong contrast to its big neighbour in the south, the People's Republic of China.

Mongolia has embraced full financial liberalization and capital account convertibility. Starting in May 1997, a zero tariff regime was implemented, except on alcohol. The country has more than fulfilled the requirements foreseen in the Multilateral Agreement on Investment (MAI). In short, Mongolia has followed the rules for success as spelled out by the Washington institutions: Mongolia has been a 'model pupil'. Why then did the 1990s bring the Mongolian economy to the brink of collapse, see real wages plummet and make 'real' jobs a rarity, while simultaneously destroying the fragile ecological balance of the sub-Arctic country, risking permanent desertification?

These problems are not of a transitory nature. In my opinion the coercive advice of the Washington institutions has unleashed classical Malthusian mechanisms leading the country into vicious circles of poverty and environmental degradation. I shall attempt to show that although nineteenth-century classical economics understood the mechanisms that today make Mongolia increasingly poorer, the economists of the Washington institutions have failed to apply the basic insights of their founding fathers, the classical economists. The Washington institutions have ignored centuries of theory and evidence testifying to the different behaviour of economic activities under international specialization: an international specialization in diminishing-return activities, without a national increasing-return sector, has never failed to be a formula for economic and social disaster.

The only strong institution in Mongolia for most of the twentieth century was the state. Other institutional pillars – such as family or clan, and religion – were consciously deconstructed under the Soviet-influenced regime. The communist regime achieved impressive scores on human development indicators, especially on social indicators such as health, education, maternal and infant mortality, and higher education. This achievement was all the more remarkable because it took place in a nation with a relatively low level of GDP and with a widely scattered rural population (see Malhotra 1998 for a discussion).

The year 1990 brought the collapse of the COMECON trading system and opened up Mongolia for trading in dollars. Mongolia's manufacturing industry, geared to adding value to the country's raw materials, immediately felt the impact of the loss of foreign markets. It is unclear to what extent the overvalued currencies of the former COMECON countries contributed to the collapse of their manufacturing industry. Exchanging the currencies of the COMECON nations at their official exchange rate rather than at their value on the black market seemed like a gesture of generosity to the

East Germans who had their marks converted 1:1 to West German marks. To the extent that this policy was followed, it brought disaster to the local manufacturing industry in the former communist countries.

Table 8.2 shows the precipitous fall in important sectors of Mongolian manufacturing industry. Table 8.3 shows an index of industrial production in all industrial branches where output is measured in quantities. (Due to problems with previous inflation, a few sectors where output is only measured in value were not included.) As can be observed, in the majority of industrial sectors (29 out of 52), output has been reduced by more than 90 per cent since 1989. No manufacturing industry other than alcohol has declined less than 50 per cent. In 15 manufacturing industries, production has either ceased completely or been reduced to less than 1 per cent of its 1989 level. The only industries showing an increase in production are mining, alcohol production (the only industry still enjoying some protection) and the collection of bird down. As we shall see, the growth of the latter category – down collection – corresponds to a general 'primitivization' of the economy back to traditional animal herding. Whereas animal herding combined with a growing manufacturing sector produced increasing standards of living under the communist regime, the virtual disappearance of manufacturing has caused a precipitous economic decline, even in the herding sector.

In real (as opposed to monetary) terms, the economic shock that hit Mongolia and the other COMECON countries was initially twofold. First, the fairly elaborate internal division of labour within the Council collapsed with the opening of borders and the dollarization of trade. This hit the export sector of all the previously centrally planned nations. Second, the industries producing for the domestic market were hit by a combination of overvalued currencies, relative inefficiency, lack of knowledge of their own costs and of marketing skills, and faltering demand from people who had lost their jobs in the export sector. In 1991 the IMF planned to increase the imports of consumer goods (International Monetary Fund 1991, p. 30).

Herein lies the enormous difference between the transitions of the 1990s and the reconstruction of a war-torn Europe after the Second World War: in the late 1940s, economists and policy-makers still internalized the seventeenth- to nineteenth-century common sense that a nation with even an inefficient manufacturing sector will be infinitely better off than a nation with no manufacturing sector at all. No one would have dreamed of demanding free trade between Europe and the United States in May 1945. It was obvious that the manufacturing sector of Europe had to be rebuilt first. This was the essence of the European Reconstruction Programme (Marshall Plan). The Washington institutions subjected Mongolia to a Marshall Plan in reverse: a fairly conscious and premeditated destruction of Mongolia's manufacturing sector, which laid the country open to the grim Malthusian mechanisms of increasing poverty.

The solution for the increasing number of Mongolians who had lost their livelihoods in the manufacturing sector was to return to the way of life of their forefathers as herdsmen. The number of herdsmen tripled during the 1990s (Table 8.8), adding 8 million grazing animals to the fragile steppe. While the number of herdsmen tripled, the number of animals increased by only 33 per cent, however. The traditional agricultural sector could only absorb the labour shed by manufacturing and by a shrinking public sector at the cost of greatly reducing the number of animals per herder. With no alternative employment, labour productivity thus becomes the first victim as the diminishing-return activity – in this case, raising animals – is pushed towards the limits of ecological sustainability. Avoiding this problem of running resource-based industries into diminishing returns was at the core of the Australian argument for building a manufacturing sector (see Reinert 1980 and 1996a for discussion). Today the economic policy of escaping the traps of diminishing returns – which was crucial for the building of European civilization for centuries – has seemingly not even been considered by the Washington institutions. The overhanging dangers of diminishing returns in a globalized economy are totally ignored in today's discussion (chapter 5 in this volume). Also gone without a trace is the common sense that rebuilt European manufacturing after the Second World War before opening those countries up for 'free trade'.

During the 1990s, many Mongolians were driven back into subsistence agriculture. The average size of the herds decreased from 182 to 94 animals between 1989 and 1998. Today 80 per cent of herdsmen possess fewer than 200 head of livestock, and 67 per cent have fewer than 100 head of livestock. 'In other words, [the] majority of herdsmen just survive without being involved in productive activities' (Batkhishig 2000, p. 45). We observe the kind of 'primitivization' of the economy that is typical when a whole community is pushed against the 'flexible wall' of diminishing returns. The same phenomenon can be observed with the depletion of fish stocks in Asian fisheries: so few fish are left that modern fishing boats can no longer be profitably used. At the same time, wages collapse, so the only way for fishermen to survive is to go back to their traditional ways: subsistence fishing (Endresen 1994, and chapter 5 in this volume). In the mines of Bolivia the same phenomenon appears when jobless miners with picks and spades manually rework the refuse from old mining activities in search of minerals.

For communities specialized in diminishing-return activities without the presence of an industrial sector, globalization will, almost as a natural law, bomb their productive sectors 'back to the Stone Age'. Without allowing for free labour migration, this is the inevitable effect of specializing in an economic activity subject to diminishing returns, be it herding, agriculture, mining or fishing. Neoclassical economics and the Washington institutions fail to distinguish between activities that, under specialization, behave like those of Microsoft and those that have one factor of production – such as land – limited by an act of God, as do the Mongolian herdsmen. The almost religious application of this simplified model is presently the source of much human suffering. The big paradox is that the politicians who are proudly featured on US paper currency – George Washington, Alexander Hamilton, Benjamin Franklin and Abraham Lincoln – all understood the need for a nation to engage in non-diminishing-return activities, and indeed they championed the nurturing and protection of increasing-return activities in the United States. The Washington institutions are not only undermining the economies of many poor nations, but by refusing to allow the Third World to follow the strategy followed by the United States they are also breaking faith with the economic ideals that built the United States.

During the mid-1990s, Mongolia experienced several mild winters. These mild winters helped to accommodate the more than 8 million additional animals on the steppe.

When a winter struck which was normal or slightly colder than normal, in 1999–2000, a disaster of biblical proportions befell Mongolia: between 2 and 3 million animals starved to death. Typical of the present mainstream Zeitgeist – never questioning the Washington institutional wisdom but possessed by fear of climatic change – the Western press without exception reported the mass starvation in Mongolia as yet another sign of changing global weather. No one even hinted at the important piece of information that the number of dead animals corresponded to the increased number of animals over the previous two to three years.

In the winter of 1999–2000, Mongolia had reached what John Stuart Mill calls 'the flexible wall of diminishing returns'. If diminishing returns are reached, for example, in fisheries, there are always a few more fish which can be caught, but at rapidly increasing costs. Diminishing returns constitute 'a highly elastic and extensible band, which is hardly ever so violently stretched that it could not possibly be stretched any more, yet the pressure of which is felt long before the final limit is reached, and felt more severely the nearer that limit is approached' (Mill 1848, p. 177). Mongolia was grazing animals at the outer limits of this elastic band, and a climatic change that was within the normal range wiped out between 2 and 3 million animals.

Crucial in Malthusian mechanisms of underdevelopment is the fact that all of nature's bounties – land, fishing areas, mines – are available in different 'qualities'. Malthus assumes that the best land is cultivated first, and as a nation specializes in a resource-based activity, poorer land, mines or fishing areas will automatically lead the nation via diminishing returns into greater and greater poverty: 'the productive powers of labour as applied to the cultivation of land must gradually diminish and as a given quantity of labour would yield a smaller and smaller return, there would be less and less produce to be divided' (Malthus 1836, pp. 273–74). This is clearly an important mechanism at work in Mongolia, as 8 million animals were added to the fragile ecosystem during the 1990s. Having forgotten both global economic history and the history of their own profession, today's economists fail to connect the age-old paradox of the economic poverty of resource-rich nations to diminishing returns. Today's explanation of this phenomenon, centred on 'Dutch disease' (Sachs and Warner 1995), totally misses the core mechanisms at work in poor nations.

These were only the first rounds of deterioration that followed Mongolia's path into Malthusian diminishing returns. The further rounds of vicious circles in Mongolia are deeply tragic, but very interesting from a theoretical point of view. We find that traditional theoretical arguments about industrialization, both from Europe and the United States, proved correct as Mongolia's development process was put into reverse. As quoted earlier, David Hume – when discussing the economic policy of Henry VII, starting in 1485 – states that 'promoting husbandry ... is never more effectually encouraged than by the increase of manufactures' (Hume 1768, vol. 3, p. 65). In Mongolia in the 1990s we could observe that the reverse is also true: as Mongolian manufacturing died out, Mongolian agriculture deteriorated. Not only did husbandry move into diminishing returns, but the productivity of the agricultural sector also deteriorated dramatically. We observe a 'primitivization' of the whole economy.

In Mongolia we also find that one historically important argument for protection of the manufacturing sector is still true: during the latter half of the nineteenth century many economists claimed that industry was of crucial importance to national wealth because if a nation specialized only in agriculture, it could not afford to import fertilizer. This was part of an important debate about the qualitative differences of agriculture and manufacturing as agents of economic development (see Esslen 1905 for a detailed discussion). Now when we find that Mongolian agriculture deteriorates for exactly the same reasons pointed out 150 years ago, it is time to unearth the same arguments, based on facts solidly observed over centuries. With the manufacturing sector gone, the Mongolian agricultural sector could no longer afford to purchase fertilizer and agricultural machinery. A very common observation in nineteenth-century Europe and the United States, along the same lines, was that the only farmers who achieved a reasonable degree of wealth were those working near increasing-return activities (see for example Leslie 1888). Again in Mongolia we see these synergies reversed.

Agricultural yield per acre in Mongolia fell by more than 50 per cent during the 1990s (Table 8.6). For cereal crops, the decline was 50 per cent, for oats 75 per cent. Yield per acre for the important animal fodder crops fell by an incredible 71 per cent, no doubt aggravating the situation for the 8 million pasturing animals added due to the collapse of the manufacturing sector.

The next turn of the screw of Malthusian/Myrdalian poverty mechanisms involves five parallel and simultaneous downward movements. In most cases these factors interact: Each one reinforces the others in a downward spiral:

1. The breakdown of the capacity to import (in Celso Furtado's terminology): as the manufacturing sector was treated to an extreme shock, almost overnight exports collapsed. Also Mongolian imports fell rapidly during the 1990s, by more than 50 per cent in current dollars (from \$963 million in 1989 to \$472 million in 1998). Exports fell even more, though, by 56 per cent (from \$722 million in 1989 to \$317 million in 1998, in current dollars). The exports left are largely from the diminishing-return sectors, mining and raw mohair and cashmere. The permanent trade deficit now amounts to 50 per cent of the value of exports.
2. Collapse of agricultural productivity: combined with the lack of foreign exchange, increasing poverty of herders and farmers follows inevitably, as more and more marginal land is used (Malthus 1836). The combined effects of these two factors on agricultural productivity in Mongolia were enormous; both total harvest and yield collapsed (Tables 8.5 and 8.6). Addressing Mongolian agriculture in general, one of the participants in the March 2000 seminar in Ulaanbaatar writes: 'Activities like fertilization and applications of herbicides were terminated due to lack of funds, fuel and petroleum. [The] majority of equipment and machinery became obsolete. 90 percent of equipment and machinery currently utilized in crop producing business were purchased before 1990' (Batkhishig 2000, p. 46).
3. Institutional collapse: institutions that previously handled agricultural extension and animal vaccination programmes disappear as government activities are reduced, further eroding animal health and agricultural productivity. The same

type of institutional collapse hits human health, particularly support to women and young children (Malhotra 1998).

4. Sharp deterioration in the terms of trade (World Bank 2000b, p. 3): Mongolia has experienced a sharp reduction in its balance of payments because of both a decline in international copper prices and the fact that, compared to before, only a very small percentage of wool and cashmere is being processed locally.
5. A collapse in real wages: estimates indicate that overall real purchasing power of the average Mongolian has been halved since 1991 (Malhotra 1998, p. 40). A wage freeze went into effect in 1996, despite 56 per cent inflation that year and 17.5 per cent inflation in 1997. This phenomenon is well known also in Latin America since the 1980s; wage freezes are kept while inflation continues. The effect of this, unfortunately, is difficult to measure, as many poor countries do not break down their GDP data into the shares of income to wages and to other factors. In the 1980s and 1990s, increasing profits of the FIRE sector (Finance, Insurance, Real Estate) often compensated for the collapse of real wages in the national data, and therefore the phenomenon of real wage decline is not picked up in GDP figures. When Peru stopped publishing these data in 1990, wages and earnings of the self-employed had fallen continuously for ten years, in the end amounting to less than 25 per cent of GDP. (The normal industrial country average is between 60 and 70 per cent.)

These factors interact and reinforce each other. As manufacturing continues to shed jobs, more and more people have to take up traditional means of livelihood. However, the productive land is not able to carry the increased number of animals and therefore marginal land is put into use. As marginal land enters into production and overgrazing increases, the animals grow more slowly and become sickly. As manufacturing exports collapse, foreign currency ceases to be available for purchase of fertilizer and agricultural machinery. As wages collapse, demand for local industrial products is severely reduced. As even more people leave their jobs in the manufacturing sector to engage in subsistence agriculture, tax income is also reduced. As tax income is reduced, the government has to cut extension services to the agricultural sector, which again reduces the productivity of the agricultural sector. And so on.

At the core of these lock-in effects are diminishing returns. There is no indication that these vicious circles will not continue indefinitely. In the 2000 seminar there was no indication that the local representatives of the Washington institutions in Mongolia understood them.

It can be argued that diminishing returns is the only factually based assumption in the whole structure of neoclassical economics. Yet, when dealing with the Third World, this fact of life is ignored by the Washington institutions. The only way out of the vicious circles – as it has been for the last 500 years of world history – is for Mongolia to engage in increasing-return activities again. This will however be impossible without some targeted support for this sector, such as, for instance, the reintroduction of a ban or a tax on the export of raw materials. Such a tax on the export of raw wool was the policy measure which moved England out of poverty, starting more than 500 years ago. In 1995, the Asian Development Bank held up $17 million of a $30 million loan to Mongolia until Mongolia had dropped its export ban (Pomfret 2000). More than 50 textile mills closed, and now the Chinese process virtually all Mongolian wool. At the same time, the European Community uncontested follows the same kind of policy that Mongolia is not allowed to follow: many raw materials – such as fresh salmon – are allowed to be imported duty-free into the European Community, whereas industrialized products from the same raw material – for example, smoked salmon – are subject to high tariffs. Through the Washington institutions, the industrialized nations prohibit the Third World from following the types of economic policies that the industrialized nations themselves follow all the time.

Whereas the Washington institutions blindly apply neoclassical economics, the economic policy actually carried out by the wealthy countries themselves is continuously mitigated by common sense. As regards US economic policy, Paul Krugman complains, 'It is not just that economists have lost control of the discourse; the kinds of ideas that are offered in a standard economics textbook do not enter into that discourse at all' (Krugman quoted in Reder 1999, p. 6). Krugman is right: standard textbook economics generally is applied only in the Third World, through the Washington institutions. Here is also where it does the greatest possible harm. In an industrialized country, which already has its comparative advantage in increasing-return activities, the failure to distinguish increasing- from diminishing-return activities is relatively harmless in the short run. To a country like Mongolia the same failure is fatal.

The targeted support of increasing-return activities has been a mandatory passage point for all economies that have raised themselves out of poverty. Now this road is closed to the Third World through the conditions imposed by the IMF: 'XXVI. IMF to continue including policies on trade liberalization, elimination of state-directed lending on non-commercial terms to favoured industries, enterprises or institutions, and provision of non-discriminatory insolvency regimes, in its conditionality.'

The rich countries have, in effect, pulled up the ladder: the Washington institutions consistently refuse to allow poor countries to employ the same development policies that the rich nations used when they moved out of poverty.

The Washington institutions appear to see themselves as managers of neoclassical black box economies, inside which all economic activities are qualitatively alike. In the theory and policy of the Washington institutions, there is no difference between the economic activities taking place in Silicon Valley and raising camels in the Gobi Desert. Today's global economy is based on a theory which 'proves' that a monoculture nation of animal herders in a sub-Arctic climate will achieve the same standard of living as the employees in Silicon Valley. I can only repeat with John Stuart Mill:

> 'It often happens that the universal belief of one age of mankind . . . becomes to a subsequent age so palpable an absurdity, that the only difficulty then is to imagine how such a thing can ever have appeared credible . . . It looks like one of the crude fancies of childhood, instantly corrected by any grown person.' (Mill 1848, p. 3)

I propose that the economic management of the Third World countries since the early 1990s is just such a palpable absurdity. While the industrialized world experiences a new wealth explosion based on the increasing returns from a new 'productivity explosion', the majority of the world's population is struggling in national economies in which all the major activities butt up against diminishing returns (see Reinert 1980). The universal belief of the economics profession that lies behind the policies of the Washington institutions – a theoretical tradition in which the observation of historical facts is absent – is that the market under all circumstances will create economic harmony.

Had it been ethically acceptable to use human beings as guinea pigs, staging an experiment like Mongolia in the 1990s would have been highly interesting. We would have been able to test a theory and observe that centuries of economic theories based on observations of the real world were correct: the removal of increasing-return activities from Mongolia would unleash vicious circles of poverty, institutional collapse and environmental degradation. It is almost too cruel to be true that this experiment was actually carried out under the supervision and coercive advice of the Washington institutions, in the belief that free trade in this situation would cause increased welfare and 'factor price equalization'.

By treating all economic activities as being qualitatively alike, the economics profession fails to recognize the age-old mechanisms which cause the nations of the world to cluster in two convergence groups. One wealthy group is engaged in Schumpeterian increasing-return activities, clustering at the top in increasing wealth. This group is mainly engaged in activities where all factors of production are expandable at costs that do not increase at the margin. The other convergence group of nations, the poor group, consists of nations that are principally engaged in activities subject to Malthusian diminishing returns, where one factor of production is limited by an act of God. The underlying mechanisms of increasing and diminishing returns will – if the process is left to the market alone – automatically produce this effect.

The notoriously inefficient communist planned economies proved the same point: their inefficient manufacturing sector provided a much higher national standard of living than what capitalism with a decimated manufacturing sector does today in the same nations. The salient feature of the 1980s and 1990s has been the loss of middle-income countries in the Second and Third Worlds. The main explanation for this loss of the middle class lies in the development of economic theory. Starting in the late fifteenth century, economic development in Europe became associated with increasing-return activities. It was recognized that not only were people working with machinery able to pay more taxes than the farmers and artisans but also that the farmers and artisans working in manufacturing communities were richer than other farmers and artisans. Although challenged by Adam Smith and David Ricardo, the increasing–diminishing returns dichotomy was a cornerstone of economic policy all through the nineteenth century. In the 1950s it was still part of the common sense behind the reconstruction of Europe.

6. A PARALLEL REALITY: THE WASHINGTON INSTITUTIONS OBSERVED

As mentioned in the introduction to this chapter, in March 2000 I was invited to Mongolia to present the paper 'The role of the state in economic growth' (Reinert

1999) at the conference 'Mongolian Development Strategy: Capacity Building'. The conference took place in the combined Parliament building and presidential palace in Ulaanbaatar. Most of the papers for this conference are reproduced in the book *Renovation of Mongolia on the Eve of the XXI Century and Future Development Patterns*, which was published both in Mongolian (in the Cyrillic alphabet) and in English (Batbayar 2000). The conference was organized by the Mongolian Development Research Center, a non-governmental organization established in 1998, financed by the Nippon Foundation, a private entity.

Very distinguished Mongolian authors presented papers. Professor D. Byambasuren, the former prime minister of Mongolia, presented 'National factors affecting development strategy of Mongolia' (Byambasuren 2000), and Professor P. Ochirbat, the former president of Mongolia, presented a paper on the role of the mining sector in Mongolian development (Ochirbat 2000).

Japanese authors at the conference contributed creatively to the evaluation of the Mongolian situation. A very positive characteristic of the Japanese experts working in Mongolia was their long experience in practical matters, for example in banking. One paper raised the issue of the damaging effect of the high-interest rates, 35 per cent in real terms at the time (Fujimoto 2000a). Another paper addressed agricultural development (Kuribayashi 2000), and one compared the development in the Republic of Mongolia with that of the Inner Mongolia Autonomous Region of China (Shinichi 2000).

Inner Mongolia (that is, China) now processes virtually all of Mongolia's cashmere and mohair. As opposed to the Soviet Union, which used to buy Mongolian manufactured goods, the Chinese purchase only raw materials: not canned meat but live animals on the hoof, and so on. In Inner Mongolia, agriculture has intensified at the expense of herding. When flying from Ulaanbaatar to Beijing, one can clearly verify this from the air. The Chinese, however, seem aware of the problem of desertification. Grass areas in Inner Mongolia are strictly managed, and Inner Mongolia's cattle management and breeding practices are modern. Inner Mongolian farmers appear to have settled permanently and have managed to increase the number of cattle per capita to almost twice that of Mongolia (Shinichi 2000, p. 4).

Towards the end of the conference, the Washington institutions – in this case also including the United States Agency for International Development (USAID) – were scheduled to present their views on the future development of Mongolia. Having spent some time perusing the extensive statistical data available on Mongolia, I was keen to hear the analyses of the 'professionals'. I was disappointed.

First, none of the expatriate experts working in Mongolia bothered to show up in person to address this conference, held for members of Mongolia's Parliament and the highest-ranking national experts and policy-makers. Instead, the Washington institutions sent their bright, well-paid Mongolian assistants to present in English.

Second, the basic message of the World Bank and IMF representatives was a declaration of victory because inflation had been stopped. There was no mention that real wages had declined by half or that agricultural productivity had declined by more than half, no mention of the collapse of the manufacturing sector and of the balance of payments, nor of the 2 to 3 million animals that at the time were dying from starvation almost outside the windows of the conference room. The Washington institutions simply presented three scenarios for the future development of Mongolia: Mongolia would grow by either 3 per cent per year, 5 per cent per year or 7 per cent per year. Graphs were presented and discussed with no mention at all of how the present downward spirals could be stopped to allow for growth. Not only had the Washington institutions lost history, but this presentation bore very little relationship with Mongolian reality; it could have been (and probably is) presented in any country whatsoever. In addition, the World Bank presented a generic document in which the problems of the financial sector in Mongolia were built in (World Bank 2000a).

References to the problems in the real economy were few, but in his paper the USAID representative derided the Mongolians for their lack of entrepreneurship. On the other hand, a local politician complained that Mongolia was becoming a nation of cafés. Entrepreneurship was surfacing in the only sector where an overvalued currency was not sucking in imports, the traditional service sector. One cannot expect an entrepreneurial spirit to arise overnight, especially not with a 35 per cent real interest rate. It took Europe centuries to build up a spirit of entrepreneurship. One Prussian king complained that he had to grab his subjects by their nostrils and lead them to profits.

The USAID representative also derided the Mongolians for 'spending today all that they have today and not worrying about tomorrow' (Bikales 2000, p. 6). This would seem fairly normal for families who have seen their real income cut in half over a few years, in a country where more than a third of families live on less than $17 per month. Too many comments on Mongolia sound like Marie Antoinette's dictum, 'If they have no bread, let them eat cake.' The USAID paper – read by a Mongolian employee – points to the need for 'fostering a dynamic private sector, which will be the engine of growth' (Bikales 2000, p. 2). USAID does not mention the virtual impossibility of creating such a sector when the real interest rate is kept at 35 per cent, conditions under which not even General Motors would be able to make money. These complaints from a US official – whose government is the main architect and supporter of IMF policy – combined arrogance and lack of perception. Reading the US economic literature (for example Carey 1869, 1876) from the time England was attempting to keep the United States from manufacturing – when the United States was trying to avoid the trap of diminishing returns and commodity competition – would have been enlightening for the USAID mission.

In the important cashmere industry, 'Chinese processors can freely borrow money at 5 per cent p.a. or less, while [their] Mongolian counterparts can borrow a limited amount at 40 per cent p.a.' (Fujimoto 2000a, p. 2). This obvious block to any development is not discussed at all in either the papers or the oral presentations of the Washington institutions, including USAID.

Like the IMF, the USAID presentation initially holds up the image of the mythical 'paths of annual growth rates of at least 5 per cent, and preferably 7–8 per cent' (Bikales 2000, p. 1). It becomes clear that the assumption underlying the presentations of the extended Washington institutions is that 'the market' will automatically grant these growth paths to all nations that follow their rules of openness, regardless of what they produce. We are back to the spectacle of an economics profession attempting to steer a vehicle by manipulating monetary phenomena, without having any interest whatsoever in its propulsion system. The undeniable historical fact is that no nation has ever reached a sustained growth path without a period of nurturing and protecting increasing-return activities.

The USAID paper also scorns the Mongolians for regretting the loss of manufacturing (incorrectly claiming that no other transition economy discusses this matter). The rhetoric is clear and straightforward, like a somewhat perverted Protestant ethic: the 'painful adjustments' imposed on Mongolia inevitably will lead to growth. The papers insist that this must all take place 'based on integration in the world economy', with no understanding whatsoever that historically no nation has ever come near the growth rates they hold up for the Mongolians without the presence of a manufacturing sector. The United States itself is the prime example of this.

Witnessing the presentations from the Washington institutions, I found myself feeling increasingly estranged. These people hardly addressed the realities of Mongolia at all, and when they did, it was with the unrealistic, careless cynicism of 'let them eat cake'. It felt like being in a theatre watching Kafka's *Prozess* being performed. Like Joseph K. – Kafka's 'hero' and victim – the Mongolians are overwhelmed by the decisions of institutions that appear to be basing their decisions on a non-existent reality. The growth paths that every country will achieve – 3, 5 or 7 per cent per year – if they just 'open up' and globalize are not real; they are illusory and completely out of reach for a country engaged only in diminishing-return activities. In the case of Mongolia, Kafka's impersonal 'Courts' are the Washington institutions which impose the laws of a 'reality' based on neoclassical economic theory. In this parallel 'reality' there is no reason why the Mongolians should not be able to create a new Silicon Valley based on goat herding. In the non-existent reality of neoclassical economics, goat herding and software engineering are qualitatively alike and equally good as carriers for economic development. In the harsh reality of Ulaanbaatar – where poverty was increasing visibly and the newspapers were filled with images of dying animals and their suffering owners – the whole scene seemed surreal.

In the same slightly surrealistic vein, Jeffrey Sachs suggested in *The Economist* that Mongolia should specialize in software, not considering that most people here do not even have electricity or telephones. The idea is a good one if we work in a neoclassical framework devoid of context and assume 'perfect information' between Mongolian herdsmen and Silicon Valley engineers. The real context is that only 4 per cent of the mainly rural population have access to electricity, and that the 1.8 million inhabitants outside the capital have only 37000 telephones between them, not to mention a lack of money for computers and education.

The imposition of impersonal outsiders and their concealed rules have effects that are just as destructive to the Mongolians as they were to Kafka's Joseph K. In *Der Prozess* there is no correlation between what the authorities (in Mongolia's case, the Washington institutions) describe, and reality. In the end Joseph K. is destroyed through laws that he was never meant to understand (Kafka 1935/1994).

7. MONGOLIA: THE MARSHALL PLAN IN REVERSE AND THE CASE FOR REPARATIONS

Modern legal traditions in the United States admirably protect its citizens from the perils of professional malpractice and corporate irresponsibility. A jury award of $2.9 million in damages for the third-degree burns suffered by an elderly woman who spilled a cup of scalding hot coffee from McDonald's in her lap may seem exaggerated (and, indeed, it was later knocked down to $640000 by the judge), but to an outsider the US legal system as it applies to medical malpractice appears more logical. In this section I shall ask the following question, which is only partly rhetorical: what would happen if we applied the legal standards imposed on the medical profession to economists?

As we have seen, the perils suffered by a society producing only in diminishing returns industries have been documented in Genesis and in European economic policy since the late fifteenth century. It was a key feature in US economic theory and policy, starting with Alexander Hamilton and Benjamin Franklin, throughout the nineteenth century, when Abraham Lincoln was a dominant politician supporting this view, and through most of the twentieth century. The core of the Economic Recovery Program (Marshall Plan) was to rebuild Europe's manufacturing industries to their pre-Second World War levels and beyond. The perils of subjecting a nation to a Morgenthau-type plan were acknowledged. The goal was to re-establish Europe in increasing returns activities in order to create enough wealth to withstand communist advances. The Marshall Plan – named after the US secretary of state George Marshall – was also in line with Alfred Marshall's suggestion of subsidizing increasing returns activities and taxing diminishing returns activities (Marshall 1890, p. 452). In 1953 George Marshall was given the Nobel Peace Prize for this work. From this perspective, the conditions imposed on Mongolia truly represent a Marshall Plan in reverse, both in the sense of the Economic Recovery Program and in the sense of Alfred Marshall's economics.

Mongolia was given assistance by the Washington institutions only on condition that the country not attempt to follow the principles of the Economic Recovery Program (Marshall Plan). A typical progress report for the Marshall Plan, published by the Economic Cooperation Administration in 1949, focused on the reconstruction of the increasing returns sector. The output of every industrial sector was recorded every month and carefully compared with previous months and with the basis year of 1936, the last 'normal' year (Economic Cooperation Administration 1949, pp. 28–29). The progress report for the Washington institutions in Mongolia, in contrast, appears to have focused narrowly on financial stability and lack of inflation. An exclusive focus on financial issues – virtually destroying the real economy by imposing a real interest rate of 35 per cent as of March 2000 – represents a total break with long-standing economic theories, with the traditional practice of good economic policy and with good judgement based on common sense.

One US college textbook in international trade theory seriously suggests that nations producing under increasing returns should pay compensation to nations specializing in diminishing returns activities:

> 'Thus the country which eventually specializes completely in the production of X (that is, the commodity whose production function is characterized by increasing returns to scale) might agree to make an income transfer (annually) to the other country, which agrees to specialize completely in Y (that is, the commodity whose production function is characterized by constant returns to scale).' (Chacholiades 1978, p. 199; see also Reinert 1980)

I would argue that the perils of forcing a nation to specialize exclusively in diminishing-return activities, especially in a fragile ecosystem such as Mongolia's, are extremely well documented both in economic theory and in economic history. 'The Tragedy of the Commons' is a well-known phenomenon, and the concept of diminishing returns continues to be one of the first introduced in introductory economics at the universities where IMF and World Bank economists are educated. How could the economists of the Washington institutions fail to see this peril? How is it possible, as James Galbraith (2000) observes, that the economists who created this economic and environmental disaster are still the only economists who are listened to?

Economic policy in the core nations is never applied dogmatically. As Lionel Robbins – later Lord Lionel – shows in his book on economic policy, the English classical economists did not follow a *laissez-faire* dogma in actual policy. These economists were sufficiently close to real life that economic policy was always filled with *ad hoc* interventions based on 'common sense' (Robbins 1952). This is even more true in the United States today, where, as we have seen, theoreticians such as Paul Krugman complain that textbook trade theory is virtually neglected as a basis for US economic policy. As the twentieth century advanced, neoclassical theory became more and more rigid and the economic practice of First World countries diverged more and more from textbook ideals. Only the Third World, and after 1990 also the Second World, became the testing grounds for the unmitigated application of 'pure theory', which had never before been tested to this extent. Joseph Stiglitz, the former chief economist of the World Bank, compared the IMF's handling of the Asian crisis of the late 1990s to the Holocaust (North 2000). The comparison could easily be extended to Mongolia.

However, even in 'pure' economic theory, diminishing returns is a core concept. After the Second World War, the United States, whose short-term business interest would have dictated free trade with Europe from May 1945, granted Europe a 15- to 20-year grace period before free trade was imposed. The European nations were for a long time permitted to look at foreign exchange as a scarce commodity, subject to rationing. In Norway the import of clothing was totally prohibited for 11 years after the Second World War in order to prepare the industry for free trade, and the import of cars for non-commercial use was freed only in 1960. European industrial tradition was much sturdier than Mongolia's, yet Mongolia was given no such grace period. Not allowing Mongolia a period of adjustment such as Western Europe received after the Second World War amounts to gross negligence and ignorance both of economic theory and of recent history.

The Mongolians are a hardy race. The huge loss of jobs in both the manufacturing sector and the government sector has left people with little choice but to go back to their old ways. The number of herdsmen – the traditional Mongolian occupation – has more than trebled since 1990. The number of animals has increased by more than one-third, by 8 million head, during the same period. But the land cannot feed the population of people who previously worked in the manufacturing and government sectors. More and more herdsmen with smaller and smaller flocks compete for a deteriorating and environmentally extremely fragile habitat. The annual population growth rate has fallen from 1.8 per cent in 1991 to 1.4 per cent in 1997, as people can no longer afford children. Support for children has gradually been withdrawn, increasing this problem (Malhotra 1998, p. 3). The support of the West will again be 'development assistance' which merely attempts to alleviate symptoms of problems that have been caused by the West in the first place.

In order to qualify for financial assistance, Mongolia was forced to give up its manufacturing sector. I have closely observed the same phenomenon in Ecuador, where assistance from the Washington institutions was given only on the condition that all assistance to increasing-return activities be terminated. In practice, no equivalent to the US government assistance to small business, subsidies to small businesses in particular sectors, assistance to high-tech industries and the like are allowed in the Third World. On the federal level, the United States gets away with many subsidies of high-tech increasing-return activities since they come under the guise of defence, but there is little doubt that if IMF conditions were imposed on the level of US states, many if not all of the 50 states would be disqualified from receiving IMF and World Bank assistance. While the World Bank follows the recommendations of the University of Chicago economists, Mayor Daley of Chicago uses city and state money to finance and subsidize an incubator that is targeted at increasing-return high-tech activities. If the United States had been a poor country, this policy would have disqualified it from receiving any assistance from the Washington institutions. It is, in my view, crucial that we understand how the industrialized countries, as part of their day-to-day economic policy, continually break the rules that they themselves force upon the Second and Third Worlds.

I would argue that there are clear parallels between the Mongolian case as it has been handled by the Washington institutions and the US court cases that the tobacco industry lost: it can be demonstrated that the institutions in question acted with the knowledge that the product they were promoting – in this case, imposing a shock therapy and restrictions which forced the closing down of increasing-return activities in Mongolia – would seriously damage the health and well-being of their customers, the Mongolian people.

A Mongolian class action lawsuit against the IMF and the World Bank in a US court could focus on five aspects:

1. The Washington institutions have showed gross negligence by not flagging the risk of forcing Mongolia into exclusive specialization in diminishing-return activities. The detrimental effects of specializing exclusively in diminishing-return activities, such as Mongolia was forced into, are well documented in economic theory and economic history, and are taught even at the elementary level of economics in all Western universities.

2. A condition, like that imposed by the IMF, refusing Mongolia the right to any kind of support in favour of increasing-return activities does not grant Mongolia the same rights as those enjoyed and practised by all US states, cities and municipalities, and is consequently discriminatory.
3. The negligence shown by the Washington institutions is considerably exacerbated because no action has been taken even now, at this very advanced stage of the problem, when the diagnosis is clearly visible to anyone showing a minimum of interest in Mongolian economic data. The arrogance shown by the Washington institutions towards Mongolian civil society and institutions, such as the Mongolian Development Research Center, indicates a complete lack of interest in the productive side of the economy as long as short-term financial goals are met. The incentive structure in the Washington institutions, which judges economic success exclusively on financial issues, has led to the collapse of all increasing-return activities and to a real interest rate of 35 per cent in Mongolia. This incentive structure is applied contrary to economic theory and to all traditions of macroeconomic management in the developed world.
4. Fundamentally this is also an issue of the human rights of the Mongolians, individually and as a nation. As one of the Japanese experts in Mongolia argues, 'As there are human rights for individuals living in a country, so should all countries have a right to live and prosper' (Fujimoto 2000b, p. 2). In view of the accumulated experience of mankind, Mongolia is the victim of an 'experiment against reality'. As the late Archbishop Helder Camara of Brazil said, these people have been made poor in the name of economics (quoted in Reinert 1980). Arbitrary abstract principles of standard economics are, in practice, given precedence over human welfare.
5. The textbook solution to assist Mongolia's failing industry, to help it become more competitive on the world market and to cure the permanent balance-of-payment deficit, would be to devalue the local currency. Today the IMF is preventing this from happening, partly by keeping the real interest rate at 35 per cent. So Mongolia gets the worst of all worlds: a 'free market' when the market destroys its productive capacity, but no free market when the forces of the market would help it regain competitiveness. In a way that Thorstein Veblen would have recognized, we observe 'financial capitalism' destroying 'industrial capitalism', a development that in the long term will prove destructive to the financial side of the economy as well.

Reparations to the Mongolian people could focus on the huge share of GDP which has permanently disappeared, on the permanent loss of 50 per cent of the Mongolian people's purchasing power, on the permanent loss of manufacturing capacity and the permanent trade deficit amounting now to 50 per cent of the value of exports (that is on the simultaneous breakdown of the country's capacity to import and its ability to produce manufactured goods itself), and on the permanent damage to the environment through increased desertification in the fragile Mongolian ecosystem.

8. TOWARDS THE GLOBAL VERSION OF 1848 AND A POSSIBLE WAY OUT

Nineteenth-century industrialization brought with it huge social ills. Books and articles addressing the 'social question' abounded in all languages well into the twentieth century. The social problems peaked in 1848, when most European nations experienced revolutions, England and Russia being the notable exceptions. Manchesterian liberalism and communism were opposite poles in the econo-political discussions, but very different forces cured the social ills. Both in the United States and in Germany, dedicated politicians and economists consciously constructed institutions to create welfare states. The German Verein für Sozialpolitik created the operative institutions of the welfare state, which were later copied throughout Europe (Verein für Sozialpolitik 1872–1932). The theoretical foundations for the economic theory undergirding the welfare state can also be found in the first 100 years of Schmollers Jahrbuch (1871–1972) and in the writings of the pre-war US institutional school of economics. On the political side, Otto von Bismarck saw that the socialists were right about the huge social problem, and the alliance between the enlightened and idealistic economists in the Verein für Sozialpolitik and Bismarck over time managed to resolve most of Europe's social ills.

More than half of the world's nations were poorer in the late 1990s than in 1990. A new technological wave is creating the 'social question' all over again. This time, however, the social question is not within each industrialized state; it is between industrialized states and the poor nations in the Second and Third Worlds. We are moving towards a new crisis in income distribution, a new 1848, but this time on a global scale. It is my firm conviction that only theories and attitudes similar to those that created the national welfare states will be able to move the world towards a global welfare state. Manchesterian liberalism had no chance of solving the social ills of nineteenth-century Europe. The present version of Manchesterianism – we could call it Washingtonianism – is based on the very same principles as Manchesterianism, and its chances of solving the world's poverty are nil.

What can bring the world out of this deadlock? Economists like those who formed the Verein für Sozialpolitik in 1872 – people who disliked communism as much as they disliked liberalism – cured the ills of Manchesterianism, the equivalent of the system today promoted by the Washington institutions. An individual whistle-blower, like Herbert Hoover in the case of Germany, no doubt helped save thousands of lives and prevented much human suffering (Baade 1955). I have mentioned that Joseph Stiglitz, the former chief economist of the World Bank, compared the intervention of the IMF in Asia to the Holocaust (North 2000). Stiglitz plays the role of the insider whistle-blower, as in Henrik Ibsen's (1882) *An Enemy of the People*. As in Ibsen's play, the very community he is in effect helping chastises Stiglitz, who makes the public aware that something is terribly wrong. This kind of whistle-blowing is unusual in the economics profession, because the appointment systems and career paths are structured in such a way that any person getting into a senior position in the system – and thus achieving credibility as a whistle-blower – will, almost by definition, have thoroughly absorbed the core assumptions of the ruling canon, in which the market is defined as a mechanism creating automatic harmony.

The fact that more than half of the world's nations were poorer in the late 1990s than in 1990 attracts as little press coverage as the German concentration camps did in the 1930s. Yet there are people who know. The report *Transition 1999* (United Nations Development Programme 1999) asserts that the transition to capitalism has 'literally been lethal for a great many people'. Compared to population projections based on demographic profiles and life expectancy recorded before 1990, 9.7 million men today are 'missing' in the transition economies. The 'transition' of Eastern Europe – in most cases from inefficient production of increasing-return products to diminishing-return economies – has been accompanied by great loss of life. As in the 1930s, those who want to know, know, but the matter is not publicly discussed.

The statistical records of the 1990s show beyond any doubt that the market fundamentalism – the quasi-religious thesis that preaches that markets are harmony-making machines – has caused great damage. A reaction is slowly mounting. Joseph Stiglitz's whistle-blowing and the refusal of the editor of the World Bank's development report to yield to the pressures from the US government to change the report are two examples of a mounting reaction. So are the protests in Seattle and Davos, and the establishment of ATTAC (the Association for the Taxation of Financial Transactions for the Aid of Citizens). These events, however, tend to be protests which do not lead to a better understanding of the problems at hand. In my opinion, a large obstacle to a better understanding of practical policy solutions is that the alterative factually based economic theory – the Other Canon theory that built the United States – has virtually disappeared. A better policy can only be produced if we have a theory of what causes development to be so uneven.

Because the economics profession today fails to distinguish categories of economic activities, it fails to understand that whereas 'openness' of an economy is a necessary and indispensable policy ingredient for a nation with a strong presence of increasing-return activities, in a backward country the same 'openness' may initiate a maelstrom of Malthusian vortices as the weak increasing-return activities wither away, bringing the economy towards the flexible wall of diminishing returns.

In 1867 the US economist Henry Carey pointed out that Ricardian economics, from which today's standard economic theory descends, has a lot in common with medical quackery: quacks live in a world without categories of diseases and remedies, and they therefore have only one medicine which they claim will cure all illnesses (Carey 1869). It was standard in the nineteenth century in Canada and the United States to argue that backward nations needed a different economic policy from that of advanced nations.

The turnaround in economic theory that is suggested by The Other Canon group is not new. The market fundamentalism that swiped the policy of the countries in the Organization for Economic Cooperation and Development (OECD) towards the rest of the world during the 1990s bears strong similarities to the Ricardian euphoria that built across Europe from the 1820s, peaking in 1846. The backlash of 1848 followed in the form of widespread revolutions. Just as in the 1840s, today's problems in economic theory originate with the abstract system of David Ricardo. In the year 1900, looking back at the human suffering caused the last time, the Ricardian system had been allowed to overrule common sense; the eminent Cambridge economics professor H.S. Foxwell wrote:

> 'Ricardo, and still more those who popularised him, may stand as an example at all times of the extreme danger which may arise from the unscientific use of hypothesis in social speculations, from the failure to appreciate the limited applications to actual affairs of a highly artificial and arbitrary analysis. His ingenious, though perhaps over-elaborated reasoning became positively mischievous and misleading when it was unhesitatingly applied to determine grave practical issues without the smallest sense of the thoroughly abstract and unreal character of the assumptions on which it was founded.' (Foxwell 1899, p. xli)

This same criticism could be levelled at neoclassical economics for its devastating effects on welfare in the Second and Third Worlds. It is this kind of theoretical 'mischief' that has caused the loss of welfare in so many countries in the 1990s. The industrialized world has, for the last 50 years, attempted to cure the symptoms rather than the causes of underdevelopment in the Third World. The Third World was 'put on the dole', like the unemployed of the European welfare states.

As it is now, non-governmental organizations move into newly impoverished countries such as Mongolia, attempting to ease economic pain. Also, the World Bank tries to alleviate the symptoms of poverty rather than spur development. We are experiencing the rise of palliative economics, a science that eases pain without even attempting to understand or address the root causes of that pain. Thus many parts of the Third World are slowly turning into gigantic hospices where the Florence Nightingales of the First World – both on the spot and through donations – do an admirable job of alleviating the pain of those dying prematurely. Our alternative is to develop the economic latecomers in the twenty-first century using the same methods as were used with the countries lagging behind England in the nineteenth century: letting the economic periphery become core by spreading increasing-return activities to them. This, however, requires understanding and distinguishing between the true causes and the mere symptoms of the phenomenon we call economic development.

The Washington conditionalities effectively make it impossible for any underdeveloped nation today to take the step into economic development. The policy of targeting increasing-return activities – whether identified under that label or not – has been a mandatory passage point for all nations without exception. The Washington institutions fail to see that a policy like the one forced on Mongolia amounts to an attempt to defy the laws of economic gravity as they have been observed since biblical times. No nation beyond the size of a city-state has ever reached economic development without targeting and cultivating 'good' economic activities (Reinert 2000a). Today's conditionality effectively outlaws the strategies that made it possible for Venice, England, the United States, continental Europe, Japan and Korea in sequence to catapult out of poverty on the virtuous circles created by increasing-return mechanisms. These mechanisms are, at any point in time, found in some activities rather than others. This makes for the activity-specific nature of economic development. Since institutions co-evolve with these economic activities, economic institutions are also activity-specific.

In order to acknowledge this crucial fact, standard economics has to go back to the roots of its own equilibrium theory, to Carl Menger. The tendency towards equilibrium must be seen as Menger and Marshall saw it: as a very rough map of the economic forces that would be at work if nothing happened, if no innovations and no economic progress were to take place. Menger saw this map as so inaccurate that no quantification should be attempted. After the economy had stopped changing, Menger envisioned a system with vacillation for decades before settling. Unfortunately the economics profession chose to work with Léon Walras's version of equilibrium theory, the theory of split-second equilibrium. The adoption of this thesis caused the economics profession to lose three important dimensions: time, space and the unevenness of economic growth.

Research in the 1990s showed that the world is converging into two groups of nations: a clustering of extremely wealthy nations and a cluster of increasing size in which the majority of nations are getting poorer. Standard economics is utterly helpless to explain this phenomenon. The Other Canon approach suggests that the forces creating the increasing gulf between the two groups of countries are two economic vortices. Nations specialized in Schumpeterian goods are catapulted towards ever-increasing welfare through a sequence of periodic productivity explosions, interspersed by quieter intervening periods of incremental innovation (Schumpeter 1942). On the other hand, nations specialized in Malthusian goods are – as in the Mongolian case – through the natural forces of the market driven into a downward spiral of increasing poverty and increasing environmental degradation. In this setting, Malthus was right: the natural wage level will be at the brink of starvation.

From the mid-eighteenth-century writings of economists such as James Steuart (1767), the rulers of Europe – the 'enlightened despots' in Wilhelm Roscher's term – understood the fundamental symbiosis between manufacturing and agriculture, between increasing-return activities and diminishing-return activities. This created the understanding that a nation with even an inefficient and undeveloped manufacturing sector would be much better off than a nation without any manufacturing sector at all. Targeting and cultivating incipient manufacturing allowed the creation of 'middle-income' countries. The sudden dismantling of any targeting and cultivating of increasing-return activities in Second and Third World countries through the shock therapy of the 1980s and 1990s in many cases effectively made their position as middle-income nations impossible.

Where do we go from here? The Washington Consensus has been through a slow learning process since the fall of the Berlin Wall. The first theory was 'get the prices right' and development would appear as out of a magician's hat. A first modification to this belief in spontaneous order saw to it that the dictum 'get the property rights right' was added. A third modification in the late 1990s was 'get the institutions right'. This position fails to grasp the activity-specific nature of economic institutions, what Richard Nelson calls the co-evolution of activities and institutions. It is virtually impossible to create among a hunting and gathering people an institution that has taken centuries to evolve in an industrial setting. On the other hand, the traditional institution of distributing wealth in a family clan of a non-market society becomes 'corruption' in the eyes of the West. Attempting to understand human institutions outside the logic provided by their respective productive systems is a key methodological flaw in today's development economics. Such understanding calls for an understanding also of non-market societies.

The next step – after 'get the institutions right' – will, in my view, have to be 'get the economic activities right'. In today's divided world, we face two possible strategic options: we can either globalize the labour market and let the poor come to where the economic activities are that are able to create prosperity, or alternatively we can follow the nineteenth-century path and spread increasing-return activities that have a potential for technological change to the countries where the poor live. In my view these are the only two real options. The third option, instant globalization combined with palliative economics, is neither ethical nor feasible.

In order to spread wealth-creating economic activities to the poor, the theoretical foundations of the Washington Consensus will have to be replaced with the principles of the Other Canon. A succinct recommendation of Other Canon economic policy can be found in Marshall's *Principles of Economics* (Marshall 1890, p. 452): tax economic activities subject to diminishing returns and give bounties to activities subject to increasing returns. As the taxable base in the Third World is not very healthy, the support to build increasing-return activities will have to come from the First World. I suggest that this 'New Deal' in development ought to be financed by extending normal US product liability and medical malpractice reparations to the nations which collectively – through the economic malpractice of the Washington institutions – were led into the precipitous fall in living standards that hit a large number of the world's nations in the 1980s and 1990s.

APPENDIX 1: ANTONIO SERRA: A NOTE ON THE HISTORY OF ECONOMIC THEORY AS IT RELATES TO UNEVEN ECONOMIC GROWTH

The first economist who explained uneven development – why the natural working of a market economy would make some nations rich and some poor – was the Neapolitan Antonio Serra, in 1613. Serra's work was republished in 1803, and the year before that a volume of eulogies was published in his honour (Salfi 1802).

Serra wrote at a time when 'public misery and crime spread [in Naples] . . . more and more people gave themselves over to public and ecclesiastic idleness . . . and assassinations increased' (Salfi 1802, p. 21). In his book, Serra explains how the poverty of Naples and the wealth of Venice originated in the fact that the economic activities in which the two states specialized behaved according to different laws: as Venice specialized in manufacturing, its unit costs fell, unleashing a virtuous circle of increasing sales, increasing production and increasing welfare. The volume-based low costs in Venice provided formidable barriers to entry for its competitors. As Naples specialized in harvesting the products of nature, the opposite phenomenon could be observed: unit costs increased and Naples was thrown into a vicious circle of falling income and poverty. European economic policy had followed Serra's principles starting in the late 1400s. They were expressed in the sixteenth- and seventeenth-century theories of 'good' and 'bad' trade (see King 1721, Pfeiffer 1764–78, Reinert 1998). However, Serra was the first to present a scientific explanation of how the mechanisms of wealth and poverty evolved around vortices moving economies up or down.

The rediscovery of Serra in 1802–03 was timely. The industrial revolution had again produced a few pockets of wealth and masses of poverty, and in 1798 Thomas Malthus had published his highly pessimistic view on the possibilities for mass welfare. Serra's idea of increasing returns delivered the opposite message, and the nineteenth-century economists who laid the theoretical foundations for mass economic welfare all based their theories on Serra's dichotomy: wealth could be created and spread only by spreading to all nations economic activities which obeyed the laws of increasing returns. Friedrich List and Wilhelm Roscher – the economists who put increasing returns back into economic theory – both repeatedly quote Antonio Serra. Based on his ideas it was possible slowly to solve the scourge of nineteenth-century Europe, the 'social question'. There is a massive amount of literature on this economic theory (for example Verein für Sozialpolitik 1872–1932, Schmollers Jahrbuch for the same period, and the writings of the US institutional school).

In terms of understanding the causes of uneven economic development, the latter part of the twentieth century was a Dark Age. In economic policy Serra's principle of distributing and rebuilding increasing-return activities was a core principle behind the Economic Recovery Program (Marshall Plan), but in economic theory this insight was lost. Just as Fordist mass production started to dominate the industrialized world – where Serra's principle of increasing returns could be observed on a scale never before seen or imagined – the dichotomy of increasing versus diminishing returns was lost in economic theory. Because the concept of increasing returns was not compatible with the arbitrary choice of making 'equilibrium' into the only economic tendency, the historically observable fact that increasing and diminishing returns produce opposite results (wealth and poverty, respectively) was thrown out of economic theory (see Reinert 1980, 1998 and chapter 5) for more detailed discussions). This opened the way for the belief that globalization would produce 'factor-price equalization', that all nations would be equally wealthy under a regime of global free trade. In fact, according to late twentieth-century theory, the poor would benefit the most, since they lagged the most behind. In this chapter, using Mongolia as an example I have attempted to describe why the opposite results were produced as the few increasing-return activities in Mongolia were closed down by sudden world competition.

With the coming of 'new trade theory' in the early 1980s (Krugman 1980), increasing returns was again put on the map. Frank Graham's 1923 article (see Appendix 3) was the basis for this revival, but although Graham, a president of the American Economic Association, showed – as Serra did – that increasing and diminishing returns would produce opposite effects, by the 1980s the idea of equilibrium was so deeply entrenched that only half of Serra's and Graham's argument was resurrected. The diminishing-return side of the argument was essentially left out. By resurrecting only half of the practice and theory that had dominated economic policy in Europe for centuries and in the United States since 1820, understanding of the mechanisms that create poverty on the one hand and wealth on the other was lost. The half of the theory that was forgotten was the half concerning the mechanisms that keep poor nations poor, and neoclassical economics continued to view the world market as a machine creating automatic harmony. In 'International trade and the economic mechanisms of underdevelopment' (Reinert 1980) both increasing and diminishing returns were resurrected, based on Serra's theoretical insights.

As already pointed out, the increasingly globalized economy produces the opposite effects of what standard economic theory predicts. Instead of a convergence of world income (towards factor price equalization), we find that the nations of the world tend to cluster in two convergence groups, one rich and one poor. In many Latin American countries, 'real' jobs are becoming a rarity and poverty is on the rise. Poverty and disease have increased sharply in sub-Saharan Africa. Most of the former communist nations are considerably poorer than they were under the inefficient centrally planned economy. I argue that a key factor in this economic deterioration in the majority of the world's nations is the failure by the Washington institutions to recognize what most nineteenth-century economists believed: a nation with even an inefficient increasing-returns sector will be infinitely wealthier than a nation with no increasing-returns sector at all. Just as the spread of increasing-return activities to all European nations starting in the sixteenth century created even development, the loss of former 'middle-income' nations originates in the wholesale closing of increasing-return activities in Latin America and in the former centrally planned economies.

The purpose of this chapter has been to use the precipitous economic decline of the Republic of Mongolia during the 1990s as an illustration of the economic mechanisms by which the conditions imposed by the Washington institutions create vortices of increased poverty. Increasing and diminishing returns are at the core of the mechanisms that make globalization a blessing – indeed a necessity for further welfare creation – for some nations, but a curse for many others. A continuation of the present policies against the Second and Third Worlds can only reinforce the present division of the world into two convergence groups steadily moving apart in wealth and income.

Twentieth-century economic theory came to conceive of economics as a *Harmonielehre* (Robbins 1952): the world economy was assumed to be a machine producing automatic harmony. This is a natural result of the basic model. A model in which all inputs are alike throughout the process will never produce anything but an equality of outcome. During the first half of the twentieth century the common sense of the past prevailed over this model in practical policy. During the second half, mainstream economics had generally lost both the collective memory of the past and the habit of checking theory against reality. 'Pure theory' had been mistaken for 'science', and being relevant gradually came to be considered 'unscientific'. While common sense and practical men continued to dominate the policy making of the industrialized North, through the Washington institutions the South was fed an unprecedented diet of neoclassical economics in its pure form, unmitigated by the common sense of the past. The simplifying assumptions of standard economics ostensibly are there to clarify the conclusion. The Mongolian case shows that the assumption that all economic activities are qualitatively alike as carriers of economic development is wrong and has caused much harm. Only by leaving the highly abstract standard theory behind, by reintroducing 'The Other Canon' of economics that produced massive wealth in the nineteenth century, will it be possible to lift the majority of the world population out of acute poverty.

Joseph Schumpeter on Antonio Serra's 1613 Treatise

'This man must, I think, be credited with having been the first to compose a scientific treatise, though an unsystematic one, on Economic Principles and Policy. Its chief merit does not consist in his having explained the outflow of gold and silver from the Neapolitan Kingdom by the state of the balance of payments, but in the fact that he did not stop there but went on to explain the latter by a general analysis of the conditions that determine the state of an economic organism. Essentially, the treatise is about the factors on which depend the abundance not of money but of *commodities* – natural resources, quality of the people, the development of industry and trade, the efficiency of government – the implication being that if the economic process as a whole functions properly, the monetary element will take care of itself and not require any specific therapy.' (Schumpeter 1954, p. 195)

'Before this, a general law of increasing returns in manufacturing industry, also in the form of a law of decreasing unit cost, had been stated explicitly and in full awareness of its importance by Antonio Serra,[3] much as it was to be stated in the nineteenth-century textbook. The restriction of increasing returns to manufacturing should be particularly noticed. Serra did not indeed assert that agrarian production was subject to decreasing returns. But the idea that *industrial and agrarian production as such follow different 'laws'* was as clearly expressed by him as if he had. Thus he foreshadowed an important feature of nineteenth-century analysis that was not completely abandoned even by A. Marshall.' (Schumpeter 1954, p. 195, emphasis added)

APPENDIX 2: STATISTICS FOR MONGOLIA, 1989–98

Table 8.2 Output of selected industrial commodities, 1989–98.

	1989	*1990*	*1995*	*1996*	*1997*	*1998*
Sawn wood (thousand metres)	553.1	509.0	61.2	70.2	36.5	35.5
Leather jackets (thousands of pieces)	212.8	264.5	18.9	6.5	1.0	0.6
Skin coats (thousands of pieces)	180.2	138.1	16.8	14.9	2.6	0.5
Canned meat (tons)	1682.3	1108.5	431.7	339.2	650.8	322.0
Salt (tons)	4818.8	3811.9	497.3	429.3	240.4	201.6
Publications (millions of pages)	376.6	312.8	50.9	36.5	38.7	79.1
Porcelain (thousands of pieces)	3747.3	3138.3	688.5	150.6	49.3	24.2
Carpet (thousand m^2)	2128.1	1971.2	595.7	667.0	643.6	587.7
Felt boots (thousands of pairs)	592.3	588.5	79.0	57.6	48.0	47.9
Suits (thousands of pairs)	182.6	201.8	1.2	1.0	1.2	1.6
Sheepskin (thousand m^2)	1151.1	1510.5	193.5	22.4	5.2	
Leather boots (thousands of pairs)	4140.0	4222.5	245.5	86.6	41.7	33.1

Source: National Statistical Office of Mongolia (1999).

3. Serra 1613, part 1, chapter 3: 'nell'artefici vi può essere moltiplicazione ... e con minor proporzione di spesa.' (In manufacturing industry, output may be increased at less than a proportional increase in expense.)

Table 8.3 Index of industrial production (1989–98) 1989=100.

Year	*1989*	*1990*	*1995*	*1996*	*1997*	*1998*
Electricity (million kW/h)	100	94	73	73	75	75
Thermo-energy thousand (Gk)	100	107	100	94	95	96
Coal (thousand tons)	100	89	61	64	61	63
Fluorspar (thousand tons)	100	79	91	98	98	106
Copper concentrate	100	101	98	100	101	102
Molybdenum concentrates (thousand tons)	100	125	116	139	126	126
Bricks (million pieces)	100	88	12	15	9	10
Cement (thousand tons)	100	86	21	21	22	21
Lime (thousand tons)	100	108	54	57	60	58
Steel and concrete blocks (thousand m^3)	100	101	8	10	8	7
Matches (million boxes)	100	76	58	36	6	3
Mineral cotton (thousand m^3)	100	90	13	11	8	6
Khurmen block (thousands of pieces)	100	111	<1	<1	4	14
Spun thread (tons)	100	77	12	6	5	2
Combed down (tons)	100	96	168	207	173	201
Camel wool blankets (thousand metres)	100	100	21	34	26	24
Scoured wool (thousand m^2)	100	96	12	8	8	5
Carpets (thousand m^2)	100	93	28	31	30	28
Knitted goods (thousands of pieces)	100	103	13	7	8	9
Felt (thousand m^2)	100	115	12	15	12	16
Felt boots (thousands of pairs)	100	99	13	10	8	8
Wool cloth (thousand running metres)	100	56	4	2	<1	<1
Overcoats (thousands of pieces)	100	121	<1	<1	2	<1
Suits (thousands of pieces)	100	111	<1	<1	<1	<1
Hides, large (thousand tons)	100	100	0	10	-	-
Sheepskin (thousand m^2)	100	131	17	2	<1	-
Chevreau (thousand m^2)	100	101	9	7	1	-
Leather boots (thousands of pairs)	100	102	6	2	1	-
Leather coats (thousands of pieces)	100	86	31	11	<1	<1
Leather jackets (thousands of pieces)	100	124	9	3	<1	<1
Skin coats (thousands of pieces)	100	77	9	8	1	<1
Meat and meat products (thousand tons)	100	94	18	14	12	11
Canned meat (tons)	100	66	26	20	39	19
Sausages (tons)	100	95	11	12	14	11
Spirits (thousand litres)	100	101	62	60	78	82
Alcohol (thousand litres)	100	131	75	73	90	102
Flour (thousand tons)	100	95	80	46	32	33
Small intestine (thousand rolls)	100	97	10	6	5	14
Salt mining (tons)	100	51	6	6	11	<1
Salt (tons)	100	79	10	9	5	4
Bakery goods (thousand tons)	100	95	55	45	29	29
Confectioneries (thousand tons)	100	91	24	25	27	23
Milk, dairy products (million litres)	100	96	3	3	3	4
Mixed fodder (thousand tons)	100	56	22	9	7	7
Washing soap (thousand tons)	100	79	9	9	9	6
Toilet soap (thousand tons)	100	100	30	30	10	0
Publications (million signatures)	100	83	14	10	10	21
Porcelain (thousands of pieces)	100	84	18	4	1	<1
Installed metal constructions (thousand m^3)	100	101	8	10	8	7
Doors and windows (thousand m^2)	100	95	2	<1	<1	<1
Railway sleepers (thousand m^3)	100	67	47	43	47	47
Sawn wood (thousand m^3)	100	92	11	13	7	6
Ceramic tiles (thousand m^3)	100	78	11	6	–	–

Source: Calculated from National Statistical Office of Mongolia (1999).

Table 8.4 Index of industrial production, new products (1995–98) 1995=100.

	1995	*1996*	*1997*	*1998*
Candles (thousands of pieces)	100	5	<1	7
Steel (thousand tons)	100	123	146	104
Metal foundries (thousand tons)	100	52	86	102
Injection syringes (million pieces)	100	214	306	151
Injection needles (thousands of pieces)	100	79	–	105

Source: Calculated from National Statistical Office of Mongolia (1999).

Table 8.5 Index of total harvest (1985–98) 1985=100.

	1985	*1990*	*1991*	*1992*	*1993*	*1994*	*1995*	*1996*	*1997*	*1998*
Total crop	100	81	67	56	54	37	29	25	27	21
Wheat	100	87	78	66	65	47	37	31	34	28
Potatoes	100	116	86	69	53	48	46	41	48	58
Vegetables	100	100	56	39	54	54	66	56	83	110
Fodder	100	88	35	23	19	5	3	3	2	2

Source: Batkhishig (2000), p. 46.

Table 8.6 Index of agricultural yields (1989–98) 1989=100.

	1989	*1990*	*1995*	*1996*	*1997*	*1998*
Cereals, total	100	88	58	53	61	50
Wheat	100	86	57	51	58	49
Barley	100	93	71	70	67	50
Oats	100	101	6	10	5	25
Potatoes	100	87	68	54	66	65
Fodder crops	100	111	43	49	56	29

Source: Calculated from National Statistical Office of Mongolia (1999).

*Table 8.7 Index of number of livestock (1989–98)*1989=100.

	Total	*Camels*	*Horses*	*Cattle*	*Sheep*	*Goats*
1989	100	100	100	100	100	100
1990	105	96	103	106	106	103
1991	103	85	103	105	103	106
1992	104	74	100	105	103	113
1993	102	66	100	101	97	123
1994	109	66	110	117	97	146
1995	116	66	120	123	96	172
1996	119	64	126	129	95	184
1997	127	64	132	134	99	207
1998	133	64	139	138	103	223

Source: Calculated from Batkhishig (2000), p. 45.

Table 8.8 Number of herdsmen and herdsmen's households.

	Herdsmen	*Index*	*Households*	*Index*
1989	135 420	100	68 963	100
1990	147 508	109	74 710	108
1995	390 539	288	169 308	245
1996	395 355	292	170 084	247
1997	410 078	303	183 636	266
1998	414 433	306	187 147	271

Source: Calculated from National Statistical Office of Mongolia (1999).

APPENDIX 3: FRANK GRAHAM'S THEORY OF UNEVEN DEVELOPMENT: INCREASING AND DIMINISHING RETURNS IN INTERNATIONAL TRADE: A NUMERICAL EXAMPLE

Stage 1: World income and its distribution before trade.

Product	*Country A*			*Country B*		
	Man-days	*Output per man-day*	*Total*	*Man-days*	*Output per man-day*	*Total*
Wheat	200	4	800	200	4	800
Watches	200	4	800	200	3	600

World production: 1600 wheat + 1400 watches. In wheat equivalents: 3200.

Country A's income in wheat equivalents: 1714 wheat.

Country B's income in wheat equivalents: 1486 wheat.

Price: 4 wheat = 3.5 watches.

Stage 2: World income and its distribution after each country specializes according to its comparative advantage.

Product	*Country A*			*Country B*		
	Man-days	*Output per man-day*	*Total*	*Man-days*	*Output per man-day*	*Total*
Wheat	100	4.5	450	300	3.5	1050
Watches	300	4.5	1350	100	2	200

World production with trade: 1500 wheat + 1550 watches. In wheat equivalents: 3271.

Country A's income in wheat equivalents: 1993 wheat.

Country B's income in wheat equivalents: 1278 wheat.

APPENDIX 4: THE MONGOLIAN VICIOUS CIRCLES CONDENSED

1991: Free trade shock and collapse of COMECON trading area > fall in exports leads to galloping deindustrialization, and loss of most activities subject to increasing returns (manufacturing) > lower demand and lower tax receipts lead to massive loss of other urban jobs, in both the services and the government sector > declining demand for people with higher education > wages collapse > lower wages reduce demand for manufactured goods even further > an overvalued currency favours imports over locally manufactured goods, increasing the crisis > return to the pastoral economy in the countryside > fast growth in diminishing returns activities, 8 million pasturing animals added by urban unemployed attempting to earn a new living > fragile ecosystem cannot support the increase in livestock (more than 2 million animals, roughly the increase in number of animals over the previous two years) starve to death during

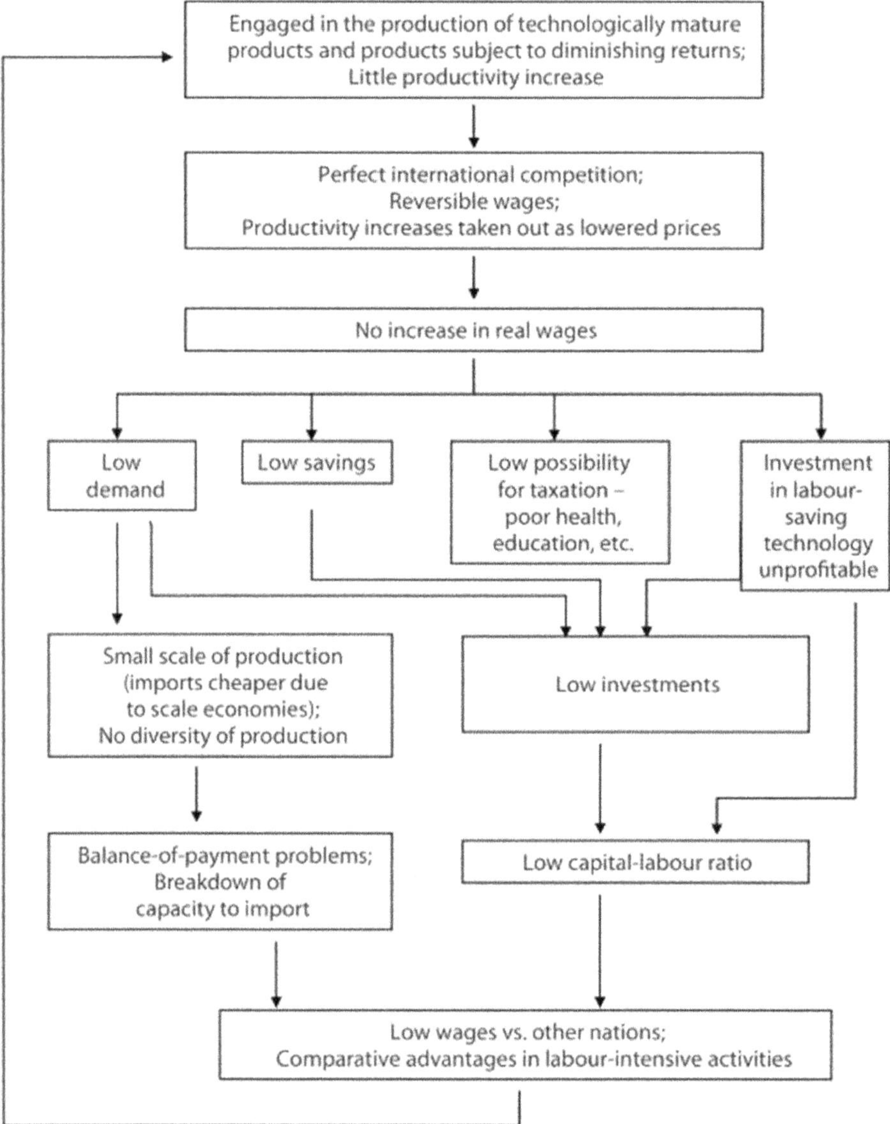

Figure 8.1 The vicious circle of Morgenthau Plans *Note:* It is futile to attack the system at any one point (for example increasing investment) when wages are still low and demand is absent. An instance of this is poor capital utilization and excess capacity in Latin American LDCs. *Source:* Reinert (1980), p. 41.

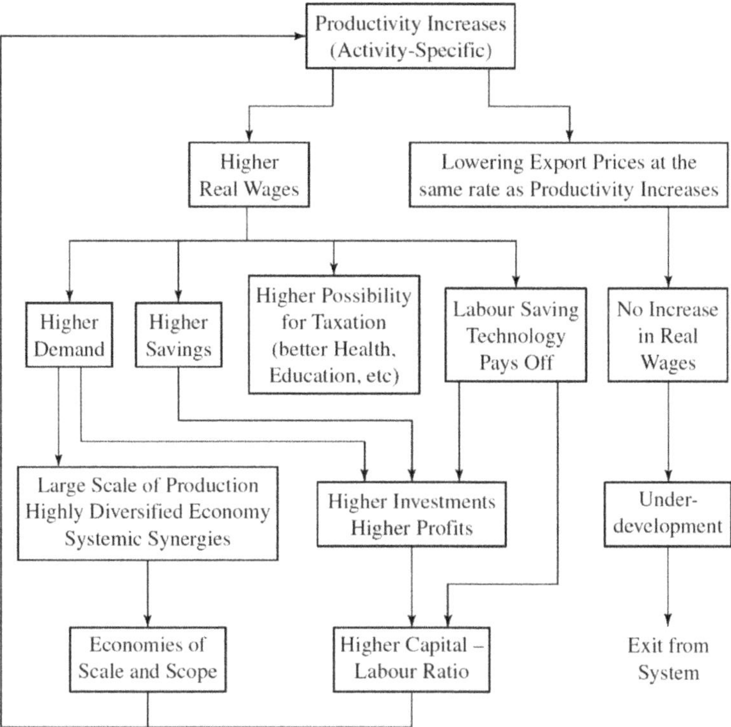

Figure 8.2 The virtuous systemic effects of a Marshall Plan *Note*: In a closed system, with constant employment rate, the only way GNP per capita can grow is through the 'virtuous circle'. However, the system can be cut-off at any one point, for example if higher demand goes to foreign goods alone, the circle will break. *Source*: Reinert (1980), p. 39.

the winter of 1999–2000) > environmental degradation, perhaps permanent desertification > exports collapse even further (exports down by 56 per cent in current dollars since 1989) > breakdown of the capacity to import (trade deficit in 1998 equal to 49 per cent of exports) > terms of trade deteriorate as exports are now raw materials > very limited foreign exchange available to agricultural sector for industrial inputs such as fertilizer > institutional collapse in agricultural sector (animal vaccines programmes, agricultural extension) > complete collapse in agricultural productivity due to lack of fertilizers and the institutional collapse (yield per acre of important fodder crops down by 71 per cent since 1989; the least affected crop is potatoes with 'only' a 35 per cent drop in productivity; all other crops decline by at least 50 per cent) > fears of inflation and of bank failures cause IMF to keep both interest rates (real interest rate is 35 per cent) and currency exchange rate high, blocking the natural mechanisms which should have made Mongolian labour and products cheap on the world market, thus blocking the market mechanisms which would have given Mongolia a chance to become more competitive in world markets. There appears to be no factor in sight to invert these causal mechanisms. (See Figures 8.1 and 8.2.)

References

Abramovitz, Moses (1956), 'Resource and output trends in the United States since 1870', *American Economic Review, Papers and Proceedings*, May.

Abramovitz, Moses (1993), 'The search for the sources of growth: Areas of ignorance, old and new', *Journal of Economic History*, **53** (2), 217–43.

Arthur, W. Brian (1994), *Increasing Returns and Path Dependency in the Economy*, Ann Arbor, MI: University of Michigan Press.

Baade, Fritz (1955), 'Gruß und Dank an Herbert Hoover', *Weltwirtschaftliches Archiv*, **74** (1), 1–6.

Balabkins, Nicholas (1964), *Germany under Direct Control: Economic Aspects of Industrial Disarmament, 1945–1948*, New Brunswick, NJ: Rutgers University Press.

Batbayar, Tsendenambyn (ed.) (2000), *Renovation of Mongolia on the Eve of the XXI Century and Future Development Patterns*, Ulaanbaatar, Mongolia: Mongolian Development Research Center.

Batkhishig, B. (2000), 'Mongolian economic reform: guidelines, results and future trends', in Tsendenambyn Batbayar (ed.), *Renovation of Mongolia on the Eve of the XXI Century and Future Development Patterns*, Ulaanbaatar, Mongolia: Mongolian Development Research Center.

Bikales, William (2000), document presented by the United States Agency for International Development, Mongolia, at the International Conference on Capacity Building for Mongolian Development Strategy, Ulaanbaatar, Mongolia, March 23–24.

Byambasuren, D. (2000), 'National factors affecting development strategy of Mongolia', in Tsendenambyn Batbayar (ed.), *Renovation of Mongolia on the Eve of the XXI Century and Future Development Patterns*, Ulaanbaatar, Mongolia: Mongolian Development Research Center.

Carey, Henry C. (1869), *How Protection, Increase of Public and Private Revenues and National Independence March Hand in Hand Together: Review of the Report of the Hon. D.A. Wells, Special Commissioner of the Revenue*, Philadelphia, PA: Collins.

Carey, Henry C. (1876), *Commerce, Christianity and Civilization versus British Free Trade: Letters in Reply to the London Times*, Philadelphia, PA: Collins.

Chacholiades, Miltiades (1978), *International Trade Theory and Policy*, New York: McGraw-Hill.

Economic Cooperation Administration (1949), *Westdeutschland im Europäischen Wiederaufbauprogramm: Eine Wirtschaftsübersicht*, Frankfurt: Economic Cooperation Administration.

Endresen, Sylvi (1994), *Modernization Reversed? Technological Change in Four Asian Fishing Villages*, PhD diss., University of Oslo, Department of Human Geography.

Esslen, Joseph (1905), *Das Gesetz des abnehmenden Bodenertrages seit Justus von Liebig: Eine dogmengeschichtliche Untersuchung*, Munich: Schweitzer.

Foxwell, H.S. (1899), foreword to Anton Menger, *The Right of the Whole Produce of Labour*, London: Macmillan.

Fujimoto, Atsushi (2000a), 'Inapplicability of the theory of positive real interest rates to highly inflationary economics', mimeograph distributed at the International Conference on Capacity Building for Mongolian Development Strategy, Ulaanbaatar, Mongolia, March 23–24.

Fujimoto, Atsushi (2000b), 'What Mongolia should do now for her mid-term and long-term economic development', mimeograph distributed at the International Conference on Capacity Building for Mongolian Development Strategy, Ulaanbaatar, Mongolia, March 23–24.

Galbraith, James (2000), 'How the economists got it wrong', *American Prospect*, http://www.prospect.org/print/V11/7/galbraith-j.html

Graham, Frank (1923), 'Some aspects of protection further considered', *Quarterly Journal of Economics*, **37**, 199–227.

Hume, David (1768), *The History of England*, 6 vols, London: T. Cadell.

Ibsen, Henrik (1882), *En Folkefiende*, Copenhagen: Gyldendal.

International Monetary Fund (1991), *The Mongolian People's Republic: Toward a Market Economy*, Washington, DC: International Monetary Fund.

International Monetary Fund (2000), *Mongolia: Statistical Annex*, IMF country staff report no. 00/26, Washington, DC: International Monetary Fund.

Kafka, Franz (1935/1994), *Der Prozess*, Frankfurt: Fischer.

King, Charles (1721), *The British Merchant, or Commerce Preserv'd.*, London: Darby.

Krugman, Paul (1980), *Rethinking International Trade*, Cambridge, MA: MIT Press.

Krugman, Paul (ed.) (1988), *Strategic Trade Policy and the New International Economics*, Cambridge, MA: MIT Press.

Krugman, Paul (1996), *Development, Geography and Economic Theory*, Cambridge, MA: MIT Press.

Kuribayashi, Sumio (2000), 'Agricultural development in Mongolia and the role of official development assistance', mimeograph distributed at the International Conference on Capacity Building for Mongolian Development Strategy, Ulaanbaatar, Mongolia, March 23–24.

Leslie, T.E.C. (1888) 'The movements of agricultural wages in Europe', in *Essays in Political Economy*, Dublin: Hodges, Figgis & Co.

List, Friedrich (1841), *Das Nationale System der Politischen Ökonomie*, Stuttgart and Tübingen: Cotta.

Malhotra, Kamal (1998), *Mongolia. Rapid Economic Assessment: A Child-Focused Perspective*, Bangkok: Global South.

Malthus, Thomas (1820/1986), *Principles of Political Economy, Considered with a View to Their Practical Application*, second edition 1836, 1986 reprint, Fairfield, NJ: Kelley.

Marshall, Alfred (1890), *Principles of Economics*, London: Macmillan.

Mill, John Stuart (1848), *Principles of Political Economy*, London: J.W. Parker.

Morgenthau, Henry, Jr (1945), *Germany Is Our Problem: A Plan for Germany*, New York: Harper.

Myrdal, Gunnar (1956), *Development and Under-Development: A Note on the Mechanisms of National and International Inequalities*, Cairo: National Bank of Egypt.

National Statistical Office of Mongolia (1999), *Mongolian Statistical Yearbook 1998*, Ulaanbaatar: National Statistical Office of Mongolia.

North, James (2000), 'Sound the alarm: Economist James Stiglitz rips Washington's "market Bolsheviks"', *Barron's*, 17 April.

Ochirbat, P. (2000), 'Development strategy of Mongolia: Minerals factors', in Tsendenambyn Batbayar (ed.), *Renovation of Mongolia on the Eve of the XXI Century and Future Development Patterns*, Ulaanbaatar, Mongolia: Mongolian Development Research Center.

Pfeiffer, Johan Friedrich von (1764–78), *Lehrbegriff sämtlicher Ökonomischer und Cameralwissenschaften*, 5 vols, Stuttgart: Johann Christoph Erhard, 1764–65 (part 1: vols 1 and 2) and Mannheim: Schwan, 1777–78 (parts 2 to 4).

Pomfret, John (2000), 'Mongolia beset by cashmere crisis; herders, mills struggle in new economy', *Washington Post*, 17 July.

Quesnay, François (1750), *Traité des Effets et de l'Usage de la Saignée*, Paris: d'Houry.

Reder, Melvin W. (1999), *Economics: The Culture of a Controversial Science*, Chicago, IL: University of Chicago Press.

Reinert, Erik S. (1980), 'International trade and the economic mechanisms of underdevelopment', PhD diss., Cornell University; Ann Arbor, MI: University Microfilms.

Reinert, Erik S. (1994), 'Catching-up from way behind: A third world perspective on first world history', in Jan Fagerberg, Bart Verspagen and Nick van Tunzelmann (eds), *The Dynamics of Technology, Trade and Growth*, Aldershot, UK and Brookfield, US: Edward Elgar (chapter 1 in this book).

Reinert, Erik S. (1996a), 'Diminishing returns and economic sustainability: the dilemma of resource-based economies under a free trade regime', in Stein Hansen, Jan Hesselberg and Helge Hveem (eds), *International Trade Regulation, National Development Strategies and the Environment: Towards Sustainable Development?* Oslo: Centre for Development and the Environment, University of Oslo (chapter 5 in this book).

Reinert, Erik S. (1996b), 'The role of technology in the creation of rich and poor nations: Underdevelopment in a Schumpeterian system', in Derek H. Aldcroft and Ross Catterall (eds), *Rich Nations – Poor Nations: The Long-Run Perspective*, Cheltenham, UK and Brookfield, US: Edward Elgar.

Reinert, Erik S. (1998), 'Raw materials in the history of economic policy; Or, Why List (the protectionist) and Cobden (the free trader) both agreed on free trade in corn', in G. Parry (ed.), *Freedom and Trade, 1846–1996*, London: Routledge.

Reinert, Erik S. (1999), 'The role of the state in economic growth', *Journal of Economic Studies*, **26** (4/5). A shorter version of this paper is published in Pier Angelo Toninelli (ed.) (2000), *The Rise and Fall of State-Owned Enterprise in the Western World*, New York: Cambridge University Press.

Reinert, Erik S. (2000a), 'Compensation mechanisms and targeted economic growth: Lessons from the history of economic policy', in Marco Vivarelli and Mario Pianta (eds), *The Employment Impact of Innovation*, London: Routledge.

Reinert, Erik S. (2000b), 'Full circle: Economics from scholasticism through innovation and back into mathematical scholasticism. Reflections around a 1769 price essay: "Why is it that economics so far has gained so few advantages from physics and mathematics?"', *Journal of Economic Studies*, **27** (4/5), 364–76.

Robbins, Lionel (1952), *The Theory of Economic Policy in English Classical Political Economy*, London: Macmillan.

Roscher, Wilhelm (1874), *Geschichte der National-Ökonomik in Deutschland*, Munich: Oldenbourg.

Roscher, Wilhelm (1882), *Principles of Political Economy*, Chicago, IL: Callaghan.

Sachs, Jeff and Andrew Warner (1995), *Natural Resource Abundance and Economic Growth*, National Bureau of Economic Research working paper 5398, Cambridge, MA: National Bureau of Economic Research.

Salfi, Franco (1802), *Elogio di Antonio Serra: Primo Scrittore di Economia Civile*, Milan: Nobile e Tosi.

Schmoller, Gustav/Schmollers Jahrbuch (1871–1972), *Jahrbuch für Gesetzgebung, Verwaltung und Rechtspflege des Deutschen Reichs* [varying titles], Leipzig: Duncker & Humblot.

Schumpeter, Joseph A. (1942), *Capitalism, Socialism and Democracy*, New York: Harper.

Schumpeter, Joseph A. (1954), *History of Economic Analysis*, New York: Oxford University Press.

Serra, Antonio (1613), *Breve trattato delle cause che possono far abbondare li regni d'oro e argento dove non sono miniere*, Naples: Lazzaro Scoriggio.

Shinichi, Kubota (2000), 'Inner Mongolian Autónomous Region: the shape of traditional production and the pressing transformation', mimeograph distributed at the International Conference on Capacity Building for Mongolian Development Strategy, Ulaanbaatar, Mongolia, March 23–24.

Steuart, James (1767), *An Inquiry into the Principles of Political Economy: Being an Essay on the Science of Domestic Policy in Free Nations*, 2 vols. London: Millar & Cadell.

United Nations Development Programme (1999), *Transition 1999: Human Development for Central and Eastern Europe and the CIS*, New York: United Nations Development Programme.

Verein für Sozialpolitik (1872–1932), *Schriften*, 188 vols.

Viner, Jacob (1937), *Studies in the Theory of International Trade*, New York: Harper.

World Bank (2000a), 'Economic and social development of Mongolia: contribution of the World Bank', mimeograph distributed at the International Conference on Capacity Building for Mongolian Development Strategy, Ulaanbaatar, Mongolia, March 23–24.

World Bank (2000b), *The World Bank and Mongolia*, country brief, Washington, DC: World Bank.

Chapter 9

INCREASING POVERTY IN A GLOBALIZED WORLD: *MARSHALL PLANS* AND *MORGENTHAU PLANS* AS MECHANISMS OF POLARIZATION OF WORLD INCOMES

1. The Problem: Marshall Plans & Morgenthau Plans

During the 1990s, a majority of the world's nations experienced falling real wages. In many cases real wages declined both rapidly and considerably; a human crisis of large proportions is evolving in some former communist countries, while in most Latin American countries, real wages peaked sometime in the late 1970s or early 1980s, and since then have fallen. The term 'state' is hardly applicable to several African countries, and this problem of 'failed states' is growing. In these nations many institutions, such as educational systems, that used to be handled by the nation state have broken down, and different areas of what used to comprise a nation are ruled over by different warlords. This is a type of political structure that a few years ago was thought of as belonging to a mediaeval past. If there is something called 'progress' and 'modernization', globalization has – particularly for many small and medium-size nations – brought with it the opposite: many are experiencing 'retrogression' and 'primitivization'. Poverty and disease increase sharply in Sub Saharan Africa, and a creeping 'Africanization' in parts of Latin America can be detected.[1]

These events profoundly challenge the present world economic order and the standard textbook economics on which this order rests. This is because the increasingly globalized economy seems to produce opposite effects of what standard economic theory predicts. Instead of a convergence of world income (towards factor-price equalization), we find that a group of rich nations show a tendency to converge, while another convergence group of poor countries gathers at the bottom of the scale. Mainstream logic is that the more backward a nation, the easier it will be to catch up to some imaginary 'frontier'. In effect, what is actually happening is very different: Nations

1. The bright spots in this development are that the two most populous nations on the planet – China and India – have not taken the same road towards increasing misery as have so many of the smaller Third World states. This is no doubt to a large extent a result of their reluctance to follow the recommendations of mainstream economics.

specialize. Some nations specialize in producing continuous flows of innovations that raise their real wages ('innovation rents'), whereas other nations specialize either in economic activities where there is very little or no technological change (*maquila*-type activities), or where technological change takes the form of process innovations (in which technical change is taken out in the form of lower prices to the consumer rather than in higher wages to the workers, who are typically unskilled – particularly in the area of raw material production).[2] We claim that economy-wide differences in wage levels originate in these specialization patterns in key areas of production, and that – as in standard trade theory – free trade reinforces the pattern of specialization: based on these innovation rents some nations specialize in being rich, others specialize in being poor. We shall return to this discussion in more detail later.

The World Bank estimates that a bus driver in Germany enjoys a standard of living 13 times higher than a bus driver in Kenya.[3] In other words, the world market rewards people with exactly the same productivity very differently. The purpose of this chapter is to explain the mechanisms and the economic policies that created this type of gap in the living standard of workers in the non-tradeable service sector. This sector, which includes most of the government sector – jobs that are all subject to a natural and total protection from international competition – provides the majority of jobs in most developed nations. Whereas increasing population pressures in an agricultural sector subject to diminishing returns were the causes of historical mass migrations,[4] a main factor behind modern mass migrations are these enormous differences in living standards between people who are essentially equally efficient.

In this chapter we shall outline a theory that explains the economic forces which have produced the enormous wage differentials between people with the same level of productivity in different countries. This alternative theory of wealth and poverty – The Other Canon Theory – differs fundamentally from mainstream economic theory. The Other Canon constituted the toolkit of the pre-Smithian mainstream around 1750, and has also been the basis of the economic strategies that have catapulted laggard countries from relative poverty to relative wealth, from fifteenth-century England, to Korea in the period 1960–80 and Ireland between 1980 and 2000.[5]

For practical purposes we have established two ideal types of economic policies. We have named economic policies that create the vortices of, respectively, wealth and poverty after two types of economic strategies that were developed and – like the atomic bomb – tried out in the field in the 1940s: Marshall Plans and Morgenthau Plans. We shall claim that virtual virtuous circles of development are the result of a set of policies that we refer to generically as Marshall Plans. The opposite effect, vicious circles, is the result of Morgenthau Plans.

---

2. See chapter 1 for a description of the two different ways technological change spreads in the economy; the classical mode – through lower prices to the consumers – and the collusive mode, through higher wages to the producers.
3. *Financial Times* 2002.
4. Alfred Marshall quotes the Bible, Genesis xii &, to emphasize this point.
5. Reinert and Daastøl 1997 and chapter 13 in this book.

The purpose of the Morgenthau Plan – named after Henry Morgenthau Jr., the US secretary of the treasury from 1934 to 1945 – was to prevent Germany, which had caused two wars in the twentieth century, from ever starting a war again.[6] This was to be achieved by de-industrializing Germany: taking all industrial machinery out of the country and filling the mines with water, thereby turning it into a pastoral state. The plan was approved in an Allied meeting in 1943 and carried out after the German capitulation in May 1945.

The Morgenthau Plan was abruptly stopped in Germany in 1947 when ex-President Herbert Hoover of the United States reported back from Germany: 'There is the illusion that the New Germany left after the annexations can be reduced to a 'pastoral state'. It cannot be done unless we exterminate or move 25.000.000 out of it'.[7] Hoover had rediscovered the wisdom of the mercantilist population theorists: an industrialized nation has a much larger carrying capacity in terms of population than an agricultural state.[8] The deindustrialization process had also led to a sharp fall in agricultural yields and partly to an institutional collapse, providing evidence of the importance of the linkages between the industrial and agricultural sector that were also a hallmark of mercantilist economics.[9] Less than four months after Hoover's alarming reports from Germany, the US government announced the Marshall Plan, which aimed to achieve exactly the opposite of the Morgenthau Plan: Germany's industrial capacity was at all cost to be brought back to its 1938 level. It cannot be emphasized enough that the Marshall Plan was not a financial plan, it was a *reindustrialization plan*.

We shall claim that Morgenthau Plans, after years of neglect, were resurrected by the Washington Consensus starting in the 1980s and, even more strongly, after the end of the Cold War in 1991. De facto Morgenthau Plans came with the label of 'structural adjustment', which very often had the effect of de-industrializing Third World nations.[10] These two ideal types of economic policy, the Marshall Plan and the Morgenthau Plan, explain the 'virtuous' and 'vicious' circles that were fashionable, but not well explained, in the heyday of development economics during the 1950s and 1960s.[11]

This chapter can only outline what Schumpeter calls a Vision.[12] Schumpeter describes vision as a 'preanalytic cognitive act' that supplies the raw material for the analytical effort, which in the case of this theory took place in the late 1970s and was expressed in my 1980 PhD thesis.[13] This particular vision developed from a profound conviction that the sources of uneven economic development had fundamentally to

6. Morgenthau 1945.
7. Hoover's Report no. 3, March 18, 1947, quoted in Baade 1955.
8. Stangeland 1966.
9. Chapter 8
10. Chapter 8
11. The crucial role of the nation state in carrying out the right type of economic policy is discussed in Reinert 1999.
12. Schumpeter 1954, pp. 41–42.
13. Reinert 1980.

be found in the realm of production rather than in the neoclassical realm of barter, trade and finance. In several articles in the 1990s, I have elaborated on the same basic understanding of the evolution of wealth and poverty.

For nearly 500 years, from the late 1400s to the 1960s, it was common knowledge that a nation with an inefficient manufacturing sector would have a higher standard of living than a nation with no manufacturing sector at all. Such was the common sense behind the reconstruction of Europe after World War II. Everyone knew that world free trade in 1945, because of the superiority of the United States, would have meant a virtual deindustrialization of Europe. Free trade was only a goal that was to be introduced after Europe had been solidly reindustrialized. The essence of the Marshall Plan was to bring back Europe's industrial production – including Germany's – to the pre-war level. Around 1750 it was generally understood that colonialism was in effect what we call a Morgenthau Plan; it was only with the appearance of barter-based economic theory – with Adam Smith and David Ricardo – that colonialism ceased to be understood as a system of poverty creation.

The contrast between the 1950s and the 1990s in terms of economic understanding is abysmal. Many Third World countries were subjected to a de facto Morgenthau Plan – a deindustrialization – in the 1990s.[14] This is because the economics profession by 1990 – having lost all sense of historical perspective – had come to believe in the Cold War propaganda version of neoclassical economics, a theory in which the market produces automatic harmony. We shall argue that understanding uneven development requires an understanding of imperfect competition, and that the mercantilist policies that laid the foundations for Europe's wealth did indeed have a developed understanding of the same type of mechanisms which created wealth and fame for Boston Consulting Group starting in the 1970s. We shall return to this argument later.

2. The two conflicting theories of globalization

It is generally not remembered that two Nobel laureates in economics have provided two largely conflicting theories of what will happen to world income under globalization.

1. Based on the standard assumptions of neoclassical economic theory, US economist Paul Samuelson 'proved' mathematically that unhindered international trade will produce 'factor-price equalization', i.e. that the prices paid to the factors of production – capital and labour – will tend to be the same all over the world.[15]
2. Based in an alternative tradition – which we broadly have labelled The Other Canon – Swedish economist Gunnar Myrdal was of the opinion that world trade would tend to increase already existing differences in incomes between rich and poor nations.[16]

14. Chapter 8.
15. Samuelson 1949, 1950.
16. Myrdal 1956.

The economic policies of the Washington Consensus – the basis for the economic policies imposed by The World Bank and the International Monetary Fund – are exclusively built on the type of theory which is represented by Paul Samuelson. The developments of the 1990s are in sharp conflict with Samuelson's type of theory, but confirm Myrdal's assertion: the rich nations as a group seem to converge into a cluster of wealthy countries, while the poor seem to converge towards poverty, with the gap between the two groups getting wider. Paul Samuelson's theory appears to explain what goes on inside the group of rich nations, while Gunnar Myrdal's theory seems to be able to explain the development of relative wealth between the group of rich nations and the group of poor nations. Samuelson's theory is not harmful to nations which already have established a comparative advantage in increasing returns, or rather in Schumpeterian activities. It is, however, extremely harmful to those nations that have not passed the mandatory passage point of a conscious industrialization policy.

The kind of theory that Myrdal proposes – a type of institutional economic theory that we call The Other Canon – is today almost extinct: it either exists only in fragments or in a perverted form tied to neoclassical economics as 'New Institutional Economics'. In its original form, it is rarely taught in the economics departments in today's leading universities. The economics profession as a group is therefore very reluctant to see that, when it comes to the relationship between rich and poor countries, Myrdal might be right instead of Samuelson.

Seeing only the broad outlines of world development, Samuelson's type of theory can claim a certain degree of success in predicting the developments *within* each group of nations. The rich nations seem to tend towards being more equally rich, while the poor seem to converge towards being equally poor. A result of this is that the 'medium-rich' – or middle-income – nations are disappearing, and the two convergence groups, rich and poor, stand out as isolated clusters in a scatter diagram. Myrdal's prediction is definitely correct when it comes to the relationship between rich and poor countries since 1990. We shall argue that the poverty of the Second and Third Worlds was an outcome of a Morgenthau Plan rather than a Marshall Plan.

3. The mechanisms at work

A paradigm can, for that matter, even insulate the community from those socially important problems that are not reducible to the puzzle form, because they cannot be stated in terms of the conceptual and instrumental tools the paradigm supplies.[17]

Thomas Kuhn, *The Structure of Scientific Revolutions.*

17. Thomas Kuhn, *The Structure of Scientific Revolutions*, p. 37.

3.1 *The absence of taxonomies and categories prevents us from seeing the causes of wealth and poverty*

We would assert that the type of theory represented by Paul Samuelson fails to account for the increasing miseries of the 1990s, in essence because this standard economic theory does not involve any theory of economic development other than that of adding capital to labour. In standard economic theory, all inputs – human beings and economic activities – are seen as being qualitatively identical and equally fit as carriers of economic growth. In this standard theory Man's wit and will, Man as a spiritual being, is also largely absent. Not surprisingly, a theory in which all inputs are qualitatively alike, all outcomes are also qualitatively alike. In other words, this is a type of theory which can only produce theoretical outcomes where all factors are as they were when they entered into the model, i.e. perfectly identical. 'Factor-price equalization' – the prediction that in a globalized economy all wage-earners will tend to have the same wages – is therefore the only possible outcome of standard economic theory: the conclusions about equality are already built into the assumptions that everything is equal.

On this basis Thomas Kuhn – in what is the most-quoted scientific book – is right when he explains how scientific paradigms may insulate the community from burning social problems such as the increasing poverty of the poor during the 1990s. The problem at hand is – as Kuhn says – not reducible to the 'language' of standard economic theory. For this reason the standard reply of the economics profession to the dramatically diminishing standards of living in many countries is 'more of the same'. Their type of theory does not contain the elements that can explain why economic development is, by its very nature, an uneven process. In this chapter we shall attempt to explain the developments of the 1990s in a 'common sense' language, that of the nearly defunct Other Canon theory of economics.

Picking up on Kuhn's point, it should be emphasized that standard economics is not a taxonomic science; the theory of the Washington Consensus is void of any possibility to observe and classify the differences in conditions that ultimately cause the differences in wealth. 'One must first observe differences in order to observe attributes', says Rousseau.[18] Its inability to observe such differences makes standard economics a theory that can only explain even economic growth.

An important explanation as to why the mainstream paradigm insulates the community from the problems created by globalization is the loss of the role of production in economic development. The roots to inequality of wealth are to be found in the realm of production. This loss of production is certainly one of the unfortunate legacies of Adam Smith, who makes no distinction between *commerce* and *industry*. Smith assimilates the process of production to that of exchange, and labour time becomes the common measuring rod of both.[19] In this way economics becomes what Lionel Robins calls a *Harmonielehre*, a system that, if left to itself, creates a system of economic harmony.

18. Quoted in Lévi-Strauss 1996, p. 247.
19. For an excellent discussion of this, see Biernacki 1995, p. 253.

During the twentieth century this weakness was exasperated, and economic theory came to lose the very cause of twentieth-century wealth: industrialism. Swedish institutional economist Johan Åkerman explains these mechanisms well:

> Capitalism, property rights, income distribution came to be considered the essential features, whereas the core contents of industrialism – technological change, mechanisation, mass production and its economic and social consequences – partly were pushed aside. The reasons for this development are probably found in the following three elements: *Firstly*, Ricardian economic theory … became a theory of 'natural' relations, established once and for all, between economic concepts (price, interest, capital). *Secondly*, the periodic economic crises are important in this respect because the immediate causes of the crises could be found in the monetary sphere. Technological change, the primary source creating growth and transforming society, disappeared behind the theoretical connections which were made between monetary policy and economic fluctuation. *Thirdly*, and most importantly, Marx and his doctrine could capitalise on the discontent of the industrial proletariat. His teachings gave hope of a natural law which led towards the 'final struggle', when the pyramid of income distribution would be turned on its head, the lower classes should be the powerful and mighty. In this ongoing process the technological change came to be considered only as one of the preconditions for class struggle.[20]

3.2 Which factors cause economic development?

Austrian Harvard economist Joseph Alois Schumpeter once criticized 'the pedestrian view that it is capital per se that propels the capitalist engine'.[21] This is indeed the basic mechanism by which standard economic theory sees economic development happening: the addition of more capital to each worker.

We would claim that this perception is fundamentally wrong. Rather, economic development is caused by new ideas and new knowledge, which produce investment opportunities and therefore create a demand for capital to invest. In this view what the Third World lacks is not capital, but investment opportunities that lead to innovations, projects in which capital may be profitably invested. For this reason, among others, we observe capital flight from the poor countries to the rich. By attempting to provide capital for the Third World without creating profitable investment opportunities, we are treating the symptoms of economic development – the lack of capital – instead of its real cause: the lack of certain types of economic activities from which growth and structural change emanate.

Two important fifteenth-century inventions made it possible to increase the supply of investment opportunities: patents and protection. These two features – one so much loved and the other so much hated by present United States trade policy – were brainchildren of the same qualitative understanding of human progress. The first patents were created in Venice in the late 1400s and enabled people to make a living

20. Åkerman 1954, pp. 26–27.
21. Schumpeter 1954, p. 468.

by generating new ideas. When ideas could no longer be immediately copied, investment in new ideas became profitable and a continuous supply of new and steep learning curves became what we now call economic development. In order for these new activities – these productivity explosions and learning curves (see sections 3.3 and 3.4) – to spread to other nations and other labour markets, protective tariffs were created in order to make profitable the introduction of new activities in more backward nations. The protective system prevented economic development from becoming a game where the winner – the first inventing country – could take all.[22] Patents vastly increased what Carlota Perez calls 'windows of opportunity' for profitable investments, and protection made it possible for laggard nations to catch on to the steep learning curves in the industries where technological change was focused. The origins of path-dependent trajectories of economic development are to be found in these early policies. These policies were all products of an administrative tradition based on civic humanism.

3.3 The productivity explosions

To use Nathan Rosenberg's terms, technical change and human learning are – at any point in time – 'focused' in certain business areas.[23] A nation with a strong concentration in the economic activities that experience high growth will experience a 'catapult effect' in real wages.

Figure 9.1 shows the first 'productivity explosion' of the first industrial revolution. In the late eighteenth century, about the time when Adam Smith was writing his *Wealth of Nations,* the productivity of cotton spinning was increasing at an incredible speed in the English manufacturing industry, reaching levels of increase up to more than 25 per cent per year.

At that time – in fact since the late fifteenth century – all European nations based their economic policy on the fact that the production from such 'leading sectors' had to take place inside the borders of every nation. From the time of Henry VII's accession to the throne of England, in 1485, the synergies observed between these 'leading sectors' and the rest of the economy (see section 3.4) were accepted wisdom in all nations. In fact, the essential difference between a colony and the Mother Country was that the colony was not allowed to produce any goods from the leading sector – from the manufacturing sector – at all. The English prohibition of most manufactures in the North American colonies was in fact a major factor behind the American Revolution in 1776. The accepted knowledge of the time – and indeed in practice until after World War II and into the 1950s – was that the export of manufactured goods and the import of raw

22. England did indeed attempt this winner-takes-it-all strategy – being the only industrial nation – well into the nineteenth century by attempting to 'kill American industry in its cradle' as a Parliamentarian expressed it.
23. Rosenberg 1975.

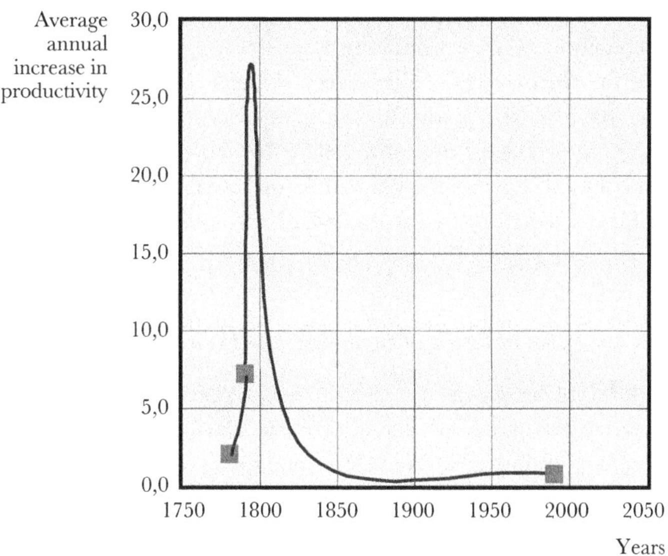

Figure 9.1 An early productivity explosion: the mechanization of cotton spinning in the first paradigm. *Source*: Carlota Perez, Calculations from Jenkins 1994.

materials was 'good trade' for a nation. By contrast, the export of raw materials and the import of manufactured goods were considered 'bad trade' for any nation. The latter was the trading pattern imposed on overseas colonies.

Interestingly, the export and import of manufactured goods was considered 'good trade' for both trading nations. The kind of economic theory which gives support to this long-practised tradition disappeared in the 1930s because increasing returns to scale – the key factor explaining the difference between manufactured goods and the production of raw materials – was not compatible with the equilibrium models that had been voted in as the core assumption of standard economic theory. It is deeply ironic that the practical implementation of the standard theory – leading to the deindustrialization of the Third World – only started in the early 1980s, at a time when the old models depicting increasing returns had been resurrected under the label of 'New Trade Theory', again 'proving' that the pre-Smithian theories (Paul Krugman, etc.) were correct. The essential problem with the new models that 'proved' that the old theories were correct, was that they were only seen as 'toy models' by the economics profession. The equilibrium models of the early twentieth century – where all economic activities are qualitatively alike as carriers of economic growth – became the sole foundations of the Washington Consensus and the policies which deindustrialized so many Third World countries during the 1990s.

Since the 1770s the world has experienced many 'productivity explosions'. These are described in the works of Christopher Freeman and Carlota Perez. Recently the so-called IT revolution has given birth to 'Moore's Law', which essentially explains the same phenomenon that is recorded in Figure 9.1. According to Moore's Law the productivity of the silicon chip doubles every eighteen months. Obviously this is not a development that can go on forever, but in the decades when this 'law' has been observed to be correct, the nations engaged in the economic activities subject to this 'productivity explosion' have moved ahead of the poor nations in fast growth without inflation. 'Productivity explosions' are deflationary: the price decreases recorded in these industries tend to reduce the general price level.

3.4 Learning and the pattern of international trade

Seen from a different angle, the productivity explosions – when plotted in terms of labour productivity per unit of product – produce 'learning curves'. These are curves that show the speed of human learning in economic activities. As a general rule, the faster the speed of learning, the faster the rate of economic growth. This is because the benefits from productivity improvements not only spread to world consumers as lower prices (a 'classical' spread of the benefits from economic change); they also spread in terms of higher wages to the workers (a 'collusive' spread of the benefits from technical change). See also section 3.5 for these 'collusive' effects.

Figure 9.2 shows the progress of human productivity, drawn as learning curves, in the production of a standard pair of shoes from 1850 to 1936. While the learning was particularly intense, from 1850 to 1900, the United States was a big producer and exporter of shoes. The United States experienced a 'productivity explosion' in the shoe industry from 1850 to 1900. As the possibilities for productivity improvements fell, the United States slowly became a net importer of shoes. This is, in effect, the 'product life cycle theory of international trade' associated with Ray Vernon and Lou Wells in the 1970s.[24]

A wealthy nation produces where the learning curve is steep – as it was in the IT industry in the 1990s – and imports products where the possibilities for learning are small and the learning curve correspondingly flat. This is the natural working of the world market: industries with fast learning capabilities use knowledge and skilled and expensive labour intensively. This is the comparative advantage of wealthy nations. Poor nations automatically specialize in economic activities where the potential for learning is low. These economic activities use inexpensive labour intensively. In this way the poor nations automatically develop a comparative advantage in providing cheap and uneducated labour. In other words, within the international division of labour they 'specialize' in being poor. This kind of perspective is lost in standard economic theory, where all economic activities are seen as being qualitatively equal.

The mercantilist economic policy that was carried out in Europe and in the United States for so many centuries found its scientific explanation in the world of business

24. Reinert 1980.

Men's Shoes

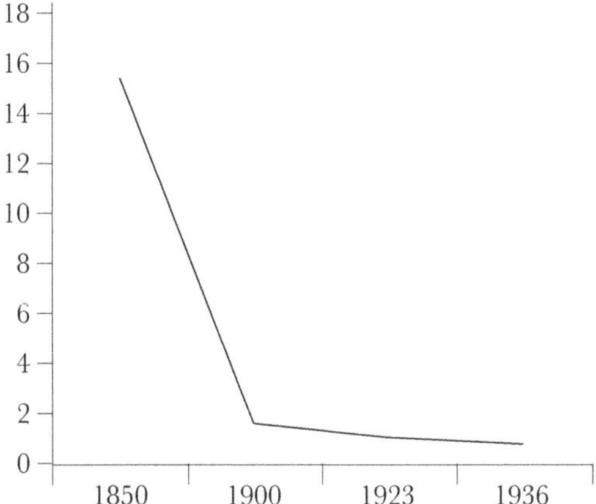

Man-Hours Required by Best-Practice Methods of Producing A Pair of Medium-grade Men's Shoes at Selected Dates in the U.S.

Year	Man-Hours Per Pair
1850	15.5
1900	1.7
1923	1.1
1936	0.9

Figure 9.2 Learning as the essence of economic growth. USA: learning curve of best-practice productivity in medium grade men's shoes. *Source*: Reinert 1980, p. 259.

during the 1970s through the work of Boston Consulting Group (BCG). This worldwide consulting firm became famous in the world of business for the creation of two tools which helped companies survive in a world dominated by dynamic Schumpeterian competition. The first tool was 'The Experience Curve', essentially a learning curve plotting total cost rather than labour hours on the vertical axis (Figure 9.2).[25] The second tool was the product portfolio, a matrix where mature cash-cows continuously finance innovations that in their turn become the cash-cows of the future.[26] In our view this theory emulates the strategy of the best mercantilists; making sure all European nations got into the cash-cows that required new skills, creating national productivity explosions and steep learning curves. The policy towards the colonies, however, caused these nations to be stuck in what BCG calls 'dog industries', activities bereft of increasing returns, with no growth and with the low profitability of commodity competition.

25. Boston Consulting Group 1972; Reinert 1980.
26. Stern and Stalk 1998, pp. 35–37.

3.5 The synergies emanating from the productivity explosions

'Husbandry ... is never more effectually encouraged than by the increase of manufactures.'
David Hume, *History of England,* 1767, vol. III.

The extremely important synergies between the leading sectors with 'productivity explosions' and the rest of the economy have been noted in England since the late 1400s. The quote above, from Adam Smith's closest friend, is typical: efficient agriculture is normally only seen in industrialized nations.

An illustration of the importance of synergies from the manufacturing sector can be observed by studying the wages of barbers or bus drivers around the world. How can we explain why the German bus driver has a standard of living 16 times higher than his counterpart in Kenya or in La Paz, Bolivia? This is essentially because, as the industrialized countries experienced wave after wave of productivity explosions in a sequence of new industries, the wages not only of the industrial workers but of the whole industrial nation were raised with rising productivity. The workers received their part of the productivity improvements not only as lower prices (in the 'classical' way) but, to a large extent, also as higher wages (the 'collusive' way).[27] In this way, each productivity explosion in the First World also jacked up the real wages of barbers and bus drivers, gaining, step by step, in real wages compared to their equally productive counterparts in the Third World.

In our opinion, the only way to raise living standards in the Third World is to repeat this procedure, the only one that has ever worked from fifteenth-century England to twentieth-century Korea. Today, the application of the rules of the Washington Consensus – essentially disallowing the historically proven procedure of artificially creating a comparative advantage in manufacturing – means that the road to development, which has been followed by all industrialized countries up until now, is completely blocked for the Third World of today. To use a nineteenth-century expression, we have 'pulled up the ladder' preventing new nations from following us on the path to development. In the meantime we address the mere symptoms of development, not the causes, through our development aid.

4. Enters taxonomy: how economic activities differ

We will never be able to understand why economic growth is so uneven unless we understand how economic activities differ. We all intuitively understand that a group of investment brokers make more money than a group of people washing dishes in a restaurant. Once this kind of pre-Ricardian common sense was part of economics. In the nineteenth century, the United States in particular emphasized the need for a 'high wage strategy': the logic was that providing the nation with jobs which paid well would make the nation rich. To the United States this meant getting out of cotton growing, which required slavery and could not support wage labour.

27. Chapter 1.

Marshall Plans: Produced by focus on **<u>Schumpeterian Activities</u>** **(= 'good' export activities)**	Morgenthau Plans: Produced by focus on **<u>Malthusian Activities.</u>** **(= 'bad' export activities if no Schumpeterian sector present)**
Increasing Returns	Diminishing Returns
Dynamic imperfect competition	'Perfect competition' (commodity competition)
High growth activities	Low growth activities
Stable prices	Extreme price fluctuations
Generally skilled labour	Generally unskilled labour
Creates a middle class	Creates 'feudalist' class structure
Irreversible wages ('stickiness' of wages)	Reversible wages
Technical change leads to higher wages to the producer ('Fordist wage regime')	Technical change tends to lower price to consumer
Creates large synergies (linkages, clusters)	Creates few synergies

Figure 9.3 How economic activities differ: only the presence of Schumpeterian activities has ever managed to raise a nation out of poverty.

4.1 Two different kinds of economic activities

We argue that there are essentially two kinds of economic activities, having very different characteristics. A nation specializing in Schumpeterian activities will find that both increasing returns and technological change will cause production costs to fall, thus opening up the way for technology-based rents that can be divided between capitalists, workers and the government. A nation specializing in Malthusian activities will find that, after a certain point, specialization will cause unit production costs to rise. This is the core of Antonio Serra's 1613 argument, in which he explained the wealth of Venice and the poverty of his native Naples. Reinert[28] showed that the main export activities of Peru, Ecuador and Bolivia were actually producing well into diminishing returns: when production was reduced, production costs were also reduced. Significantly, this mechanism explains why nations exporting raw material – in the absence of a national manufacturing sector – have never managed to get out of their poverty trap.

A nation specializing in Malthusian-type activities will stay poor, while nations that specialize in Schumpeterian-type activities will raise their wage level and standard of

28. Reinert 1980.

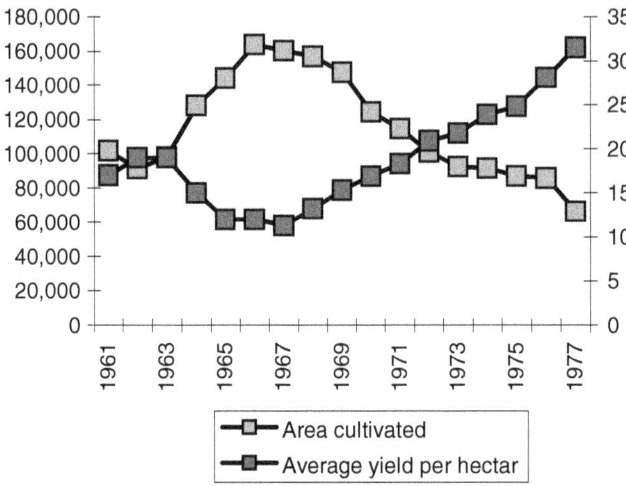

Figure 9.4 Ecuador: Diminishing Returns in Banana Production 1961–77. *Source*: Reinert 1980, page 175. Programa Nacional del Banano y Frutas Tropicales, Guayaquil. Unpublished data.

living. The growth of Malthusian activities at the expense of Schumpeterian activities is at the core of any Morgenthau Plan, as are those activities unleashed under the label of 'structural adjustment' in the 1990s.[29]

In our opinion Malthus was right when he predicted that human wages would always be around subsistence level. The historical record on this is unanimous: only Schumpeterian-type activities are able to lift nations out of poverty. This type of theory has dominated the history of economic policy, and was first advanced on a theoretical level by Antonio Serra in 1613.

Figure 9.4 shows how productivity will fall when a nation specializes in a diminishing returns activity. These activities are also subject to technical change, but this example shows how the effects of diminishing returns dwarf the effects of technical change.

Studying four waves of industrialization and deindustrialization in Peru between 1950 and 2000, Roca and Simabuco showed the same mechanism at work.[30] An extra percentage point in the share of manufacturing activities in the Peruvian economy increased white-collar real wages by 10.6 per cent and blue-collar real salaries by 15.5 per cent. This means that a growing manufacturing sector not only provides a 'catapult' for standards of living but also has a proportionally larger impact on blue-collar salaries, thus leading to a positive impact on income distribution.

29. See chapter 8 for a detailed description of these mechanisms.
30. Roca and Simabuco 2003.

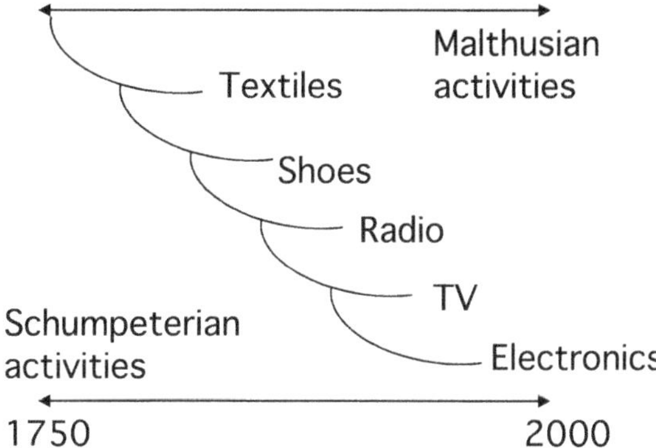

Figure 9.5 How the wage differentials between rich and poor nations were created through sequences of 'productivity explosions' translated into wage rents.

4.2 Creating the wage gap: the cumulative effect over time

A central point in the alternative vision of economic growth is how the gap between the rich and poor nations developed over time: the mechanisms which created today's situation in which the Frankfurt bus driver has a standard of living which the World Bank has calculated to be 16 times higher than that of the equally efficient bus driver in Nairobi. The developed nations have captured large rents from a sequence of productivity explosions (Figure 9.1) that have occurred since before the first industrial revolution. In addition to the obvious impact that these productivity explosions have had in making goods cheaper (what we call the 'classical' mode of distributing productivity gains), it has also had the effect of 'catapulting' the general wage level of the industrial nation to a new and higher level (what we call the 'collusive' mode of distributing productivity gains).[31]

In Malthusian economic activities, for reasons given in Figure 9.3, technological change is essentially distributed in the classical mode, i.e. in the form of lower prices to the consumer rather than higher wages to the workers, whose flat wages are represented by the top flat line. The Schumpeterian activities, on the other hand, create a sequence of steep learning curves which – every time – jacks up the wage rent in the whole labour market in the respective First World markets.[32]

Man plays two roles in the economy, as a producer and as a consumer. In order to understand the economic policies that previously made it possible for laggard countries – including, in sequence, England, the United States, Germany and Korea – to catch up, it is necessary to understand the conflicts between the economic interests of Man-the-Producer vs. Man-the-Consumer. A key feature of today's standard economics is an exclusive focus on Man-the-Consumer. Nineteenth-century US economic policy, based on the path-breaking works of Daniel Raymond in 1820 and Mathew Carey in

31. Chapter 5.
32. Reinert 1980, p. 265.

1821, explained the trade-off between the two roles. If the industrial nations have managed to jack up their wage levels in the way described in Figure 9.5, the poor nations will – after a certain point – achieve a higher national wage level by being a relatively inefficient industrial producer, rather than to continue as a supplier of raw materials. Mathew Carey succeeded in convincing US farmers of the United States that even though in the short term they would have to pay more for US-produced industrial goods than for the goods they imported from England, in the longer run they would be more than compensated for this: the rise in the general wage level in the United States would more than compensate for the higher prices which had to be paid for industrial goods. In other words, the benefits accruing to a person as a producer (in the form of higher wages) would more than outweigh the costs accruing to the same person as a consumer.

In the nineteenth-century economic debate between the United States and the UK, the English consistently refused to see the logic of Carey's argument until John Stuart Mill admitted the logic of 'infant industry protection'. Later Alfred Marshall recommended an economic policy subsidizing increasing-returns activities by taxing diminishing-return activities.[33] This is exactly the kind of policy that is at the core of creating Marshall Plans out of previous Morgenthau Plans. US economic policy was based on this principle throughout the nineteenth century. Today, the vast majority of US economists will be as blind to this argument as their English colleagues were for most of the nineteenth century.

5. Systemic effects: globalization as a Morgenthau Plan for the Third World

As a Morgenthau Plan under a different name, deindustrialization has always had the same effect. From the same problems of desperate poverty, the same remedy – industrialization – appears again and again in history. In 1613 Antonio Serra saw the wealth of Venice and the abject poverty of Naples being the result of the lack of manufacturing in Naples. 150 years later an economist in Northern Italy under French rule made the same observation there. Observers in France after the Napoleonic Wars reported the same kind of misery that Hoover saw in Germany in the spring of 1947 and that we see today in Ulaanbaatar, Mongolia or Lima, Peru: where industry is closed down, poverty enters. The 'American System' of protecting manufacturing was born in the early 1820s in a similar difficult situation. It is about time we made the same discovery again.

Figures 9.6 and 9.7 show – in circular flow-chart form – the cumulative effects of the vicious circles of deindustrialization and poverty contrasted with the virtuous circles of economic development. The main point here is that economic development is 'activity specific', that is to say, it can only occur in certain economic activities (Schumpeterian-type activities), and not in others (Malthusian-type activities). This is why, for a very long time, the term 'industrialized country' was considered synonymous with 'rich

33. Marshall 1890, p. 492.

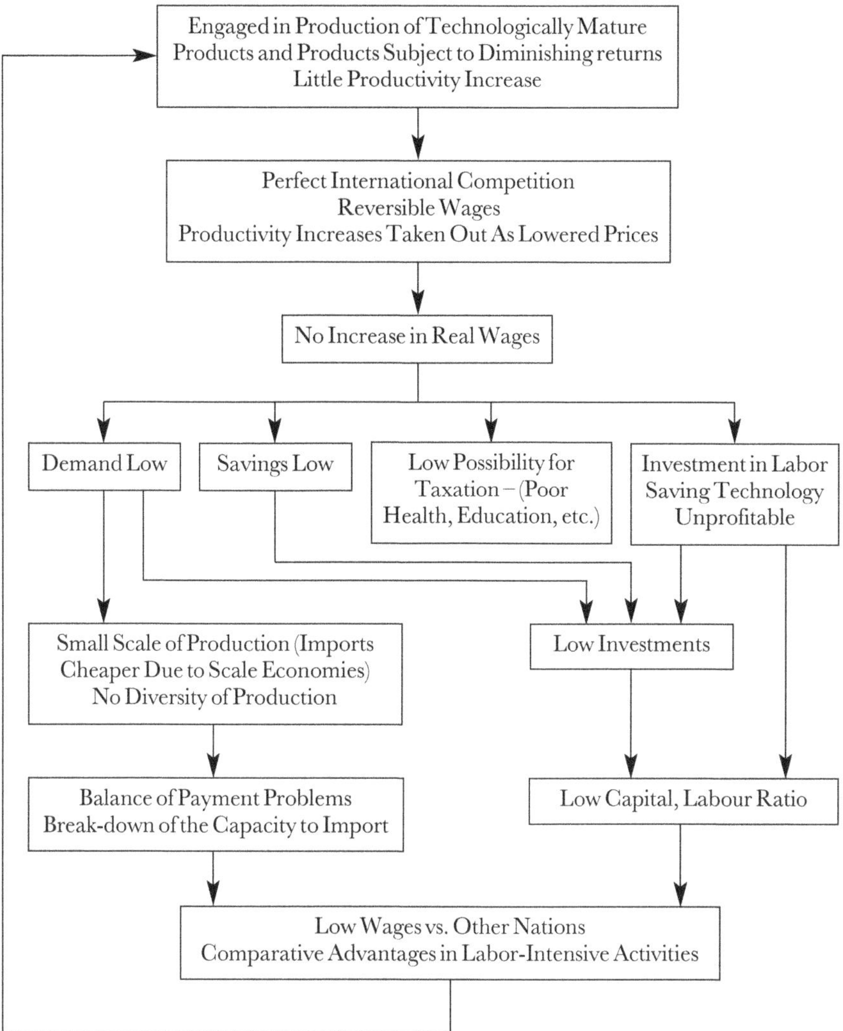

Figure 9.6 The mechanisms of a Morgenthau Plan: the 'vicious' circle of economic underdevelopment. *Note*: It is futile to attack the system at any one point, e.g., increasing investment when wages are still low and demand is absent. An instance of this is poor capital utilization and excess capacity in Latin American LDCs. *Source*: Reinert (1980), *op.cit*, p.41.

country'. The policies of the Washington Institutions have, since the late 1980s, left this traditional understanding behind.

The current fashion is to blame the poverty caused by globalization on the lack of openness on the part of industrialized countries towards agricultural imports from the Third World; in other words, the problems are seen as being created by a lack of openness to free trade. In our opinion, the historical record proves these assertions to be wrong. No nation has ever taken the step from being poor to being wealthy by exporting raw material in the absence of a domestic manufacturing sector. Malthusian activities

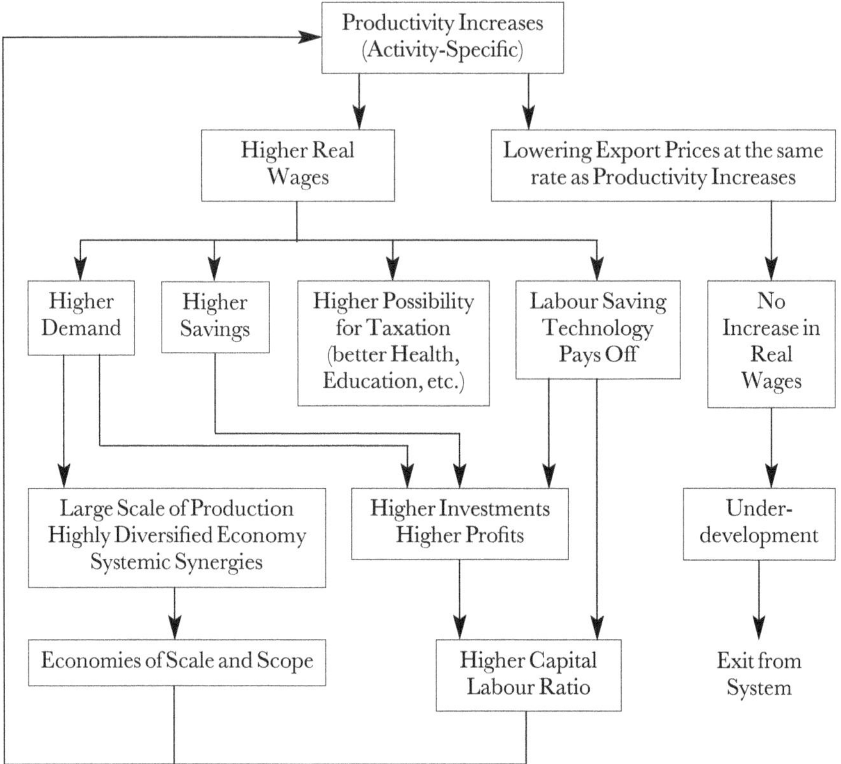

Figure 9.7 The virtuous systemic effects of a Marshall Plan. *Note*: In a closed system, with constant employment rate, the only way GNP per capita can grow is through the 'Virtuous Circle'. However, the system can be cut-off at any one point, e.g., if higher demand goes to foreign goods alone, the circle will break. *Source*: Reinert (1980), *op.cit*, p.39.

alone have never and never will in the future be able to lift a nation out of poverty without the presence of a domestic manufacturing sector. The only results of any importance that will be achieved by freeing the imports of foodstuffs from the Third World to the First World are:

a) A destruction of First World farming and of the rural areas of the First World
b) A change to industrialized farming in the Third World, where income will fall to such an extent that the local workers will not be able to afford to purchase the food they produce for the rich. This is in essence the mechanism foreseen already by Malthus.

The only way to achieve a global trading system without hunger is to strike the following deal between the rich and the poor countries: 1) The rich nations selectively commit to nourish, target and protect some of their Malthusian activities (agriculture) while 2) the Third World is allowed selectively to nourish, target and protect some of their

Schumpeterian activities (industries and advanced services subject to increasing returns) and also to protect their own food production; all under a system of internal competition. This must be done under a system of regional integration of the Third World countries.

The present policy of blind globalization coupled with increasing 'development aid' is essentially a policy of applying palliative economics: economics that addresses the symptoms of poverty without at all attacking its causes. The essence of economic development is a violent structural change leading down steep learning curves towards increased productivity. Providing a better well to subsistence agriculture is purely a palliative medicine, unrelated to the process of economic development in the real sense.

6. Conclusion

From the raw materials from Spain and the West Indies – particularly silk, iron and cochinilla (a red dye) – which cost them only 1 florin, the foreigners produce finished goods which they sell back to Spain for between 10 and 100 florins. Spain is in this way subject to greater humiliations from the rest of Europe than those they themselves impose on the Indians. In exchange for gold and silver the Spaniards offer trinkets of greater or lesser value; but by buying back their own raw materials at an exorbitant price, the Spaniards are made the laughing stock of all Europe.

Luis Ortiz, Spanish minister of finance, to Felipe II: 'Memorandum to the King to prevent money from leaving the Kingdom', Madrid, 1558.

The nations that, in sequence, have taken the step from being poor to being rich have all been through a stage of what we could call 'the cult of manufacturing'. As often happens, economic policy came before economic theory, but an early statement of this Other Canon policy is found in the quotation above, from Spain's minister of finance in 1558. The funnel of wealth coming from the New World had not been invested in the production sector, and the gold and silver had deindustrialized Spain as if it had been subject to a Morgenthau Plan. The present problems of Venezuela, and the growing problems in the productive economy of Norway, are examples of the same effect produced when monetary wealth crowds out the productive powers of an economy.

For most nations today, however, the problems are of a very different nature. As it gradually became clear during the 1990s that the basic Washington Consensus model failed to deliver its promised results, mainstream economics evolved by adding new prescriptions for the poor nations. 'Get the prices right' was initially the whole message, but it was later widened, in sequence, with 'get the property rights right', 'get the institutions right', 'get the governance right', 'get your competitiveness right' and 'get your national innovation systems right'. In our view, however, these prescriptions – these buzz-words of development – all fail on their own to get to the core of the matter. We would claim that the key to understanding unequal development is to be found in the realm of production.

From an Other Canon point of view, one formula we have been waiting for is 'get your economic activities right', i.e. some kind of policy reflecting the fact that, fundamentally, economic development is historically a process of profound structural change in which the presence of activities able to absorb new knowledge, and production under conditions of increasing returns and high barriers to entry, are conditions necessary to the achievement of economic growth. For centuries this type of economic activity was called 'manufacturing' or 'industrialization', but they are not necessarily limited to these activities. Today we have got the causalities wrong; we confuse the symptoms of development with their causes. 'It is known that a primitive people does not improve their customs and institutions later to find useful industries, but the other way around'[34] was almost common sense at the time, an understanding that was not far from that of the 1960s.

Today, there are, broadly speaking, only two possible solutions to solving the increasing poverty problems caused by globalization:

1. We can globalize the labour market, the only main institution that is not yet globalized, by allowing all the poor to move where the 'Schumpeterian' economic activities are located. This will lead to an unprecedented exodus, to enormous social problems, and to a neoclassical type 'factor-price equalization', in which world wages will tend to be equalized downwards. All will tend to get equally poor.
2. We can follow the nineteenth- and early twentieth-century path taken by all the currently rich countries – Australia is an interesting prototype for a non-export-led model – by creating national Schumpeterian sectors which initially are not competitive in the world markets, and slowly over time let the economy 'graduate' to compete on the world market. This is the only way to create dynamic 'factor-price equalization' upwards. Only in this way can we make poor countries into middle-income countries.

In our opinion, option two is the only viable solution. By a mass migration of a large number of the world's poor to the rich countries, there is an overwhelming likelihood of a factor-price equalization downwards: that the wages in the First World will fall towards the wage level of the majority of the world's population, i.e. very close to subsistence level. In this way the world will risk being caught in an underconsumption equilibrium from which the market alone will never free the economy.

The crucial transition from being a poor to being a wealthy country has, in all historical cases, involved a situation in which nations have used the market creatively as a tool to create a comparative advantage for themselves in types of economic activity which we have called 'Schumpeterian' (Figure 9.3) and 'High-Quality Activities' (Figure 9.6). In this sense, the transition from a poor to a rich nation has always been a totally artificial construct, a 'managed economy' in the sense of using private interest to artificially create a comparative advantage outside the raw materials sector. Once this

34. Meyen 1770, p. 11

threshold is overcome, the market can be left pretty much alone again. It is this transition – first made by England after 1485 and lastly by Korea in the 1960s – that is no longer possible under the Washington Consensus.

Only when the Third World has also created a comparative advantage in Schumpeterian activities will free trade be beneficial to all nations involved. This was the essential credo of US and Continental European economic theory during the nineteenth century; it was the theory behind which Europe and the US industrialized, and it is the only theory which will bring the Third World out of poverty. This type of production-based economic theory, which we have labelled The Other Canon (www.othercanon.org), has been used by all currently wealthy nations during their transition from poor to rich countries.

References

Åkerman, Johan, 1954, *Politik och Ekonomi i Atomålderens Värld,* Stockholm, Natur och Kultur.

Baade, Fritz, 1955, 'Gruß und Dank an Herbert Hoover', in *Weltwirtschaftliches Archiv,* vol. 74, no. 1, pp. 1–6.

Biernacki, Richard, *Fabrication of Labor,* Berkeley, University of California Press.

Boston Consulting Group, 1972, *Perspectives on Experience*, Boston.

Cecchini, Paolo, 1988, *The European Challenge* (aka 'The Cecchini Report'), Brookfield, Gower Press.

Kuhn, Thomas, 1962, *The Structure of Scientific Revolutions,* Chicago, University of Chicago Press.

Lévy-Strauss, Claude, 1996, *The Savage Mind,* Oxford, Oxford University Press.

Marshall, Alfred 1890, *Principles of Economics,* London, Macmillan.

Meyen, Johan Jacob, 1770, *Wie kommt es, dass die Oekonomie bisher so wenig Vortheile von der Physik und Mathematik gewonnen hat; und wie kann man diese Wissenschaften zum gemeinen Nutzen in die Oekonomie einführen, und von dieser Verbindung auf Grundsätze kommen, die in die Ausübung brauchbar sind?,* Berlin, Haude & Spener.

Morgenthau, Henry, Jr, 1945, *Germany is Our Problem. A Plan for Germany,* New York, Harper.

Myrdal, Gunnar, 1956, *Development and Under-development: A Note on the Mechanisms of National and International Economic Inequality,* Cairo, National Bank of Egypt.

Perez, Carlota, 2003, 'Technological Revolutions, Paradigm Shifts and Socio-Institutional Change', in Reinert 2003.

Reinert, Erik S, 1980, *International Trade and the Economic Mechanisms of Underdevelopment,* Ann Arbor, University Microfilm.

———, 1994, 'Catching-up from Way Behind – A Third World Perspective on First World History', in Fagerberg, Jan et al., eds, *The Dynamics of Technology, Trade, and Growth,* Aldershot, Edward Elgar. Chapter 1 in this volume.

———, 1996, 'Diminishing Returns and Economic Sustainability: The Dilemma of Resource-Based Economies Under a Free Trade Regime', in Hansen, Stein, Jan Hesselberg and Helge Hveem, eds, *International Trade Regulation, National Development Strategies and the Environment: Towards Sustainable Development?,* Oslo, Centre for Development and the Environment, University of Oslo. Chapter 5 in this volume.

———, 1999, 'The Role of the State in Economic Growth', *Journal of Economic Studies,* vol. 26, no. 4/5. A shorter version published in Toninelli, Pier Angelo, 2000, ed., *The Rise and Fall of State-Owned Enterprises in the Western World,* Cambridge, Cambridge University Press.

———, 2000, 'Globalisation in the Periphery as a Morgenthau Plan: The Underdevelopment of Mongolia in the 1990's', in Lhagva, Sakhia, ed., *Mongolian Development Strategy; Capacity*

Building, Ulaanbaatar, Mongolian Development Research Center. , also in Reinert 2003. And as chapter 8 in this volume.

——, 2003, ed., *Evolutionary Economics and Income Inequality*, Cheltenham, Elgar.

Reinert, Erik S and Arno Daastøl, 1997, 'Exploring the Genesis of Economic Innovations: The Religious Gestalt-Switch and the *Duty to Invent* as Preconditions for Economic Growth', *European Journal of Law and Economics*, vol. 4, no. 2/3, pp. 233–83.

———, 2003, 'The Other Canon: The History of Renaissance Economics. Its Role as an Immaterial and Production-based Canon in the History of Economic Thought and in the History of Economic Policy', in Reinert 2003 and chapter 13 in this volume.

Roca, Santiago and Luis Simabuko, 2003, 'Natural Resources, Industrialisation and Fluctuating Standards of Living in Peru from 1950–1997: A Case Study of Activity-Specific Economic Growth', in Reinert 2003.

Rosenberg, Nathan, 1975, *Perspectives on Technology*, Cambridge, Cambridge University Press.

Samuelson, Paul, 1948, 'International Trade and the Equalisation of Factor Prices', *Economic Journal*, vol. 58, pp. 163–84.

———, 1949, 'International Factor-Price Equalisation Once Again', *Economic Journal*, vol. 59, pp. 181–97.

Schumpeter, Joseph Alois, 1954, *History of Economic Analysis*, New York, Oxford University Press.

Stangeland, Charles Emil, 1966 [1904], *Pre-Malthusian Doctrines of Population. A Study in the History of Economic Theory*, New York, Kelley.

Stern, Carl W and George Stalk Jr, 1998, *Perspectives on Strategy from The Boston Consulting Group*, New York, Wiley.

Chapter 10

AN EARLY NATIONAL INNOVATION SYSTEM: THE CASE OF ANTONIO SERRA'S 1613 *BREVE TRATTATO*

With Sophus A. Reinert

Based on the economics of Joseph Schumpeter, National Innovation Systems have since the early 1990s emerged as a holistic and socioculturally embedded alternative approach to explaining economic growth. The idea that systemic relationships exist between different sectors of the economy that influence the production and implementation of new knowledge, and thus economic development is, however, much older than current research indicates. We will argue the Neapolitan mercantilist Antonio Serra coherently presented the kernel of a national innovation system already in his 1613 *Breve trattato*, including two of its key elements: increasing returns and synergies. The problems of establishing the institutions conducive to economic growth faced by mercantilists at the end of the Renaissance are shared today by policy-makers in the developing world, and it can therefore prove to be fruitful, if not necessary, to explore the historical roots of this early innovation system approach. Indeed, Serra's work has been brought back to light on several occasions in the past centuries, each time as a source of guidance in an era of economic turmoil: first on the eve of Italian unification, then at the dawn of German industrialization. Following the failure of the Cancun meetings in 2003 to reach a trade agreement between North and South, such turmoil is over us again as it becomes increasingly clear that the reigning economic dogma has failed to deliver on its political promises. We argue that, in the economic profession's inevitable search for new means and methods, Serra's message is again relevant.

Introduction—Mercantilism as a National System of Innovation

It has frequently been noted that static, barter-centered mainstream economics, as a collection of theoretical variants orbiting the neoclassical paradigm, is presently under siege by a wider, more dynamic and socially embedded alternative that focuses on production and innovation as mechanisms of economic growth (Broda 1996: 235; Magnusson and Ottosson 1997: 1–9; North 2001: 491). As a subset of the neo-Schumpeterian alternative, the innovation system approach—broadly conceived as the existence of institutional synergies fuelling innovative activity and economic growth—has become widely diffused in the past few years, recently, with the Globelics network meeting in Rio de

Janeiro late 2003, also entering seriously into the discourse on Third World development. With its insistence on the social and institutional embeddedness of the learning economy (Lundvall 1992; Ernst and Lundvall 2004), it seems to appeal to the dissatisfied without alienating representatives of orthodoxy. Since Christopher Freeman and later Bengt-Åke Lundvall's (Lundvall 1992) and Richard Nelson's (Nelson 1993) rendering of the concept of National Innovation Systems in the early 1990s this methodology has gradually been integrated into the policies of the OECD, the European Commission and UNCTAD (Lundvall et al. 2002: 214). One of the greatest challenges facing the theory today, however, is that much of the work done on national systems of innovation is post facto, in the sense that most research is done on systems that are already mature, already diversified and successful (Lundvall et al. 2002: 226). Theories and concepts that work wonders in countries with an industrial tradition dating back centuries, may, however, become much less productive—if not downright destructive—in the context of developing countries unless filtered through a historical lens. Identifying the necessary conditions for the successful implementation of innovation systems in impoverished nations is a project distinct from understanding how to stimulate long-industrialized economies.

It is therefore important to focus not only on the present and future of mature national innovation systems but also on their past; to identify the mandatory passage points inherent to this approach and their historical origins in terms of both theory and practice. What, in other words, did theorists in the industrialized world write about national systems of innovation as such phenomena could first be observed? The history of national innovation systems has already been traced back to the work of Friedrich List (Lundvall 1992: 16; Freeman and Soete 1997: 295–99), but its intellectual roots reach much deeper into the history of economic thought. It is clear that List [1789–1846] and Wilhelm Roscher [1817–1894], the person who put increasing returns back in the economists' toolbox, both relied on a much older tradition of political economy for many of the more synergistic aspects of their theories. Both List and Roscher quoted and referred to a certain Antonio Serra, a Neapolitan mercantilist whom Schumpeter claims was "the first to compose a scientific treatise… on Economic Principles and Policy" (Schumpeter 1954: 195), as an authority when arguing that Germany should follow England's path to industrialization (List 1841; Roscher 1881: 191). The purpose of this chapter is to outline Antonio Serra's theory of uneven economic development in the context of a national innovation systems approach to shed light on current policy concerns in the developing world. This also means putting Serra's theory in its own historical context.

Serra's work belongs to the mercantilist tradition of economic literature. "Mercantilist" is a term commonly used today to cover all economic theory and practice between the Scholastics and Adam Smith [1723–1790], and is—in modern textbooks—a decidedly derogatory term describing "bad economists" who, if one were to take the verdict of mainstream economics seriously, confused the hoarding of gold with the augmentation of national wealth: the so-called *Midas Fallacy* (Perrotta 1991).[1] When

1. The Midas Fallacy is in fact part of a collective delusion shared by many that, in the words of Foucault, economics "sprang up in Western thought, fully armed and already full of danger, at the time of Ricardo and J-B. Say" (Foucault 2002: 181).

Adam Smith wrote his *Wealth of Nations* in 1776, however, modern nation-states had been created, the Renaissance and Enlightenment had brought their huge innovations and inventions, the institutions of modern capitalism had gradually been established and the first industrial revolution was in full swing. From the perspective of modern textbooks, then, all this was believed to have been created by "bad" economists pursing "bad policies," bullionist economists who had supposedly made the fundamental mistake of confusing gold with real wealth. In reality Mercantilism, while in many ways a theoretical hydra (Magnusson 1999), provided the theoretical impetus for the creation of the early modern state, and in many cases presented the same systemic rendering of the economy as our contemporary innovation system approach. Many institutions that can be taken for granted in the industrialized world today, however, had to be constructed from scratch in the 1500s to 1700s. The developing world, lacking these institutions, thus faces many of the same challenges that Europe had to overcome in the early modern period. It is noteworthy that the important theoretical work tended not to come from the leading nations, like Venice or the Dutch Republic. Theory seems to have originated in the attempts of people in the periphery, Naples in Serra's case, to understand and copy the fortuitous conditions that caused the wealth of some cities, and the urban, maritime and manufacturing bias of this wealth accumulation. An even earlier theory to the same effect, but with much less analytical acumen, is found in France during the late 1500s (Laffemas 1597).

Only those intimately familiar with the historiography of economic analysis will know that Antonio Serra was involved in a debate very similar to that which separates economists even today. Where his rival Marc'Antonio de Santis, to whose work Serra's *Breve trattato* was a response, sought to improve the Neapolitan economy manipulating monetary and fiscal variables, Serra insisted that the unfavorable monetary and fiscal situation of Naples merely reflected underlying factors in the real economy, factors that could be influenced and developed through governmental interventions in the real, as opposed to the monetary, economy. These two conflicting ways of structuring the economic sphere—one focusing on monetary variables and the other on knowledge and production—came into conflict across Europe in the early seventeenth century, the most polemical expressions of this debate occurring within a few years of each other in London and Naples. The similarities between these two disputations have been pointed out in passing several times in the twentieth century, but the Neapolitan version of the conflict has received much less scholarly attention (Seligman 1920: ix; Schumpeter 1954: 355; Rosselli 2000). This pan-European phenomenon thus found its most renowned manifestation in the English mercantilist debates between Edward Misselden [1608?–1654] and Gerard de Malynes [1586–1641] in the early 1620s (Misselden 1622, 1623; Malynes 1622), even though the analytically much superior equivalent unfolded in Naples a decade earlier. The theoretical contributions of Antonio Serra [fl. 1613] and Marc'Antonio de Santis [fl. 1605], arguing the relative positions of Misselden and Malynes respectively, have seldom been discussed at any length, and Serra's *Breve trattato*, while often mentioned in passing in historical surveys of economic thought, thus remains largely unanalyzed in the historiography of economics.

Historically, it is interesting to note that economists who have resurrected Serra consciously have taken an interventionist stance in the methodological debate, arguing that the necessary institutional preconditions for economic growth could only be implemented by a strong state (Custodi 1803: xvii; List 1841). Innovation system theorists today often call for many of the same things (Ernst and Lundvall 2004), but Mercantilism in general and Serra in particular have not yet been re-evaluated in terms of this alternative, broader, more nuanced conception of the interface between state and economy. We will argue that Serra's theories remain relevant for the innovation system approach, particularly as regards key factors that get the virtuous circles of economic development started. Serra was, in particular, the first economist to systematically introduce two mechanisms that are at the core of the process of economic development: *increasing returns* and *cumulative causations*.

Antonio Serra and His Historical Context

Very few facts concerning Antonio Serra and his life are available to us, but enough is left to make a rough sketch of the life and times of this unfortunate and sometimes maligned economist. Antonio Serra was a doctor of law imprisoned, possibly on charges of counterfeiting, by the Spanish Viceroyalty of Naples during the monetary crisis and economic depression that marked the birth of the seventeenth century (Custodi 1803; Schefold 1994; Granata 1998). The economic crisis was not a localized phenomenon, but rather the reflection of a deeper, multilateral reconstruction of the European social and economic spheres (Gould 1955: 121–33; Wallerstein 1979; Kindleberger 1991: 149–75). The age of exploration had made many institutions antiquated, and the center of commercial gravity in Europe shifted slowly from south to north as traders and explorers commercialized the Baltic and Atlantic seaways (Schmoller 1967; Hinton 1959: 12–24; Finkelstein 2000). The counterreformation only contributed to the economic decay in the Italian peninsula (Reinert and Daastøl 1997). Based on these changes, it is not surprising that the various sciences experienced a concomitant revolution in reaction to an expanding world in flux (Ryan 1981: 519–38; Bouwsma 2000: 67–85).

We shall indeed argue that a necessary precondition for what Foucault named the "epistemologization of economics," the birth of economics as a science, was the formation of the possibility of progress, of a never-ending frontier of increasing knowledge and increasing wealth. Whereas economics had existed in practice for millennia, it only emerged in coherent theory following the "general intellectual ferment" resulting from the cosmological revolution at the end of the sixteenth century (Kuhn 1957: 1–7). This new conception of an infinitely expanding cosmos in flux (e.g., in Bruno 1584) was, one could argue, the dynamic precondition for the mercantilist reinterpretation of the economic sphere: economic activities suddenly were empowered with the ability to propagate wealth on an aggregate level. Whereas Aristotle and the Scholastics resisted economic initiatives on the grounds that they inevitably exacerbated social inequality through diverging incomes (Finkelstein 2000: 89), the mercantilists realized the economy could be directed toward increasing the material welfare of the entire population: enlightened statecraft could increase the *common good*. Mercantilist literature can thus not be properly understood without reference to their cosmological context: the understanding of an expanding cosmos brought an end to the economy as a zero-sum game. Both cosmos and the economy ceased being static and incapable of growth. At the same time a religious reinterpretation meant that *innovation* was no longer a term of heresy. In 1278 Roger Bacon was arrested in Oxford for "suspicious innovations," when Francis Bacon wrote his *Essay on Innovation* around 1605, innovation was something to be actively sought for in order to improve the lot of mankind (Reinert and Daastøl 1997). The zero-sum game *Weltanschauung* slowly disappeared and the learning economy was born.

The overriding economic question of Serra's day was why all the gold and silver that flowed into Spain from the Americas rapidly flowed out of an increasingly impoverished Spain and ended up creating unprecedented wealth elsewhere, particularly in Venice and in the Dutch Republic. To Serra the explanation of this phenomenon was to be found in the study of the real economy, not in the study of monetary phenomena. To him, the key to this mystery was that different economic sectors were subject to different economic laws; manufacturing was subject to increasing returns as production expanded, and agriculture was not. Serra explained the underlying causes in the *Realökonomie* that determined the flow of gold in and out of nations. *To Serra, a deficit of gold was but a symptom of other ills that could only be explained in the realm of production.* As Schumpeter says about Serra's work: "Essentially the treatise is about the factors on which depend the abundance not of money but of *commodities*—natural resources, quality of the people, the development of industry and trade, the efficiency of government—the implication being that if the economic process as a whole functions properly, the monetary element will take care of itself and not require any specific therapy" an argument recently revived by Alessandro Roncaglia's excellent survey of the history of economic thought (Schumpeter 1954: 195; Roncaglia 2001: 52).

As part of this epistemic shift of the late Renaissance, Antonio Serra sought to uncover the mechanisms of economic growth and, in doing so, produced the earliest known systematic treatise on political economy. Serra's theories can only be described as *avant-garde*; his insights are in many ways both valid and neglected even today, and may indeed help explain the mechanisms of uneven economic development: why some countries become richer while others become poorer in an era of globalization. Serra was the first economist to explore and establish the *rules* and *principles* governing economic expansion, and by observing and categorizing his material surroundings, Serra was able to illuminate the root causes of national wealth creation in terms of the synergies between different sectors of the economy. He was, in other words, not only the creator of the first model in the history of economic thought, he also created a theory of uneven growth and was the first exponent of what we today call a national system of innovation.

Antonio Serra in the Historiography of Economic Analysis

Serra's *Breve trattato*, while certainly being one of the more impressive analytical achievements in the history of economic thought, especially given the circumstances of its writing, was not well received by his contemporaries. After presenting his work in an audience with the Spanish viceroy in Naples, Serra was ridiculed and thrown back into jail where, as far as we know, he ended his days (Anonymous 1846: 520). The Kingdom of Naples continued to treat the symptoms of the outflow of gold and silver rather than its causes, and for a long period joined the rest of Italy in the periphery of the world system. After this, Serra and his work remained shrouded in darkness for more than a century. It was seemingly a pure coincidence that the Tuscan mathematician Bartolomeo Intieri [1678–1757] rediscovered the *Breve trattato* while stationed as administrator of the Medici estates in Naples in the middle of the eighteenth century. Intieri is best remembered for having founded the chair of political economy at the University of Naples, the first of its kind anywhere outside Germany and Sweden/Finland. The chair of political economy was given to the influential economist Antonio Genovesi[2] in 1754, and Intieri gave him the only known copy of Serra's *Breve trattato* as an inaugural gift. Genovesi later donated this book to Ferdinando Galiani, the ardent anti-physiocrat, who was the first author to write on Serra. Galiani gave the book to his student and fellow economist Giuseppe Palmieri [1721–1793], who gave it to the Neapolitan nationalist Francesco Salfi, a friend of Baron Pietro Custodi (Custodi 1803: xxviii). Custodi honored Serra's memory by including it as the first tract in his 50-volume collection of pre-nineteenth century Italian economic thought (Custodi 1803: xxviii; Ziersch 1905: 29). It is through this 1803 edition that Friedrich List and Wilhelm Roscher were so heavily influenced by Serra's work. The single known copy of the *Breve trattato* at the time thus passed, like a "proverbial lamp of life and learning"—a "*lampada di vita*"—through the hands of the greatest Italian economists of the time (Croce 1970: 151).[3]

This first known copy of Serra's tract was finally donated to the *Biblioteca Ambrosiana* in Milan, and eight more copies of the original seem to have been discovered. Several editions have appeared in Italian, but apart from a translation of a few pages in Arthur Eli Monroe's 1930 *Early Economic Thought* (Monroe 1930), the *Breve trattato* has not been available for an international audience. Around 390 years after its first publication, however, this might be in the process of change. The first complete translation of Serra's 1613 treatise, into Portuguese, was published in Curitiba, Brazil in 2002 (Serra 2002). It was predated by an article in a Brazilian student journal, *Oikos* (Padula 2002), and, given the pertinence of its message, one can hope that a critical mass of interest for Serra's work soon will be reached and an English translation published.

In addition to the translation problem, the full title of Serra's work, *A Brief Treatise on the Causes that can make Gold and Silver plentiful in Kingdoms where there are no Mines*, has been an obstacle to Serra's recognition in the historiography of economics (Perrotta 1988: 12–13). Judging from the title alone, the treatise may mistakenly be seen as an example

2. A few years later, Genovesi's brother Pietro translated the 1695 work of John Cary, a Bristol merchant, on the trade of England into three Italian volumes. Cary was the English mercantilist who most strongly emphasized the role of technological change in economic growth.
3. If one accepts Schumpeter's verdict of the standing of Italian political economy at the time, this means that these men were also the world's greatest economists during this period (Schumpeter 1954: 176–177).

of the *Midas Fallacy* of the stereotypical mercantilist, i.e. the above mentioned idea, born in Adam Smith's *Wealth of Nations,* that mercantilists confused wealth with gold. Friedrich List indeed accuses Jean-Baptiste Say [1767–1832] and John R. McCulloch [1789–1864] of judging Serra only on the basis of the title of his work (List 1841: 456, 460), and the same could be said for Lionel Robbins in the twentieth century (Robbins 1998: 49). While it is true that the title of Serra's work seems indicative of a bullionist orientation, we will argue that this may be explained in light of Serra's broader attempt to ingratiate himself with the Spanish viceroy.

The *Breve trattato* did, however, have many messages, and the work has thus led parallel, yet intertwined lives. The colonial context of its writing, as well as the unhappy fate of Serra himself, made him an icon of patriotism for Neapolitan writers prior to the Italian unification. Francesco Salfi's 1802 eulogy for Antonio Serra, while appearing in the bibliographies of most scholarship pertaining to Serra, must be read in this light. It is a lengthy, pathos-filled ode to Italian genius under Spanish oppression, and much like Serra himself, it is deeply embedded in the context of its writing. Salfi wrote approvingly of Pietro Verri, Cesare Beccaria and the entire pre-*Risorgimento* movement of Italian economic nationalism. Being part of the cenacle of intellectual forerunners of those who redefined the concept of *italianità* on the eve of unification, Salfi himself proposed an Italian federation already in 1821 (Salfi 1997: 145; Arpaia 2002: 192–214). His use of the *Breve trattato* betrays a nationalist agenda by its emphasis on the *italianità* of Serra's achievements, and there are few efforts to approach the *Breve trattato* from angles of analysis or history. Again, however, Serra's treatise is also of interest for the history of national innovation systems. The colonial legacy of the Third World remains one of the most insurmountable obstacles facing development economics. Serra's *Breve trattato,* written when Naples was a Spanish Viceroyalty, faced the very same obstacle and points to a way out. Serra's way out is essentially the same that was recommended by List and successfully followed in the nineteenth century by the United States and the European nations that industrialized after England.

We must keep in mind that the core of European colonial policy was to prohibit the establishment of manufacturing - i.e. increasing return activities - in the colonies, such activities being reserved for the Mother Country. Serra's insistence on the role of manufacturing in creating economic welfare is therefore a denunciation of colonial policies of all ages, including that of today's neo-colonialism. Serra shares a deep concern about the uneven relationships of production between nations with twentieth-century economists, with Cardoso's dependency theory and the national innovation systems approach alike (Kay and Gwynne 2000). Custodi presented Serra as "animated by the purest patriotic love," and indeed brought the *Breve trattato* forward in a conscious attempt to provide "zealots of the public good" the necessary analytical tools to catch up with England and France (Custodi 1803: xi–xvii).

The Anatomy of the *Breve Trattato*

The *Breve trattato* was formulaically dedicated to the Viceroy of Naples, the "Illustrious and Excellent" Pietro Fernandez de Castro, Count of Lemos [1587–1622], and is consistent in its praise of Catholic doctrine and authorities (Serra 1803: 3; Sumberg 1991: 370). Serra's work is furthermore not at all "brief" in comparison with contemporary economic tracts, and the bullion mentioned in the title is never considered more than a consequence of underlying economic mechanisms. The wording of the title—a brief pamphlet on how to acquire gold in nations with no mines—thus seemingly reflects clever marketing more than it reflects the actual content of the *Breve trattato*. Indeed, we find Serra framing the entire work in Spanish and Catholic admiration when he concludes the treatise by commending the pontificate of Clement VIII [1536–1605] for its sensible policies. Serra thus ironically encloses what is basically an anti-colonial argument for Neapolitan economic independence in veneration of the very forces he resists.

Summoning a literary topos of his time, Serra begins the *Breve trattato* by rhetorically asking what the causes of wonder are.[4] He quickly concludes that they are great ignorance and great intellect, and dedicates his work to the propagation of the latter in matters of national finance. Serra does not wish to discuss politics, as he doubts he can do better than the ancients. The same applies to justice and jurisprudence, for which he relies on Roman Law. He instead wishes to write on a third aspect of statecraft—the economic part on which "nobody, ancient or modern" had written with "doctrinal method before" (Serra 15–16; Schefold 1994: 14). Serra argues that "experience is master of things, to which even the most powerful reason yields."[5] Like in the later German tradition, Serra clearly defines economics as an *Erfahrungswissenschaft*, a science based on experience rather than on *a priori* assumptions. This reasoning also echoes the work of his English contemporary and creator of the modern concept of innovation, Francis Bacon [1561–1626] (Reinert and Daastøl 1997). Very much in the spirit of Bacon's *New Atlantis*, Serra also summons the vision of a "never-ending frontier of knowledge" when he complains that "there are still people who think everything they do not understand is impossible even though many such things, including ancient and modern discoveries, are now discussed that had once too been thought impossible by everyone" (177).

The *Breve trattato* itself is divided into three main parts. The first of these, and the most interesting from a purely analytical standpoint, is devoted to the mechanisms of economic growth on a generalized level and concludes with a discursive comparison between Venice and Naples meant to illuminate the power of his arguments by showing the consequences of following the right and the wrong policies, respectively. The second part is a lengthy refutation of his opponent de Santis' arguments, and the third consists of Serra's own advice on how to make Naples abound with gold and silver. He concludes the work with a detailed index of uncommon quality given the period in which it was written. It has, though, been noted that Serra's grammatical structure is awkward by seventeenth-century standards. We will, however, agree with Rodolfo Benini, who

4. Interestingly, Adam Smith's first work, on astronomy, starts with the same question (Smith 1811: 55).

5. Serra (1613: 60). In Italian: "Essendoci l'esperienza maestra delle cose, alla quale cede ogni potentissima ragione."

contends that this reflects Serra's poor familiarity with the written vernacular. Indeed, the grammatical structure of the work is consistently Latinate, rather than Italian (Benini 1892: 225).

Unlike most economic tracts predating the twentieth century, Serra's *Breve trattato* is peculiar in its generally pacifist nature. A similar extolling of peaceful trade would have to await Montesquieu's 1748 *L'Esprit de Lois*, and even after this cornerstone of the Enlightenment Project praised the "sweetness of commerce" for "breaking the back of barbarism in Europe," economics never entirely discarded its violent tenor (Montesquieu 1748 book xxi, chapter 20). It is interesting to note that Serra shared this pacifist orientation with Friedrich List, whose 1841 work is purposefully critical of Adam Smith's praise of war (Smith 1976: ii, 456). Serra's pacifism could conceivably have resulted from his attempt to get at the underlying mechanisms of economic growth, which was a project quite removed from the search for a short-term fiscal surplus characterizing some mercantilist tracts. It does, however, securely place Serra on the modern side of the epistemic shift we discussed earlier, since the *Breve trattato* no longer operates within the boundaries of a zero-sum cosmology. Far from extolling the virtues of piracy and conquest, Serra is interested in the ways of *producing* wealth rather than merely redistributing it.

Serra's Methodology

"Having considered many of Italy's cities," Serra tells us that he has "tried to investigate, in the faint light provided by [his] miniscule intellect … the causes that make gold and silver flow in Kingdoms without mines" (4-5). The goal of his endeavor, he argues, is to "arrive at the intrinsic of truth" relating to the "common good of the Kingdom" (6-6). Serra's *vision*, to use Schumpeter's terminology, clearly establishes him in what Werner Sombart calls the *activistic-idealistic* tradition of economics, rather that the *passivistic-materialistic* tradition of today's mainstream. We find Serra concluding his chapter on governmental policy by criticizing those who might find fault with him for his method, claiming instead to consciously adopt a relativist methodology in contrast to those "preferring the certainty of the thing to the nobility of the subject," (39) thus in a sense foreshadowing Amartya Sen's statement that "most economists would rather be accurately wrong than approximately right." It was the end result, rather than the method of achieving it, that Serra wanted to focus on, and echoes from Machiavelli to the German Historical School resound when he argues, "Science does not by itself have a universal method of understanding the truth," as its "subject changes across time and space" (12).

De Santis, Serra claimed, was simply attacking the symptoms rather than the causes of an underlying economic illness that had to be cured before the economic crisis could be ameliorated: "There can not be a cure, while the cause [of the illness] is still present" says Serra.[6] He is crystal clear in his conviction that while others were attacking the symptoms of Naples' poverty in the sphere of finance and monetary policy, he himself is explaining the causes of it in the real world of production. Serra's model simplified

6. Serra (1613: 135).

the economy by identifying a series of interrelated causes that produced a serendipitous clustering of economic progress. The most important cause in Serra's model was, however, always that of governance—a qualitative concept that he explicitly established as a mediator between theory and practice, between the governing effort and the various levels of abstraction. It is exactly "this cycling in and out, this continual changing of focus and perspective" which, according to Tony Lawson, is "the only way of gaining an understanding of society and economy" (Lawson 1997: 236). This indeed defines the core of the approach of the German Historical School to economics. The *Breve trattato* provided guidelines for questions of economic policy, but could not provide any detailed quantitative analysis of economic events. Many modern models, on the other hand, have, based on the *a priori* acceptance of certain assumptions ranging from the scarcity postulate to the "rational" calculation of marginal utilities, come to handle quantitative changes in aggregate models with great zeal and, to use a term from the period, perfected panurgy. The qualitative dimensions of human effort, however, have become much harder to analyze within the framework of modern models.[7] The dangers inherent to such an approach were already quite clear to Antonio Serra when he wrote his *Breve trattato* in 1613, but it has, until the recent advent of alternative approaches like the innovation system, been consciously or unconsciously forgotten in the attempt of economics to become more like the natural sciences (20; Mirowski 1989; Weintraub 2002).

Serra's Causes of Economic Growth

There are, according to Serra, two main categories of factors affecting the economic development of a nation: the *natural* and the *accidental*. Both are essentially ways of creating a "surplus," either through the bounty of nature or the toil of man. Of these, the *accidental* factors are further subdivided into subsets of *particular* and *common* causes of wealth. Particular factors, Serra argues, "may occur in only one kingdom and no others," whereas "common factors may appear in all kingdoms alike" (21). The *particular* causes are contextual and consist of the twin factors of agricultural abundance and geography. The *common* causes, on the other hand, are results, abstract ideas that can come to fruition and improve the state of affairs in any nation, constituting the most important causes of the wealth of nations; they are ***"the quantity of industry***," "***the quality of the population***," "***the extension of trading operations***" and "***the regulations of the sovereign***." Serra was quite certain that his modeling of the economic sphere included all pertinent causes of wealth, arguing "other causes besides the ones mentioned do not exist, as they are either subordinated or consequential to the ones mentioned" (39).

A synoptic model of the treatise indeed conveys a coherence of thought and an apparatus of thinking about economic matters that seems to contradict Michel Foucault's statement that economics, while present in the realms of positivity at the beginning of the seventeenth century, did not breach the threshold of epistemologization until the advent of Locke and Cantillon (Foucault 2002: 207). Serra's *Breve trattato* was far ahead of its time in the sophistication of its structure and argument when compared to

7. For a discussion of this, see Drechsler (2004).

the works of his contemporaries. In the words of Walter Ziersch, "Serra stands on the ground of reality, and we cannot find any assertions in his work that are not based on facts" (Ziersch 1905: 66). One should therefore not be surprised to find that Schumpeter argued the text was the earliest scientific treatise on economic principles and policy.

The *natural* causes, while alluded to in the full title of Serra's work, receive brief coverage, as they were of little relevance to his own context. Serra argues that "the *natural* class comprises only one situation: when there are mines of gold and silver in a country" (20). Italy was, however, generally lacking in mineral wealth, and the Tuscan silver mines operated by the Medici Grand Dukes were the only exceptions identified by Serra (20; Morelli 1976). The core of this part of the *Breve trattato* therefore deals with the various *accidental* causes of wealth.

Of these *accidental* causes, Serra first discusses the subgroup of the *particulars*. These, according to Serra, are causes of wealth that are unique to certain kingdoms and impossible to manipulate through policy. The first such factor, the abundance of agricultural surplus, might seem surprising at first, but can arguably be explained by the context of Serra's writing. Apart from the agrarian revolution in northern Europe in the sixth to the ninth centuries, agricultural technology remained largely unchanged from Roman times to the advent of agronomic theory in Britain on the eve of the industrial revolution (White 1964: 40; Duby 1974: 189). Efforts to increase agricultural surplus were therefore aimed at the expansion of tillage to less productive plots of land rather than at the refinement of technique, a typical example of the decreasing returns to scale discussed among Serra's *common* causes of national wealth (Benigno 1989: 80). The fertility of the soil and the serendipity of the climate were the principal indicators of agricultural production, and agricultural surplus could, therefore, at the time, be considered immutable by human intervention. More than 160 years later, Adam Smith—seeing progress as the result of the division of labor—asks himself why there are so few possibilities for the division of labor in agriculture (Smith 1976: i, 9).

Serra's second *particular* cause is easier to accept from today's perspective, in that it reflects the location of a nation compared to surrounding countries. Serra presents this cause as being "a potent occasion, almost a cause, for extensive trading in a kingdom" (22). While any country could theoretically become a nexus of international trade, geographical location would in practice be a crucial factor. Although there existed a long trajectory of thought relating to the fortuitous location of cities in western history from Xenophon's *Poroi* [ca. 352 B.C.] (Xenophon 1984) and the *Panathenaicus* of Aelius Aristides [second century A.D.] to Leonardo Bruni's *Laudatio Florentinae urbis* [ca. 1403–1404] (Bruni 1978) and Giovanni Botero's *Ragion di stato* [1590], Serra was the first writer to theorize about the economic advantages conveyed by geographic location in relation to other economic factors. The *Breve trattato* thus also marked the birth of economic geography, the torpid subfield of economics that Paul Krugman recently sought to revive.[8] With the next important development in economic geography, Johann Heinrich

8. While economic geography has been generally dismissed by economists, it is being kept alive at the fringes of the profession. Recent work in economic sociology has revitalized it

Gottlob von Justi [1717–1771] and later Johann Heinrich von Thünen [1783–1850] were to place Serra's increasing returns–based urban area at the center of their concentric circles of national space.

Serra's four classes of common causes—the *quantity of industry*, the *quality of the population*, the *existence of extensive trade*, and the *fortuitous regulations of the sovereign*—work dynamically and in synergetic conjunction. As a whole, they are the factors behind economic growth, since "the combination of them in any place, though it raises nothing in excess of its own needs and must procure everything from abroad, and though the place has no mines of gold or silver, these will surely make it abound in these metals" (23). Serra here alludes to the concept that German economists used to refer to as *Strukturzusammenhänge* in economics—the organic synergy of factors in relations of cumulative causation at the core of the innovation system approach, i.e. the idea that various independent factors cumulatively influence each other and the end results organically. Serra completes his analysis of this important theorem in his discussion of "the great trade." While their interaction was vital, the *common* causes had differing degrees of importance to Serra, the most essential one being the "quantity of manufacturing industry."

Serra on Manufacturing Industry and Increasing Returns

Industry, Serra argues, "ought not only to be placed at the head of the *common* ones, but in many respects should be rated higher than the particular factor of surplus produce" on the grounds that it is only dependent on the labor of man, rather than on geographic and climatic influences (23–24). Serra follows Giovanni Botero's lead in differentiating work in the agricultural and manufacturing sectors (Botero 1590: 217–22), but qualifies the distinction further by grounding the differences between these two sectors in the theories of increasing and diminishing returns to scale—whether unit production costs would rise or fall if a nation chooses to specialize in any particular activity. While Serra alluded to diminishing returns in agriculture earlier in the text when discussing the *particular* factors, he now turns his full analytical acumen to producing the first coherent statement of the effect of increasing returns. Manufactures, Serra argued, are unique because total costs decrease with increasing volumes of production:

> "There can be multiplications in manufactures which lead to a multiplication of profits, something which does not happen in agriculture as one cannot multiply it. Nobody, for example, having a territory upon which only a hundred *tomola* of wheat can be sown, will be able to have a hundred and fifty sown; but among the manufactures, it is just the other way, since they may be multiplied not only two-fold but two hundred-fold, and with proportionately less expense." (24)

Furthermore, Serra recognized, as Botero had, that the possibilities of specialization and of making profits were higher in manufactures than in agriculture; "in most cases

---

somewhat. See Krugman (1990, 1991, 1995), Saxenian (1994).

more profit is made from industry than from agricultural produce," Serra argues, because of the "infinite number" of potential trades (25–26). To put this statement in a modern language: Serra sees the multiplication of the division of labor in industries where a large market share—in form of "niches"—can be achieved through increasing returns and resulting lower unit costs of production, linking this to a potential for higher profits and higher national welfare. Serra's distinction between increasing and decreasing return activities was thus implicitly built on the theory of the division of labor as it dates back to Xenophon. To this is added a synergy argument in Serra: the greater the division of labor, the richer the city. Smith's famous statement, more than 150 years later, that "the division of labour is limited by the size of the market" is merely a pale shadow of Serra's insight, where the real cause – increasing returns – has disappeared completely. This "systemic increasing returns," which is already pointed to by Xenophon, is the core argument behind the mercantilist policy of increasing the population of cities and nations.

The possibility of increasing returns was, throughout the entire mercantilist and Cameralist traditions, seen in connection with the increased opportunity for division of labor in manufactures, and therefore highly activity-specific. As opposed to agriculture and mining, where one factor of production was determined by God's creation (in land or ore), in manufacturing all factors of production would be available in constant or increasing returns to scale as production expanded. The "cult of manufacturing" was an important part of economic policy for centuries, but only rarely, and only in the nineteenth century, does the theoretical explanation as to *why* this policy is beneficial reach Serra's level of sophistication. It should be noted that the 1776 publication of Adam Smith's *Wealth of Nations* marked a shift in the way economic activities were conceptualized. Smith's effort to formalize the science led him to simplify the varieties of labor and therefore exclude the different effects caused by increasing and diminishing returns to scale. The concepts of *production* and *exchange*, for example, intersect in Adam Smith because they both represent time spent in activities classified as "economic." While both indeed can be reduced to "time" at a certain level of abstraction, many important distinctions are lost in the process. The economic historian Biernacki argues that "an emblematic contradiction between form and content runs through the *Wealth of Nations*: the argument makes labour the font of all value, preparatory to sale, whereas the language of analysis treats the labour activity—production—as itself a vending transaction" (Biernacki 1995: 252). Indeed, we find Smith declaring that "labour was the first price, the original purchase of money that was paid for all things. It was not by gold or silver, but by labour, that all the wealth of the world was originally purchased." Biernacki further perceptively argues that Smith equates, or even confuses, "the original process of production – the creation of a good through the labor activity – with the socially organized way of acquiring goods through monetary exchange."

In Smithian economics, production and exchange become one through the nexus of labor; the various investments of time in economic pursuits—in trade or manufacture—become unified in the overriding concept of labor time, in the abstract, metric unit of economic activity. "No wonder Smith's usage makes no distinction between *commerce* and *industry*. He assimilates the process of production to that of exchange" (Smith

1976: i, 35; Biernacki 1995: 252–54). Smith's list of required factors for "putting industry into motion" is indeed indicative of this: one needs "materials to work upon, tools to work with, and the wages or recompense for the sake of which the work is done" (Smith 1976: i, 313). Where, one could ask, is the knowledge, tacit or otherwise, that makes the industrial undertaking possible? This development continued in the work of David Ricardo [1772–1823], who we all agree "more than any other single individual set the tone of modern economic theory" (Arrow 2000: 172). Ricardo indeed argued "the value of a commodity … depends on the relative quantity of labour which is necessary for its production, and not on the greater or lesser compensation which is paid for that labour." The qualitative differences between goods are thus mere reflections of the qualitative disparity present in their production; *knowledge* and *innovation* lose all meaning in a system where technological progress merely reduces a good's exchange value in terms of embodied labor (Biernacki 245–46). With this theory the core importance of Man as inventor and producer almost automatically goes overboard, establishing an economic theory based on barter and trade where the built-in result is a world of economic harmony and of factor-price equalization.

If one is to operate on the abstraction level in the works of Smith, Ricardo and Samuelson's trade theory, where production and exchange melt into the elusive concept of "labor time," one loses an entire axis of value, namely the measurement of *qualitative difference among economic activities* (Reinert 1999). The natural consequence of these standard assumptions of neoclassical economics is that prices of the factors of production—capital and labor—will tend to equalize under a system of free trade (Samuelson 1948, 1949; Samuelson 1953). It can be argued that this theorem is the very foundation of today's world economic system, and it has its roots in Adam Smith's equation of economic activities. We argue that by going back to seeing the world through the lenses of Antonio Serra, we can find the reasons why present globalization produces such different results in different countries.

The birth of neoclassical economics in the late nineteenth century dealt the theory of increasing returns its *coup de grace*. Its death can, in fact, be traced across the first nine editions of Alfred Marshall's *Principles of Economics*. Paul Krugman once observed that "economics tends … to follow the line of least mathematical resistance" (Krugman 1991: 6), and Marshall, by many considered the founder of neoclassical economics, and particularly his followers, was unable to resist this tendency. The nations dominating both the most successful innovation systems of the world and those activities most subject to increasing returns emptied economic theory both of innovation and of increasing returns – thus removing the main cause of their own success from economic theory – first England and subsequently the United States. This was the theoretical trickery that made possible what Friedrich List referred to as "kicking away the ladder," making it impossible for nations that wished to follow their paths to economic success. Princeton economist Jacob Viner had the dubious honor of finally dismissing increasing returns from the corpus of economic theory on the grounds that it was incompatible with competitive equilibrium theory—i.e. the theory of perpetually clearing markets on the assumption of perfect information (Viner 1937: 475–82). Viner, following in Adam Smith's footsteps, is also responsible for excising the concept of Mercantilism from polite economic conversation. The same economist thus dismissed Mercantilism and increasing returns, for the same reason, one may argue. The activity-specific economic protectionism so characteristic of mercantilist theory and policy—from seventeenth-century England to nineteenth-century United States and twentieth-century Japan and Korea—was thus sacrificed on the altar of simple mathematical rendering. Yet the casualties of this modeling endeavor were the factors and mechanisms that made Mercantilism so historically successful in creating prototypes of national innovation systems in the first place.

Serra on Population Theory

The "quality of the population," again a term used by Botero (1590), was the second-most important aspect of Serra's economic engine; a country would be rich if its people were "by nature industrious, or diligent and prone to inventions, and on the watch for opportunities to apply their industry and build up trade not only in their own country but in others" (27). It should be noted in this context that *industry* signified diligence and assiduousness. The word only gained its modern meaning in the nineteenth century, when it lost the qualitative dimensions it originally had (Sewell 1980: 143). Of the Italian cities, Serra asserted that the inhabitants of Genoa, Florence and Venice were renowned for their industriousness. The Genovese get the highest score here, above the Venetians. Individual economic agents, under the auspicious supervision of the state, were, as we shall see in Serra's chapter on government policy, an integral cause of economic growth

Following the 1798 publication of Thomas Malthus' [1766–1834] *Principles of Population*, a large population was generally considered a hindrance to development, though earlier economic theorists held the opposite view. This, we will argue, was not the result of their analytical ignorance, as the "Malthusian Principle" itself was well known centuries before Malthus: "Divested of nonessentials," Schumpeter wrote, "the 'Malthusian' Principle of Population sprang fully developed from the brain of Botero in 1589"[9] (Schumpeter 1954: 254–55). The *virtus generativa* was stronger than the *virtus nutritiva*, Giovanni Botero argued, and a population would therefore always grow to a limit of subsistence manipulated by negative and positive checks such as moral restraint and pestilence (Botero 1590: 222–26). Italy even had her own pessimist Malthusian economist predating Malthus, Giammaria Ortes [1713–1790].

Given Serra's material context, his conclusion regarding population, should not seem surprising. He was incarcerated in one of the most populous cities in the world, and was still surrounded by famine, poverty and suffering (Marino 1982: 226). Sheer numbers of citizens were obviously not sufficient to guarantee economic prosperity, and Serra thus qualified the reigning thoughts on population by emphasizing the role of quality in human effort—a cornerstone of the humanist, *activistic-idealistic* tradition in which he wrote.

---

9. We quote the 1590 edition.

"Great Trade" and the Theory of Cumulative Causation

The third-most important factor of economic growth was that of "great trade." By this Serra did not mean only skimming profits from long-distance trade but also the import of raw materials, to which great value was added through manufacturing, and the subsequent export of the finished product. Venice, Serra observed, had amassed great wealth for centuries by being the nexus of world trade, for "all the commodities which come from Asia into Europe pass through Venice, and from there are distributed into other parts; while commodities which go from Europe into Asia are likewise shipped from there." Naples, however, suffered from an inauspicious location "at the tip of the arm of Italy, where nobody found it convenient to trade" (32–33).

The importation of raw materials for later export of manufactured goods was one of the kernels of early modern state-building as it was defined by the German Historical School and by modern structuralists and dependency theorists. Export-led growth through import-substituting industrialization has indeed been the basis of almost every single successful industrialization policy from Solonic Athens to the Asian Tigers, a mandatory passage point of sorts on the road to the free market (Sombart 1902: ii, 55–56; E. Reinert 1999; Kay and Gwynne 2000: 52; Chang 2003). This theory was based on the view that the amount of labor invested in a good had to be maximized in the case of exports and minimized in that of imports. Raw materials were to be imported, refined and exported as finished goods and the process of adding value to a product was thus to be performed by domestic, rather than foreign labor. In this way the increasing return activities were maximized at home, while the diminishing return activities were concentrated abroad, as in the later colonial systems. Underlying this view was the clear understanding that human resources were far from being fully utilized. Cosimo Perrotta has argued, in our view correctly, that Mercantilism at its core was state-building through import-substituting industrialization (Perrotta 1988), and Serra's work appears to be the earliest theoretical explanation as to why this system is so successful. Employment and wealth were simultaneously created by this policy, and the importation of foreign human capital was a natural progression of the dictum. Serra thus argued that the viceroy should go out of his way to open Naples to the international flow of expertise by emulating contemporary Venetian policies. Christopher Freeman has argued this international exchange of knowledge to be one of the "essential features of current work on national systems of innovation" (Freeman and Soete 1997: 297).

Venice was, however, a special case due to her extremely fortuitous location, as the *particular* cause of geography amplified the *common* cause of great trade. And this is where Serra discusses one of his second great innovations in the history of economic analysis—the idea of *cumulative causation*:

> "The number of manufactures also benefits the city; a factor which brings a great many people there, not only because of the manufacturers themselves (in which case the effect would be attributed to them), but also as a result of **the concurrence of these two factors together, because one gives strength to the other**, the great concourse due to commerce and due to the geographical situation being increased by the manufactures,

and the manufactures being increased by the great concourse due to commerce, while commerce is made greater by the same concourse of people." (32)

Serra here gives the first description of cumulative causation in the history of economic analysis, or the *virtuous circle* of the innovation system approach (Lundvall 1992: 2). Although systemic effects were important in mercantilist analysis, it would be more than three centuries before another economist, Nobel Laureate Gunnar Myrdal, unknowingly resurrected Serra's idea and made it famous again (Myrdal 1956, 1957). Thorstein Veblen explicitly assumed the existence of cumulative causations as a precondition for his theory of evolutionary economic development, and the concept is today an integral part of path-dependency in evolutionary and institutional economics (Veblen 1898). The theory is, as noted, based on the organic interdependency of factors, and is crucial in the explanation of uneven international economic development. Venice grew powerful, in Serra's eyes, because she had managed to create a serendipitous cluster of industry, innovation, trade and people—an effect he very explicitly, again using a clear cumulative causation, argued was the result of good governance (48). Enforcing each other, these factors together set Venice on a very different trajectory from the one on which Naples found itself. Naples would not be able to solve her economic problems without creating a productive structure similar to that of Venice.

Government Policy

The *Breve trattato* is, in the final analysis, a policy pamphlet seeking to propagate what Serra, echoing the humanist tradition in which he writes, calls the *common good* (36). Fundamentally a relativist, Serra argues for the abandonment of all absolute principles in the formulation of legislation. Paraphrasing Thomas Aquinas, Serra warns sovereigns against oversimplifying the economy, arguing instead that the ruler should "consider carefully not one thing but many," since "the same cause generally produces different effects with respect to different subjects as the sun hardens clay and softens wax, and a light whistle rouses dogs and quiets horses" (35). These "infinite considerations" of the state, as well as the "possible inconveniences resulting from its implemented provisions," meant good statesmen were rare. Echoing the humanist tradition of the Italian Renaissance, Serra argued the only contingent constant of this shifting sea was the "will of man" (25), what Nietzsche later was to refer to as the *Geist- und Willens-Kapital* of the economy. Government policy is in the end the most potent of all causes because it, being purely based on "will," can encourage the development of other causes:

> "When this factor is found in perfection in any kingdom, there is no doubt that it will be the most potent agent of all in making it abound in gold and silver, since it may be called the efficient cause, more important than all other factors; for it can produce these, as well as an infinite number of other opportunities, keep them in good condition, remove impediments, and in other ways bring about the same result, not only in countries where there is a good situation with respect to these factors, or where they exist, but also in countries where there is no such situation and none of these factors." (36–37)

One can thus argue that Serra's conception of economic growth was based on the government's conscious manipulation of differences in contexts ranging from geography to the differing potential for innovations in various economic activities; high in manufacturing and low in agriculture (this point having been strongly made already by Giovanni Botero in 1590, a famous work which had reached many editions[10] before Serra wrote, and with which he most probably was familiar).

Sophisticated Mercantilism approached the problem of increasing national wealth from the standpoint of a state supporting individual initiative, rather than of unilateral state intervention. Unless the sheer size of the industry made it suffer from barriers that were too high for entry by individual actors in the economy—in which case Mercantilism adopted the approach of modern state capitalism—the state was seen as a guiding force, rather than an actual owner (see, in the tradition of Serra, Costantini 1742: 103–104). Following Eli Heckscher, Jürgen Habermas argued that the economic dimension of the modern public sphere could only have developed under the auspicious supervision of a guiding central authority. The collective achievement of society rested on the communal laurels of individual agents (Heckscher 1934; Habermas 1965: 34–35), and Reinhold C. Mueller's verdict of the Venetian economic miracle in the Renaissance seems to validate Serra's analysis: "The single aspect that characterizes Venetian history and historiography is the dominant role of the state in the life of the city and the symbiosis between public and private sectors of the economy, between public and private interests" (Mueller 1997: 576).

Unlike the "invisible hand" of Bernard de Mandeville [1670–1733] and Adam Smith, this tradition stressed the importance of the state taking an active role in the establishment of institutions and legislations conducive to economic development (Mandeville 1714; Smith 1976: i, 477). England's penetration of the world's markets in the sixteenth and seventeenth centuries could never have occurred without the careful superintendence of royal charters granting certain privileges to entrepreneurs in specific sectors of the economy, but the after-the-fact nature of Mandeville's and Smith's writing enabled them to take a number of productive institutions for granted (Appleby 1978: 101–102; Hintze 1975: 428). The innovation systems approach thus follows a long and venerable tradition when it argues that "the public sector plays a major role when it comes to supplement the self-organizing forces of the private sphere" (Lundvall et al. 2002: 222).

Epilogue

Throughout the 500 years of political support for industries yielding increasing returns, it is noticeable that – with the exception of the first movers Venice and the Dutch Republic – virtually no nation has ever taken the step from poverty to wealth without passing through a temporary stage of nurturing and protecting such increasing returns

10. And even an English translation, *On the Greatnesse of Cities*, published in London in 1607.

activities.[11] Serra seems to have established an "iron law of economic development." This is, however, not reflected today in the policy recommendations of the Washington Consensus. In terms of economic welfare, the de-industrialization of parts of the Third World in the past decades has been devastating and quite the opposite of what Serra would have recommended (Reinert 2003, 2004).

In our era of globalization, it should therefore not come as a surprise that neo-mercantilist methods have been resurrected by Third World economists to inspire economic growth (Kay and Gwynne 2002). Mercantilism was partly directed at establishing the institutional foundation of capitalism, and was on a certain level a very necessary consolidation of disparate factors that affected the economy. Geography, history, institutions, learning, technology, law and economics—in effect the whole society in which economics is embedded—were seen as relevant to economic theory and policy on a level impossible to comprehend within the framework of orthodox economic reductionism. Adam Smith left out the synergies, linkages, innovations and differences between increasing and decreasing return activities in the economic system. On the macro level we thus lost the dynamic systemic effects that today are called a National Innovation System.

In the early 1980s Paul Krugman had grasped the factor of increasing returns and essentially reformulated mercantilist trade theory in his "New Trade Theory" (Krugman 1990). Most models assumed symmetrical trade based on increasing returns both in importables and exportables, creating an argument for generalized free trade with which also the mercantilists would have agreed. Some of his models, however, recreated the increasing/diminishing returns asymmetry of Serra's model between Venice and Naples, and that characterizes colonial trade. Again, as with Viner's exclusion of increasing returns because it did not fit the equilibrium model, mainstream has apparently succeeded in eliminating relevance in defense of ideological and mathematical purity: Jagdish Bhagwati now triumphantly declares that Krugman's "youthful surrender to irrational exuberance" in increasing/diminishing return models is over because "the invisible hand may be frail, but the visible hand is crippled" (Bhagwati 2002: 22, 31). In other words, although faced with the resurrected theories of Antonio Serra, the economics profession of the early 1990s collectively decided not to trust governments to do what governments had done as part of a normal course of affairs continuously, and largely very successfully, from the Renaissance until the reconstruction of post–World War II Europe lasting until the 1960s. In this way science and ideology blend in an unhealthy fashion.

Partly as a response to this, the fortress of *passivist-materialist* mainstream economics now finds itself under siege by institutionalists, neo-Schumpeterian evolutionists, sociologists and historians alike. United only in their heterodox opposition to mainstream doctrine, they have so far failed to overcome the academic inertia inhibiting real and

11. The Dutch Republic did not systematically start protecting her manufacturing industries until 1725, after the decline had started, in response to the success of the tariffs in England and France.

sustained economic growth in most of the Third World. Things might, however, be changing as the damage done by mainstream economics in the Third World periphery becomes more evident. About the time of the fall of the Berlin Wall, the Commission on Graduate Education in Economics of the American Economic Association expressed concern about the state of affairs in economics. Fearing, like Serra did, that methodological rigidity had pushed the goal of analysis to the wayside, they warned that "graduate programs may be turning out a generation with too many *idiot savants* skilled in technique but innocent of real economic issues" (Krueger 1991: 1044–45).

It is now clear that the process of globalization—as managed by the Washington Institutions—was carried out by economists fitting this description very well. Their innocence in real economic issues has cost huge economic suffering in the more than 60 nations that have seen their national product and real wages fall, in some cases dramatically, during the last ten years. Until now, Mercantilism, representing the type of policy that created Europe's nation-states and the industrial revolution, has not been rethought in light of this neo-plural economic perspective. As long as we remain prisoners of the *Midas Fallacy* created by Adam Smith—that European civilization and nation-states were products of "bad social science"—we will not be able to solve the pressing problems of the Third World. The essential ingredients of Serra's national innovation system—a diversified economy with a comparative advantage in increasing returns activities, without which the cumulative causations of wealth will not start, and an enlightened government policy—will hopefully contribute to a more holistic, historically grounded and economically successful alternative to mainstream dogma. We have attempted to build a coherent theoretical alternative to standard textbook economics, incorporating Serra's vision, albeit at a lower level of abstraction than mainstream economics, at www.othercanon.org.

References

Anonymous, "Giornali del governo de Don Pietro Giron Duca d'Ossuna [1616-1620]," in *Archivio Italiano*, Florence, 1846.

Appleby, J.O., *Economic Thought and Ideology in Seventeenth-Century England*, Princeton: Princeton University Press, 1978.

Arpaia, P., "Constructing a National Identity from a Created Literary Past: Giosuè Carducci and the Development of a National Literature," *Journal of Modern Italian Studies*, Vol. 7, No. 2, 2002, pp. 192–214.

Arrow, K.J., "Increasing Returns: Historiographical Issues and Path Dependence," *European Journal of the History of Economic Thought*, Vol. 7, No. 2, 2000, pp. 171–180.

Benigno, F., "Reflections on the Seventeenth-Century Crisis: The Sicilian Experience," *Seventeenth Century*, Vol. 4, No. 1, 1989, pp. 77–87.

Benini, R., "Sulle dottrine economiche di Antonio Serra," in *Giornale degli Economisti*, 2nd series, September 1892, pp. 222–248.

Bhagwati, J.N., *Free Trade Today*, Princeton: Princeton University Press, 2002.

Biernacki, R., *The Fabrication of Labor: Germany and Britain, 1640–1914*, Berkeley: University of California Press, 1995.

Botero, G., *Della ragion di stato libri dieci: Con tre libri delle cause della grandezza, e magnificenza delle citta,* Roma: Appresso Vincenzio Pellagallo, 1590.

Bouwsma, W.J., *The Waning of the Renaissance 1550–1640,* Yale: Yale University Press, 2000.

Broda, P., "Commons and Veblen: Contrasting Ideas about Evolution," in Moss, L.S. (Ed.), *Joseph A. Schumpeter, Historian of Economics: Perspectives on the History of Economic Thought*, London: Routledge, 1996.

Bruni, L., "Panegyric to the City of Florence," in Kohl, B.G., Witt, R.G. and Welles, E.B. (Eds.), *The Earthly Republic: Italian Humanists on Government and Society*, Philadelphia: University of Pennsylvania Press, 1978.

Bruno, G., *La Cene de le ceneri*, London: John Charlewood, 1584.

Chang, H.J., (ed.), *Rethinking Economic Development*, London, Anthem, 2003.

Costantini, G.A. [Sappetti, G.], *Elementi di commerzio*, Genoa: Giambatista Novelli, 1742.

Croce, B., *History of the Kingdom of Naples*, Chicago: University of Chicago Press, 1970.

Custodi, P., "Proemio dell'Editore," in *Scrittori Classici Italiani di Economia Politica: Parte Antica, tomo 1*, Milan: G.G. Destefanis, 1803.

Drechsler, W., "Natural versus Social Sciences: On Understanding in Economics," in Reinert, E. (Ed.), *Globalization, Economic Development and Inequality: An Alternative Perspective*, Cheltenham, Edward Elgar, 2004.

Duby, G., *The Early Growth of the European Economy: Warriors and Peasants from the Seventh to the Twelfth Century*, Ithaca: Cornell University Press, 1974.

Ernst, D. and Lundvall, B.Å., "Information Technology in the Learning Economy: Challenges for Developing Countries," in Reinert, E. (Ed.), *Evolutionary Economics and Income Inequality*, London: Edward Elgar, 2004.

Finkelstein, A., *Harmony and the Balance: An Intellectual History of Seventeenth-Century English Economic Thought*, Ann-Arbor: University of Michigan Press, 2000.

Foucault, M., *The Archaeology of Knowledge*, London: Routledge, 2002.

Freeman, C. and Soete, L., *The Economics of Industrial Innovation*, London: Pinter, 1997.

Gould, J.D., "The Trade Crisis of the Early 1620's and English Economic Thought," *Journal of Economic History*, Vol. 15, No. 2, 1955, pp. 121–133.

Granata, L., *Antonio Serra: economista e meridionalista inconsapevole e il suo Breve Trattato*, Santelli, 1998.

Habermas, J., *Strukturwandel der Öffentlichkeit: Untersuchungen zu einer Kategorie der bürgerlichen Gesellschaft*, Neuwied am Rhein: Hermann Luchterhand Verlag, 1965.

Hecksher, E., *Mercantilism*, London: George Allen & Unwin, 1934.

Hinton, R.W.K., *The Eastland Trade and the Common Weal in the Seventeenth Century*, Cambridge: Cambridge University Press, 1959.

Hintze, O., "Economics and Politics in the Age of Modern Capitalism," in Gilbert, F. (Ed.), *The Historical Essays of Otto Hintze*, Oxford: Oxford University Press, 1975.

Kay, C. and Gwynne, R.N., "Relevance of Structuralist and Dependency Theories in the Neoliberal Period: A Latin American Perspective," *Journal of Developing Societies*, Vol. 16, No. 1, 2000, pp. 49–69.

Kindleberger, C.P., "The Economic Crisis of 1619 to 1623," *Journal of Economic History*, Vol. 51, No. 1, 1991, pp. 149–175.

Krueger, A.O. et al., "Report on the Commission on Graduate Education in Economics," *Journal of Economic Literature*, Vol. 29, No. 3, 1991, pp. 1035–1053.

Krugman, P.R., *Rethinking International Trade*, Cambridge, MA: MIT Press, 1990.

———, *Geography and Trade*, Cambridge, MA: MIT Press, 1991.

———, *Development, Geography, and Economic Theory*, Cambridge, MA: MIT Press, 1995.

Kuhn, T.S., *The Copernican Revolution: Planetary Astronomy in the Development of Western Thought*, Cambridge, MA: Harvard University Press, 1957.

Laffemas, B., *Reiglement (sic) general pour dresser les manufactures en ce rayaume, et couper le cours des draps de soye, & autres merchandises qui perdent & ruynent l'Estat: qui est le vray moyen de remettre la France en sa splendeur, & de faire gaigner les pauvres…*, Paris, Claude de Monstr'oil and Jean Richter, 1597.

Lawson, T., *Economics & Reality*, London: Routledge, 1997.

List, F., *Das Nationale System der Politischen Oekonomie*, Stuttgart and Tübingen: G. Cotta'scher Verlag, 1841.

Lundvall, B.Å. (Ed.), *National Systems of Innovation: Towards a Theory of Innovation and Interactive Learning*, London: Pinter, 1992.

Lundvall, B.Å. et al., "National Systems of Production, Innovation and Competence Building," *Research Policy*, Vol. 31, 2002, pp. 213–231.

Magnusson, L., *Merkantilism: Ett ekonomiskt tänkande formuleras*, Stockholm: SNS Förlag, 1999.

Magnusson, L. and Ottoson, J., "Introduction," in Magnusson, L. and Ottoson, J. (Eds.), *Evolutionary Economics and Path Dependence*, Cheltenham: Edward Elgar, 1997.

Malthus, T.R., *An Essay on the Principle of Population*, London: Printed for J. Johnson, 1798.

Malynes, G., *The Maintenance of Free Trade, According to the Three Essentiall Parts of Traffique, Namely, Commodities, Moneys, and Exchange of Moneys, by Bills of Exchanges for Other Countries*, London: Printed by I. L. for W. Sheffard, 1622.

Mandeville, B., *The Fable of the Bees: Or Private Vices, Publick Benefits*, London: J. Roberts, 1714.

Marino, J.A., "Economic Idylls and Pastoral Realities: The "Trickster Economy" in the Kingdom of Naples," *Comparative Studies in Society and History*, Vol. 24, No. 2, 1982, pp. 211–234.

Mirowski, P., *More Heat than Light: Economics as Social Physics, Physics as Nature's Economics*, Cambridge: Cambridge University Press, 1989.

Misselden, E., *Free Trade or the Meanes to Make Trade Flourish Wherein the Causes of the Decay of Trade in This Kingdom Are Discovered*, London, 1622.

Misselden, E., *The Circle of Commerce or the Balance of Trade*, London, 1623.

Monroe, A.E., *Early Economic Thought. Selections from Economic Literature Prior to Adam Smith*, Cambridge, MA: Harvard University Press, 1930.

Montesquieu, C.S., *L'esprit des Lois*, Geneva: Chez Barrillot & Fils, 1748.

Morelli, R., "The Medici Silver Mines (1542-1592)," *Journal of European Economic History*, Vol. 5, No. 1, 1976, pp. 121–139.

Mueller, R.C., The *Venetian Money Market: Banks, Panics, and the Public Debt 1200–1500*, Baltimore: Johns Hopkins University Press, 1997.

Myrdal, G., *Development and Under-Development: A Note on the Mechanism of National and International Economic Inequality*, Cairo: National Bank of Egypt, 1956.

———, *Economic Theory and Under-Developed Regions*, London: G. Duckworth & Co., 1957.

Nelson, R.R., *National Innovation Systems: A Comparative Analysis*, New York: Oxford University Press, 1993.

North, D.C., "Needed: A Theory of Change," in Meier, G.M. and Stiglitz, J.E. (Eds.), *Frontiers of Development Economics: The Future in Perspective*, New York: World Bank, Oxford University Press, 2001.

Padula, R., "Um Ensaio sobre as Politicas Públicas e o Desenvolvimento partindo do pensamento de Antônio Serra," in *Oikos*, 87–105, July 2000.

Perrotta, C., *Produzione e lavoro produttivo nel Mercantilismo e nell'Illuminismo*, Galatina: Congedo, 1988.

———, "Is the Mercantilist Theory of the Favorable Balance of Trade Really Erroneous?," *History of Political Economy*, Vol. 23, No. 2, 1991, pp. 301–336.

Reinert, E., "The Role of the State in Economic Growth," *Journal of Economic Studies*, Vol. 26, No. 4/5, 1999, pp. 268–326.

———, "Increasing Poverty in a Globalised World: *Marshall Plans* and *Morgenthau Plans* as Mechanisms of Polarisation of World Incomes," in Chang, Ha-Joon (Ed.), *Rethinking Economic Development*, London, Anthem, 2003 and chapter 9 in this volume.

———, "Globalisation in the Periphery as a Morgenthau Plan: The Underdevelopment of Mongolia in the 1990's," in Reinert (ed.), 2004. Chapter 8 in this volume.

———, (ed.), *Globalization, Economic Development and Inequality: An Alternative Perspective*, Cheltenham: Edward Elgar, 2004.

Reinert, E. and Daastøl, A.M., "Exploring the Genesis of Economic Innovation: The Religious Gestalt-Switch and the Duty to Invent as Preconditions for Economic Growth," *European Journal of Law and Economics*, Vol. 4, 1997, pp. 233–283.

Robbins, L., *A History of Economic Thought: The LSE Lectures,* Princeton: Princeton University Press, 1998.

Roncaglia, A., *La ricchezza delle idée: Storia del pensiero economico,* Rome: Laterza, 2001.

Roscher, Wilhelm, *Die Nationalökonomik des Handels und Gewerbfleisses,* Stuttgart: Cotta, 1881.

Rosselli, A., "Early Views on Monetary Policy: The Neapolitan Debate on the Theory of Exchange," *History of Political Economy,* Vol. 32, No. 1, 2000, pp. 61–82.

Ryan, M.T., "Assimilating New Worlds in the Sixteenth and Seventeenth Centuries," *Comparative Studies in Society and History,* Vol. 23, No. 4, 1981, pp. 519–538.

Salfi, F.S., *Elogio di A. Serra, primo scrittore di economia politica,* Milan: Nobile e Tosi, 1802.

———, "Minuti di Salfi a [Giuseppe Prina?] 1802," in Froio, R. (Ed.), *Salfi tra Napoli e Parigi: Carteggio 1792–1832,* Naples: G. Macchiaroli, 1997.

Samuelson, P.A., "Prices of Factors and Goods in General Equilibrium," *Review of Economic Studies,* Vol. 21, no. 1, 1953, pp. 1–20.

Samuelson, P.A. "International Trade and the Equalization of Factor Prices," *Economic Journal,* Vol 58, June 1948, pp. 163–184.

———, "International Factor-Price Equalization Once Again," *Economic Journal,* Vil. 59, June 1949, pp. 181–197.

Saxenian, A.L., *Regional Advantage: Culture and Competition in Silicon Valley and Route 128,* Cambridge, MA: Harvard University Press, 1994.

Schefold, B. (Ed.), *Antonio Serra und sein Breve Trattato—Vademecum zu einem unbekannten Klassiker,* Düsseldorf: Verlag Wirtschaft und Finanzen GMBH, 1994.

Schmoller, G. *The Mercantile System and its Historical Significance* [1884], New York: A.M. Kelley, 1967.

Schumpeter, J.A., *A History of Economic Analysis,* New York: Oxford University Press, 1954.

Seligman, E.R.A., *Curiosities of Early Economic Literature,* San Francisco: Privately Printed by John Henry Nash, 1920.

Serra, Antonio, *Breve trattato delle cause che possono far abbondare li regni d'oro, & argento dove non sono miniere. Con applicazione al Regno di Napoli. Del dottor Antonio Serra della città di Cosenza. Divisione in tre parti,* Naples: Lazzaro Scorriggio, 1613.

———, *Breve Tratado das causas que podem fazer os reinos desprovidos de minas ter abundância de ouro e prata,* Curitiba, Brazil, Segasta, 2002.

Sewell, W.H., *Work and Revolution in France: The Language of Labor from the Old Regime to 1848,* Cambridge: Cambridge University Press, 1980.

Smith, A., *An Inquiry into the Nature and Causes of the Wealth of Nations,* Chicago: University of Chicago Press, 1976.

Smith, A., *History of Astronomy,* in his *Works,* ed. Dugald Stewart, London: Cadell & Davies, 1811. Vol. 5, pp. 55–190.

Sombart, W., *Der Moderne Kapitalismus,* Leipzig: Duncker & Humblot, 1902.

Sumberg, T.A., "Antonio Serra: A Neglected Herald of the Acquisitative System," *Journal of Economics and Sociology,* Vol. 50, No. 3, 1991, pp. 365–373.

Veblen, Thorstein, *The Theory of the Leisure Class, An Economic Study of Institutions,* New York, 1898.

Viner, J., *Studies in the Theory of International Trade,* New York: Harper & Brothers, 1937.

Wallerstein, I.M., *The Capitalist World Economy,* Cambridge: Cambridge University Press, 1979.

Weintraub, E.R., *How Economics Became a Mathematical Science,* Durham: Duke University Press, 2002.

White, L.T., *Medieval Technology and Social Change,* London: Oxford University Press, 1964.

Xenophon, *Ways and Means (The Poroi),* Ed. E.C. Merchant, Cambridge, MA: Harvard University Press, 1984.

Ziersch, W., *Antonio Serra, ein Beitrag zur Geschichte der Nationalökonomie,* Bonn: Carl Georgi, 1905.

Chapter 11

INNOVATION SYSTEMS OF THE PAST: MODERN NATION-STATES IN A HISTORICAL PERSPECTIVE. THE ROLE OF INNOVATIONS AND OF SYSTEMIC EFFECTS IN ECONOMIC THOUGHT AND POLICY

With Sophus A. Reinert

'The same principle, **the same love of system**, *the same regard to the beauty of order, ..frequently serves to recommend those institutions which tend to promote the public welfare. ...When the legislature establishes premiums and other encouragements to advance the linen or woollen manufactures, its conduct seldom proceeds from pure sympathy with the wearer of cheap or fine cloth, and much less from that with the manufacturer or merchant. The perfection of police (i.e. policy), the extension of trade and manufactures, are noble and magnificent objects. The contemplation of them pleases us, and we are interested in whatever can tend to advance them. They make part of* **the great system of government**, *and the wheels of the political machine seem to move with more harmony and ease by means of them. We take pleasure in beholding the perfection of so beautiful and grand a system, and we are uneasy till we remove any obstruction that can in the least disturb or encumber the regularity of its motions.'*

The early Adam Smith, still a 'Mercantilist' before his meetings with the French physiocrats, on economic institutions and on the 'Innovation System', in *The Theory of Moral Sentiments* (1759), in *Collected Works*, London, Cadell and Davies, 1812, Vol. 1, p. 320 (our emphasis).

'There is no such thing as society. There are individual men and women, and there are families.' This famous 1987 quote by Margaret Thatcher is a logical reflection of the *methodological individualism* of both the mainstream and Austrian schools of economics. We shall argue in this chapter that early economic thought – starting at least as far back as in the 1200s – was dominated by what we could call *methodological holism.* The economy could only be properly understood as a complex system of synergies that created welfare, something closely resembling a National Innovation System. We shall argue that the later Renaissance discovery of individualism was superimposed upon this earlier synergetic view of society, creating a dualistic view of the economy in which both the viewpoint of society *and* of the individual had to be taken into consideration. At times this dualistic approach obviously created tensions between the two perspectives, and a need for conscious trade-offs arose in the political sphere. This economic tradition dominated in European social sciences for centuries – probably peaking in a virtual monopoly position around 1760 – and survived in the Continental (i.e. non-Anglo-Saxon) economic tradition well into the twentieth century. We have attempted to revive and redefine this Renaissance tradition – which we refer to as The Other Canon of economics – as regards globalization and unequal development in a collection of essays.[1]

In this Other Canon tradition the goal of creating a functioning state was in many ways synonymous with the creation of this system of synergies. In the quote above, the early Adam Smith places himself squarely in this tradition of *methodological holism* that, by gathering all theoretical approaches over a period of several centuries under the same heading, somewhat superficially has come to be known under the name of Mercantilism. In this tradition the increasing division of labour, 'the extension of trade and manufactures', were seen as goals for improving the economy *as a system.* Smith assures us that subsidies and encouragements to new manufactures were made neither in order to assist the producers nor to help the consumers – as they would be under an individualistic logic – but in order to promote the welfare of society as a whole: *the great system of government.* We shall argue that the mercantilist and cameralist tradition that was actually carried out in economic policy in Europe (as opposed to a much later post-fact rendering of Mercantilism) for centuries was fundamentally about creating innovations and synergies, and that the policy tools that were created already in the late 1400s – patents and protection in order to favour manufacturing industries – must be understood in this perspective.

Two alternative theories based on two different metaphors compete for the attention of today's economists: mainstream economics based on an equilibrium metaphor from physics, and evolutionary economics based on biology, on Darwinian evolution. Renaissance understanding of society was based on the thirteenth-century concept of *il bene comune* or *the common weal.* This Renaissance understanding of the economy and society was – dating all the way back to Roman legal tradition – based on an entirely different biological metaphor; on the *human body* as the metaphor for studying society. In the tradition of English historiography, this systemic thinking is referred to as *body politick.* The idea is clearly visualized in the frontispiece of Thomas Hobbes' *Leviathan* (1651), where Leviathan himself is depicted as consisting, literally, of a huge number of human beings. Understanding society as a body of *members* and *parts,* each specialized in different tasks, very clearly brings across the idea of *synergies, embeddedness* and *interdependencies* in human societies and in their economies. We would argue that this systemic dimension – which we find absent in *both* mainstream and evolutionary paradigms today – is reflected again both in The Other Canon approach and in the National Innovation System approach. When the biological metaphor of economics shifted from the *body politic* to Darwinian (or Lamarckian) evolution, something important was lost:

1. Reinert, Erik S. (ed.), *Globalization, Economic Development and Inequality: An Alternative Perspective,* in the series 'New Horizons in Institutional and Evolutionary Economics', Cheltenham: Edward Elgar, 2004.

the synergetic elements of the evolution of economic societies.[2] We therefore argue that the concept of National Innovation System recaptures an important feature of a long lasting, but also long lost metaphor, in the social science.

Joseph Schumpeter's role in this perspective is – as is common with him – somewhat contradictory. Schumpeter himself strongly opposed almost all 'interventionist' policies of his day, including Roosevelt's New Deal and Keynesianism, as well as activist policies with respect to science and technology.[3] It is all the more remarkable that the late Schumpeter – in the *History of Economic Analysis* – is extremely favourable to the economic theories of past interventionists, particularly the early Italian economists, whom he frequently compares favourably with Adam Smith. The young Adam Smith, as in the quote above, writes enthusiastically about interventionist policies, institutions and society as a great system. The older Adam Smith abhors with equal vehemence both institutions and interventions.[4] Interestingly, Schumpeter seems to have taken the opposite route. Late in his career the older Schumpeter of the *History of Economic Analysis* – to a large extent written in the shadow of World War II at the Kress Library of Economics at Harvard Business School – seems to find back to his Continental European roots arguing, in the long-standing continental tradition of economics, against 'A. Smith' and his successors.[5] These were the roots he to some extent had left behind more than ten years earlier by excluding the holistic and 'Germanic' chapter 7 from all the translations of the *Theorie der wirtschaftlichen Entwicklung*.

The old Schumpeter is generally also very favourable to the eighteenth-century German Cameralists, and in one case, to which we shall return, defends the interventionist and pro-development cameralist theories and policies as 'laissez-faire with the nonsense left out'. So while Schumpeter entirely neglected 'under-development' – very much a post-1945 issue anyway – we argue that he seems to have thoroughly understood and favoured the dynamic and pro-development policies of the past. Schumpeter's defence of the 'multi-level conspiracies of development' of the past is all the more remarkable because standard histories of economic thought rarely see any merit in the work of these economists.

Two purposes of this chapter are intertwined: By attempting to re-establish the pre-Smithian logic that laid the foundations for economic growth in Europe – a logic that was much supported by Schumpeter – we attempt to point out the preconditions

---

2. Reinert, Sophus, 'Darwin and the Body Politic: Schäffle, Veblen and the Biological Metaphor Shift in Economics', The Other Canon Foundation and Tallinn University of Technology Working Papers in Technology Governance and Economic Dynamics, No. 8, 2006. Also on www.othercanon.org.
3. We are indebted to Chris Freeman for this formulation.
4. Says Thomas McCraw of Harvard Business School: To Adam Smith all human institutions – private and public – 'so invariable produce "absurd" results that they have no presumptive legitimacy', in McCraw, Thomas, 'The Trouble with Adam Smith', *The American Scholar*, Vol. 61, No. 3., Summer 1992, p. 364.
5. We have previously analyzed Schumpeter's theoretical 'schizophrenia' in Reinert, Erik S., 'Schumpeter in the Context of two Canons of Economic Thought', *Industry and Innovation*, Vol. 6, No. 1, 2002.

for jump-starting National Innovation Systems (NIS). At the same time we wish to highlight the *activity-specific* and *context-specific* nature of historically successful National Innovation Systems, point to the synergies between economic activities, the role – not of innovations *per se* which in our view is not enough – but of innovations under conditions of dynamic imperfect competition and certain types of rents, and of certain policies that seem to have been *mandatory passage points* for all nations that have escaped poverty.

The aim is that such a historical perspective on innovations and economic development will facilitate the spread of the National Innovation Systems approach successfully to the Third World. The analysis of key success factors of the past should open up for a debate as to which of these policies are still open today, and/or what today's equivalent of the historical policies could be. In our view – a point to which we shall return in the conclusion – there is a risk of implementing the National Innovation Systems approach as a thin icing on a solid neo-classical cake. Our contention is that 'Schumpeterian economic geography' and 'Schumpeterian development economics' ought to embrace a wider theoretical and historical agenda than the normal neo-Schumpeterian one, an agenda that includes the visions and policies of the past that Schumpeter himself judged so favourably in his History of Economic Policy. We have tried to define this broader view of 'Schumpeterian economics' – The Other Canon[6] – as it relates to mainstream economics in Appendix II.

We should also point out that Thorstein Veblen's model of economic growth is representative of an Other Canon understanding of development, in that it both includes innovation *and* its synergetic elements. To Veblen Man's *idle curiosity* – an essentially non-economic instinct, research in its original form – was the basis for economic progress. This roughly corresponds to, or leads to, what Schumpeter later would call *invention.* This intellectual invention would have to meet *workmanship* and *capital* in order to be converted to an economic innovation. This process required an integration in and a sense of one's obligations towards 'the body of society' and history, what Veblen refers to as the *parental bend.* This trinity – idle curiosity, the parental bend and workmanship – forms the core of Veblen's theory of economic development. Compared to today's mainstream Veblen, Schumpeter and the Continental European economic tradition where they had their roots can be contrasted with today's mainstream using Schumpeter's description of the economics of John Rae – a nineteenth-century US economist: 'The essential thing is the conception of the economic process, which soars above the pedestrian view that it is the accumulation of capital *per se* that propels the capitalist engine.'[7]

This chapter consists of two separate sections, and is part of a larger work in progress. The first sections attempts to recreate the logic and policies of past innovation systems in Europe. The second part, which is more in an outline form, attempts to

---

6. Chapter 12 in this volume, also in Reinert, Erik S (ed.), *Globalization, Economic Development and Inequality: An Alternative Perspective*, Cheltenham: Edward Elgar, 2004, pp. 21-70.
7. Schumpeter, Joseph A., *History of Economic Analysis*, New York: Oxford University Press, 1954, p. 468.

present the forces that presently work against a successful implementation of national innovation systems in the Third World.

Section I: The Renaissance and the Birth of Innovation Systems

1. The liberation of time and space and the discovery of the economy as a positive-sum game

… today's 'optimum' may be very local and likely poor stuff compared to what might have been.[8]

Richard Nelson.

The compass opened, if I may so express myself, the universe.

Montesquieu

Something fundamental happened to the word 'innovation' during the Renaissance. The meaning of the word changed, from signifying something heretical and unwanted, indeed dangerous, to representing an idea of something highly desirable. In 1277, Roger Bacon, the *Doctor Admirabilis* of Oxford University, was arrested on grounds of his 'suspicious innovations': *Propter aliquas novitates suspectas.*[9] Just over 300 years later, in the early years of the 1600s, Francis Bacon – educated at Trinity College in Cambridge – published *An Essay on Innovations*, and their receptions could hardly have been more different. In order for Man to understand the potential of innovations for improving his lot, the second Bacon, Francis, wrote what he called 'feigned history', a history of the future, where such great innovations as self-propelled vehicles, submarines, microphones and new drugs would have created enormous progress and improved Man's life.[10] 'Innovation' thus went from being a threat to the established world order, God's very plan, in a society fearing commerce because 'one man's gain is the other man's loss', to become the very engine of a *desired* social and economic growth, not only for the intellectual architects of industrialization, but indeed across the entire spectrum of the European population. It was, as we shall see, not really the word itself that changed meaning, but rather Europe's relationship to *change* that shifted around it. The discovery is very similar to what the little quote from Richard Nelson above conveys: Europe slowly came to understand that their present status quo was indeed suboptimal.

In order to understand the reasons behind the growth of the West as compared to 'the Rest', we would argue that it is necessary to understand the mental *gestalt*-switch

8. Nelson, Richard, 'Recent Evolutionary Thinking about Economic Change', *Journal of Economic Literature*, Vol. XXXIII, March 1995, p. 58.
9. Compare 'To Traduce him as an Author of Suspitious (sic) Innovations' (1597), *Oxford English Dictionary*, Vol. V, p. 314.
10. One of the authors has previously discussed this gestalt-switch in Reinert, Erik S. and Arno Daastøl, 'Exploring the Genesis of Economic Innovations: The Religious Gestalt-Switch and the **duty to invent** as Preconditions for Economic Growth', *European Journal of Law and Economics*, Vol. 4, No. 2/3, 1997, and in *Christian Wolff. Gesammelte Werke, Materialien und Dokumente*, Hildesheim: Georg Olms Verlag, 1998, pp. 233–283.

behind the radical change in the meaning of the term ***innovation*** between the late 1200s and the late 1500s, between Roger Bacon and Francis Bacon. Historian of science Alexandre Koyré claims that Renaissance 'transformed Man from a spectator into an owner and master of nature'.[11] In order to understand why the National Innovation System approaches may or may not be successful in the present Third World, it is useful to explore this shift and the mentality and context that made the early innovation economies in Europe possible in the first place, i.e. the material and mental institutions present at its genesis. Schumpeter quite aptly argued 'scientific analysis is not simply a logically consistent process that starts with some primitive notions and then adds to the stock in a straight-line fashion', and to avoid whigish teleology, 'we must always leave open the possibility that, in the future, topics may be added to or dropped from any complete list that might be drawn up as of today'.[12]

Perhaps these early system builders hold pertinent answers to questions mainstream dogma long has ceased to ask, but that again have become relevant in another context. Probably those who saw the phenomenon being born – those in the 1500s and 1600s who tried to understand the fabulous economic success of Venice and The Dutch Republic and the de-industrialization and failure of Spain – could see and describe the phenomenon better than people who much later take the new system for granted.

Behind the switch in the meaning of innovation lies a complex and interwoven set of causalities, where the disturbances of status quo went from being seen as a threat to society to – frequently and for many – being its goal. From being locked in a static sphere pending the Apocalypse, Man emerged to master an infinity in flux. This change appears in early scientists' understanding of society, but it is also reflected in religion, the arts and – most importantly for our purpose – in the attitude towards innovations and technical change. Adopting Claude Lévi-Strauss' structuralist approach for the occasion, one can see how his theory of the decoding of ideas into different media is applicable to the epistemic shift we are observing.[13] The change in worldview, this reordering of the very framework that established the boundaries of conceivable agency, was a polyvalent phenomenon that both found expression in – and resulted from – a variety of languages of representation; it was deciphered in new conceptions of time, of space and of religion, as well as rendered materially in the form of maps, books, art and technology that permeated all aspects of society.

Precondition: Society as systems of synergies

Systemic relationships between parts of society had been present in explicit form for centuries, if not millennia. This connection between the human body and society occurred

11. Koyré, Alexandre, *From the Closed World to the Infinite Universe*, Baltimore: Johns Hopkins University Press, 1957, p. vii.
12. Schumpeter, Joseph, *History of Economic Analysis*, New York: Oxford University Press, 1954, pp. 4 & 10.
13. The structuralist methodological apparatus of decoding such overarching phenomena in disparate media is discussed in Lévi-Strauss, Claude, *Myth and Meaning*, p. 14, *passim*.

with a certain frequency in the Ancient Greek world, but was only systematized in Roman times. The formalization of this thinking is found in the codification of Roman Law ordered by Emperor Justinian in the sixth century. This *Corpus iuris civilis* (Body of Civil Law) came to influence, to lesser or greater extents, all Western legal systems (especially the so-called 'civil law' systems of Europe, as in Germany) and the Western tradition of political thought. The *Digest* is a compilation, organized by the *quaestor* Tribonian and a team of 16 jurists, of the legal opinions of the classical jurists of Rome culled from more than 2000 volumes of legal commentary, and it includes a much-quoted discussion on the relationships between different bodies:

> 'There are three kinds of *corpora*. The first is held together by a single spirit and is called *unitum*, such as a man, a tree, or a stone. The second consists of things joined together, that is, of many things cohering among themselves, which is called *connexum*, like a building, a ship, or a box. And the third consists of separated things, such as many whole bodies, but which are covered by one name, like a people, a legion, or a flock.'[14]

During the Middle Ages the idea of the state came to rely on the connection in Justinian's *Digest* between the individual and collective bodies. However, it was only with John of Salisbury's [ca. 1120–1180] *Policraticus* in the twelfth century that a full-scale anatomy of the anthropomorphic state was attempted.[15] The head, heart, eyes, ears, tongue and intestines of man all gain their equivalents in Salisbury's 'body of the commonwealth'.[16] From the time of the *Policraticus,* the concept of the body politic became thoroughly embedded in European thought from the Middle Ages through the Enlightenment.[17] As already mentioned in the introduction, its most celebrated manifestation is probably found in Hobbes' *Leviathan:* from its impressive frontispiece showing the incarnation of the state literally formed from its citizens to its intricate taxonomy of Man's ills and their respective counterparts in the commonwealth. As is evident from the use of physics metaphors in economics, all metaphors can easily be extended to the ridiculous and counterproductive. So also the body metaphor.

Reigning political theory at the birth of the Renaissance, in the thirteenth century, considered, then, society to be an organic unity mirroring the obvious synergies between disparate, yet interdependent parts of the human body. Michel Foucault argues Man sought to explain the unknown through analogy with more familiar concepts, the body being the perfect 'reservoir for models of visibility', as it was the only thing that

---

14. Justinian, *Digest,* 41.3.30.
15. Barkan, Leonard, *Nature's Work of Art: The Human Body as Image of the World,* New Haven: Yale University Press, 1975 p. 72.
16. *John of Salisbury, The Statesman's Book of John of Salisbury; Being the Fourth, Fifth, and Sixth Books, and Selections from the Seventh and Eighth Books, of the Policraticus, Political Science Classics, New York: A. A. Knopf, 1927 p. 65.*
17. Kantorowicz, Ernst Hartwig, *The King's Two Bodies; a Study in Mediaeval Political Theology,* Princeton: Princeton University Press, 1957.

was readily 'known, experienced, and controlled'.[18] A quote from Christine de Pizan (ca. 1364–1430) renders the idea of the strong interrelationships in society and serves as a kind of antithesis to Margaret Thatcher:

> 'For just as the human body is not whole, but defective and deformed when it lacks any of its members, so the body politic cannot be perfect, whole, nor healthy if all the estates of which we speak are not well joined and united together. Thus, they can help and aid each other, each exercising the office which it has to, which diverse offices ought to serve only for the conservation of the whole community, just as the members of the human body aid to guide and nourish the whole body. And in so far as one of them fails, the whole feels it and is deprived by it'.[19]

The idea of the 'common good', the *ben comune,* sprang partly from this organic social harmony – seeing the body as the metaphor for society – and partly from scholasticism.[20] This idea of a synergetic *common good* forms the axis around which Italian political economy was written from the Florentine chancellor Brunetto Latini (ca. 1210–1294)[21] to the important Italian economists of the Enlightenment Project, Antonio Genovesi (1712–1769) and Ferdinando Galiani (1728–1787) of the Neapolitan School of economics, and Cesare Beccaria (1738–1794) and Pietro Verri (1728–1797) of the Milanese School. This is the tradition growing out of the *civic humanism* of the Renaissance. This tradition finds its equivalents all over the European Continent. Particularly the connections between Italian and German economic thought at the time seem surprisingly strong and evidenced in the translations of economics works. Based on a study of translations of economic texts before 1850 it can be argued that a distinct 'Continental' economic tradition exists in Europe, different and separate from the Anglo-Saxon tradition.[22]

---

18. Foucault, Michel, *The Order of Things*, London: Routledge, 2002, p. 147, *passim;* Porter, Roy, 'History of the Body Reconsidered', in Peter Burke (ed.), *New Perspectives on Historical Writing*, University Park: University of Pennsylvania Press, 2001 p. 235.
19. De Pizan, Christine, *The Book of the Body Politic*, Cambridge: Cambridge University Press, 1994, p. 90.
20. Schumpeter refers to 'the old scholastic Public Good'. In *History of Economic Analysis,* New York: Oxford University Press, 1954, p. 177.
21. The concept of *buon/ben commune* is found in Latini, Brunetto, *The Book of the Treasure = Li livres dou tresor*, New York: Garland Publishing, 1993.
22. Kenneth Carpenter, retired Curator of the Kress Library at Harvard Business School – where Schumpeter wrote his *History of Economic Analysis* – possesses a huge archive recording thousands of translations of economic texts to and from European languages before 1850. Carpenter supports the hypothesis of two separate economics traditions, one continental (with frequent translations) and one English, with relatively infrequent translations between the two. A copy of this archive has been given by Mr. Carpenter to the authors, in twenty binders, for further compilation in a future project. Carpenter has addressed these issues in Carpenter, Kenneth, *Dialogue in Political Economy. Translations from and into German in the 18th Century,* Kress Library Publications No. 23, Boston: Harvard Business School, 1977 and *The Economic Bestsellers before 1850,* Bulletin No. 11, May 1975, of the Kress Library of Business and Economics, Boston: Harvard Business School, 1975. Building on Carpenter's work, this author and his wife have since published several articles on 'Economic Bestsellers'.

We also find the *common good* ideology prominently featured in the public works of art of the period. It is extremely well articulated visually in Ambrogio Lorenzetti's (ca. 1290–1348) celebrated *Allegory of Good and Bad Government* in the *Palazzo Pubblico* in Siena. Here the social and economic synergies resulting from good public policy are clearly evident.[23] The same propagation of civic well-being – the goal of the *civic humanism* – was the essence of the 'reason of state' doctrine of Giovanni Botero (1590), to which we shall return later.

These 'synergetic' civic virtues are also found a century later in the writings of San Bernardino of Siena (1380–1444), probably our most important economist-Saint. Casting his image of the perfect statesman in the iconography of Lorenzetti's fresco, San Bernardino extolled the virtues of humility, justice and mercy, as well as the will, the ability and the knowledge to ensure the propagation of Brunetto Latini's *ben comune* – the common good. San Bernardino was also instrumental in recasting economic activities as socially productive, both through his praise of guilds as conducive to the *ben comune* and in popularizing the civic humanist concept of *magnificentia*. Magnificence was the virtue, uniquely accessible to the powerful or wealthy, inherent in the making of great things (*magna facere*).

It is upon this precondition of the pre-existence of a systemic *common good* in society that the creative revolution of the Renaissance allows the individual to rise into prominence. The making of great things by the individual – his or her entrepreneurship and *magna facer*e – must be seen *in the context of the common good*. Contrasting with traditional Anglo-Saxon economics, the theories of the Italian economists mentioned above – Genovesi, Galiani, Beccaria and Verri – have as a common element with later German economics that both the interest of society ***and*** of the individual must be continuously taken into account, and occasionally traded off against one-another. These pre-Smithian economists had understood the virtues of self-interest before Adam Smith, but they did not take for granted that individual greed would necessarily contribute to the common good. Says Pietro Verri: 'Because the private interest of each individual, ***when it coincides with the public interests,*** is always the safest guarantor of public happiness.'[24]

See also Lluch, Ernest, 'Cameralism beyond the Germanic World: A Note of Tribe', *History of Economic Ideas,* Vol. V, 1997/2.

23. Lorenzetti, Ambrogio, *Mural Allegory of Good and Bad Government,* Sienna: Palazzo Pubblico, 1338–1340. Discussed in Skinner, Quentin, 'Ambrogio Lorenzetti: The Artist as Political Philosopher', *Proceedings of the British Academy* (1988), pp. 1–56. For a discussion of Lorenzetti's relation to the concept of the *buon commune* see Henderson, John, *Piety and Charity in Late Medieval Florence*, Oxford: Clarendon Press, 1994, pp. 16–20. For a discussion of Lorenzetti as he relates to modern public administration see Drechsler, Wolfgang, *Good and Bad Government: Ambrogio Lorenzetti's Frescoes in the Siena Town Hall as Mission Statement for Public Administration Today*, Budapest: Open Society Institute, 2001.
24. Verri, Pietro, *Mediazioni sulla Economia Politica,* Genoa: Gravier, 1771, p. 42 (our emphasis).

Infinite cosmology: The possibility of progress and the end of zero-sum society

When George Soros claimed that 'Globalization is not a zero sum game', he unwittingly touched upon the very problem that faced economic thinkers at the end of the Renaissance, as they indeed feared it was. The modern conception of history and economics reflected in Soros' statement is entirely dependent on our cosmological conception of 'time' as a vector of *progress*, as a linear force that potentially brings never-ending change in a space of infinite resources. Starting in the Renaissance production-centred economics – in what we refer to as The Other Canon – economic thought has been intimately intertwined with this idea of a historical progress with infinite possibilities; it indeed forms the very framework of economic thinking from the earliest stage theories to the contemporary neo-Schumpeterian approach. This conception of time is, however, a relatively recent development in what Veblen calls 'the life-history of our species'. 'Time' was for the longest time thought of in very different terms. The idea of economic *progress* is thus quite intertwined with the modern idea of time as an indicator of change, as well as the idea of spatial infinity following from the heresies of the 1500s: of the ideas of Copernicus, Bruno and Galileo.

The world was, for the longest time, a finite place, a locked system in cosmic equilibrium. This zero-sum model of the universe was an Aristotelian invention[25] channelled by St. Jerome (ca. 340–420) and Thomas Aquinas (ca. 1225–1274). The early 'Balance of Trade' was strongly related to the theory that 'one man's gain must be another man's loss'.[26] The same idea appeared again in Switzerland as an essential part of Paracelsus' work (ca. 1493–1541). Being a cosmologist rather than a scientist, Paracelsus' hermetic tradition had an enormous influence on the reigning episteme, and the influence of his work indeed is echoing across Europe into the seventeenth century and beyond.[27] In France, Michel de Montaigne (1533–1592) argued in his 1580 *Essais* that 'no profit can be made except at another's expense, and so by this rule we should condemn any sort of gain'.[28] Similarly, England saw Sir Thomas Browne's (1605–1682) 1643 *Religio Medici* hold that 'all cannot be happy at once for, because the glory of one state depends upon the ruins of another, there is a revolution and vicissitude of their greatness'.[29] The zero-sum view of the economy was, as we have seen, a pan-European phenomenon.

This is, of course, not to say that there were not earlier exponents of various aspects of this change. Indeed, positive-sum undercurrents are identifiable across the European mindscape throughout the Middle Ages, and the importance of time for economic gain

25. Aristotle, *Politics* vii, ix, 3, 1328b.
26. *St. Jerome cited in Finkelstein, Andrea, Harmony and the Balance: An Intellectual History of Seventeenth-Century English Economic Thought, Ann Arbor: University of Michigan Press, 2000, p. 89.*
27. [Paracelsus] Hohenheim, Aureolus Theophrastus Bombastus von, 'Man in the Cosmos', in Jolande Jacobi (ed.), *Selected Writings of Paracelsus*, Princeton: Princeton University Press, 1951, pp. 38–44.
28. Montaigne, Michel de., *Essays*, London: Penguin Books, 1958, p. 48.
29. Browne, Thomas, *Religio Medici*, Andrew Crooke, 1643. Book I, p. xvii.

was present in explicit form already in the tenth-century *Colloquy* of Ælfric of Eynsham.[30] It was rather the cumulative culmination of a number of these correlated factors – the new cosmology, the change in religious outlook, the understanding of an extension of the synergetic common good – that constituted the epistemic shift which made *innovation* into something desirable rather than something heretic and threatening to God's plans.

Infinite cosmology: Religious causes and effects

In a previous paper, we have treated in detail the religious aspects of the Renaissance as they relate to the birth of innovations.[31] We shall summarize the most important features here.

The emerging neo-Platonic world saw all creation in the spirit of God; it was pantheistic. The philosophers of this creed pointed out the need to explore and to better understand Nature as a necessary way to know God. They conveyed an image of God as active, rational and creative. Since Man was created in the image of God, the human being also had the potential for these same qualities, both as individuals and collectively as a 'social body'. This *permission* to seek new knowledge – to learn, explore, invent and educate – soon developed into a *duty* to do the same. Creation was not ended on the 7th day; it was God's will that Man should be creative in order to improve on the creation, and thereby improve both his own condition and that of his fellow human beings, all the members of the social body of society. It was our duty to populate the Earth, so the Lord had built in an incentive system for procreation. Likewise, would the Continental philosophers in the tradition of Leibniz (1646–1716) and Christian Wolff (1679–1754) argue the fact that it was so satisfactory to discover new things and understand the world better was a proof of our duty to do so. It became Man's *pleasurable duty* to explore, discover, invent and innovate.

Not to say that this transition was frictionless and painless. A forerunner of these thoughts, Nicholas of Cusa (1401–1464), the German-born Bishop of Brixen (Bressanone) in Italy, suffered persecutions. Giordano Bruno, one of his spiritual followers, was burned at the stake in Rome in the year 1600. Bruno laid the foundations for the works of Kepler, but also for the tradition of Galileo and Newton. The religious persecutions of new knowledge are well known.

The influences from the Byzantine Empire – the only millennium empire the world has ever seen – were very strong in these processes. This applies both to the diffusion of Plato's texts and in the religious redefinition of Man's duties on Earth, no longer as a caretaker in the garden of creation, but as a junior partner in the process itself. The fall of Constantinople to the Turks precipitated an influx of philosophers and texts

30. Wood, Diana, *Medieval economic thought,* Cambridge: Cambridge University Press, 2002, p. 117.
31. Reinert, Erik S. and Arno Daastøl, 'Exploring the Genesis of Economic Innovations: The religious gestalt-switch and the duty to invent as preconditions for economic growth', in *European Journal of Law and Economics,* Vol 4, No. 2/3, 1997, pp. 233-283, and in *Christian Wolff. Gesammelte Werke,* IIIrd series, Vol. 45, Hildesheim, Georg Olms Verlag, 1998.

from the East into Italy, and the presence of these philosophers added much prestige to the Italian city-state courts. The most influential of these Byzantine philosophers was George Gemistos Plethon[32] (ca. 1360–1450).

It was Plethon's enthusiasm for Platonism that influenced Cosimo de Medici to found a Platonic Academy at Florence, one of the earliest of the academies that were to be so important for the later growth of knowledge in Europe. In 1441 Plethon had returned to the Peloponnesus, and there he died and was buried in 1450.

Just as the young Republic of Venice snatched the body of San Mark from Alexandria to bury him in Venice, in that way adding to the power and prestige of the city, the Malatesta family of Rimini had Plethon's body removed from his resting place in the Peloponnesus to the Tempio Malatestiano in Rimini in 1465. There he can still be visited under the inscription of 'Themistius Byzantinus'. From the point of view of innovation systems it is interesting to note that Plethon emphasized the need to stimulate and protect Byzantine industry and economy faced with growing Italian competition.[33]

Rights become duties: The birth of the 'developmental state'

As the pillaging of Rome (1527) and the counterreformation extinguished the developmental furore in Italy, the ideas had already moved North. As in Italy, so in Germany, learned societies sprang up, such as the 'Donaugesellschaft' (Danubiana) in Austria and the 'Rheinische Gesellschaft' (Rhenana) in Germany around 1500. It is important to keep in mind that the 1400s and 1500s was a very cosmopolitan age in Europe, with more foreign students at the universities, percentage-wise, than today. The cosmopolitan nature of the Catholic Church hierarchy also added to mobility and to the transportation of ideas. Giovanni Botero (1544–1617), the early social scientist to whom we shall return, was born in Piedmont in Italy, but had his two first books published in Krakow in Poland and Würzburg in Germany. These were also the times of early nationalism.

In Germany the duty-based system that we have described above – the permission to invent that was converted into a duty to invent – took on a particular political flavour. The rulers' *divine right to rule* became their *divine duty to develop* the state they ruled. In Germany this becomes very clear with Veit Ludwig von Seckendorff (1626–1692) and his *Teutsche Fürstenstaat*, first published in 1656. Seckendorff adds a strong dose of duty to the right of the ruler: 'Right becomes Duty, the lord of the land becomes the first servant of the state.'[34] The context of Seckendorff's writings is significant. He was of the generation born during the Thirty-Years War (1618–48), a war that devastated large parts of Germany. In some areas up to 70 per cent of the civilian population perished, and there was a feeling that a huge effort was needed, among other things, stopping

32. His enthusiasm for Plato made him change his name to Plethon.
33. See *The Oxford Dictionary of the Byzantium*, New York: Oxford University Press, 1991. Vol. I, p. 637.
34. Lüdtke, Wilhelm, 'Veit Ludwig von Seckendorff, ein deutscher Staatsmann und Volkserzieher des 17. Jahrhunderts', *Jahrbücher der Akademie gemeinnütziger Wissenschaften zu Erfurt*, Vol. 54, 1939, p. 67.

religious wars, in order to save civilization itself. Philip von Hörnigk (1638–1712), to whom we shall return under the discussion of agriculture, wrote his best-selling book on Austrian economic policy during the years when the Turks were boycotting Vienna. This book remained in print continuously for 100 years from 1684 to 1784, passing through 17 editions. The external and internal pressures helped forge the new thinking, inspired from the South, in Northern Europe.

Being a 'philosopher-King' became the prestigious goal of Northern European royalty.[35] The connection to the prestige attached to the Byzantine philosophers at the Italian courts a century or two earlier is easy to see. Knowledge provided the king with prestige, and making the subordinates wealthy and knowledgeable added to this prestige. To this was added an admiration for the Chinese, their discoveries and their high population density (see last footnote above). Being able to feed a large population was an obvious sign of both economic success and good rule. Thus Mankind's energies could be channelled from warfare into something more constructive, building the nation.[36] However, the competitive elements remained between the states, but no longer just in warfare. This diversity of states competing on different levels has been used as an argument explaining why Europe overtook China, which was ahead in terms of inventions and government not too long before.

This was the starting point of what Albert Hirschman has called 'a multi-level conspiracy for development'. Wilhelm Roscher, the German economist of the Historical School, was to call this type of government 'enlightened despotism'.[37] It is interesting to observe how the economists at the time encouraged, flattered and cajoled their rulers into adopting the right kind of economic policy. Many of them were at the same time researchers in the most diverse subjects, teachers, government advisors, business entrepreneurs on behalf of the state and the rulers, and a one-man research council.[38]

From explorations, terrestrial and celestial, to innovations

From the advent of clocks that gave time its metric measurability and inevitability, through the astronomers who shattered Man's mental prison, to the sailors who domesticated the oceans and seaways: the period around the turn of the sixteenth century is remarkable in the synergy we can observe between *innovations* and *explorations*, between

---

35. Wolff, Christian, *The Real Happiness of a People under A Philosophical King Demonstrated; Not only from the Nature of Things, but from the undoubted Experience of the Chinese under their first Founder Fohi, and his Illustrious Successors, Hoam Ti, and Xin Num*, London: Printed for M. Cooper, at the Globe, 1750.
36. This is the core of Albert Hirschman's eminent book *The Passions and the Interests*.
37. Roscher, Wilhelm, 'Der sächsische Nationalökonom Johann Heinrich Gottlob von Justi', *Archiv für die Sächsische Geschichte*, 1868, pp. 76–106.
38. See e.g. Reinert, Erik S., 'Johann Heinrich Gottlob von Justi (1717-1771): The Life and Times of an Economist Adventurer', in Backhaus, Jürgen (ed.), *The Beginnings of Political Economy: Johann Heinrich Gottlob von Justi*, series *The European Heritage in Economics and the Social Sciences*, New York, Springer, 2009, pp. 33-74.

men of theory and men of practice, in reshaping the European worldview. Men of theory and practice joined forces to weave a new European cosmology. The late Renaissance historian William J. Bouwsma explored what he named the 'liberation' of a number of key concepts around the turn of the sixteenth century.[39] As the static Medieval worldview digested the process of new scientific breakthroughs, of geographical and scientific exploration, it was forced to broaden its horizons and accept, perhaps more than adopt, a more dynamic mentality. We would argue, on the basis of our previous qualifications, that the emancipation of two of Bouwsma's axioms – time and space – fertilized the European worldview making innovations acceptable and liberating growth and economic progress in theory as well as in practice.

Something slowly changed around the turning of the sixteenth century. Giovanni Botero and Antonio Serra – the economists of this account – testify to the gradual nature of the epistemic shift. Worldviews do not change overnight, but rather cumulatively evolve on a level of time at once dependent on and detached from that of the 'event'.[40] Giovanni Botero (1544–1617) and his writings on world geography and explorations, perhaps the earliest world geography book,[41] *The Reason of State* and *The Greatness of Cities*, was more than a symptom of altering times, but he was alone not enough to trigger drastic change.

Botero[42] warns, in a chapter on how to acquire the wealth of others, that 'to attract to oneself and acquire just possession of what belongs to another requires no less skill and judgment than to propagate what is one's own'.[43] One could, in Botero's model of the economy, produce and propagate wealth, and the Prometheus of economic growth was thus unbound from his scholastic shackles. By removing the limits of growth, as well as some of its more restrictive moral barriers, Botero effectively expanded the limits of human endeavour, fusing a Heraclitean cosmology with economics.[44] The economy went from static to dynamic, from zero-sum game to a dynamic positive-sum game. The difference between the static and dynamic conceptions of reality can be traced back to Ancient Greece: *Scholastic and modern mainstream economists* follow Zeno's belief in a reality at once static and dynamic, whereas *mercantilists and modern evolutionists* adhere to the qualitatively changing world of Heraclitus. Karl Popper points out the semantic paradox resulting from this dichotomy:

39. Bouwsma, William James, *The waning of the Renaissance, 1550-1640*, New Haven: Yale University Press, 2000.
40. Braudel, Fernand, *On History*, pp. 26–52; Kuhn, Thomas S., *The Structure of Scientific Revolutions*, p. 151.
41. Botero, Giovanni, *Le relationi vniversali di Giovanni Botero Benese, diuise in quattro parti... Nuouamente aggiuntaui la descrittione del mare*, Venice: Appresso Giorgio Angelieri, 1599.
42. Botero, Giovanni, *Della ragion di stato libri dieci: con tre libri delle cause della grandezza, e magnificenza delle città*, Venice: Appresso i Gioliti, 1589.
43. Botero, Giovanni, *Ragion di stato*, p. 157.
44. Sombart, Werner, *Die drei Nationalökonomien, Munich and Leipzig: Duncker & Humblot, 1929.*

'For the kind of society which the sociologists call "static" is precisely analogous to those physical systems which the physicists would call "dynamic" (although stationary).'[45]

Newtonian physics would consider the solar system 'dynamic', insofar as it contains motion and change, whereas social scientists would call it 'static', since it, apart from rare celestial phenomena that also can be explained within the framework of the model, never undergoes structural change. There is no 'novelty', no 'innovation'.

Botero's insight was to translate into economic terms Giordano Bruno's (1548–1600) 1584 *De l'infinito universo e mondi*, a text considered heretical by ecclesiastical authorities that contributed considerably to the eventual calling of an *auto-da-fé* against him. Bruno reinterpreted the ideas of Lucretius' (B.C. ca. 99–55) *De rerum natura* in the terms of Nicholas of Cusa (1401–1464) and Copernicus (1473–1543).[46]

A Brunian expanding cosmos was the infinite, qualitatively dynamic precondition for the mercantilist reinterpretation of the economic sphere. Economic activities were suddenly empowered with the ability to propagate wealth on an aggregate level. Whereas Aristotle and the scholastics resisted economic endeavours on the grounds that they inevitably exacerbated social inequality, the mercantilists realized the economy could be directed towards increasing the material welfare of the entire population. With reference to our hermeneutical approach, one can see that the textual theories of expanding trade in mercantilist literature cannot be properly understood without reference to their cosmological context.

The scholastic *status quo* had implications far beyond the mere allocation of wealth; however, the pursuit of knowledge was shackled by the belief in a static society. By charting the use of Icarus iconography in Europe in the sixteenth and seventeenth centuries, Carlo Ginzburg mapped, as a measure of the scientific revolution, the evolution of the Icarus iconography from an embodiment of hubris to a Promethean figure daring everything in his exploration of human possibilities as a measure of the scientific revolution.[47] Early modern economic discourse was also affected by this change; Gerard Malynes and Edward Misselden, two early English economists who debated furiously in 1622–23,[48] are separated by a *Zeitgeist* in transition. Malynes' Icarus is clearly still bound by the chains of Medievalism when he criticized Misselden for having

'undertaken (with the Artificiall wings of his supporters set on with wax) to fly so high in the discourse thereof, that this hot climate hath dissolved the wax and the splendant Beames of the Sunne of truth hath dispelled all foggy misteries of deceitfull fallacies, as aforesaid; so that he is drowned (with his Ballance) in the Sea of Exchanges.'[49]

45. Popper, Karl Raimund, *The Poverty of Historicism, London:* Routledge and K. Paul, 1957, pp. 112–13.
46. Koyré, Alexandre, *From the Closed World to the Infinite Universe*, Baltimore: Johns Hopkins Press, 1957, pp. 18, 25, *passim.*
47. Ginzburg, Carlo, 'The High and the Low: The Theme of Forbidden Knowledge in the Sixteenth and Seventeenth Centuries', in his *Clues, Myths, and the Historical Method*, Baltimore: Johns Hopkins University Press, 1989, pp. 60–76.
48. For a rendering of the debate, see chapter 12 in this volume.
49. Malynes, Gerard, *The Center of the Circle of Commerce*, London: Printed by W. Iones, 1623, p. 137.

Not until the fights of late nineteenth-century German-speaking economists was the profession to engage in such vitriolic debates as did Misselden and Malynes in England in the 1620s. However, the gentlemen in question set a record by swearing at each other in 8 or 9 different languages. Misselden in the end won the debates over English economic policy, and the subsequent Enlightenment banished the last stigma attached to the pursuit of knowledge. The imagery of the debates, however, attests to the transitional nature of their debates. Cosmologically, the Italian economic historian – and many times prime minister – Amintore Fanfani, encapsulated, without explaining, the shift we have explored: 'while scholasticism thinks of an order in equilibrium, Mercantilism thinks of an order in growth.'[50] We would claim, then, that Mercantilism and evolutionary economics fall in the same dynamic category, whereas scholasticism and neoclassical economics fall into a different static category.[51] The Medieval scholastics saw the universe as fundamentally static, while the mercantilists envisioned the cosmos as expanding, permanently in flux.

A chapter like this needs a more accurate reference to the Greek seeds of these ideas. The rhetoric of the Italian tradition of political economy, and of Antonio Serra in particular, mirrors that of Xenophon's (B.C. ca. 430–355) *Poroi* to a large extent. Writing the *Poroi – On the Ways and Means of Improving the Revenues of the State of Athens* – around the year 352 B.C., Xenophon sought both to explain and to remedy the ongoing balance of payments crisis that Athens had suffered as a consequence of the so-called 'Social War' against its former allies.[52] Xenophon refers to what we could call 'systemic increasing returns' when, in the *Poroi*, he suggests that certain problems in a city can be solved by making the city larger. The humanist Giovanni Aurispa brought all of Xenophon's works from Byzantium to Italy in 1427, and while the influence of his *Oeconomicus* on the evolution of Scholastic economic thought was considerable, the influence of the *Poroi* has never been charted.[53] Yet Xenophon's ideals of self-sufficiency, civic-mindedness and

50. Fanfani, Amintore, *Storia delle dottrine economiche dall'antichità al XIX secolo*, Milan: Casa Editrice Giuseppe Principato, 1955, p. 149. In Italian: 'mentre lo scolasticismo pensa ad un ordine in equilibrio, il mercantilismo pensa ad un ordine in accrescimento.'

51. This is discussed in Reinert, Erik S., 'Full Circle: Economics from Scholasticism through Innovation and back into Mathematical Scholasticism. Reflections around a 1769 price essay: "Why is it that Economics so Far has Gained so Few Advantages from Physics and Mathematics?"', *Journal of Economic Studies,* Vol. 27, No. 4/5, 2000. Available on www.othercanon.org.

52. Isocrates, 'On the Peace', in George Norlin (ed.), *Isocrates with an English Translation in Three Volumes*, Cambridge, MA: Harvard University Press, 355 B.C/1984. Verse 19.

53. Baron, Hans, 'Franciscan Poverty and Civic Wealth as Factors in the Rise of Humanist Thought', *Speculum*, Vol. 13, 1938, p. 25. The Latin phrase indicates that Aurispa brought the entirety of Xenophon's corpus with him from Byzantium: 'omnia quicquid scripsit'; Sombart, Werner, *Der Bourgeois: Zur Geistesgeschichte des Modernen Wirtschaftsmenschen*, Munich: Duncker & Humblot, 1913, p. 289; Bruni, Leonardo, Gordon Griffiths, James Hankins, and David Thompson, *The Humanism of Leonardo Bruni: Selected Texts*, Binghamton: Medieval & Renaissance Texts & Studies in conjunction with the Renaissance Society of America, 1987, pp. 300–11.

economic activity as factors of public welfare echo across the *activist-idealist* tradition in which Serra wrote.

The unique emphasis on Man's role in the economic system had roots in the undercurrents of neo-Platonism in late Renaissance culture, and was an integral part of Jacob Burckhardt's vision of the Renaissance as hailing the rediscovery of the individual.[54] The classical tradition of individualism in the Renaissance was, however, never divorced from the Christian ethos that saturated society. While the charitable impulse in European thought indeed may have been reinforced by the Reformation and subsequent counterreformation, it was never entirely absent. One could argue that the two axioms of classical individualism and Christian communitarianism reinforced each other synergistically, and the importance of collective individuality was integral to the tradition of Italian statecraft. It was a way of thought that favoured the organic coherence of the city-state – an anthropocentric doctrine whose legacy is clearly manifest throughout the entire trajectory of Italian political economy from the scholastics to the *Risorgimento*; Giovanni Botero (1544–1617), Tommaso Campanella (1568–1639), Antonio Serra (fl. 1613), Antonio Genovesi (1712–1769), Ferdinando Galiani (1728–1787), Pietro Verri (1728–1797) and Cesare Beccaria (1738–1794) were all touched by the communal conscience that sprang out of the 'body politic'. This school created what Werner Sombart calls the *activist-idealist* – rather than the *passivist-materialist* – tradition of economic thought.

2. *Development as paradigm shifts: stage theories in time and geography*[55]

There is a startling difference between the life of men in the most civilised province of Europe, and in the wildest and most barbarous districts of New India. This difference comes not from the soil, not from climate, not from race, but from the arts.

Francis Bacon, *Novum Organum*, 1620.

The two most important casualties of neo-classical economics are the dimensions of time and geography. History and geography were both integrated parts of pre-Smithian economics, and as we shall see in this section, in pre-Smithian economics the idea of human progress found parallel expressions both in history and geography through the *stage theories*. We would argue that these stage theories – remnants of which are still

54. These undercurrents of neo-Platonism and their influence on the role of Man in society are discussed by Kristeller in two of his essays; Kristeller, Paul Oskar, '"The Dignity of Man" and "Renaissance Platonism"', in Michael Mooney (ed.), *Renaissance Thought and Its Sources*, New York: Columbia University Press, 1979; Burckhardt, Jacob, *Die Cultur der Renaissance in Italien: Ein Versuch*, Leipzig: E. A. Seemann, 1869.

55. These aspects are discussed more in detail in Reinert, Erik S., 'Karl Bücher and the Geographical Dimensions of Techno-Economic Change', in Jürgen Backhaus (ed.), *Karl Bücher: Theory – History – Anthropology – Non-Market Economies*, Marburg: Metropolis Verlag, 2000, pp. 177-222.

found in the late Adam Smith – are theoretical tools that are similar to Perez' and Freeman's paradigm shifts.

Stage theories in time

History – it has been said – was created to prevent everything from happening simultaneously. History implies that events happen in sequence. Stage theories are attempts, based on different criteria, to organize history in sequential stages. In their most general form, stage theories postulate *that a key factor in the process of socioeconomic development is the mode of subsistence*, i.e. what, how and with which tools a society produces. Stage theories are successors to earlier historical theories that tended to be circular[56] but are frequently used in combinations. The Perez/Freeman system of paradigm shifts can be seen as a combination of both elements: progress and cyclicality combined. Stage theories are tools that can be used to study both the qualitative changes in the division of labour over time and the processes of institutional design and change that accompany these changes.

Stage theories point towards areas where the focus of human learning is concentrated at any point in time, and as such they serve as a basis for a qualitative understanding of processes of techno-economic change and of income inequality. An integrated part of this seventeenth- and eighteenth-century understanding was that the arrow of causality went from mode of production to institutional settings, not the other way around. As the quote from Francis Bacon above hints, production – *the arts* – would determine the differences in civilization and living standards. This could be contrasted with the present view that the de-industrialized or non-industrialized nations of the Third World should 'get their institutions right'. Although clearly seeing this as a process of co-evolutions, in pre-Smithian economics the mode of production would give rise to institutions, not the other way around.

Theories of periods and stages have been used in most of the social sciences. In the history profession the material from which Man's tools were made (e.g. stone or bronze) has become universally accepted as the basis for establishing early historical periods: the Stone Age (Mesolithic, Neolithic), the Bronze Age. Other criteria could have been used, e.g. based on social organization, but *the technology variable* was chosen. Not only in the history profession, but also in anthropology, the idea that technology is an important determinant for society is an old one; the discussion of the relationship between irrigation and centralized government being a classical example. In political science, the idea of stages of Man's development is born – with Jean Bodin's (1530–1596) study of the Republic – with the commencing of the science itself. If we define sociology as starting with Auguste Comte (1798–1857), the idea of stages was there from the very beginning of that science as well. In economics, theories of stages were central both to

56. A classic example of circular theories of history is the Medieval theories of Ibn-Khaldun. See Reinert, 'Karl Bücher and the Geographical Dimensions of Techno-Economic Change'.

the important French economist and statesman Robert Jacques Turgot (1727–1781) and in the teachings of Adam Smith (1723–1790).

In his book on the early stage theories from 1750 to 1800, Ronald Meek goes so far as to suggest that 'there was a certain sense ... in which the great eighteenth-century systems of 'classical' political economy in fact *arose out* of the four stage theories'.[57] In spite of this, today any idea of economic stages is peripheral, almost alien, to the economics profession. In this chapter we shall explore stage theories as they relate to economics, and discuss their usefulness from the point of view of understanding human welfare.

English Stage Theories (Eighteenth Century)	*German/US Stage Theories (Nineteenth Century)*
(Adam Smith)	*(Friedrich List/Richard Ely)*
1. Age of Hunters	1. Age of Hunting
2. Age of Shepherds	2. Age of Pasturage
3. Age of Agriculture	3. Age of Agriculture
4. Age of *Commerce*	4. Age of Agriculture and Manufacturing

This kind of stage theories is useful also in order to understand the important issues of population and sustainable development. The pre-Columbian population of North America – consisting essentially of hunters and gatherers – has been estimated at 1–2 million people, whereas the pre-Columbian population of the Andes, having reached the agricultural stage, has been calculated at 12 Million. This gives a population density 30–60 times higher in the apparently inhospitable Andes than on the fertile prairies. The concept of sustainability is not very meaningful until the technology variable is introduced.

Techno-economic paradigms should in our view be seen as continuations of this way of thinking: that the prevailing technologies and modes of production at any time will shape society and its institutions. In terms of achieving economic development, it was obvious to most pre-Smithians that it was necessary to get into the economic activities where the productivity explosions could be observed – into the paradigm-carrying industries of any period. After all, a nation finding itself with a comparative advantage in Stone Age technology – even if there were demand for their products – would be seen as specializing in staying poor and 'primitive'.

Stage theories: From time to geography

In his work on cities, German economist Johann Heinrich Gottlob von Justi (1717–1771) laid out the stage theory – which until then had been formulated along an axis of time – along a geographical axis.[58] Justi arranges economic geography in terms of

57. Meek, Ronald, *Social Science and the Ignoble Savage,* Cambridge: Cambridge University Press, 1976, p. 219. Emphasis in original.

58. Justi, Johann Heinrich Gottlob von, *Gesammelte Politische und Finanzschriften über wichtige Gegenstände der Staatskunst, der Kriegswissenschaften und des Cameral- und Finanzwesens.* 3 volumes, Copenhagen and Leipzig: Rothenschen Buchhandlung, 1761–1764, Vol. 3, p. 449 ff.

concentric circles from the centre to the periphery. At the core of a state is the city, where the increasing returns activities, manufacturing, take place. That such a manufacturing centre was the necessary core of any nation-state was obvious at the time. Outside the city walls were the areas dedicated to growing vegetables and other crops; further out lay the areas for pasturage and furthest out the areas for hunting. In essence, we see the eighteenth-century stage theories also converted into economic geography, where the economic activities are laid out with the latest and most wealth-creating activity at the centre, with the previous economic stages of economic development laid out in circles in reverse historical order: manufacturing, agriculture, pasturage and hunting.

German economist Heinrich von Thünen (1783–1850) is normally credited with the discovery and use of concentric circles and thus with the 'discovery' of human geography.[59] We would argue that economic geography was at the core of economics already with Giovanni Botero (1589) and Antonio Serra (1613), and Serra explains how increasing returns is the main reason behind the wealth of the cities.

Coupling the spatial theory of Justi and von Thünen with trade theory, we find that both in the geographical centre of their spatial construction and at the core of their development theory were the increasing returns of the manufacturing sector. Both to Justi and to von Thünen the welfare of the whole state depended on the welfare of the manufacturing sector at the centre of the economic system that was geographically spread out in concentric circles. In spite of being a gentleman farmer, von Thünen agreed that manufacturing industry needed, for a time, both targeting, nurturing and protection. Increasing returns were only to be found in the manufacturing sector that was also the urban sector.

Lately Paul Krugman had entered into the realm of both trade theory and economic geography, and essentially reformulated important elements in mercantilist economic geography and trade theory, in his works on international trade theory (1990) and economic geography (1995). Krugman's 'New Trade Theory' of the 1980s (Krugman 1990) is the trade theory also of Justi and von Thünen. Both Justi and von Thünen understood that the development machine at the core of the concentric circles – the urban increasing returns industries (manufacturing) – needed to be targeted, nourished and protected. Krugman had all these elements at hand, and – in our humble view – the logical consequence of this insight would have been to sacrifice economic equilibrium in order to gain relevance. However, Krugman failed to arrive at the same logical conclusion as Thünen and Justi.

Sacrificing equilibrium would have meant sacrificing the Archimedean Point of mainstream economics, and also the device that gives economics a claim to being more 'scientific' that the other social sciences. By introducing a situation where some nations specialize in increasing returns activities and others in diminishing returns activities – which is a core phenomenon of Mercantilism, of colonialism and of today's Third World

59. Wilhelm Roscher also recognizes Justi as being the inventor of the concentric circles that are later attributed to von Thünen (Roscher, 'Der sächsische Nationalökonom Johann Heinrich Gottlob von Justi', p. 97).

poverty problems – equilibrium and the generalized claims of economics would have to be abandoned.

3. Development as Rents

Giovanni Botero (1589) was probably the first economist and social scientist who built an economic and social theory around the observation that the world was not a zero-sum game: that the gain of one actor did not have to be the loss of another. From the very beginning, it was clear that the main force that brought the world out of the zero-sum mode was manufacturing industry. We shall later, in section 6, return to the questions of why the primary sectors were not seen as possible carriers of national wealth.

The great economic riddle of the sixteenth century was why all the gold and silver that entered Spain from its American colonies did not stay in Spain. The wealth found its way to places like the Netherlands and Venice, while Spain itself was de-industrialized. The economists of the time can roughly be divided in two groups: those who attacked the symptoms of this (i.e. the outflow of gold), and those who investigated the real economy in order to find the reasons behind the surprising reallocation of wealth. Those who investigated the causes rather than the symptoms all came to the same basic conclusion: economic wealth-creation was activity-specific; it was only possible with certain types of economic activities rather than with others. In this period – starting with Henry of Navarre in France and Henry VII in England – national economic strategies became focused on copying the conditions that clearly led to so much economic success in Venice and the Netherlands, and avoiding the type of conditions that were found in Spain.

In his *Ragion di Stato* (1589) Giovanni Botero writes that 'such is the power of industry that no mine of silver or gold in New Spain or Peru can compare with it, and the duties from the merchandise of Milan are worth more to the Catholic King than the mines of Potosi and Jalisco. Italy is a country in which … there is no important gold or silver mine, and so is France: yet both countries are rich in money and treasure thanks to industry' (Botero 1588: 152).[60] Also Tommaso Campanella, Neapolitan author of the utopian *Città del Sole*, argued for the encouragement of national industries on the basis that they were 'more prolific than mines'.[61] This same insight, that the 'real gold mines are manufacturing industry', we find 150 years later, in 1747, in the work of the first

60. Roscher, 'Der sächsische Nationalökonom Johann Heinrich Gottlob von Justi', p. 152; the use of the Potosí mines to highlight the importance of manufactures becomes a Leitmotif in early modern political economy across Europe. For example, we find Geronymo de Uztariz in 1751 proclaiming, '[Manufactures] is a mine more fruitful of gain, riches, and plenty, than those of Potosí.' Uztariz, Geronymo, *The Theory and Practice of Commerce and Maritime Affairs*, 2 vols. Vol. 1, London: John and James Rivington, 1751, p. 9.

61. Campanella, Tommaso and Edmund Chilmead, *A Discourse Touching the Spanish Monarchy: Wherein we Have a Political Classe, Representing Each Particular Country, Province, Kingdome, and Empire of the World, with Wayes of Government by Which They May Be Kept in Obedience. As Also, the Causes of the Rise and Fall of Each Kingdom and Empire. Vvritten by Tho. Campanella. Newly Translated into English, According to the Third Edition of this Book in Latine,* London: printed for Philemon Stephens and are to be sold at his shop at the Gilded Lion in Paul's Church-Yard, 1653;

Swedish professor in economics, the first professorship in economics outside Germany, Anders Berch.[62]As we shall see later, Antonio Serra (1613) was the economist who exposed the mechanisms that explain *why* this is so. Unfortunately, the non-monetary side of pre-Smithian economic policy – the part which is interesting from a National Innovation System point of view – has received very little academic attention.[63]

Rents in three types of activities

One of the more curious aspects of the present mainstream theory of capitalism is that the model depicts a very unsuccessful capitalism, one where very little profits are made, if any. 'Perfect competition' is, to a businessman, the pits, a 'hostile market'. Both with English and later US economic theory the world powers – the main beneficiaries of rents and imperfect competition – hold up to the world a picture without any such rents as the goal and standard of the economy. The 'Empires' defend themselves with a theory where all the characteristics that create an empire – imperfect markets, imperfect information, monopoly powers and the economies of scale in the use of force – are absent.

To early economists successful economies collected rents. Thorstein Veblen has compared capitalism to an advanced form of piracy, but with the Renaissance there were profits – or rents – that were not necessarily reducing the wealth of others. These rents emanated particularly from a diversified manufacturing sector (see the section on synergies). These were not the only rents, however. Our proposition is that early economic development in all the most successful European states – Venice, the Dutch Republic and England – was able to harvest three *different* kinds of rents which, to the nations in question, increased the size of the economic pie. We only have room for a brief outline.

The three kinds of rents are:

- Manufacturing rents, at the core of which are increasing returns, which are absent in agriculture (see below).
- Long-distance trading rents.
- Raw-material-based rents, which are different in each case.

In Venice the raw-material-based rent was from salt. Fredrik Lane comments that the young Venetian Republic hesitated to go to war, but was always determined in

Discussed in Fornari, Tommaso, *Delle Teorie Economiche nelle Provincie Napolitane dal Secolo XIII al MDCCXXXIV*, Milan: Hoepli, 1882, pp. 165–91.

62. Berch, Anders, *Inledning til Almänna Hushålningen, innefattande Grunden til Politie, Oeconomie och Cameralwetenskaperna*, Stockholm: Lars Salvius, 1747. For an account of Berch and the teaching of economics in eighteenth-century Sweden, see Liedman, Sven-Eric, *Den Synliga Handen* (the visible hand), Stockholm: Arbetarkultur, 1986.

63. One of the very few exceptions is Perrotta, Cosimo, *Produzione e Lavoro Produttivo nel Mercantilismo e nell'Illuminismo*, Galatina: Congedo Editore, 1988 & 'Is the Mercantilist Theory of the Favorable Balance of Trade Really Erroneous?', *History of Political Economy*, Vol. 23, No. 2, 1991, pp. 301–36. See also Magnusson, Lars, *Merkantilismen. Ett ekonomiskt tänkande formuleras*, Stockholm: SNS Förlag, 1991, English edition: *Mercantilism: The Shaping of an Economic Language*, London: Routledge, 1994.

defending the saltpans under its domination. Salt was the first non-luxury long-distance commodity traded, and the control of salt has been important from Ancient China to the Mayas of Yucatan. Due to the power that the control of salt supply brought with it, this commodity was often brought under government control, e.g. in Ancient China. The importance of salt for the finance and growth of the Venetian Republic is well documented in Jean-Claude Hocquet's *Il Sale e la Fortuna di Venezia* (Hocquet 1990).

In the Dutch Republic the raw material controlled was fish. As we shall see, there is a Schumpeterian element in this raw material in the discovery of pickling, or salting, of herring by William Buerem, who died in 1347 (Huet 1722: 25). Contemporary authors like Huet (who was born in 1630) and Uztariz, the great Spanish economist (1751), emphasize the importance of the synergies between fisheries and manufacturing in the Netherlands: that manufacturing alone would not have created the same wealth as manufacturing and fisheries do together.

In England the raw-material-based rent was wool, the control and use of which founded the basis for the economic strategy of the Tudors, starting in 1485. The export taxes put on wool were an important element in the Tudor strategy of industrializing England, insuring that her competitors had higher raw material costs than England had herself. Daniel Defoe (1728) interprets a vision of the first Tudor monarch Henry VII, who came to power in 1485, to industrialize on the basis of assuring that England's competitors had more expensive raw materials than the English manufacturers. While encouraging English woollen manufacturers, Henry VII slowly increased the export duties on raw wool. Under Elizabeth I, when sufficient manufacturing capacity had been built up, wool export was prohibited. The effect of these policies can be seen in Florence, where they caused the Medici to diversify into silk.

Triple-layer rent-seeking

These types of rents spread through the labour markets through various mechanisms. The new activities require more skill, there is more competition for labour, alternative ways of making money raise the wage level and – as in the nineteenth-century United States – a 'high wage strategy' becomes a political priority. As these rents increase, the tax-base of the nation also increases. Among German Cameralists, it was observed that people working with machinery were able to pay higher taxes that those who were engaged only in manual work, and advanced manufacturing and advanced technology therefore became a logical part of a strategy to raise the incomes of the state.

We suggest that the pie-increasing rents collected by successful businessmen spread also to the workers and to the state: thus it operates at three levels – a triple level rent-seeking: the *capitalists*, the *workers* and the *government*. It is crucial to understand why agricultural rent does not spread in the same way (see below) i.e. why – under certain circumstances – the trickle-down theory of economic development actually works. These 'rent-sharing mechanisms' are at work even today. In East Africa today, the cleaning women working in the brewery or in the tobacco factories have wages approaching the salaries of high-level public employees. The 'industrial system' 'forces', through various mechanisms, a form of rent-sharing. On the other hand, the owners of the coffee plantations in the same area are not forced to share their rent with those who pick coffee beans, who are the poorest workers in these nations. Reinert (1980 and others) explores these mechanisms.

Triple helix synergies

At the risk of overstretching the triple metaphor, we would like to refer to the concept of a Triple Helix model of knowledge production.[64] Their model describes the advancement of the endless frontier of new knowledge: relations among social, economic and scientific development in a Triple Helix of University-Industry-Government relations.

As with so many insights, the Triple Helix has clear roots in continental Mercantilism. There is strong evidence that the role of science was stronger in the consciousness of the early social scientists on the continent than in England.[65] Johann Heinrich Gottlob von Justi (1717–1771), probably the most influential German-speaking economist in the eighteenth century, made 'The inseparable connections between the flourishing of the sciences and the means which makes a nation powerful and happy' the subject of his inaugural lecture at the Theresianum University in Vienna in 1750: *Rede von dem unzertrennlichen Zusammenhang eines blühenden Zustandes der Wissenschaften mit denjenigen Mitteln, welche einen Staat mächtig und glücklich machen.*[66]

4. Development as Synergies and Path Dependency

'Promoting husbandry..is never more effectually encouraged than by the increase of manufactures'

David Hume, when discussing the Reign of Henry VII, in his: *History of England,* 1768, Vol. III, p. 65.

'So true it is, that when commerce has once changed its course, it is the most difficult thing in the World to bring it back again.'

Pierre Daniel Hüet (1630–1721), *A View of the Dutch Trade in All the States,* 1722.

'È il bene comune che fa grandi le città', says Machiavelli (1469–1527), and this 'common weal' was, as we have seen above, a natural outcome of the human body as a metaphor for society. Daniel Defoe (1660–1731) in his *Plan of English Commerce* gives us a *systemic analysis* in the same type of reasoning when he tells his readers what convinced Henry VII (1457–1509) to start an English textile industry when he came to power in 1485: While living with his aunt in France, the future king of England had observed that not only were the French

64. Leydesdorff, Loet & Henry Etzkowitz, 'Triple Helix of innovation: Introduction' *Science and Public Policy* 25(6): pp. 358-364 January 1998.
65. See e.g. Herder, Johann Gottfried, *Vom Einfluss der Regierung auf die Wissenschaften, und der Wissenschaften auf die Regierung,* 2nd edition, Berlin: Georg Jakob Decker, 1781.
66. Published in Justi, Johann Heinrich Gottlob von, *Auf höchsten Befehl an Sr. Röm. Kaiserl. und zu Ungarn und Böhmen Königl. Majestät erstattetes allerunterthänigstes Gutachten von dem vernünftigen Zusammenhange und practischen Vortrag aller öconomischen und Cameralwissenschaften; wobey zugleich zur Probe die Grundsätze der Policeywissenschaft mit denen dazu gehörigen practischen Arbeiten vorgetragen werden; benebst einer Antrittsrede von dem Zusammenhange eines blühenden Zustandes der Wissenschaften mit denjenigen Mitteln, welche einen Staat mächtig und glücklich machen,* Leipzig, 1754.

textile producers (who got all their raw materials – wool and Fuller's Earth – from England) much richer than their English providers of raw materials, but that wealth **spread to the whole community**: where there was manufacturing, also the shop-keepers were richer. There were synergetic effects between the manufacturing industry and the common weal of people ***outside*** the manufacturing sector. The quote from David Hume, Adam Smith's best friend, above, indicates that also Hume thoroughly understood the synergetic effects that Henry VII had started. Following Defoe there is a whole school of English historians who see Henry VII, or Henry Tudor, as being the launching pad from which England's greatness later developed. At the core of the Tudor strategy – later perfected by Elizabeth I – was the idea that some economic activities spread wealth, others don't. Here, as in the rest of Renaissance Europe, wealth was seen as *activity specific*.

There are several arguments founded on this kind of **systemic synergy** caused by manufacturing. The quote on the first page from Adam Smith's *Theory of Moral Sentiments* – from before his meeting with the French physiocrats – shows him as a relatively traditional mercantilist in this aspect. The reasons given by German philosophers and statesmen Leibniz and Wolff for why a State is needed include an emphasis on ***learning*** which triggers positive systemic effects. The reason why there is so little conflict between the interest of the individual and *the common weal* in their system is precisely that increased knowledge produces more of both individual and collective profits, something like: 'The incoming tide (of knowledge) raises all boats.' Wolff observes that 'Some people collect knowledge like other people collect money', and indicates the benefits to society of putting these two types of people together.

The most remarkable of all economic treatises before Adam Smith is, in these authors' opinion, no doubt the 1613 book by Antonio Serra, 'A Brief Treatise on the Causes which can make Gold and Silver Plentiful in Kingdoms where there are no Mines'.[67] The title corresponds to our stereotypes of mercantilist tracts, that they are only about gold and silver.[68] In fact Serra produces a most sophisticated model, producing – on the one hand – systemic economic development and on the other hand underdevelopment.

Serra's starting point is knowledge. On the dedicatory page he denounces 'ignorance as the cause and starting point of all evil'. He further comments on 'everybody's innate desire for knowledge'. He outlines the plan of his work as (1) understanding why some nations, even though they have no mines, are very rich, and (2) based on this understanding, to explain the apparent paradox that his own nation, the Kingdom of Naples, although abounding in natural resources has reached such an abysmal level of poverty that 'it does not leave us to breathe nor to enjoy what nature has given us'. Serra is the first economist to describe increasing returns,[69] and with the increasing returns as his

67. Serra, Antonio, *Breve trattato delle cause che possono far abbondare li regni d'oro e argento dove non sono miniere*, Naples: Lazzaro Scoriggio, 1613.
68. The title also influenced Say, who erroneously claims that to Serra only gold and silver were the sources of riches, see Coquelin and Guillaumin's *Dictionnaire de l'Économie Politique*, Paris: Guillaumin & Hachette, 1854, p. 610.
69. Both Wilhelm Roscher in his *Principles of Political Economy*, Chicago: Callaghan, 1882, and later Schumpeter recognize this, see his *History of Economic Analysis*, New York: Oxford University Press, 1951, pp. 258–59.

starting point, he describes positive feedback mechanisms which lead to virtuous circles of development in a national system.

We would argue that most mercantilists had a systemic view of society, and that – with different degrees of sophistication – they saw the synergetic and cumulative interaction of the triple factors mentioned above as being the true engines of growth and welfare. The quote from David Hume above is typical. It is also interesting to see how these ideas travelled to the 'periphery' of Europe. The subject of 'how one economic activity influences another' was the subject of a PhD thesis in Åbo (Turku) in Finland in 1772.[70] Indeed, after the first two professorships in economics had been established in Germany in 1728, the first professorships in economics outside Germany were established in the 'periphery', in Naples (Antonio Genovesi) and in Uppsala, Sweden (Anders Berch). A professorship in economics was established in Åbo, Finland, about 50 years before the first such professorship in England.

These cumulative mechanisms create strong path dependency, and therefore, as Huet says above, once commerce has changed its course, it is very difficult to get it back. Joshua Gee, in his 1729 treatise, presents a similar argument:

> The Trade of a Nation is a mighty Consequence (sic), and a Thing that ought to be seriously weighed, because the Happiness or Misfortune of so many Millions depend upon it. **A little Mistake in the Beginning of an Undertaking may swell to a very great one**. A Nation may gain vast Riches by Trade and Commerce, or for Want of due Regard and Attention, may be drained of them (emphasis added).

Antonio Serra (1613) has two types of factors which cause the wealth of nations: (1) Particular (or specific) factors (*accidenti propri*), and (2) Common (or general) factors (*accidenti communi*), which may occur in any nation:

Particular factors:

The first particular factor in Serra's system is a **surplus of products** for export. His phrase 'The surplus (*soprabbondanza*) of goods which are produced in a kingdom in excess of its own needs and conveniences' reminds us of an Adam Smith type of 'vent for surplus' theory of international trade, but this is only the beginning of Serra's long and sophisticated reasoning. Serra explains that he lists this as a *particular* factor – rather than as a *general* or *common* one, by pointing out that a surplus – or a positive balance of trade – cannot apply to all nations. His second particular factor is **the geographical position** (*il sito*) of the nation 'relative to other kingdoms and parts of the world....being a potent occasion, and almost a cause, of extensive trading of a kingdom'. Rating nations according to their geographical position, 'Venice holds the first place.'

General factors:

Serra lists four common or general factors which bring wealth, and, most importantly, *how these factors interact* with each other and with the *particular* factor of the geographical

70. Gadd, P.A., 'Försök til en politisk och economisk avhandling om näringarnes samband och medvärkan på hvarandra', Åbo (Turku), F. Brandell, PhD Thesis, Åbo Akademi, 1772.

position of a nation listed above. These 'general factors' we could refer to as man-made comparative advantages. It is worth noting that Serra sees the barrenness of a state – its lack of God-given comparative advantages – as an important trigger factor for creating the much more valuable man-made **general** comparative advantages:

1. The ***number and variety of industrial professions*** (*La quantità degli artifici diversi*). We see the 'number of professions' as fundamentally the same concept as 'the division of labour'. Clearly ***the number of industrial professions*** in a nation is a symptom – and a proxy – of a variety of economic factors: technological sophistication, a sophisticated pattern of demand, a large diversity of skills and – due to a minimum efficient scale of production in each profession – of a large market. Serra rates this factor higher than the 'vent for surplus' factor which he has listed under particular factors. This is because to Serra industrial professions, most importantly, behave differently from agriculture. The variety of employment in the Dutch Republic is frequently mentioned at the time.
2. **The *quality of the population*** (*la qualità delle genti*), or what we have later listed under Mentalité. The quality of a population is good 'when the inhabitants thereof are by nature industrious, or diligent and ingenious in building up trade not only in their own industry, but outside, and on the watch for opportunities to apply their industry'. On this factor Genoa gets the highest score, followed by Florence and, only third, Venice, which 'though it has more commerce than all the cities of Italy together, will nevertheless hold third place with respect to this factor'. Serra clearly relates the barrenness of the Genoese republic (*il loro paese sterilissimo*) to their industriousness and their wealth. We shall later see that in France Montesquieu later makes the same point, which becomes very common well into the nineteenth century.
3. ***The presence of a great commerce*** (il traffico grande). Here we find Serra's description of how the various factors creating wealth interact and mutually reinforce each other in creating virtuous circles of development. In the case of Venice, 'she is aided by her extensive manufactures; a factor which brings a great many people there, not only because of the trades themselves, in which case the effect would be attributed to them, but also as a result of **the concurrence of these two factors together, because one gives strength to the other**, the great concourse due to commerce and due to the geographical situation being increased by the manufactures, and the manufactures being increased by the great concourse due to commerce, while commerce is made greater by the same concourse of people.'[71] The starting point for the virtuous circles described by Serra is to be found in the increasing returns of manufacturing, where the Dutch Republic and Venice clearly were the world leaders at the time of Serra's writing.

---

71. '..ma ancora giova la quantità dei artifici che in essa si ritrovano, il di cui accidente causa concorso grandissimo di gente, non solo per gli artefici, mentre in tal caso a quelli si attribuirebbe la causa, ma per il **concorso di questi due accidenti insieme, poiché l'uno somministra forza all'altro**, e il concorso grande che vi é al rispetto del traffico e della ragione del sito cresce per la quantità degli artefici, e la quantità degli artifici cresce per il concorso grande del traffico, il quale per il concorso predetto diventa maggiore.'

4. **The regulations of the State** (la provvisione di colui che governa). Here Serra emphasizes the role of government policy in order to create national wealth. This is a most difficult task, he says, because one policy measure can have very different effects in different industries: 'like the sun makes clay hard, but makes wax soft, like a low whistle which irritates the dog, but quiets the horse.' (One could here e.g. think of an economic policy assisting innovation by *subsidizing research*, which would greatly benefit the pharmaceutical industry, but not at all help the printing industry, whereas a policy of *subsidizing the purchasing of advanced machinery* would help the printing industry, but hardly affect the pharmaceutical industry.) In spite of these difficulties, Serra makes it clear that economic policy is the most important factor causing the wealth of nations.

Daniel Defoe, in his *Plan of English Commerce* (1728), expresses a somewhat simpler, and perhaps more naïve, system of cumulative causation where the interactions of manufactures and navigation mutually reinforce each other:

> 'Manufacture supplies Merchandise
> Navigations supplies Shipping,
> Manufacture is the Hospital which feeds the Poor
> Navigation is the Nursery which raises Seamen
> Manufacture commands Money from Abroad.
> Navigation brings it Home
> Manufacture leads the Ships out
> Navigation loads them in
> Manufacture is Wealth
> Navigation is Strength.'

> 'To conclude, Manufacture for Employment at Home, and Navigation for Employment Abroad, **both together**, seem to set all the busy World at Work; **they seem to joyn Hands** to encourage the industrious Nations, and if well managed, infallibly make the World rich.' (Defoe 1730: 68–69, emphasis added)

A less complicated way of expressing the necessity and interrelationship of several factors at once is to refer to them as 'pillars', as does Pieter de la Court – 'The Dutch Adam Smith' – about the Dutch Republic in his *Interest van Holland*.[72] Still the metaphor of pillars clearly conveys the message that they are all necessary elements.

> 'Navigation, the fishery, commerce, and manufactures are **the four pillars of the State**; that these ought not to be weakened nor incommoded by any incumbrance whatsoever; for it is they (sic) make the inhabitants to subsist, and enrich the country, by bringing into it foreigners of all sorts &c.' (emphasis added)

Building the state and building the economy were seen as being two aspects of the same process. The mercantilist project was essentially to enlarge the territory where

72. Court, Pieter de la (Jean de Wit), *Interest van Holland*, Amsterdam: van der Gracht, 1662.

systemic synergies could be observed from the city-state to a larger economic area: the nation-state. In this process, economics, law, political science and all the auxiliary social sciences melt into one, into what in German was called the Cameral Sciences (*Cameralwissenschaften*), a term we find translated and used both in Italy, Spain and Sweden. Gustav Schmoller has described the process as follows:

> 'What was at stake was the creation of real *political* economies as unified organisms, the center of which should be, not merely a state policy reaching out in all directions, but rather the living heartbeat of a united sentiment. Only he who thus conceives of mercantilism will understand it; in its innermost kernel it is nothing but state making – not state making in the narrow sense, but state making and national-economy making at the same time; state making in the modern sense, which creates out of the political community an economic community, and so gives it a heightened meaning. The essence of the system lies not in some doctrine of money, or of the balance of trade; not in tariff barriers, protective duties, or navigation laws; but in something far greater: – namely in the total transformation of society and its organization, as well as of the state and its institutions, in the replacing of a local and territorial economic policy by that of the national state.'[73]

Nationalism was clearly an important element in this, an element to which two books contributed.[74] Creating nationalism, starting all the way back with Henry VII of England in 1485 and continuing through to Korea in the 1960s, was also a struggle against regional interests of the landed oligarchy, whose comparative advantage was in diminishing returns activities. The fight for the artisans in the towns against the feudal order, although often defeated, as in Spain in 1520–21,[75] was also the fight for those who had their competitive advantage in increasing rather than in diminishing returns sectors. Those nations with no natural resources had a clear advantage, because there the urban societies grew with no resistance.

The absence of natural resources (which would have led into diminishing returns) forced nations like the Dutch Republic and Venice into urban conglomerations, high population density (a very important element in mercantilist economics), manufacturing and increasing returns. The fact that the absence of God's gifts was actually a blessing, was observed early on by economists, along with the fact that lack of nature's gifts created a thrifty people.[76] Similarly, the involuntary protection of boycotts has played an important role historically in establishing increasing returns activities: In spite of Alexander Hamilton's theories, US manufacturing did not really take off until the Continental Blockades of the Napoleonic Wars reduced imports by between 80 and

73. Schmoller, Gustav, *The Mercantile System and its Historical Significance,* New York: Macmillan, 1897, pp. 50–51(reprinted 1967, Kelley).
74. Greenfeld, Liah, *Nationalism. Five Roads to Modernity,* Cambridge, MA: Harvard University Press, 1992 & Greenfeld, Liah, *The Spirit of Capitalism. Nationalism and Economic Growth,* Cambridge, MA: Harvard University Press, 2001.
75. The War of the *Comuneros.*
76. Montesquieu, for example, explains the backwardness – the lack of 'industry or arts' – of Africa with two factors, 'gold in abundance' and scarce population. *The Spirit of the Laws,* New York: Hafner, 1949, p. 332.

90 per cent, Latin American industrialization was kick-started by the scarcity of manufactured imports during World War II and the apartheid-related embargoes on South Africa and Rhodesia made manufacturing flourish. The fall in real wages in Rhodesia/Zimbabwe after the boycott ended was remarkable.

Giving the word to Schmoller again:

> 'The struggle against the great nobility, the towns, the corporations and provinces, the economic as well as the political blending of these isolated groups into a larger whole, the struggle for uniform measures and coinage, for a well-ordered system of currencies and credit, for uniform laws and uniform administration, for freer and more active traffic with the land – this was it (sic) which created a new division of labour, a new prosperity, and which liberated a thousand forces towards progress.'[77]

5. *Development as Synergies and Diversity: The case of Seventeenth-Century Delft*

Different fixed costs incurred in learning skills and in new tools simultaneously create *diversity* and *minimum efficient sizes* of human societies. For example, the fixed costs created by the blacksmith's fire created a minimum efficient size for human settlements. The creation of new knowledge is facilitated by the *diversity* of economic activities, all of which are subject to some type of minimum efficient size. In the words of Arthur Koestler: 'New knowledge is created by connecting previously unconnected facts.'[78] This is another element that increases both the role of a *minimum efficient size* and of *diversity* – two factors that mutually reinforce each other – in human societies. We can take for granted that with increasing diversity in an economy, the possibility of connection points for new knowledge (Koestler's *bisociation*) – both conscious and products of pure serendipity – will grow as exponentially as Malthus' assumed population growth. The larger the number of economic activities, the larger the division of labour, the larger will be the potential for spillovers.

The strong urban bias that we can observe in early economic growth supports this idea, as does Serra's (1613) idea that a larger division of labour *per se* is a starting point for cumulative causations of growth. Already Xenophon, in his *Poroi*, hinted at these 'systemic increasing returns' when he claimed that certain problems in a city may be cured by increasing the size of the city.

Historically such knowledge-creation and spillovers often leap from activities that are seemingly completely unrelated. In seventeenth-century Holland, it is possible to identify a closely-knit maritime-scientific-artistic cluster where innovations leap to and from seemingly unrelated sectors centred in the City of Delft. One interesting aspect of a case study of Delft is that it brings together, in the very same productive-scientific cluster, the sectors and elements that are traditionally seen as being the important driving forces of capitalism, all in an interwoven whole:

77. Schmoller, *The Mercantile System and its Historical Significance*, p. 51.
78. Koestler, Arthur *The Art of Creation*, London: Macmillan, 1964.

- The quest for military, in this case naval, power, as in Werner Sombart's 'Krieg und Kapitalismus'.[79]
- The quest for luxury, in this case art, as in Sombart's 'Luxury and Capitalism'.[80]
- The quest for scientific knowledge, as in Thorstein Veblen's 'idle curiosity'.

In Delft, these three forces all interact in creating economic development, and a central profession uniting all three seemingly unrelated fields is the profession of *lens grinder*.

Dutch artists invented oil painting and painting on canvases. The raw materials for these inventions – linseed oil, linen and hemp fibre – were widely used in Dutch shipbuilding and readily available. They would not be as readily available to the artists of Florence and Sienna. Whereas Venice was the centre for artistic glass, Florence under the Medici was an early centre for scientific glass production for lenses. Later Delft emerges as an important centre for lenses, making important improvements to the microscope.[81] Florence and Delft, then, shared both advanced painting and lens grinding. The two main users of lenses for scientific work, Galileo Galilei (1564–1642) from a Florentine family, and Anton van Leeuwenhoek (1632–1723) from Delft, both shared a family background in the wool business.[82] This industry was the 'paradigm carrier' of the day, of 'Kondratiev 0', indicating the ties between successful manufacturing and successful science. Galileo's father had been in the wool business, while Leeuwenhoek had himself worked in the textile industry in Amsterdam, where hand lenses were used extensively to inspect cloth. Leeuwenhoek – also an active natural scientist – was to produce more than 500 microscopes during his career,

An interesting integration of art and lens-making – bringing together the history of art and the history of science – was started by Delft painter Jan Vermeer (1632–1675), whose painting techniques included seeing his motives through lenses and a *camera obscura*, almost a primitive camera.[83] Vermeer also keenly participated in the aspects of discovery that were surrounding him in Delft: the geographical discoveries through the Dutch navy and the discoveries in the natural sciences that were made possible by the improvements of the microscope in Delft by Leeuwenhoek and his colleagues.

The navy and the merchant marine created a demand for lenses for binoculars, but lenses were also in demand by natural scientists and the producers of early microscopes at the time. Anton van Leeuwenhoek (1632–1723), who lived a couple of hundred metres

79. Sombart, Werner, *Krieg und Kapitalismus*, Munich and Leipzig : Duncker & Humblot, 1913.
80. Sombart, Werner, *Luxus und Kapitalismus*, Munich and Leipzig: Duncker & Humblot, 1913. See also Sombart's key work on capitalism, *Der moderne Kapitalismus*, Munich and Leipzig: Duncker & Humblot. First edition in 2 volumes 1902, last edition in 6 volumes 1928. Partial Spanish translation: *El Apogeo del Capitalismo*, Mexico: Fondo de Cultura Economica, 1946, 2 volumes. Partial Italian translation, *Il Capitalismo Moderno*, Turin: Unione Tipografico-Editrice Torinese, 1967.
81. Ruestow, Edward G., *The Microscope in the Dutch Republic: The Shaping of Discovery*, Cambridge: Cambridge University Press, 1996.
82. Huerta, Robert D., *Giants of Delft. Johannes Vermeer and the Natural Philosophers: The Parallel Search for Knowledge during the Age of Discovery*, Lewisburg, PA: Bucknell University Press, 2003, p. 33.
83. Steadman, Philip, *Vermeer's Camera*, Oxford: Oxford University Press, 2001.

away from the painter Vermeer, was famous for his microscope lenses and his research correspondence. Upon Vermeer's death, Leeuwenhoek was appointed to deal with his estate. The Huygens family, who later improved on the microscope, used another lens grinder in Delft, Johan van Wyck. Vermeer, the painter, who also experimented in the natural sciences, joined the microscope builders *cum* natural scientists.[84] The Delft lens grinders thus formed a core of an extremely dynamic and path-breaking cluster including such diverse activities as the Navy (binoculars), painters like Vermeer, the natural scientists and the microscope builders. The philosopher Baruch Spinoza (1632–1677), born in the same year as Vermeer and van Leeuwenhoek, but in Amsterdam, added to the Dutch knowledge system of the time. When Spinoza was excommunicated and banished from the city by the Amsterdam rabbis in 1656, also he supported himself as a *lens grinder* – as a producer of optical lenses.

Another product linking the three clusters – war (navy), luxury (art) and 'idle curiosity' (science) – in Holland at the time was mapmaking. Holland's position as a seafaring power demanded not only binoculars and naval instruments but also up-to-date maps. Vermeer's fascination with maps and explorations is clear in many of his paintings, one author commenting on his 'mania for maps'. His rendering of maps and globes are extremely accurate, and his paintings have been used to argue for the existence of certain maps before the originals were discovered.[85] In Florence this connection between art and cartography had already been developed by Filippo Brunelleschi (1377–1446), the famous architect of the cathedral *cupula* that symbolizes the city.[86] When the technology of map printing changed from woodcuts to copperplates in the late 1500s, the artisans of the Netherlands – who were skilled metalworkers – took over from the Italian mapmakers. In the working with brass and copper another aspect of the scientific-maritime-artistic cluster is reinforced. The same metalworking skills are needed for the production of naval as for scientific instruments, whereas art and metalworking meet in the production of the copperplates used in printing maps.

Such synergetic cumulative causations and the path dependency they create are no doubt at the core of knowledge-creation and the process of economic growth. They are, however, neither possible to reproduce in any meaningful way by quantitative methods nor visible through the lenses of methodological individualism.

The enormous diversity of economic activities was observed and commented on as an asset by all the contemporary economists who wrote about the Dutch Republic.[87] The role of diversity and the resulting creative serendipity brings back the issue of 'monoculture' in traditional development economics and in agricultural societies. A community of milk producers or a nation of banana producers have very little to sell to each other.

---

84. See Huerta, Robert D., *Giants of Delft. Johannes Vermeer and the Natural Philosophers: The Parallel Search for Knowledge during the Age of Discovery*, Bucknell University Press, 2003.
85. Huerta, *Giants of Delft. Johannes Vermeer and the Natural Philosophers*, p. 90.
86. Huerta, *Giants of Delft. Johannes Vermeer and the Natural Philosophers*, p. 91.
87. See Reinert, Erik S., 'The Dutch Republic (1500-1750) as seen by Contemporary European Economists', Paper presented at the conference on 'The Political Economy of the Dutch Republic', Utrecht University, April 2003.

6. Patents, protection and the mercantilist policy toolbox

Profit Opportunities as the Real Engines of Growth: Understanding Patents and Protection

Since patents and protection have a common origin, both conceptually and historically, it is difficult to understand how one of these institutions – targeting certain activities through protection – today should be seen as a mortal sin, whereas targeting the same type of activities, for the very same reason, through patents, is seen as a great feature of capitalism. Both policy measures were invented and put into systematic use between 1480 and 1500. From the point of view of the perfect competition of neo-classical economics, both institutions – patents and protection – are of course equally abominable. Why is it that economics has accepted one but not the other of these two gross inconsistencies with perfect competition?

The crucial role of patents in the 'free trade' system of today is an involuntary admission that dynamic Schumpeterian rent-seeking is essential to the capitalist system. Patents – that ingenious fifteenth-century Venetian innovation – are necessary in order to make it profitable to use new knowledge which would otherwise have easily been copied, making research and development in these areas unprofitable, and have seriously hampered economic growth. The fact that patents are of a temporary nature, just as protectionism was for the 'greatest of all protectionists' – Friedrich List – only emphasizes the similarities between patents and protection: they are both used in order to introduce new technologies and new learning into an economy; they are both there in order to create profit opportunities for businessmen in an industrial sector or in a geographical area. As long as all factors of development are globalized except the labour market, and as long as the benefits from technical change do not all translate into lower prices to foreign consumers (see our next point), the theoretical defence of patents is no better than the theoretical defence for protection. Protection is like patent focused in one geographical area, in one specific labour market.

From the point of view of the businessman or entrepreneur, the basic requirement for starting a business is a 'profit opportunity'. This must consist of a product idea and a potential market. Patents were created in order to make new inventions profitable, and protection was created in order to facilitate the transplant of the same inventions into new geographical areas. In the more backward countries, knowledge was lacking and markets were small, and the two factors had to be cultivated in parallel. It was clear at the time that basing the nation on 'competitiveness' in the agricultural sector – as we shall see under the discussion of agriculture – was not an option for growth. The logic that factor-price equalization will be achieved between a nation of subsistence farmers and an industrialized nation – or between a nation of shoe-shine boys and a nation of bio-engineers – is a modern invention that only came with the Cold War. The pre-Ricardian logic was rather that if all farmers are poorer than all those employed in manufacturing (which could be observed), the average income of the nation would go up if more manufacturing industry was added. To this came the belief – in our view realistic – that an agricultural nation would have a shortage of foreign exchange, a trade deficit, which would prevent all the necessary manufactured goods.

Figure 11.1 Schumpeterian Mercantilism: *Promoting and Protecting New Knowledge* in the Economic Policy of the Renaissance (starting in the sixteenth century).

Below we have attempted to list the 'Schumpeterian' toolbox of the mercantilists:[88]

The Establishment of Scientific Academies
- Bacon's 'New Atlantis': Salomon's House.
- Leibniz: Inspires the establishment of the academies of Berlin, Vienna and St. Petersburg.

Encouragement and Assistance to Inventors
- Bacon: 'Upon every invention of value we erect a statue to the inventor, and give him a liberal and honourable reward.'
- Wolff: 'We should forbid mockery of inventors.'

Diffusion of new Knowledge/Education
- Bacon: 'We have circuits of visits, of divers principal cities of the kingdom; where as it cometh to pass we do publish such new profitable inventions as we think good.'
- Wolff as the 'educator of the German Nation'.

Establishing an Apprentice System
- In England under Elizabeth I (1533–1603)
- In Germany as a result of the teachings of Leibniz and Wolff.

Patent Protection for new Inventions
- Showing a sophisticated understanding of the *appropriability problem* of new knowledge.

State-owned Manufactures as 'Places of Learning'
- Emphasized by Werner Sombart.

Subsidies to Firms in Industries new to the Nation or Region
- Serra: the number of different professions as a key factor in explaining the wealth of a city.

Tax Breaks and Bounties to Firms bringing in new Technology
- Systematically applied in England starting under Henry VII in 1485.
- Import of skilled labour.

Travel Restrictions for skilled Labour
- Under penalty of death for certain skills in Venice.

Prohibition against the Export of Machinery
- In force in England until the 1830s.

Prohibition against the Use of Machinery in the Colonies
- The heritage of this economic policy is still felt in many Third World counties, which, like Haiti, are specialized in the economic activities which have not yet been mechanized.

Export Duties on Raw Materials
- Ensuring that local manufacturing industries have lower prices on raw materials than foreign competitors.

Import Duties on manufactured Goods, while national Competition insured
- Machines seen as a proxy for new knowledge, this measure maximizes the flow of capital and labour to activities producing with machines, not manual power.

Strengthening the Navy
- Taking advantage of 'the economies of scale in the use of force'.

88. From: Reinert, Erik S., 'The Role of the State in Economic Growth', *Journal of Economic Studies*, Vol. 26, No. 4/5, 1999, Available on www.othercanon.org. A shorter version published in Toninelli, Pier Angelo (ed.), *The Rise and Fall of State-Owned Enterprises in the Western World*, Cambridge: Cambridge University Press, 2000.

7. The cult of manufacturing and the support of agriculture

'From the raw materials from Spain and the West Indies – particularly silk, iron and cochinilla (a red dye) – which cost them only 1 florin, the foreigners produce finished goods which they sell back to Spain for between 10 and 100 florins. Spain is in this way subject to greater humiliations from the rest of Europe than those they themselves impose on the Indians. In exchange for gold and silver the Spaniards offer trinkets of greater or lesser value; but by buying back their own raw materials at an exorbitant price, the Spaniards are made the laughing stock of all Europe.'

Luis Ortiz, Spanish minister of finance, to Felipe II: 'Memorandum to the King to prevent money from leaving the Kingdom', Madrid, 1558.

'It's the eternal paradox – the poor live in nations which are rich from Nature's bounties.',

José Cecilio del Valle, economist and vice president of the short-lived Central American Republic. About 1830.

'The higher the civilization of a people, the less does it depend on the nature of the country.'

Wilhelm Roscher, German economist and inspirer of Marx and Schumpeter, founder of the 'New Historical School' of Economics in Germany. About 1860.

Perhaps the most important assumption in neo-classical economics is what Nobel Laureate James Buchanan calls 'the equality assumption', the failure of this theoretical tradition to recognize diversity. Creating a taxonomy – a classification system – was an important task for early scientists, and we believe that it also is the case for neo-Schumpeterian economics. Economic activities are not qualitatively alike as carriers of economic growth. As was already pointed out by Giovanni Botero in 1589, the possibilities for developing new products – Carlota Perez's 'windows of opportunity' – vary considerably from one economic activity to the next. Technological trajectories evolve, leaving behind pockets of economic activities in exhausted techno-economic paradigms, technological dead-ends bereft of any scale effects or potential for change. Creative destruction may cause destruction in Bengal and creativity in Manchester; these are all factors which in our view could be built into a Schumpeterian economic geography'. In addition, when evaluating the differences between economic activities it is important to keep in mind Antonio Serra's classification of economic activities into two different groups: those where unit costs go up when a nation specializes in the activity (diminishing returns) and those where unit costs go down after national specialization, and where important barriers to entry to imitators are created (increasing returns).

A key feature of economics and state-building during the 1600s and 1700s – up until the physiocrats and Adam Smith – is what we would call the *cult of manufacturing*: the conviction that a manufacturing sector, as diversified as possible, was necessary in order for a nation to achieve economic growth. Perhaps the earliest written testimony pointing to the 'cult of manufacturing' is the 1558 report from Luis Ortiz, Spain's minister of finance, to his King (quoted above). As Friedrich List put it: 'the principle *sell manufactured goods, buy raw materials* was for centuries the English substitute for an (economic) theory.'[89] One basis for this policy was Charles King's very influential taxonomy of 'good' and 'bad' trade.[90] This policy tool reflected trade policy, not only in England but in the whole of Europe, starting in the late 1400s. In France, later a bastion of 'the cult of manufacturing', we find the earliest theoretical work with Barthélemy Laffemas in 1597.[91] 'Good trade' consisted in importing raw materials and exporting manufactured goods, 'bad trade' consisted in importing manufactured goods and exporting raw materials. Exchanging manufactured goods for other manufactured goods was also considered 'good trade'. Also from a fiscal point of view this policy was a success: the people working with machinery were able to pay higher taxes than the manual artisans. Charles King's taxonomy makes sense if manufacturing is associated with increasing returns and raw materials are associated with diminishing returns, as in Frank Graham's 1923 model and in Krugman's 'new trade theory'. [92]

In nineteenth-century US tariff policy, King's Taxonomy achieved a higher level of sophistication: Raw materials were, as in the old logic, to enter the country free of duty, but tariffs on manufactured goods were to be **gradually increased with increasing skill level of the workers.** A very clear statement of this principle is found in a resolution which was passed by the Democratic National Convention in Chicago in 1884, and which came to dominate US tariff policy:

> '*First* – The abolition of all duties on raw materials, such as wool, iron, and other ores, coal, jute, hemp, flax, dye stuffs, etc., in order that we may compete in home and foreign markets with other manufacturing nations, not one of which taxes raw materials. *Second* – The adjustment of the tariff, so that manufactures approaching nearest to the crude state will pay a lower rate, and manufactures that are further advanced, requiring more skill and labour, will pay a higher rate of duties.'[93]

89. List, F., *Das Nationale System der Politischen Ökonomie* (1841), Basel: Kyklos Verlag, 1841/1959, p. 12. This part of the foreword has not been translated in the English translation of 1885.
90. King, C., *The British Merchant; or, Commerce Preserv'd*, London: John Darby, 1721, 3 volumes.
91. Laffemas, Barthélemy, *Reiglement (sic) general pour dresser les manufactures en ce royaume, et couper le cours des draps de soye, & autres merchandises qui perdent & ruynent l'Estat: qui est le vray moyen de remettre la France en sa splendeur, & de faire gaigner les pauvres...*, Paris: Claude de Monstr'oil and Jean Richter, 1597. Reprinted with an English translation in *Fronsperger and Laffemas:16th-century Precursors of Modern Economic Ideas,* edited by Reinert, Erik S, and Philipp Robinson Rössner, London: Anthem, 2023
92. Graham, Frank, 'Some Aspects of Protection Further Considered', *Quarterly Journal of Economics*, Vol. 37, 1923, pp. 199–227. For a critical analysis on Krugman's treatment of increasing and diminishing returns, see Reinert, Erik S. and Vemund Riiser 'Recent trends in economic theory - implications for development geography' in Hesselberg, Jan (ed.) *Development Geography,* University of Oslo, Department of Human Geography, 1994. Vol. 1, pp. 1-18.
93. Quoted in Reinert, Erik S., 'Compensation Mechanisms and Targeted Economic Growth – Lessons from the History of Economic Policy', in Vivarelli, Marco and Mario Pianta (eds.), *The Employment Impact of Innovation,* London: Routledge, 2000.

This type of tariff policy is, in our view, fully consistent with a National Innovation Systems approach. In this worldview – which dominated for centuries – wages in the agricultural sector were seen as a reflection of the wages in the manufacturing sector. The research of Thomas Cliffe Leslie – an important economist of the English Historical School – confirms this: 'the chief causes of high agricultural wages are proximity to great industrial centres.'[94] This was partly because the proximity of a manufacturing sector advanced agricultural techniques, partly because of the additional demand created, and partly because the higher industrial wages increased the wages in agriculture. Today we can observe the same relationship between the manufacturing sector and the traditional service sector.

Also, modern economic historians recognize the problem of originating economic growth starting in the agricultural sector. Alexander Gerschenkron observed that the hope of developing industry from agriculture is probably not realistic.[95] Albert Hirschman put the same point in a different way by accusing agriculture for its inability to create linkage effects, the superiority of manufacturing in this respect being crushing.[96] However, Paul David found that in the US Midwest, agriculture had contributed importantly to the industrialization of Chicago.[97] Emilia-Romagna in Italy is an area where high-tech and successful agriculture share a territory, but – given the very long manufacturing traditions in the area – it is not clear at all that the synergies originally went from agriculture to manufacturing.

One important difference between agriculture and industry is their behaviour in the business cycle: agriculture is generally the sector hardest hit and the last to recover. John Kenneth Galbraith[98] reports how differently the depression in the 1930s hit manufacturing and agriculture. In industry, protected by the imperfect competition in all markets, depression created unemployment, but wages were upheld for those who kept their job. As a result wages and salaries actually increased as a percentage of GDP during the depression. In agriculture the price level and income collapsed, in addition to the employment problems. This development can be traced through the parity price relationship between prices and the cost of inputs in the agricultural sector. This index was set as base 100 in the years 1909 to 1914. In 1918, as a result of World War I, the index was at 200: agricultural prices were doubled compared to the costs of inputs. In 1929 this relationship was down to 138, and in 1932 it was down to a miserable 57. Compared to 1918 the prices the farmers got for their products compared to the costs

94. Leslie, T.E.C., 'The Movements of Agricultural Wages in Europe', in *Essays in Political Economy*, Dublin: Hodges, Figgis & Co, 1888, p. 377.

95. Gerschenkron, Alexander, *Economic Backwardness in Historical Perspective*, Cambridge, MA: Harvard University Press, 1962, p. 215.

96. Hirschman, Albert O., *The Strategy of Economic Development*, New Haven: Yale University Press, 1959, pp. 109–10.

97. David, Paul A., 'The Mechanization of Reaping in the Ante-Bellum Midwest', in Henry Rosovsky (ed.), *Industrialization in two Systems: Essays in Honour of Alexander Gerschenkron*, New York: Wiley, 1966, p. 339.

98. Galbraith, John Kenneth, *The World Economy Since the Wars*, London: Mandarin, 1994.

Figure 11.2 Industrial wages pulling the wages in the rest of the economy. Purchasing power of a median salary in primary-, secondary and tertiary sectors in 10 countries, 1928–36.[1]

Secondary (= Industrial) Sector = 100			
	Primary	*Secondary*	*Tertiary*
England, 1930	72	100	93
United States, 1935	40	100	142
France, 1930	36	100	32
Norway, 1934	24	100	58
Japan, 1934	15	100	39
Italy, 1928	70	100	114
Sweden, 1930	25	100	80
Australia, 1935-36	96	100	79
Germany, 1928	54	100	115
New Zealand 1936	113	100	78

[1]Calculated from Clark, Colin, *The Conditions of Economic Progress*, London: Macmillan, 1940.

of their inputs *was down by more than 70 per cent.* Those who have read John Steinbeck's 'Grapes of Wrath' will know the spirit of the day. Wesley Clair Mitchell, in his huge volume on Business Cycles, comments that agriculture and grazing normally are the sectors which come out of the business cycles last. He also comments on another anomaly in agriculture: the fluctuations of volumes and prices are such that sometimes a failed harvest, due to the rise in prices, causes the total value of the crop to be higher than in a large and good harvest.[99]

Figure 11.2 shows the relative wages of the three main sectors of the economy in the period 1928–36. It is evident that in most countries the wages of the industrial sector are pulling the wages in the rest of the economy. This is, of course, the reason why industrialized countries started protection of not only their manufacturing but also their agriculture. However, it is important to keep in mind that these two types of protection were born at very different periods for very different reasons: One to pull up the wages of the country, the other to protect the laggards.[100]

The mercantilist policy, however, was not *against* agriculture. To the contrary, the promotion of agriculture was in everyone's interest, and the number of texts with advice on how to improve agriculture is large. There are more translations into German of English agricultural economist Arthur Young than there are of Adam Smith.

For centuries however, agricultural productivity in Europe did not develop very much. The productivity development was nothing compared to the impressive new machinery in manufacturing and the 'productivity explosions' brought in by new techno-economic paradigms. The hope for innovation was still there, but the important thing was to use the existing land efficiently.

99. Mitchell, Wesley Clair, *Business Cycles*, Berkeley: University of California Press, 1913, p. 239.
100. See Reinert, Erik S, *International Trade and the Economic Mechanisms of Underdevelopment*, University Microfilms, 1980 for a discussion of this.

Philipp von Hörnigk,[101] the most successful economist in the German-speaking area, starts his nine points on how to improve the Austrian economy – essentially a list of how to build manufactures – like this:

> **'First**, to inspect the country's soil with the greatest care, and not to leave the agricultural possibilities of a single corner or clod of earth unconsidered. Every useful form of *plant* under the sun should be experimented with, to see whether it is adapted to the country, for the distance or nearness of the sun is not all that counts.'

Friedrich List went out of his way to explain how protection could only meaningfully be applied to manufacturing:

'The Protective System, as we understand it, can only be applied to the cultivation (*Pflanzung*) of manufacturing power. Any limitation on the import of raw materials and agricultural (food) products will in the long run hamper the development of manufactures, and is therefore against the interests of the Protective System. This is the case even if for some time such measures stimulate certain branches of agriculture and certain areas for some time. ...The development of Manufacturing Power follows completely different laws than the development of Agricultural Power.' (This is precisely Antonio Serra's argument when he explains the wealth of Venice and the poverty of Naples.) List continues: 'To make this clear, we shall for the moment only outline how differently import duties influence prices of the two branches (manufacturing and agriculture). When manufacturing is being cultivated, the prices of manufactured goods will rise (due to import duties), but as a result of the growing national manufacturing power and the increased competition resulting from this, the prices will, in time, be lower than they would have been through foreign imports.'

'Applying import duties to agricultural products, on the other hand', List says, **'does not have this invigorating power; such duties do not lead to lower prices later on.** This flaw in their reasoning (*Denkfehler*), like the mixing up of cosmopolitical with political economy, the (English) school has inherited from the physiocrats.**'**

Understanding the 'National Innovation System' that Friedrich List tried to build also requires understanding why List was in favour of free trade in agriculture:[102] this economic activity, by itself, could not build higher wages, regardless of productivity improvements. Clearly an important argument behind this is that only through manufacturing will a nation be able to create (a) the synergetic increasing returns that only could arise through a critical mass of increasing returns activities, the core of the virtuous

101. Hörnigk, Philipp Wilhelm von, *Oesterreich über alles wann es nur will. Das ist: wohlmeinender Fürschlag Wie mittelt einer wolbestellten Lands-Oeconomie die Kayserl. Erbland in kurzem über alle andere Staat von Europa zu erheben, und mehr als einiger derselben, von denen andern Independent zu machen. Durch einen Liebhaber der Kayserl. Erbland Wolfahr,* 1684.

102. See Reinert, Erik S., 'Raw Materials in the History of Economic Policy; or, Why List (the Protectionist) and Cobden (the Free Trader) Both Agreed on Free Trade in Corn', in G. Parry (ed.), *Freedom and Trade. 1846–1996*, London: Routledge, 1998.

circles of development (Antonio Serra's 1613 argument), and (b) only in manufacturing could the ratchet wheel/stickiness effect of wages be created. The imperfect competition both in the market for knowledge, for products and for labour – all protected by increasing barriers to entry created by increasing returns and cumulative learning – has been a precondition for this strategy to work, and also for what the French regulation school calls the 'Fordist' system of spreading the fruits of technological change.

To List, the fact that with the repeal of the Corn Laws in 1846 the English – by ending their protection of agriculture – seemed for a while to be able to convince the rest of the world that they should stop protecting *manufacturing*, must have seemed like a big defeat to his thinking and his life-work. The repeal of the Corn Laws was, to List, a very successful deceit which totally failed to take into account how the English themselves had got rich by employing, for centuries (since 1485), the very same policies that they were now denying to the rest of the world. This is what List sees as the English 'kicking away the ladder' from the nations that are attempting to follow their path from poor to rich nation, an argument that is still very valid. This is one connotation of the term 'free trade imperialism'. Going through List's correspondence, it seems likely that this event contributed to his suicide a few months later.

In our opinion Malthus and Ricardo and their 'dismal science' were right when only the correct circumstances are specified: human wages will for the great masses always be around subsistence level in the absence of the virtuous circles that emanate from a cluster of diversified increasing returns activities. The historical record on this is unanimous: only nations with Schumpeterian-type activities (see Figure 11.2 above) are able to work themselves out of poverty. However, nations with a manufacturing sector are able to create a decent living standard by exporting agricultural products. The existence of famines provides an interesting perspective to this. Famines are only found in nations where a high percentage of the population is engaged in agriculture. The smaller the percentage of agriculture in GDP, the smaller is the likelihood of famines. In nations where agriculture is only a small portion of GDP, people tend to die from eating too much rather than from famines. This is an illustration of the extreme synergies between agriculture and the rest of a diversified economy.

In the way of summary of this short section on a most complex issue: We argue that there are essentially two kinds of economic activities, having very different characteristics. A nation specializing in Schumpeterian activities will find that both increasing returns and technological change will cause production costs to fall, and thus open up for technology-based rents which can be divided between capitalists, workers and the government. A nation specializing in Malthusian activities will find that, after a certain point, specialization will cause unit production costs to rise. This is the core of Antonio Serra's argument from 1613, where he explains the wealth of Venice and the poverty of his native Naples. Reinert (1980) showed that the main export activities of Peru, Ecuador and Bolivia were actually producing well into diminishing returns: when production was reduced, production costs were also reduced. This is a main mechanism explaining why nations exporting raw material – in the absence of a national manufacturing sector – have never managed to get out of their poverty trap.

Figure 11.3 How economic activities differ: Only the presence of Schumpeterian Activities has ever managed to raise a nation out of poverty.

Marshall Plans: Produced by focus on Schumpeterian Activities (= 'good' export activities)	*Morgenthau Plans: Produced by focus on Malthusian Activities. (= 'bad' export activities if no Schumpeterian sector present)*[1]
Increasing Returns	Diminishing Returns
Dynamic imperfect competition	'Perfect competition' (commodity competition)
High growth activities	Low growth activities
Stable prices	Extreme price fluctuations
Generally skilled labour	Generally unskilled labour
Creates a middle-class Irreversible wages ('stickiness' of wages)	Creates 'feudalist' class structure Reversible wages
Technical change leads to higher wages to the producer ('Fordist wage regime')	Technical change tends to lower price to consumer
Creates large synergies (linkages, clusters, spillovers)	Creates few synergies

[1]'Reinert, Erik S. 'Globalisation in the Periphery as a Morgenthau Plan: The Underdevelopment of Mongolia in the 1990s', in Sakhia Lhagva (ed.), *Mongolian Development Strategy; Capacity Building*, Ulaanbaatar: Mongolian Development Research Center, 2000. See chapter 8 in this volume.

The problem today seems to be that, under a system of free trade combined with the standard IMF conditionalities, a large number of nations will not be able to build increasing returns activities that are competitive on the world market. The risk today, in our opinion, is therefore that a large number of countries will remain specialized in raw material monoculture and therefore specialize in being poor. When the United States and Australia started building their manufacturing sectors, at different times during the nineteenth century, they did not proceed with a view to competing with English manufactured goods. At the time, it is clear from their writings that they saw that as being impossible.

Today this centuries-old strategy of creating your own suboptimal and globally uncompetitive manufacturing sector in order to raise wages, employment and agricultural efficiency is no longer possible: the rule is 'be globally competitive or die'. This is in our view a situation that results in most poor countries being extremely far from their production possibility frontier: huge resources, especially labour, are unemployed. In many countries only 20–30 per cent of the population have what Europeans would call 'a job'. This extremely important fact is hardly ever discussed – the prices reflected in the market are not the true prices in this case – but only a handful of papers have ever been produced on the implications of this.[103] Under the original Bretton Woods rules, this situation entitled nations to protect their own production in order to raise employment.

103. We are indebted to Daniel Schydlowski for this point.

8. Colonialism in the framework of a National Innovation System approach

In our view it is useful to look at colonialism from a National Innovation System point of view. European colonial policy was the logical outgrowth of 'the cult of manufacturing': the essence of the colonial system was to prohibit manufacturing in the colonies, which to some extent was mirrored by the prohibition of colonial activities in the Metropolis (the growing of tobacco was e.g. forbidden both in England and Ireland).

The colonial system was a natural outgrowth of mercantilist policy:

> '... the ideal colony was one which would have freed England from importing anything from her competitors. In addition, the supplies obtained from the plantations were not to be entirely consumed in England, but their surplus was to be exported to foreign countries to the manifest advantage of the nations' trade balance. As far as it was possible the colony was to differ from England in its economic pursuits, producing nothing that interfered with the fullest development of any English industry and trade. It was to be the economic complement of the mother country, both together constituting a self-sufficient colonial empire. It naturally followed that the colony was to purchase its manufactures from England and thus employ English labour. But while its value as a market was fully recognized, chief stress was laid upon the colony as a source of supply.'[104]

To this was added what has come to be called 'The Colonial Drain', the consistent huge surplus of the balance of trade in the colonies' favour. In 1668–69, England's imports from her colonies amounted to 605.574 pounds while her export to the same colonies amounted to 107.791 pounds.[105]

Economists before Adam Smith generally understood that the colonies were getting a very poor deal economically. Some of them, as we shall see, felt the need to defend colonies morally with the argument that, yes, this is bad, but other nations do it so we have to do it as well in order not to be left behind. The reactions from the latecomer Germany are also important in this respect. While seventeenth-century German economists, like Johann Becher,[106] are pushing for Germany to have colonies of her own, the attitude 100 years later is very different. Johann Heinrich Gottlob von Justi (1771–1771),[107] the most influential German economist in the eighteenth century,[108] shares the opinion of the English that the only useful colonies are those that are only engaged in agriculture. As other economists before Smith and Ricardo, he is aware of

104. Beer, George Louis, *The Old Colonial System 1660-1754*, New York: MacMillan, 1912. Vol. I, p. 38.

105. Beer, *The Old Colonial System 1660-1754*, p. 39.

106. Becher, Johann Joachim, *Politischer Discurs*, Frankfurt: Zunner, 1668.

107. See Reinert, Erik S., 'Johann Heinrich Gottlob von Justi (1717-1771) – The Life and Times of an Economist Adventurer', on www.othercanon.org.

108. One of the persistent myths in the history of economic thought is that German Cameralism did not influence economic thinking in the rest of Europe. Of the total of 67 books written by Justi, 8 different books were translated into 5 different languages in 13 different translations.

the fact that such arrangements *are not in the interests of the colonies themselves*. Knowing that manufacturing is the key to wealth, this insight is an obvious part of the logic of the mercantilist system. Justi realizes that colonial trading arrangements hurt the colonies themselves and therefore cannot be a lasting proposition. ***It is only a matter of time before the colonies will find out that they are being deliberately kept in poverty: colonies will 'always will be in danger as soon as the foreign people start getting wiser.'***[109] No one could foresee the long-term success of Adam Smith's argument that all economic activities were equally conducive to economic growth, indirectly indicating that a successful economic agglomeration like Silicone Valley could equally well have been based on the growing of bananas.

From the point of view of pre-Smithian economics, colonialism was a kind of *winner picking* in reverse. The activity-specific view of economic growth cannot be fully appreciated without this other side of the coin – preventing 'good trade' in the colonies. Prohibition of the use of machinery in the colonies was one important and common policy measure. The English prohibition of the very successful cotton textile production in Ireland, starting in 1699, is an outstanding example of the negative targeting – the *winner-killing* rather than the *winner-picking* aspect of mercantilism. Export of cotton textiles from Ireland was prohibited, and Ireland was assigned the much more labour-intensive production of linen. One of the pamphlets lobbying for the legislation prohibiting the export of woollen textiles from Ireland, argues that since Ireland was able to produce woollen manufactures cheaper than England, woollen manufacturers in England would be unemployed and will have to go to Ireland for work, 'which means that in time the whole trade would most probably be establish'd there, and lost here'.[110] Because the colony threatened the manufacturing base of the mother country, manufacturing had to be shut down in the colony. In order to defend this *targeted underdevelopment,* the author of 1698 lists the measures of the other European colonial powers in order to show that these countries in no way treat their colonies better than the English treat Ireland. The full title of this pamphlet, in footnote 110, gives important clues to the essence of colonialism, which still today is not well understood.

As regards colonialism, Adam Smith and David Ricardo represent a real watershed in economics. It is only with their barter-based – rather than production-based – economic theories that colonialism becomes morally defensible. Perhaps the greatest novelty in Adam Smith is that he makes all economic activities ***qualitatively alike*** as carriers of economic growth. Only with this theoretical innovation can world trade – as it is today – be pictured as a system that creates automatic

109. This is supported by Roscher, Wilhelm, 'Der sächsische Nationalökonom Johann Heinrich Gottlob von Justi', p. 91.

110. Clement, S., *The Interest of England, as it Stands with the Trade of Ireland, Considered; the Arguments Against the Bill for Prohibiting the Exportation of Woollen Manufactures from Ireland to Forreign Parts, Fairly Discusst, and the Reasonableness and Necessity of England's Restraining her Colonies in all Matters of Trade, that may be Prejudicial to her Own Commerce, Clearly Demonstrated,* London: John Attwood, 1698, p. 3.

harmony. Colonialism became defensible only within an economic theory where national wealth grows independently of what the nation produces.

Adam Smith's attempts to convince his readers that all economic activities are of equal quality as carriers of economic growth, is perhaps the least convincing part of the *Wealth of Nations*. In order to create this proof, Smith has to make the creation of knowledge into a zero-sum game: 'the cost of apprenticeship accounts for the wages of manufacturers being higher than those of country labour.'[111]. There are therefore no advantages to manufacturing over agriculture, although the earnings in manufacturing 'may be somewhat greater, it seems evidently, however, to be **no greater than what is sufficient to compensate the superior expense of their education**' (emphasis added). In other words, the mercantilist tradition that nations who export the products from professions of higher skills will be wealthier than nations exporting products with low skills is here – really for the first time – strongly refuted. From the point of view of both society and the individual, adding knowledge to labour is, in Smith's system, clearly a zero-sum game.[112] Here Adam Smith's views stand in deep contrast to the eighteenth-century continental economic tradition, where the cult of new knowledge is a key feature.[113]

Sometimes Adam Smith – the mercantilist – contradicts Adam Smith, the liberalist. While the importance of knowledge is belittled throughout the *Wealth of Nations* – one of Smith's points of attack is against the apprentice system instituted by Elizabeth I – in this context, when it comes to convincing the world about the unimportance of manufacturing, the cost of knowledge, 'the superior expenses of their education' as Smith says, which is needed to get into manufacturing is so high as to make manufacturing unprofitable for other nations'. When it comes to warfare, a similar contradiction appears. In one section of his great book, Adam Smith claims that only a nation with manufacturing capacities will be able to win a war, while in another section he claims that an attempt by the American colonies to get into manufacturing will not be to their advantage. No wonder parts of Adam Smith's *Wealth of Nations* were viewed with healthy scepticism on the continent and in the United States throughout the nineteenth century.

9. Schumpeter on pre-Smithian economics

> *'The usual attitude towards what it has been agreed to call "mercantilism" is double unjust: either it is denounced for comprising a notion it continually criticised (the intrinsic value of metal as the principle of wealth), or it is revealed as a series of immediate contradictions: it is accused of defining money in its pure function as a sign while insisting upon its accumulation as a commodity; of recognising the importance of*

111. Smith ([1776]/1976), *Wealth of Nations*. Chicago: University of Chicago Press, p. 114.
112. This aspect in Adam Smith's work – making, for the first time, economic activities qualitatively alike – is discussed in Reinert, Erik, 'The Role of the State in Economic Growth', *Journal of Economic Studies*, Vol. 26, No. 4/5, 1999, pp. 268-326, A shorter version is published in Toninelli, Pier Angelo (ed.) *The Rise and Fall of State-Owned Enterprises in the Western World.*, Cambridge: Cambridge University Press, 2000, pp. 73-99
113. See Reinert, 'The Role of the State in Economic Growth', section 9, for a discussion.

quantitative fluctuations in specie, while misunderstanding their action upon prices; of being protectionist while basing its mechanism for the increase of wealth upon exchange. In fact, these contradictions or hesitations exist only if one confronts mercantilism with a dilemma that could have no meaning for it: that of money as a commodity or as a sign.'

– Michel Foucault[114]

Once the productivity explosions of the first industrial revolution had started snowballing across Europe, the painstaking groundwork of the early economists – which had taken between two and three hundred years – was expelled from what became economic theory. The welfare, the institutions, the innovations, the popular attitudes towards progress and the mechanisms of 'good governance' that these early economists had created, started to be taken for granted, as spontaneous products of an invisible hand. With 'Adam Smith Mark II', the Adam Smith of *the Wealth of Nations*, economics became *catallectics*: the science of exchange, of supply and demand of something that has already been invented and produced outside what became the narrowly defined sphere of economics. After A. Smith converted production and trade into one category, by reducing everything to 'labour time' void of any skills or other qualities, economics became, as nineteenth-century German economists would complain, a science of barter consisting of *qualitätslose Größen,* quantities void of any qualities. Economics became a science of allocation of already existing wealth rather than a science of the creation of new wealth, and a *ceteris paribus* mode of thinking abstracted from the complicated, but crucially important synergies of society.

With Adam Smith the tools used in the painstaking process of creating the productive civilization of Europe, slowly built brick by brick and institution by institution, were cancelled both from the toolbox and from the collective memory of the economics profession. As one economist put it in 1840: 'The delusion that security of life and property, the productivity of labor, and the consequent possibility of adquisition and enjoyment, and even the elevation of the spiritual and the ennobling of the moral nature – that these goods came to Man in the gift of gratuities, is itself a proof of the advanced stage of culture which the greater part of Europe at present occupies. As the grown man has long since forgotten the pains it cost him to learn to speak, so have the peoples, in the days of their mature growth of the State, forgotten what was required in order to free them from their primitive brutal savagery' (Johann Gottfried Hoffmann, quoted in Cohn 1895: 60). In this process the economists who built the institutional foundation that made the Industrial Revolution possible disappeared as 'bad economists'. This Industrial Revolution was in full swing as Adam Smith wrote his *Wealth of Nations*, but there is no indication that he was aware of it.

One generation after Hoffman, Gustav Cohn, another German economist, picks up his argument and continues: 'In point of fact, how significant was the involuntary testimony which the eighteenth Century, with its repudiation of the historic State and

114. Foucault, Michael, *The Order of Things. An Archaeology of the Human Sciences*, London: Routledge, 1966/2002, p. 192.

its yearning after the primordial state of nature, bore to the blessings of the inherited culture which it ungratefully enjoyed' (Cohn 1895: 60–61). This description – written more than 100 years ago – also fits the Zeitgeist of today, and it constitutes a serious impediment for our understanding of the continued underdevelopment of large parts of the Third World.

The 'Midas Legend' established by Adam Smith – that the economists before him were only interested in gold – became deeply entrenched in the mind of a majority of theoretical economists in the nineteenth century. Anyone who dared to comment positively on economic theory before Adam Smith could make Werner Sombart's words his own: 'I say this in spite of the risk of being branded as a neo-mercantilist, and as such to be transferred into the collection of the oddities of the profession.'[115]

Joseph Alois Schumpeter wrote what is certainly the most encyclopaedic of all histories of economic thought, *the History of Economic Analysis.*[116] Schumpeter's analysis differs from most other such works in his lack of enthusiasm for the economics of Adam Smith. Schumpeter argues, quite correctly in our view, that Adam Smith's *Wealth of Nations* – the most famous economics book ever – 'does not contain a single *analytic* idea, principle, or method that was entirely new in 1776'.[117] Schumpeter's comments on the physiocrats, the inspirers of 'Adam Smith Mark II', the school which today is considered the starting point of economics, were equally impolite: 'It's analytical merit is negligible, but all the greater was its success.'[118]

Schumpeter is right. Even the division of labour, Smith's engine of growth, can be traced back to Xenophon's *Poroi*, and William Petty, who died 99 years before the publication of *the Wealth of Nations,* describes the division of labour in a clock factory. The most remarkable, and at the same time most unknown precedent, however, is that of Ernst Ludwig Carl (1682–1743), a German economist in French service, who wrote a three-volume work on economics more than 50 years before Adam Smith (1722–23), using the pin factory as his example for describing the principle of the division of labour, the same example that made Adam Smith famous and is assumed to be his original idea.

Schumpeter is very enthusiastic about the Italian economists who continued the Renaissance tradition of the common weal. Here are some selections:

> But the honors of the field of pre-Smithian system production should go to the eighteenth-century Italians. In intent, scope, and plan their works were in the tradition that has been illustrated by the examples of Carafa and Justi; they were systems of political economy in the sense of welfare economics – the old scholastic Public Good and the specifically utilitarian Happiness meeting in their concept of welfare (*felicità pubblica).*

115. 'Ich sage das auf die Gefahr hin, als Neo-Merkantilist abgestempelt und in das Raritätenkabinett unseres Faches übergeführt zu werden', Sombart, Werner, *Der moderne Kapitalismus,* Vol. 2: *Das europäische Wirtschaftsleben im Zeitalter des Frühkapitalismus,* p. 925.
116. New York: Oxford University Press, 1954.
117. *History of Economic Analysis*, p. 184.
118. *op.cit.*, p. 175.

> 'Count Pietro Verri (1728-97) ... would have to be included in any list of the greatest economists ... he knew how to weave fact-finding and theory into a coherent tissue: the methodological problem that agitated later generations of economists he had successfully solved for himself.' (p. 178)

> 'Beccaria, the Italian A. Smith ... Both were sovereign lords of a vast intellectual realm that extended far beyond what, even then, was possible for ordinary mortals to embrace ... A. Smith's life work contains no match for *Dei delitti e delle pene*, but his *Moral Sentiments* are more than a match for Beccaria's aesthetics.' (p. 179–80, see also pp. 180–81)

Equally surprising is Schumpeter's treatment of Johann Heinrich Gottlob von Justi (1717–1771). Schumpeter heads his section on Justi in the *History of Economic Analysis* with the title 'Justi: The Welfare State'.[119] Since Schumpeter was not particularly enthusiastic about the welfare state, his later praise of Justi is all the more significant. In the comment on Justi below, Schumpeter succinctly states a typical pre-Smithian attitude to technological change and economic policy. Justi was the first to establish economic policy and public administration as a separate science – as **Policey-Wissenschaft** – the science of policy. Schumpeter's description of Justi's economics gives us a flair of the pre-Smithian mainstream, and indicates how Justi and his contemporaries integrated technology into their analysis:

> 'He (Justi) saw the practical argument for laissez-faire not less clearly than did A. Smith, and his bureaucracy, while guiding and helping when necessary, was always ready to efface itself when no guidance or help seemed needed. (Schumpeter's footnote here: "This was not merely a dream. It will be pointed out below that the bureaucracy in the typical German principality actually tried to behave like this.") Only he saw much more clearly than did the latter all the obstacles that stood in the way of its working according to design. Also, he was much more concerned than A. Smith with the practical problems of government action in the short-run vicissitudes of his time and country, and with particular difficulties in which private initiative fails or would have failed under the conditions of German industry of his time. His laissez-faire was a laissez-faire plus watchfulness, his private-enterprise economy a machine that was logically automated but exposed to breakdowns and hitches which his government was ready to mend. For instance, he accepted as a matter of course that the introduction of labour-saving machinery would cause unemployment: but this was no argument against the mechanization of production because, also as a matter of course, *his* government would find equally good employment for the unemployed. This, however, is not inconsistency, but sense. And to us who are apt to agree with him much more than we do with A. Smith, his (Justi's) vision of economic policy might look like **laissez-faire with the nonsense left out**.'(p. 172, emphasis added)

---

119. *op.cit.*, p. 170.

Section II: National Innovation Systems and Their Countervailing Forces in the International Economy: A Brief Outline

The interest in the history of economic policy reflected in the first section of this chapter is not a result of an interest in history *per se*, but part of an attempt to understand why the presently poor nations stayed poor by understanding how the rich nations got rich. In our view the concept of National Innovation Systems is also a most appropriate tool in which to understand economic successes of the past.

A future second part of this ongoing work is a description of the forces that keep the Second and Third World today from following the same path previously followed by the rich: why development in recent decades points to nations clustering in two convergence groups, one wealthy and one poor. This section gives a brief outline, almost in bullet point form, of what in our opinion prevents the success story of the First World from being repeated. In our view the National Innovation System approach – we would suggest also equipped with the extended toolbox of the German Historical School of Economics – is a useful starting point.

Schumpeter is the economist to study in order to understand the path of virtuous circles leading Mankind towards the never-ending frontier of knowledge. However, we would argue that in order to understand the situation of the Third World we must recognize that the opposite mechanisms, uncovered by the 'dismal science' of Robert Malthus and David Ricardo, are still there, alive and well, if the critical mass of increasing returns activities is removed from a nation.[120] Myrdal's mechanisms of vicious circles and 'perverse backwashes' are still working, although they are not found in the nations that have established their comparative advantage in increasing returns industries, from which the virtuous circles originate.

In a world where everything is globalized except the labour market, Friedrich List's distinction between the *Cosmopolitical* School of Economics generally focused on barter and trade, and the School of *National* Economics, focusing on production, is as valid as ever before. The policies of the Washington Consensus are open to most, if not all, the criticisms List had against the Cosmopolitical School of Economics. It is particularly interesting that List, also quoting our Renaissance hero Antonio Serra (1613), rebuilds the argument of the synergies created by the cities as the cradle of personal freedom, civil liberties, above-subsistence income, democracies, the arts – in short, of civilization as we know it.

When increasing returns activities are gone, whole economies may embark down the path of diminishing returns, creating a situation where, as David Ricardo predicted, wages will be hovering around subsistence level. As John Stuart Mill described it, the nation with natural resource monoculture hits a 'flexible wall' because one factor of

120. 'Globalisation in the Periphery as a Morgenthau Plan: The Underdevelopment of Mongolia in the 1990's', in Sakhia Lhagva (ed.), *Mongolian Development Strategy; Capacity Building*, Ulaanbaatar: Mongolian Development Research Center, 2000. Also chapter 8 in this volume.

production has its quantity and quality determined by an act of God.[121] Clearly these diminishing returns activities – now more than ever before – are subject to rapid technological change. However, technical change in an enclave economy based on the production of raw materials – in the absence of a functioning National Innovation System – spreads in a completely different way than in a nation with a critical mass of increasing returns activities.

One factor at work is that technological change in raw material production makes it profitable to utilize more marginal land and more marginal mines, so that part of the fruits of technical change is 'used up' to compensate for inferior inputs of land or ore. Another important factor is the effects of 'commodity competition' rather than 'Schumpeterian dynamic imperfect competition'. In such a situation technical change and productivity improvements are not captured in the producing nation itself. This was an essential argument of traditional development economics – probably best presented by Hans Singer, Schumpeter's student in Bonn.[122] No doubt this insight was strongly reinforced by the collapse of the agricultural prices, also in the North, during the 1930s, while prices in the industrial sector were protected from such reversals by a built-in ratchet wheel effect, created by imperfect competition both in the product markets and in the labour market ('stickiness' of prices and wages in the industrial sector).

1. National Innovation Systems vs. Global Primitivization Systems: An uphill fight

Once the idea of the possibility of progress, of improving the lot of Mankind by adding new knowledge, innovations and their institutions, has been established, it becomes clear that the opposite phenomenon – *retrogression* or *primitivization* – is also possible. Indeed the underlying idea of the Renaissance – of *re-birth* – is that the late Medieval world was in a suboptimal situation compared to previous achievements of Mankind. During the Renaissance the Greek texts that seeped into Italy after the fall of Constantinople were a proof of this. Another visible and tangible proof of retrogression was the sheep grazing among the magnificent ruins of Ancient Rome, indeed a frequent illustration also in early travel books. Early economists recognized the urban bias of early economic growth (Botero 1588, Serra 1613) just as economic historians do today, and it was clear that Rome had retrogressed from advanced urbanism to a stage of herding and pasturage.

In the economics of Gunnar Myrdal, a corollary to the virtuous circles of development were the *vicious circles* of underdevelopment and the *perverse backwashes* that were

121. Reinert, *International Trade and the Economic Mechanisms of Underdevelopment (1980)*, shows how the main export activities in twentieth-century Peru, Ecuador and Bolivia were all producing far into the realm of diminishing returns. This was shown clearly when production fell, labour productivity increased.

122. Singer, Hans W., 'The Distribution of Gains between Investing and Borrowing Countries', in *International development: Growth and Change,* New York, McGraw-Hill, 1964. (Paper originally presented in 1949 and published in 1950).

produced in the world economy. A typical perverse backwash effect in today's world economy is that capital tends to flow from the poor countries to the rich. These effects are normally not visible in nations where increasing returns and increasing diversification and their virtuous circles have achieved a strong foothold, but they are clearly present in the context of most Third World countries. In our view, it is imperative that these countervailing effects – working against the establishment of National Innovation Systems – are taken into consideration. We have argued that these effects frequently take the form of *lock-in effects;* nations may end up being specialized in economic activities at the dead-end of technological trajectories and bereft of any scale effects. We would argue that the pattern of production and world division of labour established under colonialism set most of today's poor nations on a different path than that of the North, and that there are very strong systemic effects which today reinforce their specialization in being poor. The de-industrialization of so many small and medium-sized peripheral nations over the last 20 years coupled with the present free trade ideology makes the establishment of ***genuinely wealth-producing NIS*** – as opposed to innovation systems where all the fruits of innovation go to the consumers in export markets – more difficult than ever before. This section is an attempt to identify and classify the elements of this systemic lock-in effect in poverty.

We would argue that dynamic mercantilist economic policy at best – in its combination of tools including a systemic furthering of innovation in most European countries through patents and protection (see Appendix I) – for so many centuries found its modern expression in the world of business in the 1970s through the work of Boston Consulting Group (BCG). This world-wide consulting firm became famous in the world of business for the creation of two tools which helped companies survive in a world dominated by dynamic Schumpeterian competition. The first tool was 'The Experience Curve', essentially a learning curve plotting total cost rather than labour hours on the vertical axis.[123] The second tool was the product portfolio, a matrix where mature cash-cows continuously finance innovations that in their turn become the cash-cows of the future.[124] In our view this theory emulates the cult of manufacturing and mechanization so typical of the best mercantilists; making sure all European nations got into the cash-cows requiring new skills, creating national productivity explosions and steep learning curves. The policy towards the colonies, however, caused these nations to be stuck in what BCG calls 'dog industries', activities bereft of increasing returns, with very little growth, and with the low profitability and few linkages of commodity competition.

This section of the chapter, then, presents a brief outline of the forces that make it is so difficult today to reproduce the conditions that – in the North – created functioning National Innovation Systems. We attempt to produce a taxonomy of the combined cumulative negative effects of policy decisions and market forces that mutually reinforce

123. Boston Consulting Group, *Perspectives on Experience,* Boston: BCG, 1972, Reinert, *International Trade and the Economic Mechanisms of Underdevelopment* (1980), Stern, Carl W and George Stalk Jr., *Perspectives on Strategy from The Boston Consulting Group,* New York: Wiley, 1998.

124. Stern & Stalk, *Perspectives on Strategy from The Boston Consulting Group*, p. 37. This matrix is also found in Porter 1980.

each other and in many countries have produced economic retrogression and falling national welfare. These are the mechanisms that create vicious circles that are reproduced in a market system, and against which any attempt to create National Innovation Systems in the Third World would have to fight as a form of 'economic gravity'. In short, we argue, in the spirit of Myrdal, that there are always – and particularly at present – market-, technology- and policy-based countervailing forces that work against any will and intention to introduce Nation Innovation Systems in the Third World. We would argue that since the early 1990s these forces are cumulatively so strong that they might be called a 'Global Primitivization System'. The factors outlined below must be seen as being as systemic as those of a NIS, but working ***against*** development rather than in its favour, frequently mutually reinforcing each other.

2. The Washington Consensus and the reduction of diversity: De-industrialization and the creation of de-facto Morgenthau Plans

In the NIS approach, increasing returns, innovations and economic diversity/large division of labour is at the core of the system (Lundvall 1992). In our view the phenomenon of increasing returns is at the core of these effects, being the key producer of dynamic synergies. We should keep in mind that Schumpeter coined the term ***historical increasing returns*** in order to discuss the combined effects of technological change and increasing returns; the two effects being separable in theory but frequently not in practice because previous technologies often do not exist in the old scale.[125] Technological change under diminishing returns – where the supply of one factor of production is limited and produced in different qualities by an act of God – although frequently formidable, obeys different rules, as we have argued previously.

Since the late 1980s, de-industrialization has been a key feature of a large number of developing countries, particularly small and medium-sized. Reinert (2004) contains case studies of the Mongolian and Peruvian economies documenting this phenomenon. Mongolia was the best pupil of the Washington Institutions, and opened up the country for trade almost overnight in the early 1990s. The result is that a large number of Mongolian manufacturing industries have seen their volume of output contract by more than 80 per cent, and many branches of industry have disappeared completely. In other words, the nation has both been de-industrialized and de-diversified. The only manufacturing industry that has shown an increase in production in Mongolia is the collection of bird-feathers, producing combed down. Closing steel-mills and increasing the collection of bird-feathers is in our view an example of *primitivization* of an economy.

125. This raises the issue of minimum efficient sizes of production. One could perhaps argue that the latest techno-economic paradigm has reduced the minimum efficient size of production (in the sense of batch sizes) but perhaps raised the minimum efficient size of production *systems* in many areas?

Figure 11.4 The virtuous circles of Marshall Plans.

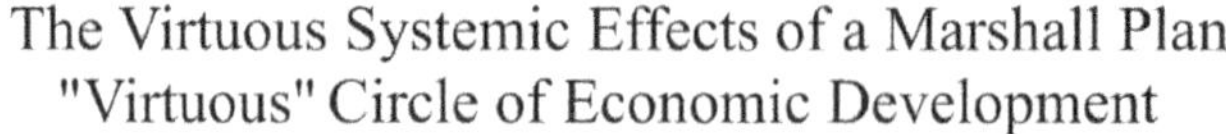

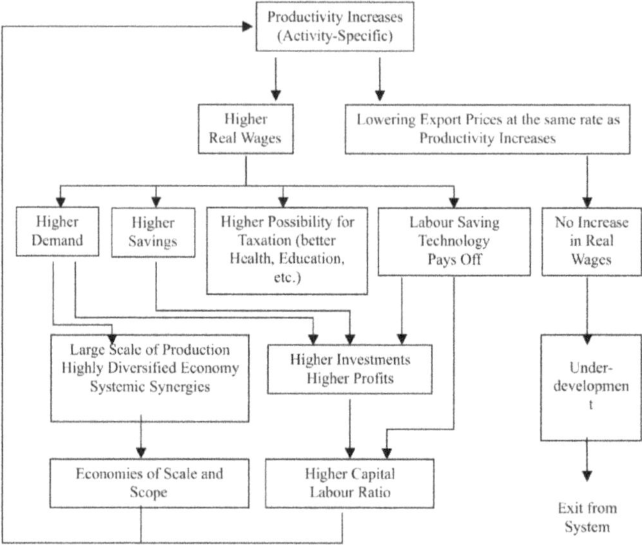

Note: In a closed system, with constant employment rate, the only way GNP per capita can grow is through the "Virtuous Circle." However, the system can be cut-off at any one point, e.g., if higher demand goes to foreign goods alone, the circle will break. *Source*: Reinert (1980) *op.cit.* p. 39.

We have argued[126] that two ideal types of economic policies may be established – one based on increasing returns activities and the other on nations without any increasing returns activities – one creating virtuous and the other creating vicious circles in the economy. We have named economic policies that create the vortices of, respectively, wealth and poverty after two types of economic strategies that were developed and – like the atomic bomb – tried out in the field in the 1940s: Marshall Plans and Morgenthau Plans. We shall claim that virtual virtuous circles of development are the result of a set of policies that we refer to generically as Marshall Plans. The opposite effect, vicious circles, is the result of the Morgenthau Plans.

The purpose of the Morgenthau Plan – named after Henry Morgenthau Jr., the US secretary of the treasury from 1934 to 1945 – was to prevent Germany, which had caused two wars in the twentieth century, ever from starting a war again. This was to be achieved by de-industrializing Germany and make it a pastoral state, taking all industrial machinery out of Germany and filling the mines with water. The plan was

126. Reinert, Erik S., 'Increasing Poverty in a Globalised World: *Marshall Plans* and *Morgenthau Plans* as Mechanisms of Polarisation of World Incomes', chapter 9 in this volume.

Figure 11.5 The vicious circles of Morgenthau Plans.

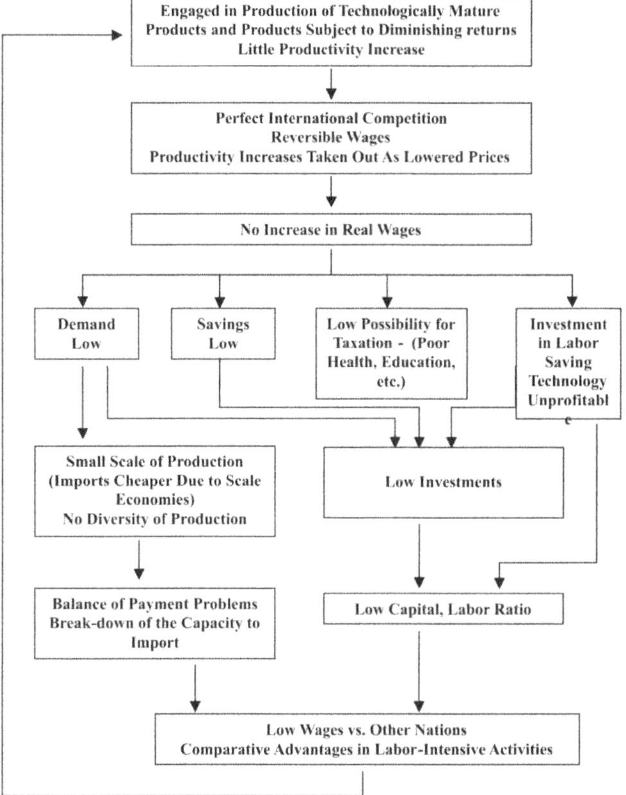

Note: It is futile to attack the system at any one point, e.g., Increasing investment when wages are still low and demand is absent. An instance of this is poor capital utilization and excess capacity in Latin American LDCs. *Source*: Reinert (1980), *op.cit*, p.41.

approved in an Allied meeting in 1943 and carried out after the German capitulation in May 1945.

The Morgenthau Plan was abruptly stopped in Germany in 1947 when ex-President Herbert Hoover of the United States reported back from Germany: 'There is the illusion that the New Germany left after the annexations can be reduced to a "pastoral state". It cannot be done unless we exterminate or move 25.000.000 out of it.' Hoover had rediscovered the wisdom of the mercantilist population theorists: an industrialized nation has a much larger carrying capacity in terms of population than an agricultural state. The de-industrialization process had also led to a sharp fall in agricultural yields and partly to an institutional collapse, giving evidence to the importance of the linkages between the industrial and agricultural sector that were also a hallmark of mercantilist economics (see section I, 7 in this chapter). Less than four months after Hoover's alarming reports from Germany, the US government announced the Marshall Plan, which aimed to achieve exactly the opposite of the Morgenthau Plan: Germany's industrial capacity was at all cost to be brought back to its 1938 level. It cannot be emphasized enough that the Marshall Plan was not a financial plan, it was a *reindustrialization plan*.

We shall claim that Morgenthau Plans, after years of neglect, were resurrected by the Washington Consensus starting in the 1980s and, even more strongly, after the end of the Cold War in 1991. De-facto Morgenthau Plans came with the label of 'structural adjustment', which very often had the effect of de-industrializing Third World nations. These two ideal types of economic policy, the Marshall Plan and the Morgenthau Plan, explain the 'virtuous' and 'vicious' circles that were fashionable, but not well explained, in the heyday of development economics during the 1950s and '60s. The crucial role of the nation-state in carrying out the right type of economic policy is discussed in Reinert (1999).

3. De-industrialization and the Vanek-Reinert Effect (winner-killing effect) of free trade

This effect is an extension both of the classical Heckscher-Ohlin model and of what in standard international trade theory is called the *Rybczynski theorem*, that – in a two-country two-factor model – the output of the commodity using extensively the factor that increases in the economy will expand and the output of the other commodity will contract. 'For instance, when only labour grows, the output of the labour-intensive commodity expands and the output of the capital-intensive commodity contracts. On the other hand, when only capital grows, the output of the capital-intensive commodity expands and the output of the labour-intensive commodity contracts.'[127]

The Vanek-Reinert effect predicts that when, following a situation of relative autarky, free trade suddenly opens up between a relatively advanced and a relatively backward nation, *the most advanced and knowledge-intensive industry* in *the least advanced country will tend to die out.* This was the case after the nineteenth-century unification of Italy and, in the 1990s, the first casualties of free trade were the Czech and Brazilian computer industries. In extreme cases of this Vanek-Reinert effect, nations become nearly completely deindustrialized as was the case of Mongolia in the 1990s.[128] The most advanced nations specialize in capital- and innovation-intensive goods, while the less advanced countries specialize in maquila-type low-technology goods. A frequent effect of this is that free trade destroys more than it contributes in terms of national wealth; we experience cases of 'destructive destruction', destruction where no regenerative activities take place.

127. Chacholiades, Miltiades, *International Trade Theory and Policy*, New York: McGraw-Hill, 1978, p. 343.

128. See chapter 9 in this volume and Reinert 2004 for a further discussion.

Trade theorist Jaroslav Vanek (of the Heckscher-Ohlin-Vanek theorem) lectured on this phenomenon as 'the herbicide effect of international trade' or 'destructive trade', and Reinert has described this as the 'winner-killing effect' (Reinert 1980). Under this 'Vanek-Reinert' effect, in a free trade regime, each nation reinforces its original comparative advantage, the wealthy First World its comparative advantage in higher skills in increasing returns industries, while the poor nations fall back on their comparative advantage in diminishing returns industries. This is what we have previously referred to as 'Schumpeterian underdevelopment'. A comparative advantage in a diminishing returns activity is a 'natural advantage', based on Nature's bounties, whereas a comparative advantage in an increasing returns activity is a 'created advantage', based on Man's inventiveness and skills. Historically a nation's transition from having a comparative advantage in resource-based diminishing returns activities to a comparative advantage in increasing returns knowledge-based activities has required extremely strong policy measures and periods of heavily managed international trade policy.

This perspective is in our view a most important one for National Innovation Systems, because it opens up for nations to specialize in economic activities which have the least possibilities for innovation and growth: activities subject to diminishing returns, activities bereft of any scale effects, dead-end activities left over from long mature paradigms, activities that are virtually unmechanizable at any reasonable cost with present technological knowledge and with cheap labour available, but for which there is still demand. In other words, it opens up for the possibility of nations to specialize in producing goods with a very limited potential for innovation, requiring very low skills, it opens up for specializing in being poor inside the international division of labour.

The problem is that once a gap in skills and wages is established, the market will automatically assign low-skill/low-wage activities to the nations that are poor and unskilled. This is the basic logic behind the new global supply chains and maquila-type activities. In our view, this represents a kind of 'economic gravity' that makes it particularly difficult to construct National Innovation Systems. This is because the areas where innovations occur will automatically be brought back to the core countries, as the low cost of labour is no longer a necessary competitive factor in this activity.

High market share is no guarantee for wealth. Honduras and Haiti dominate the world market for a manufactured product: Baseballs, produced mainly for the US market. This product illustrates in our view a classic case of Schumpeterian underdevelopment. The world's most efficient golf ball producers are located in New Bedford, Massachusetts, and are paid wages of about 12 dollars an hour. The world's most efficient baseball producers are located in Honduras and in Haiti, working 10 hours per day for an hourly wage of about 25 cents. The wage ratio between the two groups of workers, both in the same industry producing balls for sport and both being the most efficient in the world, is about 48 to 1 in nominal terms. This happens in spite of the fact that any person sewing baseballs in the United States would *not* be more efficient than the Haitians. These are the 'unequal exchange' effects of Schumpeterian underdevelopment.

The *characteristics of the product* 'baseballs' itself contain the elements of poverty and underdevelopment. No new skills are developed because there is no *demand* for new skills. No learning-by-doing takes place in Haiti, because there is no learning taking place in baseball production *anywhere.*[129] The Haitians are not working with capital and with machines, because not even all the capital of the United States has managed to mechanize baseball production. More education in Haiti will lead to migration, because there is no demand for skills. Haiti is locked into poverty,[130] specialized in being poor within the international division of labour. And, importantly, there are no market forces in sight that could conceivably change this situation. A mechanization of baseball production would simply take this industry back to the United States, just as the cutting of fabrics was removed from the Central American assembly *maquilas* the moment laser cutting became available. The mercantilists told us that economic growth was *activity-specific* – it happened in some industries and not in others. In our view they were right.

Rapid technological change of the nineteenth century created what came to be called 'the social question' in Europe, growing economic inequality and increasing misery in the middle of a technological revolution. Among the most miserable were the 'home workers', specializing in the non-mechanized routine economic activities that had not become part of the industrial factory. In our view the *maquila* system raises similar problems: global supply chains filter out the technological dead-ends and farm them out to the Third World. From a cost-reduction point of view this is perfectly logical. However, the result is that old 'inefficient' import substitution industrialization produced higher real wages in a large number of Latin American countries than the maquila activities do today.[131] These nations specialize in routine activities where the scope for innovation is minimal,[132] an important aspect of the phenomenon we have called 'Schumpeterian underdevelopment'.

The Schumpeterian Quality Index of Economic Activities ranks activities dynamically according to their potential for dynamic imperfect competition. It is our contention that a premature and too rapid globalization causes a large number of Third World countries to lose the 'high-quality' activities and to specialize in 'low-quality jobs' like baseball production.

---

129. Had the poor Haitians not been available, the high cost of sewing would probably have led to mechanization of baseball production. The availability of poor workers provides a disincentive for innovations.
130. See Arthur, Brian, 'Competing Technologies, Increasing Returns and Lock-in by Historical Events', *Economic Journal*, Vol. 99, 1989. Reinert frequently uses the lock-in concept in this context of being locked into poverty. See also Cimoli, Mario, 'Networks, Market Structure and Economic Shocks, the structural Changes of Innovation Systems in Latin America', Paper presented at the seminar 'The Other Canon in Economics', Oslo, August 2000.
131. Roca, Santiago and Luis Simabuko, 'Natural Resources, Industrialization and Fluctuating Standards of Living in Peru 1950-97: A Case Study of Activity-Specific Economic Growth, in Reinert 2004, pp. 115-156.
132. See also Audretsch, David, 'Diversity: Implications for Income Distribution', in Reinert (ed.), 2004, pp-288-308..

Figure 11.6 The Quality Index of Economic Activities.

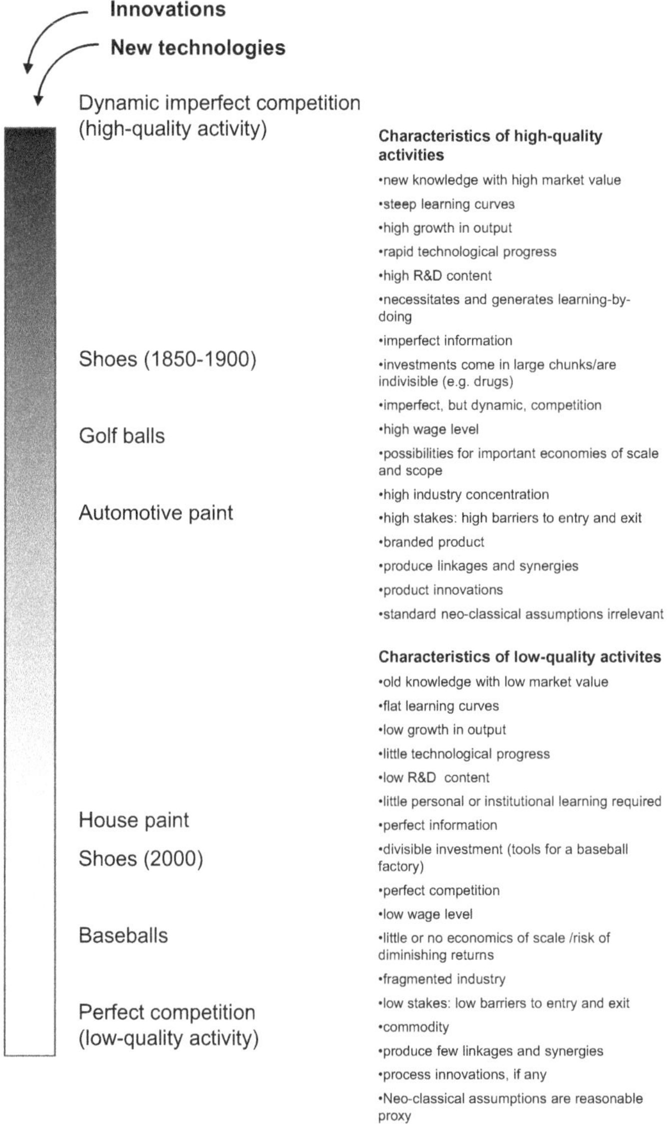

4. *De-industrialization and falling terms of trade*

The development of Terms of Trade is admittedly a complex issue, but it is remarkable that the terms of trade in some small Latin American nations peaked during the period of highest industrial development, in the 1970s. De-industrialization and falling terms of trade seem to be connected, a phenomenon that can be explained by a combination of two factors. The collapse of trade union power and the loss of industrial employment removed the floor of the labour market, creating falling wages. The pressures of the

Figure 11.7 Peru's Terms of Trade 1950–2000. 1979=100. Connecting de-industrialisation and falling terms of trade: the collapse of the industrial sector makes real wages reversible.

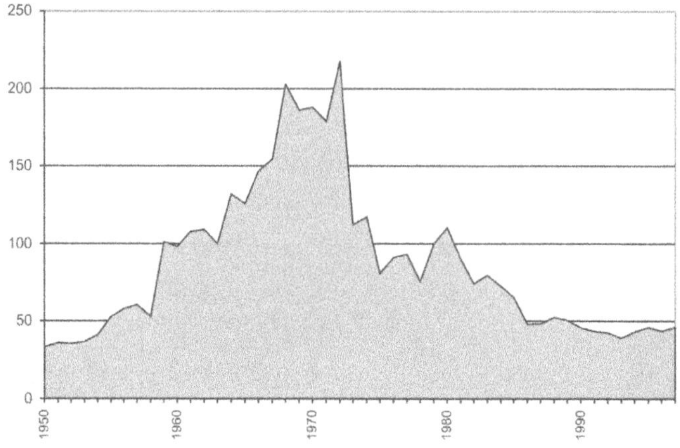

international commodity markets could then press down both the relative price of the commodity and of national wages. With no alternative employment for the workforce, commodity production could also spread into the areas of diminishing returns, reducing the marginal productivity of labour.[133] A self-reinforcing vicious circle has been created, and can only be stopped by introducing increasing returns activities to the nation.

The early twentieth-century Australian argument for the creation of an industrial sector, albeit not internationally competitive, was an argument for preventing exactly this chain of events from taking place. The existence of an alternative labour market in the manufacturing sector would prevent wool production from going into marginal areas by creating a 'wage floor', under which wages would not move, not even in the commodity sector.[134]

5. *Product life-cycles and innovation systems*

The product life-cycle theories in international trade created in the late 1960s and early 1970s by Ray Vernon and Louis Wells are in our view extremely relevant for a discussion of the construction of National Innovation Systems in the Third World.[135] These life-cycles are clearly also tied to technological trajectories. We have argued that

133. Reinert, *International Trade and the Economic Mechanisms of Underdevelopment*(1980), documents several cases of this.

134. Davidson, Frank G. *The Industrialization of Australia* (1969), Melbourne: Melbourne University Press. See also Reinert (1980), pp. 71-73.

135. Vernon, Raymond, 'International Investment and International Trade in the Product Cycle', *Quarterly Journal of Economics*, Vol. 80, May 1966, pp. 190–207. Wells, Louis, *The Product Life Cycle and International Trade,* Boston: Harvard Business School, 1972. This issue is also extensively discussed in Reinert, *International Trade and the Economic Mechanisms of Underdevelopment.*

the understanding of life-cycles both of products and technologies are important factors which must be considered when understanding what we have called 'Schumpeterian Underdevelopment'.[136]

Poor countries will automatically have a comparative advantage in mature products towards the end of the product life cycle, thus impeding the potential for innovation. This argument is closely related to point 3 above.

6. The perils of the commodity lottery

Some years ago economic historians introduced the term 'commodity lottery' when discussing economic development. We find that this is a useful term, since the characteristics of different commodities will shape national economies in many ways: the 'commodity lottery' will in many ways shape the national economy and determine the potential for cultivating a National Innovation System.

Some natural resources produce linkages to knowledge-intensive sectors more than others. In the early twentieth century, waterfalls for the production of electricity were perfect examples of these kinds of 'enforced linkages': the loss of energy was, at the time, so high per kilometre that the new industrial centres based on electricity had to be built directly under the waterfall. In contrast the smelting of Bolivian zinc was done in England for the longest time. One particularly interesting example is by Cuban social scientist Fernando Ortiz, who – in his book 'Cuban Counterpoint' – shows how sugar brings slavery, ignorance and poverty in the Eastern part of Cuba, whereas tobacco brings private smallholdings, knowledge and welfare in the Western part of the island.[137]

As the students of the Dutch Republic and of Venice of old claimed – and today one might add of Japan and Switzerland – the best draw in the commodity lottery was to have no commodity: this forced the nation directly into a man-made, rather than a nature-based, comparative advantage, subject to increasing rather than diminishing returns. Montesquieu notes:

> The barrenness of the earth renders men industrious, sober, inured to hardship, courageous, and fit for war; they are obliged to procure by labor what the earth refuses to bestow spontaneously.[138]

136. Reinert, Erik S, 'The role of Technology in the Creation of Rich and Poor Nations: Underdevelopment in a Schumpeterian System', in Aldcroft, Derek H. and Ross Catterall (eds.), *Rich Nations - Poor Nations. The Long Run Perspective*, Aldershot: Edward Elgar, 1996.
137. Ortiz, Fernando, *Cuban Counterpoint. Tobacco and Sugar*, Alfred A. Knopf, New York, 1947
138. *The Spirit of the Laws*, New York: Hafner, 1949, p. 273.

7. Technological change and diminishing returns

'The fact that there are increasing returns is wonderful news. If something gets better, as it's more used, this is great news; if something gets cheaper the more it is produced, that's wonderful. Diminishing returns made Carlyle call economics a dismal science. Increasing returns maybe makes economics a cheerful science'
W. Brian Arthur, interview in *Pretext*, May 1998.

Technological change has been very rapid in agriculture, fishing and mining. This does not, however, mean that diminishing returns are no longer in operation. We find that John Stuart Mill's term 'the flexible wall of diminishing returns' is a useful one. If diminishing returns are reached e.g. in fisheries, there are always a few more fish which can be caught, but at rapidly increasing costs. If the number of animals on the steppe is increased, there is room for more until there is a severe winter. Diminishing returns constitutes 'a highly elastic and extensible band, which is hardly ever so violently stretched that it could not possibly be stretched any more, yet the pressure of which is felt long before the final limit is reached, and felt more severely the nearer that limit is approached'.[139]

We have argued for the perils to welfare and to the environment inherent in a global economy where a large number of nations become de-industrialized without international mobility of labour.[140] These nations will constantly be butting against Mill's 'flexible wall', and as Alfred Marshall pointed out in his *Principles*, the mass migrations of world history have their origin in diminishing returns. This is, in our view, a compelling reason against the de-industrialization that has taken place in so many countries over the last decade and a half. In Mongolia de-industrialization and the return to pastoral activities have led to overgrazing. Mongolia was grazing animals at the outer limits of this 'elastic band', and a climatic change that was within the normal range wiped out between 2 and 3 Million animals during the winter of 2001–02. This was, however, only a small portion of the total number of animals that had been added to the Mongolian economy as the previously urban industrial and government workers who lost their jobs had had to return to the countryside.[141]

'Mercantilist' industrial policy – from Henry VII in 1485 through Korea in the 1960s – is, in a nutshell, essentially only a dynamic version of an industrial policy which Alfred Marshall recommends in the first edition of his *Principles*: 'A tax ...on the production of goods which obey the Law of Diminishing Returns, and devoting the tax to a bounty on the production of those goods with regard to which the Law of Increasing Returns acts sharply.'[142] In 1923, Frank Graham repeated this kind of argument, which was to become the core of 'New International Trade Theory'.[143]

139. Mill, John Stuart, *Principles of Political Economy*, London: Parker, 1848, p. 177.
140. See chapter 5 in this volume
141. Statistics are found in chapter 8 in this volume
142. Marshall, Alfred, *Principles of Economics*, London, Macmillan, 1890, p. 452.
143. Graham, Frank, 'Some Aspects of Protection Further Considered', in *Quarterly Journal of Economics*, Vol. 37, 1923, pp. 199–227.

Figure 11.8 Ecuador: Diminishing returns and productivity development in the banana industry. Production 1961–1977.

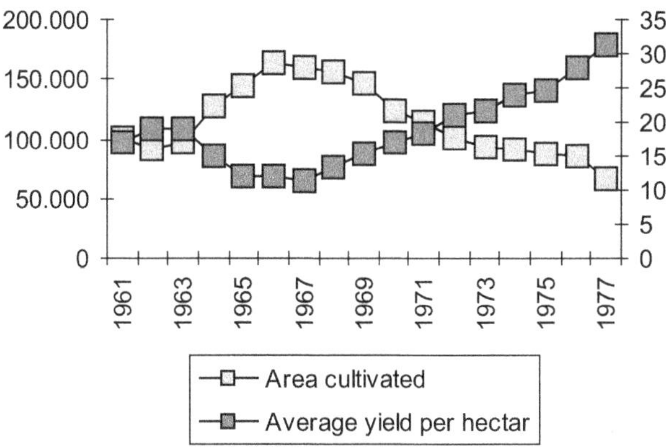

The following figure shows the fight between technological change and diminishing returns, where diminishing returns get the upper hand.

8. Resource depletion and technological retrogression

Depletion of natural resources coupled with high unemployment frequently cause technological retrogression, a phenomenon that can in some sense be seen as the opposite of a National Innovation System. The mechanisms at work are fairly straightforward: resource depletion causes expensive labour-saving technologies to be no longer profitable, and highly labour-intensive technologies requiring very poorly paid labour take over. This retrogression is strongly tied to the phenomenon of diminishing returns (see above) in combination with a lack of alternative employment opportunities.

Sylvi Endresen at the University of Oslo has worked for decades documenting technological retrogression, among them in fisheries in Sri Lanka and India.[144] When fishing resources are depleted, it is no longer profitable to use large ocean-going boats or – in the more severe cases – any boats with outboard engines, so fishing reverts to the traditional labour-intensive methods. The same phenomenon can be observed in mining industries. The miners in Potosí, Bolivia, can be seen working over the slag or refuse from previous processing in order to recuperate leftover minerals. On a visit to Tanzania, we could observe that a fall in coffee prices seemingly has had a similar 'primitivization effect' there.

The same phenomenon can of course also happen in industrialized countries, as when the consumption of diesel fuel to fish caught in certain sectors of the Norwegian coast (both measured in kilos) approached 1:1 (one kilo of diesel oil required in order

144. Endresen, Sylvi, *Technological Retrogression. A Schumpeterian Interpretation of Modernization in Reverse,* London: Anthem, 2021,

to catch one kilo of fish). The main difference is that in a developed country – where alternative employment possibilities or unemployment benefits exist – such unprofitable activities are simply shut down; they are not – as in the Third World – continued with more primitive technologies.

9. Techno-economic paradigms: central vs. peripheral effects

One underresearched aspect of Schumpeterian Development Economics is in our view how new techno-economic paradigms affect the centre and periphery differently. Carlota Perez eminently treats their cyclical aspects in terms of income distribution, and also the geographical aspects of financial crises between the core and periphery nations.[145] But in our view there are also other issues that would merit more research, issues that belong to 'Schumpeterian Development Economics'.

Human beings play two different roles in society, as consumers and as producers. When economic activities have different abilities to absorb knowledge, and when innovation in knowledge-intensive activities spread as what we have called triple-layer rent-seeking – to entrepreneurs, workers and the state – it is sometimes possible to trade off Man's role as a consumer with Man's role as a producer. By protecting knowledge-intensive industries, a nations' consumers will suffer in the short run, but in the long run their wages will rise (industrial wages are higher than agricultural wages) compared to staying in an agricultural economy. In a second round-effect goods will get cheaper again as the nation moves down the learning curve, and productivity in the agricultural sector will rise as the synergies with the manufacturing sector develop. This was the essential argument for the American System of Manufactures, which lasted in the United States from about 1820 until the end of the century.[146] In the words of Daniel Raymond, a nation could upgrade by getting more skills, just the same way a person could. For 80 years the Americans tried in vain to explain this logic to the English, but towards the end both John Stuart Mill and Alfred Marshall granted them a point.

Nations specialized in the production of paradigm-carrying activities frequently experience different effects than the consuming nations or the nations supplying the raw materials. The cotton-growing states in the United States experienced different effects than the cotton-spinning states, and in fact the friction between these two groups of states – should or should not the North try to industrialize and spin cotton – was an important element leading up to the US Civil War. The increased demand for rubber produced negative welfare effects in the rubber-producing countries. A particularly ugly case – the so-called Putumayo Affair – involving the mistreatment, slavery and brutality

145. Perez, Carlota, *Technological Revolutions and Financial Bubbles. The Dynamics of Bubbles and Golden Ages,* Cheltenham: Edward Elgar, 2002.

146. The two main authors here are Raymond, Daniel, *Principles of Political Economy*, Baltimore: Fielding Lucas, 1820 and Carey, Mathew, *Essays on Political Economy; or, the Most Certain Means of Promoting the Wealth, Power, Resources and Happiness of Nations: Applied Particularly to the United States,* Philadelphia: H.C. Carey & I. Lea, 1822. (Note the 'mercantilist' title of this US work, a collection of smaller works totalling about 550 pages.)

towards the Amazon Indian rubber collectors, created a major scandal in England and Europe in 1912–13. The sheer size of the official English documents on the affair indicates its importance at the time.[147] The North entered a new Fordist techno-economic paradigm, but the effects in the roadless Amazon periphery were mainly negative.

10. *Re-enclavization and the loss of economic diversity*

The *dual economy* was identified by early development economists as being a key characteristic of underdeveloped countries. A modern export sector – an economic enclave – was not integrated into the rest of the economy. With increasing import substitution, industrialization and a more diversified industrial sector, this contrast between the 'modern' and 'backward' sectors of the national economy was strongly reduced.

Concomitant with deindustrialization and falling protection starting in the late 1980s, many small and medium-sized poor nations saw the diversity of their productive sector strongly reduced. They were again moving towards economic monoculture based on the export of raw materials. At the same time the build-down of the state made it more difficult to monitor the (mostly foreign-owned) enclaves. One example of this was the large number of Chilean-owned mines in Peru that brought in all their needs – including food and drink – by air from Chile, bypassing any Peruvian customs. In Africa the growth of private armies seen as necessary to protect mining companies is another example of 'retrogression' taking the countries back to conditions that prevailed during the early days of colonialism. Thus many Third World countries are at present losing again developments that were seen as progress starting in the post–World War II era.

11. *Technology used for de-skilling instead of skill-creation*

This is a phenomenon which takes place in any country – both centre and periphery. New technology can be used in order to produce Burger King cashier terminals with symbols which eliminate the need for operators to be able to read and write. Such developments, however, are much more serious in developing countries where the lack of qualified jobs – the often extreme shortage of job possibilities for university graduates – is a serious problem. Not only are these countries producing far away from the production possibility frontiers, perhaps only 20–30 per cent of the economically active have what in the North would be defined as 'job', but innovations may also come in a guise which reduces the numbers of qualified jobs.

---

147. See *Report by His Majesty's Consul at Iquitos on his Tour in the Putumayo District, Presented to both Houses of Parliament by Command of His Majesty*, London: His Majesty's Stationary Office, 1913, The *Index and Digest of Evidence to the Report and Special Report from the Select Committee on Putumayo*, London: His Majesty's Stationary Office, 1913, indicates that the total number of pages in the collected reports exceed 13.000. The index itself is 90 pages folio size. There is a numerous bibliography of the events.

In a 2003 paper Mario Cimoli and Jorge Katz show these 'deskilling' effects in Argentine automotive production as regards engineers.[148] They argue that these developments 'are pushing Latin American economies into a "low development trap"'. The authors also use the term 'lock-in effects' when 'liberalization and globalization of markets in the context of competing forms under increasing returns to scale mechanism can eventually reinforce the technology gap between nations if the "destruction" of local capabilities is not compensated by technology transfers from globalised firms'.[149] This is one of the lock-in effects into relative poverty that we have referred to in several papers.

12. Increasingly footloose technological change: implications for the periphery

Geography and distance as economic factors have always worked as factors promoting the spread of production. The importance of geography as an economic factor is compounded with the factor of time: by what Alfred Chandler calls 'economies of speed'. Clearly, their relative isolation compared to the industrial powers of the world gave nineteenth-century Australia and New Zealand more 'natural protection' to native industry than did the Irish Sea for Irish industry.

Using an idea from German economist Franz Oppenheimer (1864–1943), we can imagine, as a starting point, a world void of the *costs, frictions* and *lags* created by geography and time. To this a factor representing these costs, frictions and lags of time and geography in the real world would have to be added. Oppenheimer calls this factor *Transportwiderstand*, or 'transport resistance'. Although we really intend to say 'resistance caused by time and geography', we shall stick to Oppenheimer's term, even though it sounds clumsier in English than in German. In the example above, Australia's location gives the country a higher *transport resistance* than Ireland. The transport of electricity used to have a very high transport resistance: power-intensive industries used to be located just under the waterfalls providing the electric power. Much of the turmoil in European electricity markets after 2020 has been caused by sharply reduces *transport resistance;* What previously had to be consumed below the waterfall can now be exported abroad via undersea cables.

One key feature of technological change during the last century has been the decrease of *transport resistance* – also sometimes called 'the death of distance'. This has clearly made catching up – getting the national economies into increasing returns activities – in peripheral countries more difficult. We would argue that the extreme *transport resistance* present in traditional service industries which – including public administration – provide a large percentage of First World jobs, combined with the non-globalization of the labour market, together form the main reason why the world does not experience a

148. Cimoli, Mario and Jorge Katz, 'Structural Reforms, Technological Gaps and Economic Development: A Latin American Perspective', *Industrial and Corporate Change,* Vol. 12, No. 2, 2003, pp. 387 ff.

149. p. 407.

strong trend towards factor-price equalization downwards. Only teleporting – as in the science fiction movies – would have totally eliminated *transport resistance*, opening up for international trade in traditional service industries.

A *transport and time resistance* of virtually zero makes protection meaningless in many new industries. At the same time, ideas that could previously be profitably developed within a national innovation system may often have to travel to the parts of the world where the innovative milieu and necessary venture capital can be found. The necessary focusing on core capabilities has made it much more difficult, e.g. in a small country like Norway, to integrate new innovations into an increasingly focused and specialized productive structure. When attending the annual convention of the Association of University Research Parks (AURP) in Madison, Wisconsin, some years ago, I was struck by remarks from representatives from universities in the US Midwest who complained that all the good research ideas left the Midwest to go either to the East or the West Coast where the industrial *milieus* and the venture capital were located. These forces are clearly at work – even more strongly so – in the Third World. We therefore run the risk that the good ideas produced by a peripheral National Innovation System much easier than before will be sucked into the global economy in the First World. That innovations frequently will take place in the centre, although the invention took place in the periphery, is another dimension of Schumpeterian development geography.

13. The National Innovation Systems: from independence to a core-periphery system

In his study of the Mexican National Innovation System, Mario Cimoli[150] showed that the integration between the Mexican and the US economy had gone from relative independence to a core-periphery relationship between US owners and Mexican subsidiaries. This recalls the centre-periphery dependence theories of classical developmental economics.

14. Destructive destruction and Schumpeterian Development Geography

Creative destruction is an important term in Schumpeterian economics, and we have previously argued that this term entered economics via Friedrich Nietzsche and Werner Sombart.[151] As Schumpeter, Nietzsche himself saw this process as a positive one. The eminent Renaissance historian Jacob Burckhardt – Nietzsche's friend and colleague at the University of Basel – was, however, of a different opinion. In his view 'there are (or at any rate there seem to be) absolutely destructive forces under whose hoofs no grass

150. Cimoli, Mario (ed.), *Developing Innovation Systems: Mexico in a Global Context*, London: Thompson Learning, 2000.

151. Reinert, Erik S., 'Creative Destruction in Economics: Nietzsche, Sombart, Schumpeter' (with Hugo Reinert), in Backhaus, Jürgen and Wolfgang Drechsler (eds.), *Friedrich Nietzsche 1844-1900: Economy and Society*, Series *The European Heritage in Economics and the Social Sciences*, New York: Springer, 2006, pp. 55–85.

grows'.[152] Destruction and creativity may take place in entirely different parts of the globe, as when the textile mills of Manchester replaced the weavers of Bengal. The fact that the labour market is not globalized in our increasingly globalized economy in our view opens up for this possibility, sometimes with very serious consequences, as in the case of Mongolia.

In our view, the above mechanisms work together creating formidable barriers to National Innovation Systems (NIS) that not only reduce the price of products from Third World countries but which also raise the standard of living in the Third World countries themselves. These 'perverse backwashes' – to use Gunnar Myrdal's term – in no way make the concept of National Innovation Systems less valuable as an analytical tool. They only further what is already emphasized in the NIS literature: that it is extremely important to evaluate National Innovation Systems in their context.

Conclusion: Avoiding National Innovation Systems as Schumpeterian icing on the neo-classical cake

As a response to mounting evidence of its inefficiency in promoting economic welfare, the Washington Consensus developed during the 1990s. The sequential development of the Washington policy prescriptions since the early 1990s can roughly be outlined as follows:

'get the prices right',
'get the property rights right',
'get the institutions right',
'get the governance right',
'get the competitiveness right'
'get the national innovation systems right'.

We would suggest that the next step should be 'get the economic activities right', i.e. a diversified structure of increasing returns activities.

It is not clear that these consecutive focal points really have brought us any closer to understanding why economic development by its very nature seems to be so unevenly distributed. The risk is that we have not arrived at the root causes, synergies and conditions that make institutions, innovation and good governance viable and possible. We may be continuously pointing to new symptoms rather than the root causes of development, not including in our analysis the preconditions these phenomena need to take root. For example, institutions that took centuries to develop in an industrialized Europe are not likely to be successfully transferred to a feudal mode of production or to a hunting and gathering tribe. Likewise, as far back as in the 1500s economists like Giovanni Botero were pointing to a diversified artisan and manufacturing base as a

152. Burckhardt, Jacob, *Reflections on History*, London: Allen & Unwin, 1943.

precondition both for 'good rule' and for the synergetic process that we call economic development to take place. This would explain why the very existence both of political freedom and generalized welfare was, for so many centuries, an urban phenomenon. A feudal economic structure did not lead to 'good governance'. This would also give us a hint as to why the process of de-industrialization in the 1990s – in effect removing the complex synergetic diversity and division of labour of a society – actually weakens the nation-states in question.

We argue, then, that by integrating some Schumpeterian variables into mainstream economics we may not arrive at the root causes of development. We risk applying a thin Schumpeterian icing on what is essentially a profoundly neo-classical way of thinking; trade theory is but one example here. In our view it is necessary to investigate deeper into the productive structure, into how the logic of competitive business needs to allocate routine tasks and innovative tasks internationally in order to survive, and what the consequences of these business strategies are for the possibilities of creating successful NIS in the Third World. As has already frequently been emphasized in the NIS approach, it is crucial to understand the different national contexts.

Today's problems of income polarization are similar to previous events; in Italy at the time of Serra, in France after the Napoleonic Wars, in the Italian *Risorgimento* and later in nineteenth-century Europe. Similar ideas, around the activity-specific nature of economic growth, have always surfaced. The mechanisms are similar, but the context and the necessary institutions to be created are different. We argue that nineteenth-century economic policy in the countries that industrialized in the era of English world power built on the old insights. Wilhelm Roscher and Friedrich List – the nineteenth-century economists who (directly or indirectly) put increasing returns back on the theoretical map – both quoted Antonio Serra's work (which had been reprinted in 1803). Following Botero and Serra, Friedrich List made the point that a critical synergetic mass in manufacturing (increasing returns) activities is the mother not only of welfare but also of the kind of civil liberties that are necessary both for individual freedom, the arts, civilization and democracy to flourish. According to this view, economic growth, innovation systems, good governance and democracy all depend on the same type of preconditions.

We argue, then, that the present increase of 'failed states' – the 'Somaliazation' of the Third World – ought to be seen in this light: failing states and massive deindustrialization are phenomena which develop in parallel in many poor Third World countries since the mid-1980s. They are, in our view, integrated parts of the same problem of removing the synergies that created the nation-states in the first place. Because present-day economic theory does not possess the tools to capture these effects, the situation is allowed to deteriorate further. The death of so many African refugees crossing the Mediterranean is a constant reminder of the failures of economic theory,

The world is facing a 'social question' on the world scale; various reports – among them from the UNDP – show that anywhere between 60 and 90 nations have grown poorer since 1990. The old 'social question' was only solved by creating institutions that, one by one, became building blocks of a system that produced generalized welfare: minimum wage, health and safety standards, health insurance, unemployment benefits, etc. These institutions were above all constructs of the German *Verein für Sozialpolitik* – the Association for Social Policy – working from 1872 to 1932, which received the political backing of Chancellor Bismarck at an important point. Their institutional innovations created the most important blueprints for solving 'the social question' across Europe. We are now faced with a new and global version of 'the social question', but this time the distributional problems are more *between* nations than *inside* nations. Not only do we need to acknowledge that we are facing a serious problem, we also have to build institutions that fit the new situation. And: we need a Bismarck in the political sphere to see the importance of the issue and carry through the reforms.

With the growth of evolutionary and neo-Schumpeterian economics in the 1990s, focus was again put on the production side of the economy. Evolutionary economics has been the branch of economics that has delved into the 'black box' of technology and production, into Schumpeter's *Güterwelt* – the world of goods and services. Essentially equipped with the right focus on production and innovation, evolutionary economics could, in our opinion, deliver even more to the study of uneven economic growth from the point of view of the Third World. We suggest that there is room for 'Schumpeterian Economic Geography', 'Schumpeterian Trade Theory' and 'Schumpeterian Development Economics'. The link between technology and wages – which was an important issue both for the German Historical School and the 'old' US institutionalists – has, for example, not been central in evolutionary economics.

History shows that the wealthier an economy, the less the need for government intervention. Or, as Keynes indicated, 'the more troublous the times, the worse does a laissez-faire system work.[153] The problem is that today's world economic order is working totally contrary to this principle: The wealthiest nations have the most active economic policies, both targeting, nurturing and protecting their innovation systems and picking winners, while they also protect their agricultural sectors. We claim that the present-form globalization does not allow laggard nations to catch up; it may lock in the losers into a specialization in being poor.

For centuries it was accepted common sense that a nation would be much better off with an inefficient manufacturing sector than without any manufacturing sector at all. Today increasing returns are frequently found in advanced services, but these advanced services normally need a manufacturing sector to thrive. History has shown that the synergies and the division of labour arising out of the increasing returns sectors – manufacturing and advanced services – are the core mechanisms

153. The issue was therefore not, said Keynes, one between collectivism and *laissez-faire*, but between targeted state action and a socialism which was out of date and contrary to human nature. Both quotes in Skidelsky, Vol. II, p. 152.

behind economic growth, innovation systems, good governance and democracy. As happened at the end of the first wave of globalization – about 100 years ago – this means that we again shall have to revise our attitude towards instant free trade. Although being the long-term goal, free trade is sometimes a counterproductive solution in the short run.

APPENDIX 1

Creating National Innovation Systems & The Generic Developmental State:

Continuity of policy measures and tool kit from England in 1485 (Henry VII) to Korea in the 1960s: a mandatory passage point for economic development

… the fundamental things apply, as time goes by.

Sam, the pianist, in *Casablanca.*

1. Observation of wealth synergies clustered around increasing returns activities and continuous mechanization in general. Recognition that 'We are in the wrong business'. Conscious *targeting, support and protection* of these increasing returns activities.
2. Temporary monopolies/patents/protection given to targeted activities in a certain geographical area.
3. Recognizing development as a synergetic phenomenon, and consequently the need for a diversified manufacturing sector ('maximizing the division of labour', Serra 1613 + observations of the Dutch Republic and Venice)
4. Attraction of foreigners to work in these activities (historically religious prosecutions have been important)
5. Relative suppression of landed nobility (from Henry VII to Korea). (Physiocracy as a rebellion against this policy)
6. Tax breaks for targeted activities
7. Cheap credits for targeted activities
8. Export bounties for targeted activities
9. Strong support for agricultural sector, in spite of this sector clearly being seen as incapable of independently bringing the nation out of poverty
10. Emphasis on learning/education (UK apprentice system Elizabeth I)
11. Patent protection for valuable knowledge (Venice from 1490s)
12. Frequent export tax/export ban on raw materials in order to make raw materials more expensive to competing nations (starting with Henry VII in late 1400s, whose policy was very efficient in severely damaging the woollen industry in Medici Florence).

APPENDIX II[154]

Two different ways of understanding the economic world & the wealth and poverty of nations

STARTING POINT FOR THE STANDARD CANON:	*STARTING POINT FOR 'THE OTHER CANON':*
Equilibrium under *perfect information* and *perfect foresight*	Learning and decision-making under uncertainty (Schumpeter, Keynes, Shackle)
High level of abstraction	Level of abstraction chosen according to the problem to be resolved
Man's wit and will absent	Moving force: *Geist- und Willenskapital:* Man's wit and will, entrepreneurship
Not able to handle *novelty* as an endogenous phenomenon	*Novelty* as a central moving force
Moving force: 'capital per se propels the capitalist engine'	Moving force: New knowledge which creates a demand for capital to be provided from the financial sector
Metaphors from the realm of physics	Metaphors (carefully) from the realm of biology
Mode of understanding: Mechanistic ('begreifen')	Mode of understanding: Qualitative ('verstehen'), a type of understanding irreducible only to numbers and symbols
Matter	*Geist* precedes matter
Focused on *Man the Consumer* A. Smith: 'Men are animals which have learned to barter'	Focused on *Man the Innovator and Producer.* A. Lincoln: 'Men are animals which not only work, but innovate'
Focused on static/comparative static	Focused on change
Not cumulative/history absent	Cumulative causations/'history matters'/backwash effects (Myrdal, Kaldor, Schumpeter, German Historical School)
Increasing returns to scale and its absence a non-essential feature	Increasing returns and its absence essential to explaining differences in income between firms, regions and nations (Kaldor)
Very precise ('would rather be accurately wrong than approximately correct')	Aiming at relevance over precision, recognizes the *trade-off between relevance and precision* as a core issue in the profession
'Perfect competition' (commodity competition/price competition) as an ideal situation = a goal for society	Innovation- and knowledge-driven Schumpeterian competition as both engine of progress and ideal situation. With perfect competition, with equilibrium and no innovation, capital becomes worthless (Schumpeter, Hayek)

(Continued)

154. Authors: Erik Reinert, Leonardo Burlamaqui, Ha-Joon Chang, Michael Chu, Peter Evans and Jan Kregel.

(Continued)

STARTING POINT FOR THE STANDARD CANON:	*STARTING POINT FOR 'THE OTHER CANON':*
The market as a mechanism for setting prices	The market also as an arena for rivalry and as a mechanism selecting between different products and different solutions. (Schumpeter, Nelson & Winter)
Equality Assumption I: No diversity	Diversity as a key factor (Schumpeter, Shackle)
Equality Assumption II: All economic activities are *alike* and *of equal quality* as carriers of economic growth and welfare	Growth and welfare are *activity-specific* – different economic activities present widely different potentials for absorbing new knowledge
Both theory and policy recommendations tend to be *independent of context* ('one medicine cures all')	Both theory and policy recommendations highly *context dependent*
The economy largely independent from society	The economy as firmly embedded in society
Technology as a *free good*, as 'manna from heaven'	Knowledge and technology are *produced*, have cost and are protected. This production is based on incentives of the system, including law, institutions and policies
Equilibrating forces at the core of the system and of the theory	Cumulative forces are more important than equilibrating ones, and should therefore be at the core of the system
Economics as *Harmonielehre*: The economy as a self-regulating system seeking equilibrium and harmony	Economics as an inherently unstable and conflict-rich discipline. Achieving stability is based on Man's policy measures (Carey, Polanyi, Weber, Keynes)
Postulates the representative firm	No 'representative firm'. All firms are unique (Penrose)
Static optimum. Perfect rationality	Dynamic optimization under uncertainty. Bounded rationality
No distinction made between real economy and financial economy	Conflicts between real economy and financial economy are normal and must be regulated (Minsky, Keynes)
Saving caused by refraining from consumption and a cause of growth	Saving largely results from profits (Schumpeter) and saving *per se* is not useful or desirable for growth (Keynes)

Appendix III

The Family Tree of The Other Canon

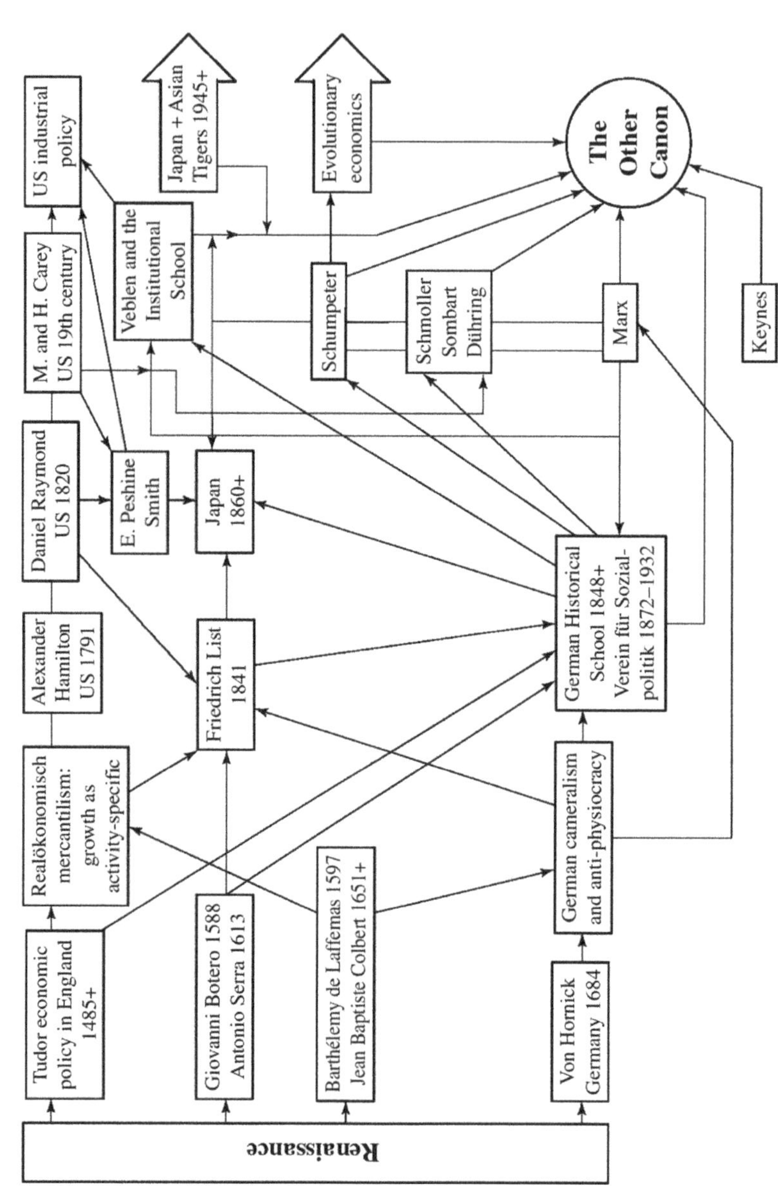

Chapter 12

THE OTHER CANON: THE HISTORY OF RENAISSANCE ECONOMICS

With Arno M. Daastøl

1. TYPOLOGIES OF ECONOMIC THEORY AND THE FOUNDATION OF THE TWO CANONS

It has been said that economics as a science – or pseudoscience – is unique because parallel competing canons may exist together over long periods of time. In other sciences, periodic gestalt-switches terminate old theoretical trajectories and initiate new ones. In a paradigm shift, the scientific world moves from a situation in which everyone knows that the world is flat to a new understanding that the world is round (Kuhn 1970). This occurs in a relatively short time. In economics, the theory that the world is flat has been coexisting for centuries with the theory that the world is round. In this chapter we shall argue for the existence of an alternative to today's mainstream theory: the continuation of the canon that dominated the worldview of the Renaissance – The Other Canon. Using a metaphor from Kenneth Arrow, 'this tradition acts like an underground river, springing to the surface every few decades'.[1]

We argue that during the Cold War, the 'underground river' of Renaissance Other Canon economics all but disappeared from economic theory, and that it is time to reintroduce it. Traditionally, The Other Canon has been resurrected in times of crisis, such as national emergencies, which bring production – not barter – into focus. This occurs, for example, when an exclusive focus on barter has caused financial bubbles that subsequently burst, when nations are engaged in serious catching up with the prevailing world leader (as the United States, Germany and Japan were in the nineteenth century, or as Korea was until later), or when a war economy forces a national political system to focus on production (of materials of war). Today the urgency of a change of focus towards the Renaissance conception of economics is particularly acute in the Third World and in formerly communist Eastern Europe. Unfortunately, this is not where economic theory is produced.

1. Quotation from Arrow's foreword to Arthur 1994. Arrow uses this metaphor to describe the place of increasing returns in economic theory. Increasing returns has, explicitly or implicitly, been at the core of the economic analysis of the Renaissance canon ever since Antonio Serra described this phenomenon in 1613. Serra explicitly associated increasing returns with manufacturing industry.

The two different canons are based on fundamentally different worldviews, which can be traced back to ancient Greece, where the term 'economics' was first used. Today's standard economics is based on a mechanistic, barter- and consumption-centred tradition – static in the tradition of Zeno – that explains human economic activity in terms of physics. Renaissance Other Canon economics is production-centred and dynamic in the tradition of Heraclitus, and tends to explain human economic activity in terms of biology rather than static physics (for a discussion of the traditions of Zeno and Heraclitus, see Popper 1997, pp. 112–13). The mainstream tradition belongs to what Werner Sombart (1930) calls *ordnende Nationalökonomie*, which is concerned with organizing the economic sphere. The Renaissance tradition is what Sombart calls *verstehende Nationalökonomie* and what Nelson and Winter (1982) refer to as 'appreciative economics'. The first tradition is represented by Malthus's dismal science, the second by Christopher Freeman's *Economics of Hope*.

Present mainstream economic theory descends in a canonical sequence from the physiocrats via Adam Smith and David Ricardo to the neoclassical tradition beginning with William Stanley Jevons, Carl Menger and Alfred Marshall. The sequence has been made clear to generations of economists as the 'family tree of economics' featured in many editions of Paul Samuelson's *Economics*. The alternative canon in economic theory runs parallel in time with the tradition of Samuelson's 'family tree'. We have named this alternative canon The Other Canon, or alternatively 'Renaissance economics', because never before or since have the values that this canon represents dominated the world picture as they did during the Renaissance. The mainstream canon is a product of the Enlightenment, in opposition to Renaissance values and outlook. Rationality and individuality during the Renaissance were based on an image of Man as a spiritual being: creative and productive. The Enlightenment had a more materialistic understanding of human rationality and individuality: mechanical and consuming. Today, the Renaissance canon disappears in the history of economic thought, as this branch of economics increasingly concentrates on the predecessors of neoclassical economics. We would claim that the absence of the history of economic policy as a branch of economics is responsible for pushing the alternative canon into virtual oblivion.

Renaissance economics is optimistic: the never-ending frontier of knowledge stands in sharp contrast with Malthus's dismal science and with the production theory of mainstream economics. Other main features of the Renaissance canon of economic theory are the following. The fundamental cause of economic welfare is human productive creativity and morality, the immaterial production factors. In order for these ideas to materialize, capital is needed. Capital *per se* is sterile. The Renaissance tradition can be contrasted with the mainstream using Schumpeter's description of the economics of John Rae, a nineteenth-century US economist of the Renaissance canon: 'The essential thing is the conception of the economic process, which soars above the pedestrian view that it is the accumulation of capital per se that propels the capitalist engine.'[2] Squarely

2. Schumpeter 1954, p. 468.

put, whereas the Renaissance canon focuses on culture as the main source of production and welfare, the mainstream canon focuses on nature. Mainstream economics defines its origins in the French school of physiocracy (that is, 'the rule of nature'),[3] where value is created by nature and harvested by Man. In Renaissance economics, value originates through man's wit and will (that is, 'ideocracy'). During the mechanization of the worldview that took place during the materialistically oriented Enlightenment, the defenders of the Renaissance tradition were the antiphysiocrats.[4] The Renaissance tradition is holistic and idealistic, not atomistic and materialistic. At the core of the system is the individual, set in a complex web of interrelations. The beneficial effects of these interrelations first became evident in Renaissance towns, giving birth to the Renaissance expression the common weal, *il bene comune* or *das Gemeinwohl* depending on the language (Latini et al. 1993, Henderson 1994) – a synergetic understanding of society as being more than the sum of its parts.[5]

Towns permitted communication, which unleashed individual freedom, creativity and diversification, which in turn engendered unprecedented wealth. Later nation-building in this tradition tried consciously to reproduce these synergetic benefits of towns on a national scale. In order to achieve this, law and administrative science had to be cultivated and promoted. Renaissance economics emphasizes the crucial role of nation-states and the duties of the ruler – that is, government – not only to regulate in order to provide incentives for the creation of welfare (in the ancient tradition of law and economics) but also to initiate projects creating a demand for knowledge-based production.

The strategy of the Renaissance Other Canon tradition included two tightly interrelated parts: (1) the promotion of new knowledge and (2) the promotion of infrastructure in its broadest sense, thereby permitting the communication of knowledge and the exchange of goods at lower transportation and/or transaction costs. These two types of investments, typically being public goods – private investors would not be able to collect the benefits of such investments – need public entrepreneurship produced by a visible hand.

An integral part of this nation-building strategy was a notion that a national market had to be created, that it did not appear spontaneously. For this reason, communication and state-initiated investments in large-scale infrastructure projects

3. Of which Schumpeter (1954, p. 175) writes: 'Its analytical merit is negligible, but all the greater was its success.'
4. In Germany, the main antiphysiocrat was Johann Friedrich von Pfeiffer; in France, Gabriel Bonnot, Abbé de Mably, Accarias de Serrionne, Jacques Necker, François Veron de Forbonnais, Jean Graslin, Ferdinando Abbé Galiani – a Neapolitan envoy at the Court of Paris – and, most critical of them all, Simon-Nicolas-Henry Linguet. For a list of works by German antiphysiocrats, see Humpert 1937, pp. 1031–32.
5. These synergetic effects are clearly described in Botero 1590 and even more so in Serra 1613. To Serra these 'virtuous circles' have their origins in the increasing returns found in the manufacturing sector, which are absent in agriculture. Machiavelli is also clear on this point: 'Il bene comune è quello che fa grandi le città.'

hold a very strong position in the Renaissance Other Canon tradition, from the dams and irrigation canals of the Sumerian kingdoms to Colbert's canals to Eisenhower's interstate highways. We could say that the strategy of Renaissance economics was to create perfect competition within national borders and dynamic imperfect competition in the export trade. Contrary to the common preconceptions of economics before Adam Smith, 'Competition was often artificially fostered [nationally] . . . in order to organize markets with automatic regulation of supply and demand'.[6] It was commonly agreed that a national competitive advantage had to be created in knowledge-intensive activities before free trade with the most advanced nations could be established.

The two canons should be seen as 'ideal types' in the Weberian sense. Through time, several distinguishing features have clearly separated them. One of these is their different conceptions of the origin of wealth:

- In the mainstream canon, wealth originates from material sources: nature (land), physical labour and capital. The accumulation of these assets takes place through trade and war. This accumulation is static – more of the same.
- In The Other Canon, wealth originates from immaterial sources: human culture, creativity and morality. The accumulation of assets takes place through innovations cumulatively changing Man's stock of knowledge and of his tools (technology). This accumulation is dynamic – something new and qualitatively different.

A second major distinguishing feature of the two canons is their analytical focus:

- In the mainstream canon, the focus of analysis is on barter, consumption and accumulation (Man as trader and consumer).
- In The Other Canon, the focus of analysis is on production and innovation, productivity being the force that unites mind and matter (Man as creative producer).

A third major difference between the canons is:

- In the mainstream canon, economic development is spontaneous and independent of any collective will. (See Viner 1972 for a discussion of the invisible hand as it relates to beliefs in Fate and Providence.)
- Since the Renaissance, economic development in The Other Canon is the result of wilful and conscious creation and policy intervention in order to promote a synergetic common weal.

At a very fundamental level, the two canons of economics are founded on two different views of how Man differs from other animals. We shall let Adam Smith represent the material and barter-based canon and Abraham Lincoln represent Renaissance economics – the immaterial and production-based canon.

6. Eli Heckshe r, quoted in Polanyi 1944, p. 278.

Adam Smith:

The division of labour arises from a propensity in human nature to . . . truck, barter and exchange one thing for another . . . It is common to all men, and to be found in no other race of animals, which seem to know neither this nor any other species of contracts . . . Nobody ever saw a dog make a fair and deliberate exchange of one bone for another with another dog. (Smith 1976[1776], p. 17)

Abraham Lincoln:

Beavers build houses; but they build them in nowise differently, or better, now than they did five thousand years ago . . . Man is not the only animal who labours; but he is the only one who *improves* his workmanship. These improvements he effects by *Discoveries* and *Inventions* . . .' (Speech of the 1860 Presidential Campaign)

There are, of course, inventions also in Adam Smith, but they are exogenous; they are created outside his economic system. The term 'innovation', which was important in English economics from Francis Bacon's 'An Essay on Innovations' (ca 1605) until and including James Steuart (1767), disappears with Adam Smith (see Reinert and Daastøl 1997 for a discussion).

We argue the existence of an immaterial and production-based canon through time. (1) The continuity of this immaterial and production-based tradition in economic theory can be traced from the 1400s to the present, and this filiation of thought and its geographical movements from nation to nation can be documented, through citations and economic policy. (2) The roots of this economic theory, both in philosophy and in economic policy, can be traced back through the Byzantine and Carolingian empires to Platonic philosophy, to Ptolemy's Egypt and the Sumerian kingdoms. In other words, our approach is mainly diffusionist. However, we do not exclude 'independent discoveries' of the rational principles of Renaissance economics, particularly in times of national crisis and war. We also see a consistent pattern of application of The Other Canon in the framework of successful economic catching up.

No nation-state has ever developed from poverty to affluence without taking the production-based canon as its fundamental guide for economic policy over long periods.[7] This was true in France (where a modern starting point for policy could be Louis XI, in 1461, and Barthélemy Laffemas (in 1597), Antoine de Montchrétien, Jean Bodin and the Duc de Sully for theory); in England (where a logical starting point for policy is the reign of Henry VII, in 1485); in Germany; in the United States (Benjamin Franklin, Alexander Hamilton, Daniel Raymond (1820), Henry Clay, Matthew and Henry Carey (1967 (1851]), E. Peshine Smith); and in Japan (the Meiji Restoration). Today we see the production-based economic strategy at work in East Asia. The Third World has never fully experienced the production-based canon.

7. With the possible exception of small city-states, such as Hong Kong and San Marino.

On the practical policy level, the two canons conflict because whereas in the Renaissance theory different economic activities offer different potentials for achieving national welfare, in the barter-centred theory (discounting the different circumstances under which the bartered goods are actually produced), all economic activities become qualitatively alike. If anything, in the standard canon, superiority is awarded to agriculture, which is more 'natural' because (1) it delivers nature's produce, and (2) competition here is more 'natural', atomistic and 'perfect'.

Tracing the Renaissance canon of economic thought presents several problems. First, the history of economic thought has to a great extent developed into a genealogy of neoclassical economics. For this reason the 'unorthodox' economists who are not part of the canonical sequence are left out. Second, the overwhelming dominance of Anglo-Saxon economists – today generally with very limited skills in languages other than English and mathematics – and of Anglo-Saxon economic policy in the post-Bretton Woods period has added an ethnocentric dimension to this development. Third, in spite of their profound impact on economic policy, the people who represented the Renaissance canon are often not classified as economists. Even Schumpeter's *History of Economic Analysis*, which is unique in this tradition in its geographical and linguistic scope, leaves out people such as Gottfried Leibniz and Christian Wolff. As economists, Leibniz and Wolff were not only very important for the economic policy of their time, but they also laid the foundation for the whole German economic tradition, which largely coincided with the US and Japanese traditions during the nineteenth century up until the Second World War. Many of these German economists tend to be classified as sociologists, particularly Max Weber. Schumpeter (1954, p. 117) writes: '[T]he great names of Leibniz and that of his faithful henchman Christian Wolff, are left out advisedly: they were polyhistors, of course, and greatly interested, among other things, in the economic events and policies of their day; but they made no contribution to our subject.' It was only in the post-Bretton Woods era that Adam Smith and David Ricardo completely won the day in economic policy, so the economists of alternative traditions who were crucial to economic policy are therefore almost entirely left out of today's history of economic thought. The last history of economics to provide good coverage of the theories behind the nineteenth-century economic policy was Spann (1926). This was translated into several languages; interestingly, the British edition was published under the title *Types of Economic Theory*, underscoring Spann's awareness that there are, indeed, different types of economics, not just one monolithic canon.

2. THE FAMILY TREE OF THE OTHER CANON

Traces of the Renaissance Other Canon can be found in pre-antiquity. Statecraft and the accumulation of knowledge – exemplified by the Library of Alexandria and the scientific academies of Sumeria under Hammurabi (2030–1995 BC) – were important features of the early Middle Eastern kingdoms of Sumeria and Egypt. These kingdoms also produced extensive literature and documents on economic and legal matters which survive today. As occurred later in Asia and in the Andes, irrigation seems to have been the first technology to create important increasing returns to scale, and consequently to require statecraft. Irrigation was therefore instrumental in the establishment of the first states. The cuneiform script of the Sumerians remained the standard for the Middle East region for the next 2000 years, and the Code of Hammurabi tells of an enlightened and humane system of law.

Later, during the Phoenician dominance of Mediterranean trade (from about 1500 to about 500 BC), there was clear practical recognition of the Other Canon principle that adding knowledge and labour to raw materials through the production of manufactured goods produces a superior standard of living to only extracting and selling the raw produce. We find this same theory clearly stated in Botero (1590), but only Serra (1613) would later explain the economic mechanisms behind this principle: why the Republic of Venice, with little or no raw materials, was so rich compared to the Kingdom of Naples, with its abundance of natural wealth. Later colonial and neocolonial projects would retain the pattern set by the Phoenicians and well expressed in the maxims of Charles King (1721): imports of raw material and export of manufactured goods are 'good trade', export of raw materials and import of manufactured goods are 'bad trade', while exchanging manufactured goods for other manufactured goods is 'good trade' for both trading partners. The 'New Trade Theory' of the 1990s again modelled Charles King's maxim, but alas with no practical consequences for the Third World.

The philosophical foundation of the Renaissance canon displays a clear continuity. Plato and other Greek philosophers were to some extent influenced by Egyptian civilization. Augustine's *De civitate dei* (413–26) was written in the Platonic spirit. Occasional rediscoveries of Plato such as this led to sporadic 'renaissances', among them the Carolingian Renaissance under Charlemagne (768–814). Charlemagne was counselled by Thomas of York, a follower of Augustine. Under Charlemagne the fondness of Renaissance economics for education, industry and infrastructure was already evident. Charlemagne was actively promoting the textile industry; in Friesland, he built roads and worked on a canal linking Europe's greatest rivers, the Danube and the Rhine; and he promoted Latin as a standard administrative language in Western Europe.

No doubt inspired by the developments in Italian city-states, France under Louis XI (1423–1483) experienced an early mini-renaissance. Louis XI established a pattern that came to typify Renaissance economics: he allied himself with the middle class against the noblemen, establishing a tax system favouring the urban, middle-class value of industriousness against the landowning upper class's feudal valuing of agriculture and trade *per se*. Renaissance economics – creating centralized nation-states – was an important factor in bringing about the decline of feudalism. In Spain, with the 1521 civil war known as the Revolt of the Comuneros, the feudal class won over the modernizing urban middle classes, thus contributing to the political foundations for Spain's deindustrialization following the inflow of precious metal from the Americas.

The Italian-born Renaissance was a rebirth of knowledge as the central engine of human change; it led to a reinterpretation of Man's place in the divine scheme. Innovations had previously been tantamount to heresy – all Man was supposed to know was already in the Holy Bible and in the writings of Aristotle. Knowledge production was confined to the interpretation of these scriptures. The influence of the

Eastern church and the inflow of refugees from the crumbling Byzantine Empire to Italy completely reversed these perceptions: Man was created in the image of God, and God's most salient feature was his rational creativity. Consequently, innovations were no longer heretical; on the contrary, Man's essential and pleasurably duty was to innovate. Figure 12.1 shows the main contributions to the Renaissance and the philosophers who helped promulgate Renaissance economic thinking in Europe.

'To me the Renaissance will always mark the high point of this millennium', says Nietzsche (2000, p. 10288). The Renaissance worldview released enormous creativity; it gave us da Vinci, Michelangelo, Raphael, Kepler and Copernicus. In all arts and sciences, the people of the Renaissance still stand out in history, whereas the statesmen and economists of the Renaissance today are represented by the caricatures Adam Smith created. In the spirit of the Renaissance, Francis Bacon – Queen Elizabeth's Lord High Chancellor – wrote *An Essay of Innovations* (ca 1605). Bacon became the 'scientific leader of the new industrialists',[8] urging the use of science to produce manufactured goods and profits.

This conviction that a society based on manufacturing is fundamentally superior to a society without a manufacturing base is an essential feature of what we label Renaissance economics. Emphasis on the 'intrinsic value of manufacturing' has been an integral part of the economic policy of all nations that have ever successfully embarked on a strategy of catching up with leading nations. Only when the catching up has been achieved, have the industrialized nations (beginning with England) embraced the classical/neoclassical tradition. In other words, no nation has ever achieved general welfare without going through a period of Renaissance economics. In England this

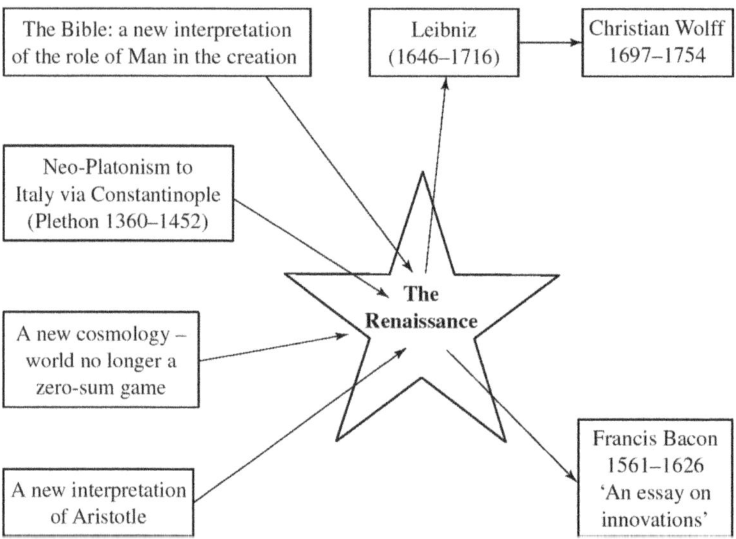

Figure 12.1 The Renaissance: influences and consequences for economics.

8. Crowther 1960, p. 97.

period lasted for more than 400 years, starting in the late fifteenth century; Korea achieved a great deal in only 40 years.

Bacon's emphasis on scientific knowledge was very similar to that of Friedrich List more than 200 years later: 'Industry is the mother and father of science, literature, the arts, enlightenment, useful institutions and national power . . . The greater the advance in scientific knowledge, the more numerous will be the new inventions which save labour and raw materials and lead to new products and processes.'[9] In this sense, there is a continuity of argument from the Renaissance through Bacon and List to today's evolutionary economics, which emphasizes the role of research and development and of innovations in improving economic welfare. As to natural resources, List (1904, p. 79) says that 'industrialisation will greatly increase the value of a country's natural resources'. This thinking was the basis for economic policy in the resource-rich nations that have achieved general welfare: Canada, Australia and New Zealand. A manufacturing sector (even though it was not competitive with England's) was needed to transform the natural resources of a nation into national wealth (Reinert 1998).

List (1904, p. 142) expressed the view of industry that prevailed among nations catching up with England during the nineteenth century:

> Let us compare Poland with England: both nations at one time were at the same stage of culture; and now what a difference. Manufactories and manufactures are the mothers and children of municipal liberty, of intelligence, of the arts and sciences, of internal and external commerce, of navigation and improvements in transport, of civilisation and of political power. They are the chief way of liberating agriculture from its chains. . . . The popular school [that is, Adam Smith and J.B. Say] has attributed this civilising effect to foreign trade, but in that it has confounded the mere exchanger with the originator.

Deindustrialization, on the other hand, has been a corollary to economic disasters and massive reductions in human welfare; examples include the deindustrialization of Holland after 1650, of Northern Italy following the French invasion, of France following the Napoleonic Wars, of Eastern Europe after the fall of the Berlin Wall and of several Third World countries after the 'adjustment policies' of the Washington Consensus (see chapter 8 on Mongolia in this volume). List, who originally had been a free trader and continued to believe that free trade was the final goal of development, recognized the crucial role of manufacturing when he saw the devastating effects of the deindustrialization of France after the Napoleonic Wars on the welfare of the nation.

In List we find again the synergy-based arguments of Renaissance economists such as Giovanni Botero and Antonio Serra. As stated earlier, the goal of the state's economic policy was to increase the common weal – the prosperity of the community. This is the starting point of virtually all economic writing of the period. To the Renaissance economists, systemic effects seem to have arisen first from the observation that widespread wealth appeared to accumulate in the cities, not in the countryside. This

9. List 1904, pp. 66–67.

was the fundamental observation of one of the earliest best-selling books in economics, *Delle Cause della Grandezza delle Città*, by Giovanni Botero (1543–1617). The English translation, published in London in 1606, is titled *The Cause of the Greatnesse of Cities.* This argument was discussed in detail by Antonio Serra in 1613, whose work is cited nine times and with extensive comments by Friedrich List.

In the best theoretical works of the time, the difference between the wealth and poverty of cities and countryside, and between cities, is explained in terms of the following main factors: (1) size and density of population; (2) different 'qualities' of economic activities, manufacturing being 'good' and agriculture alone being 'bad'; (3) the presence or absence of diversity of economic occupations; (4) the different capacities of economic activities to initiate 'virtuous circles' or positive feedback mechanisms; and (5) a steady, orderly and liberal government providing economic policy based on the above principles. The systemic effects in the economy are described by Renaissance economists at three levels of sophistication:[10]

1. Observations that higher welfare is produced by some economic activities than by others, a static and nonsystemic observation of welfare being activity-specific. (To give a modern-day example: lawyers make more money than people picking lettuce; therefore, a nation of lettuce pickers will be poorer than a nation of lawyers.)
2. Observations that certain economic activities are at the core of systemic synergies which produce and spread welfare locally or nationwide. ('Where there are many people working with machines, the shopkeepers are wealthier than in other places where machines are not used.')
3. There are degrees of understanding how these systemic synergies develop into positive feedback systems, but the most sophisticated is that of Antonio Serra (1613), who describes Venice as a true auto-catalytic system in which increasing returns and diversity – the latter expressed as the number of different professions in a nation (that is, degree of division of labour) – are identified as being at the core of virtuous circles that generate wealth. Naples represents the opposite effect in Serra's system, because the production of raw materials is not subject to increasing returns.

These synergy-based arguments are found today in the works on increasing returns by authors such as Paul David, W. Brian Arthur and James Buchanan. In our opinion these authors are reinventing the role of knowledge, synergies and path-dependence, which are main characteristics of Renaissance economics throughout history. Take, for example, List's (1841/1904) view of manufacturing's role:

> The productive powers of agriculture are scattered over a wide area. But the productive powers of industry are brought together and are centralised in one place. This process eventually creates an expansion of productive powers which grow in geometric rather than in arithmetic proportion.
>
> This is why the population of an industrialised society is brought together in a few conurbations in which are concentrated a great variety of skills, productive powers, applied

10. These arguments are thoroughly discussed in Reinert 1999.

> science, art and literature. Here are to be found great public and private institutions and associations in which theoretical knowledge is applied to the practical affairs of industry and commerce. Only in such conurbations can a public opinion develop which is strong enough to vanquish the brute force, to maintain freedom for all, and to insist that the public authorities should adopt administrative policies that will promote and safeguard national prosperity . . .
>
> In addition the manufacturers are the focus of a large, lucrative, and world wide trade with peoples of varied standards of culture who live in many distant countries. Industry turns cheap bulk raw materials, which cannot be sent long distances, into goods of low weight and high value which are in universal demand.

List was in many ways the main nineteenth-century propagandist of the Renaissance canon. He emphasized the immaterial foundations of wealth (knowledge and human 'wit and will'), the superiority of manufacturing over agriculture and raw materials, the crucial role of infrastructure, the systemic nature of economic growth (as a 'national innovation system') and free trade among nations at the same level of development. These are all typical traits in pre-First World War theories of economic policy in Germany, the United States and Japan. Later these ideas spread to Korea and Taiwan and are now the basis for China's economic strategy, where Sun Yat-Sen (Yat-Sen 1922) and Chiang Kai-shek were followers of List's system.

However, List's analysis of why these policies were so efficient is somewhat lacking. No doubt his observations were accurate, but his theoretical concepts are vague and his explanations of the economic mechanisms at work are imprecise. Werner Sombart comments: 'His concepts levitate like undelivered souls on the banks of Hades.'[11] In spite of this, List's holistic vision of the fundamentals of economic development creating national wealth or poverty is almost unprecedented.

The Renaissance theory often works through abduction – the kind of intuitive knowledge that precedes induction and deduction. Lemons helped sailors in the Mediterranean prevent scurvy 800 years before the exact mechanisms through which these lemons work were established (that is, vitamin C). Similarly, economic growth was successfully promoted in the Renaissance tradition of economics using 'new knowledge' and 'use of machinery' as proxies for the underlying factors causing systemic economic growth. The German cameralist tradition in economics recognized the superior potential of manufacturing over any other activity as a basis for collecting taxes. This was one of several reasons why manufacturing was favoured in the German states, and increased economic wealth and technical change were by-products of this policy.

We argue that there is a strong continuity in this canon (see Figure 12.2). Serra (1613) provides a theoretical framework for the mercantilist view that some specific economic activities are carriers of economic growth. He also explains the mechanisms creating the synergies which the mercantilists called the common weal. At the core of these mechanisms Serra sees increasing returns in manufacturing but not in agriculture. The purpose of Serra's treatise is to explain the wealth of Venice and the poverty of Naples,

11. '[S]eine Begriffe "schweben" umher wie die unerlösten Seelen an den Ufern des Hades', Sombart 1928, p. 929.

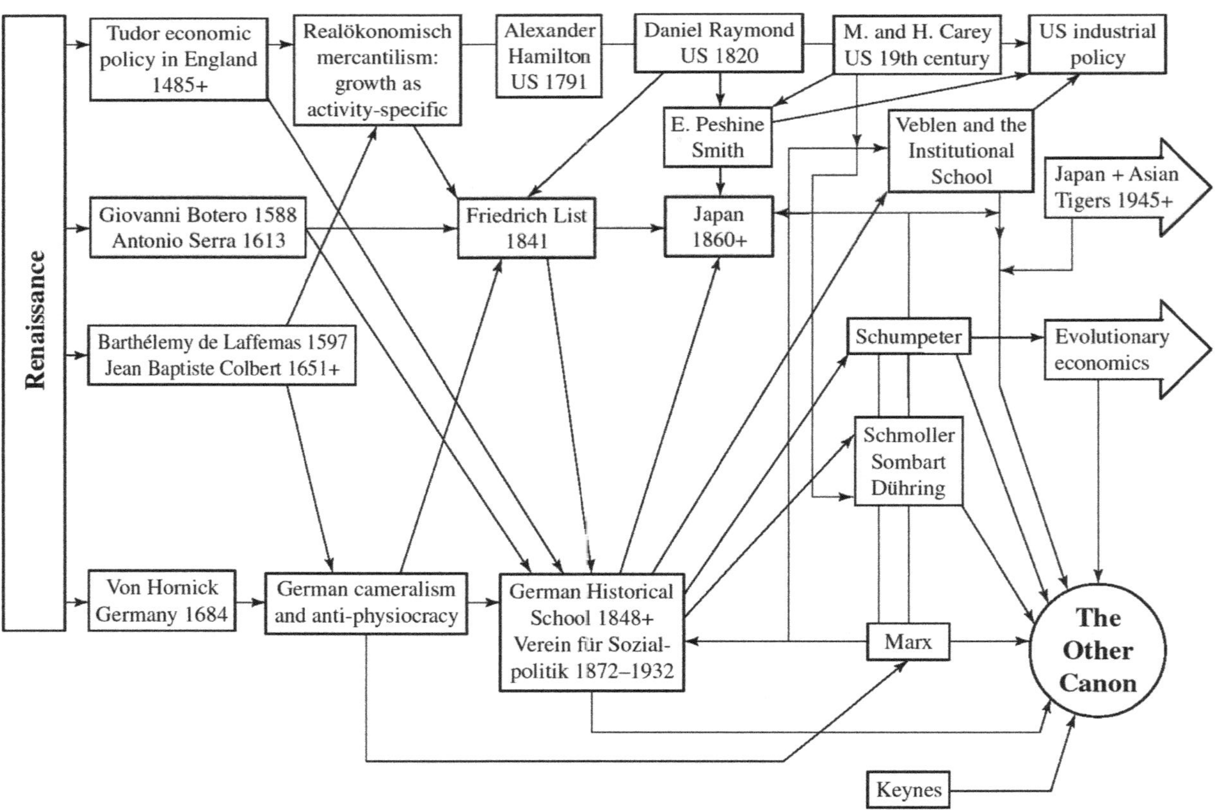

Figure 12.2 Reality economics: the knowledge- and production-based Other Canon of economics.

despite the fact that Venice had virtually no natural resources and Naples abounded in natural resources. Serra provides a theory which can explain why the English strategy, starting with Henry VII, was so successful.[12]

In France, the seventeenth-century policies of Sully and Colbert are based on the same type of reasoning. Based on the theory provided by Laffemas (1597), the voluminous letters and instructions of Colbert make clear his role as a businessman in charge of a huge empire.[13] He was faced with what historians of technology call 'reverse salients'[14] – 'dynamic bottlenecks' – retarding the system and demanding managerial attention. In the German-speaking world an early spokesman for the same principles was Philipp Wilhelm von Hörnigk, whose 1684 work *Österreich über alles wann es nur will* appeared in 16 editions, the last one as late as 1784.

The bridge between English mercantilist policies and the industrial policy of the United States can be documented by two strong pillars: Benjamin Franklin's admiring and enthusiastic footnotes to the second edition of Whatley's (1774) late mercantilist tract, and Alexander Hamilton.

It has been shown that Hamilton knew his Adam Smith but rejected the free trade conclusion. Excerpts from Malachy Postlethwayt's *Universal Dictionary of Trade and Commerce* were scattered through Hamilton's *Army Pay Book*[15] and later provided much inspiration for his 1791 *Report on the Manufactures.*

When in the 1850s Wilhelm Roscher put increasing returns on the map again as a determinant of uneven economic development, he repeatedly quoted Antonio Serra just as List had done a decade or so earlier. Serra's work had been reprinted in Italian in 1803. The German Historical School of Economics thoroughly understands and appreciates the wisdom of *realökonomisch* Mercantilism, although Sombart jokingly admits to the risk of defending any economic theory older than Adam Smith's: 'I say this in spite of the risk of being branded as a neo-mercantilist, and as such to be transferred into the collection of the oddities of our profession.'[16]

A crucial feature of nineteenth-century economic thought is the theoretical cross-fertilization between the biggest nations that were attempting to catch up with England: Germany, the United States and Japan. They were united in their opposition to the theories of Smith and Ricardo, particularly as it applied to free trade. Michael Hudson (1969, p. 45) traces the 'institutionalist (historical) school of economists which flourished in America during the final decades of the nineteenth century. The line appears to have run from the protectionist circle around Matthew Carey and Daniel Raymond, through Friedrich List to Germany and from there, via Roscher's circles, to American students such as Patten and Ely studying at German universities.' There were no graduate courses in economics in the United States at the time, and most US economists had

12. For a discussion of this strategy, see chapter 1 in this volume.
13. See Clément 1861–72.
14. For a discussion of this concept, see Bijker et al. 1989.
15. See Morris 1957, p. 285.
16. 'Ich sage das auf die Gefahr hin, als Neo-Merkantilist abgestempelt und in das Raritätenkabinett unseres Faches übergeführt zu werden', Sombart 1928, p. 925.

their PhD from Germany. This includes all the founders of the American Economic Association. The transfer of Other Canon economic ideas to Japan after the Meiji Restoration was made by German economists – and by US economists who had studied in Germany – when 'a stream of German teachers of political economy and related disciplines continually flowed in'.[17]

The mercantilist inspiration for production-based economics can also be traced to the twentieth century. The main economist behind the Third Reich was Hjalmar Schacht, who was one of the two prisoners immediately freed after the Nuremberg trials. The subject of Schacht's PhD thesis at the University of Kiel in 1900 was 'Der theoretische Gehalt der englischen Merkantilismus' ('The theoretical content of English mercantilism').[18] Schacht's skilful use of mercantilist production-based war economics, combined with a Keynesian understanding of credit, for a long time worked wonders for Hitler's Germany. Schacht's work also proves, though, the fundamental point of the Other Canon Renaissance economics – that economics cannot and must not be separated from morality. The influential German economist J.F. von Pfeiffer (1715–1787), an ardent antiphysiocrat, put it this way: 'You can make of human beings what you want. The way he is governed, commends man to good, or to evil.'[19]

3. THE TWO CANONS: SELECTIVE USE, METHODOLOGICAL SCHIZOPHRENIA AND OPPORTUNISTIC IGNORANCE

We do not imply that the world is a binary one, where all economists belong to one tradition or the other. On the contrary, a key characteristic of several important economists is their, at times, schizophrenic allegiance to both sets of theory. One example of this is the conflict between the Marshall whose 'Mecca of the economist' was based in economic biology (Marshall 1890, p. iv) and the Marshall of the appendices to his *Principles*, which were deeply steeped in 'physics envy'. In order to create the equilibrium that characterizes today's physics-based standard economic theory, Marshall paradoxically had to resort to a biological metaphor. Increasing returns had been an important argument for industrial policy, beginning with Serra (1613) and continuing through the nineteenth century. To reconcile the existence of increasing returns with equilibrium, Marshall (1890, pp. 315–16) uses a lengthy metaphor of firms growing and dying like trees in the forests. This evolutionary growth process supposedly counteracts the tendency towards uneven accumulation caused by increasing returns

17. Sugiyama and Mizuta 1988, p. 32.
18. The author's full name appears on the dissertation as Horace Greeley Hjalmar Schacht. Horace Greeley (1811–1872) was – like the important US protectionist E. Peshine Smith – a protégé of the US statesman William Seward, a secretary of state and one of the founders of the Republican Party. This party was the main proponent of 'Renaissance economics' in the United States at the time. Greeley founded the New York *Tribune* and was its editor for 31 years. One of the *Tribune*'s European correspondents was Karl Marx, whose dispatches became classics of Marxian socialism.
19. 'Man kann aus den Menschen machen, wass man will; die Art, mit der er regiert wird, entschliesst ihn zum Guten, oder zum Bösen', Pfeiffer 1777, p. 2.

to scale.[20] The argument that killed all future biological analogies in neoclassical economics was a biological analogy, which was important in making economics what it is today, a profession in which a physics-inspired equilibrium is the central gestalt.

Schumpeter emanated from the Renaissance tradition of the German historical school and spent his life on the hopeless task of formalizing the creative essence of Renaissance economics – entrepreneurship, novelty and creative destruction – into the framework of the dead equilibrium that is at the core of neoclassical economics. Schumpeter was indeed 'a living, breathing contradiction', as Mirowski (1994, p. 5) puts it. We would claim that this contradiction was a result of being steeped simultaneously in two irreconcilable paradigms (see Reinert 2002 for a discussion).

Marx was steeped in the same two irreconcilable paradigms. In his emphasis on technology and economic dynamics Marx, like Schumpeter, belongs to the Renaissance production-based canon. Marx's and Schumpeter's visions have a common basis in the German economic tradition. In Anglo-Saxon economics, these economists come across as extremely original; seen from the German side, they are both firmly rooted in that alternative canon. The one aspect of Marx's theory that belongs to the Anglo-Saxon canon is his use of Ricardo's labour theory of value. This theory is out of place in the German tradition, in which entrepreneurship, ideas, knowledge, leadership and management make vital contributions to the value added by physical labour.

Although he was – after John Locke and Bernard de Mandeville – the true founder of the mainstream canon, Adam Smith himself suffered from the same canonical mental split. In his discussion of the Navigation Act, he was clearly in favour of the protectionist policy, blocking Dutch ships and imports. His argument was to a large extent based on considerations of national defence. To Smith (1976, vol. 2, p. 219), 'The art of war . . . is certainly the noblest of all arts'.

It is of great interest to note that to Smith, the father of free trade, the mercantilist and protectionist Navigation Act was 'the wisest of all commercial regulations in England' (1976, vol. 1, p. 487). This apparent double standard and selective use of the different canons in order to suit English interests were frequently denounced by German and US economists in the nineteenth century. Their slogan was, 'Do as the English did, not as they say'. Today an appropriate strategy for the Third World would be, 'Do as the Americans did, not as they say'. Part of this use of a double standard was, and is, an 'opportunistic ignorance' (to use Gunnar Myrdal's term) of the history of one's own nation's economic policy.

Before his meeting with the French physiocrats, Adam Smith clearly expressed the Renaissance view of the common weal as the motivating force for establishing manufactures. These were established neither to assist the producer nor to assist the consumer:

> The same principle, *the same love of system*, the same regard to the beauty of order . . . frequently serves to recommend those institutions which tend to promote the public welfare . . . When the legislature establishes premiums and other encouragements to advance the linen or woollen manufactures, its conduct seldom proceeds from pure sympathy with the

---

20. This problem is discussed in Hart 1990.

> wearer of cheap or fine cloth, and much less from that with the manufacturer or merchant. The perfection of police [that is, policy], the extension of trade and manufactures, are noble and magnificent objects. The contemplation of them pleases us, and we are interested in whatever can tend to advance them. They make part of *the great system of government*, and the wheels of the political machine seem to move with more harmony and ease by means of them. We take pleasure in beholding the perfection of so beautiful and grand a system, and we are uneasy till we remove any obstruction that can in the least disturb or encumber the regularity of its motions.[21]

As we have indicated, the two alternative canons have ebbed and flowed throughout history. However, quite often we find the same nation-state applying both canons at the same time, but for different end-users. For example it is clear that, starting in the 1830s, England used Ricardo's trade theory (the barter-based classical canon) for export and Charles Babbage's works on the importance of machinery and of science (the knowledge- and production-based Renaissance canon) for domestic purposes. The United States conveniently followed this same canonic dualism in the nineteenth century. At a time when the United States was busily protecting its own industries, US commodore Matthew Perry was sent to Japan to convince that nation of the benefits of free trade. This resulted in the 'unfair treaties' that hold such a dominant position in the Japanese perception of their own history.

The same contradictory policies continued into the twentieth century. A book from the Washington-based Institute for International Economics in 1986 introduces the description of US trade policy as follows: 'With bipartisan regularity, American presidents since Franklin Delano Roosevelt have proclaimed the virtues of free trade. They have inaugurated bold international programs to reduce tariff and non-tariff barriers. But almost in the same breath, most presidents have advocated or accepted special measures to protect problem industries. Together the two strands of policy have produced a contradictory profile.'[22] On these occasions, arguments from the Renaissance-based canon – recognizing that both manufacturing and other knowledge-based activities matter – are invoked in order to protect both the national manufacturing base and the knowledge-based service sector. On the other hand the World Bank, following a strategy that 'manufacturing does not matter', carries out structural adjustment programmes which in many cases lead to the deindustrialization of whole nations, with a consequent collapse of national welfare (see chapter 8 on Mongolia in this volume). This is the paradigm of organized free trade, which in practice follows the Golden Rule: 'The one who has the gold makes the rules.'

An important feature of the opportunistic ignorance of today's leading industrialized nations is the fact that the history of their own economic policy – the policy that they used to catch up with the wealthy nations – to a surprising extent has been forgotten. This is very clear in the United States. The economists who laid the foundations for nineteenth-century US trade and industrial policy are hardly mentioned in today's history of economics, and if they are mentioned it is to point out their 'failures'. It is

21. Smith 1812, vol. 1, p. 320 (emphasis added).
22. Hufbauer et al. 1986, p. 1.

curious how today's American economists virtually unanimously declare that both the industrialization of their own country and the New Deal were carried out by 'bad economists'. Economists such as E. Peshine Smith,[23] who later played a key role in bringing the 'American System of Manufactures' to Japan, Matthew Carey, Daniel Raymond, Alexander Everett, Calvin Colton, Francis Bowen and Stephen Colwell are unknown today. Only Henry Carey is remembered by a few.

This is of course a parallel to the well-established 'fact' of economic science that the Renaissance economists who brought Europe out of the Middle Ages all belonged to the despised category of 'mercantilists'. We have collectively absorbed Adam Smith's caricature of all economists before himself: that they mistook gold for real wealth. German economist Eugen Dühring scorns *die Karikierer des Merkantilismus* – the caricature-makers of mercantilism – who 'only too often spoke as if the business people and the statesmen of the day almost believed that precious metal could be used as food for the human body'.[24] The important systemic and production-based aspects of the Renaissance theory – the creation of a national common weal – are left out of today's accounts. Recently however Cosimo Perrotta (1988) has published a book that resurrects Continental Mercantilism as a theory focused on production and employment.

The strategy of 'theory juggling' is also present in the European Community. The Cecchini Report on the single European market identifies most of the benefits from the single market as coming from economies of scale. On the other hand, EU policy towards the Third World is based on a theory which denies that economies of scale and increasing returns exist. During the nineteenth century, the existence of increasing returns in industry was an important argument for the protection of industry in all the nations that followed the English path to industrialization. Today, this argument is used only internally in the European Union, not in its policy towards the Third World. The industrialized nations are today 'pulling up the ladder' of development from those who tried to industrialize later. Only in Asia, where the activity-specific Renaissance strategy is copied from Japan, do we see real catching up.

Friedrich List saw clearly that Adam Smith's theory contradicted the policy followed by England during its ascent to world power. List's succinct and accurate summary of the history of English economic policy states: 'The principle "sell manufactured products, buy raw materials" was for centuries the English substitute for an [economic] theory.'[25]

To List (1904, pp. 368–69), English classical economic theory

> conceal[s] the true policy of England under cosmopolitan expressions and arguments which Adam Smith had discovered, in order to induce foreign nations not to imitate that policy. It is a very common clever device that when someone has attained the summit of greatness, he kicks away the ladder by which he had climbed up, in order to deprive others of the means of climbing up after him. On this lies the secret of the cosmopolitical doctrine of Adam

23. On E. Peshine Smith, see Hudson 1969. In the 1970s Hudson edited a series of reprints of the writings of nineteenth-century US economists.
24. Dühring, *Kritische Geschichte der Nationalökonomie* (1879), quoted in Sombart (1928), p. 913.
25. List 1959, p. 12. Our translation. This is part of List's foreword, which has been drastically reduced in the English edition.

> Smith, and of the cosmopolitical tendencies of his great contemporary William Pitt, and of all his successors in the British Government administrations. . . . William Pitt was the first English statesman who clearly saw in what way the cosmopolitical theory of Adam Smith could properly be made use of.

The actual historical record of free trade confirms that England carried out at home the very policies that its theoretical economists tried to prevent in the rest of the world. Conventional wisdom has it that in the nineteenth century, France was a fortress of protectionism while England was the bastion of free trade. Consulting actual trade data, however, yields the surprising conclusion that 'French average tariffs were . . . consistently below those of Britain throughout most of the Nineteenth Century, even after the abolition of the Corn Laws'.[26] The double standard is not new, but is still amazingly effective in maintaining and widening the gap between the leaders and the laggards of the world's nations.

4. COMMUNICATION, INFRASTRUCTURE AND FINANCE

In spite of its sparse treatment in economic theory, infrastructure is a key factor in any advanced economy. Infrastructure is the necessary policy response to the existence of geography and distance. Investments in transportation and communication are both productivity-enhancing and price-reducing (deflationary), and as such a prime engine of general investment. Traditional infrastructure induces investment in engineering and in the production of heavy machinery, while advanced infrastructure, as for example in telecommunications, is highly science- and innovation-driven. In both cases, transaction costs are reduced, labour productivity and employment are increased and the tax base widened.

In the Renaissance tradition, the bases for increased economic welfare are knowledge and infrastructure, broadly defined. Knowledge concerns the human ability to think, to generate hypotheses and to communicate. This communication in turn depends on the phenomenon of *consensus gentium*, which we elaborated upon in our article on Leibniz and Wolff (Reinert and Daastøl 1997).

Initial public institutions and public works focused on the need for defending society and for establishing justice; later, institutions facilitated the extension of commerce and the promotion of education. An early invention that brought wealth was the institution of the well-ordered city, with its tight communication, extended division of labour, markets, legal and political administration, and well-ordered communication with the outside world. This dates at least to the Indus civilization of 2300 BC, where Mohenjodaro was probably the first planned city in the world; it included a highly developed division of labour with many 'modern' inventions such as the wheel, the plough, intense irrigation, a sewer system, local markets and a vast international trading network.

As already mentioned, the concept of the common weal was synergetic, as had been observed already by Xenophon (Xenophon and Ambler 2001). Serra (1613) specifically

26. Nye 1991, p. 23.

relates the wealth of a city to the number of different professions contained therein, that is, to the extent and degree of the division of labour. Adam Smith's division of labour, known to the ancients and elaborated by numerous authors before him,[27] clearly implies increasing returns to scale. This is probably the reason why the division of labour has never been integrated into classical or neoclassical economic modelling. The division of labour is in some very fundamental sense not compatible with constant returns to scale; rather, it is a result of fixed costs – either of knowledge or of other tools – which automatically cause increasing returns to some degree. In the Renaissance conception of economics, therefore, returns increased with the size of population of a nation. Recreating and extending this observed urban advantage, the urban bias of development, to the whole nation-state was a central challenge to Renaissance rulers. Both List and Wallerstein point out that while England achieved this increased size through national unity, Italy, the Hansa and Holland did not develop beyond a collection of city-states, which they see as a main reason for their loss of leadership.[28]

Early municipal (city-state) mercantilists observed the beneficial effects of denser populations clustered in towns giving rise to productive synergetic effects through differentiation, personal and political freedom, and economies of scale. Having a large population was therefore regarded as a great benefit to any nation. Roscher (1882, p. 343 § 254) writes on the early policy of Henry IV that '[n]ot many had as much insight as Henry IV: la force et la richesse des rois consistent dans les nombre et dans l'opulence des sujets', and Petty 'would give up Scotland and Ireland entirely, and have the inhabitants settle in England'. For a discussion of early population theories, see Stangeland (1904). In this philosophy, building infrastructure became a key tool to later nation-building mercantilists and cameralists. State mercantilists tried to emulate on a national scale the agglomeration advantages found in urban areas through state-initiated construction of various means of infrastructure, communication and transportation. These economists and policy-makers tried to reconstruct artificially the observed benefits of the cities' high population densities in geographical areas with lower population densities. Law and order; industrial quality control; labour codes; labour discipline; standardization of language, measurements, coins and education; the construction of ports, roads, canals, postal routes and 'refuelling stations' along transportation routes were all parts of this strategy. These measures were intended to create widespread national welfare as opposed to the municipal mercantilist strategy which flourished, in the main, in coastal city-states. These city-states mostly functioned as enclave economies that were relatively isolated from the hinterland. State Mercantilism or 'statism' changed this early merchant Mercantilism. In its pursuit of public power and wealth, state Mercantilism fused the monarchic and municipal mercantilist traditions. This alliance between the king and the middle class, which opposed the feudal aristocracy, created a powerful instrument: the nation-state, an instrument that unified formerly separate towns and regions.

27. Roscher (1882, vol. 1, p. 189 § 58) refers to the works of Xenophon, Plato, Aristotle, Aquinas, Luther, Petty, Mandeville, Berkeley, Harris, Rousseau, Turgot, Diderot, Tucker and Beccaria.

28. List 1904, chapters 1, 2 and 3; Wallerstein 1978, vol. 2, pp. 90–93.

In sparsely populated areas, a policy of corridor development was pursued, similar to the old Silk Road caravan tracks between the Roman and Chinese empires established by the first Han (206 BC–220 AD) or the emperor's Grand Canal between Hangzhou and Beijing (1800 km). By creating dense populations in areas along transportation routes, construction of these arteries was made economically more worthwhile. This strategy also opened up marginal areas for development, the early railroad development of the United States being a prime example of such strategy. The purpose of the huge investments in infrastructure was in some ways similar to the purpose of the city-states itself: the realization of 'systemic increasing returns', an idea which is already very evident in Xenophon's *Cyropaedia* (§ 8.2.5, in Xenophon 2001) and in his *Poroi* (Zincke 1753). This observed 'systemic increasing returns' to the size of a city was the basis for the pro-population stance of cameralists and mercantilists.

List (1985, p. 131) notes the importance of infrastructure for greater communication between citizens. Much like the Internet today, this increased direct communication made political control of the individual more difficult, and therefore created greater political freedom and by extension increased creativity and innovation. Only in densely populated areas could a critical mass of public opinion acquire enough strength to develop into democracy and generally promote political and human rights. At the same time, the expansion of markets through improved communication allowed for greater economies of scale, greater diversification and production for niche markets, and greater production for a monetary – as opposed to a barter – market. Economies of scale allowed for improved technology and made it possible for a higher percentage of the population to engage in new activities, again contributing to diversity, division of labour and economies of scale in a positive feedback circle. The mercantilists' promotion of manufacturing also intended to emulate these positive effects of the city modelled as a huge productive machine, the factory.

A major problem with promotion of infrastructure is how to initiate and finance it. The core factors of the Renaissance policy – knowledge, innovation and infrastructure – all have the character of public goods: concentrated costs for the investor and widely dispersed benefits for society. As is well known, this results in a systematic underinvestment if left to an unregulated market. This outcome is suboptimal from a public point of view, although perfectly rational from the individual investor's point of view. The public, including the individual investors, therefore needs a coordinator, such as a municipality, a regional authority (for example, German Länder or the states in the United States), the nation or an international body (for example, the EU or the UN), to initiate and direct credit to these sectors that produce public goods. The credit directing may be done more directly through a central planning agency, such as GOSPLAN in the former USSR, or more indirectly by ordering banks to offer favourable conditions to industrialists investing in these sectors, as in the French dirigisme system up to the reign of de Gaulle. Another solution is to have many of these public goods produced under the umbrella of national defence, as in the United States where defence spending was used to finance the interstate highways (the national system of interstate and defence highways was financed 90 per cent by the Federal Government) and where military basic research that has led to innovations as diverse as the ballpoint pen (by the US airforce during the Second World War), burglar alarms (the Vietnam War), advanced cellular telephone communication (the 'Star Wars' programme) and the Internet.

From the school of the state mercantilist Colbert, then Napoleon, St. Simon and the Grandes Ecoles system came the dirigiste system with 'qualitative bank control' in various softer and harder versions (Wiles 1977, p. 215). Wiles further writes (p. 322): 'We remark here again the flexibility, speed and secrecy of such arrangements, compared with the constitutional obstacles to continual changes in taxes by the government, let alone a command economy.' There is a strong tradition of using this kind of policy among nations when endeavouring to catch up, in France, the United States, Japan and Germany. There are several ways to solve this problem of credit directing in practice. They all call for cooperation among authorities, industrialists and bankers; among people, knowledge of the physical production process and of the credit system. Such collaboration and consequent public encroachment into what is otherwise today seen as the sphere of the private market is of course against mainstream economics, but the present national innovation system of the United States is replete with institutions of this sort. The website of the US Small Business Administration, http://www.sba.gov, reveals that this institution alone channels loans of more than $58 billion of federal funds to US businesses. This government institution assisted more than one million private US companies during 2002, a most visible US government hand. On the US state level a large number of tax incentives to manufacturing companies that are 'small' (by US standards) complements this policy. The problem, however, is that the conditionalities of the Washington Institutions prevent these excellent US policies from being copied by poor nations.

Traditionally this way of thinking is accompanied by policy measures ensuring sufficient effective demand – or purchasing power – for the new production capacities thus created. The nineteenth-century US 'High Wage Strategy' was an efficient strategy, as was the 'Fordist' wage regime, lasting until about 1970, whereby production wages were increased at the same pace as productivity increases in the manufacturing sector. This would prevent depressions due to 'overproduction', 'underconsumption' or 'oversaving'. This idea is also expressed in the 'circular flow' of J.M. Keynes or the 'ecocirc' of Ragnar Frisch. In this system, increasing the standards of living of the majority of the population is not only a moral imperative, it becomes an economic necessity in order to keep the economy growing. Once the virtuous circle of increased productivity/increased real wages starts operating, increasing the real wages of the common man becomes a necessary economic policy if the system is to be perpetuated.

The leading historian and theoretician of economics in Germany in the middle of the nineteenth century was Wilhelm Roscher, whose *Principles*, book IV, is devoted to consumption. As Roscher noted, financial investments are a kind of sterile storage until channelled into consumption. This may disturb the peaceful balance and equilibrium in the perfect model of the classical school. One of Roscher's chapters has the telling heading, 'Necessity of the Proper Simultaneous Development of Production and Consumption'. After a discussion of the two areas, he writes, 'Hence, one of the most essential conditions of a prosperous national economy is that the development of consumption should keep equal pace with that of production, and supply with demand.' In a footnote he declares:

> The necessity of an equilibrium between production and consumption was pretty clear to many of the older political economists. . . . *The moderns have frequently inequitably neglected the doctrine of consumption.* Thus it appears to be a very characteristic fact that in Adam Smith's great book . . . one might think that products were not made for the sake of man but for their own sake. But on the other hand there came a strong reaction . . . And so according to Carey, *Principles*, ch. 35, § 6, the *real difficulty does not lie in production but in finding a purchaser for the products.* But he overlooks the fact here that only the possessor of other products can appear as a purchaser. From another side, most socialists think almost exclusively of the wants of men, and scarcely consider it worth their while to pay any attention to the means of satisfying them. (Roscher 1882, book VI, Chapter 1, §CCXV; emphasis added)

The core motive of Friedrich List and the American protectionists was to promote production in order to elevate wages and consumption, thereby increasing the tax base and production of public goods, and then to promote more production and consumption in a virtuous circle.

Part of this development plan must therefore also have a strategy on how to increase consumption and avoid market crises. On such crises, Roscher (1882, §CCXV) writes:

> The growth of a nation's economy depends on this: that consumption should always be, so to speak, one step in advance of production. . . . Now, the politico-economic disease which is produced by the lagging behind of consumption, and by the supply being much in advance of the demand, is called a commercial [market] crisis.

He continues (§CCXVI), 'Most theorists deny the possibility of a general glut, although many practitioners stubbornly maintain it.' In the next paragraph (§CCXVII) Roscher continues:

> All these allegations are undoubtedly true, in so far as the whole world is considered one great economic system, and the aggregate of all goods, including the medium of circulation, is borne in mind. The consolation which might otherwise lie herein is made indeed to some extent unrealizable by these conditions. It must not be forgotten in practice that men are actuated by other motives than that of consuming as much as possible. . . .
>
> There are, everywhere, certain consumption-customs corresponding with the distribution of the national income. Every great and sudden change in the latter is therefore wont to produce a great glut of the market. [Footnote: If all the rich were suddenly to become misers . . . a multitude of former consumers, having no employment, would be obliged to discontinue their demand. Overproduction would be greater yet if a great and general improvement in the industrial arts or in the art of agriculture has gone before.] (Roscher 1882, §CCXVII)

The last point about general improvement in the industrial arts is reminiscent of the recent technological revolution and the consequent financial crisis (Perez 2002). It should be noted that in this perspective the loss of purchasing power of national salaries and wages as documented in the case study of Mongolia in chapter 8 in this volume, to the order of around 50 per cent, constitute an enormous setback in the development process. Under the present economic policies there are no signs why this process should be reversed again.

The circulation problem therefore concerns not only directing credit to production but, according to Roscher, even more to channelling purchasing power to consumers in order to create a demand for this production. This brings our discussion into the age-old problem of the regulation of the financial sector as a servant of production and consumption. Such a regulation of the financial sector is found as far back as in Ancient Sumeria and in early Judaism, where sporadic debt forgiveness was an important institution. These were the Jubilee years, a financial institution that we find mentioned several times in the Bible. The famous Rosetta Stone, which made possible the deciphering of hieroglyphics, commemorates such a debt cancellation by Ptolemy V in 196 BC (Rostovtzeff 1941, II, p. 713). At one point the accumulated debt burden could cripple investment in productive activities, thereby undermining not only the ability to feed a population but also the ability to pay interest. This in turn would cripple production. Not only would the financial community fail in directing credit to productive purposes, it would also gradually become the owner of empires and people. For this reason, authors such as Marx have seen the financial community as the great culprit of derailed development, quite opposite to the positive catalyst it might have been and actually has been in some instances, such as in early industrialist Germany and Japan.

This is clearly most relevant for the Third World debt problem today. If history is to be a guide, the vicious circles of debt and poverty can only be broken by creating a virtuous circle of production in the Third World, not by debt forgiveness alone.

5. CANONICAL BATTLES: THE HEAD-ON CONFRONTATIONS

Occasionally the two canons meet head-on in what we have labelled canonical *Methodenstreite*. Next we describe six of these *Methodenstreite*.

5.1. *Canonical* Methodenstreit *1: De Santis versus Serra (1605 and 1613) and Misselden versus Malynes (1622–23)*

Today's mainstream economics was born only in the eighteenth century with Bernhard Mandeville and Adam Smith. There were, however, important earlier skirmishes between the school of barter and the school of production. An early debate is the one in Naples in the early seventeenth century between Marc'Antonio de Santis and Antonio Serra (Schumpeter 1954, p. 344; Doléjal 1921). The battle-lines between exchange and production are clearer in the debate between de Santis and Serra, but the 'English' debate between Gerard de Malynes (1622, 1623) and Edward Misselden (1622, 1623) is better represented in the historiography of economics (Seligman 1920). The latter debate is also more personal and 'acrimonious, even abusive', where 'ink was shed like water'[29] (the authors swore to each other in ten languages, Misselden mocking Malynes for not knowing the eleventh one). Malynes represents a static theory rooted in barter and Misselden represents a theory centred around learning and production. Both Misselden and Malynes were Flemish, working in London.

In the history of economic thought, the debate between Misselden and Malynes is normally interpreted as being about exchange controls and the balance of trade.[30] However, by going back to the sources, one finds that Misselden's main line of attack is against Malynes's 'mechanical' view of Man (see Mirowski 2002 for a parallel to neoclassical economics). According to Misselden, Malynes has left out Man's 'art' and 'soul'. He (Misselden 1623, p. 8) quotes Malynes's reduction of trade to three elements, 'namely, Commodities, Money, and Exchange'. Objecting to this definition, Misselden writes: 'It is against Art to dispute with a man that denyeth the *Principles* of Art.' Misselden scorns Malynes for not seeing the difference between a heap of stones and logs and a house – because Man's productive powers and his soul, which produce the house, have been left out. A similar criticism can be made of neoclassical economics.

Misselden represents the acute Renaissance awareness of the enormous territory to be covered between Mankind's present poverty and ignorance on the one hand and its enormous potential on the other. This released enthusiasm and energy. The situation recalls Keynes's frustration with the suboptimal situation of the world during the Great Depression. We shall attempt to show that to the Renaissance philosophers and economists and to Keynes, the formula needed to 'free' society from its suboptimal position was what Keynes (1930, vol. 2, p. 102) called 'Salvation through Knowledge'. The parallel with the Third World today should be clear.

In the late eighteenth century a new type of economic theory came into being, focusing on the 'natural harmony' of nature. Malynes and later Bernard de Mandeville (also a Dutchman) were the predecessors of this view. This theoretical development culminated with Adam Smith's *Wealth of Nations*, published in 1776 when the English had caught up with and forged ahead of the Dutch. Mandeville is best known for his work *Fable of the Bees* (1714, but an early version in 1705). An early parallel is that Malynes in 1655 published *The Commonwealth of Bees*. The use of bees in a harvesting economy as a metaphor for a human economy leaves out the role of creativity, novelty and intelligence. Even today, a fundamental and unresolved problem of standard economic theory is how to deal with knowledge and novelty.

This 'harvest economy' was central also to the French physiocrats: physiocracy, that is the rule of nature. As we shall see, the antiphysiocrats were defending the Renaissance tradition. In physiocracy all economic activities other than agriculture were seen as sterile. Within today's evolutionary economics, we find the same schism: part of the evolutionary school tends to substitute 'biology envy' for 'physics envy', leaving out the

29. Schumpeter (1954, pp. 344–45) discusses the controversy between the two men. See also their respective entries in the *New Palgrave*. In all cases these references are purely to the mechanics of money and exchange.

30. Buck 1942, p. 23.

creative dimension of Man. Today Adam Smith's 'invisible hand' finds its equivalent in Paul Krugman's (1996, p. 99) view of the economy as a self-organizing system: 'Global weather is a self-organising system; so surely, is the global economy.' The implications are clear: Man is at the mercy of an irrational destiny we cannot influence, particularly not on a collective level.

In his *Theory of Moral Sentiments* Adam Smith makes it clear that tampering with destiny is not Man's business:

> The care of the universal happiness of all rational and sensible beings, is the business of God and not of man. . . . Nature has directed us to the greater part of these [means to bring happiness about] by original and immediate instincts . . . [which] prompts us to apply those means for their own sake, and without any consideration of their tendency to those beneficent ends which the great Director of Nature intended to produce them.[31]

The parallel with Krugman's weather metaphor is obvious. Albert Hirschman's 1991 book *The Rhetoric of Reaction* traces the history of this theoretical school.

In our view, both Smith and Krugman fit the tradition of moral hedonism, exemplified in this quotation from Jeremy Bentham (1780, p. 11):

> Nature has placed Man under two sovereign masters, pain and pleasure. It is for them alone to point out what we ought to do, as well as determine what we shall not do. . . . [E]very effort we make to throw off our subjugation, will serve but to demonstrate and confirm it. In words a man may pretend to abjure their empire: but in reality he will remain subject to it all the while. The principle of utility – the greatest happiness or greatest felicity principle – recognises this subjugation, and assumes it for the foundation. . . . Systems which attempt to question it deal . . . in caprice instead of reason, in darkness instead of light.

Typically, proponents of the barter-centred mechanical theories of wealth appear in well-consolidated and wealthy nations where the problems of creating the institutions of a civilizing state have long been forgotten. At the time of the Misselden–Malynes controversy, Holland was the leading nation, and England and France were attempting to catch up. Many leading businessmen in England were at the time Dutch, and the same is true of many 'English' economists. We have already mentioned Misselden and Malynes. Jacob Vanderlint, an early 'English' free trader, was also a Dutchman working in London. Nicholas Barbon, another English free trader, was born in England but educated in Leiden (see Raffel 1905). In the tradition that local free traders were in reality citizens of the 'empire' of the day, the main German nineteenth-century free trader in Germany was John Prince-Smith, an Englishman (Prince-Smith 1874).

The shift of emphasis in economics from human creativity (Botero, Serra, Misselden) to 'natural harmony' and barter (Malynes, Smith) was a true paradigm shift in Thomas Kuhn's sense. It must be admitted however that in Adam Smith's England the use of some of the incentives of Renaissance economics to produce knowledge had degenerated. Patents had been established starting in the late fifteenth century in order

31. Smith 1812, chapter 3. Interestingly, this appears in a book that is said to represent the diametric opposite of *Wealth of Nations*, the first based on altruism, the latter on self-love.

to promote what we have labelled dynamic and knowledge-producing rent-seeking or Schumpeterian Mercantilism (Reinert 1999). In Adam Smith's England this system in many cases had degenerated into static rent-seeking. Patents were no longer used to promote new knowledge; monopoly patents were sold by the king in order to raise money. As was previously argued by Pieter de la Court in the case of the Netherlands (de la Court 1662), free trade and the reduction of restrictions were necessary in Adam Smith's England to reduce production costs in order for the nation to remain internationally competitive.

Whereas the optimistic theory of the Renaissance focused on the limitless potential of 'man the producer', the new economic theory came to focus on 'man the trader and consumer'. The two theories were steeped in very different realities: the old one in Man's ability to create and produce, and the new one in a world of barter, based on the mechanics of the 'natural order'. The old theory was dynamic and organic, centred around 'thought' and 'becoming'; the new theory was mechanical and static, centred around 'matter' and 'being'. In the old theory the market played the role of servant to active human beings who knew where they were going; in the new theory the market acquired many of the characteristics of 'providence', as the manifestation of the natural order (see Viner 1972). Sombart (1928, p. 919) fittingly calls the Renaissance economics activistic–idealistic, and the mainstream economics from Adam Smith onward passivistic–materialistic.

It is important to understand why such a paradigmatic shift at any historical moment may be in the interest of the leading nation, but detrimental to the laggard nations. Having created a strong nation-state and established itself in the most dynamic economic activities of the day, the hegemonic state can take the existence of such an efficient state and of its own technological capabilities for granted, and at that point – as did England and the United States in sequence – elevate the market to a goal in itself. A theory which assumes away the importance of technology and knowledge is not harmful to a nation which possesses the most knowledge and the most advanced technology, only to the laggard nations. Assuming away the existence of diminishing returns is not harmful to the nation that dominates the industries with the highest degrees of increasing returns, only to the nations specialized in activities dominated by the law of diminishing returns. Typically, the leading nations – England and the United States again in the same sequence – have produced economic theories that are void of any context.

Whereas Renaissance economics sees no limits to progress – it truly envisions 'a never-ending frontier of human knowledge' – in Adam Smith's system, which followed Malynes's, nations reach a stationary state where they can advance no further, when that 'full compliment of riches which the nature of its soil and climate . . . allowed it to require' had been reached (Smith 1976, p. 106). It is only here that we see the practical consequences of Smith's sharing the same assumptions as part of today's ecology movement: no new knowledge enters the system. The only logical consequence of a theory that does not allow for the production of new knowledge is either a stationary state (as with Smith and Ricardo) or an ecological disaster (as with Malthus). This disaster can be predicted by simple extrapolations; however, each level of knowledge carries its own level of 'sustainability'. Knowledge and institutions are the conspicuously and 'actively absent' factors in Adam Smith's system; that is, he not only ignores these factors but actively argues that they have no relevance.[32]

Whereas Renaissance economics focuses on production, neoclassical economics focuses on barter and exchange. Leibniz sees the origin of barter as being in production, and quotes Aristotle: 'Nam Maercaturs transfert tantum, Manufactura gignit' (Trade can carry only as much as the factories produce). To Leibniz, the poverty of the artisans was an important argument for the establishment of an active state: 'After all, is not the entire purpose of Society to release the artisan from his misery? The farmer is not in need, since he is sure of his bread, and the merchant has more than enough' (Leibniz 1992, p. 54).

5.2. *Canonical* Methodenstreit *2: Antiphysiocracy versus Physiocracy and Adam Smith (ca 1770–1830)*

The second *Methodenstreit* between the knowledge-based Other Canon and the predecessor of today's standard economic theory starts in the 1770s with the rise of the physiocratic school in France. It may be said that the physiocratic school in some sense was a reaction to the excesses of Colbertism. But it can also be said that it was the reaction of the landowners against Colbert's policy of systematically diverting resources from agriculture to manufacturing: The physiocrates continued the animalistic view of Man '. . . sometimes they regard Man as a browsing animal, concerned only with his nourishment, the maximum production of the fruit of the earth as his social ideal' (Higgs 1897, pp. 107–08).

The antiphysiocratic movement has received little attention in the history of economic thought. These authors, however, represented the true continuation of Renaissance economics. Interestingly, two of the main opponents of physiocracy in France were clergymen: Abbé Mably and Abbé Galiani, the Neapolitan envoy to the Court of Paris.[33] Galiani was to take a position which in many ways foreshadowed the position of the historical school in late nineteenth-century *Methodenstreit*: 'Abstract principles are no good for commercial policy. Corn laws which are good in one time or place may be bad in another. . . . The statesmen who admired Colbert should not imitate him, but ask himself, "What would Colbert do if he were here now?"' (Higgs 1897, p. 117). This criticism of a very abstract and context-free theory was similar to Richard Jones's reaction in 1820 against Ricardo's writings. Reverend Jones was the father of the English Historical School of Economics, which became very influential during the latter half of the nineteenth century.

One of the main opponents of the physiocratic school in France was Forbonnais, who refused to admit that trade and industry are sterile.[34] Forbonnais believed that the main agent creating wealth is Man, not nature: without human agency the land is doomed to absolute or relative stability. The antiphysiocracy movement was strong in France, Italy

32. This point is discussed in chapter 5.
33. A good description of Galiani and his unique standing in French society at the time is found in Pecchio 1849, pp. 80–86.
34. The antiphysiocrats are discussed in Weulersse 1910, vol. 2, pp. 256–682, and in Higgs 1897, pp. 102–22.

and Germany, but perhaps the most ardent antiphysiocrats were found in Germany. Under the heading 'Antiphysiokraten', Humpert's bibliography of the German cameralist school lists 25 works published between 1771 and 1832 (Humpert 1937, pp. 1031–32). The best known of these is Johann Friedrich von Pfeiffer's *Der Antiphysiokrat* (1780).

5.3. Canonical **Methodenstreit** *3: The American System versus the British System (Nineteenth-Century United States)*

The US opposition to English classical economic theory started with Benjamin Franklin and continued with US secretary Alexander Hamilton's report on industrial policy to the House of Representatives in 1791. This *Methodenstreit* on the policy level lasted through the 1930s, although on the theoretical level English classical economics was to be increasingly taught at the Ivy League universities in the late nineteenth century. At one point Cornell University offered parallel courses in the two traditions. Important economists in this tradition included, as already mentioned, Daniel Raymond, Matthew and Henry Carey, John Rae and E. Peshine Smith. The last great economists of this tradition were Richard Ely and Simon Patten, who had both studied in Germany.

On the policy level, the nations industrializing in the nineteenth century were to take up the example that England had set – and later abandoned when it had achieved world hegemony. The great industrial nations in their pre-take-off period shared a core theme of the activity-specific nature of growth (see Reinert 1996b). Economic growth could only be achieved by including in the nation's portfolio of industrial activities with the following characteristics: (1) fast technological change, (2) a rapid growth in output ((1)(2) representing what is normally called Verdoorn's Law), and (3) subject to increasing returns to scale. This theme can be followed in economic writings from the 1500s in Italy, England and France, and a little later in the German cameralists. It is introduced to the United States through Alexander Hamilton and his favourite economist, the English mercantilist Malachy Postlethwayt,[35] and from Friedrich List's involuntary exile in the United States it is reinforced again in the Germany of the Zollverein. In Meiji Japan, the *doitsugaku* school, which favoured the German model, became the most influential in the building of society, at least until 1945 (Yagi 1989, p. 29). The Japanese took over the autarkic views that dominated the German Historical School. As we have already commented, in Japan after 1883 'a stream of German teachers of political economy and related disciplines continually flowed in' (Sugiyama and Mizuta 1988, p. 32).

Through the centuries, one common thread of successful long-distance catching up has been a shared distrust of free trade until the nation is firmly established in what was seen to be the 'right' economic activities – the specific activities which increased the nation's 'productive powers'. Through dynamic imperfect competition (Schumpeter's 'historical increasing returns', see Schumpeter 1954 and Reinert 1980) in these specific

35. Excerpts from Postlethwayt's *Universal Dictionary of Trade and Commerce* were scattered through Hamilton's *Army Pay Book*; see Morris 1957, p. 285. Hamilton's views on the English classical economists were echoed in that of the Japanese 80 years later; see Tessa Morris-Suzuki 1989.

activities, real wages could be raised: first in the 'engine' industry and subsequently spreading through the whole national labour market. In the US tradition, adding skill to the labourer was the logical way of increasing his value (his wage). This tradition survived in the United States up to and including the economists who were taught by Ely's and Patten's generation. We would argue that in nineteenth-century US economic policy, the general view was that some economic activities were better than others. Differences in wage levels, both nationally and between nations, are to a large extent a result of varying degrees of imperfect competition, caused by both static and dynamic factors. The factors at work have long been identified both by businessmen and in industrial economics, and they are correlated. These factors were for many years discussed under the heading of 'industrialism'.

Figure 12.3 plots the 'quality' of economic activities at any given time on a scale from white (perfect competition) to black (monopoly). The whole system is constantly moving as new types of knowledge enter on top and, with varying speed, fall towards perfect information and perfect competition as they mature. We would claim that the gestalt expressed in Figure 12.3 corresponds to the nineteenth-century US view of why some nations were wealthier than others and why nations had to reach the top of the quality index before free trade would be beneficial to them. At the bottom of this hierarchy sit the world's most-efficient producers of baseballs – in Haiti – making US$0.30 per hour. This type of production has not been mechanized anywhere. Higher up sit the world's most-efficient producers of golf balls – in a mechanized production – making US$12 per hour. We maintain that no nation of any size has ever reached a high level of national welfare without going through a period of this kind of thinking, perhaps with the possible exclusion of tiny city-states. This was the vision of the *realökonomisch*-oriented mercantilist school. In English literature, Charles King's very influential 1721 volumes clearly express this thinking.

Figure 12.3 unites the economic factors that prevent factor-price equalization from ever taking place in the world economy. Within one nation – within the same labour market – the same forces are at work, but the dispersion in the wage level becomes much less pronounced. Within a nation several factors unite to create a tendency towards larger equality in wages: mobility of labour, similar education and knowledge levels, pressure from labour unions, and the like. The wage level of the traditional service sector seems to be determined by the existence or lack of 'high-quality' activities in each nation. If none are present, real wages in the service sector are low. In this sector (which includes barbers, bus drivers, chambermaids and so on), productivity levels all over the world tend to be very similar. Their real wages, however, are widely different. A barber or bus driver in Bolivia or Russia, although as efficient as those in the First World, earns real wages that are only a fraction of his Swiss or Norwegian counterparts.

The quality index of economic activities, in our opinion, answers the question of why the 'invisible hand' compensates workers of equal efficiency in the service sector so differently in different countries. We would claim that because of this mechanism, what to most people seems like a globally 'efficient' market does not maximize world welfare. By distributing the production of knowledge-intensive, high-quality products to all labour markets – not by distributing capital – the average standard of living throughout the

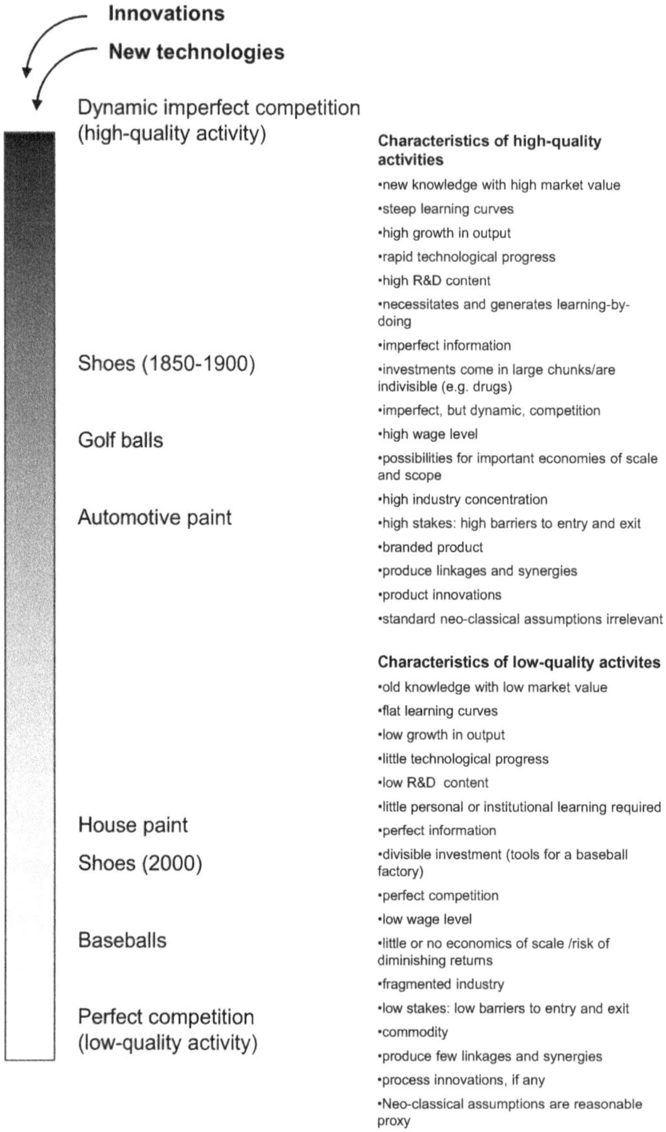

Figure 12.3 The Quality Index of economic activities.

world may be raised considerably. Our argument is very close to those of the German philosopher Leibniz and of early US economists, starting with Benjamin Franklin,[36] Alexander Hamilton, Mathew Carey and Daniel Raymond in the late eighteenth and early nineteenth centuries.

36. See particularly Franklin's comments printed as footnotes in Whatley 1774.

The pre-Mandevillean and pre-Smithian attitude towards colonialism are also worth noting. Since they knew that a nation without a manufacturing sector could not develop to any extent, pre-Smithian economists tended to acknowledge that colonialism was not in the interests of the colonies themselves. Manufacturing being a key to wealth, this is an obvious part of the logic of the mercantilist system. Johann Heinrich Gottlob von Justi (1717–1771), for example, recognized that colonial trading arrangements 'always will be in danger as soon as the foreign people start getting wiser' (quoted in Roscher 1874, p. 91). Adam Smith and David Ricardo represent a real watershed in economics, in that it is only with their barter-based, rather than production-based, economic theories that colonialism becomes morally defensible. Colonialism is only defensible within an economic theory where national wealth grows independently of what the nation produces.

5.4. Canonical **Methodenstreit** *4: The Historical School versus the Classical and Neoclassical Schools and Marginalism (1848–1908)*

The resounding success of Ricardian economics and its extreme *laissez-faire* policies during the 1840s provoked a theoretical counter-movement following the political events of 1848. The international depression in 1873 further increased opposition to the classical economic tradition all over Europe. The stronghold of the opposition was in Germany, where the older historical school founded by Bruno Hildebrand (1848), Karl Knies and Wilhelm Roscher increasingly challenged both the theoretical foundations and practical conclusions of Ricardian economics. Later a new generation of historical economists led by Gustav Schmoller – the younger historical school – dominated German academic and practical economics for a long time. Schmoller was instrumental in the founding of the *Verein für Sozialpolitik* – the Association for Social Policy – which was to build the theory and practice of the welfare state, piece by piece, between 1872 and 1932.

In 1883 Carl Menger, the founder of the Austrian marginalist school, published *Untersuchungen über die Methode der Sozialwissenschaften und der politischen Ökonomie insbesondere*. Menger dedicated his book to Wilhelm Roscher, the prominent German economist of the historical school. Menger closed the preface by praising recent German economics and hoping that his book would 'be regarded . . . as a friendly greeting from a collaborator in Austria'. Germany's reply was not friendly. Schmoller reviewed the *Untersuchungen* unfavourably in his *Jahrbuch*, and Menger responded in a small book titled *Errors of Historicism* in 1884.[37] Of all the *Methodenstreite* this, the most famous one, is paradoxically the least fundamental. Menger and Schmoller essentially shared the same critical attitude towards the mechanical and barter-based English theory. Their personalities and pride clashed, but compared to Ricardian economics the two are next of kin. This *Methodenstreit* created a debilitating civil war inside The Other Canon.

Schmoller wanted theory to be empirically founded, in opposition to the English classical tradition which founded theory on introspective assumptions and deduced far-reaching practical conclusions from these abstract structures. Schumpeter labelled this practice 'the Ricardian vice'. Today's standard explanation of this *Methodenstreit*

37. Menger 1884; see also Ritzel 1950.

generally fails to point out how similar the two men's criticism of Ricardian economics was. The New Palgrave describes the *Methodenstreit* as follows (Fusfeld 1987, p. 454):

> [Schmoller] rejected Menger's deductive method for three chief reasons: its assumptions were unrealistic, its high degree of abstraction made it largely irrelevant to the real-world economy, and it was devoid of empirical content. The theory was therefore useless in studying the chief questions of importance to economists: how have the economic institutions of the modern world developed to their present state, and what are the laws and regularities that govern them? The proper method was induction of general principles from historical–empirical studies.

However, reading through Menger's *Errors of Historicism* (1884) with the perspective of what economics has become, it becomes clear how 'Other Canon' both Schmoller and Menger were.

The historical school was steeped in the German tradition of embracing *die Ganzheit* – the whole. This search for *die Ganzheit* forced the historical school to cross the boundaries into what in the English tradition were considered unrelated academic disciplines. In the German historical tradition, it would make no sense to exclude any information relevant to the question asked – whether from the realm of climatology, pedagogy or any other branch of human knowledge. In the German tradition, economics was a science that integrated all the others and the criterion for including a factor or not was simply that of relevance. However, it is not at all clear that Menger disagreed with this. Menger formulated a model of the economic forces at work but, like Schumpeter later, he insisted that history was an 'indispensable' tool for the profession.

To Menger, the problem of the historical school was that it suffered from a kind of 'case-study syndrome': members of the school collected raw materials for a theory but failed to formalize their propositions on a higher level of abstraction. This is similar to Thorstein Veblen's view. However, this criticism is more appropriate to some members of the historical school than to others. It is crucial to define what is meant by 'theory'. The marginalist tradition came to seek 'pure theory', a formalist kind of theory that excluded from economics all the forces that in the Renaissance tradition were the driving forces of history and its auxiliary institutions: knowledge, creativity and morality. The criticism voiced by German economists at the time was similar to Misselden's accusations against Malynes: economics had become *entgeistet*, or void of human spirit. However, of all the marginalists, Menger was the closest to the historical school. As we shall discuss later, he both 'invented' marginalism and went far beyond it.

The criticism of the marginalists from the historical school was that the very source of wealth – human wit and will – had disappeared. The German ethical historical school, with its US followers such as Richard Ely and Simon Patten, followed the Renaissance tradition of seeing economics as a normative science, setting out to transform society for the benefit of the common weal. They considered morality to be rational and part of the *Ganzheit* of the economics profession. In contrast, in British empiricist philosophy and classical economics, morality was considered to be irrational and based on sympathy (feeling) in the tradition of David Hume and Adam Smith. Accordingly, to the English school morality was totally separated from science and therefore from economics.

5.5. *Canonical* Methodenstreit *5: The US Institutional School versus the Neoclassical School (Twentieth Century)*

Institutional economics presents a continuation of the US and German nineteenth-century economics tradition. Institutionalism – a term originally coined to describe the work of the Norwegian–American economist Thorstein Veblen (1857–1929) – continued the radical trend of the 'American System' in opposing the abstract structures of English theory.

The institutionalists were very critical of the established economic doctrine, but most of them did not seek to throw it out completely. Since their theory was *praxisnah* – empirical and close to the reality of practical problems – the institutionalists attracted the attention of policy-makers. Academically and in terms of influence, US institutionalism peaked in the troubled 1930s, and it may be argued that institutional policy-makers in the early 1930s anticipated the Keynesian policy prescription without his elaborate theoretical framework.

Although institutionalism declined rapidly after the Second World War during McCarthyism, its influence on economic policy-making in Washington still lingers.[38] Paul Krugman complains, 'It is not just that economists have lost control of the discourse; the kinds of ideas that are offered in a standard economics textbook do not enter into that discourse at all' (quoted in Reder 1999, p. 6). To whom have the economists lost control? Krugman lists an alliance of 'policy makers, business leaders and influential intellectuals' (ibid.). These are the groups that today defend the common sense and pragmatism of institutional economics against the unmitigated rule of standard textbook economics. To the 'Ricardian vice' labelled by Schumpeter we may add the 'Krugmanian vice': the vice of possessing more relevant economic theories – such as new trade theory – but refusing to employ these principles in real-world economic policy.

5.6. *The Coming Canonical* Methodenstreit *6: The Other Canon versus Standard Textbook Economics and the Washington Consensus*

Though neoclassicism won the day in academia and in our economic policy towards the Second and Third Worlds, the eclectic pragmatism of The Other Canon and of the old institutional school lives on in policy-making in both America and Western Europe. A clear focus on policies promoting innovations is just one indication of this. In academia today, the proponents of this school are mostly scattered in business schools and departments of government and international affairs. As a result of the virtual eradication of Other Canon economists from departments of economics, the poor countries of the world are still treated to a virtually undiluted version of neoclassical economics as administered by the Washington institutions. The centuries-old common sense – the core of the reconstruction of Europe after the Second World War – that a nation is better off with an inefficient manufacturing sector than with no manufacturing sector at all, was lost in the market euphoria following the fall of the Berlin Wall.

---

38. Two informative books (Yonay 1998; Morgan and Rutherford 1998) trace the demise of institutional economics in the United States

Over the last 50 years of the twentieth century, the mechanical model of neoclassical economics slowly gained a near monopoly position (Mirowski 2002). In a similar way Ricardian economics slowly gained prominence starting in the 1820s and culminating with the free trade movements of the 1840s. However, the 1848 revolutions that affected most Continental European nations provided an important backlash for this kind of policy, and marked the end of uncritical practical application of Ricardian theory. Between the summits in Rio in 1992 and the summit in Johannesburg in 2002, 66 developing nations had become poorer. In our view, today's increasing social problems and accompanying social protests are again caused by the uncritical application of the same Ricardian theory, now in the guise of immediate and absolute globalization of the poor world. Again a similar social reaction as that of 1848 is about to cause a similar backlash and standstill.

Enlightened economic policy, spearheaded by US and German economic theory and policy, and English social policy slowly solved the 'social question', the most burning on the nineteenth-century European agenda. It is our conviction that the same kind of Other Canon economics without equilibrium is the only type of economics that can solve the social questions of today. In 1848, the United States and Germany had a healthy stock of Other Canon economists in their economics departments. This eased the search for policy solutions. Today's global village no longer holds such a diversity of approaches to economic policy, from which a search for solutions necessarily has to start. We are therefore more dependent than ever on using history, the only laboratory of economics, and the 'gene bank' provided by the writings of past Other Canon economists as our guides towards a world less dominated by poverty and misery.

6. INTERNATIONAL TRADE POLICY AND THE TWO CANONS

A culmination of the barter-based canon – from the height of neoclassical economics – is Paul Samuelson's (1948, 1949) proof that international trade, under the usual assumptions of neoclassical economics, will produce factor-price equalization. If all nations would only convert to free trade, the price of the factors of production – capital and labour – would be the same all over the world. In response to the communist utopian idea that every man should give according to ability and receive according to need came the even more powerful neoclassical utopian idea that under capitalist free trade, all wage earners of the world would be equally rich. This theory is the foundation upon which the present world economic order rests.

The contraintuitive conclusion that all wage earners of the planet will be equally rich under free trade in our view shows the affiliation of neoclassical economics with the pedantic and circuitous reasonings of scholasticism. This danger is inherent when the language of communication is mathematics; as Wittgenstein writes: 'All mathematics is self-referential.' In its extreme form, scholasticism also 'proves' things that contradict common sense and intuition. Friedrich List accused the English classical canon of 'scholasticism'. In this same spirit the Danish economist L.V. Birck (1926) titled his article discussing the theories of Böhm-Bawerk 'Moderne Skolastik' (see Reinert 2000).

In the early nineteenth century, the immediate commonsense reply to Ricardian trade theory, such as the very influential writings of Daniel Raymond (1820) in the United States, was one intuitively appealing to the role played by knowledge, and the ability of each profession to absorb advanced knowledge. Pre-Ricardian common sense continued along this line of reasoning: if each lawyer in a nation has ten times the annual income of each person washing dishes, why should a nation of dishwashers be as rich as a nation of lawyers? Following Charles King (1721), it has been clear to The Other Canon that 'symmetrical' international trade – between nations at the same level of development – is beneficial to both nations, whereas 'asymmetrical trade' is beneficial only to the more advanced of the two trading partners. In our view – in the spirit of US and German nineteenth-century economics – symmetrical trade implies trade of goods at roughly the same level on the quality index in Figure 12.3, whereas asymmetrical trade implies trade of articles at very different positions on the quality index. Exceptions to this would be if a very large and dynamic nation or group of nations absorbed a smaller, poorer nation and upgraded its standard of living. Portugal in the EU was potentially an example of this, but the experiment was ruined by freezing the exchange rates when the Euro was introduced. Even without the exchange rate problems, Mexico's development under NAFTA may serve as an example of the same negative effects.

Samuelson, like Ricardo, failed to specify factors that were central in the Renaissance canon: (1) knowledge in and of itself, and (2) the differing capacities of economic activity to absorb knowledge. A key argument by Daniel Raymond (1820) was that because different professions have different capacities to absorb capital profitably (human or other), different professions have different 'windows of opportunity' for creating welfare. One cannot profitably add as much human capital to the job of washing dishes as to the job of being a lawyer. For this reason economists would recommend to their children professions which require a university education, although by doing this they express what – at the level of a nation – they would describe as a mercantilist preference for one profession over another. Adam Smith, however, is very consistent on this point: all risks considered, it is safer to let your son become a shoemaker's apprentice than to become a lawyer (see Reinert 1999 for a discussion).

A succinct version of the Renaissance view of the role of international trade in the creation of the common weal is found in James Steuart (1767, vol. 1, p. 336): 'If the greater value of labour be imported, than exported, the country loses.' This argument became the crusading slogan for US protectionists. The more advanced Renaissance economists also focused on this aspect, which Reinert (1980) calls the 'labour-hour terms of trade'. This was the important variable to watch if one was interested in increasing the welfare of the common man. As noted earlier, the world's most-efficient producers of baseballs (which are hand-sewn) work in Haiti, earning US$0.30 per hour today, whereas the world's most-efficient producers of golf balls (a mechanized production) in an industrialized country make at least $12.00 per hour. In the mercantilist/Renaissance view, by exporting baseballs and importing golf balls, Haiti exchanges 40 hours of labour (in baseballs) for one hour of labour (in golf balls). Haiti and Honduras together have a very large share of the world market in baseballs. The key point to remember here is that both baseball producers and golf ball producers are in this example producing with state-of-the-art technology: whereas golf ball production is mechanized, all the capital of the United States has yet to mechanize the production of baseballs. This uneven advance of technological change makes it possible for a nation to be locked into a comparative advantage of being poor and ignorant. This possibility is ignored in today's economic theory, but was clearly perceived by the more sophisticated Renaissance mercantilists, who held the variables of skill and knowledge upfront in their theoretical edifice.

Since the time of the *Methodenstreit* between Misselden and Malynes, free trade has consistently been a logical strategy of the leading technological and economic power. Protecting and building knowledge has been the pattern of nations that have caught up, and later overtaken, the leader. Only the Netherlands, having had a first-mover advantage, introduced protection at a later stage (around 1725) as a defensive measure against its neighbours who were catching up.

In our opinion it is evident that the core assumptions of standard economic theory may play a political role in protecting the vested interest of the leader against the laggards. To a nation that possesses unique technical knowledge, the assumption of 'perfect information' and 'perfect competition' is beneficial. Likewise, an assumption of constant returns to scale will benefit a nation that engages in mass production of manufactured goods, but will be very damaging to nations specializing in agriculture and extractive activities subject to diminishing returns. Therefore, in our opinion it is legitimate to talk about 'assumption-based' rents in economic theory. The rents accruing to the nation exchanging one hour of labour exporting golf balls for 40 hours of labour importing baseballs is such an 'assumption-based' rent. One may divide today's world into two groups of nations: those that at some point have been through a stage of Renaissance economics – the industrialized nations – and the others, the poor South, which continues to produce assumption-based rents for the industrialized North.

7. THE TWO CANONS IN PRESENT ECONOMICS: THEORY AND PRACTICAL POLICY

In the preliminary remarks to his *Principles of Economics*, John Stuart Mill (1987 [1848], p. 3) states:

> It often happens that the universal belief of one age of mankind – a belief from which no one *was*, nor without any extraordinary effort of genius or courage, *could*, at that time be free – becomes to a subsequent age so palpable an absurdity, that the only difficulty is to imagine how such a thing can ever have appeared credible. . . . It looks like one of the crude fancies of childhood, instantly corrected by a word from any grown person.

Today the strongest conclusion of standard economic theory is that of world factor-price equalization: if worldwide free trade is adopted, all wage earners of the world will be equally rich. In our view, this 'law' of factor-price equalization – on which our policy towards the Third World is based – qualifies as one of the beliefs which to a subsequent age will become a palpable absurdity. No doubt free trade is a cornerstone in world welfare among the rich nations. But the enormous gains from symmetrical free trade are not the static gains of Smith and Ricardo; they are the synergetic, dynamic and scale-based gains from trade to which *realökonomisch* mercantilists in the Renaissance tradition have long pointed, and which modern economists such as Paul David, W. Brian Arthur and, at times, Paul Krugman are rediscovering.

Occasionally other intuitive flashbacks from Renaissance economics appear in today's formal theory. One important example is Robert E. Lucas's (1988) article in which he argues, as in US nineteenth-century economics, that the potential to learn differs between economic activities. In his model, the nations that acquire most human capital also attract more physical capital, which will be applied more productively there. Because of this, increasing the world mobility of capital under a free trade regime will increase, not diminish, both international inequalities and international migratory pressure. We would argue that Lucas (who later won a Nobel Prize in economics) in this article has recreated a classical mercantilist argument for why vicious and virtuous circles dominate the world economy: because economic activities are qualitatively different, unrestricted free trade between nations of different stages of knowledge development will lead to significant loss of welfare for nations below a certain threshold of knowledge.

Lucas (1988, p. 8) writes, 'The consequences for human welfare involved in questions like these are simply staggering: Once one starts to think about them, it is hard to think about anything else.' One important problem in today's standard economics is that any graduate student in the profession is able to produce a model that 'proves' any pet idea he might have. As long as the profession continues to confuse theory with science – as long as models are produced with only very limited, if any, testing in the real world – the science of economics will continue to produce models that can 'prove' anything. This gives politicians a virtual smörgåsbord of alternative theories, often contradictory, to choose from and to apply according to national preferences and vested interests. Lucas's 1988 model – which is really relevant for the problems of world poverty – disappears in a sea of other elegant but, alas, irrelevant models.

Three factors have, in our opinion, led to a near-disappearance of the Renaissance tradition in the post-Second World War era. Firstly, the Cold War created an enormous demand for economic and political arguments against the totalitarian threat to the West. The perfect markets of neoclassical theory provided an ideological defence line. Communism promised that everyone would receive according to his needs. Neoclassical economics returned with an even more powerful argument: under its system all wage earners of the world would become equally rich. Although the basis for the theory was there earlier, in our view it is not merely coincidence that the influence of neoclassical formality reached its height in the Cold War. Samuelson's 'proof' of factor-price equalization came during the Berlin blockade, and Milton Friedman's 1953 defence of the use of any assumptions so long as they worked came at the height of the McCarthy era. The Cold War needed Ricardo and Smith, and they did their duty (see Mirowski 2002 for the development of post-Second World War economics).

Secondly, the mechanization of the world picture which started with the Enlightenment will probably, with the benefit of hindsight, prove to have peaked during the same post-Second World War period. The choice of mathematics as the lingua franca of economics – and the way in which the profession was mathematized – contributed to the demise of Renaissance economics. Key variables in Renaissance economics are irreducible to mathematics. Renaissance economics depends on a different form of understanding, the qualitative understanding that German philosophers call *verstehen*, as opposed to the quantitative *begreifen* which characterizes the hard sciences. Trying to bridge these two worlds was the impossible task that Schumpeter assigned himself (Reinert 2002). The creative processes underlying economic change proved impossible to reduce to linear mathematics based on nineteenth-century physics. Modern complexity theory, however, seems to be able to achieve what Schumpeter desired.

Thirdly, research and production for the Second World War produced a formidable knowledge base which fed the post-war innovation and production boom. Once the Fordist technological paradigm had been set in motion, there was no demand for the Renaissance economics idea of human creativity as the primary engine of growth. Post-Second World War society was living off the stock of human creativity which, as so often before, had been set free in a war economy. Having learned from Keynes how to even out the ruffles of the business cycle, the economics profession was confident. Paraphrasing Krugman (1990, p. 4), economic research proceeded – undisturbed by the real world – down the path of least mathematical resistance. Unfortunately, the discovery of how to iron out the business cycle was mistaken for the philosopher's stone for creating welfare. Keynesianism's emphasis on financial and monetary aspects, though justified in the crisis of the 1930s, helped financial capitalism take the upper hand over production capitalism in the late 1990s, leading to a predictable collapse (Perez 2002).

In our opinion, these three factors reinforced each other in a most unfortunate spiral to virtually eliminate The Other Canon of economics. Economics was elevated to a level of abstraction where it became unscientific to be relevant.

Today, evolutionary economics is growing as an alternative to the standard, neoclassical-based economic theory. With the TEP Programme (Technology and Economy) of the Organisation for Economic Cooperation and Development (OECD) of the early 1990s, evolutionary economics gained prominence as a policy guide in the industrialized world. At its best, this evolutionary theory captures the essence of Renaissance economics. At its worst, it merely substitutes a mechanical economic understanding based on biology ('biology envy') for the standard canon's mechanical economic understanding based on physics ('physics envy'). Evolutionary economics needs to be moved along the axis from matter to mind, not only from physics to biology. Since the early 1990s, Schumpeterian economics flourishes at the micro level, but very few attempts are made to evaluate the consequences of this kind of microeconomics at the macro level. Schumpeterian economics remains a thin icing on a thoroughly neoclassical cake, allowing the juggling of assumptions that we have criticized above.

Although the potential benefits from applying evolutionary and institutional theorizing would be much larger in the Third World than in the First World, this theory has not yet had any influence on the Third World policy of international institutions such as the International Monetary Fund and the World Bank. This is probably because the vast majority of World Bank economists, regardless of their nationality, are educated in economics departments of American and English universities, where evolutionary theory is not taught. In the same way that Renaissance knowledge was created outside the old university structure – in the scientific academies – in most countries, Schumpeterian evolutionary economics is practised mostly outside university economics departments.

Economics as it is practised in the economics departments is essentially no longer in demand in the OECD countries. These theories are too general and too abstract, and are perceived as being irrelevant to any practical purpose in the real world. Today, standard textbook theories in their pure form are applied in practical policy only in the Third World by IMF and World Bank economists who have virtually no experience in the economic policies of the wealthy nations. This is, in our view, an ethically disturbing case of selective use of economic theory, which has enormous implications for the welfare of poor countries. Although standard economics preaches the same medicine for all nations regardless of context, presently the world community is administering different medicines to the poor nations than to the wealthy nations. Perversely, however, Other Canon economics is practised in the developed nations but not contained in the prescriptions from the Washington institutions to the poor countries which need it the most. The need to resurrect Renaissance non-equilibrium economics – the Other Canon – for application in Eastern Europe and in the Third World is an urgent one.

References

Arthur, W. Brian (1994), *Increasing Returns and Path Dependency in the Economy*, Ann Arbor, MI: University of Michigan Press.

Bentham, Jeremy (1780), *An Introduction to the Principles of Morals and Legislation*, London: University Paperback.

Bijker, Wiebe, Thomas P. Hughes and Trevor Pinch (eds) (1989), *The Social Construction of Technological Systems*, Cambridge, MA: MIT Press.

Birck, L.V. (1926), 'Moderne Scholastik: Eine kritische Darstellung der Böhm-Bawerkschen Theorie', *Weltwirtschaftliches Archiv*, **24** (2), 198–227.

Botero, Giovanni (1590), *Delle Cause della Grandezza delle Cittá*, Rome: Vicenzio Pellagalo.

Buchanan, James, and Yong J. Yoon (eds) (1994), *The Return to Increasing Returns*, Ann Arbor, MI: University of Michigan Press.

Buck, Philip (1942), *The Politics of Mercantilism*, New York: Henry Holt.

Carey, Henry Charles (1967 [1851]), *Harmony of Interests: Agricultural, Manufacturing and Commercial*, New York: Augustus M. Kelley.

Clément, Pierre (ed.) (1861–72), *Lettres, Instructiones et Mémoires de Colbert*, Paris: Imprimerie Impériale/Imprimerie Nationale.

Court, Pieter de la (1662), *Interest van Holland*, Amsterdam, German translations 1665 and 1668, English translations, London 1743 and 1746.

Crowther, J.G. (1960), *Francis Bacon: The First Statesman of Science*, London: Cresset Press.

Doléjal, Oscar (1921), *Le milieu politique et économique du Royaume de Naples au XVI et au début du XVII siècle. Les doctrines économiques de Marc'Anonio de Santis, d'un Anonyme Génois et d'Antonio Serra*, PhD Thesis, Université de Poitiers, Ligugé: E. Aubin.

Freeman, Christopher (1992), *The Economics of Hope*, London: Pinter.

Fusfeld, Daniel R. (1987), 'Methodenstreit', in Eatwell, John, Murray Milgate and Peter Newman (editors), *The New Palgrave Dictionary*, vol. 3. London, Macmillan, pp. 454–455.

Hart, Neil (1990), 'Increasing Returns and Economic Theory: Marshall's Reconciliation Problem', University of Western Sydney, Discussion Paper Series, no. E9004.

Henderson, John (1994), *Piety and Charity in Late Medieval Florence*, Oxford: Clarendon.

Higgs, Henry (1897), *The Physiocrats*, London: Macmillan.

Hildebrand, Bruno (1848), *Die Nationalökonomie der Gegenwart und Zukunft*, Frankfurt: Literarische Anstalt.

Hirschman, Albert O. (1991), *The Rhetoric of Reaction: Perversity, Futility, Jeopardy*, Cambridge, MA: Harvard University Press.

Hörnigk, Philipp Wilhelm von (1684), *Österreich über alles wann es nur will*, no place (but Nuremberg).

Hudson, Michael (1969), 'E. Peshine Smith: A study in protectionist growth theory and American sectionalism', PhD diss., New York University; Ann Arbor, MI: University Microfilm.

Hufbauer, Gary C., Diane T. Berliner and Kimberly A. Elliot (1986), *Trade Protection in the United States: 31 Case Studies*, Washington, DC: Institute for International Economics.

Humpert, Magdalene (1937), *Bibliographie der Kameralwissenschaften*, Cologne: Kurt Schroeder.

Keynes, J.M. (1930), *A Treatise on Money*, 2 vols, London: Macmillan.

King, Charles (1721), *The British Merchant: Or Commerce preserv'd*, 3 vols, London: John Darby.

Krugman, Paul (1990), *Rethinking International Trade*, Cambridge, MA: MIT Press.

Krugman, Paul (1996), *The Self-Organizing Economy*, Cambridge, MA: Blackwell.

Kuhn, Thomas (1970), *The Structure of Scientific Revolutions*, Chicago, IL: University of Chicago Press.

Laffemas, Barthélemy (1597), *Reiglement [sic] general pour dresser les manufactures en ce royaume, et couper le cours des draps de soye, & autres merchandises qui perdent & ruynent l'Estat: qui est le vray moyen de remettre la France en sa splen-deur, & de faire gaigner les pauvres . . .*, Paris: Claude de Monstr'oil and Jean Richter.

Latini, Brunetto, Paul Barrette and Spurgeon W. Baldwin (1993), *The Book of the Treasure (Li livres dou Tresor)*, New York: Garland.

Leibniz, Gottfried Wilhelm (1992 [1671]), 'Society and Economy', reprinted in *Fidelio*, **2** (1), 63–9.

List, Friedrich (1904 [1841]), *The National System of Political Economy*, London: Longman.

List, Friedrich (1959 [1841]), *Das Nationale System der politischen Oekonomie*, Basel: Kyklos.

List, Friedrich (1985 [1937]), *Die Welt bewegt sich: Über die Auswirkungen der Dampfkraft und der neuen Transportmittel*, ed. Eugen Wendler, Göttingen: Vandenhoek & Ruprecht.

Lucas, Robert E. (1988), 'On the Mechanics of Economic Development', *Journal of Monetary Economics*, **22** (1), 3–42.

Malynes, Gerard de (1622), *The Maintenance of Free Trade, according to the Three Essentiall Parts . . . Commodities, Moneys and Exchange of Moneys*, London: William Sheffard.

Malynes, Gerard de (1623), *The Center of the Circle of Commerce, or, A Refutation of a Treatise . . . Lately Published by E. M.*, London: Nicholas Bourne.

Marshall, Alfred (1890), *Principles of Economics*, London: Macmillan.

Menger, Carl (1883/1963), *Problems of Economics and Sociology (Untersuchungen über die Methode der Socialwissenschaften und der Politischen Ökonomie insbesondere)*, Urbana, IL: University of Illinois Press.

Menger, Carl (1884), *Die Irrtümer des Historismus in der deutschen Nationalökonomie* (Errors of Historicism), Vienna: Alfred Hölder.

Mill, John Stuart (1987 [1848]), *Principles of Political Economy*, New York: Kelley.

Mirowski, Philip (1994), 'Doing What Comes Naturally: Four Metanarratives on What Metaphors are for', in Philip Mirowski (ed.), *Natural Images in Economic Thought*, Cambridge: Cambridge University Press, pp. 3–19.

Mirowski, Philip (2002), *Machine Dreams. Economics Becomes a Cyborg Science*, Cambridge: Cambridge University Press.

Misselden, Edward (1622), *Free Trade and the Meanes to Make Trade Flourish*, London: Simon Waterson.

Misselden, Edward (1623), *The Circle of Commerce or the Ballance of Trade*, London: Nicholas Bourne.

Morgan, Mary S. and Malcolm Rutherford (eds) (1998), *From Interwar Pluralism to Postwar Neoclassicism*, annual supplement to *History of Political Economy*, **30**.

Morris, R.B. (1957), *Alexander Hamilton and the Founding of the Nation*, New York: Dial Press.

Morris-Suzuki, Tessa (1989), *The History of Japanese Economic Thought*, London: Routledge.

Nelson, Richard and Sidney Winter (1982), *An Evolutionary Theory of Economic Change*, Cambridge, MA: Harvard University Press.

Nietzsche, Friedrich (2000), *Digitale Bibliothek Band 31: Nietzsche*, Berlin: Directmedia (CD-ROM).

Nye, John Vincent (1991), 'The Myth of Free-trade Britain and Fortress France: Tariffs and Trade in the Nineteenth Century', *Journal of Economic History*, **51** (1), 23–46.

Pecchio, Giuseppe (1849), *Storia della Economia Pubblica in Italia*, Lugano: Tipografia della Svizzera Italiana.

Perez, Carlota (2002), *Technological Revolutions and the Mechanisms of Bubbles and Golden Ages*, Cheltenham: Edward Elgar.

Perrotta, Cosimo (1988), *Produzione e Lavoro Produttivo nel Mercantilismo e nell' Illuminismo*, Galatina: Congedo Editore.

Pfeiffer, J.F. von (1777), *Lehrbegrif sämtlicher oeconomischer und Cameralwissenschaften*, vol. 3, part 1, Mannheim: Schwan.

Pfeiffer, J.F. von (1780), *Der Antiphysiokrat, oder umständliche Untersuchung des sogenannten physiokratischen Systems für eine allgemeine Freyheit und einzige Auflage auf den reinen Ertrag der Grundstücke*, Frankfurt am Main: Schäfer.

Polanyi, Karl (1944), *The Great Transformation*, Boston, MA: Beacon Press.

Popper, Karl (1997), *The Poverty of Historicism*, London: Routledge.

Prince-Smith, John (1874), *Der Staat und der Volkshaushalt*, Berlin: Springer.

Raffel, Friedrich (1905), *Englische Freihändler vor Adam Smith*, Tübingen: Laupp.

Raymond, Daniel (1820), *Principles of Political Economy*, Baltimore, MD: Fielding Lucas.

Reder, Melvin W. (1999), *Economics: The Culture of a Controversial Science*, Chicago, IL: University of Chicago Press.

Reinert, Erik S. (1980), 'International Trade and the Economic Mechanisms of Underdevelopment', PhD diss., Cornell University; Ann Arbor, MI: University Microfilm.

Reinert, Erik S. (1994), 'Catching-up from Way Behind: A Third World Perspective on First World History', in Jan Fagerberg, Bart Verspagen and Nick van Tunzelmann (eds), *The Dynamics of Technology, Trade and Growth*, Aldershot, UK and Brookfield, US: Edward Elgar, pp. 168–97. Also chapter 1 in this volume.

Reinert, Erik S. (1996a), 'Diminishing Returns and Economic Sustainability: The Dilemma of Resource-Based Economies Under a Free Trade Regime', in Stein Hansen, Jan Hesselberg and Helge Hveem (eds), *International Trade Regulation, National Development Strategies and the Environment: Towards Sustainable Development?*, Oslo: Centre for Development and the Environment, University of Oslo, pp. 119–50. (also chapter 5 in this volume)

Reinert, Erik S. (1996b), 'The Role of Technology in the Creation of Rich and Poor Nations: Underdevelopment in a Schumpeterian System', in Derek H. Aldcroft and Ross Catterall (eds), *Rich Nations – Poor Nations. The Long Run Perspective*, Aldershot: Edward Elgar, 1996, pp. 161–88. Spanish translation (2002) 'El rol de la tecnología en la creación de países ricos y pobres: El subdesarrollo en un sistema Schumpeteriano', *Cuadernos*, **7** (12).

Reinert, Erik S. (1998), 'Raw Materials in the History of Economic Policy; or, Why List (the Protectionist) and Cobden (the Free Trader) Both Agreed on Free Trade in Corn', in G. Cook (ed.), *The Economics and Politics of International Trade. Freedom and Trade: Volume II*, London: Routledge, pp. 275-300.

Reinert, Erik S. (1999), 'The Role of the State in Economic Growth', *Journal of Economic Studies*, **26** (4/5), 268–326. A shorter version was published in Pier Angelo Toninelli (ed.) (2000), *The Rise and Fall of State-Owned Enterprises in the Western World*, Cambridge: Cambridge University Press.

Reinert, Erik S. (2000), 'Full Circle: Economics from Scholasticism Through Innovation and Back into Mathematical Scholasticism. Reflections around a 1769 Price Essay: "Why is it that economics so far has gained so few advantages from physics and mathematics?"', *Journal of Economic Studies*, **27** (4/5), 364–76.

Reinert, Erik S. (2002) 'Schumpeter in the Context of Two Canons of Economic Thought', *Industry and Innovation*, **6** (1), 23–39.

Reinert, Erik S. and Arno M. Daastøl (1997), 'Exploring the Genesis of Economic Innovations: The Religious Gestalt-Switch and the Duty to Invent as Preconditions for Economic Growth', *European Journal of Law and Economics*, **4** (2/3), 233–83 reprinted (1998) in *Christian Wolff. Gesammelte Werke, Materialien und Dokumente*, Hildesheim: Georg Olms Verlag, 1998.

Ritzel, Gerhard (1950), *Schmoller versus Menger*, Offenbach: Bollwerk Verlag

Roscher, Wilhelm (1874), *Geschichte der National-Oekonomik in Deutschland*, Munich: Oldenbourg.

Roscher, Wilhelm (1882), *Principles of Political Economy*, Chicago, IL: Callaghan.

Rostovtzeff, Mikhail (1941), *Social and Economic History of the Hellenistic World*, 3 vols, Oxford: Oxford University Press.

Samuelson, Paul (1948), 'International Trade and the Equalisation of Factor Prices', *Economic Journal*, **58**, 163–84.

Samuelson, Paul (1949), 'International Factor-Price Equalisation Once Again', *Economic Journal*, **59**, 181–97.

Schumpeter, Joseph A. (1954), *History of Economic Analysis*, New York: Oxford University Press.

Seligman, Edwin A. (1920), *Curiosities of Early Economic Literature*, San Francisco, CA: John Henry Nash.

Serra, Antonio (1613), *Breve trattato delle cause che possono far abbondare li regni d'oro e argento dove non sono miniere*, Naples: Lazzaro Scoriggio.

Smith, Adam (1812 [1759]), 'The Theory of Moral Sentiments', in *Collected Works*, London: Cadell & Davies.

Smith, Adam (1976 [1776]), *Wealth of Nations*, Chicago, IL: University of Chicago Press.

Sombart, Werner (1928), *Der Moderne Kapitalismus*, vol. 2, *Das Europäische Wirtschaftsleben im Zeitalter des Frühkapitalismus*, Munich: Duncker & Humblot.

Sombart, Werner (1930), *Die Drei Nationalökonomien*, Munich: Duncker & Humblot.

Spann, Othmar (1926), *Die Haupttheorien der Volkswirtschaftslehre*, Leipzig; Quelle & Meyer. US edition (1930): *The History of Economics*, New York: Norton.

Stangeland, Charles Emil (1904), *Pre-Malthusian Doctrines of Population: A Study in the History of Economic Theory*, New York: Columbia University Press.

Steuart, James (1767), *Principles of Political Economy*, London: Millar & Cadell.

Sugiyama, C. and H. Mizuta (1988), *Enlightenment and Beyond: Political Economy Comes to Japan*, Tokyo: University of Tokyo Press.

Viner, Jacob (1972), *The Role of Providence in the Social Order: An Essay in Intellectual History*, Philadelphia, PA: American Philosophical Society.

Wallerstein, Immanuel (1978 [1974]), *Det moderne verdenssystem*, 2 vols, Oslo: Gyldendal.

Weulersse, Georges (1910), *Le mouvement physiocratique en France*, Paris: Alcan.

Whatley, G. (1774), *Principles of Trade. Freedom and Protection Are Its Best Suport* [sic]*: Industry, the Only Means to Render Manufactures Cheap*, London: Brotherton and Sewell.

Wiles, P.J.D. (1977), *Economic Institutions Compared*, Oxford: Basil Blackwell.

Xenophon and Wayne Ambler (2001), *The Education of Cyrus, Agora Editions*. Ithaca, NY: Cornell University Press.

Yagi, Kiichiro (1989), 'German Model in the Modernisation of Japan', *Kyoto University Economic Review*, **59** (1–2), 35–39.

Yat-Sen, Sun (1922), *The International Development of China*, New York: Putnam.

Yonay, Yuval (1998), *The Struggle over the Soul of Economics*, Princeton, NJ: Princeton University Press.

Zincke, Georg Heinrich (1753), *Xenophon's Buch von den Einkünften, oder, dessen Vorschläge, wie das bereiteste Vermögen grosser Herren und Staaten nach ächten Grund-sätzen des Finanz-Wesens zu vermehren*, Wolfenbüttel: Meissner.

Chapter 13

BENCHMARKING SUCCESS: THE DUTCH REPUBLIC (1500–1750) AS SEEN BY CONTEMPORARY EUROPEAN ECONOMISTS

This chapter looks at the Dutch Republic from the vantage point of the economists of the period. These pre-Smithian economists are normally grouped together in the history of economic thought under the decidedly derogatory label of 'mercantilists'. Under its standard Whig conception, any idea in the history of economic thought – as identified almost a century ago by English historical economist Ashley – instead of being judged by its relevance in a given context, is either hailed as a surprising early anticipation of a healthy neoclassical economic principle or as an example of hopelessly ill-conceived theories (Ashley 1920: II, 381).

I would argue that as a tool in order to understand the rise and fall of the Dutch Republic, mercantilism had some clear analytical advantages over neoclassical economics. Not only was the mercantilist or pre-Ricardian economists' toolbox much larger than today's, the pre-Ricardian system already included a large number of economic factors which the profession presently attempts to re-introduce to mainstream economics. Examples of what gradually was left out of economics starting with Adam Smith are innovations – part of English economics from Francis Bacon (1561–1626) until and including James Steuart's important work (1767) – technology, increasing returns, institutions, geography, synergies, path dependency, that economic activities are qualitatively different as carriers of economic growth, the idea that economic policy should be *context-specific*, and the whole fundamental question of why economic development is by nature so uneven. With the English classical economists economic theory gradually lost its previous understanding of the vicissitudes of technology and production, and came to concentrate upon trade and prices. The contemporary mercantilists are therefore likely to provide a much richer analysis of the Dutch Republic than what is found in the works of the later classical economists.

Mercantilism can productively be seen both as state- and nation-building (Schmoller 1897/1976) and as a strategy of industrial import substitution (Perrotta 1993), which at the time was seen as two sides of the same coin.[1] To the laggard countries of Europe, the Dutch Republic provided important inspiration on both these accounts. That inspiration

1. For a general discussion on Mercantilism, see chapter 14 in this volume.

did not come from Dutch policies, but by asking what policies would have to be created in order to achieve the same *results* as those observed in the Dutch productive system, but under very different circumstances and conditions; in very different contexts. The economists of the time were looking at nations much in the same way businessmen are managing companies, but instead of maximizing profit they were maximizing national value added (GDP) and employment. Just as companies may lose money and even go bankrupt, nations may lose out in this dynamic game. In this respect, from about 1550, the European theatre presented an extraordinary case of increasing poverty and failure, that of Spain (Perrotta 1993), and one or two cases, Venice and the Dutch Republic, of a resounding success that was obvious to any visitor. Later, when it became evident that the Italian city-states had fallen behind the Dutch Republic, it was clear to the Italian economists that the Dutch and others had copied them and beaten them in their own game.[2]

To the keen early observer the formula behind the wealth of the Venetians and the Dutch was reasonably straightforward, fundamentally based on observing the presence, strength and variety of those economic activities (and accompanying institutions) that dominated economic life in rich countries, but were absent or weak in the poorer ones. As Josiah Child says when explaining the purpose of his 1668 economics treatise: 'the means whereby (the Dutch) have thus advanced themselves, are sufficiently obvious, and in a great measure imitable by most other nations, which I shall endeavour to demonstrate in the following discourse' (Child 1668). In 1613 Antonio Serra had made a similar analysis, identifying the mechanisms that made Venice so wealthy and Naples so poor (Serra 1613 and chapter 10 in this volume). The methodology used by Child, Serra and their contemporaries was in its essence one of benchmarking, of attempting to generalize and theorize from the experiences of failing and successful nations. This approach is in my view a core feature of mercantilism.

1. Engines of Growth: Generalizing from the Experience of Early Economic Development in Venice and the Dutch Republic

'Mercantilism was born in response to the failure of Spain', says Perrotta (1993:19), referring to the 1500s. One could add that mercantilism further developed – during the 1600s and 1700s – as a response to the successes of the Dutch Republic, of Tudor England and of Colbert's France. The best mercantilist writers were practical men, not people dedicated to what used to be called 'metaphysical speculations'. One pragmatic

2. 'The voyages of the Italians to the Northern seas rendered Flanders a convenient place for depositing their merchandize. Awakened by their example the Flemish became the second manufacturers of Europe. Particular privileges bestowed upon their merchants by the counts of Flanders, animated them still further. But their spirit was again depressed by the revocation of these privileges. Other nations profited of this imprudence; and thus England, France, Holland and Germany by the means of the Anseatic (sic) league, came to have a share in that industry and opulence which had formerly characterized the Italians alone' (Beccaria 1769/1970: 32–33). See also S. Reinert (2005)

and logical approach in order to establish a national economic policy was to look for what had worked, or not worked, in other nations. Economics as a science was therefore not born in wealthy and successful areas – in Venice or the Dutch Republic where wealth only seemed 'natural' – but in the poorer cities and nation-states that were trying to understand what factors had created the few 'islands' of wealth in an otherwise poor Europe. This is one of the key insights from Etienne Laspeyres, the author who probably most thoroughly has studied the economic literature produced by the Netherlands' own writers during the time of the Republic (Laspeyres 1863/1961).[3]

Benchmarking with successful and less successful nations was a practice already started during the late 1400s with Henry VII and the Tudors in England (see below). Part of this process was the observation that early economic development in Europe had a very clear urban bias. Wealth accumulated in some cities, but in far from all. From a monetary point of view the basic question was a relatively simple one. Everyone knew that huge amounts of gold and silver flowed into Spain from the Americas. Starting around 1550, however, it became increasingly clear that this flow of bullion did not cause generalized wealth in Spain. The gold and silver ended up elsewhere, in nations that generally had no mines. It was clearly observable that wealth and purchasing power left the nations producing raw materials – even if the raw materials were gold and silver – and accumulated in those nations that were home to a diversified manufacturing sector. In various forms, the statement that manufacturing were the *real* gold mines, much more valuable than the gold mines themselves, is found all over Europe from the late 1500s through the 1700s, from Giovanni Botero (1590) to Tommaso Campanella (1602) and Antonio Genovesi (in the 1770s), all in Italy, to Gerónimo de Uztáriz in Spain (1724/1751:9) to Anders Berch, the first economics professor outside Germany, in Sweden (Berch 1747: 217).

In pre-Smithian economics the establishment of manufactures came to be seen as part of a wider mission of *civilizing society*. The Italian economist Ferdinando Galiani (1728–1787) – whom Friedrich Nietzsche called the most intelligent person of the eighteenth century – stated that 'from manufacturing you may expect the two greatest ills of humanity, superstition and slavery, to be healed' (Galiani 1770/1959: 116). The following statement from Johann Jacob Meyen in 1769 summarized the zeitgeist of the day: 'It is known that primitive nations do not improve their customs and habits later to find useful industries, but the other way around…'[4]

As we shall see, part of this *zeitgeist* was an understanding that only in barren areas lacking natural resources and with few possibilities for food production – such as in Venice and in the Dutch Republic – such development would come 'naturally'. In other areas the transition from diminishing returns activities (agriculture) to increasing returns activities (manufacturing) – as they were identified by Serra (1613) – from 'natural activities' to 'artificial activities' – using the terminology of Thomas Mun (1621/1664) – required heavy-handed government policies. Here again, what the Dutch

3. On Laspeyres' book, see Drechsler (2000).
4. See also Montesquieu (1748) and Hirschman (1977) for discussions of this issue.

Republic had achieved – rather than the policies of the Dutch Republic – was the object of attention of foreign economists and foreign rulers alike.

Successful business and its profits were also viewed very differently at the time of the Dutch Republic than in neoclassical economics. Businessmen and traders of all times and ages have sought profit. It is therefore somewhat illogical to find that at the core of today's economic theory of capitalism is a situation where no profit, or very little, is made, that of 'perfect competition'. The kind of economic success that creates national wealth is in effect Schumpeterian dynamic imperfect competition, the kind of rents that increase the size of the economic pie. The success of Bill Gates should in my view be described as an example of such successful dynamic Schumpeterian rent-seeking. It is my claim that the same is the case of early economic development. In this perspective economic development is a situation that is tied to successful rent-seeking of a particular kind. If capitalism is about making profits, then economic development is successful profit-making – not merely 'normal' profits – when and if these profits, through markets and policy measures, result in *an increase in the standard of living of the nation's population.* If the purpose of the actors of the economic system is to create 'rents', it is not meaningful to label rent-seeking in general as something 'wrong'. My approach to mercantilism is therefore very different from that of Ekelund and Tollison (1981), but closer to that of Thorstein Veblen, whose distinction between 'good' and 'bad' capitalists, and implicitly 'good' and 'bad' rent,[5] was whether they increased the size of the economic pie available for distribution. Many of the rents created and collected in the Dutch Republic did.

In my view, the study of early successful economic development – of early successful rent-seeking – is also useful in order to explain differences in economic growth today. Some of the most powerful economic mechanisms – like compound interest and increasing and diminishing returns – are timeless. As Alfred Marshall (1890) points out, diminishing returns appears very early in the history of Mankind, in the Genesis of the Bible, when 'the land was not able to carry them all'. The existence of diminishing returns made economics into 'the dismal science'. I would similarly claim that the opposite mechanism – increasing returns – is at the core of the synergetic and cumulative mechanisms that made early economic development possible in Europe. A study of the economists contemporary with the Dutch Republic shows that these mechanisms were operating in the Republic and were – with varying degrees of clarity and sophistication – known to them.

2. Imperfect Competition, Schumpeterian Rents and Synergies in Early Economic Development

2.1. Dynamic Rents and Rising Incomes

Perhaps the most significant economic breakthrough marking the end of scholasticism and the birth of the Renaissance was the recognition that economic wealth was not

5. To Veblen 'good' capitalists base their income on *production*, whereas the 'bad' capitalists base their income on *vendibility*. It may be argued that Veblen did not see the importance of finance for innovations.

a zero-sum game. A new worldview of an expanding economic world gained ground parallel to the expanding geography of the great discoveries and the expanding cosmos of Giordano Bruno (see chapter 13). Italian economic historian (and many times prime minister) Amintore Fanfani encapsulated the shift from scholasticism to mercantilism: 'while scholasticism thinks of an order in equilibrium, mercantilism thinks of an order in growth' (Fanfani 1955: 149).

Giovanni Botero (1590), from Piedmont in Italy, was one of the first economists and social scientists who clearly saw that the world was not a zero-sum game, and that the gain of one actor did not have to be the loss of another. From the very beginning, it was clear that the main force that brought the world out of the zero-sum mode was manufacturing industry. In his *Ragion di Stato,* Botero himself writes: 'such is the power of industry that no mine of silver or gold in New Spain or Peru can compare with it, and the duties from the merchandise of Milan are worth more to the Catholic King than the mines of Potosí and Jalisco. Italy is a country in which … there is no important gold or silver mine, and so is France: yet both countries are rich in money and treasure thanks to industry' (Botero 1590: 152).

There were, then, profits – or rents – which were seen to not necessarily reduce the wealth of others. This was particularly the case with manufacturing-based rents rather than feudal rents. My proposition is that early economic development in all the most successful European states – Venice, the Dutch Republic and England – were able to harvest three *different* kinds of rents which, to the nations in question, increased the size of the economic pie.

The three kinds of rents were:

- Manufacturing rents, at the core of which are increasing returns which are absent in agriculture (Serra 1613)
- Long-distance trading rents
- Raw-material-based rents, which were different in each case

In Venice the raw-material-based rent was from salt. Fredrik Lane comments that the young Venetian Republic hesitated to go to war, but was always determined in defending the saltpans under its domination (Lane 1973: 58). Salt was the first non-luxury long-distance commodity traded, and the control of salt has been important from Ancient China to the Mayas of Yucatan. Due to the power that the control of salt supply brought with it, this commodity was often brought under government control, e.g. in Ancient China. The importance of salt for the finance and growth of the Venetian Republic is well documented in Jean-Claude Hocquet's *Il Sale a la Fortuna di Venezia* (Hocquet 1990).[6]

6. Also in the Dutch Republic salt refining, essential to the fishing industry, was among the important processing industries or *trafieken* (de Vries and van der Woude 1997), but did not reach the strategic importance it earlier had in Venice.

In the Dutch Republic the raw material controlled was fish. There are important Schumpeterian elements attached to the development of the Dutch fisheries. The first one is the discovery of pickling, or salting, of herring. The importance of pickling is emphasized by Huet, who puts the date of its invention at the first part of the fourteenth century. Huet names the inventor as William Buerem, who died in 1347 and to whom Charles V (1500–1558) later erected a statue (Huet 1722: 25). In order to fully utilize this new invention, a second innovation was needed: a large vessel, the herring *buss* carrying from eighteen to thirty men – a 'factory ship' gutting and salting the fish while at sea – that could remain at sea for up to eight weeks (de Vries and van der Woude 1997: 244). This technology was fully developed by 1600 and remained stable for the next 200 years.

In England the raw-material-based rent was wool, the control and use of which founded the basis for the economic strategy of the Tudors, starting in 1485. The export taxes put on wool were an important element in the Tudor strategy of industrializing England. Daniel Defoe (1728) interprets a vision of the first Tudor monarch Henry VII, who came to power in 1485, to industrialize on the basis of assuring England's competitors having more expensive raw materials than the English manufacturers. Growing up with his aunt in Burgundy, Henry VII (1457–1509) observed the general wealth there, created by the manufacturing of woollen cloth with English raw materials (Defoe 1728 and chapter 1 in this volume). After conquering the throne of England, Henry started encouraging their own woollen manufacturers, while slowly increasing the export duties on raw wool and the import duties on finished cloth. Under Elizabeth I, when sufficient manufacturing capacity had been built up, wool export was prohibited. The effect of these policies can be seen in Florence, where they caused a general economic decline and an attempt by the Medici to diversify into silk.

These types of rents spread through the labour markets by various mechanisms. A larger division of labour is increased, the new activities require more skills, possibilities for technological spillovers are created (see under point 4), there is more competition for labour, alternative ways of making money raise the wage level, and – as in the nineteenth-century United States – a 'high wage strategy' becomes a political possibility. As these rents increase, the tax-base of the nation also increases. Among German cameralists, it was observed that people working with machinery were able to pay higher taxes than those who were engaged only in manual work, and advancing manufactures and advanced technology therefore became a logical part of a strategy to raise the income of the state.

I suggest that the pie-increasing rents collected by successful businessmen spread also to the workers and to the state, thus operating at three levels in a triple rent-seeking: the *entrepreneurs/capitalists*, the *workers*, the *government*. It is crucial to understand why agricultural rent does not spread in the same way (see below), i.e. why – under certain circumstances – the trickle-down theory of economic development works. The *industrial system* (Sombart 1902/1928), through various mechanisms, forces a form of rent-sharing. Reinert (1980 and 1996) explores these mechanisms.

2.2. Path Dependency and Synergies

'So true it is, that when commerce has once changed its course, it is the most difficult thing in the World to bring it back again.'

Pierre Daniel Huet (1630–1721), *A View of the Dutch Trade in All the States*, 1722.

The advanced mercantilists had a systemic view of society, and – with different degrees of sophistication – they saw the synergetic and cumulative interaction of the factors mentioned above as being the true engines of growth and welfare. These cumulative mechanisms create strong path dependency, and therefore, as Huet says above, once commerce has changed its course it is very difficult to get it back. Joshua Gee, in his 1729 treatise, presents a similar argument:

> 'The Trade of a Nation is a mighty Consequence (sic), and a Thing that ought to be seriously weighed, because the Happiness or Misfortune of so many Millions depend upon it. **A little Mistake in the Beginning of an Undertaking may swell to a very great one**. A Nation may gain vast Riches by Trade and Commerce, or for Want of due Regard and Attention, may be drained of them' (emphasis added).

The mercantilists discussed the 'stickiness' and cumulativeness of national wealth much in the same way a business strategist today will discuss the importance of industry market shares. In both cases, *volume* is a key to lower costs and consequently to more market power. The nations that attempted to copy the Dutch Republic were acutely aware that the Dutch strategy was one of high volume and low margins (e.g. Uztáriz 1724/1751), and this strategy created considerable barriers to entry for would-be competitors. In the countries that were attempting to catch up with the Dutch Republic, the accumulated learning and economies of scale in Dutch trading and manufacturing needed to be compensated not only through tariffs and subsidies; laggard countries also faced considerable barriers caused by the leading nation's 'increasing returns from the use of force as an economic service' (Lane 1979: 45–48).

The most sophisticated model of economic growth at the time is that of Antonio Serra (1613) who analyzes the wealth of Venice and the poverty of Naples, a model that also fits the Dutch Republic very well. Serra's is a system where 'the number and variety of industrial professions' (i.e. the degree of division of labour), 'the quality of the population', 'the presence of a great commerce', economic policy ('the regulations of the State') – under the presence of increasing returns to scale in manufacturing (but not in the production of raw materials) – create a self-reinforcing system of growth where each factor reinforces the others (chapter 10 in this volume):

> 'Venice 'is aided by her extensive manufactures; a factor which brings a great many people there, not only because of the trades themselves, in which case the effect would be attributed to them, but also as a result of **the concurrence of these two factors together, because one gives strength to the other**, the great concourse due to commerce and due to the geographical situation being increased by the manufactures, and the manufactures being increased by the great concourse due to commerce, while commerce is made greater by the same concourse of people.' (Serra 1613, translated in Reinert 1999)

Daniel Defoe, in his *Plan of English Commerce* (1728), expresses a simpler system of cumulative causation where the interactions of manufactures and navigation mutually reinforce each other:

> Manufacture supplies Merchandise
> Navigation supplies Shipping,
> Manufacture is the Hospital which feeds the Poor
> Navigation is the Nursery which raises Seamen
> Manufacture commands Money from Abroad
> Navigation brings it Home
> Manufacture leads the Ships out
> Navigation loads them in
> Manufacture is Wealth
> Navigation is Strength
>
> To conclude, Manufacture for Employment at Home, and Navigation for Employment Abroad, **both together**, seem to set all the busy World at Work; **they seem to joyn Hands** to encourage the industrious Nations, and if well managed, infallibly make the World rich'. (Defoe 1730: 68-69, emphasis added)

A different way of expressing the necessity and interrelationship of several factors at once is to refer to them as 'pillars' that are all needed to sustain the economic structure, as does Pieter de la Court about the Dutch Republic in his *Interest van Holland* (1662/1702). The metaphor of pillars effectively conveys the message that all the elements are necessary.

> 'Navigation, the fishery, commerce, and manufactures are **the four pillars of the State**; that these ought not to be weakened nor incommoded by any incumbrance whatsoever; for it is they (sic) make the inhabitants to subsist, and enrich the country, by bringing into it foreigners of all sorts &c.' (emphasis added).

Contemporary authors like Huet (born in 1630) and Uztáriz (born in 1670) emphasize the importance of the synergies between fisheries and manufacturing in the Dutch Republic: that manufacturing alone would not have created the same wealth as manufacturing and fisheries do together. This argument is found again today when modern scholarship emphasizes the numerous backward and forward linkages from the fishing industry in the Republic to the rest of the economy (de Vries and van der Woude 1997: 236, 268). The importance of this kind of linkages for agricultural development, seeing the benefits accruing to agriculture from the proximity of manufacturing, was perhaps the most important new insight in economics during the early 1700s. 'Husbandry … is never more effectually encouraged than by the increase of manufactures', says David Hume in his *History of England* (1767, vol. III). The Dutch fisheries and manufacturing sectors combined may indeed have played the same role of modernizer of the agricultural sector as so many eighteenth- and nineteenth-century economists attributed to the manufacturing sector alone. Agricultural labour productivity in the maritime sector of the Republic was double that of the inland sector, partly reflecting a greater capital intensity in the maritime zone (J. L. van Zanden referred to in de Vries and van der Woude 1997: 230–31). Economists at the time would attribute this important synergy to the proximity of agriculture to diversified manufacturing; an insight lost both to the English classical economists and to today's development economists. The agricultural output in the rest of the Dutch Republic was comparable to the rest of Europe: the productivity in the maritime areas was exceptional.

Already Giovanni Botero (born 1544) commented on the strength of Dutch inventions, imitations and manufacturing as well as on the strength of Dutch husbandry. The pastures and cows 'produce a lot of milk', and 'it is assumed that cheese and butter bring in more than one million in gold annually because large quantities are exported to the surrounding countries, to Germany, England and Spain'. The Dutch sheep 'produce three or four lambs at the time, and the cows often two calves; the cows produce so much milk that one who has not seen it would not believe it' (Botero 1596/1622: 48).

3. The Dutch Republic and the Contemporary Economists

Historians of economic thought generally point to the lack of 'high theory' in the Dutch Republic. Laspeyres (1863/1961) discusses 644 texts on practical economic and administrative issues from the time of the Republic, but finds they contain little theory. However, from the late 1500s through the 1700s political economists from outside the Netherlands frequently comment on the economic success, and later decline, of the Dutch Republic, and attempt to draw lessons from the Dutch experience for domestic use. The economic success of the Dutch Republic and its mirror image in the failed economic policies of Spain during the same period provided inspiration to economists of many nations. The gold from the Americas flowed into Spain while 'no Nation in the World has so little Gold and Silver as the Spaniards' (Huet 1722: vii). What were the mechanisms at work? Gold and silver in this connection should be seen as wealth in terms of purchasing power, not 'treasure'.

'The worse the situation, the less laissez-faire works', says Keynes. The Dutch Republic, having an early mover advantage both in trade and manufacturing, could achieve economic success with much less policy intervention than with the nations that followed. Dutch policy and Dutch economics were by nature fairly pragmatic, essentially responding to the policy of its neighbours and, as Laspeyres says, it is not easy to find consequent principles behind the policies, as it was in France (Laspeyres 1863: 134). I would argue, though, that the goals behind Dutch policy were not much different from those of Colbert's France. Having had a first mover advantage it was, however, not necessary for the Dutch to use customs duties extensively in order to promote manufacturing until into the eighteenth century, when the catching-up policy of their neighbours was successful to the point of seriously wounding Dutch manufactures. However, the primacy the Dutch Republic put on manufacturing is clear, as when de la Court says: 'So desirous were the people of Amsterdam to increase their manufactures, that in 1614 they offered large sums of money to the employers and artisans of Aix and other places to induce them to come and settle in their city, and their offers, we are told, were accepted' (quoted in McCullagh 1846: 267). The goals of the Dutch and the goals of the French, English and later German mercantilist writers that followed were essentially the same, but the contexts were different, and consequently also the policies.

The wealth of the Dutch Republic – their 'great treasures' and 'how they have made themselves absolute owners of all the commerce in Europe' as declared in the title of one book on the subject (Goyeneche 1717) – was of great interest to the other European nations. Much as the Chinese were seen in the eighteenth century to have found the *philosophers' stone*, the Dutch were, long before that, seen as having found an *economists' stone*, a key to producing national wealth. The policies of the mercantilists were based on the following understanding.

- Economic development is activity-specific, created by some economic activities (manufacturing) rather than others (due to agriculture's stagnant productivity, diminishing returns and monoculture without synergies.)
- Economic development is a synergetic process: the greater the division of labour and the number of professions, the greater the wealth (very clear already in Serra 1613).
- The targeting, support and protection of manufacturing is argued both in terms of
  a) its ability to create wealth,
  b) its ability to create employment,
  c) its ability to solve balance-of-payment problems,
  d) its ability to increase the velocity of circulation of money.
- Starting in the 1700s great emphasis is put on the beneficial synergies between manufacturing and agriculture: only where there is manufacturing there is successful agriculture (Leibniz and Justi in Germany, Galiani in Italy, Hume in England).

The **French** observed the development of their neighbours in the Dutch Republic with much interest. The rudimentary tariff legislation under Henry IV specifically targets Dutch cloth (France, Edict 1581), and so do the policies of the first French mercantilist (Laffemas 1597). The voluminous correspondence of Colbert, who by his contemporaries all over Europe is almost unanimously referred to as 'the great Colbert', contains literally hundreds of references to the political economy of the Dutch (Clément 1861–72). One of Colbert's complaints is the Dutch prohibition of imports from France, and also – a complaint echoed by Huet – the role of the Dutch in 'copying and falsifying' French products. However the early Dutch protectionist measures seem to have been directed at France at times of conflict and/or war. As Laspeyres comments, Dutch trade policy is distinguished by the fact that systematic protection only occurs in the period of decline, starting around 1725.

Pierre Daniel Huet (1630–1721) is in my view the most interesting and clearly the most influential French observer of the economy of the Dutch Republic. In *A View of the Dutch Trade* Huet traces the history of beneficial Dutch economic policy back to before the turn of the first millennium, giving an account of Dutch inventions and innovations. Huet also quotes Julius Caesar on the industrious nature of the Dutch. Huet was a collaborator of Colbert and a teacher of the French princes, and his study of the economy of the Netherlands was made at Colbert's request. Huet had been bishop of Avranches, but retired to the Jesuits in Paris in 1699, where he spent the last 22 years of his life. Several translations indicate the influence of Huet's book on the Dutch Republic (originally published in 1712). There is a Spanish translation (Goyeneche 1717) and a second edition of the English translation already in 1722 (Huet 1722). A German edition from 1717 is thoroughly commented by the most influential German cameralist at the time, Georg Heinrich Zincke (1692–1769), who also provides a biography of the distinguished author (Zincke 1748: 552–78).

Charles Dutot, a cashier in the *Compagnie des Indes*, in his *Political Reflections upon the Finances and Commerce of France* (1739), ends the book with the quote from Pieter de la Court's found under point 2.2 above: 'Navigation, the fishery, commerce, and manufactures are the four pillars of the State.' These elements – navigation, fishery, commerce and manufacture plus the role of foreigners – are common for most of the foreign commentators when they attempt to explain the wealth of the Dutch, however with different emphasis.

In **England** William Petty (1623–1687) studied two years in the Dutch Republic as a young man, and even wrote a 'Collection of the Frugalities of Holland' that was lost at sea. What was later to become 'Petty's Law', the stages of growth of various economic sectors, was based on his observations of Holland. Petty saw initially the primary sector of an economy dominating, later to be followed by growth of the secondary (manufacturing) sector, and finally the tertiary service sector would be dominant. As did virtually all pre-Smithian economists, Petty saw the transition from agriculture to manufacturing as a necessary evolution. For the latecomers, this required tariffs. It is important to note that at the time, the term 'free trade' was used to describe the absence of trade monopolies, not the absence of tariffs (Seligman 1920: ix).

The obvious urban biases of early economic development made Petty suggest that England, like Holland, should industrialize and buy its foodstuffs abroad. By observing Holland it became clear that density of population obviously was one of the secrets of riches; Petty – as did so many of his contemporaries – not only wanted population to rise as rapidly as possible but also wanted to diminish the population of the already thinly populated areas of Britain and bring as many as possible to London.

Few English mercantilists of the 1600s and 1700s fail to mention the Dutch, almost always as an example to imitate. Josiah Child opens his 1668 book with a comment on 'the prodigious increase of the Netherlanders which is 'the envy of the present and may be the wonder of all future generations' (Child 1668). In his 1681/1693 book, Child returns to the Dutch as being the example to imitate: 'If we intend to have the Trade of the World, we must imitate the Dutch, who make the worst as well as the best of all manufactures, that we may be in a capacity of serving all Markets, and all Humors' (Child 1693: 90).

Italian economists were the first to recognize the synergetic growth of the cities as a product of division of labour and the inventions that were only possible in manufacturing, not in the production of raw materials. An early and much-quoted work on the Netherlands was written by the Florentine Lodovico Guicciardini (1521–1589): *Descrittione di tutti i Paesi Bassi, altrimenti detti Germania inferiore* (Guicciardini 1567)

Lodovico was the nephew of Francesco Guicciardini (1483–1540), the famous historian of the Italian peninsula. Giovanni Botero's *On the greatnesse of Cities (Sulle Grandezze delle Città,* 1588, English translation 1607) sees cities not only as the cradle of manufacturing but also of freedom, culture and wealth in Europe.

In what is a very early book on geography and ethnology at a world level – *Relationi Universali* (first edition 1596) – Giovanni Botero partly uses Guicciardini as a source, but has clearly also visited the Netherlands himself. Botero gives an account of the 'Schumpeterian' qualities of the Dutch both as inventors and imitators, and lists some of the things they have invented. In the style of the early Italian economists, Botero emphasizes 'the quality of the people': the Dutch 'drink immoderately' and 'believe lightly' and 'even the women have very great abilities in commerce' (Botero 1596/1622: 49). During the *settecento* Italian economists like Antonio Genovesi and Cesare Beccaria analyze how Italy has fallen behind the Dutch Republic and other countries that have taken over Italy's previous strength in manufacturing and trade. This comparative analysis provides important inputs into the intellectual ferment that created the Italian *risorgimento* (S. Reinert 2005).

Spanish economists were naturally very interested in the economic success of the Dutch Republic, whose sixteenth- and seventeenth-century success provided such a contrast to the decadence of Spain during the same period (from about 1550). The economic decadence of Spain did not occur for lack of competent economic advice from its native economists (Hamilton 1932). Spanish economist Gerónimo de Uztáriz (1670–1732) is of particular interest not only because his very influential *Teórica y practica de comercio y de marina* (1724/1751) contains many references to the Dutch Republic but also because of Uztáriz's personal knowledge of the Netherlands during a period of a military career of almost 20 years. He attended the Royal Academy at Brussels and served in the Low Countries both during his military service and later as captain in the infantry, before becoming prime minister to the Spanish viceroy of Sicily in 1705 (Hamilton 1935, Fernandez Durán 1999). Also with Uztáriz we can observe how ideas travelled in Europe at the time. His book was translated into English, French and Italian. Uztáriz's first publication was the foreword to the 1717 Spanish translation of Huet's *Commerce de Holland* mentioned above (Goyeneche 1717). Uztáriz's conclusion is in line with the contemporary mainstream: '[Manufactures] is a mine more fruitful of gain, riches, and plenty, than those of Potosí,[7] and he presents a long list of policy measures aimed at making the Spanish economy more like that of the Dutch Republic.

In **Germany**, Veit Ludwig von Seckendorff (1626–1692) has been called the 'Adam Smith of Cameralism' (Small 1909), and justifiably so. His times were violent and extremely difficult for Germany. In the reconstruction of Germany after the Thirty Years' War (1618–48), Seckendorff – in the service of Duke Ernst *der Fromme* (the Pious) of Sachsen-Gotha – came to set an example for the management of the many small German states. Seckendorff travelled to the Netherlands, accompanying Count Ernst,

7. Potosí, at about 4,000 metres in present Bolivia, was the richest of all mines in the world. At the time it was the second-largest city in the world after London.

and the wealth and religious tolerance he observed there made a huge impression on him (Stolleis 1995:158). To Seckendorff, the Dutch appear as 'examples of the wisest and in production and trade (*in Gewerb*) the most experienced people' (Seckendorff 1665). From his travels in the Dutch Republic, Seckendorff came to understand the crucial need for manufactures and the importance of population density. Economic activities needed to be clustered rather than spread, an argument that Antonio Serra had already raised at a theoretical level in 1613. Seckendorff's economic measures therefore included the promotion of manufactures and the resettlement of artisans from the countryside in the cities, where they were likely to make much better livings. He also promoted the extension of agriculture and activities adding value to the produce of the land.

Later in the seventeenth century, authors like Philipp Wilhelm von Hörnigk (1684) follow up the cameralist tradition with more emphasis on purely economic factors. As William Petty in England at that time, Hörnigk was an early proponent of 'political arithmetic' and, among other things, he calculated the income from artisans in a successful Dutch city. In the early economics journals, references are continuously made to Dutch institutions and practical affairs (Zincke 1746–1767, Bergius 1767–1780, Beckmann 1770–1806). German economists Jakob Friedrich von Bielfeld (1717–1770) and Johann Heinrich Gottlob von Justi (1717–1771) provide insights and descriptions of the reasons for the *decay* of states in general (Bielfeld 1760) and of the Dutch Republic in particular (Justi 1760) (see section 6 of this chapter).

4. Development as Synergies and Diversity: The Case of Seventeenth-Century Delft

The strong urban bias that we can observe in early economic growth supports the idea that a larger division of labour *per se* is a starting point for cumulative causations of growth (Serra 1613 and chapter 10 in this volume). Already Xenophon hinted at these 'systemic increasing returns' when he claimed that certain problems in a city may be cured by increasing the size of the city. A large division of labour maximizes the potential of learning across disciplines. The foreign economists whose knowledge of the Dutch Republic is the most intimate, Huet and Uztáriz, do not tire in listing the different industries of every Dutch city and the importance of the enormous diversity.

A case study of the Dutch city of Delft in the seventeenth century shows how synergies created by a diversified base of activities produced knowledge and spillovers between seemingly unrelated activities. No doubt other Dutch cities also exhibit similar cases of cross-activity learning. In Delft it is possible to identify a closely-knit maritime-scientific-artistic cluster, where innovations leapt to and from very different sectors of the economy. The case of Delft brings together, in the very same productive-scientific cluster, the sectors and elements that, in the German tradition, are seen as being the important driving forces of capitalism, all in an interwoven whole:

- The quest for military power, in this case through the navy, as in Werner Sombart's 'War and Capitalism' (Sombart 1913a);

- The quest for luxury, in this case art, as in Sombart's 'Luxury and Capitalism' (Sombart 1913b);
- The quest for scientific knowledge, as in Sombart's work on capitalism (Sombart 1902/1928) and Thorstein Veblen's 'idle curiosity'.

These three forces interact in creating serendipitous economic development in Delft, and a profession curiously uniting the three seemingly unrelated fields – woollen industry, maritime warfare, art and scientific development – is that of the producer of glass lenses, *the lens grinder.*[8]

Dutch artists invented oil painting and painting on canvases, a fact emphasized already by Botero (1588). The raw materials for these inventions – linseed oil, linen and hemp fibre – were widely used in Dutch shipbuilding and readily available, but would not be as readily available to the artists of other schools. Taking over the leadership from Florence, in the seventeenth century, Delft emerged as a centre for the scientific glass production of lenses. Important improvements to the microscope were also made here (Ruestow 1996). The Delft natural scientist and microscope maker, Antoni van Leeuwenhoek (1632–1723), found a synergy between the production of woollen cloth, the main industry of the day, and his scientific work, because the hand lenses he developed were used extensively to inspect woollen cloth (Huerta 2003:33). Similarly, lens-making was integrated with the development of Flemish art – bringing together the history of art and the history of science – through the work of the Delft painter Johannes Vermeer (1632–1675). Vermeer's painting technique included seeing his motifs through lenses and a *camera obscura*, an apparatus similar to a primitive camera (Steadman 2001). Vermeer also keenly participated in aspects of the discoveries surrounding him in Delft: the geographical discoveries of the Dutch navy and the discoveries in the natural sciences resulting from the improved microscopes made by Leeuwenhoek and his colleagues.[9] Leeuwenhoek 'also had extensive, indeed intimate, contacts with the artistic community, for his microscopic researches involved years of close interaction with the artists who served as his draftsmen' (Ruestow 1996: 182n). The navy and the merchant marine constituted the largest demand for lenses for binoculars, but as mentioned, lenses were also in demand in the textile industry and among natural scientists and producers of early microscopes. The Delft lens grinders thus formed the core of an extremely dynamic and path-breaking cluster including such diverse actors as the navy, the woollen industry, painters like Vermeer, natural scientists and their draftsmen, and the microscope builders.

Another product linking the three clusters – war (navy), luxury (art) and 'idle curiosity' (science) – in Holland at the time was mapmaking. Holland's position as a seafaring power demanded not only binoculars and naval instruments but also up-to-date maps.[10]

8. This analysis builds on chapter 14 in this volume.
9. Leeuwenhoek was to be the executor of his neighbour Vermeer's estate.
10. With the technology of mapmaking changing from woodcuts to copper plates, the same copper used by instrument makers, the Dutch took over its production from the Italians.

Vermeer's fascination with maps and explorations is clear in many of his paintings, one author commenting on his 'mania for maps'. Such synergic cumulative causations, and the path dependency they created, were no doubt at the core of knowledge creation and the process of economic growth.

The enormous diversity of economic activities was observed and commented on by most contemporary continental economists who wrote about the Dutch Republic. This is also apparent in the early economic journals (Zincke 1746–1767). The role of diversity and the resulting creative serendipity bring back the problem of 'monoculture' as identified in traditional development economics, where such creative linkages as those observed in seventeenth-century Delft do not occur. Agricultural communities normally have little to sell to each other. By emulating Dutch economic structure, rather than necessarily Dutch economic policies, and by avoiding the pitfalls of Spain, the mercantilists constructed their economic policies.

5. Factors and Issues

5.1. Scarcity of Natural Resources as a Prime Mover

This factor is mentioned by virtually every author as a fundamental reason behind the success of the Dutch, and de la Court – himself a Dutchman – devotes a whole chapter to the miserable natural conditions of Holland. 'Our country yields almost nothing out of its own bowles', he says (part 1, ch.9), also quoted by McCullagh (1846, Vol. 2: 270). Joshua Gee (1729: 128) is among the many writers who ascribe the Dutch engagement in trading as a result of the deficiency of valuable land.

Botero (1590/1622) comments on Holland's lack of resources, but wealth in products. The absence of raw materials creates abundance the goods made from the same raw materials: 'Holland, without vines, without flax, without wood and with very little cultivated soil, abounds incredibly with wine, linen, ships, and grain' (Botero 1590/1622: 57). Not only did the Netherlands lack natural resources, the ports were also 'positively bad' (McCullagh 1846: 12). Uztáriz comments in this way on the connection between Dutch barrenness, its lack of possibilities for food production and its specialization in other areas:

> 'Its inhabitants are so skilful in theory, and vigilant in the practice of this important maxim of state, that other nations must acknowledge an inferiority. For it is notorious that in spite of a small sandy district, which nature has allotted them, they singly carry on more trade in all the four quarters of the world, than the great powers of France and England united. To attain this, they avail themselves of very active principles, and a plan of traffick different from that of other states, and which the barrenness of their country obliges them to. And yet, by the help of commerce, they are become so populous, that were all their broad rivers, arms of the sea, gulphs, marshes, and waste land, converted into fruitful pastures, all would not suffice to maintain the inhabitants with food. But as a fourth part of that district is not cultivated, and its pastures are about another fourth, the rest being water, or land that yields neither fruit, grass, trees, or anything useful in life, some writers insist that their harvests cannot support a fourth of their own consumption, the worst circumstance a people can labour under' (Uztáriz 1751: 149–50)

A late English author comments, bordering on the heroic, on how the harsh surroundings moulded the Dutch character:

> 'That undismayed and undisheartened the early Frisian race should have lived on amid their often-broken, but as often-mended dykes, learning by each new catastrophe how to improve on former expedients, with no rash confidence that even these repairs would prove effectual, is the first and, on the whole, perhaps the greatest fact in the book of their national life. From it all the rest of their dauntless venture, daring and endurance, seems to grow naturally and credibly. What work could they be put to do harder than this? Day and night, all the year round, from sire to son, to keep wakeful watch lest their country should sink into the sea!' (McCullagh 1846: 8)

5.2. The People

> *'Caesar observes in his Commentaries, that the People of the Low Countries were very laborious and industrious, both for Invention and Imitation. His Words are, Est summae genus solertiae, atque ad ad omnia imitanda quae a quoquo traduntur aptissimum.'*
>
> Huet, *A View of the Dutch Trade*, 1722.

Early economists paid much attention to what Serra (1613) calls 'the quality of the people'. In Serra's book, the Genovese work harder than the Venetians, but other factors (like geographical position) cause the Venetians to come out as being the wealthiest. In the 'quality of the people', the Dutch score very high with early economists, but – most importantly, in my view – the industriousness of the people is normally mentioned in connection with the scarcity of resources: the one is almost a result of the other. That necessity is the mother of inventions (and imitations) was obvious to most of the contemporary economic observers (Montesquieu 1748).

Because the mentality was recognized as being so important, a mandatory passage point for laggard nations was its conscious changing and moulding. Profit-seeking was understood as not being *nature* but an acquired *culture*. As Frederick the Great of Prussia impatiently says in Lowe's translation: 'The plebs will never give up their humdrum tune, unless you drag them by their noses and ears to their profits' (Lowe 1988: 21). Manufacturing and trade were seen as the carriers of the 'right' habits (Hirschman 1977).

Botero (1590: 49) comments on the Dutch that 'They have an inclination towards music …, they rapidly and easily imitate everything they see. They have invented the art of painting in oils and to colour glass and many other noble things'. He also says that:

> 'The peoples of Holland surpass all other nations of Europe in size and their women all others in beauty, and they do not lag behind them in politics or wealth. They have maintained their ferocity and bravery of old, and in possession of an abundant country, in continuous contact with the Sea, they respect no foreign power or force'.

If one wishes to subscribe to a cyclical idea of history (Kindleberger 1996: 14 ff), the Dutch are here described as still forcefully ascending, while 200 years later a German author would observe the same characteristics declining in the Dutch Republic (an anonymous Italian traveller (1786) and Bielfeld (1760), see section 6 of this chapter).

Botero admires the skill of the Dutch women: 'Also the women have a great intelligence in commerce and trade, and almost all of them know reading and writing and several languages' (1590: 49). However, he also describes the Dutch as pragmatic and relatively unemotional: 'They forget easily both insults and benefits, they neither hate nor love firmly.' Adam Smith says that 'It is there (in Holland) unfashionable not to be a man of business' (Smith 1776/1976, I, 108).

A late contribution to this discussion, from Sweden, sums up the mercantilist argument with emphasis on *population density*. The author is a student of Anders Berch, who held the Chair of Economics in Uppsala:

> 'How things really are in national economics, is nowhere clearer than in the case of the United Netherlands. They have virtually no domestic (resources), but still, through the industry of its large population, exceed in strength the immense but sparsely populated and idle Spain. (The Netherlands) knows well how to use the folly of others to its own benefit. We see how poor Spain is with all its gold and silver mines, the best ports and the best soil in the world, because of its lack of inhabitants. On the other hand how its large number of inhabitants make the United Provinces mighty, with their miserable ports and the worst climate on earth.' (Westbeck 1747: 4–5)

The importance of foreign immigration – particularly through the skills that they bring in – is a constant theme starting already in the Byzantine Empire and in Xenophon's *Poroi* (Zincke 1753). The immigration of foreign skills was often helped by religious and other prosecutions, a fact that both Holland and England – starting with the Tudors – consciously used to their advantage. Conversely, the Venetian Republic prohibited the migration of skilled workers under the threat of death penalty (Reinert 1999). Carlo Salerni (1782/1996) comments on how already Edward III of England, in 1331, recruits a certain John Kemp from Flanders in order to obtain the skills of producing fine woollens while his conational Brevver brought the art of fine dyeing to England in 1667 (Salerni: 1782/1996: 81).

In his first work – *Het Welvaeren der Stad Leyden* – Pieter de la Court indeed puts immigration at the centre of the engine of growth in that city. Leyden's welfare is neither the result of wise laws promoting manufacturing nor of the guilds, but a result of warring neighbours. The policy here must be not to tax foreigners more than the locals. This principle must also be extended to the students. If costs – rents, luxury taxes etc. – are too high, manufacturing will be forced into the countryside (Laspeyres 1863: 185–86).

'Not only were strangers of every race and creed sure of an asylum in Holland, but of a welcome; and singular pains were taken to induce those whose skill enabled them to contribute to the wealth of the state to settle permanently in the great towns', says McCullagh (1846, Vol.2: 267). The different immigrants would also contribute different skills; at one point the Flemish Protestants brought in skills in laces and ribbons, and the Jews skills in dyeing and chemistry in general.

The Dutch institutions and their 'organisational capability', their reliability as suppliers of goods and shipping services, is commented on by the early economists. The institution-building seems to have been very conscious at many levels. Grotius's 'Mare Liberum' (1609) had as its immediate objective to overthrow the claims of the crown of Spain to the exclusive navigation of the Indian and Pacific Oceans (McCullagh 1846, Vol. II: 334). Johann Beckmann, professor of economics in Göttingen at the time of Adam Smith, makes the following observation in his *History of Inventions* (London 1797): 'In the year 1404 the magistrates of Bruges, in Flanders, requested the magistrates of Barcelona to inform them what was the common practice in regards to bills of exchange' (Beckmann 1797, Vol. 2: 462). The Dutch ability to learn from others, as Colbert complained about when it came to copying French products, has clearly been an important feature across time.

5.3. Industries and the Cult of Manufacturing

> 'From the raw materials from Spain and the West Indies – particularly silk, iron and *cochinilla* (a red dye) – which cost them only 1 florin, the foreigners produce finished goods which they sell back to Spain for between 10 and 100 florins. Spain is in this way subject to greater humiliations from the rest of Europe than those they themselves impose on the Indians. In exchange for gold and silver the Spaniards offer trinkets of greater or lesser value; but by buying back their own raw materials at an exorbitant price, the Spaniards are made the laughing stock of all Europe'. Luis Ortiz, Spanish Minister of Finance, to Felipe II: 'Memorandum to the King to prevent money from leaving the Kingdom', Madrid, 1558

This statement by Luis Ortiz is an early expression of what I have called 'the cult of manufacturing' in Europe. Almost 200 years later, when discussing Germany's import of manufactured goods, Zincke repeats the same argument: 'Above all Holland is the country which, through its manufacturing- and trading-arts, brought it to the point that in addition to importing from them many raw materials, which they themselves do not produce, we also import an indescribable quantity of their own and imported goods. Even goods that we could acquire directly and nearer ourselves, are delivered to us through the hands of the Dutch. One example of this is camel hair. The most unbelievable and ridiculous is that we receive our own produce, i.e. from our own raw materials on which we have already worked, only improved and perfected, from the hands of the Dutch: i.e. cloth made from our wool and yarn, the canvas made from our own linen yarn, lace, yarn etc.' (Zincke 1750: 306). The importance of the *variety and diversity* of the Dutch manufactures is frequently mentioned (e.g. McCullagh 1846, Vol. II: 267–69).

Huet lists page after page of the manufactures in which the different cities of the Dutch Republic specializes, but sees the impossibility of giving a complete account:

> 'I do not pretend to give an exact Particular of all the Manufactures of the United Provinces; it would be too prolix for the Brevity of this Treatise. I shall only say, that it is certain, that in no Kingdom, State, or Country in the World, they are so numerous and flourishing as in Holland. I shall take Notice only of some of the most considerable, and such as sell best in other Countries'.

Then follow page after page of listings of towns and their industries. The importance of the fisheries in explaining the success of the Dutch is emphasized both by Huet and Uztáriz (1751, Vol. 1: 168 ff). Hume reports that Greenland was discovered by the English under the reign of James I, 'and the whale-fishery was carried out with great success. But the industry of the Dutch, in spite of all opposition, soon deprived the English of this source of riches' (Hume 1767, Vol. 5: 125).

The sources also stress the long Dutch tradition in shipbuilding, since before the Crusades. When Count William in 1217 sailed from the Meuse, 'The troops of France and Germany were transported to Palestine in Venetian and Genovese vessels; the Dutch were borne thither in their own' (McCullagh 1846, Vol. 2: 79).

Already in 1590 Botero comments that more than 800 large ships can be seen outside the walls of Amsterdam (Botero 1590/1622: 57). On this branch of industry Huet (1722) says:

> 'Sardam, not far from Amsterdam, is certainly the only Place in the World, where all Sorts of Ships are built for the Use of Merchants, not only of the United Provinces, but of other Countries, which causes a prodigious Consumption of Wood, Cordage, Masts, Sails, and other Necessaries for Shipping, of which great Numbers are daily sold to Strangers, ready built, and fit for Launching.'

5.4. Technology, Inventions, Imitations and Competitiveness

I have already quoted Julius Caesar – as quoted by Huet – on the skills of the Dutch both in inventing and in imitating. The Dutch also have a long history of manufacturing. Huet starts his account on Holland in the year 1000, but McCullagh goes further back. After all, his volume on Holland is Volume II of a work entitled *The Industrial History of Free Nations*, where Volume I is an account of the industries in Ancient Greece. McCullagh notes that the Dutch manufacturers around the year 750 were 'held in high repute among the people of other countries where comparatively little progress in the peaceful arts had as yet been made'. He also notes their dependence on English wool, which made Charlemagne (742–814) scrupulously protect the Anglo-Saxon merchants although he was at war with England.

There are clearly many elements of both inventions and imitations in Dutch economic history. I have already mentioned the crucial Schumpeterian elements behind the success in fishing, and the synergies created between fishing, manufacturing and trading:

> 'About the year 1400, the Art of Salting, or Pickling of Herrings, was found out by a Fleming of Pierulem, which much encouraged this Sort of Fishery, as being of very great Advantage, and together with the Manufactures, made Navigation flourishing in that large Province, and of Consequence very much increased their Trade and Commerce.' (Huet 1722: 9)

The French under Colbert emphasized the Dutch skills of imitation rather than that of invention. However, the index of Zincke's *Leipziger Sammlungen* (1761: 561–63) gives us an indication of the many inventions and products which reached Germany from Holland, still at this late stage: *Holländerey* is another term for *Viehzucht* or husbandry; *Holländische Alleen* was a way of planting fruit trees, and *Holländische Erbsen* are 'field peas'. Among the many things discussed and praised in Zincke's journal over the years are *Holländisches Manufakturwesen;* the Dutch manufacturing system, the Dutch maxim of finance, the Dutch printing houses and their books, Dutch fisheries, Dutch inns, Dutch paper mills, Dutch horses, Dutch policy institutions, the Dutch constitution, the Dutch way of building ships, Dutch silk manufactures, Dutch cloth, Dutch flax cultivation, Dutch herring fisheries, Dutch clover, Dutch scarlet, Dutch turf, Dutch paper, Dutch gunpowder and Dutch navy. Similarly the *Oxford English Dictionary* (Vol. III: 729) provides an impressive list of objects and institutions that have been used in the English language with the prefix 'Dutch'. The word 'dutchify' seems, at one point, to have had similar connotations as the term 'americanize' today.

Zincke (1750: 338) is worried about the inability of the Germans to be inventive, and is forced to admit 'that few Germans have achieved fame from inventing something entirely new' He attributes this to the 'German *Phlegma*' and the love of old habits. Because of this, he says, the Germans overestimate the value of imported goods, Italian, French or Dutch, so that often goods which are produced in Germany are sold as imports (1750: 339).

Uztáriz emphasizes the cost effectiveness of Dutch shipping as an important success factor (Uztáriz Vol. 1: 170). He recommends a similar high volume/low margin strategy for Spain. Also according to Adam Smith, the Dutch 'trade upon lower profits than any people in Europe' (1776/1976: 102). Important elements in Dutch 'competitiveness' were the low interest rates in the Republic, and the ease with which capital could be raised. John Law (1750) is the author who clearly understands these mechanisms best (Child 1668: 13, 15, Law 1750: 26–30, Smith 1776/1976: 102). Child elevates low interest rates to the main cause of the wealth of a nation (1668: 7), while many continental economists would typically see the low costs of capital as a result of the abundance and profitability of manufacturing and trade; factors mutually reinforcing each other and creating 'virtuous circles' of cumulative causations.

The level of costs was frequently a concern with early economists, including the cost of articles that would indirectly determine the price of common labour, and – in the last instance – determine the nation's ability to compete with foreign manufactures. Along this line of reasoning Johann Heinrich Gottlob von Justi was worried about the high price of firewood in Germany, and in England an important motive behind Richard Cobden's campaign for free trade in corn was the very high influence of corn prices on the cost of feeding English manufacturing labour (Reinert 1998). In France Colbert saw that in order to enable France to compete internationally, 'an easy and sure subsistence had to be provided for the working population' (Kaplan 1976: Vol. 1, 2.). The Dutch prohibition of export of freshwater fish, which as opposed to the luxury product herring was food for 'the lesser sort of folk' (de Vries and van der Woude 1997: 237), most certainly served the same purpose of keeping costs down by keeping down the cost of feeding and maintaining the common man.

I would argue with Laspeyres that the Dutch criticism of monopolies also should be seen in this light: they make Holland less competitive through high costs

(Laspeyres: 93). On the other hand, the huge profits in overseas trade would no doubt have fallen if the Dutch monopolies had been given over to an army of independent traders. More 'perfect competition' would have brought both profits and prices down considerably. So the Dutch Republic was faced with a trade-off: de-monopolizing trade would increase the competitiveness of local production at the cost of the profits of the trading companies. Monopoly prices for luxury articles were not the main problem; these did not influence the wage level of the common man, and the huge profits from re-exports from Holland in the end would benefit the Republic through 'trickle-down'. For the articles consumed by the common man, on the other hand, regulations of various sorts aimed to reduce the negative effects of the monopolies (Laspeyres: 94–95).

Beckmann's section on 'Garden Flowers' in the *History of Inventions* gives perhaps one typical role of the Dutch as innovators and traders. Beckmann first informs us that flower bulbs were first brought to Europe by the Spaniards, but then 'the full tuberoses were first produced from seeds by one le Cour, of Leyden, who kept them scarce for some years by destroying the roots, that they might not become common' (Beckmann 1797, Vol. 3: 3).

A discussion of the Dutch Republic also invites the reopening of the huge debate on luxury that lasted for centuries in Europe. Early economists, like Botero (1590) and Laffemas (1597), attack luxury, but – as is well known – Bernhard Mandeville (1714) turns the argument around: luxury is the demand that keeps the wheels of business growing. In the end the consensus of the eighteenth century boiled down to a general agreement that luxuries were tolerable if they created employment at home. We must keep in mind that full employment and a positive balance of payments cannot be taken for granted in most European states at the time. We are far from any 'production possibility frontier', and through its de-industrialization and accompanying capital shortage, unemployment and poverty, Spain has set an example of *what not to do.*

Bernhard Mandeville, a Dutchman by birth and education, wrote his *Fable of the Bees* in 1714 (an early fragment in 1707) as if he were English. While many writers comment on the frugality of the Dutch, Mandeville examines the contradictions of frugality and luxury in the Dutch Republic: 'In Holland the People are only sparing in such things as are daily wanted, and soon consumed; in what is lasting they are quite otherwise: In Pictures and Marble they are profuse; in their Buildings and Gardens they are extravagant to Folly.'

Mandeville also sees the combination of encouragement of luxury consumption and high excise taxes being a conscious Dutch 'strategem'. When the sailors from the East India ships come home, the sailors 'squander away in wine, women and music, as much as people of their taste and education are well capable of', and they become 'the Lords of six weeks'. 'In this stratagem', says Mandeville, 'there is a double policy': first, their squandering insures that they have to go to sea again, solving the problem of manning the ships, and secondly. 'the large sums so often distributed among those sailors, are by this means made immediately to circulate throughout the country, from whence, by heavy excises and other impositions, the greatest part is soon drawn back into the public treasure' (Mandeville 1714/1806: 112).

6. The Decline of the Dutch Republic

Starting in the 1630s, Dutch envoys and authors started reporting on other nations' growing willingness to promote and protect their own shipping and manufacturers (Laspeyres 1863: 125). The English navigation acts of 1655 and Colbert's acts protecting French manufacturing (1664 and 1667) supported the transfer of production and trade from Dutch to English and French hands. These measures were clearly hurting the Dutch interests, and in Holland the discussion at the time focused on whether the English or the French policy was the most harmful to the nation (Laspeyres 1863: 127).

However, among foreign economists commenting on Holland in the early eighteenth century, like Huet, there is little sign of a decline. Being born in 1630, Huet's frame of reference would naturally be the 1600s. But as the eighteenth century advances, we start finding comments about the decay of Holland in the economic literature. An important reason for the decline is seen as other nations' attempts at taking over the activities that create most profit for the Dutch, a successful policy of 'import substitution' both in shipping and manufacturing (Mandeville 1714/1806: 109 and Steuart 1767).

Adam Smith, returning to the discussion above, sees the deindustrialization of Holland as a result of high taxation on bread and other necessities of the common man.[11] 'These and some other taxes of the same kind, by raising the price of labour, are said to have ruined the greater part of the manufactures of Holland' (Smith 1776/1976: I: 405). Typically of economics as it was to become, starting with A. Smith, the decline of Holland was to him a) self-imposed by internal mistakes (indirectly by too big government) b) tended to be reduced to a single factor of explanation, understood at the level of *prices*, rather than in the realm of production and c) void of any analysis of power relations, so important to the mercantilists. England's success in 'blowing the Dutch out of the waters' played no role in Smith's analysis (see Lane (1979) on military power below).

As already mentioned, the Italian city-states had been subject to similar problems of de-industrialization and loss of political power as those now faced by the Dutch Republic.[12] That trade was warfare in another form was clear to the mercantilists. The analysis across the Italian peninsula was similar to that in the Dutch Republic: the foreigners are beating us at our own game.

Asking if the decline of the Dutch Republic was inevitable is a tempting exercise in counterfactual history. One could ask if an earlier reversal of the policy of free trade and small duties, rather than only in the 1720s, would have given a different outcome? As O'Brien, Griffiths and Hunt (1991:418) say, 'Apart from Switzerland, few states followed Holland in allowing attachment to commerce and free trade to undermine national industries.' An anonymous Italian visitor to Holland in 1786 makes an additional interesting point: 'Why do not the Dutch, who are so skilled in commercial affairs, establish an easy remedy to the decadence of their manufactures? They do still have poor

11. 'In Holland the money price of the bread consumed in towns is supposed to be doubled by the price of such taxes' (Smith 1776/1976 I: 405).

12. See S. Reinert (2005). Van der Wee (1988) addresses the industrial decline both in Italy and the Low Countries.

provinces that are maintained by the charity of the other provinces. Why do they not establish the manufactures in these (poor) provinces, copying the English who have established the greatest part of their manufactures where money is scarce, and, as a consequence, food is cheaper?' (Anonymous 1786: 110–11).[13]

Probably the key element here is that the industrial developments in England at the time were qualitatively entirely different from the industries that were dying out in the Dutch Republic. The late 1700s in England represent the birth of a new techno-economic paradigm (Perez 2002 and 2004): during this period the technological improvements in cotton spinning, the leading industry, increased English labour productivity by more than 25 per cent *per year*. Having lost touch with the technological frontier, as the Dutch Republic clearly had, competing against areas where such rare 'productivity explosions' take place is virtually impossible. Any attempt to meet the challenge of English cotton spinning, which was well ahead on the learning curve, would have required firm policies and high tariff barriers. One hundred years later, the United States built its steel industry against English competition behind tariff barriers of up to 100 per cent. Such policies would have been completely alien to the principles that the Dutch Republic had inherited from the Golden Age, a time when the Republic itself had been in the position where England now was: the main beneficiary riding and cashing in on the waves of new technologies.

To the extent our anonymous Italian himself provides an answer to the question, this development is due to the 'laziness' of the Dutch inhabiting 'this coffee house of Europe'. He admires the past achievements of the Dutch, and recognizes the classical mercantilist argument that commerce 'domesticates Man and forms him to society'. But he argues that the Dutch Republic at this point suffers from an overdose, where commerce dominates over everything else and exhausts society rather than perfecting it further (*ibid*: 117). In a phrase that recalls the analysis of the decadence of Spain 200 years earlier, our Italian traveller refers to people who are so wealthy that they feel they would lose their honour if they worked. Although manufacturing is decaying all over the Republic, the situation in Utrecht – which is the refuge of the national nobility – is worse than elsewhere: manufacturing has disappeared almost completely (*ibid.* 110).

The data surrounding the decline of the Dutch Republic are controversial, but the sequential decline of the Hanseatic League, the Italian city-states and the Dutch Republic indicate that an era of small city-states is over. Two overriding factors seem to combine, irreversibly increasing the *minimum efficient size* of capitalism: Larger nations, like France and England, have themselves built manufactures and overseas trade, and these nations consciously attempt to extend the synergies of the city-state to a larger geographical territory.[14] The idea of a *minimum efficient size* of an economic system, reflect-

---

13. There were attempts to prevent the migration of industry to the poorer areas of the Republic (de Vries and van der Woude 293, 337). However, it is argued that this would not have improved the situation very much because 'the lower costs did not enlarge the market', and this policy would therefore only have delayed the deindustrialization (ibid. p. 337).

14. This aspect of capitalist development is described by Eli Heckscher (1931) and Karl Polanyi (1944).

ing *systemic increasing returns*, was not new at the time. I have already mentioned that in Xenophon such 'systemic increasing returns' were seen as curing the problems of a city by increasing its size. One could argue that the present trend towards globalization is just a further move in this same direction.[15] Regarding the decay of the Dutch Republic, we find this type of analysis confirmed by contemporary economists.

In his 'Nature and Character of States' *(Natur und Wesen der Staaten)* (1760), Johann Heinrich Gottlob von Justi (1717–1771) provides some very perceptive comments on the decay of Holland. Justi uses the fact that Holland is built on water to create a metaphor conveying the message that a certain era – a certain way of producing wealth – has come to an end. Holland is like a house on pillars on water, where the pillars are rotting:

> '....the example of Holland can be held against me: a country that lacks almost all the gifts of nature and that even in its little corner of the world must keep up the most expensive dikes in order not to be swallowed by the sea; but in spite of that, due to the industrious inhabitants, is a flourishing state. To this I reply that while I recognise that the poverty of the soil can be compensated by the industriousness of the inhabitants, that will still only be on borrowed and artificial ground. This is a structure that has been erected on piles that have been driven into the seabed, in which it is possible to live comfortably for a while. In the end, however, these piles will decompose, and the structure will collapse. Such an artificial ground have all nations that have flourished only by virtue of the comfort of their navigation and their hard work, without any natural wealth. **This ground will only exist as long as other nations are so naïve that they do not see that, with their own industriousness, they could busy themselves with the production that they have (previously) left to be done by that hard-working people.** As soon as these nations grow wiser, the artificial ground will rot and they will have nothing but the bad soil that nature has given them. In my opinion, during this present century the artificial ground of the Dutch has already started to decompose considerably, and probably it will increasingly go into decomposition as the wisdom and industriousness of the other European peoples increases, in particular that of the people of the North (*nordisch*). ... A republic is much better off when it has constructed its structure of welfare on its own natural soil.' (Justi 1760: 35–36, emphasis added)

In other words, as other nations learned to follow the Dutch strategy, she would 'fall behind'. We can assume this to happen both in trade and in manufacturing. In my opinion Justi is here pointing to several things: a) there is a catching-up, foreign nations understand that they will be better off if they increase their manufacturing and shipping, b) the rules of the game are changing; city mercantilism is no longer enough as a larger *Hinterland* is needed. Interestingly, at the time when the decay of the Dutch Republic was becoming increasingly evident, the mercantilists start emphasizing the important synergies between manufacturing and agriculture. Although Botero had already commented on the successful Dutch husbandry in the 1500s, agriculture had tended to be disregarded as a source of wealth during the time of the city-states. Now agriculture,

15. The theories of German economist Karl Bücher in this respect are discussed in Reinert (2000).

but *only if manufacturing was present*, increasingly started to be seen as a source of wealth. We may speculate that the small weight of agriculture in the city-states, which had once been their important strength, became a weakness as nation-state mercantilism gradually gained force. Part of the explanation would be the importance of the farming population – who represented the vast majority of the population in most European countries – as a home market at a time when industrialization increasingly addressed the needs of ordinary people while rural self-sufficiency diminished.

Justi changes the rules in Serra's model (1613): nature-given comparative advantage (geographical position) has diminished in importance, and man-made comparative advantage has increased in importance. Recreating and extending the observed urban advantage became a central challenge as city mercantilism gave way to nation-based mercantilism. Justi's comments here are in line with later observations by Friedrich List and Immanuel Wallerstein, who both point out that while England achieved this increased size through national unity, the failure of the Hanseatic League, the Italian city-states and Holland did not develop beyond a collection of city-states, which they see as a main reason for their loss of leadership (List 1841, chapters 1–3; Wallerstein 1978, vol. 2: 90–93).

The work of Jakob Friedrich von Bielfeld (1717–1770) contains an extensive typology on the reasons for the decadence of states. Bielfeld's book (1760) was an economic bestseller with a total of 12 editions, and one chapter (Chapter XV in Vol. 2) treats the decadence of states. To Bielfeld there are two types of causes of decadence, *Foreign* and *Intrinsic*. Among the twelve foreign external causes are large-scale migrations (barbarian invasions), wars, too much quarrel and warfare with neighbours ('it can take one century of war to obtain the same result as a couple of written treaties'), too large geographical extension of the empire (the Roman Empire is one example), loss of independence (Portugal's dependence on England is one example), too ambitious and vain national projects (like Carl XII's plans for Sweden), civil wars which carve up the empire, dividing the power between two rulers, and the weakening of authority and loss of control of the territories (Portugal's loss of control over Brazil and Genova's loss of control over Corsica are Bielfeld's examples).

The *intrinsic* reasons for the decadence of a state are 20: a 'vicious Constitution', a king unfit to rule (*un Souverain incensé*), minorities which weaken the ruler, ministers who betray the ruler, lax law enforcement, contempt for religion, *fanatisme*, 'exaggerated despotism', too much liberty, negligence of useful production in favour of the frivolous (the Portuguese who take their manufactured goods from England, only to play the guitar and fill up the churches to pray in front of some Saint is the example of horror here), a useless nobility too proud to work (see also Justi 1756), ridiculous laws, depopulation of the state (celibacy being one of the causes), colonies that become too strong (the Spanish possessions in the Americas being the example), epidemic diseases, alcoholism, lenient military discipline, too high debts, internal strife in the state administration, and changing the basic principles of the constitution.

Which of these 20 different intrinsic causes of decadence did Holland suffer from, in Bielfeld's view? Bielfeld mentions Holland in two cases: He sees too much liberty – *Liberté dégénere en libertinage* – being the cause of 'the lethargy of Holland' in 1760. Bielfeld's use of the word 'lethargy' in describing the Dutch contrasts sharply with Botero's use of the words 'ferocity and bravery' about the Dutch 170 years earlier, adding that they 'respect no foreign power or force'. These statements support a 'life cycle' theory of economic development (Kindleberger 1996). This also resembles the very early theories of history represented by twelfth-century Arab historian Ibn Khaldun, where a dynamic desert tribe invades and occupies a city, only slowly to degenerate, and in turn to be taken over by a new 'brave tribe'. Adding to this the eighteenth-century idea of the stages of economic development – hunting and gathering, pasturage, agriculture and industry (Reinert 2000) – we may superimpose world-wide cycles of technological change and progress on a cyclical theory of growth and decay in specific geographical areas.

Although representing decidedly different schools of thought, Bernhard Mandeville (1714/1806: 109) and James Steuart (1767) both anticipate Adam Smith's point about the high level of taxation as an important reason for the decay of the Dutch. So does, later, McCullagh (McCullagh 1846, Vol. 2: 358). Observers of the decline of Spain point to the fact that the productive people tended to be highly taxed, but the passive *rentiers* were not. To James Steuart (1767) the worst kind of taxes are those levied on private production for private use (i.e. goods not entering the market): His example here is 'Holland, where a man cannot kill his own pig, or his own calf, without paying a tax'.

The factors that present themselves as candidates for the decline of the Dutch Republic are many, and – as in the case of the much slower rise of the same Republic – we must assume that the economic, political and institutional factors collude and mutually reinforce each other. Kindleberger presents a long list of factors causing the decline of the Dutch Republic: 'wars; foreign mercantilism; foreigners copying Dutch techniques; the shift of Europe away from using Amsterdam as an entrepôt, first in trade, then in finance; the loss of capital in loans to France in the Revolution; and the levying of indemnities by France', all external. Internal factors listed are 'withdrawal from trade and industry by finance, high taxes on consumption (i.e. Mandeville's point); provincial resistance to central directions, especially in matters of taxation; the persistence of guilds; loss of skilled workers; conspicuous consumption (which Mandeville had seen as a reason for growth, not decline); skewed income distribution, and many more' (Kindleberger 1996: 103–04).

Like Florence and many Italian city-states, the Dutch Republic seems, then, to have failed to successfully convert from 'city mercantilism' to 'national mercantilism', a centralized system where the benefits observed in the cities were extended, through a central government, to a larger geographical territory. This failure in the long term to build synergies created by economies of scale in trade and production to the extent later done by its rivals, had probably also been responsible for the decline already of coalition which was much than that of the Dutch states; the Hanseatic League (compare Kindleberger 1996: 83–84).

Like Florence – whose industries suffered from the English Tudor strategy of import substitution and high export taxes on wool – the Dutch Republic may have been unable to respond to the economic challenges posed first from England and France, and then from Germany. I would argue that the virtuous circles created cumulatively by the triple rents; *long-distance trade, fisheries* and *manufacturing* seem to have been weakened in parallel. The mutually reinforcing factors of high profits in these three types of economic activities degenerated synergetically – through cumulative causation – in much the same way as they had been generated, but in a much slower process, over the centuries building up to the Golden Age. The final result was the parallel loss of economic, military and political power that throughout history seems to hinge on what Frederick Lane (1979: 45–48) – the great historian of Venice – calls '*increasing returns* from the use of force as an economic service'.

References

Anonymous (1786), *Relazione di una scorsa per varie provincie d'Europa del M. M.... a Madama G.. in Parigi,* Pavia, Nella Stamperia del Monastero di S. Salvatore.

Ashley, William (1920), *An Introduction to English Economic History and Theory,* New York, Putnam.

Beccaria, Cesare ([1769] 1970), Elementi di Economía Pubblica, in, *Opere dei Classici Italiani,* Vol 2. Milan, Società Tipografica de' Classici Italiani.

Beckmann, Johann, editor (1770–1806), *Physikalisch-ökonomische Bibliothek worinn von den neusten Büchern, welche die Naturgeschichte, Naturlehre und die Land- und Stadtwirtschaft betreffen, zuverlässige und vollständige Nachrichten ertheilet warden,* Göttingen, im Verlag der Wittwe Vandenhoeck und im Vandenhoek und Ruprechtschen Verlage, 23 volumes.

Beckmann, Johann, (1797) *A History of Inventions and Discoveries,* London, J. Bell. 3 volumes.

Berch, Anders (1747), *Inledning til Almänna Hushålningen, innefattande Grunden til Politie, Oeconomie och Cameralwetenskaperna,* Stockholm, Lars Salvius.

Bergius, Johann Heinrich Ludwig, editor (1767–1780), *Policey- und Cameral-Magazin (1767–1774) & Neues Policey- und Cameral-Magazin (1775–1780),* Leipzig, bey M. G. Weidmanns Erben und Reich.

Bielfeld, Jakob Friedrich (1760), *Institutions politiques,* The Hague, Pierre Gosse Junior. 2 volumes.

Botero, Giovanni (1590), *Della Ragione di Stato. Libri Dieci,* this work also contains *Delle Cause della Grandezza delle Città, libri tre,* Rome, Vicenzio Pellagalo. English translation 1706.

Botero, Giovanni (1596/1622), *Relazioni Universali,* Venice, Alessandro Vecchi.

Child, Josiah (1668), *Brief Observations Concerning Trade and Interest of Money,* London, Elizabeth Calvert and Henry Mortlock.

Child, Josiah (1681/1693), *A Treatise Concerning the East-India Trade,* London, Printed for the Honourable the *East India Company.*

Clément, Pierre, editor (1861–1872), *Lettres, Instructiones et Mémoires de Colbert,* Paris, Imprimerie Impériale/Imprimerie Nationale, 7 volumes in 10 + 1 volume 'Errata Général et Table Analytique.'

Drechsler, W. (2000), 'Etienne Laspeyres' History of the Economic Thought of the Netherlanders: A Law & Economics Classic?', *European Journal of Law and Economics,* vol. 10, no. 3 (November), pp. 235–242.

Dutot, Charles, *Political Reflections upon the Finances and Commerce of France,* London, A. Millar, 1739.

Ekelund, Robert B. and Robert D. Tollison (1981), *Mercantilism as a Rent-Seeking Society: Economic Regulation in Historical Perspective,* Texas A&M University Press, College Station.

Fanfani, Amintore (1955), *Storia delle dottrine economiche dall'antichità al XIX secolo,* Milan, Giuseppe Principato.

Fernández Duran, Reyes (1999), *Jerónimo de Uztáriz (1670–1732). Una Política Económica para Felipe V,* Madrid, Minerva.

France, Edict (1581), *Edict du Roi, contenant establissemét d'un Bureau de Douane en chascune ville de ce Royaume à la semblance de celuy qui est long temps y a estably à Paris,* Paris, Federic Morel.

Gee, Joshua (1729), *Trade and Navigation of Great Britain Considered,* London, Bettesworth & Hitch.

Goyeneche, Pedro Francisco (1717), *Comercio de Holanda, o el gran thesoro historial y político del floreciente comercio, que los holandeses tienen en todos sus estados y señoríos del mundo. Qual es el modo de hazerle, su origen, sus grandes progresos, sus posesiones y gobierno en la Indias. Como se han hecho dueños absolutos de todo el Comercio de Europa, y cuales son las mercaderías convenientes para el trato Marítimo. De donde las sacan, y las considerables ganancias queen él hacen,* 'traducido del francés', Madrid, Imprenta Real, por J. Rodríguez Escobar. Comments by Uztáriz.

Guicciardini, Lodovico (1567), *Descrittione di tutti i Paesi Bassi, altrimenti detti Germania Inferiore,* Antwerp, Silvio.

Hamilton, Earl (1932), 'Spanish Mercantilism before 1700', in Cole, Arthur H. (editor) *Facts and Factors in Economic History, Articles by former Students of Edwin Francis Gay,* Cambridge, MA, Harvard University Press, pp. 214–239.

Hamilton, Earl (1935), 'The Mercantilism of Gerónimo de Uztáriz: A Reexamination', in Himes, Norman (editor), *Economics, Sociology and the Modern World. Essays in Honor of T. N. Carver,* Cambridge, MA, Harvard University Press, pp. 114–129.

Heckscher, Eli (1931), *Merkantilismen. Ett led i den ekonomiska politikens historia,* Stockholm, Norstedt.

Hirschmann, Albert O (1977), *The Passions and the Interests. Political Arguments for Capitalism before Its Triumphs,* Princeton, Princeton University Press.

Hocquet, Jean-Claude (1990), *Il Sale e la Fortuna di Venezia,* Rome, Jouvence.

Hörnigk, Philipp Wilhelm von (1684), *Oesterreich über alles wann es nur will. Das ist: wohlmeinender Fürschlag Wie mittelt einer wohlbestellten Lands-Oeconomie die Kayserl. Erbland in kurzem über alle andere Staat von Europa zu erheben. Durch einen Liebhaber der Kayserl. Erbland Wolfahrt.*

Huerta, Robert D (2003), *Giants of Delft. Johannes Vermeer and the Natural Philosophers: The Parallel Search for Knowledge during the Age of Discovery*, Lewisburg, Bucknell University Press.

Huet, Pierre Daniel (1722), *A View of the Dutch Trade in all the States, Empires, and Kingdoms of the World,* London, C. King and J. Stagg. Second edition, first edition 1717. Original French edition 1712.

Hume, David (1767), *The History of England from the Invasion of Julius Caesar to the Revolution in 1688,* London, A. Millar, 1767. 6 volumes.

Justi, Johann Heinrich Gottlob von (1760), *Die Natur und das Wesen der Staaten, als die Grundwissenschaft der Staatskunst, der Policey, und aller Regierungswissenschaften, desgleichen als die Quelle aller Gesetze, abgehandelt,* Berlin, Johann Heinrich Rüdigers.

Kaplan, Steven L. (1976), *Bread, Politics and Political Economy in the Reign of Louis XV,* The Hague, Nijhoff.

Kindleberger, Charles (1996), *World Economic Primacy 1500–1900,* New York, Oxford University Press.

Laffemas, Barthélemy (1597), *Reiglement (sic) general pour dresser les manufactures en ce rayaume, et couper le cours des draps de soye, & autres merchandises qui perdent & ruynent l'Estat: qui est le vray moyen de remettre la France en sa splendeur, & de faire gaigner les pauvres…,* Paris, Claude de Monstr'oil and Jean Richter.

Lane, Frederick (1973), *Venice. A Maritime Republic,* Baltimore, Johns Hopkins.

Lane, Frederick (1979), *Profits from Power. Readings in protection-rent and violence-controlling enterprises,* Albany, State University of New York Press.

Laspeyres, Etienne (1863/1961), *Geschichte der Volkswirtschaftlichen Anschauungen der Niederländer und Ihrer Literatur zur Zeit der Republik,* Nieuwkoop, de Graaf. (reprint)

Law, John (1705/1750), *Money and Trade Considered,* Glasgow, R & A. Foulis (French, German and Dutch contemporary translations).

List, Friedrich (1841), *Das Nationale System der Politischen Ökonomie*, Stuttgart, Cotta.

Lowe, Adolph (1988), *Has Freedom a Future?,* New York, Praeger.

Magnusson, Lars, editor (1993), *Mercantilist Economics*, Boston, Kluwer.

Mandeville, Bernard (1714), *The Fable of the Bees or Private Vices, Public Benefits*, London, J. Roberts.

McCullagh, W. Torrens (1846), *The Industrial History of Free Nations, Considered in Their Relation to Their Domestic Institutions and External Policy*, volume I, The Greeks, volume II, The Dutch, London: Chapman & Hall.

Montesquieu, Charles de Secondat, Baron de (1748), *De l'esprit des loix, ou, du rapport que les loix doivent avoir avec la constitution de chaque gouvernement, les moeurs, le climat, la religion, le commerce, &c*, Genève, Chez Barrillot & fils.

Mun, Thomas (1621), *A Discourse of Trade, from England unto the East-Indies*, London, Nicholas Okos for Ion Pyper.

Mun, Thomas (1664), *England's Treasure by Forraign Trade*, London, J. G. for T. Clark.

O'Brien, Patrick, Trevor Griffiths and Philip Hunt (1991), 'Political Components of the Industrial Revolution: Parliament and the Cotton Textile Industry, 1660–1774', *The Economic History Review*, New Series, vol. 44, no. 3, pp. 359–423.

Perez, Carlota (2002), *Technological Revolutions and Financial Capital: The Dynamics of Bubbles and Golden Ages*, Cheltenham, Edward Elgar.

Perez, Carlota (2004), 'Technological Revolutions, Paradigm Shifts and Socio-institutional Change', in Reinert, Erik S. (editor), *Globalization, Economic Development and Inequality: An Alternative Perspective*, Cheltenham, Edward Elgar, pp. 217–242.

Perrotta, Cosimo (1993), 'Early Spanish Mercantilism: The First Analysis of Underdevelopment', in Magnusson (1993), pp. 17–58.

Polanyi, Karl (1944), *The Great Transformation*, New York, Rinehart.

Reinert, Erik S. (1980), *International Trade and the Economic Mechanisms of Underdevelopment*, Ann Arbor, MI,, University Microfilms.

Reinert, Erik S. (1994), 'Catching-up from way Behind - A Third World Perspective on First World History', in Fagerberg, Jan et al. (editors), *The Dynamics of Technology, Trade, and Growth*, Aldershot, Edward Elgar, pp. 168–197 + chapter 1 in this volume.

Reinert, Erik S. (1996), 'The Role of Technology in the Creation of Rich and Poor Nations: Underdevelopment in a Schumpeterian System', in Aldcroft, Derek H. and Ross Catterall (editors), *Rich Nations - Poor Nations. The Long Run Perspective*, Aldershot, Edward Elgar, pp. 161–188.

Reinert, Erik S. (1998), 'Raw Materials in the History of Economic Policy; or, Why List (the Protectionist) and Cobden (the Free Trader) Both Agreed on Free Trade in Corn.', in Parry, G. (editor), *Freedom and Trade. 1846–1996*, London, Routledge, pp. 275–300.

Reinert, Erik S. (1999), 'The Role of the State in Economic Growth', *Journal of Economic Studies*, vol. 26, no. 4/5, pp. 268–321.

Reinert, Erik S. (2000), 'Karl Bücher and the Geographical Dimensions of Techno-Economic Change', in Backhaus, Jürgen, (editor), *Karl Bücher: Theory - History - Anthropology - Non-Market Economies*, Marburg, Metropolis Verlag, pp. 177–222.

Reinert, Erik S. ed. (2004), *Globalization, Economic Development and Inequality: An Alternative Perspective*, Cheltenham, Edward Elgar, series 'New Horizons in Institutional and Evolutionary Economics'.

Reinert, Erik and Arno Daastøl (1997), 'Exploring the Genesis of Economic Innovations: The Religious Gestalt-Switch and the Duty to Invent as Preconditions for Economic Growth', *European Journal of Law and Economics*, vol 4: no. 2/3, pp. 233–283.

Reinert, Erik S. and Sophus Reinert (2003), 'An Early National Innovation System: the Case of Antonio Serra's 1613 *Breve Trattato*', *Institutions and Economic Development/Istituzioni e Sviluppo Economico*, vol. 1, no. 3, pp. 24–47. Also chapter 10 in this volume.

Reinert, Sophus (2005), 'The Italian Tradition of Political Economy: Theories and Policies of Development in the Semi-Periphery of the Enlightenment', in Jomo, K.S. and E.S. Reinert (editors), *The Origins of Development Economics*, London and New York, Zed Books.

Ruestow, Edward G. (1996), *The Microscope in the Dutch Republic: The Shaping of Discovery*, Cambridge, Cambridge University Press.

Salerni, Carlo (1782/1996). *Riflessioni sull'economia della provincia d'Otranto,* Lecce, Centro di Studi Salentini.

Schmoller, Gustav (1897/1967), *The Mercantile System and its Historical Significance,* New York, Macmillan, Kelley (translated from articles in *Schmoller's Jahrbuch*).

Seckendorff, Veit Ludwig von (1665), *Additiones oder Zugaben und Erleuterungen zu dem Tractat des Teutschen Fürstenstaats,* Frankfurt, Gotzen.

Seligman, E.R.A. (1920), *Curiosities of Early Economic Literature,* San Francisco, Privately Printed by John Henry Nash.

Serra, Antonio (1613), *Breve Trattato delle Cause che Possono far Abbondare l'Oro e l'Argento dove non sono Miniere,* Naples, Lazzaro Scorriggio.

Smith, Adam (1776/1976), *The Wealth of Nations*, Chicago, Chicago University Press.

Sombart, Werner (1913a), *Krieg und Kapitalismus*, Munich & Leipzig, Duncker & Humblot.

Sombart, Werner (1913b), *Luxus und Kapitalismus*, Munich & Leipzig, Duncker & Humblot.

Sombart, Werner (1928), *Der moderne Kapitalismus,* Munich & Leipzig, Duncker & Humblot. 6 volumes.

Steadman, Philip (2001), *Vermeer's Camera*, Oxford, Oxford University Press.

Steuart, James (1767), *An Inquiry into the Principles of Political Economy: being an Essay on the Science of Domestic Policy in Free Nations. In which are Particularly Considered Population, Agriculture, Trade, Industry, Money, Coin, Interest, Circulation, Banks, Exchange, Public Credit, and Taxes,* London, A. Millar & T.Cadell. 2 volumes.

Stolleis, Michael ed. (1995), *Staatsdenker in der Frühen Neuzeit,* Munich, Beck.

Uztáriz, Gerónimo de (1751), *The Theory and Practice of Commerce and Maritime Affairs,* London, Rivington & Croft.

Van der Wee, Herman, editor (1988), *The Rise and Decline of Urban Industries in Italy and in the Low Countries,* Leuven, Leuven University Press.

Vries, Jan de and Ad van der Woude (1997). *The First Modern Economy. Success, failure and perseverance of the Dutch economy, 1500–1815,* Cambridge, Cambridge University Press.

Wallerstein, Immanuel (1978), *Det Moderne Verdenssystem*, 2 volumes, Oslo, Gyldendal.

Westbeck, Gustaf (1747), *Tankeförsök om Särskilda Näringars Särskilda Idkande*, Uppsala.

Zincke, Georg Heinrich, editor (1746–1767), *Leipziger Sammlungen von Wirthschafftlichen Policey-, Cammer- und Finantz-Sachen*, Leipzig, Erster (bis) Sechzehender Band (und) General-Register, 192 numbers in 17 volumes.

Chapter 14

MERCANTILISM AND ECONOMIC DEVELOPMENT: SCHUMPETERIAN DYNAMICS, INSTITUTION BUILDING AND INTERNATIONAL BENCHMARKING

With Sophus A. Reinert

In most arts and sciences – from astronomy to zoology – the Renaissance represents a qualitative watershed in human history, and historians are generally united in considering it a period of unprecedented intellectual ferment. Echoes of da Vinci, Galileo and Machiavelli still resound in the way we approach art, science and human coexistence, and it is noticeable how these developments came 'out of Italy' (Braudel 1991). As a precondition for this, the Renaissance was also a period when the productive powers of small European city states allowed a large part of the population to live free from poverty. Where feudalism had provided wealth for the very few and misery for most, the city states of the Renaissance for the first time witnessed a situation where artisans, merchants and public employees filled the ranks of a new middle class.

The Debate on Mercantilism: A Brief Overview

In this picture, the economics profession stands out with a completely different view of the period. The fact that 300 years of economic theory and practice tend to be lumped together under the label of 'mercantilism', as if it were a homogeneous mass, alone points to a rather superficial treatment of a long period with much variety. The common view today is that mercantilism was 'an irrational social order' (Ekelund & Tollison 1981: 6), the basic feature of which was that economists collectively made the serious mistake of confusing gold with wealth. This practice is referred to as the 'Midas Fallacy' (*chrysohedonism*), after the mythological king whose touch converted everything to gold. Starting with Adam Smith, this Midas Fallacy has been the common interpretation of mercantilism, the one also found in today's histories of economic thought. The Midas Legend had, however, been known as a warning since Roman times, and the mercantilists themselves used it to explicitly refute this view of wealth (Barbon 1696). Two American authors have offered what appears to be an alternative interpretation of mercantilism, that of a society seeking rents, presumed to be non-productive (Ekelund & Tollison 1981).

Both these standard interpretations, of mercantilism, and of pre-Smithian economics in general, present us with serious problems. How is it possible that human civilization as we know it, from the birth of modern cities to the Industrial Revolution, is recognized as the product of genius in all human endeavours but economics? A field whose practitioners supposedly 'did not rely on any "true" empirical knowledge of economic reality whatsoever' (Magnusson on Heckscher, in Magnusson 1993: 15), but were committed to hideous methodological errors, wrong economic policies and false goals? Mercantilism has, in a sense, been set up like an irrational 'hell', a strawman against which classical and neo-classical economic rationality increases its splendour. But, is it possible that the Industrial Revolution, which Adam Smith lived through without even noticing, came into being *in spite of* the stupid and irrational economic policies of the preceding period? Only in the bigoted historiographical tradition of 'manifest destiny', that the greatness of the United States is God-given regardless of policy, is it possible to ignore the fact that the US economy was built on key principles of mercantilism for well over 100 years, starting with Alexander Hamilton in 1791.[1] The titles of the most influential US economics books at the time testify to their mercantilist origins (Carey 1822).

Or, do we dare think that the mercantilist policies actually carried out, to a large extent, were in fact wise policies, given the circumstances? In this chapter, we shall claim the latter is the case; indeed, we argue that the production-focused mercantilist policies have been a mandatory passage point for nations that have taken the step from poor to wealthy, from England starting in 1485 to South Korea in the 1980s. This 'mercantilist' toolbox of the generic developmental state, the basic principles of which, we claim, have changed very little over the years – gaining somewhat in sophistication over time, but keeping to the same basic doctrines – is reproduced in Appendix 1. We argue that this represents a collection of economic principles and policy tools typical of mercantilism across Europe, including its local variants – Cameralism in Germany and Colbertism in France.

One fundamental problem of interpreting mercantilism is that few historians of economic thought actually read the original texts. Magnusson (1993: 50), discussing the previously mentioned work of Ekelund and Tollison, argues, 'They also seem totally uninterested in what the mercantilist writers actually wrote', a criticism that may be extended to many histories of economic thought. Furthermore, the analysis of mercantilism frequently suffers from what Perrotta (1993: 21) calls 'percursorism', that any idea – instead of being judged by its relevance in a given context – is either hailed as a surprising early anticipation of a healthy neo-classical economic principle, or as an example of hopelessly ill-conceived theories (Ashley 1920: II, 381).

Additionally, few studies of mercantilism cover more than one or two language areas. The truly pan-European distribution of common principles and policies, particularly in the period from 1650 to 1770, is therefore seldom noticed. The matter is further complicated by the fact that the long-recognized authority on the mercantilist system,

1. Even the chapter on this issue in the *Cambridge Economic History of the United States* must be considered as belonging to the 'manifest destiny' tradition (Engerman & Sokoloff 2000).

the Swede, Eli Heckscher (1931),[2] made a rather static analysis of a tradition, for which he had little sympathy, and therefore depicted as primitive and pre-analytical. Likewise, the first compiler of Spanish mercantilist literature, Manuel Colmeiro, was a recent convert to economic liberalism, and was therefore also fundamentally opposed to the system he was attempting to describe. All in all, the modern history of Mercantilism has largely been written as if Attila and his Huns had been put in charge of writing the history of the Roman Empire.

Our interpretation of Mercantilism relies on the insights provided when the mercantilist texts themselves are studied in the historical context in which they were written. This interpretation coincides with views from the European periphery, by Cosimo Perrotta (1988, 1991, 1993) in Italy, Ernest Lluch (1973, 1997, 2000) and others in Spain, and Lars Magnusson (1991, 1993) in Sweden. This 'new' and context-specific interpretation largely corresponds to the view of mercantilism held by the German Historical School, in that most of them acknowledge the interdependency of Mercantilism and state-building.[3]

We shall, however, grant some validity to the two other theories of Mercantilism because – although both arrive at conclusions that, in our view, are fundamentally incorrect – they grab different tails of the problems that mercantilists attempted to address. This applies both to Smith's Midas Fallacy approach and to the Ekelund & Tollison rent-seeking approach. Indeed, the outflow of bullion in the form of gold and silver was an acute *symptom* of a set of economic problems that affected most nations, and therefore, a matter contemporary writers had to attend to.[4] Early mercantilist policy advice falls into two broad categories – the simplistic and populist ones that attempted to cure the symptoms evident in the financial sphere, simply by manipulating financial variables, and what we have called the 'mercantilists of the real economy' (*realökonomische Merkantilisten*) who sought the underlying causes of the problems in the sphere of production.[5] The most heated of all mercantilist debates were between these two types of theorists – 'monetarists' and 'productionists' – between de Santis and Serra in Naples (1610–13) and between Misselden and Malynes in England (1622–23). By the late 1600s, however, the emphasis was clearly more on the 'real economy'. John Locke (1691/1696) was one of the latest pure monetarists. Recurrent financial bubbles nevertheless recreated relatively short-lived floods of books on speculation, as was the case in the 1720s.

In this chapter, we focus on the 'productionists' who were everywhere the great majority; in fact, most mercantilists are extremely clear in their analysis that the key to

2. Also the father of the Heckscher-Ohlin trade theory.
3. Brentano (1827–1829), Eisenhart (1881), Laspeyres (1863/1961), Schmoller (1897/1967), (Sombart 1902/1928, 1913a, 1913b).
4. This would be similar to a balance-of-payment problem in Third World countries today, of what Celso Furtado once called 'the break-down of the capacity to import'.
5. Schumpeter's recognition of Antonio Serra's 1613 treatise is particularly clarifying on this point: 'the implication being that if the economic process as a whole functions properly, the monetary element will take care of itself and not require any specific therapy' (Schumpeter 1954:195).

wealth lies in the sphere of production, rather than finance.[6] In this sense, present-day economics suits the standard accusation made against Mercantilism, due to its predominant focus on financial and monetary values, much better than does Mercantilism itself. The handling of the economic crisis in Argentina in the 1990s, de-industrializing the nation and halving its wage bill in order to pursue an arbitrarily chosen monetary goal, is the kind of policy against which the majority of mercantilists would have protested vehemently.

One of the more curious aspects of capitalist economic theory is that it does not allow for other than a 'normal' profit, identifying 'perfect competition' or 'commodity competition' as both the normal state of affairs and the goal of the system. The 'normal' participant in the economy is the farmer who has no influence over price, and the success stories of history, from the steel magnates to Henry Ford and Bill Gates, are in this view abhorred as 'rent seekers', by definition, a negative concept. The Ekelund & Tollison view of Mercantilism can only be understood from this neo-classical/neo-Austrian point of view, and in a sense, they do identify an important aspect of Mercantilism: the 'perfect competition' of the farmers did not and still does not produce significant wealth. Even the most efficient farmers in the world today, those in the United States and in the European Community, need heavy subsidies in order to achieve a decent income. Pre-Smithian economics can only be understood as system-building, 'Schumpeterian', dynamic imperfect competition. Two of its most successful economic institutions, *patents* and *protection* (for industrialization, rather than for revenue), were both created during the late 1400s in order to achieve this dynamic imperfect competition through artificially creating time-limited market power. As any businessman today, the mercantilists understood that 'perfect competition' is a situation where serious wealth cannot be accumulated, and economic development cannot take place.

It is argued in chapter 12 that dynamic rents spread in the economy at three levels:

1) to the entrepreneur in the form of profit, 2) to the employee in terms of employment and 3) through the government in terms of increased taxes. Under conditions of rapid technological change – as with the 'productivity explosions' of new technologies (Perez 2004) – this 'triple level rent-seeking' represents a hugely positive-sum game in the producing country. We argue that a core objective of Mercantilism was achieving this 'triple-level rent-seeking'. Institutions like patents, protection and apprenticeship, created 300 years before Adam Smith, and scientific academies, created almost a century before his writings, would help increase the size of the economic pie, increasing profits, the wage bill and the governments' ability to tax.

Changing Mentality and the Origins of Renaissance Wealth Creation

The very idea of economic development, however, was an early mercantilist innovation. When George Soros recently claimed that 'globalization is not a zero sum game' (Soros

6. See Seligman (1920) and Reinert & Reinert (chapter 10 in this volume) for a discussion of these debates between the monetarists and 'the mercantilists of the real economy'

2002), he unwittingly touched upon the very problem that faced economic thinkers as the idea of development emerged at the end of the Renaissance. For the longest time, the world was considered a finite place, locked in a cyclical system of cosmic equilibrium. This traditional zero-sum model of the universe was codified by Aristotle (politics 1328b, vii, ix, 3) and, channelled by the scholastics, came to dominate the European cosmology into the early modern period.[7] Sir Thomas Browne [1605–1682] encapsulated this view when he argued that 'all cannot be happy at once for, because the glory of one state depends upon the ruins of another, there is a revolution and vicissitude of their greatness' (Browne 1643: xvii), and the early 'balance-of-trade' argument was strongly related to this theory that 'one man's gain must be another man's loss' (St. Jerome in Finkelstein 2000: 89). Economic thought and, in many ways, economic development were thus shackled by fear of social instability. This, however, slowly eroded in the late Renaissance.

Several factors combined to unlock this zero-sum worldview.[8] Many of the necessary elements can be traced far back in time, but only during the Renaissance, did they achieve a critical mass sufficient to profoundly change society in the whole Italian peninsula, and later, the rest of Europe. First of all, the undeniable urban bias of wealth creation was, at the time, identified as the result of *synergic effects*, what Florentine chancellor Brunetto Latini (ca. 1210–1294) had called the 'common good'. This *ben comune* that made some cities so wealthy (Machiavelli in Reinert & Daastøl 1997) sprang from an organic social harmony – seeing the body as the metaphor for society – which was also an inheritance from the scholastics.[9] This idea of a synergic *common good* forms the axis around which many mercantilists wrote. It must be emphasized that the important discovery of the role of the individual during the Renaissance was superimposed upon the idea of a synergic common weal of society. Mercantilism, as later German economics, had a dual vision where the interests both of society and of the individual had to be considered, and at times had to be traded off against one another.

Secondly, the Aristotelian view of society as a zero-sum game slowly gave way to an understanding that new wealth could be *created* through innovations. Indeed, the very meaning of the word *innovations* changed, from being a potentially heretical activity – as when Roger Bacon was arrested for 'suspicious innovations' in 1277 in Oxford – to being the new carrier of human welfare and happiness when Francis Bacon wrote *An Essay on Innovations* a little more than 300 years later (Reinert & Daastøl 1997). New scientific breakthroughs and geographical and scientific explorations slowly changed the static medieval worldview. This growing understanding of an infinite and expanding cosmos was the precondition for the mercantilist reinterpretation of the economic sphere: as cosmos expanded unendingly, so could the economy. There was a remarkable

7. See, for example, the important and influential works of Paracelsus (1951: 38–44) and Michel de Montaigne (1580/1958: 48).
8. We discuss the factors in more detail in chapter 10.
9. Schumpeter (1954:177) refers to 'the old scholastic Public Good'. See also Sophus Reinert (2003).

synergy observable between *innovation* and *exploration*, between theory and practice, in weaving the new European cosmology.

Thirdly, religion loosened its grip on society and opened up to innovations. With the fall of Constantinople to the Turks, Byzantine philosophers moved to Italy and brought with them religious views that were more open to Man's role as a co-creator, rather than merely a caretaker, in God's plan. Man's creation in the image of God indeed made a life of invention and innovation *a pleasurable duty* (Reinert & Daastøl 1997). Thus, around 1600, as in Francis Bacon's *New Atlantis*, a never-ending frontier of new knowledge was drawn up for Mankind, that had been transformed 'from a spectator into an owner and master of nature' (Koyré 1957: vii).

The Italian economic historian – and, many times, prime minister – Amintore Fanfani, encapsulated the shift from scholasticism to mercantilism: 'while scholasticism thinks of an order in equilibrium, mercantilism thinks of an order in growth' (Fanfani 1955: 149). We would argue that neo-classical economics, with its focus on the allocation of scarce resources and equilibrium, in many ways, represents a return to scholasticism (Reinert 2000a).

Observing Spain and the Dutch Republic: Mercantilism as National Benchmarking

'Mercantilism was born in response to the failure of Spain', says Perrotta (1993:19), referring to the 1500s. We could add that Mercantilism further developed – during the 1600s and 1700s – in reaction to the successes of the Dutch Republic and Colbert's France. The best mercantilist writers were practical men, not people dedicated to what used to be called 'metaphysical speculations'. One logical approach to establishing a national economic policy was to look for what had worked, and not worked, in other nations. The European scene provided examples of both poor and rich areas, and the observations of these successful and unsuccessful economies became a major source of inspiration for the economic theory and policy of laggard nations. Economics as a science was therefore not born in wealthy and successful areas – in Venice or in the Dutch Republic, where wealth only seemed 'natural' – but in the poorer cities and nation-states (Laspeyres 1863/1961) that were trying to understand what factors had created the few 'islands' of wealth in an otherwise poor Europe (some were islands in more than one sense, which is part of the clue).

We argue, then, that one of the key tools of Mercantilism, as well as its inspiration, was benchmarking successful and less successful nations, a practice already existent during the late 1400s (Defoe 1728). Starting from around 1550, Europe provided one outstanding experience of national economic failure, Spain, and two examples of unquestionable economic success, Venice and the Dutch Republic. The basic question was a relatively simple one. Everyone knew that huge amounts of gold and silver flowed into Spain from the Americas. Starting around 1550, however, it became increasingly clear that this flow of bullion did not cause generalized wealth in Spain. The gold and silver ended up elsewhere, in nations that generally had no mines. Wealth left the nations producing raw materials – even if the raw materials were gold and silver – and accumulated in the nations housing a diversified manufacturing sector.

Spain became increasingly indebted to foreign bankers after about 1550, and gradually lost its financial independence. The monopolies of Spanish agricultural supplies, like wine and olive oil for the American colonies, caused very high food prices in the peninsula and, with the inflow of species, contributed to rampant inflation. Spanish industries, which had previously been competitive in European markets, like silk, iron and steel, died out. The country was de-industrialized and flooded with imports, which caused the species that flowed in from the American colonies to leave the country at the same speed, or even faster. Wealthy farmers, protected by a monopoly and a very inelastic supply of wine and oil, could purchase noble titles that exempted them from paying taxes. Church property and organizations were also exempt from taxes, leaving the tax burden on the few artisans and industrialists who survived the flood of imports. The powerful *Mesta*, the organization of sheep farmers, fortified its power with loans to the Crown, and worked like a state within the state. Large tracts of mortmain[10] land belonging to the church remained uncultivated. A huge clerical class added to a general contempt for manual work; huge unemployment, underemployment and large numbers of beggars complete this brief picture of Spain in rapid decay. Money was made in Spain from financial transactions that did not promote the productive system, from *censos,* i.e. financial loans and mortgages, and from *juros,* i.e. privileges, titles and rights granted by the king in exchange for loans. A very interesting aspect here is the extent to which Spanish economists at the time clearly saw the forces behind the economic ills of the country and provided theoretical and practical remedies. 'History records few instances of either such able diagnosis of fatal social ills by any group of moral philosophers or of any such utter disregard by statesmen of sound advice', said American historian Earl Hamilton (Hamilton 1932:237).

On the other side of the European economic spectrum, we find the united Dutch provinces. Many mercantilist tracts, starting with Giovanni Botero (1590, 1622), contain descriptions of their wealth, and, after the death of 'the Great Colbert' in 1683, similarly, of the success of French policies. In various forms, the statement that manufactures were the real gold mines, much more valuable than the actual gold mines themselves, is found all over Europe during the 1600s and 1700s, from Giovanni Botero (1590), Tommaso Campanella (1602) and Antonio Genovesi (1770s) in Italy, to Anders Berch, the first economics professor outside Germany, in Sweden (Berch 1747). The Spanish mercantilist Gerónimo de Uztariz (1724/1752, and foreword to Goyeneche 1717), whose main work was translated into both French and English, commented from a particularly good vantage point, being a Spaniard and having lived in Holland and Italy for 23 years. Uztariz's conclusion is in line with the contemporary mainstream: '[Manufactures] is a mine more fruitful of gain, riches, and plenty, than those of Potosí.'[11]

Josiah Child, a governor of the British East India Company and one of the more famous mercantilists, encapsulates this benchmarking attitude to economic policy by

10. Mortmain is land that cannot be sold.
11. Potosí, at about 4.000 metres above sea-level in present-day Bolivia, was the richest of all mines in the world. At the time, it was the second-largest city in the world after London.

arguing, 'If we intend to have the Trade of the World, we must imitate the Dutch, who make the worst as well as the best of all manufactures, that we may be in a capacity of serving all Markets, and all Humors' (Child 1693: 90). Similarly, Child opens his 1668 book with a comment on 'the prodigious increase of the Netherlanders' which is 'the envy of the present and may be the wonder of all future generations'. 'And yet', he adds, 'the means whereby they have thus advanced themselves, are sufficiently obvious, and in a great measure imitable by most other nations ..., which I shall endeavour to demonstrate in the following discourse' (Child 1668). The French observers of the period, Huet (1712/1722) perhaps being the most detailed, found not only a country specialized in manufacturing – where close to 30 per cent of the labour force was already engaged in manufacturing in the early 1500s – but also a system of synergies which brings to mind the old Italian idea of a *ben comune*. It was clear to most astute observers that the wealth of Holland rested on the synergic interdependence of manufacturing, long-distance trade and fisheries, where 'one factor gave strength to the other and vice versa', as Antonio Serra explained the Venetian system.

A brief case study of the Dutch city of Delft in the seventeenth century shows how synergies created by a diversified base of activities created knowledge and spillovers between seemingly unrelated activities. In Delft, it is indeed possible to identify a closely-knit maritime-scientific-artistic cluster, where innovations leapt to and from very different sectors of the economy. The case of Delft brings together, in the very same productive-scientific cluster, the sectors and elements that, in the German tradition, are seen as being the important driving forces of capitalism, all in an interwoven whole:

- The quest for military power, in this case through the navy, as in Werner Sombart's 'War and Capitalism' (Sombart 1913a).
- The quest for luxury, in this case art, as in Sombart's 'Luxury and Capitalism' (Sombart 1913b).
- The quest for scientific knowledge, as in Sombart's work on capitalism (Sombart 1902/1928) and Thorstein Veblen's 'idle curiosity'.

These three forces interact in creating serendipitous economic development in Delft, and a profession curiously uniting the three seemingly unrelated fields – maritime warfare, art and scientific development – is that of the producer of glass lenses, *the lens grinder*.

Dutch artists invented oil painting and painting on canvases. The raw materials for these inventions – linseed oil, linen and hemp fibre – were widely used in Dutch shipbuilding and readily available, but would not be as readily available to the artists of other schools. Taking over the leadership from Florence, in the seventeenth century, Delft emerged as a centre for the scientific glass production of lenses. Important improvements to the microscope were also made there (Ruestow 1996). Delft natural scientist and microscope maker, Antoni van Leeuwenhoek (1632–1723), found a synergy between the production of woollen cloth, the main industry of the day and his scientific work, because the hand lenses he developed were used extensively to inspect cloth (Huerta 2003:33). Similarly, lens-making was integrated with the development of Flemish art – bringing together the history of art and the history of science – through the work of the Delft painter Johannes Vermeer (1632–1675), whose painting techniques included seeing his motifs through lenses and a *camera obscura*, an apparatus similar to a primitive camera (Steadman 2001). Vermeer also keenly participated in aspects of the discoveries surrounding him in Delft: the geographical discoveries of the Dutch navy and discoveries in the natural sciences made possible by improvements of the microscope by Leeuwenhoek and his colleagues.[12] The navy and the merchant marine constituted, however, the largest demand for lenses for binoculars, but as mentioned, lenses were also in demand among natural scientists and producers of early microscopes. The Delft lens grinders thus formed the core of an extremely dynamic and path-breaking cluster, including such diverse actors as the navy, the woollen industry, painters like Vermeer, natural scientists and microscope builders.

Another product linking the three clusters – war (navy), luxury (art) and 'idle curiosity' (science) – in Holland at the time was mapmaking. Holland's position as a seafaring power demanded not only binoculars and naval instruments but also up-to-date maps.[13] Vermeer's fascination with maps and explorations is clear in many of his paintings, with one author commenting on his 'mania for maps'. Such synergic cumulative causations, and the path dependency they created, were no doubt at the core of knowledge creation and the process of economic growth (Arthur 1989). They were, however, neither possible to reproduce in any meaningful way by quantitative methods only, nor apparent through the lenses of methodological individualism.

The enormous diversity of economic activities was observed and commented on by all contemporary economists who wrote about the Dutch Republic. This is also apparent in the early economic journals (Zincke 1746–67). The role of diversity and the resulting creative serendipity bring back the issue of 'monoculture' in traditional development economics and in agricultural societies, where such creative linkages do not appear among professions that trade with each other. A community of milk producers and a nation of banana producers have very little to sell to each other. By emulating Dutch economic structure, rather than Dutch economic policies necessarily, and by avoiding the pitfalls of Spain, the mercantilists revealed their conviction in common economic principles:

- Economic development is *activity-specific*, created by some economic activities (manufacturing), rather than others. (Due to stagnant productivity, diminishing returns and monoculture, without synergies in agriculture.)[14]

12. Leeuwenhoek was to be the executor of his neighbour Vermeer's estate.
13. With the technology of mapmaking changing from woodcuts to copper plates, the same copper used by instrument makers, the Dutch took over its production from the Italians.
14. The wisdom of taxing diminishing returns activities and paying bounties to increasing returns activities was also recognized by Alfred Marshall, the founder of neo-classical economics (Marshall 1890: 452). Similarly, the different effects of technological change in agriculture (lower prices) and industry (higher wages) in Hans Singer (1950/1964) supported arguments for the key role of manufacturing industry in development. See also Reinert (1980, and chapter 5 in this volume).

- Economic development is a *synergic* process: the greater the division of labour and the number of professions, the greater the wealth (already very clear in Serra 1613).
- The targeting, support and protection of *manufacturing* were argued in terms of
  a. its ability to create wealth
  b. its ability to create employment
  c. its ability to solve balance-of-payment problems
  d. its ability to increase the velocity of circulation of money
- Starting in the 1700s, great emphasis was put on the beneficial synergies between manufacturing and agriculture: only where there was manufacturing, was there successful agriculture (Justi in Germany, Galiani in Italy, Hume in England)[15]

The mercantilists are generally accused of not having a 'model' for development. In our view, the model comes out clearly and consistently both across time – from the first Spanish and Italian writers in the 1500s to Friedrich List in the 1840s – and across the European continent. The economic essence of Mercantilism was to line up private and public vested interests by getting nations into increasing returns industries that create virtuous circles of development.

We would argue that adherence to the above principles has been a *mandatory passage point* for all nations progressing from poor to rich, including Korea in the 1960s and 1970s. When classical and neo-classical economics disallowed their *de jure* or *de facto* colonies from following these principles, they were – as Friedrich List put it – in reality, 'kicking away the ladder', which they themselves had used to climb to wealth.

The most fundamental difference between mercantilist economics and neo-classical economics is that the mercantilist policy recommendations were highly context-dependent – protecting manufacturing industry could be the right thing to do in one context, while promoting free trade could be right in another – whereas the policy recommendations of neo-classical economics are independent of context.

Mercantilist Dynamics and Institutions: Activity-Specific Growth and Context-Specific Policy

Economic institutions have been brought to the forefront of the development debate during the recent decades. It is generally agreed that economic activities and their institutions co-evolve, and attempts at establishing causality – to what extent institutions are created through *demand-pull* or *supply-push* – can therefore easily run into a chicken-and-egg type of problem. The mercantilist view of institutions was, from very early on, that institution-building was fundamentally a *demand-pull* phenomenon, that *the mode of production of a society* would determine its institutions. In 1620, Francis Bacon formulated a view that was to dominate in the social sciences for almost the next two centuries:

15. Modern economic historians agree with the mercantilist explanation of causality here: 'The bulk of the evidence points to urbanization being the cause of agricultural productivity gain, not a result.' Philip Hoffman quoted in Prak (2001).

'There is a startling difference between the life of men in the most civilised province of Europe, and in the wildest and most barbarous districts of New India. This difference comes not from the soil, not from climate, not from race, but from *the arts*.' Francis Bacon is crystal clear on the causality in question: Man's activities – his mode of production – determine his institutions. In a similar vein, Carlota Perez (2004) has argued the relationship between technological change and human institutions.

When Johann Jacob Meyen, a German scientist, stated in 1769 'It is known that a primitive people does not improve its customs and institutions, later to find useful industries, but the other way around' (Reinert 2000a), he expressed an understanding of causality considered common sense at the time. This view would appear to run counter to the standard World Bank view that the lack of institutions *per se* can be blamed for the poor performance of so many Third World countries. To the mercantilists, it would not be meaningful to attempt to understand the institutional development of Europe independently of the underlying strategy of industrialization that prompted the establishment of so many key institutions. The patent system was invented in Venice in the late 1400s for this purpose, and the establishment of an apprentice system in England under Elizabeth cannot be understood outside the context of a highly successful Tudor strategy of building English woollen manufactures during the 1500s. The establishment of scientific academies in the 1700s, promoted particularly by Gottfried Wilhelm von Leibniz and Christian Wolff, cannot be understood independently of their strategy of building German economic activities outside agriculture. The success of these diversification strategies, in turn, created new institutional arrangements.

These mercantilist institutions cannot be understood outside a context of nations seeking to escape a comparative advantage in producing raw materials, a strategy which cannot be understood in the neo-classical framework of the Washington Consensus. We would argue that the present focus on institutions views institutions as outside the context of what they were created to accomplish. In reality, a large number of these institutions are part of a much broader process of economic development that is incompatible with the internal logic of current mainstream economics. Seeing institutions independently of the productive system they support and sustain is not meaningful, and attempting to establish scientific academies in hunting and gathering tribes is therefore attacking the problem from the wrong end. History shows that only societies that have achieved a certain level of manufacturing and/or other increasing return activities have ever achieved the 'right' institutions or any degree of 'competitiveness'. Hundreds of years of accumulated experience show that today's maxim of 'getting institutions right' cannot be solved independently of 'getting into the right kinds of economic activities'.

Perhaps, the most fundamental methodological difference between Mercantilism and neo-classical economics is that the mercantilists, in the same way as any successful businessman today, see economic activities as being qualitatively different. The whole colonial system was based on this crucial insight. 'Linen industry is proper only for countries where they can have flax and hemp cheap, and where the common people work at very easy rates', wrote the English mercantilist Charles Davenant (1696). The woollen industry, on the other hand, was able to maintain much higher wages. When the English king prohibited the Irish from exporting woollen manufactures in 1699, he therefore knew that England was 'underdeveloping' its Irish colony. As Davenant (1699: 275) said, 'No Wise State, if it has the Means of preventing the Mischief, will leave its Ruin in the Power of another Country'.

The mercantilists were clearly aware that they were keeping the colonies poor. Most saw this as a natural part of the world power game, while a few defended the practice by saying that since everyone else did so, England had to follow the same policy. Some, like Justi in Germany in the 1750s, thought colonialism would soon end because the people in the colonies knew they were being fooled. This was, of course, what happened in the United States, who suffered from not being allowed to establish manufacturing industries.

By establishing themselves as the workshop of the world, importing raw materials and exporting manufactured goods, England experienced the most dramatic increase in wealth the world had yet seen. It was therefore of vital importance to keep things that way:

> That all Negroes shall be prohibited from weaving either Linnen or Woollen, or spinning or combing of Wooll, or working at any Manufacture of Iron, further than making it into Pig or Bar iron: That they be also prohibited from manufacturing of Hats, Stockings, or Leather of any Kind. ... Indeed, if they set up Manufactures, and the Government afterwards shall be under a Necessity of stopping their Progress, we must not expect that it will be done with the same Ease that now it may. (Gee 1729: 81)

When the colonies demanded to establish their own manufactures, their attention could be diverted by allowing them to export their raw materials to other European countries:

> Because People in the Plantations, being tempted with a free Market for their Growths all over *Europe*, will all betake themselves to raise them, to answer the prodigious Demand of that extensive Free Trade, and their Heads be quite taken off from Manufactures, the only thing which our Interest can clash with theirs... (Decker 1744/1751)

In our view, the parallel to today's situation is clear. A large number of Third World countries have been de-industrialized during the last decades (chapters 8 and 9), but they are kept politically at bay with promises of being able to export their agricultural products to Europe and the United States.

As already mentioned, two important mercantilist institutions – both invented in the late 1400s – have been *patents* (in order to protect new knowledge) and *protection* (for industry-building, rather than for revenue purposes). Both institutions, of course, go against the basic tenets of neo-classical economics. It is curious how the twin institutions, *patents* and *protection* – children of the same basic understanding of the dynamics of a knowledge-based economy – are today considered to be heroes and villains, respectively. Patents and their rights, creating artificial rents in order to promote new knowledge, are heralded as an indispensable ingredient of world growth, while protection, creating manufacturing rents in order to spread this production into new geographical areas, is considered the greatest of all evils. This is particularly problematic since all historically successful catching-up strategies – starting with England's in 1485 and lasting there for more than 300 years – have depended on the nourishing, promotion and protection of economic activities subject to increasing returns. The Washington Institutions now defend the mercantilist institution that helps rich countries (i.e. patents), but seek to eliminate its twin institution that could help the poor (i.e. protection).

The main institution that the mercantilists built was, of course, the state (Reinert 1999). Cosimo Perrotta saw Mercantilism as an import substitution strategy, while Gustav Schmoller saw Mercantilism as an exercise in state-building and nation-building. These are complementary, rather than contradictory views of Mercantilism. As Schmoller describes mercantilism: 'The essence of the system lies not in some doctrine of money, or of the balance of trade; not in tariff barriers, protective duties, or navigation laws; but in something far greater: – namely in the total transformation of society and its organizations, as well as of the state and its institutions, in the replacing of a local and territorial economy by that of the national state' (Schmoller 1897: 51).

Mercantilist economic policy therefore became highly context-specific, whereas from a mercantilist standpoint, neo-classical economic policy suffers from the same weakness as cure-all medicines in the old US West; they come across as what used to be referred to as 'snake oil'.

Why Successful Mercantilism Carries the Seeds of Its Own Destruction, or Adam Smith, the Misunderstood Mercantilist

We agree with Cosimo Perrotta that Mercantilism, at its core, is an import substitution policy (Perrotta 1988, 1993), a policy aimed at establishing national comparative advantage in increasing returns areas.[16] In the language of Thomas Mun (1664), the transition is from 'natural activities' to 'artificial activities', or in the language of Michael Porter, from a 'natural comparative advantage' to a 'created comparative advantage'. Porter (1990) provides a stage theory of economic development that is perfectly compatible with mercantilism (Reinert 2000b).

If this was the strategy, we should expect mercantilists to stop arguing for protectionism once this goal of industrialization has been reached. And indeed, this is what we see. Most mercantilists, and all the most sophisticated ones from Jean-Baptiste Colbert (1619–1683) to Friedrich List (1789–1846) and the nineteenth-century American economists,[17] saw the end of industrial protection and, indeed, argued that international trade between nations specialized in manufactures was a positive-sum game. After the Tudor Plan in England, the first successful system – originating in the writings of Laffemas (1597) – was that of Colbert during the reign of Louis XIV. The many volumes of Colbert's collected papers (Clément, (ed.) 1861–1872) show the manager of

16. This is a fundamental *Leitmotif* in sixteenth, seventeenth and eighteenth economic thought, and formed the basis of successful industrialization policies across Europe. It appears in English mercantilist texts, e.g. Misselden (1623), Mun (1664), Child (1693: 3, 18, 100–01), Cary (1695: 1), Barbon (1696), Davenant (1696), abd King (1721)
17. See Hudson (2004) for a discussion of nineteenth-century US industrial strategy.

'France Inc.' building manufacturing and infrastructure, facilitating internal trade, and attempting to recreate, on a national level, the synergies which earlier observers (Botero 1590) had confined to city states (Cole 1931, 1937). Already, however, Colbert saw mercantilist policies as temporary, and 'spoke of protective duties as crutches by the help of which manufacturers might learn to walk and then throw them away' (Ingram 1888: 41). The contemporaries could observe that for long periods of time, the leading nation of the period, the Dutch Republic, had relatively low tariffs, raising their tariff barriers only when their decay was obvious and advanced in the 1720s.

The English mercantilists John Cary (1695), Theodore Janssen (1713) and Charles King (1721) spelled out a system of 'good' and 'bad' trade, which is completely in line with Paul Krugman's (1980) trade theory – later recanted[18] – based on increasing and diminishing returns (see also Graham 1923). Janssen and King's system was very influential throughout the eighteenth century. This was judged on a nation-by-nation basis. 'Good trade' is with nations from which you import raw materials and export manufactured goods, 'bad trade' is with nations from which you import manufactured goods and export raw materials. And finally, exchanging manufactured goods for other manufactured goods is 'good trade' for both nations involved. This is also Friedrich List's principle (List 1841), which explains why List is, at the same time, both an important mercantilist and the first supporter of a European Union with free trade between manufacturing nations (Reinert 1998). List too saw Mercantilism as a mandatory passage point on the road towards global free trade among equals. In other words, successful mercantilism carried with it the seeds of its own destruction: the type of protection that would initially help manufacturing, would later, by limiting production only to the national market, be an obstacle to manufacturing success. The assumption of increasing returns in manufacturing underlies most mercantilist writings, and is clearly spelled out by Antonio Serra (1613). It was James Steuart (1767), however, who produced the most mature mercantilist work in England, integrating important elements like technology, innovations and institutions in his analysis of economic development – elements that were later to be removed from economics by Adam Smith. Two immediate translations into German testify to Steuart's international popularity and influence at the time.

Throughout the early modern 'mercantilist' period, it was clear to all that universal free trade was only in the interest of the wealthiest nations, Venice and the Dutch Republic in the sixteenth and seventeenth centuries, England later. In the United States, the same type of economic analysis that recommended industrial protection in the 1820s (Raymond 1820; Carey 1822) recommended free trade for that country in the 1880s and 1890s. The new and changed message is already clear from the book title, 'The Destructive Influence of the Tariff upon Manufacture and Commerce' (Schoenhof 1885). Writing in the United States, Friedrich List already foresaw this development around 1830: some time in the future, when the United States had industrialized after a century of protection, when its population had reached 100 million, and its navy was the most powerful in the world, then, the period would come when the United States

18. Bhagwati (2002:31) confirms '(Krugman's) firm retreat back to free trade'.

would proclaim free trade to the world (Reinert 1998). It is impossible to understand Friedrich List's work without seeing that his 'Mercantilism' was only a mandatory passage point towards free trade, which would be desirable when a symmetrical situation had been created in which all nations have a comparative advantage in dynamic, increasing returns activities.

Normally, one would see Friedrich List and Adam Smith as opposite poles when it comes to economic policy, one the archetypical protectionist, and the other the archetypical free trader. However, Adam Smith can be read in a variety of ways, and he is an author who is more quoted than read. Not only are there important differences between Adam Smith's views before and after his meetings with the French physiocrats, the *Wealth of Nations* also contains passages that are more or less 'mercantilist'. The inconsistencies between the early and later Smith have, since the mid-nineteenth century, led to a debate under the German heading, *Das Adam Smith Problem*. The variation within *the Wealth of Nations* opened the way for selective translations, as in the case of Sweden, where the most mercantilist Smith was translated first. As a result, there is at least one Adam Smith interpretation for every European nation.

In his early work, *The Theory of Moral Sentiments* (Smith 1759/1812), Adam Smith argued passionately for 'the great system of government' which is helped by adding new manufactures. Interestingly, Smith argued that new manufactures are to be promoted, neither to help suppliers nor to help consumers, but in order to improve 'the great system of government' (Smith 1759/1812, vol. 1: 320)

In fact, it is possible to argue that Adam Smith was also a 'misunderstood mercantilist', someone who firmly supported the mercantilist policies of the past, but then argued that they were no longer necessary for England. In other words, Adam Smith played the same role later played by Schoenhof (see above) in the United States. Policies, like patents and protection, that had once been established in order to further innovation, were in the 1770s partly used to hinder innovations and sold to finance the Crown. Adam Smith praised the Navigation Acts protecting English manufacturing against Holland, arguing 'they are as wise ... as if they had all been dictated by the most deliberate wisdom' and holding them to be 'perhaps, the wisest of all the commercial regulations of England' (Smith 1776/1976: I, 486–87). All in all, Smith described a development that had become successfully self-sustained, a kind of snowballing effect, originating in the wise protectionist measures of the past. Only once did Smith use the term 'invisible hand' in the *Wealth of Nations*: when it sustained the key import substitution goal of mercantilist policies, when the consumer preferred domestic industry to foreign industry (Smith 1776/1976: 477). This is when 'the market' had taken over the role previously played by protective measures, and national manufacturing no longer needed such protection. If one cared to look, Adam Smith also argued for mercantilist policies as a mandatory passage point, as did Charles King and Friedrich List.

But Adam Smith is contradictory, and it is possible to read British vested interests into his contradictions. Undoubtedly, Alexander Hamilton – the first US treasury secretary– who had read Smith – noticed that, at one point, Smith argued that it would be very foolish for the people of the United States, with whom England was at war when his book appeared, to attempt to establish manufactures. In a different part of the same book, Smith convincingly argued that only nations with manufacturing industries are able to win wars. English classical economists are first Englishmen and then economists, is the implication of a remarkable passage by Lord Lionel Robbins: '..we get our picture wrong if we suppose that the English Classical economists would have recommended, because it was good for the world at large, a measure which they thought would be harmful to their own community' (Robbins 1952: 10–11). It is not surprising then, that Alexander Hamilton (1791) let the English mercantilists (in particular, Malachy Postlethwayt), and not Adam Smith, be his inspiration for US industrial policy (Hamilton 1791). 'Don't do as the English tell you to do, do as the English do' became a maxim in the young United States. Today, a wise maxim for economic policy would similarly be 'Don't do as the Americans tell you to do, do as the Americans did'.

Conclusion: Mercantilism as a *Mandatory Passage Point* for Development

Most economists show clear mercantilist tendencies when they advise their own children. Even the most convinced neo-classical economist will not tell his or her children that it does not matter what profession they choose – picking tomatoes or becoming a lawyer – because factor-price equalization, when wages and interest rates will be equal across the planet, is around the corner. However, when pontificating on children in the Third World, the same economists recommend that nations specialize according to their comparative advantage, which will normally mean specializing in providing cheap labour to produce raw materials for simple assembly operations. If a job is available at all, that is.

When the future of their own children is at stake, economists understand that a career picking cucumbers and tomatoes will provide much less wealth than a skilled job in industry or services. Why, then, is the mercantilist argument so unheard that a nation where *everyone* specializes in picking cucumbers and tomatoes – growth industries in Mexico today – will be poorer than a manufacturing nation? We are tempted to refer to Thorstein Veblen, who claimed that education tends to contaminate and ruin many healthy human instincts. Of course, the enlightened economist today will add that Mexico should invest more in education. But Mexico's comparative advantage lies in economic activities that do not require much knowledge. Hence, its comparative advantage lies in providing cheap and uneducated labour. Investing in education therefore means training either for unemployment or for migration.

In this chapter, we have argued that the mercantilists who influenced economic policy were obsessed with strengthening domestic production. It must be kept in mind that the 1500s was a particularly cosmopolitan era, when the percentage of foreign students in European universities was much higher than today. As early as 1550, this cosmopolitan European theatre presented economic theorists and policy makers with two fascinating and revealing case studies of success and failure, respectively. 'A spectre haunted Europe in the mercantilist period', says Perrotta, 'the fear of ending up like Spain, rich in gold, poor in production, and with a frighteningly unfavourable balance of trade' (Perrotta 1993: 18). Fortunately, two other cases – Venice and the Dutch Republic – as successful as Spain's case was unsuccessful, were also at hand.

Daniel Defoe (1728) tells how the first and hugely successful import substitution strategy, the English Tudor Plan during 1485–1603, was based on King Henry VII benchmarking the poverty of England and the wealth of Burgundy, a wealth based exclusively on English raw material. The success of England's 'Tudor Plan' in building a woollen manufacturing sector showed the world that even if the success of Venice and the Dutch Republic, in a certain sense, were products of an invisible hand of Providence – a lack of raw materials had forced them into manufacturing – it was possible, through enlightened policy, to achieve the same results, even from a very different starting point.

Standard business strategy aims at maximizing market share without necessarily spelling out the theory of increasing returns and lowered unit costs, in everything from production to finance and advertising, that underlies this strategy. In the same way, the mercantilists did not necessarily explain the underlying mechanisms behind the success or failure they observed. The identification of cumulative and synergic elements behind wealth creation is what makes Antonio Serra's 1613 work so remarkable, and, we would argue, theoretically much superior to other theorists, like Myrdal, who worked on the same problems much later. In order to learn from the mercantilists, it is therefore necessary to spell out the mechanisms that they utilized, but often did not explain.

We argue that some basic economic mechanisms are as timeless as gravity. The effects of compound interest were the same in Babylonia in 2000 B.C. as with Third World debt today.[19] The conditions of a commercial enterprise with cash-flow problems would be fairly similar today as 500 years ago, and whether costs of production would increase (diminishing returns) or fall (increasing returns) as a nation specialized will have very similar results today as when Serra wrote in 1613.[20] In fact, we would argue that all the basic policy recommendations of *realökonomisch* Mercantilism – investment in manufacturing, an extensive division of labour, importing raw materials and exporting manufactured goods, increasing the population of the cities – all aim at creating dynamic synergies based on what Schumpeter called 'historical increasing returns'[21] in order to create sustainable wealth, employment and balance of payments.

Martin Wolf (2003: 49), associate editor and chief economic commentator for the *Financial Times*, recently wrote an article for *Foreign Policy* where he argued the 'gap' between rich and poor countries 'reflects the success of those countries that embraced capitalism and the failure of those that did not'. The fact that mercantilism lies at the

19. When asked what power could be stronger than the atomic bomb, Albert Einstein reputedly answered 'compound interest'. It can, in fact, be argued that the ancient Babylonians institutionalized a better solution to this problem than we have today. At varying and unforeseeable intervals, the king would cancel all non-commercial debt, thus creating a 'clean slate' for everyone. Remnants of this practice, the Jubilee Years, are found in the Old Testament, becoming the basis for the Jubilee 2000 movement to forgive Third World debt.
20. Reinert (1980) documents that developing countries tend to produce well into the area of diminishing returns, revealed when costs decrease as production is reduced. See also chapter 5.
21. With this term, Schumpeter refers to the combined effects of technological change and increasing returns, which are separable in theory, but often not in practice, because new technology is not available in the former scale

root of all successful capitalism is not considered. Harvard economist Robert J. Barro, writing for *Business Week*, has dismissed worries about unemployment resulting from China's growing textile exports by arguing, 'we should not be swayed by 17th century mercantilism, which viewed imports as bad and exports as good'. When taken together, these statements, appearing in two of the world's most influential publications on economic policy matters, frame real historical fallacies fuelling contemporary economic debates: liberalism is always 'right' and protectionism is always 'wrong'. Mercantilism, probably the most contested 'ism' in the historiography of economic analysis (Magnusson 1993), is mostly summoned as a straw man of irrational folly representing a system of destructive rent-seekers that supposedly made the fundamental mistake of confusing gold with wealth. The diffusion of this view reflects the extent to which the economics profession is virtually united in a common misconception of its own past, both as regards theory and policy.

We argue that the basic mercantilist insights – in the right contexts – have been proved right, again and again. These are: 1) national wealth cannot be created or based on raw material production in the absence of a manufacturing/increasing returns sector. 2) an inefficient manufacturing/increasing returns sector provides a much higher standard of living than no manufacturing sector. Large-scale deindustrialization is therefore a crime to posterity (chapters 8 and 9). Time after time, these principles have been resurrected in times of need: with increasing poverty in Spain after 1550, with the economic downturn of Italy in the following century, during the famines in Paris in the 1770s, with the misery in France following the Napoleonic Wars, as the basis for solving serious economic problems in the United States in the early 1820s, solving the 'social problem' in nineteenth-century Continental Europe, aiding Korea, poorer than Tanzania in 1950, in creating wealth, and after the devastation of the Morgenthau Plan in Germany after World War II. We argue that although increasing return activities partly may shift from manufacturing to services, the fundamental insights about the activity-specific and synergic nature of economic development remain valid. These are, however, blind spots in standard economics. The blind spots are products of David Ricardo's approach to economic theory – based on *a priori* assumptions rather than on factual observations as in the Baconian method – today fossilized into an ideology impervious to observations of economic reality. To those nations that have not yet been through a successful mercantilist phase, generally due to a colonial past, these blind spots of economic theory create untold human suffering on a daily basis.

Appendix 1. 'Mercantilist' Economic Policies of the Generic Developmental State: Continuity of Policy Measures and Tool Kit from England in 1485 (Henry VII) to Korea in the 1960s: A Mandatory Passage for Economic Development

... the fundamental things apply, as time goes by.

Sam, the pianist, in 'Casablanca'.

1. Observation of wealth synergies clustered around increasing returns activities and continuous mechanization in general. Recognition that 'We are in the wrong

business'. Conscious *targeting, support and protection* of these increasing returns activities.

2. Temporary monopolies/patents/protection given to targeted activities in a certain geographical area.
3. Recognizing development as a synergic phenomenon, and consequently, the need for a diversified manufacturing sector ('maximizing the division of labour' (Serra 1613) plus observations of the Dutch Republic and Venice).
4. Accumulated empirical evidence shows that the manufacturing sector solves three policy problems endemic to the Third World in one go: increasing national value added (GDP), increasing employment and solving balance-of-payments problems.
5. Attracting foreigners to work in targeted activities (historically, religious prosecutions have been important).
6. Relative suppression of landed nobility (from Henry VII to Korea). (Physiocracy as a landowners' rebellion against this policy).
7. Tax breaks for targeted activities.
8. Cheap credit for targeted activities.
9. Export bounties for targeted activities.
10. Strong support for the agricultural sector, in spite of this sector being clearly seen as incapable of independently bringing the nation out of poverty.
11. Emphasis on learning/education (UK apprentice system under Elizabeth I, Child (1693); Leibniz, Wolff and Justi in Germany).
12. Patent protection for valuable knowledge (Venice from 1490s).
13. Frequent export tax/export ban on raw materials in order to make raw materials more expensive to competing nations (starting with Henry VII in the late 1400s, whose policy was very efficient in severely damaging the woollen industry in Medici Florence).

Bibliography

Arthur, Brian (1989). 'Competing technologies, increasing returns and lock-in by historical events'. *Economic Journal* 99 (394): 116–31.

Ashley, William (1920). *An Introduction to English Economic History and Theory*. Putnam, New York.

Barbon, Nicholas (1696). A *Discourse Concerning Coining the New Money Lighter*. Richard Chiswell, London.

Berch, Anders (1747). *Inledning til Almänna Hushålningen, innefattande Grunden til Politie, Oeconomie och Cameralwetenskaperna*. Lars Salvius, Stockholm.

Bhagwati, Jagdish (2002). *Free Trade Today*. Princeton University Press, Princeton.

Botero, Giovanni (1590). *Della Ragione di Stato. Libri Dieci*, this work also contains *Delle Cause della Grandezza delle Città, libri tre*. Vicenzio Pellagalo, Rome.

Botero, Giovanni (1622). *Relazioni Universali*. Alessandro Vecchi, Venice.

Braudel, Fernand (1991). *Out of Italy, 1450-1650*. Flammarion, Paris.

Brentano, Lujo (1827-1829). *Eine Geschichte der wirtschaftlichen Entwicklung Englands*. 3 volumes, Gustav Fischer, Jena.

Browne, Thomas (1643). *Religio Medici*. Andrew Crooke, London.

Campanella, Tommaso (1653). *A Discourse Touching the Spanish Monarchy: Wherein We Have a Political Classe, Representing Each Particular Country, Province, Kingdome, and Empire of the World, with Wayes of Government by Which They May Be Kept in Obedience*, Printed for Philemon Stephens and are to be sold at his shop at the Gilded Lion in Paul's Church-Yard, London.

Carey, Mathew (1822). *Essays on Political Economy; or, the most certain means of promoting the wealth, power, resources and happiness of nations: applied particularly to the United States.* H.C. Carey & I. Lea, Philadelphia.

Cary, John (1695/1745). *A Discourse Concerning the East India Trade.* T. Osborne, London.

Child, Josiah (1668). *Brief Observations Concerning Trade and Interest of Money.* Elizabeth Calvert & Henry Mortlock, London.

Child, Josiah (1693). *A New Discourse on Trade.* John Furringham, London.

Clément, Pierre ed (1861-1872). *Lettres, Instructions et Mémoires de Colbert.* 7 Volumes in 10 + 1 Volume 'Errata Général et Table Analytique'. Imprimerie Impériale/Imprimerie Nationale, Paris.

Cole, Charles Woolsey (1931). *French Mercantilist Doctrines Before Colbert.* R.R. Smith, New York.

Cole, Charles Woolsey (1937). *Colbert and a Century of French Mercantilism.* Columbia University Press: New York.

Davenant, Charles (1696/1995). *An Essay on the East-India Trade.* n.p., London.

Davenant, Charles (1699). *An Essay upon the Probable Methods of Making a People Gainers in the Balance of Trade.* James Knapton, London.

Decker, Mathew (1744/1751). *An Essay on the Causes of the Decline of the Foreign Trade.* George Faulkner, Dublin.

Defoe, Daniel (1728). *A Plan of English Commerce.* Printed for Charles Rivington, London.

Eisenhart, Hugo (1881). *Geschichte der Nationaloekonomie.* Gustav Fischer, Jena.

Ekelund, Robert B. and Robert D. Tollison (1981). *Mercantilism as a rent-seeking society: economic regulation in historical perspective.* Texas A&M University Press, College Station.

Engerman, Stanley L. and Kenneth L. Sokoloff (2000). 'Technology and Industrialisation, 1790-1914'. In Engerman, Stanley L & Robert E. Gallman. *The Cambridge Economic History of the United States.* Cambridge University Press, Cambridge: 367–401.

Fanfani, Amintore (1955). *Storia delle dottrine economiche dall'antichità al XIX secolo.* Giuseppe Principato, Milan.

Finkelstein, Andrea (2000). *Harmony and the Balance: An Intellectual History of Seventeenth-Century English Economic Thought.* The University of Michigan Press, Ann Arbor.

Gee, Joshua (1729). *Trade and Navigation of Great Britain Considered.* Bettesworth & Hitch, London.

Goyeneche, Pedro Francisco (1717). *Comercio de Holanda, o el gran thesoro historial y político del floreciente comercio, que los holandeses tienen en todos sus estados y señoríos del mundo.* Imprenta Real, por J. Rodríguez Escobar, Madrid.

Graham, Frank (1923). 'Some Aspects of Protection further considered'. *Quarterly Journal of Economics* 37: 199–227.

Hamilton, Alexander (1791). A Report on the Manufactures of the United States. On http://www.juntosociety.com/i_documents/ah_rom.htm

Hamilton, Earl (1932). 'Spanish Mercantilism before 1700'. In *Facts and Factors in Economic History, Articles by former Students of Edwin Francis Gay.* Harvard University Press, Cambridge, Mass: 214–239.

Heckscher, Eli Filip (1931). *Merkantilismen: Ett Led i den Ekonomiska Politikens Historia.* P.A. Norstedt, Stockholm.

Hudson, Michael (2004). 'Technical progress and obsolescence of capitals and skills: theoretical foundations of nineteenth-century US industrial policy'. In Erik S. Reinert [ed.] (2004).

Huerta, Robert D. (2003). *Giants of Delft. Johannes Vermeer and the Natural Philosophers: The Parallel Search for Knowledge during the Age of Discovery.* Bucknell University Press, Lewisburg, PA.

Huet, Pierre Daniel (1722). *A View of the Dutch Trade in All the States, Empires, and Kingdoms of the World.* C. King and J. Stagg, London. Second edition, first edition, 1717. Original French edition, 1712.

Hume, David (1767). *The History of England from the Invasion of Julius Caesar to the Revolution in 1688,* 6 volumes. A. Millar, London.

Ingram, John Kells (1888). A *History of Political Economy*. Black, Edinburgh.

Janssen, Theodore (1713). 'General Maxims in Trade, Particularly Applied to the Commerce between Great Britain and France'. In King (1721).

Justi, Johann Heinrich Gottlob von (1760). *Die Natur und das Wesen der Staaten, als die Grundwissenschaft der Staatskunst, der Policey, und aller Regierungswissenschaften, desgleichen als die Quelle aller Gesetze, abgehandelt.* Johann Heinrich Rüdigers, Berlin.

King, Charles. (1721). *The British Merchant; or, Commerce Preserv'd.* 3 volumes. John Darby, London.

Koyré, Alexandre (1957). *From the closed world to the infinite universe.* Johns Hopkins University Press, Baltimore.

Krugman, Paul (1980). *Rethinking International Trade.* MIT Press, Cambridge.

Laspeyres, Etienne (1863/1961). *Geschichte der volkswirtschaftlichen Anschauungen der Niederländer und ihrer Litteratur zur Zeit der Republik.* de Graaf, Nieuwkoop.

Laffemas, Barthélemy (1597). *Reiglement (sic) general pour dresser les manufactures en ce royaume, et couper le cours des draps de soye, & autres merchandises qui perdent & ruynent l'Estat: qui est le vray moyen de remettre la France en sa splendeur, & de faire gaigner les pauvres...* Claude de Monstr'oil and Jean Richter, Paris.

Latini, Brunetto (1284/1993). *The Book of the Treasure (Li livres dou tresor).* Garland Publishing, New York.

List, Friedrich (1841/1959). *Das nationale System der Politischen Ökonomie.* Kyklos Verlag, Basel: 12. (This part of the foreword was not translated in the English translation of 1885.)

Lluch, Ernest (1973). *El pensament econòmic a Catalunya.* Edicions 62, Barcelona.

Lluch, Ernest (1997). 'Cameralism beyond the Germanic World: A Note of Tribe'. *History of Economic Ideas.*5 (2): 85–99.

Lluch, Ernest (2000). 'El cameralismo en España' in Enrique Fuentes Quintana (ed) *Economia y Economistas Españoles,* Vol. 3, Galaxia Gutenberg, Barcelona, pp. 721–728.

Locke, John (1691/1696). *Some considerations of the Consequences of the Lowering of Interests, and Raising the Value of Money.* Awnsham & Churchill, London.

Magnusson, Lars (1991). *Merkantilismen. Ett ekonomiskt tänkande formuleras,* Stockholm, SNS Förlag, English edition: *Mercantilism: The Shaping of an Economic Language.* Routledge, London.

Magnusson, Lars [ed.] (1993). *Mercantilist Economics.* Kluwer, Boston.

Marshall, Alfred (1890). *Principles of Economics.* Macmillan, London.

Misselden, Edward (1623). *The Circle of Commerce or the Balance of Trade.* Printed by John Dawson for Nicholas Bourne, London.

Montaigne, Michel de (1580/1958). *Essays*; translated by J.M. Cohen. Penguin, London.

Mun, Thomas (1664). *England's Treasure by Forraign Trade.* J. G. for T. Clark, London.

[Paracelsus] Hohenheim, Aureolus Theophrastus Bombastus von (1951). *Selected Writings of Paracelsus.* Jacobi, Joland [ed.]. Princeton University Press, Princeton.

Perez, Carlota (2004). 'Technological Revolutions, Paradigm Shift and Socio-Institutional Change'. In Erik S. Reinert [ed.]. *Globalization, Economic Development and Inequality: An Alternative Perspective.* Edward Elgar, Cheltenham.

Perrotta, Cosimo (1988). *Produzione e Lavoro Produttivo nel Mercantilismo e nell'Illuminismo.* Congedo Editore, Galatina.

Perrotta, Cosimo (1991). 'Is the Mercantilist Theory of the favorable balance of trade really erroneous?' *History of Political Economy* 23 (2): 301–336.

Perrotta, Cosimo (1993). 'Early Spanish Mercantilism: The First Analysis of Underdevelopment'. In Magnusson (1993): 17–58.

Porter, Michael (1990). *The Competitive Advantage of Nations.* Macmillan, London.

Praak, Maarten (2001). 'Early Modern Capitalism: an Introduction'. In Maarten Prak [ed.]. *Early Modern Capitalism: Economic and Social Change in Europe 1400–1800.* Routledge, London: 1–21.

Raymond, Daniel (1820). *Principles of Political Economy.* Fielding Lucas, Baltimore.

Reinert, Erik S. (1980). *International Trade and the Economic Mechanisms of Underdevelopment.* University Microfilms, Ann Arbor.

Reinert, Erik S. (1996). 'Diminishing Returns and Economic Sustainability: The dilemma of resource-based economies under a free trade regime'. In Stein Hansen, Jan Hesselberg and Helge Hveem [ed.]. *International Trade Regulation, National Development Strategies and the Environment: Towards Sustainable Development?*. Centre for Development and the Environment, University of Oslo, Oslo. Chapter 5 in this volume.

Reinert, Erik S. (1998). 'Raw Materials in the History of Economic Thought: or, Why List (the Protectionist) and Cobden (the Free Trader) Both Agreed on Free Trade in Corn. In Geraint Parry, Asif Qureshi, and Hillel Steiner [eds.]. *Freedom and Trade, 1846-1996.* Routledge, London.

Reinert, Erik S. (1999). 'The Role of the State in Economic Growth'. *Journal of Economic Studies* 26 (4/5). A shorter version was published in Pier Angelo Toninelli [ed.]. *The Rise and Fall of State-Owned Enterprises in the Western World.* Cambridge University Press, Cambridge (2000).

Reinert, Erik S. (2000a). 'Full Circle: Economics from Scholasticism through Innovation and back into Mathematical Scholasticism. Reflections around a 1769 price essay: "Why is it that Economics so Far has Gained so Few Advantages from Physics and Mathematics?"'. *Journal of Economic Studies* 27 (4/5).

Reinert, Erik S. (2000b). 'Karl Bücher and the Geographical Dimensions of Techno-Economic Change'. In Jürgen Backhaus [ed.]. *Karl Bücher: Theory, History Anthropology, Non-Market Economies.* Metropolis Verlag, Marburg.

Reinert, Erik S. (2003). 'Increasing Poverty in a Globalised World: Marshall Plans and Morgenthau Plans as Mechanisms of Polarisation of World Incomes'. In Chang Ha-Joon [ed.]. *Rethinking Economic Development.* Anthem, London. Chapter 9 in this volume.

Reinert, Erik S. (2004). *Globalization in the Periphery as a Morgenthau Plan: The Underdevelopment of Mongolia in the 1990's.* In Reinert [ed.], 2004. Chapter 8 in this volume.

Reinert, Erik S. [ed.] (2004). *Globalization, Economic Development and Inequality: An Alternative Perspective.* Edward Elgar, Cheltenham.

Reinert, Erik S. (2004). 'Benchmarking Success: The Dutch Republic (1500-1750) as seen by Contemporary European Economists'. In Oscar Gelderblom [ed.]. *The Political Economy of the Dutch Republic.* Chapter 13 in this volume.

Reinert, Erik S. & Arno Daastøl (1997). 'Exploring the Genesis of Economic Innovations: The Religious Gestalt-switch and the Duty to Invent as Preconditions for Economic Growth'. *European Journal of Law and Economics* 4 (2/3): p. 233–283.

Reinert, Erik S. & Arno Daastøl (2004). 'The Other Canon: The History of Renaissance Economics. Its Role as an Immaterial and Production-based Canon in the History of Economic Thought and in the History of Economic Policy'. In Reinert [ed.] (2004)

Reinert, Sophus (2003). 'Darwin and the Body Politic: Schäffle, Veblen and the biological metaphor shift in economics'. Paper presented at the 17th Heilbronn Conference in the Social Sciences, June. On www.othercanon.org.

Reinert, Sophus & Erik S. Reinert (2003). 'An Early National Innovation System. The Case of Antonio Serra (1613)'. *Institutions and Economic Development* 2 (1). Chapter 10 in this volume.

Robbins, Lionel (1952). *The Theory of Economic Policy in English Classical Political Economy.* Macmillan, London.

Ruestow, Edward G. (1996). *The Microscope in the Dutch Republic: The Shaping of Discovery.* Cambridge University Press, Cambridge.

Schmoller, Gustav (1897/1967). *The Mercantile System and its Historical Significance.* Macmillan, New York, 1897: 50–51 (reprinted Kelley 1967).

Schoenhof, Jacob (1885). *The Destructive Influence of the Tariff upon Manufacture and Commerce and the Figures and Facts Relating Thereto.* 2nd edition, New York Free Trade Club, New York.

Schumpeter, Joseph Alois (1954). *The History of Economic Analysis.* Oxford University Press, New York.

Seligman, Edwin (1920) *Curiosities of Early Economic Literature.* John Henry Nash, San Francisco.

Serra, Antonio (1613). *Breve Trattato delle Cause che Possono far Abbondare l'Oro e l'Argento dove non sono Miniere.* Lazzaro Scorriggio, Naples.

Singer, Hans W. (1950/1964). 'The Distribution of Gains between Investing and Borrowing Countries'. In *International Development: Growth and Change.* McGraw-Hill, New York.

Smith, Adam (1759/1812). *The Theory of Moral Sentiments.* In *Collected Works.* Cadell and Davies, London.

Smith, Adam (1776/1976). *The Wealth of Nations.* Chicago University Press, Chicago.

Sombart, Werner (1913a). Krieg und Kapitalismus. Duncker & Humblot, Munich & Leipzig.

Sombart, Werner (1913b). *Luxus und Kapitalismus.* Duncker & Humblot, Munich & Leipzig.

Sombart, Werner (1902/1928). *Der moderne Kapitalismus.* Duncker & Humblot, Munich & Leipzig.

Soros, George (2002), *George Soros on Globalization.* Public Affairs, New York.

Steadman, Philip (2001). *Vermeer's Camera.* Oxford University Press, Oxford.

Steuart, James (1767). *An Inquiry into the Principles of Political Economy: being an Essay on the Science of Domestic Policy in Free Nations. In which are particularly considered population, agriculture, trade, industry, money, coin, interest, circulation, banks, exchange, public credit, and taxes.* 2 Volumes. A. Millar & T. Cadell, London.

Uztariz, Gerónimo (1724/1751). *The Theory and Practice of Commerce and Maritime Affairs.* 2 vols. John and James Rivington, London.

Wolf, Martin (2003). 'The Morality of the Market', *Foreign Policy,* September-October: 47–50.

Zincke, Georg Heinrich, editor (1746–1767). *Leipziger Sammlungen von Wirthschafftlichen Policey-, Cammer- und Finantz-Sachen.* 192 issues in 17 volumes. Erster (bis) Sechzehender Band (und) General-Register, Leipzig.

Chapter 15

DEVELOPMENT AND SOCIAL GOALS: BALANCING AID AND DEVELOPMENT TO PREVENT 'WELFARE COLONIALISM'

'... just as we may avoid widespread physical desolation by rightly turning a stream near its source, so a timely dialectic in the fundamental ideas of social philosophy may spare us untold social wreckage and suffering.'

Herbert S. Foxwell, Cambridge economist, 1899

The Millennium Development Goals (MDGs) are noble goals for a world sorely in need of urgent action to solve pressing social problems. They rest, however, upon completely new principles whose long-term effects are neither well thought through nor well understood. In this chapter, I shall attempt to explain why the MDGs do not represent good social policy in the long run.

One novelty of the MDG approach lies in the emphasis on foreign financing of domestic social and redistribution policies rather than on domestic financing by the developing countries themselves. Disaster relief, which used to be of a temporary nature, now finds a more permanent form in the MDGs. In countries where more than 50 per cent of the government budget is financed by foreign aid, huge additional resource transfers are being planned. This raises the question of the extent to which this approach will put a large number of nations permanently 'on the dole', a system similar to 'welfare colonialism', which will be discussed at the end of the chapter.

The pursuit of the MDGs may appear as if the United Nations institutions have abandoned the effort to treat the causes of poverty and have instead concentrated on attacking its symptoms. In this chapter, I shall argue that palliative economics has, to a considerable extent, taken the place of development economics. Indeed, the balance between development economics (radically changing the productive structures of poor countries) and palliative economics (easing the pains of economic misery) is key to avoiding long-term negative effects.

How we used to deal with problems of development

In less than one generation, a stark contrast has emerged between the type of economic understanding underlying the Marshall Plan, on the one hand, and the type of economic theory behind today's multilateral development discourse and the Washington institutions, on the other. The Marshall Plan grew out of recognition of the flaws of its precursor, the Morgenthau Plan. While the goal of the Morgenthau Plan was to deindustrialize Germany, the goal of the Marshall Plan was not only to reindustrialize Germany but also to establish a *cordon sanitaire* of wealthy nations along the borders of the communist bloc in Europe and Asia, from Norway to Japan. The self-enforcing mechanisms that maintain the vicious circles of a Morgenthau Plan are outlined in Figure 15.1 while the virtuous circles of a Marshall Plan are outlined in Figure 15.2.

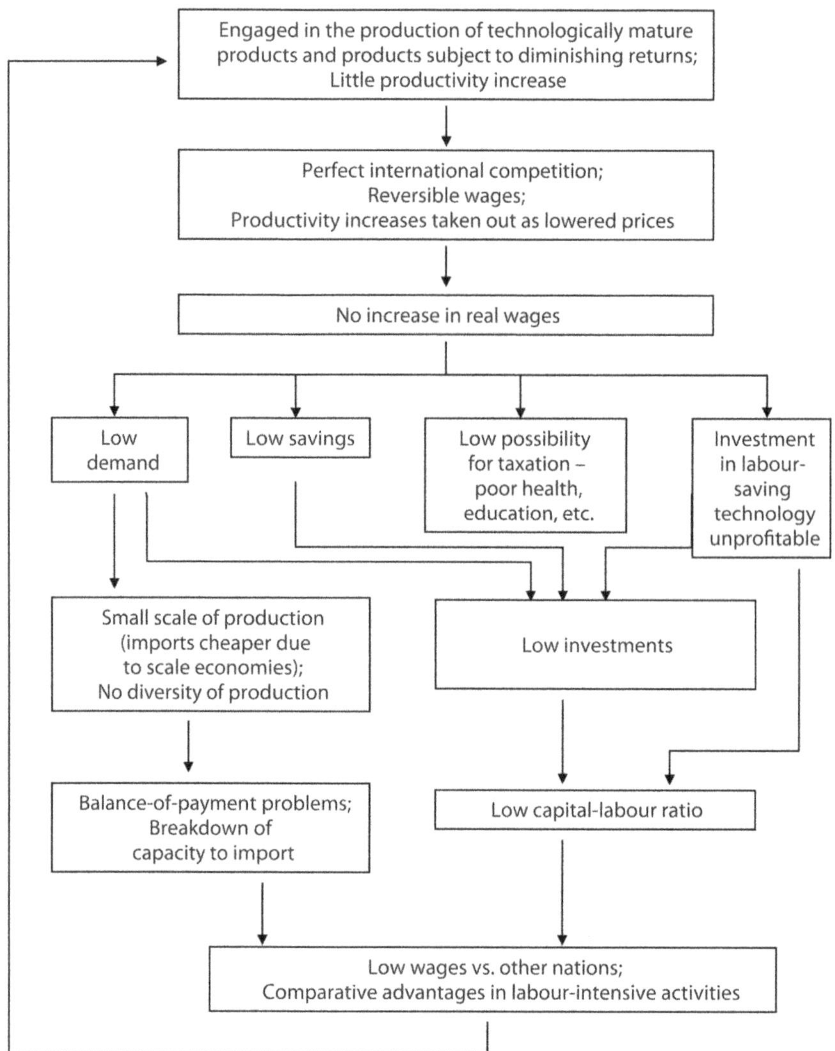

Figure 15.1 The mechanisms of a Morgenthau Plan: the 'vicious circle' of economic underdevelopment *Source*: Reinert (1980:.41). *Note*: It is futile to attack the system at any one point, e.g., by increasing investment when wages are still low and demand is absent. An instance of this is poor capital utilization and excess capacity in Latin American least developed countries.

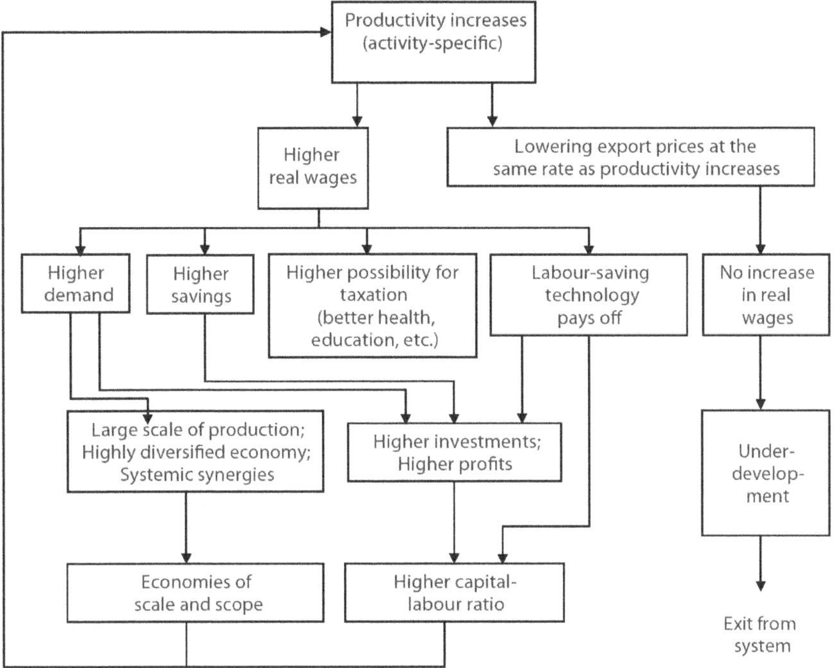

Figure 15.2 The systemic effects of a Marshall Plan: the 'virtuous circle' of economic development *Source*: Reinert (1980: 39). *Note*: In a closed system, with a constant employment rate, the only way that GNP per capita can grow is through the "virtuous circle'. However, the system can be cut off at any one point, e.g., if higher demand goes to foreign goods alone, the circle will break.

Judging from the number of nations lifted out of poverty, this reindustrialization plan was probably the most successful development project in human history. The fundamental insight behind the Marshall Plan was that the economic activities in the countryside were qualitatively different from those in the cities. In his famous June 1947 speech at Harvard, US secretary of state George Marshall (later awarded the Nobel Peace Prize) stressed that 'the farmer has always produced the foodstuffs to exchange with the city dweller for the other necessities of life'. This division of labour, i.e., between activities with increasing returns in the cities and activities with diminishing returns in the countryside, 'is the basis of our modern civilization', said Marshall, adding that at the present time it was threatened with breakdown. In this way, he recognized the relevance of the cameralist and mercantilist economic policies of previous centuries.

Economists and statesmen from Antonio Serra and Alexander Hamilton to Abraham Lincoln and Friedrich List would certainly have agreed that civilization requires activities generating increasing returns. The principles behind the 'toolbox' used by nations going from poverty to wealth, through the creation of 'city activities' (Appendix 1), have been surprisingly consistent. Yet, many of today's problems are due to the conditionalities imposed by the Washington Institutions that outlaw the use of the policy measures contained in this toolbox.

After World War II, these general principles did not produce the same success in every country. Some of the most successful countries (e.g., the Republic of Korea (South Korea)) temporarily protected new technologies for the world market, while some of the least successful ones permanently protected mature technologies, often for small home markets, by limiting competition (e.g., the small countries of Latin America). Appendix 2 classifies 'good' and 'bad' protectionist practices. In many countries, however, real wages were considerably higher when this inefficient industrial sector was in place than they are today with a much weakened industrial sector (see, for example, Figure 15.3). For centuries it was understood that having an 'inefficient' industrial sector produced higher real wages than having no industrial sector at all, and that this 'inefficient' sector ought to be made more efficient rather than be closed down. Figure 15.3 suggests that we may have established a world economic order that maximizes international trade rather than international welfare.

In its simplest form, this argument is born out of the role of increasing and diminishing returns in trade theory as the starting points for virtuous and vicious circles of growth or poverty. A praxis ignoring these mechanisms may cause factor price polarization rather than factor price equalization. Serra (1613) first established increasing returns, virtuous circles and large economic diversity as necessary elements for wealth creation. This principle was used almost continuously – with brief interruptions – until it was abandoned with the emergence of the 'Washington Consensus'. Since the 1980s, 'structural adjustment' has deindustrialized many poor peripheral countries and produced falling

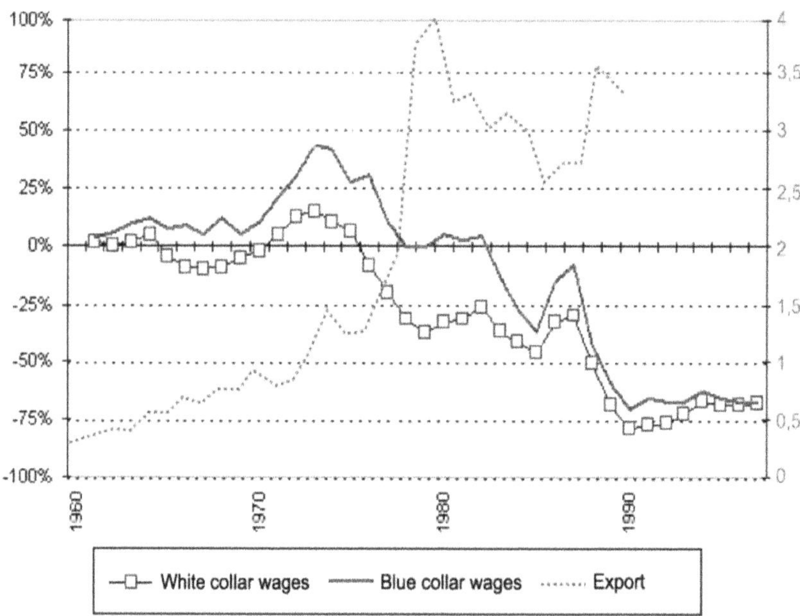

Figure 15.3 Peru: diverging trends of real wages and exports, 1960–90.

real wages.[1] Mainstream theory has long claimed that deindustrialization does not matter. On the contrary, according to the first World Trade Organization (WTO) director-general, Renato Ruggiero, free trade would unleash 'the borderless economy's potential to equalize relations between countries and regions'.

In the 1930s, maintaining the gold standard and balancing the budget were viewed as economic fundamentals which locked the world into a suboptimal equilibrium and prevented Keynes' policies from being carried out. Similarly, having free trade as the ideological centrepiece of development policies since the debt crises of the 1980s has locked the less industrialized countries into a suboptimal equilibrium.

Rather than continuing policies based on the most simplistic version of mainstream trade theory, the conflict between free trade and real wages in non-industrialized countries must be considered seriously. Specialization in activities with diminishing returns in the face of increasing population pressures also has serious environmental consequences (chapter 5).

Poverty in many Third World and former Second World countries is not caused by transitory problems but rather by the permanent features of nations that have different economic structures. Historically, few nations had the ambition to compete with the world industrial leaders of the day. But they understood that compared to being a supplier of raw materials, the nation could massively improve its welfare by industrializing, even if the industrial structure created would end up being less efficient than that of the world leader. The logic is like that of an individual who, instead of being London's most-efficient shoeshine boy, raises his income by choosing to become a mediocre lawyer.[2] Thus, when the United States started industrializing, its leaders merely wanted to create a (less-efficient) version of the production structure in England, a process which required tariffs. Successful industrialization under protection, however, carries the seeds of its own destruction. By the 1880s, US economists – invoking the same arguments based on scale and technology that were used to protect industries in the United States in the 1820s – argued for free trade. The same tariff that created a manufacturing industry for a period of time was now hurting the same industry (Schoenhof, 1883). This is why Friedrich List, a prominent protectionist, was in favour of global free trade only after all countries had achieved their comparative advantage outside the diminishing returns sector (Reinert, 1998). In other words, he disagreed not over the principle of free trade as such, but rather over its timing.

If one reads Adam Smith, an icon of free trade and laissez-faire, on economic development at an early stage, one finds his views are very much in line with those of classical development economists who advocate industrialization. In his earlier work, *The Theory*

1. This analysis is complicated by the fact that the incomes of employees and the self-employed as a share of GDP has been falling in most countries, while profits and earnings – particularly of the FIRE sector (finance, insurance, real estate) – have been growing. This wage/self-employed share of GDP has been close to 70 per cent in Norway and around 23 per cent in Peru.
2. The idea that a nation upgrading its skills in the same way a person could do, was part of the US industrialization strategy from the 1820s (Raymond, 1820).

of Moral Sentiments (Smith, 1759/1812), Smith argued for 'the great system of government', which is helped by adding new manufactures. Interestingly, he argued that new manufactures are not to be promoted to help suppliers or consumers but in order to improve the 'great system of government'.

It is also possible to argue that Adam Smith was a misunderstood mercantilist, who strongly supported the mercantilist policies of the past, but argued that they were no longer necessary for England. He praised the Navigation Acts protecting English manufacturing and shipping against Holland, arguing 'they are as wise … as if they had all been dictated by the most deliberate wisdom' and holding them to be 'perhaps, the wisest of all the commercial regulations of England' (Smith, 1776/1976: I, 486–87). All in all, Smith described a development that had become self-sustaining – a kind of snowball effect – originating in the protectionist measures of the past. Only once did Smith use the term 'invisible hand' in *The Wealth of Nations* – when it sustained the key import-substitution goal of mercantilist policies, and the consumer preferred domestic to foreign industry (Smith, 1776/1976: 477). This was only possible when 'the market' took over the role previously played by protective measures, and national manufacturing no longer needed such protection.

The praxis of economic development has been to assimilate and produce less-efficient 'copies' of the economic structure of wealthy nations. The key features of the economic structure of wealthy nations – a large division of labour (with a large number of different industries and professions) and a sector with increasing returns (industry and knowledge-intensive services) – were codified by economists such as Antonio Serra (1613), James Steuart (1767), Alexander Hamilton (1791) and Friedrich List (1841/1909). These principles are, at times, unlearned – as in France in the 1760s, Europe in the 1840s and the world in the 1990s.

These periods ultimately came to an end because of their great social costs, however. Physiocracy in France created shortages and scarcity of bread, contributing to the onset of the French revolution (see, for example, Kaplan, 1976). The free trade euphoria of the 1840s met its backlash in 1848, with revolutions in all large European countries except England and Russia. David Ricardo's trade theory has been proven wrong every time it is applied asymmetrically to increasing and diminishing returns industries.[3] He is right, however, in saying that the 'natural' wage level is subsistence. The trade liberalization euphoria of the 1990s has increased poverty in several peripheral countries, but our response to this has also been wrong. We have been focusing too much on the symptoms – rather than the causes – of the problem.

The present situation

Standard economics tends to see development as a process largely driven by *accumulation* of investments in physical and human capital (Nelson, 2006). Standard economic

3. This asymmetry is the core of the argument in Frank Graham's 1923 article, a basis for Krugman's New Trade Theory.

theory underlying today's development policies is generally unable to recognize qualitative differences between economic activities. Almost none of today's failed or failing states could pass George Marshall's test for what brings about modern civilization, as they have very weak manufacturing sectors and are unable to generate the virtuous exchange between city and rural activities. They also have very little diversity in their economic base, a limited division of labour and specialize in activities subject to diminishing returns.

Historically, modern democracy began in nations where this civilizing trade between urban and rural areas had already been established, e.g., in the Italian city states. In the most successful city states – including states with a scarcity of arable land, such as Venice and the Dutch Republic – power did not lie with the landowning class. In Florence, 40 or so landowning families were banned from political life in the thirteenth century, thus enabling Schumpeterian 'cronyism' where political and economic interests 'colluded' in ways that created widespread wealth. Dependency on raw materials encouraged feudalism and colonialism, neither of which leads to political freedom. Similarly, the US Civil War was essentially between the South, where landowners had vested interests in agriculture and cheap labour, and the North, which had vested interests in industrialization. The history of Latin America has been, in many ways, similar to the history of the United States, except that the outcome was analogous to the South's winning the Civil War.

In the alternative economic paradigm – which could broadly be called evolutionary and historical – the process of development is driven by *assimilation*: learning from more advanced countries by 'copying' both their economic structure and their institutions.[4] Key elements in this assimilation strategy are institutions such as patent protection, scientific academies and universities. In this model, economic growth tends to be activity-specific, tied to 'clusters' of economic activities characterized by increasing returns, dynamic imperfect competition and rapid technological progress. In addition to capital, the process requires transferring and mastering skills and, above all, creating a viable market for activities with increasing returns where the absence of purchasing power and massive unemployment tend to go hand in hand. By generally using models assuming full employment, the Washington institutions avoid a key issue that locks nations in poverty – the lack of formal employment. Since sixteenth-century Holland and Venice, only nations with healthy manufacturing sectors have achieved anything close to full employment without massive rural underemployment.

The dominant economic theory today represents what Schumpeter called 'the pedestrian view that it is capital *per se* that propels the capitalist engine': development is seen as largely driven by the accumulation of capital, physical or human. According to Richard Nelson, 'The premise of neoclassical theory is that, if the investments are made, the acquisition and mastery of new ways of doing things are relatively easy, even automatic' (Nelson 2006). More importantly, a core assumption of standard economics that is seldom acknowledged is that economic structure is irrelevant, as capital *per se*

4. Historical evidence of this practice in Europe can be found in chapter 13.

will lead to economic development, regardless of the economic structure within which investment is made. The alternative theory suggests that economic activities have very different windows of opportunity as carriers of economic growth. In other words, we have to rid ourselves of what James Buchanan calls 'the equality assumption' in economic theory, which is probably its most important, but least discussed assumption.[5] The ability, at any time, to absorb innovation and knowledge – and consequently to attract investments – varies enormously from one economic activity to another.

The problem

Viewing capital *per se* as the key to growth, loans are given to poor nations with productive/industrial structures that are unable to absorb such capital profitably. Interest payments often exceed the rate of return on investments made. 'Financing for development' may therefore take on the characteristics of a pyramid scheme, the only ones to gain being those who started the scheme and who are close to the door (see Kregel, 2004). Similarly, investments in human capital, made without corresponding changes in the productive structure to create demand for the skills acquired, will tend to promote emigration. In both cases, Gunnar Myrdal's 'perverse backwashes' of economic development will be the result: more capital – both monetary and human – will flow from the poor to the rich countries. One explanation for this lies in the type of economic structure – locked into a vicious circle with a lack of supply and demand and an absence of increasing returns – that characterizes poor nations. United States' industrial policy from 1820 to 1900 is probably the best example for Third World countries to follow today until these nations are ready to benefit from international trade.

Recommendation

As with the Marshall Plan, funds must be matched by the establishment of industrial and service sectors that can absorb the physical and human investments. Diversification from raw material production is necessary to create a basis for democratic stability and increased welfare, even if the new sectors are initially unable to survive world market competition. This incipient industrialization will need special treatment of the kind afforded by the Marshall Plan and will require interpreting the Bretton Woods agreement in the same manner as in the immediate post-World War II era.

The neoclassical economists' poor understanding of how businesses operate also contributes to the problem. At the core of their economic theory of capitalism is perfect competition and equilibrium, a state which produces very little profit. Any successful and profitable business enterprise rests, almost by definition, on some kind of

5. At its core, the Enlightenment project was one of ordering the world by creating taxonomies or classification systems, of which Linnaeus' is the best known. Neoclassical economics achieves analytical precision precisely by lacking any taxonomy: everything is qualitatively alike. Therefore its conclusions, like factor price equalization, are essentially already built into its assumptions.

rent-seeking. The poverty-stricken Third World probably most closely corresponds to conditions of diminishing returns and perfect competition, while the rich countries, whose exports are produced under conditions of Schumpeterian-dynamic imperfect competition, are 'rent seekers', whose rents lead to higher wages and a higher tax base. This failure to understand development as Schumpeterian imperfect competition is at the heart of the arguments against industrial policy. Anything that causes imperfect competition tends to be seen as contributing to corruption and 'cronyism'.

Keynes saw investments as resulting from what he called 'animal spirits'. Without 'animal spirits' – the will to invest in uncertain conditions – capital is sterile in the worlds of both Joseph Schumpeter and Karl Marx. The motivating force behind 'animal spirits' is the desire to maximize profits, thus upsetting the equilibrium of perfect competition. From a businessman's point of view, poor countries often suffer from low investments because of a lack of profitable investment opportunities, largely due to low purchasing power and high unemployment. Subsistence farmers are not profitable customers for most producers of goods and services. Tariffs can create incentives to move production to the labour markets of the poor. Historically, this has been seen as a conscious trade-off between the interests of 'Man-as-a-wage-earner' and 'Man-as-a-producer'. The idea that industrialization would rapidly increase employment and wages – which would more than offset the temporarily higher cost of manufactured goods – was at the core of Prebisch's import-substitution industrialization, as well as of US economic theory around 1820 (see, for example, Raymond, 1820).

The idea that greater 'openness' would improve the lot of the poor countries is both counter-intuitive and contrary to historical experience. In many cases, the sudden 'opening' of a backward economy killed off the little manufacturing activity that existed, thus exacerbating the situation (see chapters 8 and 9). From the unification of Italy in the nineteenth century to the integration of Mongolia and Peru (see Roca and Simabuco 2004) in the 1990s, historical experience shows that free trade between nations of very different levels of development tends to destroy the most-efficient industries in the least-efficient countries (the Vanek-Reinert effect). Figure 15.3 shows how the export increases that followed the opening up of the Peruvian economy were accompanied by falling real wages. In Peru, as in many other Latin American countries, real wages peaked during the period of 'inefficient' import substitution. The ports, airports, roads, power stations, schools, hospitals and service industries created by this inefficient industrial sector led by rent-seekers were *real* and could not have been created without the demand for labour and infrastructure that this sector generated.[6]

The timing of opening an economy is also crucial. Opening up an economy too late can seriously hamper growth, while opening up an economy too early will result in deindustrialization, falling wages[7] and increasing social problems. An anonymous traveller, who observed the effects of economic policy in different European countries in 1786, reached this conclusion: 'Tariffs are as harmful to a country after the arts

6. I am grateful to Carlota Perez for having formulated this insight.
7. Though not necessarily falling GDP per capita (see footnote 1).

[manufacturing industry] have been established there, as they are useful to it in order to introduce them' (Anonymous, 1786: 31).

Southern Mexico experienced this destructive sequence of deindustrialization, de-agriculturalization[8] and depopulation. That large numbers of subsistence farmers should be made 'uncompetitive' by subsidized First World agriculture is a relatively new, but alarming, trend that may persist even after the subsidies are removed. In India, there are around 650 million farmers, a large proportion of whom will be as 'uncompetitive' as their Mexican colleagues if and when free trade opens up. In the poorest countries today, a trade-off exists between maximizing international trade – which is what present policies achieve – and maximizing human welfare (see Figure 15.3). This trade-off needs to be addressed in a manner different than that of merely compensating the losses of the poor countries through increased aid.

History has shown that the vicious circles of poverty and underdevelopment can be effectively attacked by changing the productive structure of poor and failing states. This entails increasing diversification away from sectors with diminishing returns (traditional raw materials and agriculture) to sectors with increasing returns (technology-intensive manufacturing and services), in the process creating a complex division of labour and new social structures. In addition to breaking away from subsistence agriculture, this will create an urban market for goods, which will induce specialization and innovation, bring in new technologies and create alternative employment as well as the economic synergies that unite a nation-state. The key to coherent development is an interplay between sectors with increasing and diminishing returns in the same labour market.

Arguments against industrial policy

Malthusian vs. Schumpeterian cronyism

2005: A Filipino sugar producer uses his political influence to get import protection for his products.

2000: Mayor Daley of Chicago (ignoring the advice of University of Chicago economists) provides subsidies to already wealthy high-tech investors through an incubator programme.

1950s and 1960s: Swedish industrialist Marcus Wallenberg uses his close contacts with Labour Party minister of finance, Gunnar Sträng, to win political support to carry out his plans for the Swedish companies Volvo and Electrolux.

1877: Steel producers in the United States use their political clout to impose 100 per cent duty on steel rails (Taussig, 1897: 222).

1485: Woolworkers use their connections to King Henry VII to influence the state to give them subsidies and to impose an export duty on raw wool so as to increase raw material prices for their competitors on the continent, thus slowly killing the wool industry elsewhere, e.g., in Florence.

8. As imported and subsidized United States food takes over from local maize and wheat production.

The above examples all involve crony capitalism and rent-seeking behaviour that mainstream economic theory tends to abhor. A crucial difference separates the first example from the rest, however. The Filipino crony differs from the other cronies in that he gets subsidies for a raw material with diminishing returns that competes in a world market facing perfect competition. In other words, he is a Malthusian crony, leading his country down the path of diminishing returns (in spite of technological change which counteracts this). The others are Schumpeterian cronies, producing under what Schumpeter called historical increasing returns (a combination of both increasing returns and fast technological change). If we couple this with trade theory, we see that the tilted playing fields of Schumpeterian cronyism produce vastly different results than those of the Malthusian crony.

Keynes indicated that laissez-faire would be suboptimal under difficult circumstances. If we insist on abandoning industrial policy because moving away from perfect competition will cause some cronies to get rich, we have totally misunderstood the nature of capitalism. After all, capitalism *is* about getting away from perfect competition.

Economic development is caused by structural changes which break the equilibrium, creating rents. Insisting on the absence of rents is insisting on a steady and stationary state. There is still a need to choose which activities to protect, however, which in turn creates cronies. Abraham Lincoln protected the steel cronies – by paying a little more for steel;[9] the United States created a huge steel industry with many high-paying jobs that also provided a base for government taxation. Economic development is about aligning the public interests of the nation with the private vested interests of the capitalists. The failure of standard economics to understand the dynamics of the business world will lead to a failure to understand the economic essence of colonialism. By preventing colonies from having their own manufacturing industries, economic activities with high growth potential and mechanization remained in the mother country, whereas activities with diminishing returns went to the colonies.

The immense transfers that accompany the MDG process will necessarily also lead to cronyism. Through this initiative, some will get wealthy, since crony-free economics only exists in neoclassical models. By opting for Schumpeterian cronyism, instead of aid-based cronyism, it will be possible for poor countries to extricate themselves from economic dependency.

We seem to have unlearned the logic behind policy tools for economic development. Patents and modern tariffs were created at about the same time, in the late 1400s. These rent-seeking institutions were created using the very same understanding of the process of economic development in order to protect knowledge (in the case of patents) and to produce in new geographic areas (in the case of tariffs). Both patents and tariffs represent legalized rent-seeking to promote goals not achievable under perfect competition.

9. That the steel tariff later got as high as 100 per cent was a result of technological change and rapidly falling prices in a situation where the tariff was not based on value, but weight (dollars per ton).

Why are the rent-seeking and cronyism arguments not applied to patents, but only used against tariffs and other policy instruments used in poor countries? With some justification, it can be said that the wealthy countries are establishing rules that legalize constructive rent-seeking in their own countries but prohibit similar ones in the poor countries.

The Washington Consensus and sequential single-issue management

Following the fall of the Berlin Wall, variations of neoclassical economics became the only game in town. Neoclassical economics was, however, in Nicholas Kaldor's term, an *untested theory*. Although neoclassical theory had provided an effective ideological shield during the Cold War, no nation had ever been built on this theoretical framework. In its most extreme form, as practised around 1990, if nations 'got their prices right', economic growth would follow automatically, regardless of economic structures. By 1990, policy recommendations were formulated around Samuelson's 'law' of factor price equalization and neglected other important theoretical contributions, including key insights by the founding father of neoclassical economics, Alfred Marshall. Marshall had not only described taxes on activities with diminishing returns in order to subsidize activities with increasing returns as being a good development policy, but he had also emphasized the importance of a nation's producing in sectors where most technical progress was to be found, as well as the role of synergies (industrial districts).

In the 1990s, as the world economy failed to deliver results following trade liberalization, the search began for other explanations based on the premises of neoclassical economics. The search for a factor which would ensure factor price equalization with free trade resulted in various policy fads:

- 'getting prices right';
- 'getting property rights right';
- 'getting institutions right';
- 'getting governance right';
- 'getting competitiveness right';
- 'getting national innovation systems right';
- 'getting entrepreneurship right'.

This vision of 'the borderless economy's potential to equalize relations between countries and regions' was based on erroneous theory, and instead became a nightmare in many poor countries. As economic growth is an uneven process by nature, only wise political intervention can even out factor price polarizations. Attributing poverty to a lack of entrepreneurship comes across as being particularly uninformed. In contrast to most people in wealthy countries who can make a living on their largely routine jobs, the poor of the world have to use their entrepreneurial talents every day in order to secure sustenance.

This sequence of policy fads failed to address several fundamental blind spots in neoclassical economics:

a) Its inability to register qualitative differences, including the different potentials of economic activities as contributors to economic growth;
b) Its inability to acknowledge synergies and linkages;[10] and
c) Its inability to cope with innovations and novelties, and how these are differently distributed among economic activities.

Together, these blind spots of contemporary mainstream economics prevent many poor countries from developing. China and India – probably today's most successful developing countries – have, for decades, followed the recommendations of the Marshall Plan, rather than the Washington Consensus.

While learning is a key element in development, it may also be passed on in the economy simply as falling prices to foreign consumers. The key insight by Schumpeter's student Hans Singer was that learning and technological change in the production of raw materials, particularly in the absence of a manufacturing sector, tend to lower export prices rather than increase the standard of living in the raw material–producing nation (Singer, 1950). Learning tends to create wealth for producers only when they are part of a close network, once called 'industrialism' – a dynamic system of economic activities subject to increasing productivity through technical change and a complex division of labour. The absence of increasing returns, dynamic imperfect competition and synergies in raw material–producing countries are all part of the mechanisms that perpetuate poverty.

Since the 1990s, huge resources have been increasingly employed by well-intentioned governments along the largely sterile 'mainstream' path of inquiry, without exploring alternative theoretical approaches. The best social policy, however, is to create development, but not by the rich creating subsidized reservations where the poor are kept, largely underemployed and 'underproductive'. The Indian reservations in North America are a sad example of policies that subsidize without changing productive structures. Similarly, the MDGs are far too biased towards palliative economics rather than structural change, i.e., towards treating the symptoms of poverty rather than its causes. While such policies may be needed under current critical conditions, they will remain poor social policies in the longer term unless the deeper roots of the problem are confronted.

Although malaria was endemic to Europe for centuries, present not only in the South but also in the Alpine valleys all the way to the Kola peninsula in north-western Russia, Europe rid itself of the disease through industrialization and development. Advanced and intensive agriculture, irrigation systems, huge public health efforts and eradication

10. The slogan 'get national innovation systems right' proved to be an exception as it refers to a synergistic phenomenon. However, this does not lead very far because of the theory's inability to distinguish between different windows of opportunity, e.g., for innovation in Microsoft, under hugely increasing returns, and in a goat herding firm in Mongolia, under critically diminishing returns. In standard analysis, Schumpeterian economics tends to be added like thin icing on a thoroughly neoclassical cake.

plans enabled Europe to eradicate malaria. Europe's development over time also enabled European states to honour their debts.

Instead of embarking on a similar economic development model, Africa continues to preserve colonial economic structures, exporting raw materials and maintaining underdeveloped industrial sectors. Debt cancellation and free mosquito nets merely address the symptoms of these problems.

Creating 'welfare colonialism'

Current policies risk inadvertently undermining the development potential of aid with its palliative effects. What we may be creating is a system that could be described as 'welfare colonialism', a term coined to describe the economic integration of the native population in Northern Canada (Paine, 1977). The essential features of welfare colonialism are:

1) A reversal of the colonial drain of the old days, the net flow of funds going to the colony rather than to the mother country;
2) Integration of the native population in ways that radically undermine their previous livelihoods; and
3) The placing of the native population on unemployment benefits.

In Paine's view, welfare colonialism identifies welfare as the vehicle for stable 'governing at a distance' through exercise of a particularly subtle, 'non-demonstrative' and dependency-generating form of neocolonial social control that pre-empts local autonomy through 'well-intentioned' and 'generous', but ultimately 'morally wrong', policies. Welfare colonialism creates paralyzing dependencies on the 'centre' in a peripheral population, a centre exerting control through incentives that create total economic dependency, thereby preventing political mobilization and autonomy. The social conditions in which the native inhabitants of North American reservations find themselves today show us that, in their case, the final effect of massive transfer payments has been to create a dystopia rather than a utopia.

The discussion on whether or not aid to Ethiopia should be cut as a sanction against the Ethiopian government illustrates the kind of dilemmas which will necessarily accompany 'welfare colonialism'. The rich countries will always be in the position to cut off aid, food and livelihood sources of poor countries if they disapprove of their national policies. As long as 'development aid' remains palliative, rather than developmental, seemingly generous and well-intentioned development aid will inevitably become extremely powerful mechanisms by which rich countries end up controlling poor countries. Rather than promoting global democracy, such policies will lead towards global plutocracy.

We already see aid and other transfers creating passivity and disincentives to work in poor nations. Haitian observers point to family transfer payments from the United States, which create disincentives to work for a going rate of US$0.30 an hour in Haiti. A Brazilian research project on the highly laudable Zero Hunger Project, carried out at different government levels (national, state and local) for various programmes targeted to fight hunger, concludes that these projects are, to a large extent, ineffective since they treat the symptoms of poverty by distributing food or subsidizing food prices rather than by creating situations where the poor can become breadwinners (Lavinas and Garcia, 2004). These are welfare colonialism effects that result from treating the symptoms, rather than addressing the causes of poverty.

The idea of nations producing under increasing returns (industrialized nations) paying annual compensation to nations producing under constant or diminishing returns (raw material producers) is not a new one. It is a logical conclusion of standard trade theory and has been present in US college textbooks since the 1970s.[11] Until recently, the favoured option was to industrialize the poor countries, even if it meant that their industries would not be competitive in the world market for a considerable period of time. Making free trade the linchpin of the world economic system – one to which all other considerations must yield – has made welfare colonialism appear as the only option. The alternative option of developing the poor world is presently absent because many do not wish to abolish free trade as the core of the world economic order. The long-term and cumulative effects of having this group of nations specialize in pre-industrial economic structures will be staggering, however.

In 1947, political pressure due to the spectre of communism resulted in successful development practices. The free traders in Washington had to yield to the political need for protectionist development policies encircling the communist bloc, which led to the astonishing success of the Marshall Plan in Europe and the East Asian miracle. It is perhaps a faint hope that today's terrorist threat will yield a similar situation where free trade is temporarily abandoned in order to promote development as a *political*, rather than a *social*, goal.

During the Enlightenment, civilization and democracy were understood to be products of a specific type of economic structure. The origins of this understanding can be found more than 100 years earlier; according to Francis Bacon (1620), 'There is a startling difference between the life of men in the most civilized province of Europe, and in the wildest and most barbarous districts of New India. This difference comes not from the soil, not from climate, not from race, but *from the arts*.' When German economist Johann Jacob Meyen stated in 1770, 'It is known that a primitive people does not improve their customs and institutions, later to find useful industries, but the other way around', he expressed something which was considered common sense at the time. Nineteenth-century thinkers, from Abraham Lincoln to Karl Marx, shared the idea that civilization is created by industrialization. As Marx put it, 'Industrialization draws all, even the most barbarian, nations into civilization'.

11. 'Thus the country which eventually specializes completely in the production of X (that is, the commodity whose production function is characterized by increasing returns to scale) might agree to make an income transfer (annually) to the other country, which agrees to specialize completely in Y (that is, the commodity whose production function is characterized by constant returns to scale)' (Chacholiades, 1978: 199). See also Reinert (1980).

We ought to use our understanding of policies that have been successful in the past to solve today's challenges, while remaining firmly grounded in an understanding of the present technological and historical context. The connection between production and civilization must be understood, and the theoretical focus should shift from trade to production. Different technological developments affect different economic activities, creating huge variations in the windows of opportunity to innovate. Hence, core issues – like economies of scale, specialization, lock-in effects, the effects of diminishing returns, the *assimilation of knowledge* and the economic structures of poor countries – should not be ignored. We should read not only Schumpeter on technical change and 'creative destruction' but also open our eyes and minds to the type of 'destructive destruction' that can be observed in the peripheral countries of the world.

Europe's present problems reflect the problems of globalization

As mentioned earlier, our present failure to understand why so many countries stay poor is intimately tied to a number of blind spots that make it extremely difficult, if not impossible, to create a theory of uneven economic development. As Lionel Robbins warned us long ago, the basic features of the neoclassical paradigm produces a *Harmonielehre*, where economic harmony is already built into the assumptions on which the theory rests. Today, this paradigm hinders, rather than helps, our understanding of the reasons behind poverty. As Thomas Kuhn (1962: 37) said, 'A paradigm can, for that matter, even insulate the community from those socially important problems that are not reducible to the puzzle form, because they cannot be stated in terms of the conceptual and instrumental tools the paradigm supplies'.

Any long-term solution for Africa and other poor regions will have to rest on a theory of uneven development. This theory, which allowed for successful economic policy for 500 years – from Henry VII's England in 1485 to the integration of Spain and Portugal into the European Union (EU) in 1986 – is now virtually extinct. Although a complete outline of this theory and its accompanying policy measures lies beyond the scope of this chapter, some core elements can be mentioned here.

The present approach towards the poor is very much tilted in favour of *palliative economics* to ease the pains of poverty rather than to permanently eradicate it through economic development. In addition, the current approach makes it possible to continue and even extend (as in the World Trade Organization (WTO) negotiations) present practices without investigating the problems with globalization in the periphery. The same myths – based on ideology rather than experience – and the same policies are still in place. Keeping in power the same people who introduced the neoclassical shock therapy measures responsible for much of the problem has been a mistake. It virtually guarantees that we do not engage in a fundamental discussion of *what went wrong*. Instead, what is needed is a theory that explains why economic development, by its very nature, is such an uneven process. Only then can the appropriate policy measures be put in place.

The problems created by the currently dominant economic theory are not limited to the Third World countries. In the case of the EU, most developed nations have experienced increasing economic inequalities internally. The same problems are thus experienced on three levels – globally, within the EU and within most developed nations. The cause behind these developments is essentially the same: theories that worked for centuries have been abandoned. Tensions within the European Community are the result of the same economic forces that create poverty around the world. Those in the old member states of the EU feel betrayed because their welfare is being eroded, while those in the new member states feel betrayed because their welfare is not improving as fast as expected. Not surprisingly, this unexpected situation has caused many to ask what went wrong.

Although German economist Friedrich List (1789–1846) is hardly mentioned in today's economic textbooks, his economic principles not only industrialized Continental Europe in the nineteenth century but also facilitated European integration from the early 1950s up to and including the successful integration of Spain and Portugal into the EU in 1986. It was not until the introduction of the Stability and Growth Pact that List's principles were abandoned in favour of the kind of economics that dominates the Washington Consensus. The result has been increasing unemployment and poverty in the old core countries, inflaming the debate that resulted in the rejection of the proposed new European constitution (see Reinert and Kattel, 2004).

Below are three of List's key principles, which contrasted with standard textbook economics. In order to develop Africa and other poor countries, the present neoclassical economic principles must be abandoned in favour of the old Listian principles.

- ***Listian principle*:** A nation first industrializes and is then gradually integrated economically into nations at the same level of development.

  Neoclassical principle: Free trade is the goal *per se*, even before the required stage of industrialization is achieved. The 2004 EU enlargement was directly at variance with Listian principles. First, the former communist countries in Eastern Europe (with the exception of Hungary) suffered dramatic deindustrialization, unemployment and underemployment. These countries were then abruptly integrated into the EU, creating enormous economic and social tensions. From the point of view of Western Europe, the factor price equalization promised by international trade theory proved to be an equalization *downward.*
- ***Listian principle*:** The preconditions for wealth, democracy and political freedom are all the same: a diversified manufacturing sector subject to increasing returns[12] (which historically means manufacturing, but also includes knowledge-intensive services). This was the principle promoted by the first US secretary of the treasury, Alexander Hamilton (1791), upon which the US economy was built. It was rediscovered by George Marshall in 1947, as mentioned above.

  Neoclassical principle: All economic activities are qualitatively alike, so what is produced does not matter. The ideology is based on 'comparative advantage', without recognizing that it is actually possible for a nation to specialize in being poor and ignorant, engage in economic activities that require little knowledge and operate under perfect competition and diminishing returns and/or bereft of any scale economies and technological change.

---

12. The works of Jane Jacobs on the role of the cities arrive at the same conclusion as List, albeit from a different starting point.

- ***Listian principle***: Economic welfare is a result of synergy. The thirteenth-century Florentine Chancellor, Brunetto Latini (1210–1294), explained the wealth of cities as a *common weal*, 'un ben comune' (see chapter 5).

  Neoclassical principle: 'There is no such thing as society', Margaret Thatcher (1987).

As Kuhn described above, these Listian principles cannot be captured by the tools of the reigning economic paradigm. Understanding List requires the recognition of qualitative differences between economic activities, diversity, innovations, synergies and historical sequencing of processes – all of which are blind spots in standard economics.

Working with economic tools that prevent them from understanding List's points, today's mainstream economists grope for explanations of continued poverty. They return to factors that have been studied and discarded, like race and climate, and refuse to see how historical experience demonstrates that the economic structure of wealthy countries has certain characteristics that poor nations lack, e.g., increasing returns, innovation, diversity and synergies. The collapse of the first wave of globalization led economists to eugenics and racial hygiene.[13] Africans were not seen as poor because of the colonial economic structures that had been imposed on the continent, but rather because they were black. Today, the ostensibly more politically correct version of this type of theory is that Africa is poor because blacks are corrupt.

Diversity as a precondition for development

Another blind spot of economics is its inability to understand the importance of diversity for economic growth. Diversity is a key factor in development for a variety of reasons. First, a diversity of activities with increasing returns – maximizing the number of professions in an economy – is the basis for the synergy effects called economic development. This was the standard understanding from the 1600s (see chapter 13). Second, modern evolutionary economics point to the importance of diversity as a basis for selection between technologies, products and organizational solutions, all of which are key elements in an evolving market economy (see Nelson and Winter, 1982). Third, diversity has been an important explanation for European 'exceptionalism', where a large number of nation-states, in competition with one another, created tolerance and a demand for diversity. A scholar, whose views were not popular with a particular king or ruler, could find employment in a different nation, thus creating a greater diversity of ideas.

Fourth, religious diversity was emphasized by Johann Friedrich von Pfeiffer (1718–1787), one of the most influential German economists of the eighteenth century. While some economists believe that more rapid economic growth is promoted by some religions, rather than others,[14] Richard Tawney (1926), the famous English historian, emphasized

13. Irving Fisher was both a leading economist and the leader of the eugenics movement in the United States in this period. For a discussion, see Ross (1998).
14. Werner Sombart emphasized the role of Judaism, and Max Weber the role of Protestantism.

the declining importance of religion in propelling capitalism. About 150 years earlier, Pfeiffer argued that when a diversity of 'competing' religions exists within a state, religion, as an institution, will lose much of its power over the inhabitants. The existence of alternatives will remove fear and other factors that contribute to fanaticism, and a new tolerance will open up for a desirable diversity of its population and skills (Pfeiffer, 1778).

We live in an age of great ignorance today, where established qualitative arguments exploring the process of economic development have been abandoned. The importance of diversity is just one of these arguments. The banality of today's explanations about poverty being a result of climate and corruption amply testifies to this ignorance, which is fortified by the absence of historical knowledge and of an interest in proven principles that have brought nation after nation from poverty to wealth over five centuries. As Paul Krugman has pointed out, previous economic insights tend to fade away, only to be rediscovered later. In a situation similar to the one we are in now, an enlightened group of nineteenth-century German economists caught the ear of Chancellor Bismarck and were allowed to design that country's developmental and welfare state. Similarly, just after World War II, the world understood that economic development was the result of synergies and increasing returns. Combined with the political threat of communism, this understanding made it possible to overrule the free trade ideologies in Washington and reindustrialize Europe and industrialize parts of Asia. In order to restart growth, it is necessary to reinvent this type of economic theory.

Policy implications

Aiming for increasing returns, diversity and the common weal

From an economic point of view, the poor populations on the world periphery may be seen either in terms of *consumption* or in terms of *production*. From the consumption point of view, there are two billion people whose extremely low purchasing power causes them to live on the brink of famine and disease. One suggestion would be to give them more purchasing power through aid, and it is this suggestion that has inspired the MDGs and traditional development assistance. Since many of the victims of poverty are farmers, another normal reaction would be to make their farming more efficient.

These policies, however, go squarely against successful development policies of the past. Only the presence of manufacturing industry produces efficient agriculture. As David Hume (1767) said in his *History of England*, 'Promoting husbandry...is never more effectually encouraged than by the increase of manufactures'. The conscious creation of such synergies and the economic diversity that makes them possible have been mandatory 'passage points' for all nations going from poverty to wealth since the late 1400s (see chapter 14).

From a production point of view, incorporating insights from David Hume to George Marshall, we get a very different picture which shows a world suffering from a huge *underutilization of resources*, with around two billion people who are severely underemployed or unemployed, engaged in economic activities that are far from 'efficient'. This is the logic found in the original Bretton Woods agreement: poor nations are operating very far from their production possibility frontier, many resources being underutilized.

The Marshall Plan was based on the principle of fully utilizing underutilized resources to protect and create industrialization, diversity and activities with increasing returns in all the nations involved. The post-war interpretation of poverty included assigning a social cost to the underutilization of resources, e.g., unemployment that could be measured using shadow prices, and justified temporary protection to achieve both full employment and a diversified industrial structure. Today, the Washington Consensus uses models assuming full employment, assigning no social or other costs to the fact that human resources in Third World countries are hugely underemployed. Viewing *palliative economics* as the only solution is thus a natural consequence of this view.

In an expanding world economy, where many raw materials are rapidly becoming strategic commodities, the poor 'stand in the way' of access to these raw materials, not unlike the native American 'Indians' being a hindrance to the settlers' use of land. For some US conservatives, placing the poor on 'reservations' is an option to be seriously considered. Only a decade ago, two American authors recommended the establishment of a *custodial state* in a much publicized book: 'by custodial state, we have in mind a high-tech and more lavish version of the Indian reservation for some substantial minority of the nation's population, while the rest of America tries to go about its business' (Herrnstein and Murray, 1994: 526). The MDGs are uncomfortably close to combining the consumption-based view of poverty with the idea of establishing reservations where the basic needs of the poor are taken care of while the rest of the world gets along with its business.

In the original Bretton Woods agreement, unemployment and underemployment justified the protection of national economies until full employment was reached. National development plans – e.g., to industrialize a country – were legitimate reasons for tariff protection under the original Bretton Woods agreement. Similarly, today, it is necessary to temporarily let the free trade principle yield to the principles of economic development and structural change. In short, the conditionalities of the Washington institutions must be subordinated to the original Bretton Woods agreement, as interpreted during its first decades.

In order to implement such policies, we must understand that the process of catching up for very poor countries involves a trade-off between the interests of 'Man-the-producer' and 'Man-the-consumer'. In addition, we need to realize that static absolute efficiency may differ considerably from long-term income-maximizing efficiency. As Paul Samuelson once said, "You need more temporary protection for the losers. My belief is that every good cause is worth some inefficiency' (*Süddeutsche Zeitung/New York Times*, 2004: 10).

At the time when England was the only nation to have industrialized, any consideration of *static efficiency* meant that no other nation ought to follow its path to industrialization. All of the nations that followed England's path to wealth did so only by sacrificing *static efficiency* in order to achieve a higher long-term *dynamic efficiency*. Industrializing the United States by targeting and protecting certain industries at that time was just as statically inefficient as protecting Africa's industries is today. The very rapid increase in real wages after the boycotts of the United States (during the Napoleonic Wars), and of South Africa and Rhodesia, testifies to the beneficial effects of protectionism, even when imposed from the outside. It is important to keep in mind, however, that – unlike many Latin American countries after World War II – it is essential to combine protection with national or regional competition. Appendix 2 establishes guidelines for 'good' and 'bad' protection based on historical experience.

In the poorest periphery, targeting economic diversity has to begin with economic activities that already exist. In the original spirit of Bretton Woods or Keynesian doctrine, one starting point for increasing real employment would be to identify the smallest tariffs which would maximize economic results in terms of employment and national value added, while minimizing the profitability of smuggling. For example, many poor countries import large quantities of poultry from developed countries. A small tariff on poultry could easily create much more employment and value added than the cost of the tariff. It should be kept in mind that tariffs have always played the dual role of producing revenues while creating more productive economic structures. In weak states, ports were often the only territories fully under government control, and tariffs were the easiest form of revenue to collect.

Free trade among nations at the same level of development has always been beneficial. Regional integration is, therefore, key to development. The problem, however, is that poor neighbouring countries often have little to sell to each other. In Africa, pressures from the United States and the EU, together with the spaghetti bowl of regional integration schemes (Common Market for Eastern and Southern Africa (COMESA), East African Community (EAC), Southern African Customs Union (SACU), Southern African Development Community (SADC)) and cross-membership of countries in these schemes, present difficulties for development and discourage policies promoting industrialization under local competition. The pressures to export faced by developing countries undermine, rather than advance, the Listian principle of regional integration that must precede any successful globalization. The EU presses for market access for their apples in Egypt, thereby destroying the century-old tradition of Egypt's buying apples from Lebanon. The present carving up of Africa into different economic spheres is exactly the opposite of what Africa needs, which is stronger economic integration within Africa and a certain degree of development before opening up for globalization.

A unifying characteristic of the 50 poorest countries in the world today is an almost total absence of manufacturing industries. The key insight that having an inefficient manufacturing sector produces a higher standard of living than having no manufacturing sector at all, will have to be recognized in order to transform poor into middle-income nations. Only this insight can stop the parallel race to the bottom in terms of democracy and economic welfare. After all, it was common knowledge in the eighteenth century that democracies were products of diversified economic structures, and not the other way around.

During the last decades, the United Nations Industrial Development Organization (UNIDO) and other United Nations institutions, such as the United Nations Conference on Trade and Development (UNCTAD), the United Nations Development Programme (UNDP), the International Labour Organization (ILO), the Economic Commission for Latin America and the Caribbean (ECLAC), the United Nations Research Institute for Social Development (UNRISD) and the United Nations Children's Fund (UNICEF), have been overshadowed by the aggressiveness of the Washington Institutions. The

United Nations institutions have virtually been bullied into silence, and the political turmoil around the 2003 UNDP report *Making Global Trade Work for People* testifies to this censorship. The report – financed by civil society foundations – was almost withdrawn because of political pressure and was only salvaged due to the intervention of these same foundations. It is indeed time for United Nations agencies to start working together in a more coordinated way in order to be heard.

In 1956, Nobel Economics Laureate Gunnar Myrdal advised Third World leaders on the subject of economic theory (Myrdal, 1956: 77). He stated that:

> They should be aware of the fact that very much of these theories are partly rationalizations of the dominant interest in the advanced and rapidly progressing industrial countries. … it … would be pathetic if the young social scientists of the under-developed countries got caught in the predilections of the thinking in the advanced countries, which are hampering the scholars there in their efforts to be rational but would be almost deadening to the intellectual strivings of those in the under-developed countries. I would instead wish them to have the courage to throw away large structures of meaningless, irrelevant and sometimes blatantly inadequate doctrines and theoretical approaches and to start out from fresh thinking right from their needs and their problems. This would then take them far beyond the realm of both outmoded Western liberal economics and Marxism.

Appendix 1

'Mercantilist' economic policies of the generic developmental state

Continuity of policy measures and toolkit, from England in 1485 (under Henry VII) to South Korea in the 1960s: a mandatory passage point for economic development.

> ***… the fundamental things apply, as time goes by.***
>
> Sam, the pianist, in *Casablanca*.

1. Recognition of wealth-creating synergies clustered around activities with increasing returns and continuous mechanization. Recognition that 'we are in the wrong business'. Conscious *targeting, support and protection* of activities generating increasing returns.
2. Granting of temporary monopolies/patents/protection to targeted activities in certain geographical areas.
3. Recognition of development as a synergetic phenomenon and, consequently, of the need for a diversified manufacturing sector, 'maximizing the division of labour' (Serra, 1613) – drawing on observations of the Dutch Republic and Venice.
4. Accumulation of empirical evidence showed that the manufacturing sector solved three policy problems endemic to the Third World: increasing national value added (GDP), increasing employment and balance-of-payment problems.
5. Attraction of foreigners to work in targeted activities (historically, religious persecution was important).
6. Weakening of landed interests (from England under Henry VII to South Korea). (Physiocracy as a reflection of the landowners' rebellion against this policy.)

7. Tax breaks for targeted activities.
8. Cheap credit for targeted activities.
9. Export subsidies for targeted activities.
10. Strong support for the agricultural sector, in spite of its clearly being seen as incapable of independently bringing the nation out of poverty.
11. Emphasis on learning and education (United Kingdom apprentice system under Elizabeth I).
12. Patent protection for valuable knowledge (Venice from the 1490s).
13. Export taxes/bans on raw materials to make them more expensive for competing nations (starting with Henry VII in the late 1400s, whose policy was very effective in severely damaging the wool industry in Medici Florence).

Appendix 2

Two ideal types of protectionism compared

East Asian: 'good'	Latin American: 'bad'
Temporary protection of new industries/ products for the world market.	Permanent protection of mature industries/ products for the home market (often very small).
Very steep learning curves compared to the rest of the world.	Learning that lags behind the rest of the world.
Based on a dynamic Schumpeterian view of the world – market-driven 'creative destruction'.	Based on a more static view of the world – planned economy.
Domestic competition maintained.	Little domestic competition.
Core technology locally controlled.	Core technology generally imported from abroad/assembly of imported parts/'superficial' industrialization.
Massive investment in education/industrial policy created a huge demand for education. Supply of educated people matched demand from industry.	Less emphasis on education/type of industries created did not lead to huge (East Asian) demand for education. Investment in education therefore tends to feed emigration .
Meritocracy – capital, jobs and privileges distributed according to qualifications.	Nepotism in the distribution of capital, jobs and privileges.
Equality of land distribution (South Korea).	Mixed record on land distribution.
Even income distribution increased home market for advanced industrial goods.	Uneven income distribution restricted scale of home market and decreased competitiveness of local industry.
Profits created through dynamic 'Schumpeterian' rent-seeking.	Profits created through static rent-seeking.
Intense cooperation between producers and local suppliers.	Confrontation between producers and local suppliers.
Regulation of technology transfer oriented towards maximizing knowledge transferred.	Regulation of technology transfer oriented towards avoiding 'traps'.

References

Anonymous (1786). *Relazione di una scorsa per varie provincie d'Europa del M. M.... a Madama G.. in Parigi.* Nella Stamperia del R. Im. Monastero di S. Salvatore, Pavia.

Bacon, Francis (1620). *Novum Organum.* Joannem Billium, Typographum Regium, London.

Chacholiades, Miltiades (1978). *International Trade Theory and Policy.* McGraw-Hill, New York.

Graham, Frank (1923). 'Some Aspects of Protection further considered'. *Quarterly Journal of Economics*, 37, 199–227.

Hamilton, Alexander (1791). *Report on the Subject of Manufactures.* Excerpt in Frank Taussig (1921). *Selected Readings in International Trade and Tariff Problems.* Ginn & Company, Boston.

Herrnstein, Richard J. and Charles Murray (1994). *The Bell Curve: Intelligence and Class Structure in American Life.* Free Press, New York.

Hume, David (1767). *History of England.* Vol. III. Millar/Cadell, London.

Kaplan, Steven (1976). *Bread, Politics and Political Economy in the Reign of Louis XV.* Martinus Nijhoff, The Hague.

Kregel, Jan (2004). 'External Financing for Development and International Financial Stability'. G-24 Discussion Paper No. 32, UNCTAD, Geneva, October.

Kuhn, Thomas (1962). *The Structure of Scientific Revolutions.* University of Chicago Press, Chicago.

Lavinas, Lena and Eduardo Henrique Garcia (2004). *Programas Sociais de Combate à Fome. O legado dos anos de estabilização econômica.* Editora UFRJ/IPEA, Coleção Economia e Sociedade, Rio de Janeiro.

List, Friedrich (1841/1909). *The National System of Political Economy.* Longmans, London.

Myrdal, Gunnar (1956). *Development and Underdevelopment.* National Bank of Egypt, Cairo.

Nelson, Richard R. (2006). 'Economic Development from the Perspective of Evolutionary Economic Theory'. Working Papers in Technology Governance and Economic Development, No. 2, Tallinn University of Technology, Estonia/The Other Canon Foundation, Norway. http://hum.ttu.ee/tg.

Nelson, Richard R. and Sydney Winter (1982). *An Evolutionary Theory of Economic Change.* Harvard University Press, Cambridge, MA.

Paine, Robert (ed.) (1977). *The White Arctic. Anthropological Essays on Tutelage and Ethnicity.* Institute of Social and Economic Research, Memorial University of Newfoundland, St. Johns.

Pfeiffer, Johann Friedrich von (1778). *Vermischte Verbesserungsvorschläge und freie Gedanken.* Vol. 2. Esslinger, Frankfurt.

Raymond, Daniel (1820). *Thoughts on Political Economy.* Fielding Lucas, Baltimore.

Reinert, Erik S. (1980). 'International Trade and the Economic Mechanisms of Underdevelopment'. PhD Thesis, Cornell University, New York.

Reinert, Erik S. (1996). 'Diminishing Returns and Economic Sustainability: The Dilemma of Resource-based Economies under a Free Trade Regime'. In Stein Hansen, Jan Hesselberg and Helge Hveem (eds.), *International Trade Regulation, National Development Strategies and the Environment: Towards Sustainable Development?* Centre for Development and the Environment, University of Oslo, Oslo, 119–150. Chapter 5 in this volume.

Reinert, Erik S. (1998). 'Raw Materials in the History of Economic Policy; or, Why List (the Protectionist) and Cobden (the Free Trader) Both Agreed on Free Trade in Corn'. In Gary Cook (ed.), *The Economics and Politics of International Trade: Freedom and Trade. 1846–1996.* Vol. 2. Routledge, London, 275–300.

Reinert, Erik S. (1999). 'The Role of the State in Economic Growth'. *Journal of Economic Studies*, 26 (4/5), 268–321.

Reinert, Erik S. (2003). 'Increasing Poverty in a Globalised World: Marshall Plans and Morgenthau Plans as Mechanisms of Polarisation of World Incomes'. In Ha-Joon Chang (ed.), *Rethinking Development Economics*, Anthem, London, 453–478. Chapter 9 in this volume.

Reinert, Erik S. (2004a). 'Benchmarking Success: The Dutch Republic (1500-1750) as seen by Contemporary European Economists'. In *How Rich Nations got Rich. Essays in the History of*

Economic Policy. Working Paper No. 1, SUM - Centre for Development and the Environment, University of Oslo, 1–24. Chapter 13 in this volume.

Reinert, Erik S. (2004b). 'Globalisation in the Periphery as a Morgenthau Plan: The Underdevelopment of Mongolia in the 1990s'. In Erik Reinert (ed.), *Globalization, Economic Development and Inequality: An Alternative Perspective.* Edward Elgar, Cheltenham, 157–214. Chapter 8 in this volume.

Reinert, Erik S. and Rainer Kattel (2004). 'The Qualitative Shift in European Integration: Towards Permanent Wage Pressures and a "Latin-Americanization" of Europe?'. Working Paper no. 17, Praxis Foundation, Estonia. http://www.praxis.ee/data/WP_17_2004.pdf.

Reinert, Erik S. and Sophus Reinert (2005). 'Mercantilism and Economic Development: Schumpeterian Dynamics, Institution Building and International Benchmarking'. In K. S. Jomo and Erik S. Reinert (eds.), *Origins of Development Economics.* Zed Books, London. Chapter 14 in this volume.

Roca, Santiago and Luis Simabuco (2004). 'Natural Resources, Industrialization and Fluctuating Standards of Living in Peru, 1950-1997: A Case Study of Activity-Specific Economic Growth'. In Erik S. Reinert (ed.), *Globalization, Economic Development and Inequality: An Alternative Perspective.* Edward Elgar, Cheltenham, 115–156.

Ross, Eric (1998). *The Malthus Factor: Poverty, Politics and Population in Capitalist Development.* Palgrave Macmillan, London.

Schoenhof, Jacob (1883). *The Destructive Influence of the Tariff upon Manufacture and Commerce and the Figures and Facts Relating Thereto.* New York Free Trade Club, New York.

Serra, Antonio (1613). *Breve Trattato delle Cause che Possono far Abbondare l'Oro e l'Argento dove non sono Miniere.* Lazzaro Scorriggio, Naples.

Singer, Hans W. (1950). 'The Distribution of Gains between Investing and Borrowing Countries'. *American Economic Review*, 40, 473–485.

Smith, Adam (1759/1812). *The Theory of Moral Sentiments,* in *the Works of Adam Smith. With an account of his life and writings,* 5 Vols. T. Cadell and W. Davies &c, London.

Smith, Adam (1776/1976), *An Inquiry into the Nature and Causes of the Wealth of Nations,* University of Chicago Press, Chicago.

Steuart, James (1767). *An Inquiry into the Principles of Political Economy: being an Essay on the Science of Domestic Policy in Free Nations. In which are Particularly Considered Population, Agriculture, Trade, Industry, Money, Coin, Interest, Circulation, Banks, Exchange, Public Credit, and Taxes,* 2 Vols. A. Millar & T. Cadell, London.

Süddeutsche Zeitung/New York Times (2004). September 20, 10.

Taussig, F.W. (1897). *The Tariff History of the United States.* Putnam's, New York.

Tawney, Richard (1926). *Religion and the Rise of Capitalism: A Historical Study.* J. Murray, London.

Printed in the USA
CPSIA information can be obtained
at www.ICGtesting.com
JSHW021101200124
55754JS00003B/8

9 781839 98297